GW00686250

MODERN STUDIES IN PROPERTY LAW: VOLUME 7

This book contains a collection of peer-reviewed papers presented at the ninth biennial Modern Studies in Property Law conference held at the University of Southampton in March 2012. It is the seventh volume to be published under the name of the conference. The conference and its published proceedings have become an established forum for property lawyers from around the world to showcase current research in the discipline. This collection reflects both the breadth of modern research in property law and its international dimensions. Incorporating a keynote address by Lord Walker of Gestingthorpe, retired Justice of the Supreme Court, on 'The Saga of Strasbourg and Social Housing', a number of chapters reveal the burgeoning influence of human rights in property law. Other contributions illustrate an enduring need to question and explore fundamental concepts of the subject alongside new and emerging areas of study. Collectively the chapters demonstrate the importance and relevance of property research in addressing a wide range of contemporary issues.

Modern Studies in Property Law

Volume 7

Edited by

Nicholas Hopkins

·HART·
PUBLISHING
OXFORD AND PORTLAND, OREGON
2013

Hart Publishing
16C Worcester Place Oxford OX1 2JW
United Kingdom
Telephone: +44 (0)1865-517530
Fax: +44 (0)1865-510710
E-mail: mail@hartpub.co.uk
Website: http://www.hartpub.co.uk

Published in North America (US and Canada) by
Hart Publishing
c/o International Specialized Book Services
920 NE 58th Avenue, Suite 300
Portland, OR 97213-3786
USA
Tel: +1 (503) 287-3093 or toll-free: +1 (800) 944-6190
Fax: +1 (503) 280-8832
E-mail: orders@isbs.com
Website: www.isbs.com

British Library Cataloguing in Publication Data
Data Available

ISBN: 978-1-84946-321-8

Typeset by Compuscript Ltd, Shannon
Printed and bound in Great Britain by
TJ International Ltd, Padstow

Preface

This volume contains refereed papers from the ninth Biennial Modern Studies in Property Law Conference that took place at the University of Southampton in March 2012. The conference series has its origins in the Centre for Property Law at the University of Reading, which held its first conference in 1996. These conferences gave rise to the book *Modern Studies in Property Law*, the volumes of which have, since 2001, been the medium for refereed publication of the conference proceedings. The conferences provide a snapshot of debates and developments in property law research for an international audience of speakers, delegates and readers of the proceedings. Collectively, they provide a representation of recurring and emerging themes in property jurisprudence. It is a testament to the vitality of the research in the field that the inaugural Postgraduate Research Student stream of the conference that took place on the final day in Southampton attracted speakers from the UK, Asia and South Africa.

This published volume opens with the text of the keynote address given by Lord Walker of Gestingthorpe. In his speech, 'The Saga of Strasbourg and Social Housing', Lord Walker reviews the case law on social housing and Article 8 of the European Convention on Human Rights (ECHR) and the 'clash of the Titans' between the English domestic courts and the European Court of Human Rights. He describes the saga as 'the most important concluded struggle, so far, between our courts and Strasbourg'. The remaining chapters in Part I of this collection, 'Property and Housing', focus on what is perhaps the most socially, politically and practically significant use of property; its use as a home. In Chapter 2, Susan Bright, Nicholas Hopkins and Nicholas Macklam continue the theme of human rights and social housing in the specific context of English shared ownership schemes. The authors consider how human rights and domestic public law can be used to protect those who 'own part' but risk 'losing all' as a result of the legal model used to deliver this form of low-cost home ownership. In Chapter 3, Warren Barr considers the impact of the Big Society initiative for charities involved in social housing provision. He suggests that despite the shared rhetoric of the Big Society and charitable providers of social housing, the initiative has ultimately provided more of a challenge than an opportunity. Part I concludes with an analysis of the regulation of private residential tenancies in Ireland by Áine Ryall. Written against the background of an increased demand for private residential housing as the 'dream' of home ownership has ended for many in the global economic crisis, Ryall examines the Residential Tenancies Act 2004. Against the background of proposed reform of the Act, she argues that the legislation is in urgent need of substantial amendment.

The contributions in Part II are themed around 'Challenging Perceptions of Property and Trusts'. In Chapter 5, Adam Hofri-Winogradow examines the phenomenon of 'shapeless trusts': those arising through legislation which does not require title to the trust assets to vest in the trustees. His focus is on two jurisdictions; Israel, whose shapeless trust is set to come to an end, and China. By setting the 'old' alongside the 'new', he suggests that shapeless trusts do have their use, particularly in making trusts more accessible outside the Anglo-Saxon legal tradition. In Chapter 6, Leslie Turano-Taylor challenges the assumptions that underpin the decision in *Hammersmith and Fulham LBC v Alexander-David* and the statutory regime that imposes a trust on the grant of a legal lease to a minor. She highlights the practical and theoretical difficulties caused by the trust against the substantively different relationship between a landlord and tenant and a trustee and beneficiary. In Chapter 7, Magdalena Habdas takes us to condominium schemes in Poland and examines the competence of the 'community of owners' in respect of common parts. Common parts remain the focus for Sarah Blandy in Chapter 8. Drawing on empirical research undertaken in 'cohousing' developments, she challenges the perception of property as being confined to externally imposed 'rights' and argues that recognition should be given to a property regime that emerges from the 'lived experience' of residents. Underlying both of these chapters is the difficulty presented to property law by any move away from individual, private property. In Chapter 9, written by Sue Farran, the division between private and public property is seen to have become increasingly blurred as people go 'back to the land'. Tracing a growth in collective use of land, Farran questions whether the property law 'menu' (the *numerus clausus*) needs to be reviewed to reflect a move away from individualism.

Part III of the collection, 'Intersections between Private Property, the Public and the State', picks up on the themes emerging from Part II. The preceding chapters by Habdas, Blandy and Farran have taken us away from the idea of property rights as individual rights to collective rights and uses of land. In Chapter 10 by John Page, which opens Part III, we move from collective ownership to public property. Page seeks to help fill the gap in the lack of theoretical understanding of such property. Janet Ulph's contribution in Chapter 11 then considers the sometimes controversial issue of the sale and transfer of items in museum collections. She argues that the guidance provided by law is inadequate, but that the gap should be filled by ethical principles. A theme thus recurs between Parts II and III as to the limits of property law, which appears an inadequate expression for the values and interests in issue beyond wholly 'private' rights.

In Chapter 12, Frankie McCarthy poses the challenging question of whether terrorists are entitled to peaceful enjoyment of their possessions. She considers whether anti-terrorist finance measures, designed to stop the flow of money to fund terrorist activities, would and should be found compatible with Article 1 of Protocol 1 of the ECHR. Part III concludes with two chapters focused on property and planning. In Chapter 13, Rachael Walsh explores planning law to cast light on the relationship between property and participation. She argues that the major role afforded to participation in the English planning system is evidence of the increasing 'democratisation' of property. In Chapter 14, Peter Williams considers the rise of property and development rights in Australia and the implications for urban planning policy and law.

The final part of the collection, Part IV, is entitled 'The Nature, Content and Acquisition of Property' and opens with a contribution by Simon Gardner in Chapter 15. Gardner's audio-visual keynote address presented at the conference is not one that could translate to writing. Instead, Gardner uses his contribution to this collection to provide an appraisal of the theory of 'persistent rights' developed principally by Ben McFarlane. It is particularly appropriate for Gardner to choose this collection to do so, as one of the key texts of the theory is published in the previous volume of *Modern Studies in Property Law*. Gardner rejects the theory, but not without praise for its ambition. Chapters 16 and 17 address the 'content' of property. In Chapter 16, Simon Douglas raises the question of whether a freeholder has 'a right to use' land. He concludes that while a freeholder has 'liberties to use' land, it remains unclear to what extent these liberties impose duties on others. In Chapter 17, Scott Grattan focuses attention on the right to alienate. Locating his discussion in the broader inquiry of the relationship between property and rights, Grattan considers different contexts in which the right to alienate is absent *ab initio* or has been removed. The final two chapters are each concerned with the 'acquisition' of property. In Chapter 18, written by Robin Hickey, the original acquisition of title to personal property by theft is examined. Hickey questions the use of standard actions for interference with goods in situations of 'wrongful' possession and argues that rather than recognising a relative title, in some instances the objects of the law may be better served by the imposition of a personal right. In Chapter 19, written by Emma Waring, the 'acquisition' has taken the form of compulsory purchase, but for private purposes. Waring places current concerns with private takings in the US and the UK in their historical context. She argues for the need for modern private takings to be 'scrutinised carefully and used sparingly' to ensure that their benefits do not come at the expense of the stability of the property regime.

Collectively, the contributions to this volume demonstrate the breadth, depth and variety of modern property scholarship. One of the great benefits of the *Modern Studies in Property Law* series is the ability to bring together a rich diversity of research at an international gathering. The conference owes this to the vision of Professor Lizzie Cooke and her colleagues at the University of Reading and, in no small part, to Richard Hart for his ongoing commitment to the series. On a personal level, I would like to thank my fellow members of the series' Editorial Board for entrusting the ninth conference to me. I am extremely grateful to the keynote speakers, Lord Walker of Gestingthorpe and Professor Simon Gardner, and to the Rt Hon Sir Terence Etherton, who addressed the conference at its dinner. At Southampton, special thanks are due to my colleagues Emma Laurie and Sarah Nield for their continuous support and involvement in the organisation of the conference. To preserve the integrity of the process, Emma and Sarah also arranged for Chapter 2, on which I am co-author, to be refereed. It would not have been possible to hold the event at Southampton without the backing of Professor Natalie Lee as Head of School, whose support was wholehearted and enthusiastic. Finally, the practical administrative burden of organisation was handled with the utmost efficiency by Jo Hazell.

As this book goes to press, we look forward to the tenth *Modern Studies in Property Law* conference that will take place at the University of Liverpool in 2014.

Nicholas Hopkins
Professor of Law, University of Southampton
January 2013

Table of Contents

PART III: INTERSECTIONS BETWEEN PRIVATE PROPERTY, THE PUBLIC AND THE STATE

PART IV: THE NATURE, CONTENT AND ACQUISITION OF PROPERTY

Table of Cases

United Kingdom

Australia

Canada

China (People's Republic)

Ireland

Israel

New Zealand

Poland

Singapore

South Africa

United States

European Commission and Court of Human Rights

European Court of Justice

European Court of First Instance

Table of Legislation

United Kingdom

Australia

Ireland

Israel

Jersey

Luxembourg

New Zealand

Poland

Part I

Property and Housing

1

The Saga of Strasbourg
and Social Housing

LORD WALKER OF GESTINGTHORPE*

W HEN THE HUMAN Rights Act 1998 was enacted, the Lord Chancellor's
Department predicted that the Act would cause a wave of litigation for
about three years, but that the wave would then subside and the waters
would be calm again. This prediction may have been based on the experience in
New Zealand, which enacted its Bill of Rights in 1990. But as we all know, it has
not worked out like that. There was indeed a wave of litigation, but in the twelfth
year since the Act came into force, the waters are far from calm and the Act is still—
indeed more than ever—the subject of acute political controversy.

The four most contentious areas have been the impact of the Act on criminal
justice, on anti-terrorist legislation, on immigration law and on the law of social
housing. The first of these topics is concerned with fair trial rights under Article 6
of the European Convention on Human Rights, including issues as to the reverse
burden of proof,[1] trial within a reasonable time,[2] hearsay evidence[3] and the right
of access to a lawyer while in police custody.[4] The second topic, engaging rights to
personal liberty and fair trial under Articles 5 and 6, is the contentious litigation
over detention without trial of foreign national suspects, followed by the control
order regime.[5] The third topic is concerned with the right to respect for family life
under Article 8,[6] which has had a huge influence on decisions about the deporta-
tion of failed asylum-seekers and other immigrants, and led last November to an
unusually candid exchange of views between the Home Secretary and the Secretary
of State for Justice.

The fourth topic, social housing, is my subject today. Part of its particular interest and difficulty is that it raises issues on both Article 6 and Article 8. Article 6

---

* Retired Justice of the Supreme Court.
[1] *Sheldrake v DPP* [2004] 1 AC 264; *O'Halloran v United Kingdom* (2008) 46 EHRR 397.
[2] *Re Attorney General's Reference (No 2 of 2001)* [2004] 2 AC 72.
[3] *Kawaja v United Kingdom*, Grand Chamber, 13 December 2011.
[4] *Cadder v HM Advocate* [2010] 1 WLR 2601.
[5] *A v Secretary of State for the Home Department* [2005] 2 AC 68; *Secretary of State for the Home
Department v AF (No 3)* [2010] 2 AC 269.
[6] *Huang v Secretary of State for the Home Department* [2007] 2 AC 167; *ZH (Tanzania) v Secretary
of State for the Home Department* [2011] 2 AC 166; *R (Quila) v Secretary of State for the Home
Department* [2011] UKSC 45, [2012] 1 AC 261; (extradition) *Norris v Govt of USA* [2010] 2 AC 287.

gives everyone the right to have his civil rights and obligations determined by an independent and impartial tribunal. This has raised issues where decisions as to the management of the community's stock of social housing are in effect divided between housing authorities (which may be impartial but are not independent) and a district judge faced with a long list of summary applications for possession. At the same time, Article 8 raises the issue of how (if at all) a housing authority's obligation to show respect for its tenant's home adds to its general obligation to manage its housing stock for the benefit of the community. These are the issues that have led to something of a stand-off between the Strasbourg Court and our highest tribunal, ending (at any rate for the present) a year ago with the decision of the Supreme Court in *Powell*.[7]

There was nothing confrontational about the earliest cases on the impact of the Human Rights Act on social housing. Twelve years ago, the Strasbourg jurisprudence on the subject was much sparser than it is today, although it was already well established[8] that in Article 8 'home' (or in other European languages, 'domicile', 'domicilio' or 'Wohnung') is an autonomous concept that has very little to do with different forms of ownership or tenure under the property laws of different states. One of the first housing cases to reach the Court of Appeal, in April 2001, was concerned with possession proceedings commenced soon after the coming into force of the Act. In the *Poplar Housing Association* case,[9] the Court of Appeal held that the association was (for the relevant purposes) a public authority and that Article 8 was engaged, but that the eviction of an assured shorthold tenant was justifiable under Article 8(2), despite the mandatory terms of section 21(4) of the Housing Act 1988. The court held that section 21(4), which effectively deprived the county court of any discretion to refuse a possession order, was not incompatible with Article 8, and rejected the argument that it should be creatively construed under section 3 of the Human Rights Act by reading in the requirement that the court considered it reasonable to order possession.

To my mind, the judgment of the Court of Appeal showed, at what was a very early stage in our jurisprudence on the Human Rights Act, an impressive grasp of the new problems that it poses. In a key passage, the Court emphasised not the housing authority's proprietary title, but its function in carrying out Parliament's enacted policy for allocation of the limited stock of social housing:

> The Court has to pay considerable attention to the fact that Parliament intended when enacting section 21(4) of the 1988 Act to give preference to the needs of those dependent on social housing *as a whole* over those in the position of the defendant. The economic and other implications of any policy in this area are extremely complex and far-reaching. This is an area where, in our judgment, the courts must treat the decisions of Parliament as to what is in the public interest with particular deference. The limited role given to the court under section 21(4) is a legislative policy decision ... the Human Rights Act 1998 does not require the courts to disregard the decisions of Parliament ... when deciding whether there has been a breach of the Convention.[10]

---

[7] *Hounslow LBC v Powell* [2011] 2 AC 186.
[8] *Buckley v United Kingdom* (1996) 23 EHRR 101 [63].
[9] *Poplar Housing and Regeneration Community Association Ltd v Donoghue* [2002] QB 48.
[10] Ibid [69].

I feel able to commend this judgment without any fear of appearing condescending, since at the time I was in the Court of Appeal and was a party to one of its least successful early decisions on the Act, *Aston Cantlow*.[11] This was the case about chancel repairs, in which the House of Lords held that we had fallen into error on just about every point in the case. But our misguidedness was not quite so complete as that of another constitution of the Court of Appeal in *Wilson v First County Trust Ltd (No 2)*.[12] This was an appeal from the county court in a small consumer credit case in which the Court of Appeal of its own motion raised an incompatibility issue and proceeded to make a declaration of incompatibility. This was appealed to the House of Lords by the Secretary of State for Trade and Industry (the original parties having lost any appetite for the fight) and argued on behalf of interveners including the Attorney General on behalf of the Speaker of the House of Commons (on *Pepper v Hart*[13] implications) and numerous trade bodies. As in *Aston Cantlow*, the House of Lords allowed the appeal on numerous grounds. I mention the case not simply as a diversion but because, in the context of incompatibility, Lord Nicholls made some general remarks about it being open to Parliament to lay down clear general rules, which the court is bound to follow, even if this produces individual hard cases. Lord Nicholls said:

> Considered overall, this course may well be a proportionate response in practice to a perceived social problem. Parliament may consider the response should be a uniform solution across the board. A tailor-made response, fitting the facts of each case as decided in an application to the Court, may not be appropriate.[14]

One way of putting the Strasbourg Court's message on our social housing legislation—to which I now return—is that this 'one size fits all' attitude may be good enough for a trader doing business under the Consumer Credit Act 1974, but that it is not good enough for a public sector tenant with an Article 8 right to respect for his or her home.

Another early Court of Appeal case explored the other aspect: that of the housing authority as decision-maker. In the *McLellan* case[15] heard in October 2001, a tenant with an introductory tenancy of a flat in Bracknell sought judicial review of the borough council's decision to serve on her notice of proceedings for possession. In such a case, the county court had no discretion to refuse a possession order, provided that the proper procedure had been followed. This was the effect of sections 127 and 128 of the Housing Act 1996, and any review under section 129 was conducted by the housing authority itself, not by the county court. The court's only discretion was, in a case of exceptional hardship, to extend the 14-day period for giving up possession to six weeks. This procedure was challenged as contrary to Article 6 on the ground that it amounted to the determination of the tenant's civil rights otherwise than by an independent and impartial tribunal.

---

[11] *Aston Cantlow Parochial Church Council v Wallbank* [2002] Ch 51; [2004] 1 AC 546.
[12] *Wilson v First County Trust Ltd (No 2)* [2004] 1 AC 816.
[13] *Pepper v Hart* [1993] AC 593.
[14] Ibid [74].
[15] *R (McLellan) v Bracknell Forest Borough Council* [2002] QB 1129.

The Court of Appeal rejected this challenge. It followed the decision of the House of Lords in the *Alconbury* case.[16] These two decisions, together with that of the House of Lords in *Ruma Begum*[17] early in 2003, mark the beginning of the slow and uncertain unfreezing of the rigidity of the judicial review process where human rights are concerned. In *Alconbury*, Lord Slynn said of proportionality:

> I consider that even without reference to the Human Rights Act 1998 the time has come to recognise that this principle is part of English administrative law, not only when judges are dealing with Community Acts but also when they are dealing with Acts subject to domestic law. Trying to keep the *Wednesbury* principle and proportionality in separate compartments seems to me to be unnecessary and confusing.[18]

Lord Hoffmann, both in *Alconbury* and in *Ruma Begum*, was less inclined to favour a general extension of judicial review principles to include proportionality. He preferred a nuanced approach (reflecting Strasbourg's margin of appreciation) to the nature of the particular administrative decision subject to review and the character of the particular decision-maker.

These themes—whether it is compatible with the Human Rights Act for the court's discretion to be restricted to vanishing point and whether the possibility of resort to judicial review of the housing authority's decision is a sufficient answer—dominate the leading cases to which I now turn. But to complete the preliminaries, it is appropriate to refer to one other early case, which is the decision of the House of Lords in the *South Bucks* case.[19] It was heard with two other appeals, all of them planning cases concerned with unauthorised development by gipsy communities, and the significance of Article 8 in that context. The point actually decided was a fairly limited one, relating to the width of the court's discretion[20] to grant an injunction in aid of an enforcement notice issued by a local planning authority. But the speeches contain a recognition of the complexities of these problems. Lord Bingham[21] quoted a saying of the late Vaclev Havel that 'the Gipsies are a litmus test not of democracy but of civil society'. Gipsies feature in three of the leading cases.

The first social housing appeal to go to the House of Lords was *Qazi*.[22] Mr Qazi and his wife had a secure tenancy of a two-bedroom council house in Harrow Weald. In 1998, there were matrimonial troubles and his wife moved out with their daughter. A few months later, she gave notice to the council, effectively terminating the joint tenancy. Mr Qazi applied for a new tenancy, but it was not granted because the accommodation was more than a single man needed. The council claimed possession in March 2000. At a preliminary hearing in June 2000, Mr Qazi told the Court that he was living with his new wife and her child. By November 2000, she was pregnant and by the trial in June 2001, there were two adults and two children living in the house. The recorder held that as Mr Qazi had no legal or equitable

---

[16] *R (Alconbury Developments Ltd) v Secretary of State for the Environment, Transport and the Regions* [2003] 2 AC 295.
[17] *Ruma Begum v Tower Hamlets LBC* [2003] 2 AC 430.
[18] *R (Alconbury Developments Ltd)* (n 16) [51].
[19] *South Bucks DC v Porter* [2003] 2 AC 558.
[20] Town and Country Planning Act 1990, s 187B.
[21] *South Bucks DC v Porter* [2003] 2 AC 558 [31].
[22] *Harrow LBC v Qazi* [2004] 1 AC 983.

rights in the house, it could not be his home. In December 2001, the Court of Appeal allowed the appeal and remitted the case to the county court to consider whether the landlord's interference with Mr Qazi's Article 8 rights was justified under Article 8(2).

Harrow appealed on two main grounds. The first, that the house was not Mr Qazi's home, was unanimously rejected. But the House of Lords was deeply divided as to whether a public sector landlord with an immediate right to possession could be required to justify its claim by a balancing exercise under Article 8(2). Lord Bingham and Lord Steyn were firmly of the view that Article 8 was engaged and justification under Article 8(2) was required. Lord Bingham emphasised:

> The Strasbourg authorities have adopted a very pragmatic and realistic approach to the issue of justification. Counsel were agreed that even if the argument for Mr Qazi were accepted, the occasions on which a court would be justified in declining to make a possession order would be highly exceptional.[23]

These words 'highly exceptional' were to be revisited more than once. Later cases have recognised that they cannot be a principle on which to decide cases, but only a prediction as to how many cases will be decided in a particular way—and as a prediction, they have not proved to be particularly reliable.

Lord Hope, Lord Scott and Lord Millett took a very different view. A public sector landlord with an immediate, unqualified right to possession under English property law could not be required to justify the enforcement of that right. Lord Scott was characteristically forthright:

> There is no case in which a balance has been struck between the tenant's interests and the landlord's rights. In every case the landlord's success has been automatic. And so it must be unless Article 8 is to be allowed to diminish or detract from the landlord's contractual and proprietary rights.[24]

All three law lords in the majority stressed the potency of the landlord's proprietary rights under English law, rather than relying, as the Court of Appeal had in the *Poplar Housing Association* case, on the carefully differentiated system of tenure (shorthold, secure, introductory and demoted) that had emerged from almost a century of housing legislation.

In May 2004, the Strasbourg Court gave judgment in *Connors*.[25] This case concerned the eviction of a gipsy family from a gipsy caravan site owned and run by Leeds City Council. This occurred in August 2000, before the Human Rights Act came into force. The Strasbourg Court held unanimously that the UK was in breach of Article 8 and did not find it necessary to decide on a separate complaint about discrimination under Article 14. But the fact that it was a gipsy family that was evicted from a caravan site specially provided for gipsies was important. Because of an exception in the Mobile Homes Act 1983, licences to occupy plots on these sites had only four weeks' security of tenure. This exception was defended by the UK government on the ground that it was in the public interest for local authorities to

---

[23] Ibid [25].
[24] Ibid [146].
[25] *Connors v United Kingdom* [2004] 40 EHRR 189.

have special flexibility in the management of gipsy caravan sites. But the Strasbourg Court did not accept this as sufficient justification.

However the judgment also contains some important general observations as to the inadequacy of the UK model of judicial review for the resolution of factual disputes. In the *Connors* case, Leeds City Council had indicated in correspondence and in witness statements that Mr Connors and his extended family were anti-social troublemakers, but at the court hearing, the council simply relied on the notice to quit without those allegations being supported by evidence. This is a real dilemma in many of these cases. In practice, housing authorities are slow to evict their tenants, even when there are substantial arrears of rent, because they know that eviction may well lead to other more difficult and more expensive problems in other parts of the social security system. But they may feel bound to evict tenants whose seriously anti-social conduct makes life intolerable for their neighbours. The burden of proving anti-social behaviour is a much heavier one (especially if neighbours are intimidated from giving evidence) than simply giving notice to quit in a case where the county court has little or no discretion about making a possession order.

That is one general point that we can take from *Connors*. The other is that in this, as in the later Strasbourg cases in this area, the Chamber included the UK judge, Sir Nicolas Bratza. It is easy to detect his hand in the full and clear judgment, which shows a real understanding of the problems as seen from the domestic side. I believe that there has been a real dialogue—difficult but salutary—between London and Strasbourg on this issue, and Bratza, recently elected as President of the Strasbourg Court, can take much of the credit for this. I add that I must declare an interest in the matter, since over 40 years ago he was my first pupil in chambers in Lincoln's Inn.

Nearly two years after *Connors*, the problem was reconsidered by seven law lords in *Kay* and *Price*.[26] In *Kay*, the appellants were seven individuals who had believed that they had secure tenancies granted by a housing trust, but found (as a result of a notice given to the trust by Lambeth) that they were in the position of trespassers. They might be thought to have had much more in the way of merits than the Maloney family, the effective appellants in *Price*, who had unlawfully sited their caravans on part of a recreation ground belonging to Leeds City Council and had been in occupation for only two days when proceedings were commenced against them.

The House of Lords was unanimous in concluding that both appeals should be dismissed, but there was an important split, four to three, as to the reasons. The majority (led by Lord Bingham) held that in all these cases, Article 8 is engaged and may be relied on to resist an order for possession in the county court, even though it would require—the same form of words again[27]—'highly exceptional circumstances before Article 8 would avail the occupiers'. Neither appeal met this requirement: *Price* obviously failed, and in *Kay* the appellants had not pleaded or put forward evidence in support of any special claim.

The tenant's right to raise an Article 8 defence was supported, in Lord Bingham's view,[28] by the express terms of section 7(1)(b) of the Human Rights Act. It was also

---

[26] *Kay v Lambeth BC, Leeds CC v Price* [2006] 2 AC 465.
[27] Ibid [36].
[28] Ibid [36].

supported by the decision of the House of Lords, made over 20 years earlier, in the *Winder* case.[29] In that case, Wandsworth Borough Council, which in the days of Mrs Thatcher claimed to be one of the most efficient local authorities in the country, raised some of its tenants' rents by half within a year—an increase of about 35 per cent followed by 13 per cent on top of that a year later. Mr Winder, a secure tenant of a council flat, refused to pay the increase. When he was sued for arrears of rent and possession, he defended the claim on the ground that the rent increases were unreasonable and thus unlawful. The House of Lords unanimously and forthrightly rejected the council's argument that it was an abuse of process for Mr Winder to raise this defence in the county court rather than by way of judicial review.

The majority, led by Lord Hope and Lord Scott, considered that *Qazi* should not be departed from. *Connors* was treated as a special case. Lord Hope countered Lord Bingham's reliance on section 7 by referring to section 6(2)(b) of the Human Rights Act.[30] This provision disapplies a public authority's duty not to act incompatibly with Convention rights where some provision of primary legislation is itself incompatible and 'the authority was acting so as to give effect to or enforce those provisions'. The precise scope of section 6(2)(b) has still not been fully resolved, but in *Pinnock*,[31] the unanimous judgment of the nine-strong Supreme Court did not accept Lord Hope's view.

Lord Hope went on[32] to set out what he called 'gateways' as the only circumstances in which the county court could refrain from making a possession order, where the statutory requirements were satisfied and the court had no statutory discretion. These were: (a) by applying section 3 of the Human Rights Act, if possible, to avoid incompatibility, or alternatively transferring the case to the High Court, which has the power to make a declaration of incompatibility; or (b) by considering (on the *Winder* principle) any seriously arguable issue as to what Lord Hope called 'an improper exercise of its powers at common law'.

The most moderate majority speech (which is not of course to suggest that the others were immoderate) was that of Lady Hale, who observed:

> My Lords, I myself do not think that the purpose of Article 8 was to oblige a social landlord to continue to supply housing to a person who has no right in domestic law to continue to be supplied with that housing, assuming that the general balance struck by domestic law was not amenable to attack and that the authority's decision to invoke that law was not open to judicial review on conventional grounds. It should not be forgotten that in an appropriate case, the range of considerations which any public authority should take into account in deciding whether to invoke its powers can be very wide.[33]

She then referred to some well-known observations of Sedley LJ[34] about local authorities taking account of 'considerations of common humanity, none of which can properly be ignored when dealing with one of the most fundamental human needs, the need for shelter with at least a modicum of security'. Here Lady Hale was

---

[29] *Wandsworth LBC v Winder* [1985] AC 461.
[30] *Kay; Price* (n 26) [86].
[31] *Manchester City Council v Pinnock* [2010] 3 WLR 1441 [93]–[103].
[32] Ibid [110], a paragraph which has been the subject of much discussion and controversy.
[33] Ibid [190].
[34] *R v Lincolnshire CC, ex p Atkinson* (1995) 8 Admin LR 529, 534.

saying, in effect, that Article 8 did not add anything to a local authority's existing public responsibilities.

Qazi had not been considered by the Strasbourg Court in *Connors* (perhaps, Lord Bingham suggested in *Kay*,[35] because the reasoning of the majority did not support the case that the UK government wished to put forward), but both *Qazi* and *Kay* were considered by the Strasbourg Court in *McCann*,[36] in which judgment was given in March 2008 (by then *Kay* was itself on its way to Strasbourg).

McCann resembled *Qazi* in that a married couple had been secure tenants of a council house. In 2001, after incidents of domestic violence, Mrs McCann moved out with the children and they were rehoused by Birmingham City Council. At the landlord's suggestion, Mrs McCann gave notice to quit, terminating the tenancy of the former home, where her husband was still living. Following the House of Lords' decision in *Qazi*, the Court of Appeal dismissed Mr McCann's appeal from the county court. An application for judicial review also failed and Mr McCann was evicted. The Strasbourg Court's evaluation was very clear:

> It is, for present purposes, immaterial whether or not Mrs McCann understood or intended the effects of the notice to quit. Under the summary procedure available to a landlord where one joint tenant serves notice to quit the appellant was dispossessed of his home without any possibility to have the proportionality of the measure determined by an independent tribunal. It follows that, because of the lack of procedural safeguards, there has been a violation of Article 8.[37]

The next step in the saga (for me it seems like retracing a via dolorosa) is the decision of the House of Lords in *Doherty*.[38] This was another case concerning gipsies, the essential facts of which were similar to those in *Connors*, except that Mr Doherty and his family were not said to be troublemakers. The appeal was argued in March 2008, before the Strasbourg Court's decision in *McCann*, but the speeches (delivered at the end of July 2008) took account of that decision. There were five law lords sitting, so there was no real possibility of the House departing from *Kay*. But there was some hope of a degree of clarification, especially as Carnwarth LJ had made clear (when *Doherty* was in the Court of Appeal)[39] what that Court thought about the number, length and opacity of the speeches in *Kay*.

The speeches in *Doherty* may be said to have provided clarification 'up to a point, Lord Copper'. Lord Hope[40] set out to explain and modify the 'gateways' that he had expounded (with the concurrence of the majority) in *Kay*. Lord Mance and I both expressed regret at the restriction of gateway (b) to 'traditional' or 'conventional' grounds of judicial review, especially as the thinking behind it seemed to be based on a questionable view of the scope of section 6(2)(b) of the Human Rights Act. This led into a further question as to whether the exception of gipsy caravan sites from protection under the Mobile Homes Act 1983 meant that Birmingham City

---

[35] *Kay; Price* (n 26) [23].
[36] *McCann v United Kingdom* (2008) 47 EHRR 913.
[37] Ibid [55].
[38] *Doherty v Birmingham City Council* [2009] 1 AC 367.
[39] *Doherty* [2007] LGR 165 (CA).
[40] *Doherty* (n 38) [36]–[55].

Council was relying on a common law rather than a statutory right. If I may venture to quote from my own opinion on this point:

> At common law, a landlord is entitled to possession of the demised premises if the tenant's lease or tenancy has expired or been validly terminated, and similarly a fortiori if there was only a licence. To that extent the first defendant and the Secretary of State are correct in saying that the city council was, in seeking possession, relying on a common law right. That is part of the picture, but it is far from the whole picture, and in my opinion it would be unrealistic, and productive of error, not to look at the whole picture. The fact is that the city council's common law right was surrounded on all sides by statutory infrastructure, like a patch of grass in the middle of a motorway junction.[41]

The last important case is *Pinnock*,[42] decided by a nine-strong Supreme Court in November 2010. It is, in domestic terms, the most important case of all, since *Qazi*, *Kay* and *Doherty* were all departed from. Other recent developments—the Strasbourg Court's decision in *Kay*[43] six weeks before *Pinnock*, and *Powell*[44] in the Supreme Court in February 2011—are little more than footnotes. *Pinnock* was remarkable not only for departing from three recent decisions of the House of Lords, but also for the fact that the Supreme Court gave a single unanimous judgment delivered by Lord Neuberger MR. The judgment recorded, correctly, that all members of the court had contributed to it. But it is unmistakeably the work of Lord Neuberger, who produced a judgment (if I may say so) combining comprehensiveness with clarity, and showing sensitivity both to the Strasbourg jurisprudence and to the social problems that are the staple fare of social landlords and county court judges.

The judgment deals with four issues of increasing specificity. The facts are considered in detail at the end of the judgment. It is sufficient to say that Mr Pinnock was the long-term secure tenant of a council house occupied by himself and his female partner, and—sporadically and at different times—by some or all of his adult or teenage children. Mr Pinnock was a pensioner and was not himself accused of anti-social behaviour, but his partner and his children were found to have been guilty of very serious anti-social behaviour. Lord Neuberger described it as a 'history of crime, nuisance and harassment ... extraordinary in its extent and persistence'.[45]

In March 2005, Manchester City Council applied for possession or alternatively a demotion order under section 82A of the Housing Act 1985 (as inserted by the Anti-social Behaviour Act 2003). Neither order could be made unless the judge was satisfied that it was reasonable to do so. In June 2007, after a six-day hearing, the judge declined to make an order for possession, but made a demotion order. It seems to have had little effect on the behaviour of the tenant's family, and within the year before the order would have lapsed, the Council gave notice to terminate the tenancy. Mr Pinnock exercised his right to require a review, but the notice was upheld by the review panel. In these circumstances, under sections 143D, 143E and 143F of

---

[41] Ibid [100].
[42] *Pinnock* (n 31).
[43] *Kay v United Kingdom* (2012) EHRR 30, noted in [2011] *European Human Rights Law Review* 105.
[44] *Hounslow LBC v Powell (No 1)* [2011] 2 AC 104.
[45] *Pinnock* (n 31) [162].

the Housing Act 1996 (as inserted by the 2003 Act), the county court was obliged to order possession if it thought the correct statutory procedure had been followed.

Many of you will be very familiar with Lord Neuberger's judgment, and I will not attempt a full summary here. On the first issue,[46] he discussed the domestic authorities and the Strasbourg jurisprudence, citing a key passage from the *Connors* judgment.[47] He concluded, with a reference to *Ullah*,[48] that *Qazi*, *Kay* and *Doherty* could not stand with the 'clear and constant line of decisions' of the Strasbourg Court. He referred to Lord Bingham's observation that cases of disproportionate claims for possession would be 'very highly exceptional' and stated firmly[49] that it is 'both unsafe and unhelpful to invoke exceptionality as a guide'.

On the second issue, Lord Neuberger dealt with the application of proportionality to different types of tenancy, and in particular demoted tenancies.[50] On the third issue, he concluded that section 3 of the Human Rights Act must be applied so as to read section 143D(2) of the Housing Act 1996 'as allowing the court to exercise the powers which are necessary to consider and, where appropriate, to give effect to any article 8 defence which the defendant raises'. This part of the judgment also contains an important passage[51] discussing (but not expressing final and comprehensive views on) section 6(2)(b) of the Human Rights Act.

By the time the Supreme Court gave judgment, it was over five years since the council had originally sought possession and over two years since it gave notice to terminate the demoted tenancy. Rather than remit the matter to the county court, the Supreme Court thought it best to resolve the proportionality issue itself. After a detailed review of the evidence and findings, it upheld the possession order made by the county court judge.

The most recent Supreme Court case, *Powell*,[52] was little more than a footnote. The Court (sitting with seven Justices) applied the principles laid down in *Pinnock* to the cases of two tenants with introductory tenancies (Mr Hall and Mr Frisby) and one homeless person in insecure accommodation (Ms Powell). Introductory tenancies are subject to statutory provisions similar to those applied to demoted tenancies, under which the county court's discretion is severely limited once the landlord gives notice to terminate the tenancy. The Supreme Court gave effect to section 3 of the Human Rights Act so as to read into the key provision (section 127(2) of the Housing Act 1996) the same requirement of reasonableness as had been read into section 143D(2) in *Pinnock*. So the two early Court of Appeal decisions that I mentioned, *Poplar Housing Association* and *McLellan*, have both been reversed in relation to section 3. But the Supreme Court felt unable to use section 3 to alter the natural meaning of section 89 of the Housing Act 1980, under which an order for possession in respect of a non-secure tenancy cannot be postponed for more than 14 days (or six weeks in circumstances of exceptional hardship). As Lord Hope

---

[46] Ibid [22]–[54].
[47] Ibid [81]–[83].
[48] *R (Ullah) v Special Adjudicator* [2004] 2 AC 233.
[49] *Pinnock* (n 31) [51].
[50] Ibid [55]–[64].
[51] Ibid [93]–[103].
[52] *Powell* (n 44), heard with *Leeds City Council v Hall* and *Birmingham City Council v Frisby*.

observed,[53] the language ('shall not in any event') could hardly be more explicit. To read it in another sense would be to cross a constitutional boundary, as Lord Nicholls put it in *Ghaidan v Godin-Mendoza*.[54]

What is the significance of the whole social housing saga? It is probably too early to draw definitive conclusions, especially as reform of the European Court of Human Rights is very much on the agenda for the UK's current chairmanship of the Council of Europe. But on any view it can be seen as the most important concluded struggle, so far, between our courts and Strasbourg. I emphasise 'concluded' because the other three topics that I mentioned—criminal justice, national security and immigration—are certainly no less important. But they are still unfinished business. On social housing, by contrast, the unanimous judgment in *Pinnock* is a clear acknowledgment that in this area, the 'clear and constant' jurisprudence of the Strasbourg Court (best exemplified by its judgment in *Connors*) must prevail. As Lord Rodger put it in a judgment about control orders, referring to Strasbourg by its ancient Roman name, 'Argentoratum locutum, judicium finitum'.[55]

If further issues arise under shared ownership schemes[56] or under Part 7, Chapter 2 of the Localism Act 2011, I would expect the principles in *Pinnock* to provide the basis for resolving them.

There are several other points of general interest. First, the majority in *Qazi* may be thought to have taken a wrong turning in the development of the law by a rather nineteenth-century adherence to the potency of property rights and freedom of contract. It might have been more helpful to have examined (as the House of Lords did in *Ruma Begum*) the important social functions which Parliament has deliberately entrusted to local authorities and housing associations in managing and allocating the limited supply of social housing available to meet ever-growing needs. These functions are going to become even more important and difficult with the new restrictions on housing benefit.

Second, the litigation has shown that although the Human Rights Act is for the most part admirably drafted, the very compressed terms of section 6(2)—and especially paragraph (b) of that subsection—conceal some complex problems for local authorities with a multiplicity of statutory duties and powers. I suspect that there will be quite a lot more litigation before all these complexities have been sorted out.

Third, there is a quite a striking contrast between the Supreme Court's application of section 3 of the Human Rights Act in construing sections 127(2) and 143D (2) of the Housing Act 1996 in *Powell* and *Pinnock*, and its inability to apply section 3 to the time limits in section 89 of the Housing Act 1980. It might be argued that to apply section 3 to any of these provisions goes against the 'grain of the legislation' (Lord Rodger's expression in *Ghaidan*).[57] Lord Neuberger and the other justices in *Pinnock* recognised it as a difficult point.[58] But the fact that the court felt able to

---

[53] Ibid [61] and [62].
[54] *Ghaidan v Godin-Mendoza* [2004] 2 AC 557 [33].
[55] *Secretary of State for the Home Department v AF* (No 3) [2010] 2 AC 269 [98].
[56] *Richardson v Midland Heart Ltd* [2008] L & TR 31, discussed by S Bright and N Hopkins [2009] *Conv* 337 (on the unusual facts of that case, they suggest reliance on Article 1 of the First Protocol rather than Article 8).
[57] *Ghaidan* (n 54) [121].
[58] *Pinnock* (n 31) [75].

apply section 3 to sections 127(2) and 143D(2) avoided the need for declarations of incompatibility, which would otherwise have been inevitable. If such declarations had been made, affecting the status of many hundreds of thousands of public sector tenants, the political and social consequences would have been incalculable.

Finally, and on a lighter note, it is a comfort to me, and I hope to many practitioners, legal scholars and law students, that in *Pinnock* the Supreme Court has shown that it is capable of functioning in a truly collegiate way. I sincerely hope that it will not prove to have been a one-off event.

2

Owning Part but Losing All: Using Human Rights to Protect Home Ownership

SUSAN BRIGHT, NICHOLAS HOPKINS
AND NICHOLAS MACKLAM[*]

I. INTRODUCTION

IN ENGLAND THE majority of householders live in homes that they own, with surveys demonstrating repeatedly the population's strong preference for home ownership over renting.[1] Home ownership has been actively promoted by successive governments for a mix of ideological and political reasons, and the Coalition government continues to present the opportunity to own as central to its housing strategy.[2] Ownership is sold as providing the opportunity for wealth accumulation, a financial buffer, collateral that can be borrowed against, and supporting a sense of security and stability.[3] Yet rising housing prices mean that traditional home ownership—the purchase of a home funded through the buyer's own resources and commercially available mortgage finance—has become the impossible dream for many.[4] As a result, successive governments have sought to make this dream a reality by filling the affordability gap through Low Cost Home Ownership (LCHO) schemes.

[*] Professor of Land Law, University of Oxford; Professor of Law, University of Southampton; student member of Lincoln's Inn, respectively. The authors are grateful for the helpful comments received at the conference, and for the comments and assistance of Sarah Nield, Alistair Mills and the anonymous referee.

[1] A report issued by the Department for Communities and Local Government states that 86 per cent would choose to buy if they had a free choice. See Department for Communities and Local Government, *Public Attitudes to Housing in England: Report Based on the Results from the British Social Attitudes Survey* (July 2011) 5.

[2] 'For too long, millions have been locked out of home ownership. We want to build an economy that works for everyone, one in which people who work hard and play by the rules can expect to own a decent home of their own.' See Department for Communities and Local Government, *Laying the Foundations: A Housing Strategy for England* (November 2011) v (Foreword by the Prime Minister and the Deputy Prime Minister).

[3] For a more detailed discussion, see S Bright and N Hopkins, 'Home, Meaning and Identity: Learning from the English Model of Shared Ownership' (2011) 28 *Housing, Theory & Society* 377.

[4] The problem of affordability is recognised in the government's housing strategy; see Department for Communities and Local Government (n 2) 1–2.

One legal model for such schemes is 'shared ownership', known colloquially as 'part-buy, part-rent'.[5] Shared ownership schemes aim to offer the purchaser the opportunity to get a foot on the housing ladder, but are in fact a misnomer; there is no sharing of ownership at all. In return for an initial premium paid to a housing provider (most typically a housing association),[6] the purchaser (referred to throughout this chapter as the 'shared owner') is granted a 'shared ownership lease' of a 99-year term. The premium paid for the lease (which may be funded using commercially available mortgage finance) is calculated according to the percentage of the market value of the property that the purchaser is able to afford (generally between 25 and 75 per cent);[7] this is the share of the property that the shared owner is said to 'own'. A sub-market rent is then paid on the unpurchased share.[8] The lease contains provisions which allow the shared owner to expand her 'ownership' interest in the property through additional capital payments to the housing provider, known as 'staircasing up'—the idea being that eventually the shared owner will have paid 100 per cent of the market value of the property. It is only at this time that the shared owner will be entitled to have the freehold to the property transferred to her by the housing provider.[9]

The shared ownership lease will usually be an assured tenancy under section 1 of the Housing Act 1988.[10] This can be surprising; the assured tenancy regime is generally associated with short-term or periodic tenancies. Most long leases granted in exchange for an initial premium will be at a rent that excludes them from the assured tenancy regime,[11] but the rent payable for a shared ownership lease will be above the level of the low-rent exclusion. This means that a shared ownership lease can be ended only by court order on one of the grounds provided in Schedule 2 to the Housing Act 1988,[12] including Ground 8, which entitles the landlord to a possession order if two months' rent is unpaid.[13] Possession under Ground 8 is mandatory; provided

---

[5] This is the most commonly used form of part ownership. In 2009–10 shared ownership accounted for 65 per cent of affordable housing sales; see Homes and Communities Agency, *Data Compendium: A Collation of Published Data about Affordable Home Ownership* (June 2011) [28].

[6] Although the Tenant Services Authority now uses the term (Private) Registered Provider of Social Housing (PRPSH), following the Housing and Regeneration Act 2008, and housing associations previously were briefly known as Registered Social Landlords (RSLs), we refer to them throughout this chapter as housing associations, as the Department for Communities and Local Government continues to do.

[7] The average stake for purchases in 2009–10 was 38.4 per cent: see Homes and Communities Agency (n 5) [22].

[8] The initial rent must not exceed three per cent of the value of the unpurchased share: see Homes and Communities Agency, *Capital Funding Guide: Housing for Sale—Shared Ownership—Rents and Service Charges* (2012–13) [4.1.2].

[9] Where shared ownership concerns a flat, staircasing to 100 per cent has the effect that the rent reduces to a minimum rent and the clauses of the lease connected to shared ownership cease to have effect. The shared owner is therefore left with a standard long lease of the flat.

[10] Lettings by social landlords come within the Housing Act 1988; it is only local authority lettings that are secure tenancies governed by the Housing Act 1985.

[11] Tenancies let at a low rent (£1,000 or less a year in London, £250 or less a year elsewhere) are not assured tenancies: Housing Act 1988, sch 1, para 3A(b). Some long residential leases granted in recent years will also be above the low rent limit and thus, perhaps unexpectedly, come within the assured tenancy regime.

[12] Housing Act 1988, s 5.

[13] The entitlement based on two months' unpaid rent is for rent payable monthly; if payable weekly, the requirement is eight weeks' unpaid rent; if payable quarterly or annually, the requirement is one-quarter's rent in arrears of more than three months and three months' rent in arrears of more than three months respectively.

the rent arrears exist both at the time that notice is served and at the date of the hearing, the court must order possession, even if it appears unreasonable on the particular facts. Research has shown that district judges dislike the mandatory nature of Ground 8,[14] but it is particularly unfair if used in the shared ownership context.

Richardson v Midland Heart[15] shows how Ground 8 can shatter the dreams of shared owners. In 1995 Miss Richardson paid £29,500 (representing 50 per cent of the market value of the property) for a 99-year shared ownership lease. Her husband was sentenced to eight years' imprisonment in 2003, and shortly after that she began receiving threats from his former associates. This led to her fleeing the property and residing at a women's refuge. As she no longer lived in the house, her housing benefit was stopped in February 2005 and rent arrears began to accrue. She unsuccessfully attempted to sell the property,[16] which was then worth £151,000, and in the meantime arrears continued to build up. Finally, in January 2006, the housing association was granted possession of the property under Ground 8.[17] At the time when the possession order was granted, Miss Richardson owed 16 months' rent arrears, amounting to £3,009.

Miss Richardson subsequently sought to recover her 50 per cent share in the property, which by 2005 was valued at around £75,000. Her claim was based on arguments of private law, all of which were rejected—albeit with regret—by Jonathan Gaunt QC, sitting as a Deputy High Court Judge. Miss Richardson did not, in fact, have any 'ownership' of the home at all.

Miss Richardson lost everything—her home and her capital. The housing association received an unanticipated and unjust windfall: it did not simply get back the property, but also got to keep the value of Miss Richardson's share in the house.[18] If this had been a forfeiture case, there would have been the possibility of relief against forfeiture, and in considering whether to grant relief, courts take account of proportionality as well as the justice of the landlord retaining any advantage received from forfeiture.[19] Alternatively, the court may have decided to order sale in preference to forfeiture (enabling Miss Richardson to retain her share of the value).[20] Instead, the lease was ended and Miss Richardson got nothing.

Some may argue that there is no injustice here. Miss Richardson got the lease she bargained for. Possession and its consequences were part and parcel of that bargain;

---

[14] C Hunter et al, 'The Exercise of Judicial Discretion in Rent Arrears Cases', DCA Research Series 6/05 (October 2005) 90.

[15] *Richardson v Midland Heart* [2008] L & TR 31.

[16] Although the judge noted that there was no evidence to support this view, he commented that it may not have sold because of 'the state of repair and decoration ... [as] the house had suffered a degree of vandalism in Miss Richardson's absence'. See ibid [6].

[17] Midland Heart is not alone in using Ground 8 in shared ownership cases: see H Pawson et al, *Rent Arrears Management Practices in the Housing Association Sector* (Tenant Services Agency, March 2010) 81.

[18] In *Richardson*, the housing association made an ex gratia payment to Miss Richardson of her initial premium, with rent arrears deducted. But, as noted by the judge (at [24]), this did not take into account Miss Richardson's share in the uplift of the property's value (£45,000), which went to the housing association as a windfall.

[19] See *Southern Depot Co Ltd v British Railways Board* [1990] 2 EGLR 39, 44.

[20] See *Khar v Delbounty Ltd* (1998) 75 P & CR 232; the landlord would have to account to the shared owner for the balance of the sale proceeds after deduction of costs and arrears.

Miss Richardson ran the risk of possession if she became unable to pay the rent. We consider this argument to be inadequate as it does not take into account either the fact that there may be alternative options to possession that adequately protect the landlord's interests (which we raise in Part II of this chapter) or the wider context in which shared ownership has been promoted by governments as a means of enabling those on low incomes to get onto the housing ladder, with the attendant prospect of asset appreciation and security.

Bright and Hopkins have previously shown that private law arguments are unlikely to enable Miss Richardson, and other shared owners in her situation, to recover the value of lost shares.[21] Accordingly, this chapter focuses primarily on the question of whether public law can protect a shared owner's 'investment value'[22] in her property. This could be achieved by postponing possession temporarily to give the shared owner the opportunity to sell the property herself. Shared owners enjoy rights of alienation, albeit that the leases are drafted to encourage the shared owner to sell the property to a purchaser nominated by her landlord rather than on the open market. Crucially, however, on a sale of the property, the shared owner is entitled to receive the proceeds of the sale in proportion to the share owned. Therefore, shared owners have an expectation of receiving both their initial investment and any uplift arising through increases in the market value of the property (and carry the risk of a fall in property values). If possession has already been granted, then the question is whether public law can protect the investment value by enabling the shared owner to recover her share of the property's market value from the landlord. While our principal concern is with protecting the shared owner's investment, we also acknowledge that in some circumstances it might be (more) appropriate for the shared owner to be able to stay in the house, that is, for the 'use value'[23] to be protected.

This chapter is structured as follows. Part II considers whether Article 8 of the European Convention on Human Rights (ECHR) (the right to respect for the home) or Article 1 of the First Protocol to the ECHR (A1-P1) (the right to peaceful enjoyment of possessions) could be utilised to defend possession proceedings. In Part III we consider whether possession proceedings could be defended in the alternative through administrative law by questioning whether the decision to seek possession using Ground 8 could be said to be irrational or could constitute a breach of a legitimate expectation. Part IV considers the scenario where a housing association has already recovered possession of shared ownership property and examines whether human rights arguments provide the basis for a claim which would allow the shared owner to recoup her share of the market value of the property, thereby protecting the investment value.

---

[21] See S Bright and N Hopkins, '*Richardson v Midland Heart Ltd*: Low Cost Home Ownership— Legal Issues of the Shared Ownership Lease' [2009] *Conv* 337, discussing resulting and constructive trusts, *Pallant v Morgan* trusts, estoppel and unjust enrichment.

[22] This term and 'use value' (to which we refer below) are discussed in more depth in Bright and Hopkins (n 3). Put briefly, by 'investment value' we mean the shared owner's financial interest in the property.

[23] By this we mean the importance attached by the shared owner to using the property as 'home', as shelter, as the centre of community and so on.

II. DEFENDING POSSESSION PROCEEDINGS: THE ECHR

This Part looks at whether the shared owner can defend possession proceedings by using human rights law. We are not (necessarily) arguing that she should be able to stay in the property for the longer term—given that non-payment of rent involves the breach of important lease obligations, this may be inappropriate. Instead, we are using the argument to buy time, preventing possession so that the shared owner has the chance to recoup the investment value of the property through sale.

The Human Rights Act (HRA) 1998, through which the ECHR is given domestic effect, applies only to public authorities. In publicly funded shared ownership schemes, the landlord is likely to be a housing association rather than a local authority, but the provisions of the HRA 1998 will usually still apply. Section 6(3)(b) of the HRA 1998 provides that a 'public authority' for the purposes of the Act includes what some call 'hybrid' public authorities, defined by the Act as 'any person certain of whose functions are of a public nature'. The leading case on what may constitute a 'hybrid' public authority is *R (Weaver) v London Quadrant Housing Trust*,[24] in which the Court of Appeal formulated a number of factors which are indicative of a body that exercises 'public functions'. These include: whether the body is in receipt of public funds; whether the body may exercise statutory powers; whether the body provides a public service; and whether the body undertakes a role similar to that of central government or a local authority. The court also stated that the concept of a hybrid public authority is to be given a 'broad and generous interpretation'.[25]

Many non-profit housing associations receive social funding in the form of social housing grants, provide subsidised housing (which is a governmental function), have charitable status and act in the 'public interest', as well as being able to exercise certain statutory powers, such as applying for Anti-Social Behaviour Orders.[26] Following *Weaver*, it is therefore likely that non-profit housing associations which offer shared ownership leases will be classified as 'hybrid' public authorities under section 6(3)(b) of the HRA 1998.

However, it is not sufficient that the housing association performs a public function and is a hybrid public authority; the particular act in question (allocation of housing, termination, etc) must also be a public act rather than a private one.[27] Following *Weaver*, seeking possession is highly likely to constitute a public act: the act of terminating a social tenancy[28] is so bound up in the function of providing social housing that, if the latter constitutes a 'public function', the former must constitute a 'public act'.[29] This chapter therefore proceeds on the basis that a shared ownership lease may only be terminated in a way which is consistent with the shared owner's rights under the ECHR.

---

[24] *R (Weaver) v London Quadrant Housing Trust* [2009] EWCA Civ 587, [2010] 1 WLR 363.
[25] Ibid [72].
[26] Crime and Disorder Act 1998, s 1(1A)(ca).
[27] Human Rights Act 1998, s 6(5).
[28] The Housing and Regeneration Act 2008, ss 68 and 70 classifies shared ownership as social housing.
[29] See *Weaver* (n 24) [76]–[80]. Although *Weaver* involved the termination of an assured tenancy, the argument applies equally to the allocation and termination of LCHO products.

A. Article 8 of the ECHR

Article 8 has in recent years been used frequently to challenge possession proceedings brought by social landlords. A sustained clash between the European Court of Human Rights (ECtHR) and domestic courts[30] was finally brought to an end by the Supreme Court in *Manchester City Council v Pinnock*, where a panel of nine Justices held that any 'person at risk of being dispossessed of his home at the suit of a local authority should in principle have the right to raise the question of the proportionality of the measure, and to have it determined by an independent tribunal in the light of article 8'.[31] Soon afterwards came the seven-person Supreme Court decision in *Hounslow LBC v Powell*,[32] which focused on the practical application of *Pinnock*.

There has yet to be a reported decision on whether an Article 8 defence raised in the context of proceedings brought under Ground 8 requires the court to consider proportionality in deciding whether to order possession. However, the results of *Pinnock* and *Powell* suggest that it does. In both cases, the tenants had no security,[33] and although the relevant statutory provisions seemingly gave no discretion to the court (like Ground 8), it was held that they must be read in such a way as to enable a court to take account of proportionality if Article 8 was raised.[34] Therefore, following *Pinnock* and *Powell*, it appears that where a mandatory ground for possession (such as Ground 8) is relied upon, proportionality must be considered if the tenant relies on Article 8 as an arguable defence.

i. The Substantive Challenge under Article 8

Article 8 reads:

Everyone has the right to respect for his private and family life, his home and his correspondence.

There shall be no interference by a public authority with the exercise of this right except such as is in accordance with the law and is necessary in a democratic society in the interests of national security, public safety or the economic well-being of the country, for the prevention of disorder or crime, for the protection of health or morals, or for the protection of the rights and freedoms of others.

---

[30] See S Nield, 'Clash of the Titans: Article 8, Occupiers, and their Home' in S Bright (ed), *Modern Studies in Property Law: Volume 6* (Oxford, Hart Publishing, 2011).

[31] *Manchester City Council v Pinnock* [2011] UKSC 6, [2010] 3 WLR 1441 [45].

[32] *Hounslow LBC v Powell* [2011] UKSC 8, [2011] 2 WLR 287.

[33] *Pinnock* concerned a demoted tenancy; *Powell* involved introductory tenancies and a tenant housed under pt 7 of the Housing Act 1996.

[34] In *Pinnock* this was achieved by using s 3 of the HRA 1998 to 'read in' to the legislation a requirement that the notice procedure had to be 'lawfully followed', which allowed consideration of 'whether the procedure had been lawfully followed, having regard to the defendant's article 8 rights' (see Lord Neuberger at [2011] UKSC 6, [2010] 3 WLR 1441 [77]). This approach was followed by Lord Hope in *Powell* (at [2011] UKSC 8, [2011] 2 WLR 287 [56]). However, Lord Phillips (who wrote a minority concurring judgment in *Powell*) appeared to approach the task of interpretation in a different manner. He stated (at [2011] UKSC 8, [2011] 2 WLR 287 [98]) that 'the precise formulation of the proviso required by article 8 is of no significance ... compatibility can be achieved ... by implying the phrase "provided that article 8 is not infringed"'.

Where a public authority seeks possession of a person's home, Article 8 is engaged due to the interference with the tenant's 'home' rights.[35] Any measure which interferes with Article 8 rights must pursue a legitimate aim in accordance with the law by answering a 'pressing social need' and the measure used to pursue that aim must be 'necessary in a democratic society'. In practice, this is now taken to mean that it is necessary to show both that possession pursues a legitimate aim and that it is a proportionate means of achieving that aim.

ii. Pursuit of a Legitimate Aim

In *Pinnock*, it was said that 'there will be no need, in the overwhelming majority of cases, for the local authority to explain and justify its reasons for seeking a possession order'.[36] This view was based on the fact that, in the majority of cases, the twin aims identified in *Pinnock* were satisfactory for the purposes of Article 8. These twin aims were: first, vindicating the authority's ownership rights; and, second, enabling the authority to comply with its public duties in relation to the allocation and management of its housing stock.[37]

But shared ownership operates very differently from the social housing statutory regimes under consideration in the *Pinnock* and *Powell* cases.[38] In *Powell*, Lord Hope placed emphasis on the fact that Parliament had already carefully decided who is to have security and who is not under the Housing Act 1985 to reflect the perceived housing management needs of local authorities.[39] This is not the case with shared ownership. First, no particular parliamentary attention has been given to the way in which shared ownership is structured legally.[40] Second, shared owners have not been deliberately placed into a class of occupiers for whom there is no security, unlike the occupiers under consideration in *Pinnock* and *Powell*. The absence of security is probably an unanticipated consequence of the legal model used to deliver shared ownership. It is likely that prior to *Richardson*, most people would have assumed that termination of a shared ownership lease would be governed by the usual rules on forfeiture, giving the possibility of relief against forfeiture being available. Indeed, it is notable that only after the decision in *Richardson* was a 'key information' sheet annexed to the standard model leases, which includes the warning:

> You need to be aware that if the Leaseholder fails to pay the rent reserved by the Lease and/or fails to observe and perform his or her obligations in the Lease the Landlord may be entitled to terminate the lease (subject to the Landlord obtaining any necessary court

---

[35] See *Kay v United Kingdom* (2012) 54 EHRR 30 [68]: 'The loss of one's home is the most extreme form of interference with the right to respect for the home.'

[36] *Pinnock* (n 31) [53].

[37] Ibid [52].

[38] The demoted and introductory tenancies under consideration in *Pinnock* and *Powell* were set up to deal with the problem of anti-social behaviour; the licence granted under the homelessness legislation in *Powell* was part of the response to the need for housing authorities to be able to respond flexibly and quickly to homelessness situations.

[39] *Powell* (n 32) [10].

[40] As we note in Part I above, it is surprising that the shared ownership lease falls within the assured tenancy regime.

order). If the lease is terminated the Leaseholder will lose (and will not be entitled to any compensation for) any shares in the property which he or she had acquired.[41]

Third, the first aim in *Pinnock* is to do with vindication of ownership—in shared ownership cases, ownership itself is split between the housing association and the tenant.[42] Fourth, account should be taken of the aim of shared ownership: unlike rental social housing, it is about more than simply providing a roof over one's head; it is also intended to enable a capital asset to be built up.[43]

In practice, both the European and domestic courts readily find that there is a legitimate aim, and in *Pinnock* and *Powell*, the Supreme Court, although cautious about the use of the language of 'exceptionality', clearly thought that in 'virtually every case' a possession order would be proportionate.[44] However, this evaluation was, as the Justices were careful to note, context-specific. In the context of the kind of housing management issues involved in those cases and the statutory schemes involved, it is unsurprising that very strong weight would be attached to the two legitimate aims identified and that when it came to the balancing exercise involved in proportionality, only very special (exceptional) personal circumstances were likely to lead to a finding of disproportionality.

In shared ownership cases, quite different considerations are involved; shared ownership properties are not part of the regular rented housing stock that is seen as available for housing those in need or on waiting lists. Rather, they are made available to facilitate entry into the home ownership market and involve potential loss of housing stock if the purchaser eventually 'staircases' up to a full equity share.

If the shared owner is in arrears with rent, although it may appear reasonable to recover possession in order to vindicate the landlord's ownership rights and to protect the economic well-being of the country,[45] there may be other, less intrusive measures that could be taken in order to achieve these legitimate aims. This includes, most obviously, allowing the shared owner to sell the property or alternatively using the more flexible remedy of forfeiture (as against a mandatory ground for possession like Ground 8). More imaginative means of protecting the landlord's financial interests could also be explored: for example, utilising a sale and rent-back arrangement or converting the rent arrears into a larger equity share for the landlord. This raises a further issue: although the aims of possession are legitimate, is it proportionate that the housing association should acquire a windfall at the expense of the shared owner?

---

[41] The Key Information sheet is available at: www.homesandcommunities.co.uk/cfg?page_id=6169 &page=155.

[42] For more detailed information on this point, see Bright and Hopkins (n 3).

[43] See Part I above.

[44] *Pinnock* (n 31) [54]. In *Powell* (n 32) [41], Lord Hope said that the twin aims identified in *Pinnock* 'should always be taken for granted' and only if a 'seriously arguable' defence is put forward, based on 'factual objections' and 'personal circumstances', will the court need to adjourn the case to consider issues of 'lawfulness or proportionality'. It is also worth noting the 'margin of appreciation' doctrine developed by the ECtHR. This is essentially an area of discretion within which a state is entitled to operate when, among other things, deciding whether a certain legitimate aim exists. If a court finds that a state has operated within its margin of appreciation when making a decision, the ECtHR will not usually substitute its judgment for that of the state. For more information on this concept, see R Clayton and H Tomlinson, *The Law of Human Rights: Volume 1*, 2nd edn (Oxford, Oxford University Press, 2009) paras [6.42] and following.

[45] This combination of legitimate aims was accepted by the ECtHR in *Kryvitska and Kryvitskyy v Ukraine* (App No 30856/03) (unreported) [56].

iii. Proportionality

As Hickman notes, despite having now accepted proportionality as a principle of English public law, domestic courts have yet to formulate a clear and principled approach to proportionality.[46] In *Powell*, the Supreme Court was invited to adopt the structured approach to proportionality developed in the leading immigration case of *Huang v Secretary of State for the Home Department*.[47] This would have required consideration of whether the grant of possession, taking full account of all considerations weighing in favour of the occupant, would prejudice the occupier's right to respect for the home in a manner sufficiently serious to amount to a breach of the fundamental rights protected by Article 8. In *Powell*, this was expressly rejected by Lord Hope due to fears that it would give rise to the risk of prolonged and expensive litigation and therefore, 'in the context of a statutory regime that has been deliberately designed by Parliament', it would be wholly inappropriate. But, as noted above, the statutory regime that governs shared ownership leases has not been 'deliberately designed by Parliament', unlike those being considered in *Powell*. As a result, it could be said that the structured approach to proportionality developed in *Huang* may well be appropriate for shared ownership cases, notwithstanding its rejection in *Powell*.

In the more usual (non-shared ownership) tenancy possession cases, the argument that possession would be disproportionate would have to take into account the particular context in which the possession claim is being made, including considerations such as how long the occupier has been living in the home, whether there are children involved, the health of the occupier, particular vulnerabilities and so on.

Of course, some of these personal and context-specific considerations may be equally applicable to the shared owner's claim that possession will be disproportionate. But the primary argument for the shared owner is a bigger one: that it will always be disproportionate to use Ground 8 where shared ownership is in issue. In the shared ownership context, when the landlord recovers possession, the occupier does not merely lose the roof over her head (the use value).[48] Home ownership offers financial benefits, in particular the investment value, as well as non-financial benefits, such as providing a sense of place and permanence.[49] For the shared owner, the ability to build a capital asset is integral to the meaning of 'home'. It is this combination of impacts that makes it likely that mandatory termination of the lease, with the concomitant loss of the shared owner's share in the property, will be found to be disproportionate and in breach of the shared owner's Article 8 rights.

Admittedly, this argument relies on an expansive understanding of 'home' within Article 8. Existing ECtHR case law shows that 'home' has an autonomous meaning,

---

[46] T Hickman, 'The Structure and Substance of Proportionality' [2008] *PL* 694, 695.

[47] *Huang v Secretary of State for the Home Department* [2007] UKHL 11, [2007] 2 AC 167. The approach to proportionality in *Huang* was itself developed from the Privy Council's formulation of proportionality in *De Freitas v Permanent Secretary of Ministry of Agriculture, Fisheries, Lands and Housing* [1999] 1 AC 69, which requires that the means used to impair the right must go no further than is necessary to accomplish the legitimate aim. This formulation, known as the 'minimal impairment test', has been cited with approval in numerous House of Lords cases and has been described as 'firmly established as the test of proportionality in domestic law': Hickman (n 46) 701.

[48] In the *Richardson* case, Miss Richardson had had to leave her home and so it no longer provided 'use value' to her, but the other values associated with home ownership remained.

[49] For fuller discussion, see Bright and Hopkins (n 3).

as a place of residence with which the individual has 'sufficient and continuing links',[50] and it has also been given a broad interpretation at the domestic level.[51] These links are not dependent on, or limited by, property rights, but look to the social and psychological attachment that a person has with a dwelling and its location.[52] A home is 'not just a place where one lives but also the place where one feels one belongs'.[53] While 'home' may begin with the physical structure, it also embodies values closely associated with personhood. The idea of home within Article 8 can thus readily encompass the non-financial benefits that flow from home ownership. Our argument is that, in addition, taking account of the policy reasons underlying the promotion of LCHO and the emphasis placed by successive governments on the idea of it providing a secure nest egg, the courts' interpretations of 'home' could—and should—be developed to reflect the investment value.

B. Article 1 of the First Protocol of the ECHR

In contradistinction to Article 8, the investment value connected to home ownership, but not the non-financial benefits, fits readily within the ambit of A1-P1.

A1-P1, entitled 'protection of property', reads:

> Every natural or legal person is entitled to the peaceful enjoyment of his possessions. No one shall be deprived of his possessions except in the public interest and subject to the conditions provided for by law and by the general principles of international law.

> The preceding provisions shall not, however, in any way impair the right of a State to enforce such laws as it deems necessary to control the use of property in accordance with the general interest or to secure the payment of taxes or other contributions or penalties.

The protection of 'possessions' in the first sentence of A1-P1 guarantees, in substance, the right to property.[54] Within its scope fall all rights and interests constituting assets, broadly understood, as explained by the ECtHR in *Stretch v United Kingdom*:

> The Court recalls that, according to the established case law of the Convention organs, "possessions" can be "existing possessions" or assets, including claims, in respect of which the applicant can argue that he has at least a "legitimate expectation" of obtaining effective enjoyment of a property right.[55]

In order for a shared owner to use A1-P1 to prevent the lease being ended, it would have to be shown that termination is an interference with 'possessions' (the 'interference' question), which is not 'in the public interest' (the 'justification' question).

[50] *Gillow v United Kingdom* (1986) 11 EHRR 335.

[51] *R (Countryside Alliance) v Attorney General* [2007] UKHL 52, [2008] 1 AC 719, 745, citing *Niemietz v Germany* (1993) 16 EHRR 97 to illustrate that 'home' can 'cover premises other than the place where a person lays his or her head at night'.

[52] A Busye, 'Strings Attached: The Concept of Home in the Case Law of the ECHR' (2006) *European Human Rights Law Review* 294.

[53] Ibid, 296.

[54] *Marckx v Belgium* (1979) 2 EHRR 330 [63].

[55] *Stretch v United Kingdom* (2004) 38 EHRR 12 [32].

In substance, the justification question leads to a proportionality analysis. The 'possession' that we argue is interfered with is the shared ownership lease and all the rights of ownership flowing from the lease as a legal estate. This includes the power to sell and to recoup the investment at the current market value. In this way, the shared owner's interest in the investment value of the property is brought into play directly, rather than requiring it to be introduced indirectly as an element of the shared owner's home rights under Article 8.

Although in *Pinnock* and *Powell* the Supreme Court was considering Article 8 only, it follows as a matter of principle that the domestic courts must be similarly required to consider whether making a possession order would breach the occupier's A1-P1 rights where it is engaged and an arguable defence is raised.[56]

i. The 'Interference' Question

Although this is not evident from the wording of A1-P1, the ECtHR has treated A1-P1 as containing three rules:

The *first* rule, which is of a general nature, enounces the principle of peaceful enjoyment of property; it is set out in the first sentence of the first paragraph.

The *second* rule covers deprivation of possessions and subjects it to certain conditions; it appears in the second sentence of the same paragraph.

The *third* rule recognises that states are entitled, amongst other things, to control the use of property in accordance with the general interest, by enforcing such laws as they deem necessary for the purpose; it is contained in the second paragraph.[57]

The approach of the ECtHR is to classify an interference with possessions under one or more of these three rules. The second rule ('deprivation' of possessions) is said to apply to someone who is deprived of ownership, meaning 'the extinction of all the legal rights of the owner by operation of law or the exercise of a legal power to the same effect'.[58] In contrast, the third rule ('control of use' of possessions) typically involves the elimination of one of the incidents of ownership, thus constituting interference with possessions, but not to the extent required under the second rule.[59]

---

[56] In the same manner as discussed in section A of Part II in relation to art 8.

[57] *Sporrong and Lonnroth v Sweden* (1983) 5 EHRR 35 [61] (emphasis added).

[58] See Clayton and Tomlinson (n 44) para [18.104], citing *Lithgow v United Kingdom* (1986) 8 EHRR 329 [107].

[59] There is, of course, a considerable literature about the nature of ownership. Harris argues that there is an 'ownership spectrum', which ranges from 'mere property' to 'full-blooded ownership'. Where one falls on this spectrum depends upon the nature and extent of the 'property-limitation' and 'expropriation' rules to which a particular item of property is subject, and the nature and extent of the 'open-ended' use privileges and powers to control the 'owner' is said to enjoy in relation to that property (see JW Harris, *Property and Justice* (Oxford, Oxford University Press, 1996)). However, the 'bundle of rights' view is still the dominant theoretical view. This sees property as comprised of a multiplicity of rights rather than a single, unitary right of 'property' or 'ownership', ie a right to possess, a right to use, a right to manage, a right to the income, a right to the capital, a right to alienate, a right to security and so on. See AM Honoré, *Making Law Bind: Essays Legal and Philosophical* (Oxford, Clarendon Press, 1987). For supporters of this approach, see: J Waldron, *The Right to Private Property* (Oxford, Clarendon Press, 1998) 47–53, 59–60; L Becker, *Property Rights: Philosophic Foundations* (London, Routledge, 1977) 11–21; S Munzer, *A Theory of Property* (Cambridge, Cambridge University Press, 1990) 22–36. Adopting this analogy, taking one of these sticks from the bundle is likely to be a control of use; taking all of the sticks will be a deprivation. Where the line is to be drawn is unclear.

Examples of measures which have been held to constitute a 'control of use' include planning controls[60] and rent control.[61]

The analytical value of approaching A1-P1 on the basis of three separate rules has been questioned, and in some cases the ECtHR has considered it unnecessary to decide whether an interference falls within the second or third rules, pointing out that the second rule is merely a specific example of the general principle enunciated in the first rule.[62] However, in other cases, the classification as to which 'rule' the case falls under has been influential on the outcome, because interferences falling under the second rule may be subject to a proportionality inquiry of a greater intensity than those falling within the third rule[63]—in particular, in the absence of compensation to justify a deprivation of possessions, the ECtHR will almost always find that A1-P1 has been breached.[64]

On first impressions, it may seem obvious that the termination of a lease which results in a shared owner losing her home and—importantly—losing the 'share' that she has bought in the property will be a deprivation of possessions and will therefore not be justified in the absence of compensation. However, it is far from clear that this is the case, and there are two particular difficulties in the analysis.

The first difficulty relates to classification: under the ECtHR's A1-P1 jurisprudence, it is not straightforward into which of the rules any particular interference will fall. This is illustrated by *JA Pye (Oxford) Ltd v United Kingdom*.[65] The majority in the Grand Chamber of the ECtHR held that the English scheme of adverse possession constituted a 'control of use' of property under the third rule.[66] This contrasts with the analysis of the Chamber which had held that the cumulative effect of the statutory provisions of the Land Registration and Limitation Acts was to transfer beneficial ownership of the land from one individual to another and therefore constituted a deprivation of possessions (within the second rule).[67] The fact that the Grand Chamber preferred the analysis that there was a control of use (the third rule) demonstrates the difficult task in drawing a line between the three rules.

---

[60] *Pine Valley Developments v Ireland* (1991) 14 EHRR 319.

[61] *Mellacher v Austria* (1990) 12 EHRR 391.

[62] See Clayton and Tomlinson (n 44) para [18.99], citing *Beyeler v Italy* (2001) 33 EHRR 52 [106] and *Broniowski v Poland* (2005) 40 EHRR 21 [135]–[136]. See also *Gladysheva v Russia* [2012] HLR 19 [71].

[63] See Clayton and Tomlinson (n 44) para [18.131].

[64] See section B(ii) of Part II below.

[65] *JA Pye (Oxford) Ltd v United Kingdom* (2008) 46 EHRR 45 (Grand Chamber).

[66] The case concerned adverse possession as it operated within the regime of the Land Registration Act 1925 (the later Land Registration Act 2002 operates differently). It was decided on the basis that the proportionality test was satisfied: a fair balance *had* been struck between the interests of the individuals and the community. However, the court was split 10:7, with a dissenting judgment arguing that a fair balance *had not* been struck, in large part down to the absence of compensation for the holder of the paper title. The majority considered that compensation was only an important factor in second rule (deprivation of possessions) cases; the dissenting judgment disagreed. Arguably, if the case were categorised as falling within the second rule, the absence of compensation would have tipped the balance in the proportionality inquiry.

[67] *Pye* (n 65) [60].

Domestic courts have not devoted much attention to the issue of what exactly constitutes 'control of use'.[68] Instead, a common-sense approach has been taken; it has been stated (in a context outside of A1-P1) that 'whether a law or exercise of an administrative power does amount to a deprivation of property depends of course on the substance of the matter rather than upon the form'.[69] This suggests that a domestic court would treat the termination of a lease as falling within the second rule of deprivation of possessions. Indeed, subject to the discussion below on the 'inherent limitation' difficulty, it is hard to see how it could be seen as anything other than a deprivation of possessions. *Pennycook v Shaws (EAL) Ltd* implicitly supports this view, as the Court of Appeal held that the service of a counter-notice under the Landlord and Tenant Act 1954 which had the effect of denying the tenant of the opportunity to renew its lease (effectively bringing the leasehold relationship to an end) was a deprivation of possessions, albeit one justified on the facts.[70]

The second difficulty relates to a doctrine known as 'inherent limitation':[71] when the interference reflects a burden or qualification to which the possession was already subject at the point of acquisition, this will not count as an interference with possessions and as a result A1-P1 will not be engaged. An example might be that if a purchaser acquires land which is subject to a right of way, she cannot then complain that her land is interfered with when that right of way is exercised.[72] The challenge is to explain where the line is drawn between an interference, such as the exercise of an easement, that should not engage A1-P1 and an interference that should.

As Harris points out, all ownership rights in land are subject to property limitation rules and expropriation rules; for example, the risk of compulsory purchase.[73] If land is bought and later taken by compulsory purchase, this is something that should be treated as an interference with possessions so as to engage A1-P1 (although as compensation is paid under compulsory purchase laws, the interference will most likely be justified). To argue that compulsory purchase is not an interference on the basis that the land (possession) was inherently limited by this possibility even when originally bought would be a nonsense, as it denudes A1-P1 of any sensible

---

[68] Although they have followed the Strasbourg jurisprudence in treating adverse possession as a 'control of use'. See *Ofulue v Bossert* [2008] EWCA Civ 7, [2009] Ch 1.

[69] See *Grape Bay Ltd v Attorney General of Bermuda* [2000] 1 WLR 574 (PC) 583. This concerned a complaint that a legislative provision preventing the applicant from running a franchise in Bermuda was a deprivation of property without compensation under the Constitution of Bermuda.

[70] *Pennycook v Shaws (EAL) Ltd* [2004] EWCA Civ 1000, [2004] Ch 296. On the other hand, it is difficult to distinguish the Grand Chamber's decision in *Pye*: there are clearly differences between *Pye* and *Pennycook*/shared ownership cases at a formal level, but it is hard to see the substantive differences as the practical outcome in each is the removal of all ownership powers from the (former) owner/tenant.

[71] This term is not intended to refer to the doctrine of implied limitations on Convention rights, which provides that certain rights which appear 'absolute' under the Convention are in fact subject to implicit limitations. This doctrine appears most frequently in the ECtHR's case law on access to the courts under art 6 of the Convention. For example, in *Golder v United Kingdom*, the ECtHR said: 'The Court considers ... that the right of access to the courts is not absolute. As this is a right which the Convention set forth without, in the narrower sense of the term, defining it, there is room, apart from the bounds delimiting the very content of any right, for limitation permitted by implication.' See Clayton and Tomlinson (n 44) paras [6.202] and following.

[72] See *Aston Cantlow and Wilmcote with Billesley Parochial Church Council v Wallbank* [2003] UKHL 37, [2004] 1 AC 546.

[73] See Harris (n 59) 33–38.

content.[74] Yet, as Goymour and Gardner both illustrate, there is no convincing way to articulate exactly when the 'inherent limitation' argument will prevent there being an interference with possessions and when it will not.[75] At the end of the day, it may come down to little more than a legally based intuition that termination of a shared ownership lease is the sort of interference that engages A1-P1.

ii. The 'Justification' Question

Any interference with the rights protected by A1-P1 must be justified. In *Stretch v United Kingdom*, the ECtHR explained that 'an interference must strike a "fair balance" between the demands of the general interests of the community and the requirements of the individual's fundamental rights'.[76]

There are two connected issues here. First, any deprivation must be in the public interest; legislative measures which interfere with possessions must be subject to conditions provided for by law and must pursue a legitimate aim. As discussed above in relation to Article 8, a housing association would most likely seek to advance as its legitimate aims for taking possession proceedings against a shared owner the protection of its ownership rights coupled with protecting the economic well-being of the country.[77]

The second connected issue is that the interference must strike a 'fair balance' between the interests of the community and individual rights. In substance, this amounts to a proportionality analysis: the means employed must be proportionate to the aims pursued and must not impose an excessive burden on an individual. The provision of compensation is relevant to the fair balance inquiry: a 'deprivation of possessions' under the second rule is unlikely to be proportionate if no compensation is paid.[78] The presence of procedural safeguards is also relevant: the ECtHR has stated that A1-P1 requires that the individual must be given a reasonable opportunity to put her case forward, 'for the purpose of *effectively* challenging the measures interfering with the rights guaranteed'.[79]

The mandatory nature of Ground 8 is important in this context.[80] Similarly, if the termination of a shared ownership lease invokes the second rule of A1-P1, the

---

[74] In *Wilson v First County Trust Ltd (No 2)* [2003] UKHL 40, [2004] 1 AC 816 [41]–[42], Lord Nicholls commented that the proposition that A1-P1 is not engaged where a property is acquired subject to limitations under the national law which subsequently bite would mean that a 'convention right guaranteeing a right to property would have nothing to say. That is not an attractive conclusion'.

[75] See A Goymour, 'Property and Housing' in D Hoffman (ed), *The Impact of the UK Human Rights Act on Private Law* (Cambridge, Cambridge University Press, 2011); and S Gardner, *An Introduction to Land Law*, 3rd edn (Oxford, Hart Publishing, 2012) 32–33.

[76] *Stretch* (n 55) [37].

[77] See section A(ii) of Part II above.

[78] See *James v United Kingdom* (1986) 8 EHRR 123 [54].

[79] *Jokela v Finland* (2003) 37 EHRR 26 [45] (emphasis added).

[80] In *Zehentner v Austria* (2011) 52 EHRR 22 [73], the ECtHR said: 'Moreover, the Court reiterates that although art 1 of Protocol No 1 contains no explicit procedural requirements, the proceedings at issue must afford the individual a reasonable opportunity of putting his or her case to the relevant authorities for the purpose of effectively challenging the measures interfering with the rights guaranteed by this provision. In ascertaining whether this condition has been satisfied, the Court takes a comprehensive view.'

absence of any compensation means that to grant possession, and thereby terminate the lease, is likely to be found to be disproportionate. Even if termination of the lease is (improbably) categorised as falling under the third rule, the absence of compensation may nevertheless violate the fair balance requirement.[81]

C. The Likelihood of Success

Both Article 8 and A1-P1 present challenges, quite apart from predicting how a judge would decide the issue of proportionality. Success under Article 8 would rely upon the court giving 'home' an expansive definition incorporating not just 'use value' but also the 'investment value'. A1-P1 requires no such judicial creativity—the protection afforded to 'possessions' under A1-P1 can encompass both.[82] However, although A1-P1 might seem a more natural Convention right to apply in the shared ownership context, the intensity of review differs from that under Article 8. Certainly, at the level of the ECtHR, it is recognised that national authorities should have space to choose how to protect Convention rights, but that this space or 'margin of appreciation' will be narrower when a right of central importance, such as the right to respect for the home, is concerned.[83] As a result, domestic courts are likely to adopt a stricter intensity of review when dealing with an argument based on Article 8.[84] Nonetheless, using a mandatory statutory ground for ending the shared ownership lease, with all of the emotional and financial consequences that this entails, is likely to be disproportionate even in the light of the more relaxed scrutiny of A1-P1, particularly since the housing association may have less intrusive means of advancing its legitimate aims.[85] This then leads on to the question of remedies: where granting the possession order would be disproportionate, what should a judge do?

D. The Outcome of a Successful Human Rights Defence

Where the heart of the proportionality argument is that the shared owner should not lose the investment value of the property, it may be appropriate to delay possession in order to give the shared owner time to sell the property. Once arrears have been repaid, this would leave the shared owner with a significant portion of her

---

[81] In *Di Palma v Victoria Square Property Co Ltd* [1984] Ch 346, 361–62, a long lease was forfeit because of service charge arrears amounting to £299.36, together with a bailiff s fee of £15. The flat, at the time of forfeiture, was worth around £30,000. The judge commented (obiter) that such a loss was a wholly disproportionate penalty .

[82] See *Gladysheva* (n 62).

[83] *Connors v United Kingdom* (2005) 40 EHRR 9 [81]–[83].

[84] The rights contained in arts 8–11 of the ECHR allow interference with Convention rights only if objectively 'necessary in a democratic society'. This text is not replicated in A1-P1; as a result, where A1-P1 is engaged but art 8 is not, the national legislature is afforded a wider margin of appreciation in tailoring the legislation to the pursuit of the legitimate aim. Indeed, the ECtHR has expressly rejected a test of strict necessity in the context of A1-P1: see *James* (n 78) [51].

[85] See the discussion above in section A(ii) of Part II.

share in the property intact. The issue of remedies was discussed by Lord Neuberger in *Pinnock*, where he said:

> [I]f domestic law justifies an outright order for possession, the effect of article 8 may, albeit in exceptional cases, justify (in ascending order of effect) granting an extended period for possession, suspending the order for possession on the happening of an event, or even refusing an order altogether.[86]

His Lordship also noted[87] that this may require certain statutory provisions to be revisited, referring to section 89 of the Housing Act 1980. Section 89 limits the period for which a mandatory possession order can be postponed to 14 days, but in cases of 'exceptional hardship', this period can be extended to six weeks. In *Powell*, Lord Hope said that it is not possible to read down section 89 to extend this period further, but that, as no evidence had been given to show that six weeks was insufficient to meet cases of exceptional hardship, he declined to make a declaration of incompatibility.[88] When discussing section 89, Lord Phillips noted that the effect of the strict section 89 time limit may 'in rare cases' cause a judge to refuse possession when it would otherwise have been granted with a longer postponement.[89]

Given that more than a six-week delay will almost certainly be needed in order to give the tenant of a shared ownership property time to sell, the effect of section 89 is that a court may need to refuse possession (or issue a declaration of incompatibility under section 4 of the HRA 1998). It is not yet possible to discern a common approach taken by the lower courts to successful arguments of proportionality. Unhelpfully, some judges continue to refer to the old Gateways (a) and (b) (and indeed also appear to confuse or conflate the two), a distinction which is no longer helpful post-*Pinnock*.[90] However, it does appear that the lower courts are willing to refuse possession orders where defences based on proportionality are successful.[91]

Of course, if the effect of the argument is to prevent possession at all, this will mean that the housing association is stuck with an occupier who is not paying her dues. It may be that after a certain length of time, a court would say that it would now be proportionate to order possession, given that the shared owner has been given adequate time to sell the property, or it could simply issue a declaration that legislative change was needed to deal with the problem.

III. DEFENDING POSSESSION PROCEEDINGS: ADMINISTRATIVE LAW

In English public law, the principle of legality requires that public bodies must act lawfully when exercising their powers. This principle is enforced through the grounds of judicial review found in the speech of Lord Diplock in *Council of Civil Service*

---

[86] *Pinnock* (n 31) [62].
[87] Ibid [63].
[88] *Powell* (n 32) [64].
[89] Ibid [103].
[90] For more detail on the gateways, see Part III below.
[91] See *Chesterfield Borough Council v Bailey* [2011] EW Misc 18 (CC); *London Borough of Southwark v Hyacienth* (unreported, 22 December 2011) (CC); *Southend-on-Sea v Armour* (unreported, 12 March 2012); a transcript of the judgment is available at www.gardencourtchambers.co.uk/imageUpload/File/SouthendvArmourJudgment.pdf; affirmed by the High Court (unreported) on 18 October 2012.

Unions v Minister for the Civil Service:[92] illegality, irrationality and procedural impropriety.

In most cases, judicial review must be brought in the Administrative Court,[93] but in *Wandsworth LBC v Winder*,[94] the House of Lords confirmed that a defendant to a civil action may challenge a public law decision in the course of defending that action, and may do so outside of the judicial review procedure.[95] This allows tenants to raise defences to possession in the county court based on the principle of legality (provided, of course, that the body seeking possession is subject to the legality principle; in other words, that it is amenable to judicial review).[96]

This type of defence was formerly known as Gateway (b), following Lord Hope's classification of the two grounds for defending a possession order in *Kay v Lambeth LBC*:

(a)   that the law which requires the court to make a possession order despite the occupier's personal circumstances is Convention-incompatible; and

(b)   that, having regard to the occupier's personal circumstances, the local authority's exercise of its power to seek a possession order is an unlawful act within the meaning of section 6 [of the HRA 1998].[97]

The *Pinnock* and *Powell* cases discussed above focused on the availability of a defence based on Gateway (a); the Supreme Court held in *Pinnock* that even when the ground for possession was mandatory, the law should be read (if possible) as allowing a consideration of proportionality. *Pinnock* and *Powell* also reaffirmed the availability of defences based on principles of public law (formerly Gateway (b)),[98] and that they could be used to challenge any prior decision on which the possession claim was founded (for example, the decision to serve a notice to quit) as well as the decision to bring possession proceedings.[99]

It is therefore open for a shared owner to utilise any argument based on the principle of legality that can be supported by the facts of her case. For instance, a shared owner may wish to argue that there is an element of procedural impropriety in the way in which the housing association has brought proceedings. Alternatively, she may wish to claim that the decision to bring possession proceedings is irrational, or that by doing so, the housing association has acted in a way which goes against a legitimate expectation held by her. Under the following two headings, these latter two arguments are considered.

---

[92]   *Council of Civil Service Unions v Minister for the Civil Service* [1985] AC 374, 410.

[93]   Senior Courts Act 1981, s 31. See also *O'Reilly v Mackman* [1983] 2 AC 237. Judicial review is governed by pt 54 of the Civil Procedure Rules.

[94]   *Wandsworth LBC v Winder* [1985] AC 461.

[95]   See also *Clark v University of Lincolnshire and Humberside* [2000] 1 WLR 1988.

[96]   In *R (Weaver) v London Quadrant Housing Trust* [2008] EWHC 1377 (Admin), [2009] 1 All ER 17, the Divisional Court approached in the same way the questions of whether a body is subject to the HRA 1998 as a hybrid public authority and of whether that body was also subject to judicial review. This approach was approved by the Court of Appeal (see [2010] EWCA Civ 587, [2010] 1 WLR 363 [83]). Therefore, this chapter proceeds on the basis that housing associations which provide shared ownership leases are amenable to judicial review on conventional public law grounds.

[97]   *Kay v Lambeth LBC* [2006] UKHL 10, [2006] 2 AC 465 [39].

[98]   *Pinnock* (n 31) [81].

[99]   *Powell* (n 32) [42]. See J Luba et al, 'Defending Possession Proceedings' (2011) *Legal Action Group* (online update) 3, available at: www.lag.org.uk/files/93674/FileName/DPP7onlineupdateforweb.pdf.

A. Irrationality

The principle of legality requires that discretionary powers—such as the decision to bring possession proceedings—must be exercised rationally. Traditionally the test for whether a public body has acted rationally is whether the exercise of power is *Wednesbury unreasonable*.[100] However, in *Kay v Lambeth LBC*[101] and *Doherty v Birmingham City Council*,[102] this ground of review was expanded to what is now known as *Wednesbury plus*, which provides for a greater intensity of review. The precise scope of *Wednesbury plus* is unclear.[103] It appears to allow a wider range of factors to be taken into account when considering whether the impugned decision was 'one which no reasonable person would consider justifiable'.[104] For instance, Lord Hope in *Doherty* stated that the considerations that can be taken into account under *Wednesbury plus* include, for example, longevity of occupation.[105]

Applying this to the shared ownership context, an argument could be made that the decision to bring possession proceedings is *Wednesbury unreasonable* in light of the potential consequences of the possession order being granted: the shared owner will lose not only her home but also her share in the market value of the property. The difficulty with this argument is, of course, that the shared owner is in default with her rent and therefore, whilst the consequences of the possession order are unfortunate, the decision to bring proceedings cannot be said to be irrational.

Furthermore, *Pinnock* and *Powell* emphasise that the focus of a defence based on judicial review principles is primarily on the decision-making process rather than on the potential effect that a possession order may have on the shared owner. Where an argument is based on the latter, the more appropriate defence is based on Article 8 (or, in the shared ownership scenario, A1-P1), whereby the specific factual circumstances of the claim can be dealt with through a proportionality inquiry. This makes the potential for a successful defence based on rationality review limited in scope in the shared ownership context, as it will inevitably play second fiddle to challenges based on Convention rights of the type discussed above.

B. Legitimate Expectations

An alternative defence based on administrative law principles could be founded on the doctrine of legitimate expectations. This is a device used to prevent public authorities from defeating, without good reason, expectations of procedural or substantive rights they have created in citizens. The doctrine of legitimate expectations aims to prevent an abuse of power by a public body and balances the individual's

---

[100] Named after the case of *Associated Provincial Picture Houses v Wednesbury Corporation* [1948] 1 KB 223.

[101] *Kay* (n 97).

[102] *Doherty v Birmingham City Council* [2008] UKHL 57, [2009] 1 AC 367.

[103] *Liverpool City Council v Doran* [2009] EWCA Civ 146, [2009] 1 WLR 2365 [50]. See also Nield (n 30).

[104] *Doherty* (n 102) [55].

[105] Ibid.

expectations against the wider public interest. A legitimate expectation that has been generated can be defeated, but only where it is proportionate for the public authority to do so, having regard to a legitimate aim pursued in the public interest.[106]

A potential claim under legitimate expectations would require a tenant to demonstrate that a public authority generated a legitimate expectation which is then defeated. One possible avenue to establish the expectation is through the shared ownership literature, which advertises 'the normal rights and responsibilities of a full owner-occupier'.[107] The argument would be that this expectation was defeated by the loss of the home and the consequent loss of the investment value, which illustrate clearly that the tenant did not have the 'normal rights and responsibilities' of a true owner. Potentially, this could be used to quash the decision to use a mandatory ground for possession as opposed to seeking forfeiture of the lease for non-payment of rent. However, given that Bright and Hopkins have doubted whether Miss Richardson would have succeeded with a private law claim to estoppel,[108] it is improbable that a legitimate expectation claim would get very far: the threshold for generating a legitimate expectation is at least as high as that for an assurance of rights for estoppel. In *Weaver*, the court noted that a legitimate expectation required a 'clear, unambiguous and unqualified promise',[109] whereas in *Thorner v Major*, the House of Lords variously described estoppel as requiring an assurance that is 'clear and unequivocal' or simply 'clear enough'.[110] In the absence of a housing association expressly informing a shared owner that it will not take possession proceedings against her and then seeking to do so, it is difficult to see how a legitimate expectation could be generated in this context.

However, if a legitimate expectation were established, the issue would then become one of proportionality, akin to the ECHR arguments discussed above. The question would be whether the housing association acted to pursue a legitimate aim in a manner that is proportionate, balancing the defeat of the tenant's expectations against the wider public interest.

C. The Outcome of a Successful Administrative Law Defence

The remedies available where a rationality or legitimate expectations argument is used to defend successfully possession proceedings are those of public law: the decision to use Ground 8 would be quashed, leaving the housing association to make the decision as to how to proceed against the tenant again. Public law claims do

---

[106] See *R (on the Application of Nadarajah) v Secretary of State for the Home Department* [2005] EWCA Civ 1363.

[107] Homes and Communities Agency, Council of Mortgage Lenders and National Housing Federation, *Shared Ownership: Joint Guidance for England* (November 2010) para [5]. The same statement has appeared in previous versions of the Joint Guidance and, notably, has been retained even after the decision in *Richardson* (n 15). In contrast, a Key Information sheet annexed to model leases provides only that the leaseholder has 'the normal responsibilities of a full owner': the sheet is available at: www.homesandcommunities.co.uk/cfg?page_id=6169&page=155.

[108] See Bright and Hopkins (n 21).

[109] *Weaver* (n 96) [87].

[110] *Thorner v Major* [2009] UKHL 18, [2009] 1 WLR 776.

not generally provide a route to financial compensation. Damages are only usually available in judicial review proceedings where they could have been claimed in private law at the time that the judicial review was sought,[111] or a private law claim may arise following a successful judicial review (for example, where the effect of finding a public authority's conduct unlawful is that a tort has been committed). The latter possibility may have particular pertinence in relation to Ground 8. If judicial review of a decision to use Ground 8 is successfully obtained after repossession has been granted, the landlord's possession of the property would be a trespass from the time of the repossession for which damages would be available.

IV. RECOVERING THE SHARE OF THE PROPERTY'S MARKET VALUE

The arguments canvassed in Parts II and III of this chapter assume that the shared owner can defend the possession claim and thus protect the 'use value' of the property, at least long enough to enable her to attempt a sale of the property. But once the lease has been terminated and the shared owner has lost the home, is there any way in which she can recover the 'investment value'? Perhaps surprisingly, the shared owner is unlikely to be able to recover her investment value under private law principles, as Bright and Hopkins have discussed elsewhere.[112] Therefore, this chapter turns once more to arguments of human rights, and also briefly mentions the potential role that could be played by ombudsmen.

A. Article 8 and A1-P1

Assuming that ending the lease involves a breach of A1-P1 and/or Article 8, section 8(1) of the HRA 1998 gives a court broad powers to award 'such relief or remedy, or make such order, within its powers as it considers just and appropriate'. Section 8(4) of the HRA 1998 states that when determining whether to award damages, domestic courts must take into account the principles applied by the ECtHR in relation to the award of compensation under Article 41 of the ECHR. Article 41, which was introduced by the Eleventh Protocol to replace Article 50, reads as follows:

> If the Court finds that there has been a violation of the Convention or the protocols thereto, and if the internal law of the High Contracting Parties allows only partial reparation to be made, the Court shall, if necessary, afford just satisfaction to the injured party.

It is therefore appropriate to consider, first of all, the ECtHR's approach to remedies under Article 41.

i. The Approach of the ECtHR to Remedies

Typically, the approach of the ECtHR to a violation of Convention rights has been to issue a declaration to that effect. This reflects the fact that the ECHR is an

---

[111] Senior Courts Act 1981, s 31(4).
[112] Bright and Hopkins (n 21).

international human rights treaty—in many cases, the applicant's primary aim in bringing proceedings is put to an end the violation of her rights. In these situations, 'just satisfaction' can be afforded without the payment of monetary compensation.

However, it is clear that the ECtHR retains a discretionary jurisdiction to award compensation in order to afford just satisfaction to the injured party. The principle of compensation is *restitutio in integrum*: the applicant is to be put back in the position she would have been in had the violation not occurred. It should be noted in this respect that in the jurisprudence of the ECtHR, compensation awarded pursuant to the principle of *restitutio in integrum* is a loss-based award, in contradistinction to a gain-based *restitutionary* one.[113]

The case law of the ECtHR in respect of its approach to the quantification of damages is not at all helpful. Practitioners and commentators searching for principles in this area are frequently frustrated. Lester and Pannick argue that the court simply makes an equitable assessment of the facts of the individual case,[114] and a former judge of the ECtHR has been reported as stating privately that the court has no principles when it comes to assessing compensation.[115] A report by the English and Scottish Law Commissions[116] distilled from the court's jurisprudence the following factors which may be taken into consideration when deciding whether to award compensation:

— the other measures taken by the public authority in remedying the breach;
— whether a finding of a breach can constitute 'just satisfaction' without the need for compensation;
— whether the loss suffered is sufficient to render an award necessary;
— the seriousness of the violation;
— the conduct of the respondent;
— the conduct of the applicant.

There may be cases where not even the payment of compensation can afford just satisfaction to the applicant. For example, in *Gladysheva v Russia*, the applicant was evicted from her flat by the state, in violation of Article 8 and A1-P1. In assessing her damages under Article 41, the Court reiterated the principle of *restitutio in integrum* and went on to state:

> Consequently, having due regard to its findings in the instant case, and in particular having noted the absence of a competing third-party interest or other obstacle to the restitution of the applicant's ownership, the Court considers that the most appropriate form of redress would be to restore the applicant's title to the flat and to reverse the order for her eviction. Thus, the applicant would be put as far as possible in a situation equivalent to the one in which she would have been had there not been a breach of Article 8 of the Convention and Article 1 of Protocol No. 1 to the Convention.[117]

---

[113] Law Commission and Scottish Law Commission, *Damages Under the Human Rights Act 1998* (Law Com No 266/Scot Law Com No 180, 2000) paras [3.19]–[3.21].

[114] A Lester, D Pannick and J Herberg, *Human Rights Law and Practice*, 3rd edn (London, LexisNexis, 2009) para [2.8.4]. See also J Varuhas, 'A Tort-Based Approach to Damages under the Human Rights Act 1998' (2009) 72 MLR 750, 756.

[115] Clayton and Tomlinson (n 44) para [21.30].

[116] Law Commission and Scottish Law Commission (n 113).

[117] *Gladysheva* (n 62) [106].

A similar award was made by the Grand Chamber in the context of an A1-P1 violation in *Brumarescu v Romania*[118] and *Papamichalopoulos v Greece*.[119] In the latter case, the Court ordered the properties in issue to be returned to the applicants (and, failing that, compensation reflecting the current market value of the houses was to be paid).

Therefore, it is clear that the ECtHR has at its disposal a wide range of remedial orders which it can utilise when seeking to afford 'just satisfaction' to the applicant. The principles that can be taken from the case law of the Court are that: first, in principle it is for the national authorities to decide the means by which *restitutio in integrum* is to be achieved—whether by compensation or otherwise;[120] and, second, where the national authority fails to afford just satisfaction to the applicant, the ECtHR is willing to make whatever order for redress that it feels appropriate.

ii. Damages under the HRA 1998

The leading English case on damages under the HRA 1998 is *R (Greenfield) v Secretary of State for the Home Department*, where a unanimous appellate committee of the House of Lords held that domestic courts were *not* free to depart from the scale of damages applied by the ECtHR (the argument was run by counsel that the courts could use domestic comparators in awarding damages).[121] Therefore, domestic courts now operate a 'mirror' approach to assessing damages under the HRA 1998, both in terms of how the discretion to award damages is to be exercised and the scales of damages applied.

iii. Application to the Shared Ownership Scenario

Where a tenant has failed to defend possession proceedings (at all, or at least successfully) and has therefore lost her home in breach of A1-P1 and/or Article 8, section 8 of the HRA 1998 requires the court to assess what relief or remedy should be granted. There appear to be two main options.

First, the court could follow the type of award made by the ECtHR in *Gladysheva*. This would involve quashing the possession order and restoring the shared owner's title. This could then enable the shared owner to sell the property (in the situation where retention is not financially viable) and by doing so recoup her investment. The shared owner may additionally seek compensation for non-pecuniary losses and

---

[118] *Brumarescu v Romania* (2001) 33 EHRR 36.

[119] *Papamichalopoulos v Greece* (1996) 21 EHRR 439.

[120] See *Dixon v United Kingdom* (App No 3468/10) (unreported), in which the ECtHR accepted that the national authority had provided the applicant with just satisfaction following a compensatory payment of £3,000, despite the applicant's argument that if art 8 had been correctly applied in his case, a possession order would never have been made.

[121] *R (Greenfield) v Secretary of State for the Home Department* [2005] UKHL 14, [2005] 1 WLR 673. HRA 1998, s 8(4) obliges domestic courts to take account of ECtHR principles in relation to the award of compensation under art 41 of the Convention. The *Greenfield* decision is unpopular: the English and Scottish Law Commissions have recommended that the principles of tort law should be drawn upon when awarding damages: Law Commission and Scottish Law Commission (n 113). See also Varuhas (n 114).

costs and expenses.[122] However, such an award may not be possible or practicable. For example, the property may have been resold following repossession or the shared owner may now be settled in a new home for which she has financial and contractual commitments as the tenant. It is worth noting that in *Gladysheva*, the court considered important the fact that there was no competing third party interest that would have been prejudiced by the reversal of the order for eviction.

Second, the court could award damages. This is subject to section 8(3) of the HRA 1998, which provides that damages can only be awarded if, after consideration of:

(a) any other relief or remedy granted, or order made, in relation to the act in question (by that or any other court), and

(b) the consequences of any decision (of that or any other court) in respect of that act,

the court is satisfied that the award is necessary to afford just satisfaction to the person in whose favour it is made.

As previously mentioned, following section 8(4) of the HRA 1998 and *Greenfield*, the domestic courts draw heavily upon ECtHR principles when assessing whether to make an award for damages (and, if so, to what amount). In the shared ownership context, the nature of the loss suffered means that compensation would be required to provide just satisfaction to the shared owner. As regards the shared owner's pecuniary loss, the principle of *restitutio in integrum* requires that the tenant be restored to the position she would have been in if the violation had not occurred. This would seem to allow an award for the tenant's share of the market value of the property at the time of the repossession (the time of the violation), less arrears owed to the housing association.[123]

B. Ombudsmen

If *Richardson v Midland Heart*[124] represents the legally correct outcome, it may nonetheless be that there remains an 'injustice' of the sort an ombudsman could investigate. Both the Housing Ombudsman[125] and the Parliamentary Ombudsman might potentially have jurisdiction. The Housing Ombudsman may well be able to investigate, for example, the decision to seek possession under Ground 8 and the accuracy of information provided by the housing association in respect of a shared ownership scheme.[126]

---

[122] 'Just satisfaction' is not confined to pecuniary loss: Law Commission and Scottish Law Commission (n 113) para 3.22.

[123] This also seems to follow the award in *Brumarescu* (n 118), save to the extent that the ECtHR based the award on the current market value.

[124] *Richardson* (n 15).

[125] The Housing Ombudsman Service was created by the Housing Act 1996, s 51 and sch 2. Under the Localism Act 2011, the jurisdiction of the Service extends to incorporate local housing authorities from 1 April 2013.

[126] The jurisdiction includes the power to order the payment of compensation: Housing Act 1996, sch 2, paras 7(1) and 7(2)(a).

There is not space here to consider these possibilities further. In any event, the ombudsman service hardly seems the appropriate forum through which to seek redress for the fundamental issues relating to the rights of shared owners, given that they stem from problematic law rather than poor administration.

V. CONCLUSION

Shared ownership has used a legal model—the long lease—that was not designed for the *sharing* of ownership. This has had unanticipated consequences, which are exposed by the injustice of the *Richardson v Midland Heart* case. It is unlikely that had anyone given serious consideration to the issue in advance, they would have intended shared owners to be vulnerable to repossession on the grounds given in the Housing Act 1988. It is much more likely that the usual termination provisions for long leases—forfeiture, with the accompanying possibility of relief against forfeiture on terms—would have been considered appropriate. It is also the case that the source of the injustice is the failure to deliver what shared ownership promises— 'the normal rights and responsibilities of a full owner-occupier'. This includes, at its core, an expectation that the financial investment in the home is 'their capital'. The product has been mis-sold and the responsibility for this is spread amongst the government and social landlords. But even if this is recognised, it does not solve the problem that arises under the model that has been used. Hence, our aim in this chapter has not been to consider alternative models for LCHO, or ways in which the existing model could be improved upon. It has a much more limited goal of finding a way to remedy the injustice that Miss Richardson and others in her position have suffered. It may be considered surprising that private law cannot help and that there is more promise in human rights arguments. The application of Article 8 and A1-P1 is not beyond doubt, but if, as we suggest, they apply to possession proceedings in the shared ownership context, we are left with the question of whether it is disproportionate to deny Miss Richardson the opportunity to recover her investment. The answer to us is clear: she should at least get back her share of the property's value.

3

The Big Society and Social Housing: Never the Twain Shall Meet?

WARREN BARR*

I. INTRODUCTION

T HE BIG SOCIETY concept or initiative has 'eluded any kind of pithy definition' since its introduction by the Coalition government in 2010,[1] but it has
remained a key element of policy ever since.[2] In simple terms, the three core
aims are: (i) empowering communities; (ii) opening up public services; and (iii) promoting social action.[3] These aims are to be met by a myriad of schemes, including
encouraging volunteering in communities, supporting charities and other voluntary
organisations or cooperatives to have a greater involvement in running public services, and increasing charitable giving.[4]

Charities are championed as the 'backbone'[5] of the Big Society as key implement-
ers and exemplars of the aims of local communities operating to implement local,
community solutions and better, more focused public services. Charities have an
enviable track record in this area,[6] and many 'successful charities [had] already
embraced the principles of Big Society, before it acquired that label'.[7]

Even the most fanatical adherent of the Big Society initiative would be forced to
admit that it has had a troubled childhood. Born at a time of deep, global recession and
wet-nursed against the backdrop of the most swingeing public sector funding cuts seen

* Senior Lecturer, Liverpool Law School. Thanks to my colleagues, Dr Ruth Lamont and Ms Debra
Morris, for their helpful comments. I am also indebted to Dr Karen Atkinson for proofreading the final
version of this piece. The usual responsibility for errors applies. This chapter states the law as at 1 August
2012. Email: wbarr@liv.ac.uk.

[1] D Morris, 'Charities and the Big Society: A Doomed Coalition?' [2012] *Legal Studies* 132.
[2] Cabinet Office, *Building the Big Society* (May 2010).
[3] Cabinet Office, *Building a Stronger Civil Society. A Strategy for Voluntary and Community Groups,
Charities and Social Enterprises* (October 2010).
[4] Cabinet Office (n 2).
[5] A Holt, 'The Big Idea' (2011) *Solicitors Journal, Charity & Appeals Supplement*, February.
[6] The first hospitals, for example, were set up by charities before the state intervened through the
National Health Service, and a significant number of charities are already involved in public service
delivery. See R Macmillan, 'The Third Sector Delivering Public Services: An Evidence Review' *Third
Sector Research Centre Working Paper 20* (Birmingham, 2010).
[7] Morris (n 1) 133.

in a generation,[8] the initiative has lost many of its advocates.[9] It has also failed to fuel the public imagination.[10] Nevertheless, the underlying principle of shrinking centrally provided services and pushing the burden onto voluntary and charitable organisations remains. It is clear that there is great unease in the charitable sector as a whole, and a strong impression that providers are being asked to do more with less through the supposedly enabling framework of the Big Society,[11] so that many charities (and other voluntary sector organisations) see the future as more challenge than opportunity.

This chapter will consider the impact of changes for charities involved in social housing provision wrought by the Big Society, either in their role as general providers taking over from retreating government functions or those providing specialist services, such as for the vulnerable. Oft-discussed changes to the shape of the regulatory framework in the social housing sector,[12] coupled with significant alterations to charity funding,[13] have fundamentally altered the basis on which these organisations operate and mean that the impact of the Big Society on such organisations cannot be considered in a vacuum.

In seeking to meet the stated aims, the chapter will consider the structural impact of the Big Society initiative on charities that are involved in the provision of social housing; the ability of charities as organisations to meet the demands of shouldering direct provision of services across the country.[14] It will seek to argue that many of the challenges faced by charities in this respect are not new, as the idea of charities providing frontline public services was a feature of the 'Third Way' initiative of the Blair government,[15] but have been brought into relief by the combination of shrinking funding and state involvement in social housing under the auspices of the Big Society and are the more potentially damaging for it.

It goes further to suggest that Big Society thinking has indirectly informed legislative change. It identifies that one of the key strands underpinning the Big Society is 'localism' or, more accurately, seeking to make decisions at a local, and sometimes individual, level.[16] To illustrate the impact of Big Society thinking, it takes this theme of 'individual decision making' as a focus of the Localism Act 2011 and

---

[8] HM Treasury, *Spending Review 2010*, Cm 7942, October 2010.

[9] Philip Blond (head of the think tank credited with the idea behind the Big Society) and Steve Hilton (then Director of Strategy) have both thrown cold water on the concept. See, for example, 'Big Society Under Pressure' *The Guardian* (24 January 2011).

[10] Liverpool, once considered a vanguard area, withdrew from the Big Society in February 2011.

[11] The impact of funding cuts and changes in taxation suggest that charities, alongside the rest of the voluntary sector, 'stand to lose an estimated £1.2bn per year' for the rest of the current Parliament (John Trickett, Labour Shadow Cabinet Office Minister, 4 April 2012; www.bbc.co.uk/news/business-17602323).

[12] See D Cowan, *Law in Context: Housing Law and Policy* (Cambridge, Cambridge University Press, 2011) ch 5 for a good summary of the debates.

[13] These changes are discussed later in the chapter.

[14] What this chapter does not seek to do is provide an ideological critique of the Big Society concept; that has been done elsewhere—see, for example, P Alcock, 'Building the Big Society: A New Policy Environment for the Third Sector in England' [2010] *Voluntary Sector Review* 379. It is instead concerned with how charitable social housing providers deal with the impact of it. It also does not deal with issues of 'homelessness', which would be deserving of an article of its own.

[15] See, eg, A Gamble, *The Third Way Revisited* September 2008 www.policy-network.net/publications; Ian Harden, *The Contracting State* (Open University Press, 1992).

[16] See Cabinet Office *Building the Big Society* (May 2010).

demonstrates how it may complicate issues of tenure for charitable social housing providers.

In conclusion, it will be suggested that despite an apparent companionship of rhetoric between the goals of the Big Society and the purposes of charitable organisations engaged in providing social housing, there are concerns that, in fact, never the twain shall meet.

II. THE ROLE OF CHARITIES IN SOCIAL HOUSING

In order to conduct any meaningful analysis, it is first necessary to outline the exact details of the role charities play within social housing and how the sector is regulated and funded.[17]

A. Charities and Social Housing

Charitable bodies are not-for-profit organisations that are both part of, and distinct from, the third sector at large, which includes many non-charitable voluntary organisations.[18] Charities must normally be registered with the Charity Commission,[19] enjoy the fiscal and other privileges associated with charitable status,[20] and be subject to regulation by the Charity Commission.[21] Charities still play an important role in social housing, though they are no longer the principal vehicle for meeting social needs in this area,[22] but are of more than residual importance.[23]

Broadly, social housing is a service for those in housing need, either by local authorities or by private housing associations (now referred to as 'private registered providers').[24] Social rented housing has a statutory definition under the

---

[17] The treatment here is necessarily limited. For a more detailed introduction to the social housing sector, including the debates and policy that shape it, see Cowan (n 12). For a more detailed treatise, see M McDermont, *Governing, Independence and Expertise: The Business of Housing Associations* (Oxford, Hart Publishing, 2010).

[18] Together, charities and other not-for-profit organisations, including cooperatives and mutual societies, make up the third sector (as opposed to the private and public sectors). They are also increasingly referred to as together constituting civil society.

[19] To be eligible for registration as charities, under the Charities Act 2011, such organisations must have as their object a recognised charitable purpose (s 3), must demonstrate that they carry on their purposes for the benefit of the public (s 4) and must be wholly and exclusively charitable (s 2). See further H Picarda, *Law and Practice Relating to Charities*, 4th edn (London Bloomsbury, 2010); R Pearce, J Stevens and W Barr, *The Law of Trusts and Equitable Obligations*, 5th edn (Oxford, Oxford University Press, 2010) ch 19.

[20] In the year 2007–08, the Inland Revenue estimated that the value of tax reliefs for charities was around £2.19 billion (HMRC, *Annual Report Tables & Statistics 2007–2008*, Table 10.2). For a brief summary of the key advantages of charitable status, see Pearce, Stevens and Barr (n 19) 576–79.

[21] For details of the nature of this regulatory framework, see Pearce, Stevens and Barr (n 19) 854–69.

[22] For a penetrating analysis of the evolving role of charities in social housing, including the impact of the housing association model, see M McDermont (n 17) ch 3.

[23] See N Glover-Thomas and W Barr, 'Re-examining the Benefits of Charitable Involvement in Housing the Mentally Vulnerable' (2008) *Northern Ireland Legal Quarterly* 177.

[24] Previously, many of these organisations were known as Registered Social Landlords. The taxonomy was changed under the Housing and Regeneration Act 2008 (Consequential Provisions) Order 2010, SI 2010/866.

Housing and Regeneration Act 2008.[25] Organisations must be registered bodies[26] that provide low-cost rental accommodation,[27] which is available for rent below a market rate.[28] In addition, private registered providers must operate in 'accordance with rules designed to ensure that it is made available to people whose needs are not adequately served by the commercial housing market'.[29] Both not-for-profit and profit-making bodies can assume the mantle of private registered providers, though profit-making providers are subject to different rules and more stringent regulation.

It is already well documented that the social rented sector is increasingly seen as a 'sector of last resort' due to the encouragement by successive governments of owner-occupation and a failure by central government to finance the construction of new social housing stock.[30] Demand for social housing far exceeds supply. Provision has become fragmented and lacking in coherence following the shift from local authorities housing individuals to the discharge of their duties through private registered providers.[31] Market pressures have meant that larger providers have become general housing providers, leaving specialist services (such as housing the vulnerable with particular physical or mental health needs) to smaller, more specialised providers.[32]

Charities are one such provider, stepping in to provide either specialist housing directly or supply specialised services to mainstream providers.[33] Charities may also be registered private providers of general social housing, and, to add complexity,[34] social housing may be only one aspect of provision offered by charities as part of their charitable purposes. It is therefore as service providers and/or partners to other housing bodies and as direct service providers that the role of charities is best understood.

B. The Regulation and Funding of Charitable Social Housing

The regulation of all social housing used to be conducted by two separate bodies: the Homes and Communities Agency (HCA), which regulated the funding of organisations, and the Tenant Services Authority (TSA), which dealt with other

---

[25] This is normally referred to as the 'social rented sector', which links both local authority and non-local authority housing. This chapter is not concerned with local authority housing, though reference will be made to it where appropriate.

[26] To be registrable, an organisation must intend to provide or provide social housing in England and satisfy the registration authority that it is financially viable, appropriately constituted and has a management structure in place. See Housing and Regeneration Act 2008, s 112.

[27] Ibid, ss 68(1)(b) and 69.

[28] Ibid, s 69(b).

[29] Ibid, s 69(c).

[30] See Housing Corporation, *The Impact of the Large Scale Voluntary Transfer of Local Authority Housing Stock on the HA Sector* (London, 2002).

[31] See D Cowan and M McDermont, *Regulating Social Housing: Governing Decline* (Abingdon, Routledge-Cavendish, 2006).

[32] For a succinct summary of the phenomenon, see Glover-Thomas and Barr (n 23).

[33] Ibid, 180.

[34] See N Glover-Thomas and W Barr, 'Enabling or Disabling? Increasing Involvement of Charities in Social Housing' [2009] 73 *Conv* 209.

aspects of regulation.[35] Section 178 of the Localism Act 2011 saw the establishment of a new, independent Regulation Committee of the HCA and the abolition of the TSA.[36] Essentially, this sees a rebalancing of regulatory functions, such that the HCA will have a proactive role in relation to economic matters, but will have more of a 'backstop role' in relation to consumer regulation standards and functions, with other parties and agencies acting locally to take over the monitoring and improvement roles that previously sat with the TSA. There are also some significant changes from the old regulatory framework,[37] not least of which are the creation of some new standards, such as the Tenant Involvement and Empowerment consumer standard, which places a greater focus on local mechanisms to resolve complaints and disputes,[38] and the continuation of a risk-based approach to intervention, alongside a cooperative approach to regulation with organisations at local levels, underpins the new framework.[39] There are also significant changes in the substance of regulation of tenure, 'the most radical since the introduction of security of tenure to social housing in 1980',[40] which will be considered below.

Charities are, as noted, also subject to regulation by the Charity Commission. In the past, many social housing charities escaped full regulation under charity law if they were registered as industrial and provident societies, as such charities were considered exempt charities[41] and were mostly formed for the purpose of relief of poverty, under which public benefit was presumed to be present.[42] Such organisations were instead regulated by the Financial Services Authority and by the Tenant Services Authority. Today, these organisations will be required to be registered for a distinct charitable purpose,[43] and must demonstrate that they carry out such purposes for the benefit of the public[44] and would fall within the remit of the Charity Commission as regulator. The National Housing Federation provides a model objects clause for charities that are either private registered providers of social

---

[35] These institutions replaced the Housing Corporation, which was the principal regulator under the Housing Act 1998.

[36] This followed a long consultation period and the TSA conducted a consultation exercise before passing into regulation history. The Localism Act 2011 also makes significant changes to nomination schemes and the duties of local authority and private registered providers of social housing in relation to such lists. For a good summary, see Cowan (n 12) 200–02.

[37] TSA, *The Regulatory Framework for Social Housing in England from April 2010* (March 2010). This was the last governing regulatory document issued under the old regime.

[38] *The Regulatory Framework* (March 2012) 17–18.

[39] *The Regulatory Framework* (March 2012) 8–9.

[40] Shelter, *Local Decisions on Tenure Reform: Local Tenancy Strategies and the New Role of Local Housing Authorities in Leading Tenure Policy* (July 2012).

[41] See Charity Commission CC23, *Exempt Charities* (March 2012).

[42] There is now a requirement that all charities demonstrate that they are carrying out their charitable purposes for the benefit of the public: Charities Act 2011, s 4. The requirement of public benefit has not changed—see, for example, P Luxton, *Making Law? Parliament Versus the Charity Commission* (POLIETIA, 2009).

[43] Providing social housing or services to social housing providers would likely fall under one or more of the following charitable purposes set out in s 3 of the Charities Act 2011: s 3(2)(a) (prevention or relief of poverty), (j) (the relief of those in need), (e) (the advancement of citizenship or community development) and (d) (the advancement of health) of the Charities Act 2011.

[44] Charities Act 2011, s 4(3).

housing or assist such providers in delivering services,[45] which many will follow. Charitable private registered providers are thus subject to two regulatory regimes: by the HCA in relation to the discharge of their social housing functions and by the Charity Commission in relation to the carrying out of their charitable purposes.

The funding of charitable social housing organisations is dependent on the size of the organisation and the services it offers. Put simply, it is usually a mix of state income through delivering public service contracts and other statutory sources such as local authority nominations,[46] or general charitable fundraising activity, including donations and, at times, loans on assets. The largest source of income, though, is the first: state income.[47] Sustainable funding of activity is a sectorial concern, especially in the prevailing economic climate, as will be discussed later in this chapter.

III. THE BIG SOCIETY AND ITS IMPACT ON CHARITABLE SOCIAL HOUSING PROVIDERS

Now that the general shape of charitable social housing provision and the regulatory framework within which it operates have been outlined, the impact of the Big Society on the operation of charitable private registered providers can be considered.

A. Big Society and Charities: Surface Synergies

The key concepts of the Big Society have already been introduced; namely, empowering communities, opening up public services and promoting social action. The five key principles through which is it hoped this will be achieved are identified as follows: (i) give communities more power; (ii) encourage people to take an active role in their communities; (iii) transfer power from central to local government; (iv) support cooperatives, charities, mutual and social enterprises; and (v) publish government data.[48] Of particular interest in relation to social housing is principle, (iii) as this seeks to support the creation and expansion of charities and other social enterprise groups, and supporting these groups to have a much greater involvement in the running of public services. Funding should come from the Big Society Capital (a Big Society bank) by way of an investment loan.[49] This organisation was finally

---

[45] NHF Model Rules 2011 (model objects clause). The NHF is a body whose mission is to support and promote the work that housing associations do and campaign for better housing and neighbourhoods.

[46] Charities, as part of the wider third sector, delivered £9.1 billion of public service contracts in 2007/08. J Clark et al, *The UK Civil Society Almanac 2010* (London, NCVO, 2010).

[47] *Ibid*, 43, where it was identified that around 36 per cent of the total income of charities was state-derived.

[48] Cabinet Office, *Building the Big Society* (May 2010).

[49] This is an independent financial institution, registered with the Financial Services Authority. It is tasked with developing and shaping a sustainable social investment market in the UK by funding organisations to carry out relevant societal purposes and increasing confidence and awareness of social investment—see *Big Society Capital: Transforming Social Investment* at www.bigsocietycapital.com.

established in April 2012, with £600 million of funds to invest to support such schemes.[50]

On the surface, charitable organisations do seem well placed to play an active role in the Big Society. They tend to work locally (even, to varying extents, the national organisations), an important underlying theme of the Big Society. They are seen as offering greater institutional efficiency than many other organisations and have considerable expertise in carrying out their functions. Charities have a degree of political insulation, as they are purpose-driven organisations, focusing on carrying out their charitable purposes. It is also worth noting that, for many successful charitable organisations, the Big Society may simply be a new label for initiatives and working practices that already existed—cooperation and the sharing of working practices are endemic to the charity sector, as are the use and promotion of the community as volunteers in running the charity or providing its services.

Charities are also felt to have an ability to meet the competing and conflicting demands of a heterogeneous society, and have an enviable track record of filling gaps in the provision of services. The current role that charities play within social housing provision, where they provide more specialist services, is an excellent example of this. Similarly, as already noted, charities already play a significant role in the delivery of public services, so growth in this area would seem to be an axiomatic benefit to all.

These perceived benefits of charities undertaking public services such as social housing are neither novel nor surprising. Much of the groundwork of utilising charities and other third sector organisations to enhance or deliver frontline public services was undertaken by the Labour government through its 'Third Way' concept,[51] which saw charities as a 'key partner in a mixed economy of public service provision'.[52] The identified benefits of utilising charities in the Big Society are also eerily similar to those proposed under the Third Way. Characteristics such as charitable organisations being value-driven, independent, responsive and innovative in delivery, as well as the recognised track record of charities filling gaps in mainstream provision, were all suggested as reasons for involving charities in public service provision under the Third Way.[53]

In this context, the Big Society could be seen as a further step along the path of moving provision away from government-funded services, delivered centrally, to services being delivered locally, by charities and other voluntary or community groups. It is not fanciful to suggest that the Localism Act 2011 is to some extent the statutory embodiment of many of the principles identified in the Big Society relating to community involvement in local decision making, and the changes outlined earlier in relation to social housing regulation are clearly intended to facilitate many of the ideals identified under the umbrella concept of the Big Society. Charities also have a history of working with other agencies to achieve outcomes, not least

---

[50] This is drawn from £400 million from dormant bank accounts and circa £200 million from investment from four high street banks (Barclays Bank plc, HSBC, Lloyds Banking Group and the Royal Bank of Scotland).

[51] See, eg, Cabinet Office, *Partnership in Public Services—An Action Plan for Third Sector Involvement* (2006); *Partnership in Public Services—The Public Services Action Plan One Year On* (2007).

[52] DTI, *Social Enterprise: A Strategy for Success* (2002) 7.

[53] See Glover-Thomas and Barr (n 34) 221–24, which discusses these benefits in more detail.

in social housing, where charities (for example, those providing specialist services to vulnerable people) are necessarily involved in working with multiple agencies to manage the different care requirements of such individuals.[54]

B. Problems with the Implementation of the Big Society

There is, however, good reason to question many of the proposed benefits of the Big Society and charities in delivering social housing.[55] Without delving into a detailed critique of the Big Society concept, it is suggested that much of it is predicated on the fallacy that there is a sharp division in the provision of services between the public and charitable sectors. It has already been demonstrated that the public and charitable sectors are deeply entangled, with charities supplementing the delivery of public services or delivering public services directly through public service contracting. Hence, it would be easy to conceptualise the Big Society as an attempt to cut not only supply but also demand for the state, with the private and third sectors stepping in as the government retreats.

The major concern, though, with the Big Society as it relates to social housing is funding, or, more accurately, the lack of adequate funding. The Big Society was introduced, as noted above, at a time of deep, global recession. In response, the government introduced a series of swingeing budget cuts, which, at the time of writing, have failed to significantly stimulate growth. This has had a very negative impact on both unemployment figures and growth in the housing market in the UK, with the former rising and the latter shrinking over the past few years. One of the sectors most affected by these budget cuts has been the public sector.[56] Ironically, this has increased demand for social housing services, as the general housing market is failing to meet the needs of a growing number of the population, so that demand is rising at a time when funding is falling away. This extends to charitable providers as well, who are being expected to come forward and deliver these housing services in local communities, despite a reduction in public and private funding to the charities themselves.

The extent of the funding loss is staggering. The National Council for Voluntary Organisations estimated that charities will have to absorb a cut in public funding of £3.3 billion by 2016.[57] In an internal document,[58] the Association of Chief Executives of Voluntary Organisations (ACEVO) estimated the loss to be somewhere between £1 and 5.5 billion.[59] Charities are also said to be losing staff at twice the rate of the public sector.[60]

---

[54] See Glover-Thomas and Barr (n 23) 190–91.

[55] See Morris (n 1), which presents a convincing critique of the proposed benefits of the Big Society to charities.

[56] HM Treasury (n 8). The extent of the cuts has been a subject for discussion in the UK media on a daily basis—see, for example, www.guardian.co.uk/society/2011/mar/25/public-sector-cuts.

[57] D Kane and J Allen, *Counting the Cuts: The Impact of Spending Cuts on the UK Voluntary and Community Sector* (London, NCVO, 2011).

[58] Reported in the *Sunday Times* (4 March 2012).

[59] This is an umbrella organisation, with funds of £100 million to aid charities facing financial difficulties.

[60] Reported in *The Times* (5 March 2012).

Against this funding shortfall, it is to be expected that the success of the Big Society is under threat[61] and that it has been 'largely heralded as a smoke-screen for implementing massive public sector cuts and then expecting an army of volunteers to fill the gaps as the state retreats'.[62] Social funding measures, such as the social investment funds available through Big Society Capital, will likely be ineffective to fill the gap for all but the largest charities as smaller charities have neither the free cash reserves nor the capacity to access loan or investment funding.[63] This is of particular resonance in charitable social housing, as it has already been identified that many registered social providers exist as smaller organisations.

There are other, more structural concerns about the ability of charities to deliver the perceived benefits of involvement in social housing through the Big Society.

C. The Structural Impacts of the Big Society on Charities

The capacity of (social housing) charities to deliver frontline public services has already been considered in the context of increasing demand through the Third Way for those charities dealing with mentally vulnerable individuals.[64] It has been argued that there are fundamental impediments in the structural nature of charities which mean that the proposed benefits of using charities may not be realised and:

> [T]hat charities have neither the ethos nor the infrastructure to support the volume of work involved. Services would inevitably become homogenised and public confidence and trust would be further compromised, with potentially serious consequences.[65]

Similar concerns have been identified for all charities operating within the Big Society, observing that certain legal constraints inherent in the nature of charities, such as the need to maintain their independence and act according to their objects, mean that 'the assumed natural alliance of symbiotic aims is sadly lacking'.[66]

Indeed, it is possible to identify five common structural issues that threaten the efficacy of charities in carrying out public services under these two analyses, suggesting that the increased demands of the Big Society bring the existing concerns of charities providing social housing into sharp relief. These are: (i) concerns over the independence of charities;[67] (ii) barriers to volunteering;[68] (iii) the legal consequence of mission drift;[69] (iv) the fragility of funding regimes;[70] and (v) the capacity of

---

[61] Liverpool City Council cited a lack of funding as one of the major reasons for its withdrawal as a Big Society vanguard area.

[62] Morris (n 1) 136.

[63] Ibid, 136–37.

[64] See Glover-Thomas and Barr (n 23) and Glover-Thomas and Barr (n 34).

[65] Glover-Thomas and Barr (n 34) 234–35.

[66] Morris (n 1) 152.

[67] Morris (n 1) 144–47; Glover-Thomas and Barr (n 34) 226–33; Glover-Thomas and Barr (n 23) 195–97.

[68] Morris (n 1) 138–41; Glover-Thomas and Barr (n 23) 187–88. These include both legal and practical barriers, each of which help explain a lack of growth in volunteering activity.

[69] Morris (n 1) 147–48; Glover-Thomas and Barr (n 23) 192–94. The consequences include intervention by the Charity Commission as regulator and, potentially, removal from the Register of Charities.

[70] This has already been considered above, but see further Morris (n 1) 135–38; Glover-Thomas and Barr (n 34) 217–20; Glover-Thomas and Barr (n 23) 194–95.

smaller charities (as opposed to larger charities) to undertake effective provision.[71]
Two examples should suffice to illustrate the impact and importance of these issues:
concerns over independence and the capacity of smaller charities.

i. Independence

Independence is seen as a core value of charities[72] and relates to independence in
both governance and decision making. Charity trustees (or governing boards) must
have the freedom to make decisions in the best interests of the charity as a whole
in carrying out their charitable purposes and must be free of the influence of any
third party or the state.[73] They must also be free to voice opinions about policy and
provision in the sectors in which they work, which is seen as one of the strengths of
charities as organisations.

Questions over independence arise because of the increased reliance on charities
to procure public funding and to carry out public services. While permissible,[74] it
is for each organisation to demonstrate that it is focused purely on carrying out its
charitable purposes or objects, rather than carrying out activities under the direction
of a public authority. Meeting these concerns could be difficult, particularly given
the increased demands the Big Society will place on charities. Charities already
believe that funders, for example, can compromise their independence.[75] Funders
can also have a less direct impact in shaping how the organisation carries out its
objects to secure funding.[76]

These difficulties in ensuring independence are compounded by the fact that
charities must not just be independent, but must be seen to be independent in how
they operate if public confidence in them is to be maintained. This is a significant
concern in the light of the Big Society as:

> [T]he public already believes that professionalised organisations have compromised
> their independence to obtain funding from government, and that it is only the smaller
> organisations, which retain their independence as they have little or no relationship with
> government.[77]

A lack of actual independence could led to severe legal consequences for a charity,
and ultimately removal from the register, while a perceived lack of independence
could lead to a loss of funding as the public loses confidence in charities, which 'may

---

[71] Morris (n 1) 150–52; Glover-Thomas and Barr (n 34) 224–26; Glover-Thomas and Barr (n 23) 198–99.

[72] See, eg, Charity Commission, *The Hallmarks of an Effective Charity* CC10, July 2008.

[73] See A Blackmore, *Standing Apart, Working Together: A Study of the Myths and Realities of Voluntary and Community Sector Independence* (London, NCVO, 2004) 17.

[74] In the sense that the Charity Commission will allow a charity to be created or to change its purposes to provide government functions—see Charity Commission, *Independence of Charities from the State* RR7, February 2001.

[75] Research undertaken by the Charity Commission found that only 26 per cent of charities that delivered public services felt they had freedom from funders to make decisions—see Charity Commission, *Stand and Deliver—the Future for Charities Providing Public Services* RS15, February 2007.

[76] See J Garton, 'Charities and the State' [2000] 14 *Trust Law International* 93.

[77] See Blackmore (n 73).

well be an insurmountable hurdle for charities seeking to play an enhanced role in the Big Society'.[78]

ii. The Capacity of Small Charities

The ability of smaller, more localised charities (a category into which many charities involved in social housing fall) to either access or provide the benefits of the Big Society concept are open to question. Research by the Charity Commission suggests that only larger organisations could cope with direct involvement in tendering for and delivering frontline public services.[79] In the context of a social housing charity, the economies of scale in governance, workforce, overheads and housing stock are obvious in larger organisations, and they are also more likely to have access to appropriate legal advice when tendering for public contracts than smaller organisations. They are also more likely to have the necessary capital reserves to be able to access loan and investment funding.[80] The larger providers offer more general housing and are likely to tender for (less expensive) general services. Such organisations may be far from the ideal of local organisations making local decisions.

Smaller charities, by contrast, though they may be best placed to deal with local issues at a local level, may lack either the income or the structural capacity to realise these potential benefits in providing services. One way to meet concerns would be to pool resources, either through working with other organisations and submitting joint bids or by merging to become a bigger organisation. Again, research suggests that either approach can lead to difficulties, especially if the motivation for the change is forced upon the organisations concerned rather than arising from shared goals and aspirations.[81] The issue of funding remains of concern for those organisations wishing to provide specialist social housing to the vulnerable, as they will have difficulty funding such services if they find that they also have to provide the general housing itself, given the fact that other organisations may no longer be in a position to provide the necessary housing. Coupled with competition from profit-making social housing providers, such small organisations may find it difficult to survive in the Big Society and, as has already been discussed, accessing social investment may not help these organisations. Indeed, there is a risk that private sector bodies will be better placed to meet needs than the charitable and wider voluntary sectors.

From these two examples, it is clear that there are significant hurdles in the way of charities providing the very benefits that the Big Society suggests they will. In fact, the Big Society, as implemented, may actually make it more difficult for charitable

---

[78] Morris (n 1) 147.

[79] Charity Commission CC37, *Charities and Public Service Delivery—An Introduction and Overview* (February 2007).

[80] This has not gone unnoticed by the government or bodies that support charities, though there are solid reasons to believe that measures introduced to assist smaller groups will not work—see Morris (n 1) 147.

[81] Charity Commission, *Strength in Numbers—Small Charities' Experience of Working Together* RS24, 2010.

organisations to carry out social housing functions and may exacerbate problems that were already extant in the sector, but under-appreciated.

IV. THE BIG SOCIETY AND LOCALISM: TENURE AND SOCIAL HOUSING

There are also concerns for social housing providers at a narrower level due to the influence of Big Society thinking. It has already been noted that localism, in the sense of local decision making, is a key theme and tenet of the Big Society concept. The reforms to social housing introduced by the Localism Act 2011[82] are designed to ensure that decisions about housing are taken locally,[83] and this has been seen to underpin the whole of the new regulatory framework for registered private providers. It is the changes relating to tenure that highlight the unintended consequences of pursuing localism as an ideal.

A. Tenure: The Pre-Localism Act 2011 Position

In the social housing rented sector,[84] the perceived standard for the length of tenure that a private registered provider should give a tenant was normally a tenancy for life.[85] This followed from guidance issued by the Tenant Services Authority that tenants should be granted the 'most secure form of tenure compatible with the purpose of the housing and sustainability of the community'.[86] For private registered providers, this was the assured tenancy or, in exceptional circumstances, the assured shorthold tenancy.[87]

This approach, predicated on laudable concerns such as the importance of providing a stable home environment for service users, nonetheless caused problems for charities letting social housing in certain circumstances.[88] Broadly, it was argued that the guidance of the TSA was open to a more liberal interpretation than it

---

[82] The Act contains a raft of provisions that tackle a number of major issues. These are outside the remit of this chapter. Some housing issues, such as changes to nomination listing procedures to allocate housing, duties on homelessness and the affordable rent product, are also outside the scope of this chapter.

[83] See Centre for Local Government, *A Plain English Guide to the Localism Act* (November 2011) 19. The changes are contained in the Localism Act 2011, pt 7.

[84] For a good discussion of what tenure is and the different meanings that can be ascribed to it, see Cowan (n 12).

[85] This arose from a tenant guarantee scheme, instituted by the Housing Corporation (the precursor to the TSA)—see W Barr, 'Leases: Rethinking Possession against Vulnerable Groups' in E Cooke (ed), *Modern Studies in Property Law: Volume 4* (Oxford, Hart Publishing, 2007) ch 7, 119.

[86] TSA Reg Code 2010a, 25.

[87] See the Housing Act 1988. The regime for local authority tenants was different—they could offer secure tenancies under the Housing Act 1985 or, exceptionally, introductory tenancies. For a discussion of the development and operation of the regime, see Law Commission, 'Renting Homes 1: Status and Security', Consultation Paper No 162 (April 2002) pt II.

[88] Barr (n 85) 136–38 and 145–46. Against, see, for example, S Fitzpatrick and H Pawson, 'Security of Tenure in Social Housing: An International Review' (Shelter, May 2011), where it is argued that a reduction in tenure does not improve management or availability of stock.

had been given,[89] and it was important for the charitable purposes pursued by an organisation to match tenure to purpose in every circumstance to avoid complicated legal problems in the future. People with a mental illness, for example, may have changing needs, so that it may be necessary to move them from a property to meet their needs. In situations where this could not be managed consensually, legal action would require eviction, which, if the level of tenure was set too high, could be difficult to achieve.[90] Similarly, even for general needs tenants, charities must keep tenancies under review. A person who was in social housing owing to financial distress would no longer qualify as an object of charity if he or she won a substantial sum of money on the National Lottery. Again, it could be difficult to evict this person if tenure was too great, even though it would be essential to do so if the charity was to continue carrying out its charitable purposes.[91]

B. The Localism Act 2011 and Tenure

The Localism Act 2011 changes the guidance and regulation on the length of tenure that both local authorities and private registered providers should offer tenants. This follows recognition that the interpretation of the previous tenancy regime could act as a straitjacket for organisations and may allow some people to remain in social housing who now had the means to move on.[92] For local authority providers, a new form of tenancy is created, the flexible secure tenancy with a fixed term of a minimum of two years.[93] These tenancies can only be granted following publication of a Tenancy Strategy outlining the circumstances in which these and other tenancies may be granted.[94] This strategy both influences private registered providers by providing a strategic lead from the local authority and, as a nod to localism, requires registered social providers to be given a reasonable opportunity to comment on proposals before adopting or making a major modification to a Tenancy Strategy so that they can help shape the strategy.[95]

Private registered providers are given the equivalent of flexible tenancies, as they are now allowed to grant fixed-term assured shorthold tenancies to all general needs tenants, meaning that it can be ended by notice at the end of the fixed

---

[89] The continued adherence to granting the greatest form of security of tenure possible, except in very exceptional circumstances, suggested that the wording may have changed with the new guidance issued by the TSA, but the operation of many organisations did not.

[90] This could depend on the grounds relied on to evict, as well as the summary nature of the eviction hearing. See Barr (n 85) 145–46.

[91] Similar concerns were expressed by Sir John Vinelott in *Gray v Taylor* [1998] 1 WLR 1093, in which he found that a letting by an almshouse created a licence, not a tenancy, and thereby escaped statutory protection. This can be contrasted with the judgment of Lord Hoffmann in *Bruton v London & Quadrant Housing Trust* [2000] 1 AC 406, in which his Lordship considered the charitable purposes of the letting irrelevant to determining whether a lease or licence had in fact been granted.

[92] The changes were well signposted. See CSG, *Local Decisions: A Fairer Future for Social Housing* (November 2010); CSG, *Local Decisions: Next Steps Towards a Fairer Future for Social Housing* (28 February 2011); CSG, *Implementing Social Housing Reform: Directions to the Social Housing Regulator* (July 2011). They have not been universally welcomed—see, for example, Shelter (n 40).

[93] Localism Act 2011, ss 154–55, inserting s 106A into the Housing Act 1985.

[94] Ibid, ss 150–53.

[95] Ibid, s 151(1).

term.[96] The new tenant standards require that tenancies should be granted that are compatible with 'the purpose of the accommodation, the needs of individual households, the sustainability of the community, and the efficient use of their housing stock'.[97] If a fixed-term assured shorthold is granted, it will normally be for five years, but exceptionally it may be for a period of no less than two years.[98] It is also a requirement that each private registered provider publish a Tenancy Policy,[99] which references the local authority Tenancy Strategy and sets out, inter alia, the circumstances in which it will grant tenancies of different types and what happens on the expiry of a tenancy.[100] Options on expiry include whether to grant another fixed-term assured shorthold, let on another form of letting or regain possession on the expiry of the fixed term. There is no right of appeal against decisions to grant a fixed-term tenancy as there is with local authority flexible secure tenancies.[101]

C. Assessing the Impact

At face value, this seems like a useful change for charitable (and other) private registered providers, and would appear to meet many of the concerns expressed about matching tenure and charity objectives more effectively. The guidance in the new tenancy standard is much more open than in the past and actively encourages providers to have a clear policy in place to deal with tenure issues. Similarly, requiring each organisation to have its own tenancy policy would seem to be the purest expression of localism in decision making, bringing the issue down to the level of the individual organisation, especially when coupled with the ability of organisations to shape the local authority strategy for housing in their area through consultation on the local authority Tenancy Strategy.

There are practical hurdles to overcome. It is clear that the grant of tenancy will have to be justified on the basis of the four tenancy standards outlined above and on the terms of the Tenancy Policy. Essentially, a registered social provider wishing to utilise fixed terms needs to set out policies and procedures as to: (a) why a fixed-term tenancy is being used and the duration of that tenancy; and (b) what will happen at the end of the tenancy.

How, then, does a provider set out about deciding the terms on which to grant particular individuals a particular form of tenure, be it an assured tenancy for life

---

[96] Possession has also been altered under s 164 of the Localism Act 2011, which adds sub-s 1B to s 21 of the Housing Act 1988 and introduces an additional notice requirement, which must be served containing the listed information on the tenant not less than six months before possession.

[97] *The Regulatory Framework For Social Housing in England From April 2012* (March 2012) ch 4, 23–24.

[98] Ibid.

[99] At the time of writing, so soon after the implementation of the new law, few such tenancy policies are available for further analysis.

[100] Funding for this new type of tenancy, whether flexible or assured shorthold, comes from an Affordable Rents funding model—see HCA, *The Regulatory Framework for Social Housing in England from April 2012* (March 2012).

[101] See Localism Act 2011, s 154, inserting s 107B (grant) and s 107E (termination by landlord) into the Housing Act 1985. The content of the review is governed by the Flexible Tenancies (Review Procedures) Regulations 2012.

or a fixed-term tenancy? Guidance has recently been published by both the Local Government Association and the Chartered Institute of Housing on producing Tenancy Strategies and Policies respectively,[102] but in both cases this is at a high level of generality.[103] Would all lettings start as flexible lettings to avoid the inconsistency? If they did, how could this be justified in line with the required tenancy standards, or would stating it in the tenancy policy be sufficient? How would the provider decide on the length of the fixed term of a flexible tenancy? If it is set, say, at a minimum of five years, will it be the same tenancy arrangement for everyone? Will it apply to all housing stock owned or managed by the charitable registered provider, or may it be, in different geographical areas, subject to different conditions? If so, why? How, including costing of time and money, does a provider make available the necessary resources to carry out end-of-fixed-term assessments and reviews as part of its housing management policy?

Doubtless, these questions will be answered in time, but there is a more fundamental concern raised by such policy documents. In requiring providers to make individual decisions about housing tenure and to publish a policy detailing how and when they will grant and manage such tenancies, a consequence is that the decisions of the charitable private registered provider may be open to legal challenge,[104] including possible human rights claims.

D. Legal Challenges and the Tenancy Policy

It now appears clear that a charitable private registered provider of social housing would be classed as a 'hybrid' public body under section 6(3)(b) of the Human Rights Act 1998 as a body providing a public service or a role similar to a local authority and in receipt of public funds.[105] Not all acts of the registered provider will be classed as 'public', but acts such as the grant of tenure are likely to be so, considered as they are integral to the housing function.

It is unlikely that the grant of a tenancy will prove 'incompatible with a Convention right' under section 6(1) of the Human Rights Act 1988, but, as a public function, it may be open to judicial review.[106] Broadly, it would be necessary to prove that the decision is not unreasonable,[107] the decision did not take account of irrelevant

---

[102] LCA, *Writing an Effective Tenancy Strategy* (May 2012); CIH, *How to Develop Your Tenancy Policy* (May 2012).

[103] For a critique of the likely effectiveness of these Tenancy Agreements and for a suggested approach to making them work best in social housing, see also Shelter (n 40).

[104] While it is not discussed here, the nature of social housing provision undertaken by charities, particularly those dealing with vulnerable people, may leave them open to a challenge on the basis of discrimination under the Equality Act 2010 over one of the protected characteristics—see Equality Act 2012, s 5 (age); s 6 (disability).

[105] See *R (Weaver) v London and Quadrant Housing Trust* [2010] 1 WLR 363 (CA). For a detailed discussion of this case, see S Bright. N Hopkins and N Macklam, ch 2 in this volume.

[106] See *R (McIntyre) v Gentoo Group Ltd* [2010] EWHC 5, where it was said that the management functions of a social landlord in relation to stock may be open to judicial review. Note, however, that for judicial review to be available as a cause of action, there must be no adequate alternative remedy.

[107] The test applicable is 'Wednesbury' unreasonableness (*Associated Provincial Picture Houses Ltd v Wednesbury Corporation* (1948) 1 KB 223).

matters or fail to consider relevant factors and that no procedural irregularities arose from a failure to follow the written strategy on lettings.[108] This also suggests that adequate resources should be made available to review panels as a matter of course. It is worth remembering that if a decision is quashed on administrative grounds, the matter can be reconsidered and a fresh conclusion reached, which can be the same conclusion, provided that it is arrived at lawfully. The importance of acting according to the stated policy is clear.

A private registered provider seeking to terminate a tenancy would be a public act[109] and may be in breach of Article 8 of the European Convention on Human Rights (the right to non-interference with private and family life). Challenges to possession proceedings under Article 8 have been the subject of much litigation in the UK, and the position is now governed by two Supreme Court cases—*Manchester City Council v Pinnock*[110] and *Hounslow LBC v Powell*.[111] Detailed critiques of the operation of such claims and how they operate can be found elsewhere,[112] but in essence the challenge is one of proportionality of the action to seek eviction set against the person's rights to stay in the home. If a challenge is successful, no new claim can be brought without a change of circumstances.

Without rehearsing the legal arguments in detail,[113] the effect of the Supreme Court decisions is that while the right to possession is no longer determinative in itself and may be open to a proportionality claim, it is only in cases where the case is 'seriously arguable' that the claim will be considered. Moreover, as Lord Neuberger opined:

> [I]n virtually every case where a residential occupier has no contractual or statutory protection, and the local authority is entitled to possession as a matter of domestic law, there will be a very strong case for saying that making an order for possession would be proportionate ... However, in some cases, there may be factors which would tell the other way.[114]

In practice, it is suggested that the decision of a private registered provider to seek possession of a fixed-term tenancy will only be open to a human rights challenge based on proportionality in truly exceptional cases, as the nature of the tenancy means that there is a low threshold to cross before justifying termination of the arrangement and there are significant procedural safeguards already in place before termination is ordered, including both the notice procedure and the tenant management agreement.

Nevertheless, while the Supreme Court made it clear that there was no duty for a landlord to give reasons for his decision to evict an individual, it is strongly

---

[108] For a detailed and persuasive treatment of the judicial review process, see M Elliot and R Thomas, *Public Law* (Oxford, Oxford University Press, 2011) pt IV.

[109] This was the case in *Weaver* itself—see the discussion at para [76] onwards.

[110] *Manchester City Council v Pinnock* [2010] 3 WLR 1441.

[111] *Hounslow LBC v Powell* [2011] 2 WLR 287.

[112] See, for example, D Cowan and C Hunter, '"Yeah but, no but": Pinnock and Powell in the Supreme Court' (2012) *MLR* 75 and Bright, Hopkins and Macklam, ch 2 in this volume.

[113] For an excellent comment on the *Pinnock* case, see M Thompson, 'Case Comment: Possession Actions and Human Rights' [2011] *Conv* 421.

[114] *Pinnock* (n 110) [54].

suggested that registered social providers should do just that and should make sure that these reasons accord with the written tenancy policy. This is particularly true where the charitable provider is dealing with vulnerable tenants, as the claim for proportionally may be more relevant in such situations.[115]

A good point is worth repeating. In all cases, to avoid any challenge, a charitable social housing provider should give reasons before service of any notice, possession proceedings or decision to grant a type of tenancy, and should make sure that these decisions are based on evidence within the provider's tenancy policy. This presupposes that the tenancy policy is written to the requisite standard and provides a strong incentive to take the drafting of such documents seriously. It would also be a major change in practice for most organisations, which, in the absence of a duty to give reasons, may not do so.

The potential for challenge is a necessary consequence of making individual decisions at a local level and, it is suggested, is an unintended consequence of the 'localism' theme in the Big Society.[116]

V. CONCLUSIONS

It has been argued over the course of this chapter that the Big Society has presented more of a challenge than an opportunity for charitable social housing providers. It has been demonstrated that the implementation of the concept against a backdrop of a funding crisis has proved seriously problematic for charities, and that the demands placed upon organisations in providing frontline housing services exposes structural problems within such organisations. The impact of these factors means that some charities, particularly smaller ones, may fail or lose their coherence and value as they are forced to merge with other organisations to attain a critical mass to carry out their functions. This is particularly worrying for charitable housing providers, who are often small in terms of size and specialised in terms of scope. In a sense, many of these warnings were evident under the Third Way, which did not have the funding crisis attached. It is natural that the Big Society, in bringing charities out into the limelight as key actors, exacerbates these structural issues, but it is apparent that this has been lost on many of the proponents of the Big Society.

Even attractive aspects of Big Society thinking, such as localism in decision making, are causing unforeseen problems for charitable (and other) private registered providers. Few in the charity sector or the wider community would question the benefit of moving from central to local decision making about issues of service delivery. Yet, as ever, the devil is in the detail and, as has been demonstrated through the issue of tenure, while the concept of individual decision making is sound, as implemented by the Localism Act 2011 it leaves charities vulnerable to challenge, something that doubtless was not foreseen at the time.

---

[115] See *Holmes v Westminster CC* [2011] EWHC 2857 (QB), which dealt with the issue in the mental health context. Perhaps the best solution is not to evict at all and to pursue other remedies first—Barr (n 85) ch 7.

[116] This issue, identified as part of the costs of management that the use of fixed-term assured shorthold tenancies will incur, is discussed in Shelter (n 40) ch 2.

This is not to say that all is lost. There have been some worthwhile reforms under the Localism Act in terms of regulation of the sector, and many of the challenges posed by the Big Society can be met by proper management, both of the organisation and its social housing functions. Many, but not all, as some of the structural issues such as independence are such that they threaten the very value of charities as organisations, not just as key players in the Big Society.

So, returning to the title of this chapter, shall the twain ever meet? This would be too simplistic an analysis, but it is clear that in the concept as currently implemented, the proposed synergy between the Big Society, charities and a good social housing sector is less than clear. It would be tempting to think that the major issue is a lack of finance, and while this is undoubtedly a fundamental factor, it is not conclusive. Yes, providing the money for charities to provide the relevant services would at least counter arguments that the Big Society is a smokescreen for cutting public funding, and would at least put the policy emphasis back on the quality of provision, something which has been lost in the ether. It will also provide some much-needed capital to improve or build housing stock—the Big Society does not build houses, money does. However, an injection of funding would not deal with many of the other structural issues identified—in demonstrating independence, for example, money, sadly, provides no panacea.

It may be that the Big Society concept is remembered only as a label, one used to champion those organisations which embody the tenets of the concept. If so, it is likely that such organisations were doing this before someone thought of the concept of the Big Society, and in such cases it is unlikely that the advent of a worked concept has advanced the cause of these organisations. For example, a large and well-managed charitable registered private provider might provide a framework and discussion forum for smaller organisations in its local area engaged in social housing, and, as such, would embody some of the ideals of the Big Society. In providing no additional funding or support, unless through a tendering process to the Big Society bank, and in changing the legal landscape of regulation through informing the changes wrought by the Localism Act 2011 with the unintended consequences identified, it is hard to see how such an organisation has benefited from the Big Society.

So, what of the future? Charities have proved nothing if not resilient over the last few hundred years, and they will survive the Big Society, even if they emerge smaller in number and with a different social housing focus. Likewise, the social housing sector will survive the Big Society, but it will be interesting to see what shape the sector is in once the Big Society, along with the radical changes to housing tenure that it has brought in its wake, recedes from view.

Localism, in the sense of a move towards local decision making, may well prove to be the greatest legacy of the Big Society, and it is too early to say whether this is to the benefit of charities seeking to be involved in social housing or to the social housing sector itself. It is suggested that there is something of a tension in trusting the local community or organisations to make decisions based on the best interests of that community, with a requirement to regulate that trust to provide some objective comparability and certainty in decision making and the application of policies between organisations. Housing tenure is just the first ground where this tension is felt through the new tenancy regulation system and it will doubtless not be the last. The unintended consequence of this—that housing providers may have to give reasons for tenancy decisions, in the absence of a legal duty to do so—demonstrates the potential impact of localism on social housing. Interesting times lie ahead, whatever the eventual fate of the headline Big Society concept.

4

Regulating Residential Tenancies in Ireland: Rights, Responsibilities and Enforcement

ÁINE RYALL*

I. INTRODUCTION

FOR STRONG HISTORICAL and cultural reasons, including a bitter and violent Land War during the late 1800s, the vast majority of Irish people generally aspire to home ownership. This ambition was stoked further over the years by a housing policy that vigorously promoted home ownership via a range of financial incentives. The net result is that, in Ireland, other forms of tenure are still perceived as a 'second best', notwithstanding the current government's commitment to a more tenure neutral approach to housing policy.[1] Apart from the deeply entrenched national obsession with home ownership, another reason for the traditional lack of enthusiasm for private renting was the almost complete lack of meaningful regulation of the sector. For many years, successive governments claimed that legislative intervention on security of tenure and rent control was off-limits due to the strong protection afforded to private property rights in the Irish Constitution. However, an objective analysis of the relevant constitutional provisions, and the modern Supreme Court jurisprudence, confirms that these fears were overstated and were deployed as an excuse for non-intervention in this politically sensitive area.[2]

The long-standing regulatory gap was eventually tackled in the late 1990s when a climate of rapidly rising rents, together with a spate of tenancy terminations due to a lack of security of tenure, exposed the vulnerability of tenants who sought to make their home in the private rented sector. The government of the day responded to the clamour for action to protect tenants by establishing an expert Commission to undertake a thorough analysis of the legal framework and to make

---

* Senior Lecturer, University College Cork. Thanks are due to my colleague Professor John Mee and to an anonymous referee for very helpful comments and suggestions on an earlier draft of this chapter.

[1] Department of Environment, Community and Local Government, *Housing Policy Statement* (June 2011), www.environ.ie/en/DevelopmentHousing/Housing/PublicationsDocuments/FileDownLoad, 26867,en.pdf.

[2] On property rights and the Irish Constitution, see generally G Hogan and G Whyte, *J M Kelly: The Irish Constitution*, 4th edn (Dublin, Tottel Publishing, 2003) ch 7.7; and D O'Donnell, 'Property Rights in the Irish Constitution: Rights for Rich People, or a Pillar of Free Society?' in O Doyle and E Carolan (eds), *The Irish Constitution: Governance and Values* (Dublin, Thomson Round Hall, 2008).

recommendations for a new regulatory scheme. The Commission on the Private Rented Residential Sector reported in July 2000[3] and proposed a series of sweeping reforms which later formed the basis of the Residential Tenancies Act 2004 (RTA).[4] One of the most significant innovations in the RTA was the establishment of a new body, the Private Residential Tenancies Board (PRTB), which is charged with a wide range of regulatory functions, including determining disputes between landlords and tenants instead of the courts.

While impressive on paper, important aspects of the current regulatory framework are seriously flawed and fail to deliver in practice. Significant practical problems stem from the complexity of the legislative scheme and the multi-layered nature of the dispute resolution mechanism, which is plagued by long delays. The PRTB is under intense pressure due to an ever-increasing demand for its services and the fact that its resources continue to decline due to sharp cutbacks in public sector expenditure and tight controls on recruitment.[5] It has recently invested significant resources in developing its Information Communication Technology (ICT) strategy, including a sophisticated Tenancy Management System (TMS).[6] However, the move to online delivery of core PRTB services (including applications for tenancy registration and dispute resolution services) will take some time to bed down and it is plainly not a panacea for an inherently defective legislative framework.

Current problems and challenges in the regulation of residential tenancies have emerged at a time when an increasing number of people are seeking to make their home in the private rented sector. Data from *Census 2011* revealed a significant increase in the number of rented households and confirmed that between 2006 and 2011, the rate of home ownership dropped sharply (from 74.7 per cent to 69.7 per cent).[7] The expansion of the private rented sector is based on a number of factors,

---

[3] Department of Environment and Local Government, *Report of the Commission on the Private Rented Residential Sector* (2000) (hereafter the 'Commission report').

[4] The text of the RTA (as originally enacted) is available at: www.irishstatutebook.ie/2004/en/act/pub/0027/index.html. The RTA was amended pursuant to pt 7 of the Housing (Miscellaneous Provisions) Act 2009, which came into force on 15 July 2009. In brief outline, the amendments concerned: a new exception for tenancies where the term is more than 35 years was added (s 3, scope of the RTA); a new obligation to provide receptacles for the storage of refuse outside the dwelling (s 12(1)); clarification of the circumstances in which the landlord may retain all or part of the deposit (s 12(1)(d), concerning the landlord's obligation to repay the deposit); the removal of the requirement that both the landlord and the tenant must sign the registration form (s 135, concerning the rules governing tenancy registration). Finally, a new s 147A was added governing exchange of information between the PRTB and the Revenue Commissioners. The Residential Tenancies (Amendment) Act 2009 should also be noted. This short Act deals with one specific issue. It deems the appointment, or purported appointment, of certain members of the PRTB Dispute Resolution Committee to be valid. A Tenancy Tribunal constituted, or purported to have been constituted, under s 102, and every act done or purported to have been done by the Dispute Resolution Committee or a Tribunal before the passing of the 2009 Act, is also deemed to be valid and effective for all purposes. These emergency measures were necessary when it was discovered on 9 December 2008 that the appointment of Board members to the Dispute Resolution Committee in December 2007 was technically invalid due to non-compliance with s 159(3).

[5] Under the Employment Control Framework, the PRTB must reduce its staff significantly—from 70 to 33—by the end of 2013.

[6] PRTB, *Annual Report and Accounts 2010*, pp 468 and PRTB, *Annual Report and Accounts 2011* 38. The PRTB website—www.prtb.ie—is the gateway to the online services offered by the Board.

[7] Central Statistics Office, *Profile 4—The Roof over our Heads: Housing in Ireland* (August 2012), www.cso.ie.

in particular the reduced level of social housing provision by local authorities and the fact that many prospective home buyers encounter problems securing mortgage finance due to a combination of a lack of job security, falling incomes and stricter lending criteria. It is also apparent that many people continue to rent rather than buy in the hope that house prices, which have been on a sharp downward spiral since the Irish property bubble burst dramatically in 2007, will continue to fall in the future. In sum, the market is crippled due to a lack of certainty as to what the future holds for house prices. Another striking feature of the contemporary private rented sector is the emergence of the 'accidental' landlord. During the property boom, it was common for individuals to invest in property with a view to realising a significant capital gain in the short to medium term. Many of these individuals became landlords by default, so to speak, when they let out their 'investment' property (or properties). They were often unaware of the sophisticated legal framework that applies to the business of renting dwellings.[8] Lack of knowledge, expertise and experience among certain landlords led to a range of problems and disputes in practice that could have been avoided by a more conscientious and professional approach to the business of letting property. A similar situation arises where individuals, who can no longer afford to pay their mortgage, opt to rent out their home and live elsewhere with a view to reducing their expenditure. Again, it is doubtful if these reluctant, 'amateur' landlords are always well-versed in the intricacies of residential tenancies legislation. In light of this new reality, it is more important than ever that the private rented sector is regulated in an effective but relatively straightforward fashion.

This chapter examines the contemporary regulation of private residential tenancies in Ireland, with particular emphasis on the practical impact of the RTA. Part II opens by sketching the background to the RTA, including the main triggers for reform and the most significant legislative influences from other jurisdictions. The rather unusual law reform process by which the RTA was crafted, and the impact of this process on the overall quality of the legislative scheme, is also considered. Part III explains the core elements of the RTA and the pivotal role played by the PRTB. This review is followed by an assessment of the regulatory framework. Part IV considers the proposals for revision of certain aspects of the RTA set out in the Residential Tenancies (Amendment) (No 2) Bill 2012, which was published in July 2012. At a more general level, it considers how contemporary issues and problems might be remedied with a view to building greater confidence in the PRTB and in the opportunities offered by the private rented sector. The chapter concludes that, while there have been significant improvements in the regulation of residential tenancies since the enactment of the RTA, the legislation is in urgent need of substantial amendment to address a range of practical problems that currently undermine its effectiveness. Beyond the legislative framework, the PRTB must be provided with adequate resources to deliver its statutory mandate. In addition to its core work in the areas of tenancy registration and dispute resolution, the PRTB requires significant resources to provide clear, user-friendly information on rights and obligations for landlords and tenants, together with a range of education and awareness-raising

---

[8] 'The Snaglist for Accidental Landlords' *Sunday Business Post* (4 March 2012).

initiatives, in order to sharpen the impact of the RTA and to reduce the scope for disputes in the first instance.

II. THE FUNDAMENTAL OVERHAUL OF RESIDENTIAL TENANCY LAW AND THE EMERGENCE OF THE RTA

The main trigger for reform of residential tenancy law was the high-profile problems encountered by tenants (and especially tenants with low incomes) when rents suddenly began to rise rapidly in the late 1990s. An acute shortage of good-quality, reasonably priced accommodation for rent fuelled a situation where landlords regularly sought to terminate periodic tenancies in the certain knowledge of finding new tenants who would pay a higher rent. This state of affairs, which was highlighted by organisations representing tenants' interests, revealed the lack of control over the frequency of rent increases and the hopelessly limited provision for security of tenure. The government-appointed Commission on the Private Rented Residential Sector (established in June 1999) was charged with delivering proposals to address the problems encountered by tenants and to consider how best to promote and develop the private rented market. Membership of the Commission comprised representatives of landlords and tenants, together with property professionals, letting agents, lawyers, government officials, students and other interested parties. It was not surprising to find that two fundamental issues proved to be sharply divisive: rent regulation and security of tenure. The Commission failed to reach agreement on how best to address these two problems, with the result that relatively moderate proposals emerged which were subsequently enacted in the RTA. A majority of the Commission recommended that the rent payable for a dwelling should be the 'market rent'[9] and that any change in the rent should only be permissible once in every 12-month period of tenancy.[10] As regards security of tenure, the Commission's inability to agree on a specific proposal led to a compromise recommendation whereby, after six months' continuous occupation, a tenant should quality for a further three-and-a-half-year period of occupancy (ie a four-year tenancy in total), with the possibility for further four-year periods of tenancy on a rolling basis.[11] This limited right to security of tenure after six months' continuous occupation is described in the RTA as a 'Part 4 tenancy'.[12] This modest settlement fell far short of the demands made by tenants' representatives, in particular Threshold (the National Housing Charity), which had pushed hard for a greater measure of rent regulation and security of tenure. In fact, the Commission split down predictable lines, with landlords' representatives implacably against any form of rent regulation and enhanced security of tenure, and tenants' advocates clamouring for robust

---

[9] The concept of 'market rent' is essentially the rent that a tenant who is not already in possession would offer and a landlord would accept for the premises on the basis of vacant possession and having regard to the terms of the tenancy and the letting values of similar dwellings situated in a comparable area.

[10] Commission report (n 3) [8.6].

[11] Ibid [8.5].

[12] The label 'Part 4 tenancy' reflects the fact that the rules governing security of tenure are found in pt 4 of the RTA.

statutory intervention on these fundamental issues.[13] Another important practical issue for the Commission was the need to ensure that landlords and tenants would have access to an efficient and effective dispute resolution mechanism. There was general agreement that the courts system was expensive, complex and off-putting, and was unsuited to residential tenancy disputes.[14] The Commission recommended that a new body—in the form of the PRTB—should take over the role of resolving disputes.[15] This particular proposal was influenced by developments in other jurisdictions, especially Australia and New Zealand, where expert tribunals for residential tenancy disputes are well established.[16] Beyond dispute resolution, the Commission made a series of recommendations around the rights and obligations of landlords and tenants, and also called for an improved tenancy registration system to facilitate the enforcement of statutory rights and obligations.[17] The RTA reflected most of the Commission's recommendations and its enactment was widely anticipated as heralding the emergence of a more robustly regulated and professional private rented sector.

The long title to the RTA confirms the core objectives of legislative intervention in this area as being to provide for, inter alia: 'a measure of security of tenure for tenants of certain dwellings'; amendments to the law in relation to the basic rights and obligations of landlords and tenants; the establishment of the PRTB with the aim of allowing disputes to be resolved 'cheaply and speedily'; and the registration of tenancies. From the outset, there were high expectations of the PRTB among landlords and tenants, in particular as regards the new dispute resolution service. It was also anticipated that the RTA would lead to a higher profile for tenants' rights more generally and that these rights would be enforced vigorously by the PRTB.

Part 8 of the RTA provides for the establishment of the PRTB and sets out its composition and principal functions. The PRTB was established formally on 1 September 2004 and commenced its dispute resolution function under the RTA on 6 December 2004.[18] It soon become clear that the legislative framework was defective and that the RTA had established a labyrinthine scheme involving a degree of complexity that baffled landlords, tenants, regulators, lawyers, the judiciary and everyone else involved in the private rented market. In *Canty v Private Residential Tenancies Board*,[19] Laffoy J of the High Court observed that the RTA was 'an extremely complex piece of legislation' and described the rules governing termination of a Part 4 tenancy in the case of alleged non-payment of rent as being 'very technical and confusing'. Subsequently, in *Canty v Private Residential Tenancies Board*,[20] Kearns J of the Supreme Court observed that section 123(4) of the RTA (governing the scope

---

[13] Commission report (n 3) [8.11].

[14] Ibid [4.4], [4.8] and 8.3.

[15] Ibid [8.3] and [8.4].

[16] An overview of the comparative study undertaken on behalf of the Commission on the Private Rented Residential Sector by Professor Yvonne Galligan, which embraced Australia, Canada, New Zealand, the Netherlands and the UK, is provided in Appendix C to the Commission report.

[17] Commission report (n 3) pt II, Conclusions of Commission's Deliberations, www.environ.ie/en/Publications/DevelopmentandHousing/Housing/FileDownLoad,1994,en.pdf.

[18] Residential Tenancies Act 2004 (Commencement) Order 2004 (SI 505/2004) and Residential Tenancies Act 2004 (Commencement) (No 2) Order 2004 (SI 750/2004).

[19] *Canty v Private Residential Tenancies Board* [2007] IEHC 243.

[20] *Canty v Private Residential Tenancies Board* [2008] IESC 24.

of the right to appeal to the High Court on a point of law from the decision of a Tenancy Tribunal) was 'unsatisfactorily drafted in a number of respects' and its meaning was obscure. This complexity is due, in part, to the rather unusual law reform process that lay behind the RTA, which left the draftsman in the position of having to give effect to the Commission's intricate recommendations, including the compromise reached on rent regulation and security of tenure. The draftsman therefore faced considerable challenges in attempting to deliver the elaborate legislative scheme envisaged by the Commission. The level of detail presented in the RTA is at times overwhelming for lawyers and practically impossible for laypersons to comprehend. Identifying the rules that apply in a particular case usually involves extensive cross-referencing between different parts of the RTA and a range of other legislative measures. The RTA was superimposed on a series of existing rules governing the basic aspects of residential tenancies, including the rent books regulations[21] and the minimum standards regulations,[22] as well as fire safety rules and building control regulations. The scope for error in identifying and isolating the relevant rules is considerable, even for seasoned practitioners. It is regrettable that a piece of legislation that aimed to clarify the rights and obligations of landlords and tenants and to enable disputes to be resolved 'cheaply and speedily', and without the need for legal representation, was not drafted in a more coherent and user-friendly manner.

III. THE CORE ELEMENTS OF THE RTA, THE ROLE OF THE PRTB AND CONTEMPORARY ISSUES IN PRACTICE

A. The RTA: Basic Structure

The RTA, which is divided into nine parts,[23] is a tortuous piece of legislation which practitioners have compared to Deasy's Act[24] (another convoluted, yet highly significant piece of legislation from the 1800s) in terms of its sweeping impact on the law and practice governing the relationship of landlord and tenant.[25] This brief overview disguises the complexity that lies at the heart of the RTA, but aims to provide a general flavour of the statutory scheme. The RTA applies to what is usually described as the 'mainstream' private rented sector; pursuant to section 3(1),

---

[21] Housing (Rent Books) Regulations 1993 (SI 146/1993) as amended by Housing (Rent Books) Regulations 1993 (Amendment) Regulations 2004 (SI 751/2004) and Housing (Rent Books) (Amendment) Regulations 2010 (SI 357/2010).

[22] Housing (Standards for Rented Houses) Regulations 2008 (SI 534/2008) as amended by Housing (Standards for Rented Houses) (Amendment) Regulations 2009 (SI 462/2009).

[23] RTA, pts 1, 4, 5 (other than ss 17 and 72), 7, 8 (other than s 159(1)), 9 (other than ss 182, 189 and 190, paras (a) and (d) of s 193, and sub-ss (4) and (5) of s 195), and the Schedule came into operation on 1 September 2004: Residential Tenancies Act 2004 (Commencement) Order 2004 (SI 505/2004). The remaining provisions of the RTA came into operation on 6 December 2004: Residential Tenancies Act 2004 (Commencement) (No 2) Order 2004 (SI 750/2004).

[24] Landlord and Tenant Law Amendment Act Ireland 1860 (23 & 24 Vict Cap 154), known in Ireland as 'Deasy's Act' after Rickard Deasy, Attorney General for Ireland, who steered the Bill through Westminster.

[25] On Deasy's Act, see generally K Deale, *The Law of Landlord and Tenant in the Republic of Ireland* (Dublin, Incorporated Council of Law Reporting, 1968) pt I; and JCW Wylie, *Landlord and Tenant Law*, 2nd edn (Dublin, Butterworths, 1998) paras [1.08]–[1.09] and [2.07]–[2.10].

it applies to every dwelling which is the subject of a tenancy, including a tenancy created before the passing of the Act. This is subject to section 3(2), which lists nine categories of dwellings excluded from the RTA. In general terms, these exemptions embrace: business lettings; formerly rent controlled dwellings;[26] a dwelling let by or to a public authority or an approved body;[27] a dwelling where the occupier is entitled to acquire the fee simple;[28] a dwelling occupied under a shared ownership lease; a holiday letting; a dwelling where the landlord is also resident; a dwelling where the landlord's spouse, parent or child resides and no written tenancy agreement has been entered into by any person resident in the dwelling; and a dwelling the subject of a tenancy granted under Part II of the Landlord and Tenant (Amendment) Act 1980.[29] An amendment introduced in 2009 confirmed that the RTA does not apply to a tenancy where the term is more than 35 years.[30] This amendment was necessary because the RTA, as originally drafted, had not expressly excluded long leases of dwellings at low rents which are commonly used in conveyancing practice when transferring ownership on the sale of apartments.[31]

i. Obligations of Landlords and Tenants

The core obligations of landlords and tenants are found in Part 2 of the RTA. Section 12 lists the landlord's obligations, which include: to allow the tenant 'to enjoy peaceful and exclusive occupation of the dwelling'; to carry out specified repairs; to return or repay promptly any deposit paid by the tenant; and to reimburse the tenant for all reasonable and vouched expenses that may be incurred by the tenant in carrying out repairs to the dwelling which are the landlord's responsibility. The tenant's obligations are set down in section 16 and include: to pay the rent and any other agreed charges; to avoid causing, and to make good, any damage beyond 'normal wear and tear'; to notify the landlord of any defects in the dwelling that require repair; not to engage in or allow 'anti-social' behaviour;[32] and not to assign or sub-let, alter, improve or

---

[26] A rapidly declining category of private rented dwellings, the legacy of former rent control legislation which was found to be unconstitutional in 1982. The formerly rent controlled sector is regulated under a separate statutory scheme. For an overview, see M de Blacam, *The Control of Private Rented Dwellings*, 2nd edn (Dublin, Round Hall, 1992).

[27] 'Public authority' is defined in broad terms in s 4(1) of the RTA. An 'approved body' includes, for example, voluntary or cooperative housing associations approved under s 6 of the Housing (Miscellaneous Provisions) Act 1992. Note that the Residential Tenancies (Amendment) (No 2) Bill 2012, considered in Part IV below, proposes to extend the scope of the RTA to embrace dwellings let by voluntary and cooperative housing associations.

[28] On the entitlement of certain lessees to acquire the fee simple, see generally Wylie (n 25) ch 31.

[29] This relates to the entitlement of certain tenants to apply for a new tenancy based on business use, long occupation or improvements. See generally Wylie (n 25) ch 30. In practice, the entitlement to apply for a new tenancy would arise only very rarely in the context of a residential tenancy. In any event, s 192 of the RTA provided for this entitlement to be phased out in the case of tenancies to which the RTA applies in light of the right to security of tenure set down in pt 4 of the RTA.

[30] RTA, s 3(3), inserted by the Housing (Miscellaneous Provisions) Act 2009, s 100(2)(b).

[31] The failure to exclude long leases at low rents was problematic because owners of apartments will usually have a long lease with a nominal rent and provision for service charges. In *Private Residential Tenancies Board v Her Honour Judge Linnane* [2010] IEHC 476, the High Court confirmed that this category of long leases fell within the scope of the RTA as originally enacted—although plainly this was never the intention of the *Oireachtas* (Parliament).

[32] To behave in a way that is 'anti-social' is defined in broad terms in s 17(1) of the RTA to include: (a) engaging in behaviour that constitutes the commission of an offence which is reasonably likely to

change the use of the dwelling without the landlord's written consent. It is not possible to contract out of the terms of section 12 or 16, but the parties are free to agree more favourable terms for the tenant beyond those articulated in section 12.[33] Obligations over and above those set down in section 16 may be imposed on the tenant, but only where any such additional obligations are consistent with the RTA.[34] The RTA will override any conflicting provisions in a lease or tenancy agreement.[35] Section 14 provides that a landlord may not penalise a tenant for taking certain steps to enforce his rights (for example, where a tenant refers a dispute to the PRTB or complains to the local housing authority in relation to any matter concerning the occupation of the dwelling). A novel provision is found in section 15, pursuant to which a landlord owes a duty to enforce the tenant's obligations under the tenancy to every person 'who could be potentially affected' (for example, a neighbouring occupier who may be affected by noise or some other disturbance caused by the tenant).

ii. Rent and Rent Reviews

The rules governing rent and rent reviews are set out in Part 3 of the RTA and include rent setting, the definition of 'market rent',[36] rent review (including the right to a rent review even where this is not provided for expressly in the lease or tenancy agreement) and the formalities that apply when the landlord notifies the tenant of a new rent. The basic rule is that the rent may not be set at a level greater than the 'market rent' and rent reviews may not take place more frequently than once in every 12-month period, subject to limited exceptions.[37] Rents may be revised upwards or downwards depending on the prevailing market rent at the time of the review.

iii. Security of Tenure

Part 4 of the RTA concerns security of tenure and reflects the complicated, com-promise proposal on this fundamental issue recommended by the Commission on the Private Rented Residential Sector. Essentially, Part 4 provides that where the tenant has been in possession of a dwelling for a continuous period of six months, then he is entitled to remain in possession for a further period of three and a half years—amounting to a four-year period in total—known under the RTA as a 'Part 4 tenancy'. In cases where the tenancy in question is periodic, or any fixed term agreed

---

affect directly the well-being or welfare of others; (b) engaging in behaviour that causes or could cause fear, danger, injury, damage or loss to any person living, working or otherwise lawfully in the dwelling concerned or its vicinity (including violence, intimidation, etc); and (c) engaging persistently in behaviour that prevents or interferes with another person's peaceful occupation of the dwelling or a dwelling in the vicinity of the rented dwelling.

[33] RTA, s 18(1) and (2).

[34] Ibid, s 18(3).

[35] This is the position even in the case of a tenancy agreement entered into before 6 December 2004 (the date of commencement of pt 2 of the RTA).

[36] 'Market rent' is defined in s 24(1) of the RTA as 'the rent which a willing tenant not already in occupation would give and a willing landlord would take for the dwelling, in each case on the basis of vacant possession being given, and having regard to (a) the other terms of the tenancy and (b) the letting values of dwellings of a similar size, type and character to the dwelling situated in a comparable area to that in which it is situated'.

[37] RTA, s 20(3).

between the parties has expired, the landlord may prevent a Part 4 tenancy from arising by serving a valid notice of termination before the expiry of the initial six-month period.[38] Where the tenant has qualified for a Part 4 tenancy, the landlord may only move to terminate the tenancy and regain possession of the dwelling in the specific circumstances set out in the table to section 34. There are six grounds for termination covering the following situations: breach of tenancy obligations by the tenant; where the dwelling is no longer suited to the accommodation needs of the occupants; where the landlord intends to sell within three months of termination of the tenancy; where the landlord requires the dwelling for his own occupation or for occupation by a family member;[39] where the landlord intends to substantially refurbish or renovate the dwelling; and where the landlord intends to change the use of the dwelling. This comprehensive catalogue of grounds covers the practical situations where a landlord would need to recover possession of a rented dwelling.

Where a Part 4 tenancy continues to the expiry of the four-year period, without the landlord serving a valid notice of termination before that period expires, then a new tenancy will come into being on that expiry. Any such new tenancy is referred to in the RTA as a 'further Part 4 tenancy'.[40] This statutory entitlement reflects the rolling nature of the security of tenure rights established in Part 4 of the RTA. However, during the first six months of any 'further Part 4 tenancy', a landlord may terminate the tenancy by serving a notice of termination giving the period of notice required under the RTA.[41] Once the initial six-month period expires without a valid notice of termination being served by the landlord, the landlord may only seek to terminate the 'further Part 4 tenancy' on the basis of one of the six grounds for termination set down in the table to section 34.

iv. Tenancy Terminations

The rules governing tenancy terminations are set down in Part 5 of the RTA, which prescribes statutory notice periods and other mandatory procedural requirements. The most significant change brought about by Part 5 is that it is no longer open to a landlord to deploy traditional mechanisms such as forfeiture and re-entry to recover possession of a dwelling to which the RTA applies.[42] It is important to note that in the case of a Part 4 tenancy, the requirements set down in Part 5 for the valid termination of a tenancy are *in addition* to the rules established in Part 4 concerning the right to security of tenure.[43] The awkward interaction between Parts 4 and 5 has proven problematic in practice due to the complexity of the relevant provisions and

---

[38] Ibid, s 28(3).

[39] A 'family member' in this context is defined in s 35(4) of the RTA (as amended) as meaning any spouse, civil partner, child, stepchild, foster child, grandchild, parent, grandparent, step-parent, parent-in-law, brother, sister, nephew or niece of the landlord or a person adopted by the landlord under the Adoption Acts 1952 to 1998.

[40] RTA, s 41(2).

[41] Except in cases where the landlord is bound by a fixed-term tenancy agreement with the tenant.

[42] Section 59 of the RTA excludes existing rules of law and enactments from application in the case of termination of a tenancy of a dwelling. This provision is subject to s 60, which provides that where a greater period of notice than that specified in pt 5 of the RTA is required to be given under the terms of any lease or tenancy agreement, then the greater period of notice continues to apply (subject to s 65(4)).

[43] RTA, s 57(b).

the fact that poor draftsmanship means that the two parts do not interlock neatly. The procedural requirements to terminate a Part 4 tenancy in the case of non-payment of rent remained in a state of considerable uncertainty until a High Court decision attempted to make sense of the relevant provisions.[44] It is heartening to see that the Residential Tenancies Amendment (No 2) Bill 2012 proposes to address this important point by adding a new ground to the table to section 34 dealing with the specific case of alleged non-payment of rent.[45]

Section 62 specifies the detailed contents of a valid notice of termination. The notice must be in writing, signed by the landlord (or his agent) and must specify both the date of service and the termination date. It must also state that any issue as to the validity of the notice must be referred to the PRTB within 28 days of the date of receipt. Moreover, where the landlord seeks to terminate a tenancy which has lasted for more than six months, the notice must state the reason for termination. Section 66, which contains two tables, prescribes the periods of notice that must be given to terminate a tenancy (Table 1 concerns termination by the landlord and Table 2 governs termination by the tenant). The notice periods specified in the tables are linked to the duration of tenancy. In the case of termination by the landlord, the notice periods range from 28 days to 112 days depending on the length of the tenancy in question. The notice periods that apply where the tenant seeks to terminate range from 28 days to a maximum of 56 days, again depending on the length of the tenancy. Special provision is made for abridged periods of notice where it is alleged that either party has failed to comply with his obligations under the tenancy.[46] Where a tenancy is being terminated due to the alleged default of one of the parties, mandatory procedural requirements are prescribed.[47] In most cases, the party in default must be given notice of the alleged breach, and an opportunity to remedy the situation, before the party seeking to terminate can proceed to issue a valid notice of termination. Failure to comply with any of the mandatory requirements set down in Part 5 of the RTA (in addition to Part 4, in cases where this also applies) will invalidate a notice of termination and a fresh notice will need to be served in order to terminate the tenancy lawfully. In the early days of the RTA, a significant number of landlords remained unaware of the detailed requirements prescribed in section 62 and in Part 4, with the result that notices of termination were successfully challenged by tenants before the PRTB on a regular basis.[48] Although the rules have now bedded down to a considerable extent, the detailed and prescriptive nature of the statutory regime governing tenancy termination remains a trap for the unwary landlord or tenant.

v. Dispute Resolution

The vast majority of residential tenancy disputes are now dealt with by the PRTB under Part 6 of the RTA rather than in the courts.[49] Pursuant to section 109 of the RTA, the PRTB has published detailed rules governing its dispute resolution

---

[44] *Canty* (n 19).
[45] See Part IV below.
[46] RTA, ss 67 and 68.
[47] Ibid.
[48] PRTB, *Annual Report 1/9/2004–31/12/2005*, 22.
[49] Subject to the jurisdictional limits set down in s 182(1) of the RTA.

procedure.[50] The initial fee to engage the Board's dispute resolution service is only €25 and, since May 2012, an application may be made online via the PRTB website. During 2011, the PRTB received 2,060 applications for dispute resolution; 59 per cent of applications were made by tenants, 38 per cent by landlords and 3 per cent by third parties.[51] The Annual Report for 2011 confirms a 25 per cent increase in the number of disputes referred to the PRTB since 2008. It is difficult to identify the specific reasons behind this dramatic rise in referrals, but it is most likely due to a greater awareness of the PRTB and its services, together with the fact that the current, very difficult, economic climate has led to more incidents of rent arrears. In line with the consistent trend since the entry into force of Part 6 of the RTA in December 2004, the two most significant categories of disputes referred to the PRTB in 2011 involved deposit retention (39 per cent) and rent arrears (32 per cent), followed by validity of notice of termination (9 per cent) and standard and maintenance of the rented dwelling (5 per cent).[52] It is striking that in the deposit disputes determined by adjudicators in 2011, the landlord was required to refund all or part of the deposit in 78 per cent of cases.[53] Deposit disputes consume a major portion of the PRTB's limited resources and it is obvious that in a substantial number of these disputes, the landlord's claim is unsustainable. This state of affairs confirms that nine years after the enactment of the RTA, many landlords remain ignorant of their obligations concerning the deposit and fail to comply with the law. The persistent nature of the deposit retention culture, and the difficulties it creates for tenants who need access to a deposit to move to new premises, led to calls for the establishment of a 'Tenancy Deposit Protection Scheme' in line with similar schemes in place in a number of common law jurisdictions, including, for example, England and Wales,[54] New South Wales (Australia),[55] New Zealand,[56] Scotland,[57] and, most recently, Northern Ireland.[58] The current *Programme for Government 2011* contains an express commitment to 'establish a tenancy deposit protection

---

[50] *Section 109 Rules: Private Residential Tenancies Board Dispute Resolution Procedure* (11 May 2011), http://public.prtb.ie/disputes.htm.

[51] PRTB, *Annual Report and Accounts 2011*, 23. Typical third parties would include neighbours seeking redress pursuant to s 15 of the RTA where they allege that the landlord has failed to enforce the tenant's obligations and, in particular, the obligation not to engage in anti-social behaviour.

[52] PRTB, *Annual Report and Accounts 2011* p 23.

[53] PRTB, *Annual Report and Accounts 2011* p 24 (a full refund was ordered in 45 per cent of cases and a part refund was ordered in 33 per cent of cases).

[54] Sections 212–15 of the Housing Act 2004, as amended by s 184 of the Localism Act 2011, provides for tenancy deposit schemes for deposits received in connection with assured shorthold tenancies. For an overview of the difficulties that beset the initial legislative provisions aimed at protecting deposits, see J Morgan, 'Tenancy Deposits: Better Late than Never' [2011] *Conv* 240.

[55] In New South Wales, pursuant to the Residential Tenancies Act 2010, the Rental Bond Board receives and holds rental bonds (deposits).

[56] In New Zealand, pursuant to the Residential Tenancies Act 1986 and the Residential Tenancies Amendment Act 2010, the Department of Building and Housing Group Tenancy Division (within the Ministry of Business, Innovation and Employment) receives and holds rental bonds (deposits) and administers the RTA.

[57] Pursuant to the Tenancy Deposit Schemes (Scotland) Regulations 2011 (SI 2011/176), landlords and letting agents are required to lodge deposits with a government-approved tenancy deposit scheme.

[58] The Tenancy Deposit Schemes Regulations (Northern Ireland) 2012 (SI 2012/373). From 1 April 2013, a landlord is obliged to protect any deposit relating to a private residential tenancy in an approved tenancy deposit scheme.

scheme to put an end to disputes regarding the return of deposits'.[59] Organisations representing tenant interests, and in particular Threshold (the National Housing Charity) and the Union of Students in Ireland (USI), have long campaigned for such a scheme and continue to urge the government to deliver on its express commitment in this regard.[60] Meanwhile, the Irish Property Owners' Association (IPOA) has expressed its strong opposition to this proposal.[61] A study commissioned by the PRTB to examine the feasibility of establishing a residential tenancy deposit protection scheme was published in November 2012.[62] This much-anticipated study identified and evaluated a range of options for an Irish deposit protection scheme and concluded that a custodial scheme, with the management and administration undertaken by a private sector provider, would be the best option. However, the report highlighted that any such scheme would not be financially viable without government subsidies or significant legislative amendments aimed at reducing the costs currently involved in processing disputes. Measures to address the problem of non-compliant landlords were also identified as being crucial to its financial viability. Notwithstanding these reservations, it is clear that there is a strong political commitment on the part of government to press ahead with the introduction of a deposit protection scheme. However, the form and structure of any such scheme, how it will interact with the RTA, and when it is likely to materialise, are all issues that remain uncertain at the time of writing.

vi. The Mechanics of the PRTB Dispute Resolution Process

The dispute resolution mechanism established in Part 6 of the RTA may involve two distinct stages, depending on the particular factual scenario: (1) mediation (which is voluntary) or adjudication; and (2) a hearing before a Tenancy Tribunal. Where the parties agree to mediation, a mediator is appointed from the PRTB's panel of mediators to assist the parties in resolving the dispute themselves. However, the rate of take-up of the mediation service offered by the PRTB has been very low to date (less than two per cent of the cases referred) and there is no indication that this situation is likely to change significantly, at least in the short term. Where either of the parties decides not to engage in mediation,[63] an adjudicator is appointed from the PRTB's panel of adjudicators to examine the parties' evidence, to investigate the dispute and to determine how it should be resolved. Mediation and adjudication are confidential to the parties, although Determination Orders issued by the PRTB following adjudication are published on its website.[64] At the time of writing,

---

[59] *Programme for Government 2011*, p 16, <www.taoiseach.ie.>

[60] Threshold, presentation to the Joint Oireachtas Committee on Environment, Transport, Culture and the Gaeltacht, 4 October 2011 and USI, *Deposit Protection Scheme*, Submission to the Joint Oireachtas Committee on Environment, Transport, Culture and the Gaeltacht, 4 October 2011. See also Threshold, *Annual Report 2010*, p 16.

[61] IPOA, *A Rental Deposit Protection Scheme Discussion*, Submission to the Joint Oireachtas Committee on Environment, Transport, Culture and the Gaeltacht, 4 October 2011.

[62] Indecon International Economic Consulstants, *Indecon's Assessment of the Feasibility of a Tenancy Deposit Protection Scheme in Ireland* (November 2012) <www.prtb.ie.>

[63] Or where the PRTB takes the view that, in the particular circumstances of the case, a dispute is not suitable for mediation.

[64] The adjudicators' reports are issued only to the parties to the dispute and are not published.

the average processing time for a dispute, from the initial application to the PRTB until a Determination Order is issued following mediation or adjudication, is 8–10 months. However, it is PRTB policy to prioritise certain urgent disputes, including, for example, rent arrears cases where the tenant is overholding, illegal eviction and serious 'anti-social' behaviour. At the time of writing, the average processing time for priority cases is 4–5 months.

A dispute may be referred to a Tenancy Tribunal in a number of circumstances: first, where mediation is unsuccessful and any of the parties requests a tribunal hearing; second, where a party wishes to appeal an adjudicator's determination; and, third, the PRTB may refer a dispute *directly* to a tribunal where it considers that mediation or adjudication would not be appropriate, for example, in the case of alleged illegal eviction or serious 'anti-social' behaviour. In the case of an appeal to the Tribunal from an adjudicator's ruling, the tribunal deals with the matter de novo. Each Tenancy Tribunal is made up of three persons drawn from the PRTB's Dispute Resolution Committee. In light of the formal procedures that apply before the Tribunal and the complexity of the statutory scheme, it is surprising to find that the RTA does not mandate that at least one member of the Tribunal must be a lawyer. The fee for a referral to the Tribunal is €100[65] and each of the parties is entitled to be heard, to present evidence and witnesses to the Tribunal, and to be represented. However, there is very limited provision for the award of legal and other costs and expenses in relation to proceedings before the PRTB, and costs are only rarely awarded to parties to disputes in practice.[66] Civil legal aid is not available for disputes arising under the RTA.[67] According to the PRTB Annual Report for 2010, the majority of parties before the Tribunal were not represented (55 per cent), while 16 per cent of landlords and 6 per cent of tenants engaged a solicitor.[68] A further 22 per cent of tenants were represented by Threshold (the National Housing Charity).[69] Proceedings before the Tribunal are more formal than adjudication hearings and are conducted in public, subject to limited exceptions.[70]

The rate of appeal to the Tenancy Tribunal from adjudicators' decisions is in the region of 33.5 per cent.[71] During 2010, 340 Tenancy Tribunals were convened, representing a dramatic 93 per cent increase in the number of Tribunal hearings when compared to the 2009 figure.[72] The figure for 2011 was 179, representing a 47 per cent decrease in Tribunal hearings from 2010 to 2011.[73] The PRTB has explained

---

[65] The PRTB increased this fee from €40 to €100 as from 11 July 2011. The rationale behind this sharp increase was presumably an attempt to discourage vexatious and frivolous appeals that are lodged solely for the purpose of delaying the conclusion of PRTB proceedings.

[66] RTA, s 5(3) and (4).

[67] Section 27(2)(b) of the Civil Legal Aid Act 1995 provides that legal aid is not available for proceedings before administrative tribunals unless the particular tribunal is prescribed by the Minister for Justice and Equality.

[68] PRTB, *Annual Report and Accounts 2010*, 36. It is notable that the 2011 Annual Report does not include any data on representation before the Tenancy Tribunal.

[69] PRTB, *Annual Report and Accounts 2010* 37.

[70] RTA, s 106(2).

[71] K Ward, Assistant Director, PRTB, 'How to Make the Best Use of PRTB Services', presentation to PRTB Stakeholder Consultation Meeting, 15 December 2011 (transcript on file with author).

[72] PRTB, *Annual Report and Accounts 2010* 32.

[73] PRTB, *Annual Report and Accounts 2011* 25.

that the striking reduction in the number of Tribunals convened during 2011 is due to the implementation its new Tenancy Management System during that period and the significant reduction in its staffing levels noted earlier. At the time of writing, the average waiting time for a tribunal hearing is in the region of 2–3 months. In 2010, adjudicators' determinations were upheld in 26 per cent of cases and varied in 68 per cent of cases.[74] The fact that over two-thirds of decisions were varied on appeal is striking and raises concerns over the quality of decision making at first instance. However, an analysis of Tenancy Tribunal reports indicates that this state of affairs is due to a complex mix of factors and it is not simply a case of adjudicators getting it 'wrong' at first instance and decisions being overturned on appeal.[75] The reality is that a significant number of parties to disputes fail to appreciate that they must present cogent and credible evidence to support their claim before the PRTB. Having learnt this lesson at first instance before the adjudicator, it is open to a party to appeal an adverse decision and to present fresh evidence to the Tribunal with a potentially very significant impact on the outcome of the proceedings. Similarly, parties who fail to appear at the adjudication hearing may appeal to the Tribunal in order to revive the proceedings. Apart from the 21-day time limit and the €100 referral fee, there is currently no restriction on the right to appeal to the Tribunal.

Tenancy Tribunal determinations are binding on the parties unless appealed to the High Court on a point of law within 21 days of the order being issued to the parties. The High Court may direct the PRTB to cancel the Determination Order concerned or to vary it in such manner as specified by the court, and the determination of the High Court is final and conclusive. There is no general right of appeal to the courts from a tribunal determination. When compared with other statutory schemes governing de novo administrative appeals, it is surprising to find that the RTA does not confer the Tribunal with the power to refer a point of law arising in the course of a hearing to the High Court for determination. This option would enable the Tribunal to have novel and difficult points of law, including thorny questions of interpretation of the RTA, determined definitively as they arise in practice.

The forms of redress that may be granted under Part 6 of the RTA are set out in section 115 and a wide variety of declarations or directions may be made in respect of a dispute. An adjudicator, or the Tribunal, may also grant interim redress pending the final determination of the dispute.[76] This provision is separate from the PRTB's entitlement to apply to the Circuit Court pursuant to section 189, on being requested to do so by the person who referred (or who is referring) the dispute to the Board, for interim or interlocutory relief (for example, in the case of threatened illegal eviction or serious 'anti-social' behaviour). An adjudicator, or the Tribunal, may award damages of up to €20,000 and rent arrears of up to €20,000 or twice the annual rent (whichever is the greater), subject to an upper limit of €60,000 for rent arrears.[77] A mediated agreement, or a determination of an adjudicator or

---

[74] Ward (n 71).
[75] Ibid.
[76] RTA, s 117.
[77] Ibid, s 115(3). Disputes involving amounts greater than these thresholds must be pursued through the courts.

of a tribunal, will result in a Determination Order being prepared and issued by the PRTB. Determination Orders are based on reports submitted to the PRTB by a mediator or an Ajudicator, or on the determination of the Tribunal.[78] They are published in the 'Dispute Resolution' section of the PRTB website.[79]

vii. Tenancy Registration

Part 7 of the RTA governs tenancy registration and section 134(1) requires the landlord to apply to register each tenancy with the PRTB within one month of its commencement. The registration process, which can now be completed online via the PRTB website, costs €90 per tenancy and involves the landlord providing detailed information about each tenancy to the PRTB. The most recent data indicates that as at 31 December 2012, there were 264,434 active tenancies registered on the PRTB system (comprising 212,306 landlords and 593,383 tenants).[80] It is notable that the PRTB cannot deal with a dispute referred to it by a *landlord* if the tenancy is not registered under Part 7.[81] However, this prohibition does not impact on the right of a tenant or a third party to refer a dispute concerning an unregistered tenancy.

B. The RTA: General Assessment

The enactment of the RTA, together with the establishment of the PRTB, has brought about dramatic changes in the regulation of private residential tenancies in Ireland. In many respects, the RTA has improved the situation for both landlords and tenants. Pre-RTA, a blend of common law and statute law (including many archaic and little-known statutory provisions) provided some basic rights for tenants, including, for example, a minimum period of four weeks' notice to quit, the right to a rent book and minimum standards of rented accommodation.[82] Tenants rarely engaged in litigation to enforce their (limited) rights and, in many cases, simply opted to 'cut their losses' rather than pursue a potential remedy through the costly and intimidating courts system. In a major advance on the previous position, the RTA sets out a comprehensive and detailed catalogue of the rights and obligations of landlords and tenants, while the PRTB provides an accessible, specialist dispute resolution mechanism. Tenants now regularly pursue claims against their landlords for a wide variety of alleged breaches of the RTA.

---

[78] A Determination Order embodying the terms of a mediated agreement or the determination of an adjudicator is binding on the parties concerned once the order is issued to them. A Determination Order embodying the terms of a determination made by a Tenancy Tribunal becomes binding once the time limit for an appeal to the High Court on a point of law has expired.

[79] Apart from Determination Orders embodying the terms of a mediated agreement, which remain confidential to the parties.

[80] It is necessary to treat these figures with a note of caution, however, as the RTA does not require landlords to notify the PRTB that a tenancy no longer exists.

[81] RTA, s 83(2) and (3).

[82] See generally Á Ryall, 'Recent Developments in Residential Tenancy Law (Part I)' (1997) 2 *Conveyancing and Property Law Journal* 51 and 'Recent Developments in Residential Tenancy Law (Part II)' (1998) 3 *Conveyancing and Property Law Journal* 4.

While deposit disputes are by far the most common in practice, an analysis of the Determination Orders issued by the PRTB confirms that tenants have been awarded significant sums in damages for illegal eviction,[83] breach of the right to peaceful and exclusive occupation of the dwelling,[84] sub-standard accommodation and failure to carry out repairs.[85] Neighbours who are adversely affected by a tenant's 'anti-social' behaviour have also secured remedies against landlords under section 15, including significant damages awards.[86] As awareness of the RTA and the potential remedies available to tenants grows, demand for the PRTB's dispute resolution service will continue to expand rapidly, creating further pressure on its already-stretched resources.

Notwithstanding the availability of an accessible and specialist dispute resolution service via the PRTB, the RTA has failed to live up to expectations. In particular, the complex, multi-layered dispute resolution mechanism prescribed in the RTA, together with resource constraints within the PRTB, has resulted in long delays in processing disputes to a conclusion. Even then, there is no guarantee that the respondent will comply with the Determination Order issued by the PRTB and enforcement action via the courts may be required.

Enforcement has emerged as a serious problem in practice which poses a real threat to the PRTB's credibility among landlords and tenants. It is frustrating in the extreme for a party who has successfully negotiated the PRTB dispute resolution process to find that the respondent refuses to comply with the Determination Order and that further action is required to secure compliance. The RTA provides for specific enforcement measures in this scenario. The PRTB, or any party mentioned in a Determination Order, may apply to the Circuit Court to direct the respondent to comply with the terms of an order.[87] The main drawback here is that civil enforcement requires the PRTB, or the party seeking enforcement, to engage with the courts system, thereby triggering further costs, uncertainty and delay. The PRTB's enforcement powers are discretionary and the RTA does not place any obligation on the Board to enforce its Determination Orders. Failure to comply with a Determination Order is an offence[88] and the PRTB may bring criminal proceedings in the District Court where a maximum fine of €4,000 and/or a period of imprisonment of up to six months may be imposed on conviction.[89] There is a growing problem of non-compliance with Determination Orders issued by the PRTB and this situation

---

[83] See, eg, TR34/DR1549/2011, *Vincent Cosgrave v Marek Swiderski and Ryszard Molenda* (the Tenancy Tribunal awarded damages of €15,000 for illegal eviction) and TR323/DR11/2010, *Al-Sadik KH Jaly v Phyllis O'Donnell* (the Tenancy Tribunal awarded €15,000 for the unlawful termination of the tenancy).

[84] See, eg, TR49/DR1509/2009, *Landlord X v Edmund Monaghan*.

[85] See, eg, TR62/DR1045/2008, *John Ironside v Michael Allen* (the Tenancy Tribunal awarded the tenant €1,950 in damages for 'stress and diminished enjoyment of the tenancy' due to the landlord's failure to carry out promised works) and TR50/DR1206/2009, *Avril Trayer v Patrick O'Neill*.

[86] See generally Á Ryall, 'Landlords, Neighbours and Misbehaving Tenants: Dispute Resolution Mechanisms under the Residential Tenancies Act 2004', paper presented at conference on Contemporary Housing Issues in a Changing Europe (NUI Galway, 21 April 2012).

[87] RTA, s 124(1).

[88] Ibid, s 126.

[89] There is provision for a further fine of no greater than €500 a day for continuing non-compliance.

is compounded by the fact that the PRTB's resources are limited and enforcement activity is both expensive and time-consuming.

The PRTB received 561 enforcement requests in 2010, an increase of 82 per cent on the figure for the previous year. The main problems experienced by landlords concerned rent arrears and related matters (234 enforcement requests), while deposit retention was the main issue for tenants (221 enforcement requests). Demand for enforcement action by the PRTB remains high, with 589 new requests for enforcement of Determination Orders received in 2011—representing a 5 per cent increase on the 2010 figure. The PRTB attributes the sharp increase in enforcement requests to the financial consequences of the economic downturn (which has led landlords to refer an increased number of rent arrears disputes) and to the fact that demand for the PRTB's dispute resolution service has risen exponentially in recent years as awareness of the service has grown. There is a strong view among landlords, tenants and their representative organisations that the PRTB is not proactive in enforcing its Determination Orders.[90] Given the vocal critique of its enforcement role, it is disappointing that the PRTB has not published an enforcement policy to date. Instead, a summary of enforcement activity is presented in its Annual Reports. In the first instance, the PRTB attempts to secure compliance via non-legal means and during 2011, direct intervention by its Enforcement Unit led to 'compliance or settlement' without the need for legal proceedings in 65 of the enforcement requests received.[91] In the same period, the PRTB approved 81 cases for enforcement action: 61 for civil action in the Circuit Court and 20 for criminal proceedings in the District Court.[92] Fifty four court orders were obtained in 2011, 42 from the Circuit Court and 12 from the District Court.[93]

It is difficult to quantify the extent of the enforcement deficit, but the PRTB data for 2010 and 2011 confirms that it is a significant problem and anecdotal evidence suggests that the situation continues to deteriorate. There is a striking lack of information around the current levels of enforcement activity (the most recent PRTB data relates to 2011) and the extent to which the PRTB prioritises certain categories of cases for enforcement action. A more proactive stance on enforcement matters, and greater transparency around enforcement activity, is vital if landlords and tenants are to have confidence in the regulatory framework. If the regulatory framework lacks teeth, then landlords and tenants have no incentive to

---

[90] The enforcement challenge was mentioned on a number of occasions during the hearings involving the PRTB and stakeholders, including the IPOA, Threshold and the USI, before the Joint Oireachtas Committee on Environment, Transport, Culture and the Gaeltacht, 4 October 2011. The enforcement deficit was highlighted in a RTÉ *Prime Time* programme—*Unwelcome Home*—broadcast on 10 May 2012, which presented a number of striking case studies that revealed the PRTB's reluctance and tardiness in pursing enforcement action in a number of specific cases (including in the case of serial unlawful deposit retention by one particular landlord and a serious illegal eviction involving physical violence and sustained threats by another landlord against his tenants).

[91] PRTB, *Annual Report and Accounts 2011*, 36.

[92] Ibid.

[93] Ibid.

comply with the law and are more likely to be tempted to take the law into their own hands.

IV. THE WAY FORWARD

If the RTA is to underpin an effective and responsive regulatory framework for the private rented sector, then action is required on two fronts. First, the RTA must be amended to address a range of problems that have surfaced in practice over the past nine years. Second, adequate resources must be made available to the PRTB to enable it to fulfil its statutory mandate more efficiently.

A. The RTA: Review and Revision—the Residential Tenancies Amendment (No 2) Bill 2012

At the time of writing, moves are under way to amend the RTA. Following a number of (unpublished) reviews of the RTA by the Department of Environment, Community and Local Government (DECLG), the Residential Tenancies Amendment (No 2) Bill 2012 was published in July 2012.[94] This section considers the proposed amendments that are likely to impact most significantly in practice on landlords and tenants in the private rented sector.[95] Other important aspects of the Bill, including Part 2, which proposes to extend the RTA to certain dwellings let by approved voluntary and cooperative housing bodies, lie beyond the scope of this chapter.[96] It must be stressed at the outset that the provisions considered here relate to the text of the Bill *as initiated* and that there are likely to be important changes and additions to the original text as the Bill makes its way through the *Oireachtas*. The Press Release issued by the DECLG on the publication of the Bill confirmed that the Minister intends to bring forward additional amendments at a later stage.[97] Specifically, it is anticipated that amendments will be forthcoming to address the significant problem of landlords unjustifiably withholding tenants' deposits, potentially involving the establishment of a tenancy deposit scheme. The Minister has also pledged to bring forward an amendment to the Bill to address non-payment of rent

---

[94] The text of the Bill (as initiated) and the Explanatory Memorandum is available at: www.oireachtas. ie/documents/bills28/bills/2012/6912/b6912d.pdf.

[95] By way of summary, there are essentially four elements to the Bill. First, it extends the scope of the RTA, including the registration requirement, to include certain tenancies in the voluntary and cooperative housing sector. This is a very positive development, given the expanding role that this sector plays in the provision of social housing. Second, it provides for a series of amendments to the RTA, including, inter alia, clarification of the rules governing tenancy termination and simplification of the mediation process. Third, it provides for the dissolution of the Rent Tribunal and for the transfer of its functions to the PRTB. Fourth, it amends s 84 of the Housing (Miscellaneous Provisions) Act 2009 to ensure consistency with the provisions in the Bill relating to the inclusion of the voluntary and cooperative housing sector within the scope of the RTA.

[96] As a result of this very significant development, the Bill proposes to change the name of the PRTB to the Residential Tenancies Board (s 8(1) of the Bill).

[97] Department of Environment, Community and Local Government, Press Release, 'Minister O'Sullivan Publishes Legislation to Significantly Reform Landlord and Tenant Law', 19 July 2012, www. environ.ie/en/DevelopmentHousing/Housing/News/MainBody,30752,en.htm.

by tenants who are overholding following termination of their tenancy. As things stand, where a notice of termination is served after a dispute has been referred to the PRTB, the RTA prevents the tenancy from being treated as terminated, notwithstanding the expiry of the relevant notice period.[98] The net result is that termination is, in effect, suspended pending determination of the dispute. This state of affairs is obviously a source of immense frustration for landlords, which is compounded by the fact that at the time of writing it can take 12 months or more to have a dispute determined by the PRTB. It is vital that the Bill addresses this unacceptable situation so as to prevent tenants from abusing their position and taking advantage of the current delays in the PRTB dispute resolution process. At the same time, however, careful drafting is required to achieve an appropriate balance between the rights and interests of landlords and tenants while a dispute is still pending before the PRTB.

In its current form, the Bill proposes to address the following issues.

i. Tenancy Termination

The rules governing tenancy termination are one of the most convoluted and impenetrable aspects of the RTA. The current rules are far from being user-friendly and the scope for error, particularly as regards the contents of a notice of termination, is considerable. The Bill makes some attempt to clarify and improve the current rules, but the proposed amendments are rather limited in scope. First, section 11 of the Bill amends section 33 of the RTA in order to clarify that the provisions of Part 5 of the RTA also apply to the termination of a Part 4 tenancy. This has always been the case, but this amendment is useful in that it flags this fundamental point expressly in the text of Part 4 of the RTA (currently, this point is mentioned only in Part 5 of the RTA, specifically in section 57(b), which is drafted in such an opaque manner that it could easily be overlooked and/or misunderstood). Second, section 12 of the Bill introduces important amendments to the table to section 34 of the RTA. It will be recalled that this table sets out the six grounds on which a landlord may seek to terminate a Part 4 tenancy. Serious deficiencies in the drafting of Ground 1 in the table (which applies where the tenant has failed to comply with any of his obligations in relation to the tenancy, including non-payment of rent)[99] have resulted in significant problems in practice and the text of Ground 1 has been criticised sharply by the High Court.[100] Section 12 aims to address these deficiencies by creating a new, separate ground for termination of a Part 4 tenancy in the specific case of non-payment of rent (Ground 1A). A landlord may seek to rely on the new Ground 1A where: (1) the tenant has failed to comply with the obligation to pay the rent and the landlord has notified the tenant in writing under section 67(3) that an amount of rent due has not been paid;

---

[98] RTA, s 86(1)(c).

[99] Section 16(a) of the RTA sets out the tenant's obligation to pay the rent and, where the lease or tenancy agreement so provides, any charges or taxes payable by the tenant.

[100] *Canty* (n 19). Laffoy J observed that the provisions of the RTA governing termination of a Part 4 tenancy for non-payment of rent 'are very technical and confusing'. The High Court found it difficult to understand why, as regards non-payment of rent, the notification under Ground 1, para (a) in the table to s 34 was not made coterminous with the notification required under s 67(3).

(2) 14 days have elapsed from the receipt of the notification under section 67(3); and (3) the tenant has not paid the amount of rent due. As a result of this amendment, Ground 1 will now only apply in the case of a breach of tenancy obligation *other than* non-payment of rent and the Bill amends the text of Ground 1 to reflect this position. The text of Ground 1 is also amended by the addition of an express obligation on the landlord to notify the tenant 'in writing' of the alleged failure to comply with his obligations relating to the tenancy. Section 12 also amends the text of Ground 5 in the table to section 34. In brief terms, Ground 5 enables a landlord to seek to terminate a Part 4 tenancy on the basis that he intends to substantially refurbish or renovate the dwelling and requires vacant possession for this purpose. In addition to serving a valid notice of termination, a landlord who seeks to invoke Ground 5 must provide the tenant with a statement (either contained within the notice of termination or accompanying it) which sets out certain information. This information must specify the nature of the intended works and must explain that, in certain circumstances, the landlord is obliged to offer the tenant a tenancy of the dwelling if the dwelling becomes available for re-letting following refurbishment. In sharp contrast with Ground 4[101] and Ground 6[102] in the table to section 34, Ground 5 does not set any time limit on the landlord's obligation to offer the former tenant a tenancy of the refurbished dwelling. Section 12 addresses this omission by stipulating that this obligation arises within the period of 12 months from the expiry of the period of notice required to be given by the notice of termination, or in the event of a dispute as to the validity of the notice of termination being referred to the PRTB, the final determination of the dispute. Third, section 13 of the Bill amends section 70 of the RTA to clarify that where the landlord wishes to terminate both a head-tenancy and any sub-tenancy created out of the head-tenancy, then it is the landlord who must serve notice of termination on the sub-tenant.

ii. Dispute Resolution

The Bill proposes a number of amendments to the rules governing dispute resolution by the PRTB, including a number of significant changes designed to make mediation more attractive. Currently, there is a very low take-up of the mediation service offered by the PRTB (less than two per cent of the disputes referred). The key amendments to the rules governing mediation are found in sections 16–19 and sections 21–22 of the Bill.[103] Essentially, the proposed amendments aim to simplify and streamline the mediation procedure: for example, section 19 of the Bill amends section 98(1) of the RTA by providing that the 'cooling-off' period following a mediated agreement is reduced from 21 days to 10 days. Furthermore, section 16(1)

---

[101] Ground 4 may be invoked where a landlord requires the dwelling (or the property containing the dwelling) for his or her own occupation or for occupation by a family member.

[102] Ground 6 may be invoked where a landlord intends to change the use of the dwelling (or the property containing the dwelling) to some other use and has obtained any planning permission required for that change of use.

[103] The Bill also provides for a number of other amendments that are consequential to these changes to the mediation provisions.

of the Bill amends section 93 of the RTA to provide that the PRTB may not charge a fee in respect of mediation services. The amendments to the mediation provisions will not operate retrospectively. Beyond mediation, the Bill provides for various amendments to the rules governing dispute resolution. First, section 15 amends section 86 of the RTA to clarify that this section only applies in cases where a tenancy has not been terminated. It also confirms that, pending the determination of a dispute that has been referred to the PRTB, the rent remains payable by the tenant, sub-tenant or multiple tenant (as the case may be). Second, section 23 of the Bill amends section 115 of the RTA to clarify that the reference to an award of damages in section 115(3)(a) or 115(3)(c)(i) includes damages in relation to a failure by a tenant to comply with his obligations under section 16(f) or 16(g) of the RTA. These provisions relate to the tenant's obligation not to damage the dwelling (subject to any deterioration due to 'normal wear and tear') and the obligation to restore the dwelling to the appropriate condition, or to defray the landlord's costs in this regard, where any such damage is caused.[104]

iii. Tenancy Registration

Section 27 of the Bill amends section 136 of the RTA, which sets down the particulars that must be specified in an application to register a tenancy with the PRTB under section 134 of the RTA. Pursuant to this amendment, a landlord will no longer be required to include particulars concerning: (1) the number of occupants of the dwelling; (2) the estimated floor area of the dwelling; and (3) the number of bed spaces in the dwelling.

B. Assessment of the Proposed Amendments to the RTA

The limited scope of the amendments to the RTA proposed in the Bill is disappointing. The amendments relating to termination of Part 4 tenancies are a welcome and long-overdue response to the problem identified in *Canty v Private Residential Tenancies Board*.[105] However, it is surprising that the Bill makes no attempt to simplify the general rules governing the contents of a valid notice of termination. These rules, which are found in section 62 of the RTA, have attracted persistent criticism and are certainly not user-friendly. Section 62 should be reworked to reduce the number of mandatory requirements for a valid notice of termination and to make it more comprehensible to persons who do not have legal training. Furthermore, a standard form notice of termination should be prescribed, as envisaged by section 62(1)(d). It is remarkable that the Bill does not address the ambiguity that surrounds the termination of fixed-term tenancies, given the confusion in practice as to whether or not a notice of termination is required in order to validly terminate a fixed-term

---

[104] Section 24 of the Bill provides for an amendment to s 119(1) of the RTA that is consequential on the amendment to s 115 of the RTA.
[105] *Canty* (n 19).

tenancy.[106] This point should be put beyond doubt by including a specific provision in the Bill confirming that a fixed-term tenancy terminates automatically on expiry of the fixed term (although, of course, this will not impact on any rights that a tenant may have acquired under Part 4 of the RTA).

It is curious that the Bill does not address certain issues that were identified by the previous government as requiring attention. In November 2009, following a review of the operation of the RTA, the then Minister for Housing and Local Services, Michael Finneran TD, announced a number of proposed amendments to the RTA, including simplification of the rules governing registration and tenancy termination. It was also anticipated at that time that issues around third party complaints and the RTA's engagement with 'anti-social' behaviour would be addressed. Subsequently, in November 2010, Minister Finneran flagged a possible shift in the focus of the registration obligation from 'tenancies' to 'dwellings' with a view to improving compliance by landlords with regulatory requirements.[107] In light of the proposals floated by the previous government, it is interesting to note that the Bill (as initiated) makes only minor changes to the registration provisions and leaves the general rules governing tenancy termination largely unchanged. It contains no proposals on third party complaints or 'anti-social' behaviour, nor does it attempt to set any statutory timeframe within which a Determination Order should be issued following an application to the PRTB for dispute resolution. Apart from the proposed amendments to the rules on mediation, there are no current proposals to streamline the dispute resolution process more generally or to address the significant problems that arise in practice around the enforcement of PRTB orders.

It remains to be seen what amendments will be made to the Bill as it works its way through the *Oireachtas*. Given the extremely complex legal, economic and policy issues arising, it is unclear at this stage whether specific provisions to establish a deposit protection scheme will be included in the forthcoming amendments to the Bill, or whether a separate legislative proposal on this particular issue will be presented at a later stage. Should the government decide to press ahead and establish such a scheme, it will have dramatic consequences for the way in which landlords and their agents go about their business. At a more general level, any proposed amendments to the Bill that may be introduced at a later stage should be published in sufficient time to facilitate proper consideration and robust debate by all interested parties. In this context, it is surprising that the results of the review of the RTA undertaken during 2009, and the various submissions received in the course of that review, were never published on the DECLG website. In the interests of

---

[106] Relying on s 59 of the RTA, Cassidy and Ring maintain that, since the enactment of the RTA, the common law rule by which a fixed-term tenancy terminated on expiry of the fixed term 'no longer applies to a tenancy which comes within the scope of the RTA 2004': Ú Cassidy and J Ring, *Landlord and Tenant Law: The Residential Sector* (Dublin, Round Hall 2010) para [8-102]. However, this is not the approach adopted by the Tenancy Tribunal, as is clear from its published case law. See, eg, TR55/DR368/2010, *O'Donnell v Lane*, 21 April 2010, text available at: http://public.prtb.ie/2010%20 Disputes/Tribunals%202010/TR55.DR368.2010/Tribunal%20Report.pdf.

[107] Department of Environment, Heritage and Local Government, Press Release, 'Minister for Housing and Local Services Announces Plan to Address Regulatory Non-compliance by Landlords', 8 November 2010, www.environ.ie/en/DevelopmentHousing/Housing/PrivateRentedHousing/News/MainBody,24700,en.htm.

transparency, and with a view to promoting informed debate on proposed amendments to the RTA during the Bill's progress though the *Oireachtas*, this material
should be published on the DECLG website as a matter of urgency.

The proposed amendments to the RTA, if enacted, will necessitate considerable cross-referencing between various Acts of the *Oireachtas* in order to identify
the current legal rules. With a view to facilitating access to the law, the DECLG
should arrange for the online publication of an unofficial, consolidated version of
the amended Residential Tenancies Act 2004 as soon as practicable after the Bill is
enacted. Serious consideration should also be given to producing a standard form
(precedent) letting agreement (that would be freely available on the PRTB website)
as envisaged by section 152 of the RTA.

In summary, the Bill presents the opportunity to address the many problems that
have emerged in the day-to-day operation of the RTA. The government cannot
afford to squander this opportunity by simply tinkering with selected elements of
the legislation. More fundamental revisions are required along the lines outlined
above.

C. PRTB Resources

Resources are the key to any real improvement in the quality of service offered by
the PRTB. This is a difficult issue at a time when the public finances are in crisis,
and hard choices will have to be made to ensure value for money and the maximum impact from any investment. The experience of the RTA in action over the
past nine years confirms the existence of persistent information gaps and a striking
lack of awareness of rights and obligations among landlords and tenants. It seems
clear, therefore, that greater emphasis should be placed on information, education
and awareness-raising, together with a range of other measures aimed at avoiding
disputes in the first instance. The PRTB website is currently under-utilised as a
mechanism for disseminating accessible, high-quality and up-to-date information
on the RTA and related matters. The layout of the website is poor and it is difficult
to locate particular items of information. At the very minimum, one would expect
the information on the website to be updated regularly, but this is not happening in
practice. The lack of up-to-date statistical data on registration levels and enforcement activity is a particularly striking omission. Furthermore, it is surprising that
the PRTB has not prepared a model tenancy agreement and published it on its website for the benefit of landlords, tenants and their advisors.

There are also issues relating to how information is presented for public con-
sumption. For example, there is a vast amount of important and useful information
in the reports produced by the Tenancy Tribunal. The full text of all of these reports
is published on the PRTB website, but it is necessary to trawl through each report
to identify any points of interest. Summaries of the key points of interpretation of
the RTA emerging from the Tribunal determinations, together with a series of case
studies covering a wide range of common types of dispute, should be posted online
on a regular basis to inform interested parties of how the Tribunal works in practice.
As noted earlier in this chapter, the PRTB has never published a formal enforcement policy, with the result that there is an unacceptable lack of predictability

and transparency around its enforcement activities. If the RTA is to be effective in practice, the PRTB must convince landlords and tenants that any breach of the law carries serious consequences.

V. CONCLUDING REMARKS

The effectiveness of the RTA was compromised from the outset by the absence of support structures tailored to enable landlords and tenants to avoid disputes in the first instance and, where this proved impossible, to assist them to resolve disputes informally before turning to the PRTB. If an intricate system such as that established in the RTA is to work in practice, it is vital that landlords and tenants have access to independent, free or low-cost expert advice on the relevant law and related matters.[108] Given its quasi-judicial function, the PRTB is obviously prohibited from providing any advice to the parties to a dispute. This state of affairs is compounded by the fact that civil legal aid is not available for disputes before the PRTB. Landlords and tenants are therefore left to fend for themselves if a lack of resources prevents them from engaging legal or other expert representation. Threshold (the National Housing Charity), which has offices in Dublin, Cork and Galway, has emerged as a significant provider of free, expert advice to tenants on matters relating to the RTA. It also represents tenants in proceedings before the PRTB, but there is no equivalent service available to landlords. The lack of an accessible, expert advice service that is open to all landlords and tenants is a serious shortcoming in the current regulatory system. Accurate advice and information at an early stage in a dispute can have a profound influence on the parties' mindsets. Moreover, it can identify strengths or weaknesses in a particular case in advance of parties engaging the PRTB dispute resolution service. Intervention by an expert neutral third party may facilitate a settlement without recourse to formal dispute resolution proceedings, thereby reducing the PRTB's workload and saving scarce resources. Threshold has deployed this model to good effect since its establishment in 1978—albeit firmly from the tenant's perspective. The potential impact of support structures of this nature should not be lost sight of in the course of the debate that will take place around the proposed amendments to the RTA.

As things stand, the PRTB is hamstrung by a regulatory framework that is not fit for purpose. Legislative amendments alone will not bring about the change in mindset that is required to deliver a culture of compliance. There are obvious limits to the law in this regard. Information, education and awareness of rights and obligations, backed up with proactive enforcement to command respect for the law, will gradually deliver a more professional private rented sector based on mutual respect and the rule of law. Until policy makers and the PRTB accept this reality, the RTA will continue to have a limited impact in practice.

---

[108] Á Ryall, 'An Assessment of the Recommendations of the Commission on the Private Rented Residential Sector' (2001) 6 *Conveyancing and Property Law Journal* 5 and 'Residential Tenancies Bill 2003: A Commentary from the Tenant's Perspective' (2003) 8 *Conveyancing and Property Law Journal* 54.

Part II

Challenging Perceptions of Property and Trusts

5

Shapeless Trusts and Settlor Title Retention: An Asian Morality Play

ADAM S HOFRI-WINOGRADOW*

I. THE CHINESE SHAPELESS TRUST

THE FIRST 11 years of the present century have seen several jurisdictions formulate and enact new trust regimes, including the French statutory *fiducie*,
the British Virgin Islands' VISTA trust, the Uruguayan *fideicomiso,* the
affidamento fiduciario of the Republic of San Marino and the trust chapters of the
new draft civil codes of the Hungarian and Czech Republics.[1] From a comparative
perspective, the most challenging of the new regimes may be the People's Republic
of China's Trust Act of 2001.[2] In not specifying who of the three main protago-
nists of the trust—the settlor, the trustee or the beneficiary—must hold title in the
trust assets, and permitting the settlor's retention of title in those assets without his
declaring himself a trustee, China has produced a truly 'shapeless' trust.

The 'shapeless trust' moniker was coined by Maurizio Lupoi, one of Italy's great
trust scholars, for the definition of the trust in the Hague Convention on the Law

---

* Lecturer, Hebrew University of Jerusulem.

[1] See: (a) France: loi n°2007-211 du 19 février 2007 instituant la fiducie, amending several codes,
including the Code Civil, to which new Articles 2011–31 were added; see discussion in F Barrière,
'The French Fiducie, or the Chaotic Awakening of a Sleeping Beauty' in L Smith (ed), *Re-imagining
the Trust: Trusts in the Civil Law* (Cambridge, Cambridge University Press, 2012) 222–57; P Crocq,
'National Report for France' in SCJJ Kortmann et al (eds), *Towards an EU Directive on Protected Funds*
(Deventer, Kluwer, 2009) 99–113; (b) the British Virgin Islands: Virgin Islands Special Trusts Act 2003;
see discussion in G Thomas and Ar Hudson, *The Law of Trusts*, 2nd edn (Oxford, Oxford University
Press, 2010) 1167–79; (c) San Marino: Law of 1 March, 2010, no. 43, on the affidamento fiduciario; see
discussion in M Lupoi, 'The New Law of San Marino on the "Affidamento Fiduciario"' (2011) 25 *Trust
Law International* 51–59; (d) Uruguay: Ley de Fideicomiso, No 17.703; see discussion in DWM Waters,
'The Future of the Trust—Part I' (2006) 13 *Journal of International Trust and Corporate Planning* 179,
197–98; (e) Hungary: 2009 évi CXX. Törvény a Polgári Törvénykönyvről (Law no 120/2009 on the
Civil Code [not yet in force]) ss 5:583–95; see discussion in N Csizmazia, 'National Report for Hungary'
in Kortmann et al (cited above) 175, 184–91; (f) Czech Republic: see discussion of the new draft civil
code in T Richter, 'National Report for the Czech Republic' in Kortmann et al (cited above) 59, 65–70.

[2] Trust Law of the People's Republic of China, 28 April 2001, Order of the President of the People's
Republic of China (No 50), with effect from 1 October 2001 (official translation at www.npc.gov.cn/
englishnpc/Law/2007-12/10/content_1383444.htm), hereinafter 'the Chinese Trust Law'.

Applicable to Trusts and on their Recognition.[3] This defined the trust as 'the legal relationships created—*inter vivos* or on death—by a person, the settlor, when assets have been placed under the control of a trustee for the benefit of a beneficiary or for a specified purpose', adding that it is a characteristic of trusts that 'title to the trust assets stands in the name of the trustee or in the name of another person on behalf of the trustee'.[4] Lupoi substantiated his description of the Convention definition as 'shapeless' by noting that as it does not require, as American, English and Commonwealth trust law does, that title to the trust assets vest in the trustee, the definition seems to include under the term 'trust' a great many types of relationships, both bilateral and trilateral, including relationships leaving the settlor as owner of the trust fund despite his having appointed, rather than become, a trustee.[5]

The definition of the trust in the Chinese Trust Act is no less shapeless than that in the Hague Convention. The Chinese definition provides 'that the settlor, based on his faith in trustee [*sic*], *entrusts* his property rights to the trustee and allows the trustee to, according to the will of the settlor and in the name of the trustee, administer or dispose of such property in the interest of a beneficiary or for any intended purposes'.[6] The precise meaning, in this context, of the term 'entrusts'—*weituo*—is obscure. It does not, according to Professor Lusina Ho of the University of Hong Kong, amount to a requirement that settlors transfer title in the trust assets to their trustees; the Chinese term for 'transfer' is *zhuanyang*. Chinese courts, having started to interpret and apply the Act, have similarly ruled that the Act does not mandate the transfer of title in the trust assets from the settlor to the trustee.[7] Ho and others note that Chinese law uses *weituo* in describing the relationship of principal and agent.[8] The phrase 'allows the trustee ... [to administer or dispose of the property] according to the will of the settlor' also carries considerable echoes

---

[3] M Lupoi, 'The Shapeless Trust' (1995) 1 *Trusts & Trustees* 15; and see full discussion in M Lupoi, *Trusts: A Comparative Study* (S Dix trans, Cambridge, Cambridge University Press, 2000) 327–67.

[4] Convention on the Law Applicable to Trusts and on their Recognition, concluded 1 July 1985, entered into force 1 January 1992 (hereinafter 'the Convention'), art 2.

[5] Such situations should be distinguished from 'declaration of trust' situations, where the settlor declares that he holds assets on trust, thereby making himself into a trustee and transforming his ownership of the trust assets into fiduciary ownership. For Lupoi's discussion, mentioning several further points of doctrine on which the Convention stakes no position at all, thus rendering its trust concept 'shapeless', see Lupoi, 'Shapeless Trust' (n 3) 16–17, and Lupoi, *Trusts* (n 3) 339.

[6] Chinese Trust Law, s 2, emphasis added.

[7] *Beijing Haidian Science & Technology Development Co Ltd v Shenzhen Xinhua Jinyuan Touzi Fazhan Youxian Gongsi and others* (First Instance Civil Cases, Chongqing High People's Court, 19 March 2007), discussed, eg, in L Ho, 'China: Trust Law and Practice since 2001' (2010) 16 *Trusts & Trustees* 124, 126–27.

[8] My discussion of the Chinese Act in the following paragraphs draws on the following materials: L Ho, 'Trust Laws in China: History, Ambiguity and Beneficiary's Rights' in Smith (n 1) 183–221; L Ho, 'The People's Republic of China' in J Glasson and G Thomas (eds), *The International Trust*, 2nd edn (Bristol, Jordans, 2006) 825–38; L Ho, 'Reception of the Trust in Asia: Emerging Asian Principles of Trust?' (2004) *Singapore Journal of Legal Studies* 287–304, 293–303 (referring, at 294, n 35 and text thereto, to the use of the term *weituo* in an agency or mandate context in the General Principles of Civil Law of China, Order no 37 of the President of the People's Republic of China, adopted on 12 April 1986, arts 64 and 65); L Ho, *Trust Law in China* (Hong Kong, Sweet & Maxwell Asia, 2003); Ho (n 7); D Hayton, 'The Core of the Chinese Trust Law 2001' (2005) 3 *Trust Quarterly Review* 24–27; R Lee, 'Conceptualizing the Chinese Trust' (2009) 58 *ICLQ* 655–69; Waters (n 1) 219–22; FH Foster, 'American Trust Law in a Chinese Mirror' (2010) 95 *Minnesota Law Review* 602–51.

of agency. English law, noticeably, uses the verb 'entrust' to describe fiduciary relations generally, rather than a trust.[9]

The Chinese Act includes several other provisions that appear to envision a continuing connection between the settlor and the property he has already transferred into trust. The Act provides that 'the trust shall be differentiated from other property that is not put under trust by the settlor'.[10] Under most trust regimes, such differentiation is achieved by transferring title in the trust assets from the settlor to the trustee. Where such transfer is a fundamental feature of any trust, a provision enjoining differentiation of trust property from the settlor's non-trust property is unnecessary, other than, perhaps, in 'declaration of trust' situations. Rules of law enjoining the *trustee* to keep trust and non-trust property separate are far more common.[11] Yet the Chinese provision just quoted is not restricted to 'declaration of trust' scenarios.[12]

The Act gives the settlor of an already-constituted trust an impressive array of powers, demonstrating an understanding of the trust as a continuing contractual relationship between the settlor, the trustee and the beneficiary.[13] It provides, for example, that 'the settlor shall have the right to know the administration, use and disposition of, and the income and expenses relating to, *his* trust property, and the right to request the trustee to give explanations in this regard';[14] that 'if, due to special reasons unexpected at the time the trust is created, the methods for administrating [*sic*] the trust property are not favorable to the realization of trust purposes or do not conform to the interests of the beneficiary, the settlor shall have the right to ask the trustee to modify such methods';[15] that 'where the trustee's appointment is terminated, a new trustee shall be appointed according to the provisions in the trust documents; where there are no such provisions in the documents, the settlor shall make the appointment';[16] and that under certain circumstances, 'after a trust is created, the settlor may replace the beneficiary or dispose of his right to benefit from the trust'.[17]

In the decade since its enactment, the unique approach of the Chinese Trust Act has drawn the attention of numerous scholars, both in China and elsewhere.[18] Much of the discussion has centred on the Act's not requiring that the settlor

---

[9] In *Reading v The King* [1949] 2 KB 232 (CA), Asquith LJ explained, at 236, that 'a "fiduciary relation" exists (a) whenever the plaintiff *entrusts* to the defendant property ... and relies on the defendant to deal with such property for the benefit of the plaintiff or for purposes authorised by him' (emphasis added).

[10] Chinese Trust Law, s 15.

[11] See, eg, Restatement of Trusts, 3rd, §84 and cmt b (enjoining trustees 'to keep the trust property separate from the trustee's own property'); Chinese Trust Law, s 16 (providing that 'the trust property shall be segregated from the property owned by the trustee').

[12] See discussion of s 15, quoted earlier in the present paragraph, and its implications for the Chinese Act's fundamental trust model in Ho, 'Reception of the Trust in Asia' (n 8) 295, nn 42–43 and text thereto.

[13] See, eg, Ho (n 7) 125; H Wang, L Ho and Y Zhou, 'Contract or Trust: Examining the First Trust Decision of the Chinese Courts' (2007) 5 *Trust Quarterly Review* 11–14, 12, 14.

[14] Chinese Trust Law, s 20, emphasis added.

[15] Ibid, s 21.

[16] Ibid, s 40.

[17] Ibid, s 51.

[18] See the sources in n 8 above.

transfer title in the trust assets to the trustee.[19] As the principal point was recently put by Scottish property scholar Kenneth Reid, 'the location [under Chinese trust law] of title [in the trust assets] is a matter of choice—an arrangement unparalleled, so far as I know, in any other country'.[20] A shapeless trust indeed.

In commenting on the Chinese Act, Professors Ho and Reid noted that trusts the trustees of which do not own the trust assets raise several difficulties. Following recent comparative trusts literature, Reid admitted that trustees' ownership of trust assets cannot be described as 'an essential feature of a trust', further admitting that 'the difficulties of [placing ownership in the settlor or beneficiary] are practical rather than doctrinal'.[21] The difficulties raised by Reid and Ho are as follows:

(i)   'A trustee who derives powers indirectly, from the ownership of others, will have the tiresome burden of proving these powers to the satisfaction of third parties.'[22]

(ii) If ownership of the trust assets is placed in settlors or beneficiaries rather than trustees, situations may arise where trust assets have no owner, or where the identity of some or all of their owners is disputed. The settlor or beneficiary might die or be dissolved. While the Chinese Act provides a mechanism for replacing a dead or dissolved trustee,[23] no such mechanism is provided for replacing a dead or dissolved settlor or beneficiary.[24] Some

---

[19] See, eg, Ho's criticism of this feature of the Act in her 'Reception of the Trust in Asia' (n 8) 293–96.

[20] KGC Reid, 'Conceptualising the Chinese Trust: Some Thoughts from Europe' in Remco van Rhee and Lei Chen (eds), *Towards a Chinese Civil Code: Historical and Comparative Perspectives* (Leiden, Brill, 2012); University of Edinburgh School of Law Working Paper Series No 2011/06, at 9.

[21] Ibid, 9, internal quotes omitted. For comparative trusts scholarship counting the 'essential features of trusts' and finding that trustees' ownership of the trust assets is not one of them, see Ho, 'Reception of the Trust in Asia' (n 8) 289–90; T Honoré, 'Trust: The Inessentials' in Joshua Getzler (ed), *Rationalizing Property, Equity and Trusts—Essays in Honour of Edward Burn* (London, Butterworths, 2003) 1–2, 4, 12 ('[the South African and Quebec trust regimes show that] the essential relation of a trustee to the trust assets is one not of ownership but of control'); T Honoré, 'On Fitting Trusts into Civil Law Jurisdictions', available at: ssrn.com/abstract=1270179, at 7 ('it does not matter where the title to the trust property is located. To locate it in the trustee, as in Anglo-American trust law, is convenient but not essential'), and see also at 12; L Thévenoz, 'Trusts—The Rise of a Global Legal Concept' in M Bussani and F Werro (eds), *European Private Law: A Handbook*, available at: papers.ssrn.com/sol3/papers. cfm?abstract_id=1723236, at 22–23 ('The actual legal owner of the trust property also appears not to be critical. It is the trustee in Scotland; it can be either the trustee or the beneficiary under South African law; but there is no legal owner under the recent codification of Quebec. One should infer that the vesting of legal title with the trustee is inconsequential'). For the view that trustees' ownership of the trust assets is an essential feature of all trusts properly so called, see GL Gretton, 'Trusts without Equity' (2000) 49 *ICLQ* 599, 603 ('though it functions as a trust, the *bewind* is not trust, for a simple reason: the location of legal title is the reverse of the trust'); M Lupoi, 'The Civil Law Trust' (1999) 32 *Vanderbilt Journal of Transnational Law* 967, 970 (noting that 'the transfer of property to the trustee, or a unilateral declaration of trust' is part of the 'definition of the trust in comparative law terms').

[22] Reid (n 20) 7; the same point was noted by Ho, 'Reception of the Trust in Asia' (n 8) 295–96; Ho, 'Trust Laws in China' (n 8) 200–01.

[23] Chinese Trust Law, s 40; under s 52, a trust is not terminated by the death, insolvency or incapacity of its settlor or trustee.

[24] Section 15 provides that where a settlor is not also a beneficiary, on his death, dissolution, cancellation or bankruptcy, 'the trust shall subsist, and the trust property shall not be his legacy or liquidation property'.

trusts have no living, identified or identifiable beneficiaries, for a time or permanently. The identity of a trust's beneficiaries can also be disputed.[25]

(iii) Settlors who never parted with ownership in the trust assets seem, under Chinese law, to owe no fiduciary duties. Thus:

> [I]f the settlor misappropriates the trust assets, and it is very easy for him as the owner to do so, there is very little the beneficiaries could do. As the property is not owned by the trustee, any action against him will face the difficulty of proving lack of prudence on his part in not pre-empting the conduct of the settlor, who is after all the legitimate owner of the trust assets ... any direct action against the settlor will meet the even greater difficulty that the Chinese Trust Law does not subject him to any duties.[26]

Are those difficulties enough to condemn trust regimes under which title to the trust assets is left in the settlor, despite his having appointed, rather than become, a trustee, as inferior to the conventional model, under which that title is in the trustee? And what of the 'shapeless trust' itself? Is the Chinese Act's silence on the locus of title in the trust assets inferior to a trust regime positing one—any one—of the three points of the 'eternal triangle of the trust'[27] as the locus of that title?[28] Or is it inferior only to the conventional model locating that title in the trustee?

It is the task of the present chapter to begin an examination of the relative efficacy of 'shapeless' trust regimes, which permit, among other configurations, trusts the assets of which remain in the settlor despite his having appointed, rather than become, a trustee. Empirical data on the operation of such regimes is limited, however, due to their small number. The Chinese regime is still too recent for empirical data to be available in useful quantities. As late as 2010, even judicial decisions interpreting or applying the 2001 Act appear to have been rare.[29] While South Africa, Germany and the Netherlands, as well as Quebec and its Uruguayan and Czech offshoots, offer examples of regimes placing title to the trust assets elsewhere than in the trustee, their trust models are the opposite of shapelessness—they are clear, definite and concrete regarding the locus of title.[30] Alone among this group,

---

[25] Reid (n 20) 7, 10–12.

[26] Ho, 'Reception of the Trust in Asia' (n 8) 296.

[27] *Cf* M Mautner, 'The Eternal Triangles of the Law: Toward a Theory of Priorities in Conflicts Involving Remote Parties' (1991) 90 *Michigan Law Review* 95–154.

[28] Lupoi's criticism of the 'shapeless trust' was confined to its use in the Hague Convention's description of the class of legal instruments to which it applies as a matter of conflicts law. His criticism did not extend to the adoption of a 'shapeless' definition of the trust as part of a specific jurisdiction's substantive trusts regime. See his 'The Shapeless Trust' (n 3) 16–17 and his *Trusts* (n 3) 339.

[29] Ho, 'Trust Laws in China' (n 8) 202–03; Ho, 'China: Trusts Law and Practice' (n 7) 126.

[30] South Africa and the Netherlands both allow the *bewind*, according to which title to the assets is in the beneficiary, though the *bewindvoerder* (in the Netherlands) or *bewindhebber* (in South Africa) enjoys an exclusive right to administer and dispose of them. For the Netherlands, see SCJJ Kortmann and HLE Verhagen, 'National Report for the Netherlands' in David Hayton, SCJJ Kortmann and HLE Verhagen (eds), *Principles of European Trust Law* (The Hague, Kluwer, 1999), 195–215, 199–200. For South Africa, see Trust Property Control Act, Act 57 of 1998, s 1, s. v. 'trust', and E Cameron et al, *Honoré's South African Law of Trusts*, 5th edn (Lansdowne, Juta Law, 2002) 272–77. The Civil Code of Quebec provides that 'the trust patrimony ... constitutes a patrimony by appropriation, autonomous and distinct from that of the settlor, trustee or beneficiary and in which none of them has any real right' (art 1261). Studies of the Quebec trust are many. See, for example, JB Claxton, *Studies on the Quebec Law of Trust* (Toronto, Thomson, 2005) especially ch 2. Uruguay has adopted, and the Czech Republic is apparently about to adopt, the Quebecois solution; see sources cited in n 1. For Germany, see the next two notes and text thereto.

the German *unechte treuhand* is notable for leaving title in the settlor (who *treuhand* law assumes to also be the beneficiary);[31] shapeless, however, it is not.[32] I hope to examine its operation in a future article.

Fortunately, however, the efficacy of shapeless trusts, a question made urgent by the Chinese Trust Act, may be illuminated by the annals of a jurisdiction at the other end of continental Asia: Israel. Pre-dating the Hague Convention by a few years, the Israeli trust regime under the Trust Act of 1979[33] seems to have been the world's first shapeless trust regime. In Part II, I discuss this regime, focusing on express private trusts. I first describe the regime's shapelessness, and then the courts', practitioners' and academics' responses to this shapelessness. Finally, I describe the Israeli shapeless trust model's impending demise with the upcoming enactment of the Israeli Civil Code, which will rearrange the local trust model, expressly granting title in the trust assets to the trustee. In Part III, I conclude the chapter by trying to tease out the lessons of the Israeli experience for the general viability of 'shapeless' trust regimes, permitting, among other configurations, 'settlor title retention trusts'. The upshot is that despite the flaws of existing Chinese and Israeli legislation, as well as the many doctrinal difficulties created by those innovative trust models grating against established doctrine, which reflects the traditional trust model, both 'shapeless trusts' and 'settlor title retention trusts' could have their uses, particularly, perhaps, in making trusts more understandable and accessible for populations foreign to traditional Anglo-Saxon trust culture.

II. THE ISRAELI SHAPELESS TRUST: THE TRUST ACT OF 1979

A. The Israeli Shapeless Trust Regime

The Israeli Trust Act of 1979 is designedly vague regarding several key aspects of the trust relationship, not defining either the trustee's or the beneficiary's rights in the trust property. It rests content with a definition of a 'trust' as 'a relationship to property by which a trustee is bound to hold the same or act in respect thereof, in the interest of a beneficiary or for some other purpose'.[34] The notion of 'trustee' implicit in this definition includes fiduciaries such as executors, administrators, guardians and liquidators.[35] The beneficiary's rights in the trust property not being

---

[31] S Grundmann, 'Trust and Treuhand at the End of the 20th Century: Key Problems and Shift of Interests' (1999) 47 *American Journal of Comparative Law* 401–28, 402–03, n 8 and text thereto.

[32] See D Krimphove, 'National Report for Germany' in Kortmann et al (n 1) 115–43, 116–17.

[33] Trust Act, 5739-1979, 941 *Statutes*, 3 August 1979 at 128 (hereinafter 'the 1979 Act' or 'the Act').

[34] 1979 Act, s 1. An unofficial English translation of the Act, as promulgated in 1979, was published in the (1980) 15 *Israel Law Review* 418 ff. While the Act was thrice amended since then, these amendments are not material to our discussion.

[35] The application of statutory trust regimes beyond trustees on the common law trust model by an extended use of the terms 'trust' or 'trustee' is not unheard of in England. The English Trustee Act 1925 (15 and 16 Geo 5 c 19), for example, provides in s 68(17) that 'the expression ... "trust" ... extend[s] to ... the duties incident to the office of a personal representative, and "trustee" where the context admits, includes a personal representative'. The difference is that in England, this extended application of rules principally applicable to trustees is not achieved by transforming the traditional trust concept.

defined, it appears that the common law, split ownership model of trusteeship, characterizing the beneficiary as the 'owner in equity' of the trust property, is not part of Israeli law; rather, an Israeli beneficiary has, like Indian, Scottish and Chinese beneficiaries, an obligatory right vis-a-vis the trustee.[36]

Following this general definition, the Act contains two distinct trust regimes. One applies only to 'trusts created by an instrument of endowment', which, where not created by will or by beneficiary designation under an insurance policy or pension plan, must be created by the settlor signing a trust instrument before a notary.[37] The other, focused largely on trustees' duties and powers, applies to any fiduciary relationship involving property which the fiduciary must hold, use or 'act in respect of', applying the term 'trust', unconventionally, to this large class of relationships. Imposing duties which traditional common law trust law made specific to trustees on a much wider class of fiduciaries, this second regime serves as a common background to specific Israeli statutory regimes governing fiduciary situations such as those of the executor, administrator, guardian, liquidator, trustee in bankruptcy, banker and legal practitioner.[38]

Many familiar rules of common law trust law appear in the 1979 Act only as regards 'trusts created by an instrument of endowment'. A key example is the requirement that where the settlor and trustee are different persons or entities, in order for the trust to be constituted, the trust's initial assets must be transferred from the settlor to the trustee. Applied only to trusts created by an instrument of endowment, this fundamental rule does not apply where a trust is created 'by contract with a trustee' or 'by statute'—the two other ways in which a trust may be created under the 1979 Act.[39] Significantly, even where a trust is created by an instrument of endowment, only control of the property, not title, must be transferred.[40] Many of the Act's other fundamental provisions, such as the provisions governing the appointment of trustees,[41] their resignation and removal,[42] the modification

---

[36] For beneficiaries' rights under Indian trust law, see BM Gandhi, *Equity, Trusts and Specific Relief* (Lucknow, Eastern Book Company, 1983) 372–77; for their rights under Scots law, see K Reid, 'National Report for Scotland' in Hayton, Kortmann and Verhagen (n 30) 67–84, 69–72; for their rights under Chinese law, see Ho, 'Trust Laws in China' (n 8) 210–19. See discussion of some of the 1979 Act's unconventional features in I Rabinovich-Brun, 'The Trust and Private International Law: An Israeli Perspective' in A Gambaro and AM Rabello (eds), *Towards a New European Ius Commune* (Jerusalem, Sacher Institute, 1999) 685, 688–94.

[37] This regime is contained in ss 17–24. Formal requirements regarding the creation of trusts 'by an instrument of endowment' are contained in s 17(a); see discussion in S Kerem, *Trusts*, 4th edn (Tel Aviv, Perlstein-Ginossar, 2004) 633–76.

[38] See discussion of this second, more general 'trusts' regime as 'a general framework applicable to any trust ... [including] trust relationships governed by other legislation', in *ibid*, 142–43.

[39] 1979 Act, s 2. Post-1979 cases eventually provided that the s 2 list of ways in which trusts may be created is not exhaustive: Application for Permission to Appeal 5715/95 *Weinstein v Fuchs* Piskei Din (hereinafter 'PD') 54(5) 792 (2000). For the transfer requirement in English law, see *Knight v Knight* (1840) 3 Beav 148, 173; 49 ER 58, 86; *Milroyd v Lord* (1862) 4 De GF & J 264, 274; 45 ER 1184, 1189; internationally, see P Panico, *International Trust Laws* (Oxford, Oxford University Press, 2010) 16–27.

[40] See Discussion in A Alter, 'Taxation of Ordinary Trusts in Israel' (PhD Thesis, Tel Aviv University, 1985) 38, n 86.

[41] 1979 Act, s 21.

[42] Ibid, s 22.

and termination of the trust,[43] and revocability,[44] as well as the provisions that the court may issue directions to the trustee[45] and that the settlor or another may, at any time, add to the trust property,[46] appear in the Act's second chapter, entitled 'A trust under an instrument of Endowment'. It is thus, at best, unclear if they apply to trusts created in the other ways recognised by the Act—by contract or by statute.[47]

Both trust regimes in the 1979 Act appear to be strikingly shapeless. Even Lupoi's original 'shapeless trust', the trust concept which appears in the Hague Convention, is not quite as vague as the trust concept under the 1979 Act. The Convention's definition of a trust as 'the legal relationships created—*inter vivos* or on death—by a person, the settlor, when assets have been placed under the control of a trustee for the benefit of a beneficiary or for a specified purpose' shares with the general definition of a trust in the 1979 Act the catch-all description of the trust as an unspecific 'legal relationship'.[48] The Convention is, further, content to refer, as the 1979 Act does in discussing trusts created by an instrument of endowment, to assets being placed 'under the control' of a trustee, not requiring that title pass from the settlor, or indeed that title pass at all.[49] The 1979 Act, however, is of still broader application, in that under trusts created other than by an instrument of endowment, trustees do not even need to have the trust property 'under their control', but may merely 'act in respect of' that property.[50] The Convention's concept of a trust is also rather more specific than the sentence I have just quoted from it implies, for it also provides, unlike the 1979 Act, that among the 'characteristics' of a trust is the fact that 'title to the trust assets stands in the name of the trustee or in the name of another person on behalf of the trustee'.[51] Israeli trustees, contrastingly, can be reduced to 'acting in respect of' property title to which is not even in another on their behalf.

Further, the definition in the 1979 Israeli Act is even more 'shapeless' than the Chinese definition of 2001. The former does not require, as the latter does, that trustees necessarily administer or dispose of the trust property, or that they do so 'in their [the trustees'] name'.[52] An Israeli trustee may merely 'act in respect of' the trust property, in the settlor's name or in the name of any other person.

Title in the trust assets may thus, under the 1979 Act, remain in the settlor. Appropriately, the Act gives settlors of already-constituted trusts powers which traditional common law trust law does not give them, while stopping short of the

---

[43] Ibid, s 23.

[44] Ibid, s 18(b).

[45] Ibid, s 19.

[46] Ibid, s 18(a).

[47] Kerem believed that they do not: Kerem (n 37) 139.

[48] The Convention, art 2. See Lupoi's critique of the convention in his *Trusts* (n 3) 327–67; and see further criticism of art 2 in Hayton, Kortmann and Verhagen (n 30) 38–40.

[49] The Convention, art 2. Lupoi noted the 'closeness' of the definition in s 1 of the 1979 Act to that in the Hague Convention: Lupoi, *Trusts* (n 3) 279, 334. See also 305, n 228, where Lupoi described the Israeli definition as 'the only legislative formulation which defines the relationship without indicating its source'. The Israeli definition lost its exclusiveness in 2001 with the enactment of the Chinese Trust Law. Lupoi's statement appears to have been correct when he made it: the original (Italian) version of his book appeared in 1994.

[50] 1979 Act, s 1.

[51] The Convention, s 2.

[52] Chinese Trust Act, s 2; see the discussion in Part I above.

panoply of powers that the Chinese Act grants settlors. The 1979 Act provides that the court, on the application of the settlor, may modify or strike out provisions of trusts created by an instrument of endowment.[53] However a trust is created, the settlor may always apply to the court in any matter concerning the trust. These provisions contrast with the English rule that holds the settlor to have no standing regarding the trust, without express provision to the contrary, once the trust has been launched and the trust property transferred to the trustee.[54]

The 1979 Act thus provided not one but two trust regimes: one a 'shapeless', generalised scheme of fiduciary duties, applicable to any fiduciary who must hold property or act in respect thereof, the other a regime for donative trusts, complete with several features reminiscent of the trust regimes Caribbean island jurisdictions offer non-residents, such as the possibility of creating trusts for non-charitable purposes,[55] and even a statutory default spendthrift clause.[56] How have the two regimes been received since their introduction in 1979?

B. Responses to the 1979 Israeli Trust Regime: Courts, Practitioners and Academics

Significantly for our examination of the efficacy of shapeless trust regimes, the reception of the 1979 Israeli Act, especially of those of its features which contradict common law trust orthodoxy, has been mixed. In brief, the *courts*, having only fairly recently started to produce a sizeable body of case law on the 30-year-old Act, now read it literally, acknowledging its not requiring that title in the trust assets vest in the trustee. While the Act has seen use in practice, some *practitioners*, especially those creating sophisticated family and tax-planning trusts, continue their pre-1979 practice of using other legal systems' trust regimes, though this practice appears to have nothing to do with the 'shapelessness' of the Act's trust regime. However, the Act has met with significant *academic* criticism, which has been focused on its

---

[53] 1979 Act, s 23(a). See discussion in Alter (n 40) 33. Under English trust law, once a trust has been created, its provisions may be modified by agreement between the trustees and beneficiaries, or, under the rule in *Saunders v Vautier* (1841) 4 Beav 115, 115 ER 282 (M.R.), aff'd Cr & Ph 240, 41 ER 482 (LC), by agreement of the (ascertainable, *sui juris*) beneficiaries alone: see discussion of the English law of trust modification in G Moffat, G Bean and R Probert, *Trusts Law: Text and Materials*, 5th edn (Cambridge, Cambridge University Press, 2009) 323–55.

[54] Moffat et al, ibid, at 14.

[55] Section 1 defines a trust as 'a relationship to property by virtue of which a trustee is bound to hold the same or to act in respect thereof, in the interest of a beneficiary *or for some other purpose*'. Section 17 defines an 'endowment' as 'the dedication of property in favor of a beneficiary *or for some other purpose*' (emphasis added). Both sections leave the nature of the purpose referred to open. See the discussion in Alter (n 40) 32–33.

[56] Section 20 provides that beneficiaries' rights under a trust created by an instrument of endowment may not be transferred, charged or attached. A court may transfer, charge or attach a beneficiary's entitlement under such a trust, without an express exclusion of the statutory default spendthrift clause, only in order to satisfy maintenance, child support or taxes due from that beneficiary, or, 'under special circumstances', in order to collect other debts due from him or her. One commentator believes this power of the court, as to debts other than maintenance or taxes, to run only to property the time to distribute which has come according to the terms of the trust: Kerem (n 37) 706–07.

deviating from common law orthodoxy. Let me describe the reaction of each of these three components of the legal community in more detail.

More than legal practitioners, who often can, so far as trusts are concerned, choose a foreign trust regime of their liking, or academics, who can criticise the local law as they wish, it has been the *courts* that, at length, have recently started to breathe life into the Israeli shapeless trust regime. While reasoned judicial discussions of this regime have long been few and far between, they have seen a modest renaissance in the last decade or so. That judicial consideration of the 1979 Act has been slow to appear is a consequence of the long life of many trusts, of the time problems take to develop, come to light and be litigated, of limitation periods only starting to run, in trust cases, once beneficiaries are aware of trustees' breach,[57] as well as of many Israeli practitioners often employing trust regimes other than that of the 1979 Act. Many of the early post-1979 cases dealt with trusts subject to pre-1979 law.[58] Cases applying the 1979 Act started to appear in the mid-1980s. Most direct judicial discussion of the Act's innovations has focused on the shapelessness of its trust model—its seeming omission of the common law requirement that title in the trust assets vest in the trustee. Israeli courts have, until recently, tended to ask themselves whether the Act really meant to let go of this requirement. Several decisions sought refuge in indecision, refusing to pick a side.[59] Those that did stake a position, however, tended to follow the Act's vague definition of the trust as 'a relationship to property by which a trustee is bound to hold the same or act in respect thereof', holding that trustees under Israeli law do not necessarily have title in the trust assets.[60] They thus recognised and gave effect to the Israeli trust regime's shapelessness.

---

[57] For this rule in Israeli law, see Civil Appeal 5964/03, *Estate of the Late Edward Aridor v Petah-Tikva Municipality* 60(4) PD 437 (2006) 467 and the older cases cited there. In England, see the Limitation Act 1980 c 58, s 21(1), providing that no limitation period shall apply to a beneficiary's action in respect of the trustee's fraud or fraudulent breach of trust, or to recover trust property which the trustee has converted to his use.

[58] Civil Appeal 34/88, *Josephina Rutenberg Reis v Estate of Hanna Eberman* 44(1) PD 278 (1990); Civil Appeal 410/87, *Estate of the Late Mrs. Liberman v Junger* 45(3) PD 749 (1991); Civil Appeal 369/84, *Michael Beril v Ran Bar Lev* (decided June 1988, published online); Civil Appeal 414/87, *Assessing Officer for Large Factories v Kiryat Nordau Development Company Ltd* 46(5) PD 387 (1992); Civil Case (Tel Aviv) 688/87 *'Ramatayim', a Cooperative, Ltd v Popular Housing Ltd* District Court Decisions 510 (1988(2)); Application (Beer-Sheva) 48/88, *Ben Gurion University of the Negev v Beer-Sheva Municipality* District Court Decisions 353 (1992(3)).

[59] Civil Appeal 654/82, *Mediterranean Car Agency Ltd v C D Chayut*, Adv 39(3) PD 80 (1985); Civil Appeal 3829/91, *Wallace v Gat* 48(1) PD 808 (1994); Civil Appeal 8068/01, *Ayalon Insurance Corporation Ltd v Executor of the Late Chaya Ofelger* 59(2) PD 349 (2005); Civil Appeal 9225/01, *Zayman v Komeran* (decided 13 December 2006, published online). This last decision was a draw rather than a fudge. Procaccia J chose the broader, 'shapeless' view, writing that 'the trust is a duty imposed on a person given control over an asset, so that he may use that control in order to achieve a certain purpose' (para [9] of her opinion). Barak CJ adhered to the common law trust model, identifying the trustee's ownership of the trust assets as a sine qua non of trusts and sharply distinguishing trusts from other fiduciary relations (paras [3]–[4] of his opinion, repeating a view he expressed in Aharon Barak, *The Agency Act, 5725–1965*, 2nd edn (Srigim-Leon, Nevo, 1996) 1121–22). Grunis J refused to join either of his colleagues on the point of principle, ensuring the draw.

[60] Application (Tel Aviv) 12844/86, *El Al v Balas*, District Court Decisions 45, 50 (1989(1)); Civil Appeal 4660/94, *Attorney-General v Moshe Lishitzki* 55(1) PD 88 (1999) 108, 124–25, 129 (both the majority and minority opinions seem to reject the restriction of trusteeship to scenarios where title in the trust assets is in the trustee, with Cheshin J emphasising in his majority opinion both that the Israeli courts should be wary of adopting the details of foreign trust regimes and that there was in the instant

Two District Court decisions of 2009 and one Supreme Court decision of 2011 seem to represent a watershed in Israeli decisional law on express private trusts, regarding both its depth and its fully conscious endorsement of the 1979 Act's shapeless trust regime. The three contain by far the longest, most elaborate discussions of this legal institution and the law governing it yet penned by Israel's judiciary.[61] All three decisions enforced beneficiaries' rights—one vis-a-vis the breaching trustee,[62] the other two, addressing the same case at the trial and appellate levels, vis-a-vis the trustee's personal creditors, annulling an attachment of what was proven to be a trust asset.[63] All three conceived of the trust quite independently of common law trust orthodoxy. The first District Court decision followed the literal meaning of the 1979 definition, noting that trustees can be given the necessary control over trust assets either by receiving title in those assets or by being permitted to act thereon.[64] The other District Court decision identified beneficiaries as the sole owners of trust property, describing even trustees registered as titleholders as mere nominees.[65] Interestingly, this understanding of the 1979 Act, though not obvious on the face of the statutory text, is reminiscent of at least one Chinese court's understanding of the 2001 Chinese Trust Act, this court positing that even where ownership of the trust assets has been transferred to a trustee, either the settlor, the beneficiary or both were those assets' substantive owners.[66] Both the Chinese and Israeli courts gave shape to what the statutes they applied left shapeless. They assimilated their systems' trust regimes into those systems' general—civilian—frameworks of private law by reading the former as a type of agency, nomineeship or, in the Israeli case, a Dutch or South African *bewind*; the Chinese court was excused from choosing between the settlor and the beneficiary by their being one and the same in the case before it. The recent Israeli Supreme Court decision followed both the letter of the 1979 Act and the majority of earlier decisions in holding that Israeli law does not currently require, as a condition for the constitution of a trust, that trustees be given title in the trust property.[67]

---

case no need to formally decide the question whether the Israeli trust concept was so restricted); Civil Appeal 1631/02, *Gorban et al v Tshuva Yitzchak Association for Solving the Housing Shortage* (decided 31 July 2003, published online); Civil Appeal 6406/03, *Endowment Trustees of the Sephardi Community in the Holy City of Sephad and Meiron v Kamus* (decided 16 June 2005, published online) (deciding, in para [6], that trusts created by an instrument of endowment could leave the settlor as the registered owner of the trust property); Application (Tel Aviv) 548/06, *Yigal Arnon v Shlomo Pyotrkovski* (decided 1 March 2009, published online); Bankruptcy (Jerusalem) 4044/07, *Hoffmann v The Official Receiver—Jerusalem District* (decided 24 June 2009, published online); Civil Appeal 5955/09, *Ya'acov Amster, Receiver v Marsha Tauber Tov* (decided 19 July 2011, published online).

[61] The three are *Arnon*, *Hoffman* and *Amster* respectively (ibid). *Arnon* involved a celebrated dispute between two of Israel's top lawyers, one of whom, Pyotrkovski, held stock on bare trust for Arnon, so that the stock would not be included in the wealth pool Arnon was then dividing between himself and the wife he was in the process of divorcing. When large dividends beckoned, Pyotrkovski forgot that he held some of his stock on trust.

[62] *Arnon* (n 60) [36]–[39].

[63] *Hoffmann* (n 60) [42]–[43].

[64] *Arnon* (n 60) [18].

[65] *Hoffmann* (n 60) [13], [28].

[66] *Beijing Haidian* (n 7), discussed by Ho (n 7) 126.

[67] *Amster* (n 60) [6]. Even while consolidating Israeli law's independent approach to trustees' rights in the trust property, however, *Hoffmann* and *Amster* drew the local system into closer conformity with common law trust orthodoxy regarding the vulnerability of trusts to trustees' non-trust creditors.

Trustees', accountants' and *legal practitioners'* responses to the Act's innovations, including the shapelessness of its fundamental framework, have been lukewarm. Until 1979, Israeli lawyers were uncertain regarding the express private trust's very availability under Israeli law. This uncertainty made local practitioners, who were nevertheless acting as trustees in myriad factual contexts, subject some of the express trusts they created to foreign legal systems under which private trusts were clearly available. Sometimes foreign trustees were used. While the 1979 Act removed all doubt regarding the existence of the express private trust as part of the local legal system, practitioners continued and continue to use foreign legal systems' trust regimes side by side with the local regime. The local trust regime is used in contexts such as nominee arrangements and trusts for disabled family members, while foreign trust regimes continue to be used for more complex family trusts, as well as where practitioners and their clients are interested in bypassing elements of Israel's fiscal or regulatory regime, such as taxation and (until 2003) exchange control.[68] Alon Kaplan, a leading Israeli trust practitioner and President of the local branch of the Society of Trusts and Estates Practitioners (STEP), explained why Israeli professionals prefer foreign trust regimes to the 1979 Act when creating elaborate family and business trusts:

> Israeli professionals tend to use foreign law trust structures for organizing private and business affairs where an Anglo-Saxon type of trust is required. Sometimes, the continental foundation entity is also used. One can identify several reasons for the above usage:
>
> ... The legal structures available under the Trust Law 1979 are mostly insufficient. The establishment of a trust which would 'skip' generations, often available under foreign trust structures, is not available in Israel. Therefore there is a need for probate of the will in order to achieve the settlor's goal of creating a trust that will exist for a number of generations.[69]

Israeli practitioners have thus found that despite the existence of the 1979 Act, the 'Anglo-Saxon type of trust' is still sometimes 'required'. In private communication, Kaplan made clear that the key difficulty in local law, which results in the continuing

---

Rejecting earlier case law, which construed the 1979 Act to say that where the existence of a trust was not noted on a public register, third parties having no actual or constructive knowledge of the trust could acquire the trust property free of trust (*Mediterranean Car Agency* (n 59); Civil Appeal 371/89, *Orit (Shechter) Ford v Chaim Shechter* 46(1) PD 149 (1992)), the two recent decisions held that even in such a scenario, trustees' non-trust creditors could not reach trust property (*Hoffmann* (n 60) [28]; *Amster* (n 60) [7]–[13]). See discussion, prior to the recent decisions, in N Cohen, 'A Minor's Contract for Purchasing a Flat, Confronted by a Creditor of the Seller's' (1993) 41 *HaPraklit* 161, 176–79; M Deutsch, *Property*, vol 4 (Tel Aviv, Bursi, 2007) §§25.20–25.

[68] This paragraph is based on interviews with three experienced Israeli trust practitioners active in the trusts field since the 1960s: interview with Shlomo Kerem, 1 May 2011; interviews with Advocate Alon Kaplan, 10 January 2010 and 11 May 2011; interview with Meir Minervi, 5 May 2011. For Israeli exchange control and its end on 1 January 2003, see M Michaely, 'Liberalization of the Israeli Foreign Currency Market, 1950–2002' in N Levitan and H Barkai (eds), *The Bank of Israel: Fifty Years' Striving for Monetary Control*, vol 2 (Jerusalem, Bank of Israel, 2004) 79–110.

[69] A Kaplan, 'The Use of Trusts and Offshore Structures in Israel and Major Changes in Israeli International Taxation' (2002) 8 *Trusts & Trustees* 14. See the similar language in A Kaplan, L Eyal and L Harris, 'Israel Launches Trust Tax Amnesty' (2004) 10 *Trusts & Trustees* 21. Similar sentiments were expressed by another leading Israeli trusts practitioner, Michael Shine, in an interview held on 12 May 2011.

use of foreign trust regimes, is not the shapelessness of Israel's trust regime, but rather Israel's anti-perpetuity policy, which is apparently both strict and effective, despite the absence of an explicit rule against perpetuities from the 1979 Act.[70] The nub of this policy lies in the provision of the Succession Act that gifts which are to reach their recipients on or after the donor's death are void unless made by will under that Act.[71] Multi-generational family trusts must thus be testamentary to be valid. Wills must be probated, however, and the personnel of the Israeli Public Custodian, who are involved in the administration of every estate,[72] have been known to be unsympathetic towards attempts to create trusts.[73] The Succession Act places strict limits on multi-generational bequests: testators may only bequeath their property to persons alive at their death or born within 300 days afterwards.[74] Though subject to this restriction, one may bequeath one's property to a series of successive donees, the same Act provides that each donee may consume the full value of the inherited asset, thereby eliminating the value the donor meant later donees of the same asset to receive.[75] These restrictions are strictly enforced by Public Custodian personnel. Israeli practitioners creating complex family trusts thus seem to avoid Israel's *trust* regime due to the perpetuity-unfriendly character of its *succession* regime, which prevents even the extent of perpetuity permitted under the traditional rule against perpetuities, not to mention the boundless extent now permitted by perpetuity-friendly jurisdictions.[76] These practitioners do not generally object to the local trust regime permitting title to the trust assets to be elsewhere than in the trustee.

Academic criticism of the 1979 Act started before its enactment. Ze'ev Zeltner, a judge and contract law professor at Tel Aviv University, attacked the 1974 bill which preceded the Act in a scathing article of 1976. As the bill did not require that trust property be transferred to the trustee, the institution it introduced, wrote Zeltner, would seem to 'have nothing in common with the English trust'.[77] Believing the split ownership trust model to be the only trust model properly so called, Zeltner wrote that where such transfer is not required, 'the trustee would simply appear to be an administrator of the settlor's property'.[78] Zeltner's identification of common law trust law as the only true trust model made him doubt the wisdom of receiving the

---

[70] Communication with the author, 22 May 2011. For Joshua Weisman's criticism of the absence of an explicit rule against perpetuities from the 1979 Act, see his 'Shortcomings in the Trust Law, 1979' (1980) 15 *Israel Law Review* 372, 381–89.

[71] Succession Act, 5725-1965, 446 *Statutes*, 10 February 1965, p 65, s 8(b).

[72] Following reform of the Succession Act in 1998 (s 65A, inserted in the Succession Act (Amendment No 7), 5758-1998, 1670 *Statutes*, June 30, 1998, p 240), probate is now granted by Succession Registrars, who are appointed from among Public Custodian personnel. Additionally, executors, where appointed, must submit an inventory of the estate (Succession Act, last note, s 84) as well as periodical accounts (s 86) to the Public Custodian.

[73] Alon Kaplan, communication with the author, 22 May 2011.

[74] Succession Act, s 3.

[75] Ibid, s 42(a), (b) and (d).

[76] For the classical rule against perpetuities, see JC Gray, *The Rule Against Perpetuities* 4th edn (Roland Gray (ed), Boston, Little, Brown, 1942) § 201; for its recent decline in many US and offshore jurisdictions, see J Dukeminier and JE Krier, 'The Rise of the Perpetual Trust' (2003) 50 *UCLA Law Review* 1303; RH Sitkoff and MM Schanzenbach, 'Jurisdictional Competition for Trust Funds: An Empirical Analysis of Perpetuities and Taxes' (2005) 115 *Yale Law Journal* 356.

[77] Z Zeltner, 'The Trusts Bill, 1974' (1976) 2 *Tel Aviv University Studies in Law* 88–97, 88, n 3.

[78] Ibid.

trust at all, considering the modeling of Israel's private law legislation of the 1960s and 1970s on civil law models, having, for example, abolished equitable rights in property and granted beneficiaries of contracts to which they were not parties standing to sue for their entitlements.[79] He preferred an approximation of the trust by way of contract, agency, gifts and succession mechanisms to the bill's departure from the hegemonic trust model.

The next to critique the bill in print was a banker, Ze'ev Brochstein of the Bank Union, who expressed that body's reaction to the bill.[80] Brochstein focused on the bill's omission of a requirement that title in the trust assets be transferred to the trustee. Noting that the legislature emphasised the managerial aspects of the trust relationship, ignoring its temporal aspects and their consequences regarding the distribution of property rights in the trust assets, Brochstein suggested that this single-minded focus be reconsidered.[81] Though his criticism of the draft Act was far milder than Zeltner's, Brochstein's outlook too was based on an identification of the trust with its hegemonic, common law version. Puzzling over the causes of the Israeli legislature's unconventional approach, he noted the local system's then-recent turn to a civilian, unitary ownership outlook, adding that unitary ownership systems such as those of Japan, South Africa, Quebec and Louisiana did manage to fully import the English trust model.[82]

Enacted amid such inauspicious augurs, the Act was met, almost immediately on its entry into force, with further critical scholarship. Joshua Weisman, the Hebrew University of Jerusalem's distinguished property law expert, entitled his article on the new statute 'Shortcomings in the Trust Law, 1979'.[83] Joining Zeltner and Brochstein in his belief that the traditional common law split ownership trust model was the crux of the trust, Weisman, who acquired a part of his legal education in King's College, London, rejected the possibility of a looser model such as that envisaged in the Act. A loose definition of the trust having nevertheless entered the statute book, Weisman suggested that it be read to require that title in the trust assets be transferred to the trustee.[84] Less critical of the Act, but no less attached to the hegemonic trust model, was Nili Cohen of Tel Aviv University. Identifying split ownership as 'the most significant characteristic of the trust',[85] she noted that beneficiaries' rights under the Act can, despite their having been left undefined, be presumed to have in rem characteristics, as there was no particular point in its enactment where those rights were merely in personam.[86] Cohen's strict distinction between trusts, meaning split ownership trusts, on the one hand, and other fiduciary relationships involving property on the other, made her strain to conclude that the Act applies to the latter

---

[79] Ibid, 88, 95–96.
[80] Z Brochstein, 'The Trust Bill, 5735-1974 and its Influence on the Israeli Banking System' (1977) 18 *Banking Quarterly* 63.
[81] Ibid, 71.
[82] Ibid, 66.
[83] Weisman (n 70).
[84] Ibid, 378–81.
[85] N Cohen, *Interference in Contractual Relations* (Tel Aviv, Ramot, 1982) 34.
[86] Ibid, 56, n 49.

as well as to the former.[87] This conclusion would have been easier to attain had she adopted the more relaxed approach to the trust concept evident in the Act itself.

Other academics proved less attached to the hegemonic trust model: Gualtiero Procaccia and Daniel Friedman of Tel Aviv University both read the Act as permitting the creation of trusts where title in the trust assets was not in the trustee.[88] Friedman rejoiced in the Act's liberal approach, noting that the protection it extends to beneficiaries of all fiduciary relationships involving property will remedy the difficulties created by the abolition of equitable rights in land in the Land Act of 1969.[89] Most partial to the wider reading of the Act was Shlomo Kerem, who, though a practitioner rather than an academic, published a Kommentar on the Act.[90] In each of four editions, Kerem insisted that the term 'trust', as used in the Act, means any fiduciary relationship involving property;[91] that every trustee, in that wider sense, is subject both to the Act and to a more specific, often statutory, legal framework, such as the law regulating executors, guardians or corporate directors;[92] and that beneficiaries under the Act have no rights in the trust property, such rights having been rendered superfluous by the Act's granting beneficiaries a right of action vis-a-vis their trustees.[93] Taking an intermediate position between the two camps, Avraham Alter acknowledged, in an extensive doctoral thesis largely concerned with the taxation of trusts, that the Act applies both to trusts on the common law model and to other fiduciary relationships concerning property, insisting, however, that the Act did grant beneficiaries of both common law and other trusts rights in the trust property.[94] Alter's dissertation having remained unpublished and Kerem's treatise being practitioner-oriented, Weisman's scathing attack of 1980 remained the most extensive purely academic treatment of the Act in print.

C. Shapelessness Abolished? The Draft Civil Code of Israel

Just as Israel's courts have finally started to more thoroughly apply and interpret the 1979 Act, fully acknowledging its non-committal approach to the location of title in the trust assets, Israel's shapeless trust may be about to be swept away. June 2011 saw the publication in formal 'blue book' form, following more than 25 years

---

[87] Ibid, 102–03.

[88] G Procaccia, 'The Agent as Trustee' (1982) 34 *HaPraklit* 479, 482; D Friedman, *The Law of Unjust Enrichment* (Jerusalem, Bursi, 1982) 332–33.

[89] Land Act, 5729-1969, 575 *Statutes*, 27 July 1969, s 161; Friedman (n 88) 334. By his next edition of 1998, he retreated to a less distinct position, noting that it is unclear whether the Act requires, as a precondition for the creation of a trust, that title in the trust assets be transferred to the trustee: Friedman, *The Law of Unjust Enrichment* 2nd edn (Tel Aviv, Aviram, 1998) 535–36. He still hinted, however, that the wider reading of the Act is preferable: 154, n 60.

[90] S Kerem, *Trusts*, 1st edn (Gad Tedeschi (ed) Jerusalem, Sacher Institute, 1983); 4th edn—Kerem (n 37).

[91] Ibid, 1st edn, 20; 4th edn, 37–39.

[92] Ibid, 1st edn, 28, 61; 4th edn, 42.

[93] Ibid, 1st edn, 26, 50; 4th edn, 80–84; see also S Kerem, 'Guaranteeing Trust Assets and the Beneficiary's Rights' (1984) 35 *HaPraklit* 52.

[94] Alter (n 40) 22–62; A Alter, 'The Cestui Que Trust's Right in the Trust Property' (1984) 35 *HaPraklit* 307. Following Alter's unpublished dissertation and his article of 1984, the quantity of Israeli academic treatments of trust law questions started declining rapidly, excepting Kerem's later editions. For a few later treatments, see Cohen (n 67) and Deutsch (n 67); Rabinovich-Brun (n 36).

of drafting, of the Israeli Draft Civil Code, which, if enacted, will replace the private law legislation of the 1960s, 1970s and 1980s, including the Trust Act of 1979.[95] The trusts chapter of the Draft Code[96] moves Israeli trust law much closer to common law orthodoxy: it redefines a trustee as 'the owner of property, who must act regarding it for the benefit of a person or another purpose'[97] and unifies the two trust regimes of the 1979 Act into one, applying to every trust provisions the current Act applies only to trusts created by an instrument of endowment.[98] If and when the Draft Code is enacted, Israel will have retreated from its shapeless trust model to a more traditional model.[99]

Responses to the Israeli shapeless trust seem, then, to have followed the same pattern that responses to the Chinese shapeless trust seem to be following: the courts have largely accepted the local trust regime's deviation from common law trust orthodoxy,[100] while many academics[101] have remained attached to the hegemonic trust model, which requires, in both its English, American, Commonwealth and civilian versions, that title in the trust assets be vested in the trustees.[102] The Israeli Draft Civil Code's return to the hegemonic trust model is another expression of this continuing attachment: it was composed by a committee of (mostly) professors, who, during the very first committee meeting dedicated to the trusts chapter of the Code, expressed their unanimous opinion that trustees must be clearly declared to own the trust assets.[103] The 1979 Act, contrastingly, was largely composed by Ministry of Justice personnel, with later interventions by Bar representatives and politicians.

III. SHOULD SHAPELESS TRUSTS HAVE A FUTURE?

What are the lessons of Israel's experience with the world's first shapeless trust regime for the efficacy of such trust regimes elsewhere?[104] The key lesson seems to

---

[95] Civil Law Act, 5771-2011, 595 *Bills*, 15 June 2011, 699.

[96] Consisting of ss 563–93.

[97] Ibid, s 563.

[98] See the explanatory remarks to the bill: introductory remarks to the trusts chapter and remarks to s 564. See also, on the trusts chapter of the draft code, M Deutsch, *The Civil Code Interpreted*, vol 1 (Tel Aviv, Bursi, 2005) 138–40.

[99] The trusts chapter of the Draft Code still bears some signs of its civil law environment: the common law split ownership trust model is absent and, as in the 1979 Act (s 3(b)), trust creditors have direct access to the trust assets (s 568).

[100] See, for the Chinese courts, Ho (n 7) 126–27. For the Israeli courts, see text to nn 57–67 above.

[101] And academics-turned-judges, such as Professor (later Chief Justice) Barak; see his position in *Zayman* (n 59). For China, see especially the position of Ho in her publications cited in nn 7–8 above; for Israel, see my discussion of the academic response at text to nn 77–94 above.

[102] For civilian versions of the dominant trust model, see, eg, the Scottish regime (Reid (n 36)) and the French (Barrière (n 1) and Crocq (n 1)).

[103] Protocol of Codification Committee Meeting no 81, held on 27 January 1994 (Ministry of Justice archives). At the second committee meeting dedicated to trusts, held on 8 February 1994, Shlomo Kerem made a last stand for the looser trust model evident in the 1979 Act, to little avail. See Protocol of Meeting no 82 (Ministry of Justice archives).

[104] One commentator believed that 'the lesson to be drawn ... is that in today's increasingly integrated international system, it is ever more difficult to insulate one's legal system. We can define legal institutions as we wish for internal purposes, but if we want them to be recognised on the international level, it is best to bring into account the customary international definitions and requirements. In the case of the trust,

be that such regimes are workable, for Israel's courts have, at length, come to accept and apply the 1979 Act's shapeless trust regime, without reading the hegemonic trust model into the Act.[105] The Israeli shapeless trust was born as a result of two phenomena, one socio-legal, the other doctrinal. The former was Israeli legal professionals' casual use of the term 'trust', extending to any fiduciary situation involving property, a use facilitated by the absence, until the 1979 Act, of any positive source of Israeli law delineating the limits of the trust label. The latter was a conscious attempt on the part of some of the Act's many drafters to domesticate the trust into Israel's then-recent system of private law, which has been modelled on the civil law systems of continental Europe. Many of the views and preferences of the Israeli shapeless trust's most persistent advocate, practitioner Shlomo Kerem, make a notably snug fit with civilian trust regimes such as those of Luxembourg or France. Like the latter regimes, which both post-date the 1979 Act, Kerem focused on the trust's functions as a commercial and investment vehicle; like them, he disregarded the constructive trust.[106] A similar domestication effort may be apparent in the Chinese Trust Act of 2001. Some Israeli and Chinese courts have reinforced this effort by effectively absorbing even trusts where title to the trust assets is in the trustee into their respective systems' regimes governing agency, nomineeship and mandate. This was achieved by declaring the settlor or beneficiary, who may be one and the same, to be the substantive owner of the assets of such trusts.[107]

As noted above, the habit of some Israeli practitioners of using foreign trust regimes adhering to common law trust orthodoxy rather than the Israeli regime appears not to be a product of any distaste for the local regime not mandating that title in the trust assets vest in the trustee. This habit, born decades ago as a result of Israel's not having formally received, until 1979, any private trust regime of general application, was, rather, sustained largely as a result of Israel's highly effective perpetuities regime. As the Draft Civil Code softens the perpetuities regime applicable to inter vivos trusts, exempting them from probate and merely positing a 100-year perpetuities period,[108] we may expect the local trust regime—no longer 'shapeless'—to be increasingly used by practitioners if and when the Draft Code is enacted into law. It may well be a mistake, however, to attribute such an increase,

---

this does not mean that Israel must adopt the customary concept of trust lock, stock and barrel, but it does mean that the internal debate on this issue should take it into account': Rabinovich-Brun (n 36) 689–90. The 'customary concept of trust' was brought into account by the drafters of both the Israeli and Chinese Acts, and again by the drafters of the Draft Civil Code of Israel, with various results. The international recognition of shapeless—or other—local trust regimes is beyond the ambit of the present chapter.

[105] Barak CJ attempted such a reading in his brief remarks in *Zayman* (n 59). Most recent case law reads the 1979 Act literally, recognising the shapelessness of its definition of the trust (n 60).

[106] For Kerem's views, see his 'Trust Law in Israel' (1977) 31 *HaPraklit* 233, 238–39. For the French *fiducie* of 2007, see sources cited in n 1 above. For the Luxembourgeois *fiducie* regime, installed in 1983 and improved in 2003, see Règlement grand-ducal du 19 juillet 1983, Mém 29.7.1983 (n 59) 2; Law of 27 July 2003; and see discussion in André Prüm, 'National Report for Luxembourg' in Kortmann et al (n 1) 239–55.

[107] *Beijing Haidian* (n 7); *Yanxin Co Ltd v Huabao Trust and Investment Co Ltd*, Shanghai High People's Court, 16 March 2005, Decision No 226 of 2004; both discussed in Ho, 'Trust Laws in China' (n 8) 203–06; *Hoffmann* (n 60); and see discussion at nn 65–67 above.

[108] Section 702(b) of the Draft Code excepts trusts from the rule, stated in sub-s (a), that undertakings to transfer one's property on or after one's death are void; the 100-year perpetuity period is stated, as regards trusts, in s 588(b).

if it materialises, to the Code's adhering to common law trust orthodoxy regarding the location of title in the trust assets.

Given that neither the Israeli courts nor practitioners now generally object to the Israeli trust regime's shapelessness, its coming demise in the Draft Code is striking. The protocols of the codification committee reveal the change of course to have been a result of academic opinion. Academic lawyers appear to have disapproved of the shapelessness of Israel's 1979 trust regime more than their practising and adjudicating brethren. Such disapproval is evident, for example, in the similar suggestions of Joshua Weisman and Lusina Ho, each of them a key academic trusts expert in his or her respective jurisdiction, that the Trust Acts of 1979 and 2001 respectively be construed so as to require the vesting of title to the trust assets in the trustee. Both Weisman and Ho disapproved of the shapelessness of their respective jurisdictions' trust regimes.[109]

Considering the state of academic opinion on shapeless trust regimes, it is appropriate to close the present study with a preliminary examination of their advantages and disadvantages. Let me begin with the latter. As noted in Part I above, recent literature on the Chinese Trust Act has exposed three difficulties raised by the Act's facilitation of trusts where the settlor, despite his having appointed a trustee, retains title in the trust assets. One such difficulty is non-owner trustees' 'tiresome burden of proving [their] powers to the satisfaction of third parties',[110] a difficulty applicable to *bewind*-type arrangements, whose beneficiaries own the assets, as well. It appears to the present writer that shouldering the burden of obtaining and brandishing a power of attorney should not be impossible, given that American law, for example, provides, by statute, both rules protecting persons who in good faith accept and rely upon acknowledged powers of attorney and rules mandating the acceptance of such powers.[111]

The second difficulty, or group of difficulties, which has been raised is what happens to the assets when owner-settlors or owner-beneficiaries die or are dissolved, when the identity of all or some owner-beneficiaries is disputed, or when trusts the assets of which are owned by their beneficiaries go through periods when no living, identified or identifiable beneficiaries exist.[112] These difficulties too do not appear insurmountable, at least if one's trust model is 'shapeless', that is, if one allows the trust assets to be owned by any one of the trust triangle's three points. The workability of trusts the assets of which are owned by their settlors or beneficiaries would require that arrangements governing several aspects of these trusts' functioning be supplied, either by statute law, case law or the trust instrument. The workability of trusts where trustees own the assets requires no less. While rules requisite for the smooth operation of trusts on the conventional model have already been developed, the extension of the trust concept to trusts the assets of which are owned by their settlors or beneficiaries would require that new rules be supplied. Some preliminary propositions governing the issues raised follow.

---

[109] Weisman (n 70) 378–81; Ho, 'Trust Laws in China' (n 8) 200–01.
[110] See the text to n 22 above.
[111] See Uniform Power of Attorney Act 2006, §§119 and 120 respectively.
[112] See the text to nn 23–25 above.

The problem of owner-settlors and owner-beneficiaries passing away or being dissolved is less likely to arise in shorter-term trusts, such as many commercial and investment trusts. In cases where it is more likely to arise, settlors' or beneficiaries' ownership of the trust assets could presumably pass according to the rules of law usually applicable to the devolution of a deceased or dissolved rightholder's property, namely the law of inheritance and company liquidation. Unless otherwise provided in the trust instrument, the segregated trust fund would survive the settlor or benefi-ciary's death or dissolution: his, her or its executor, administrator, heirs or liquidator would hold the trust fund on trust for the relevant beneficiaries or purpose, trust assets being answerable to trust debts alone. Or ownership of the trust assets could be vested in a fluctuating group of beneficiaries: much as the law provides a means for the appointment of new trustees when none remain, the law or trust instrument could similarly provide for the appointment of new owner-beneficiaries in a manner tracking the settlor's express or implied intentions. Where the primary motivation behind the creation of a trust is avoiding probate or minimising a settlor's exposure to creditors (assuming that 'asset protection trusts' are allowed), trustees, a benefi-ciary other than the settlor, or beneficiaries as a class, could serve as owner of the trust assets. Where the inexistence, for a time, of any beneficiaries, or disputes as to their identity are realistic possibilities, title in the trust assets could be granted to either the settlor, the trustee or, again, 'the beneficiaries of X trust' as a class, which could have zero members for a while. It thus appears that all three points of the trust triangle could have their uses as owners of the trust assets, depending on the type of trust envisioned, its goals, its lifespan and the circumstances likely to occur during its existence.

The final difficulty raised in recent literature regarding the retention of title in the trust assets by their settlors is that under current Chinese law, such settlors owe no fiduciary duties and could thus act in breach of trust, leaving the beneficiaries largely defenceless.[113] While the current Chinese Act may not be perfect and could require amendment, including the imposition of fiduciary or other duties on settlors retaining ownership of the trust assets, its current imperfections could hardly serve as arguments for rejecting the very idea of trusts the settlors of which retain title in the trust assets. Unlike settlors who have declared that they themselves hold assets on trust, settlors who merely retain title in the trust assets, having appointed another as trustee, could be subjected to duties sufficient to protect the trust and its assets without being granted powers to either manage or dispose of the trust assets. The very lack of such powers could provide some of the necessary protection.

It seems, then, that the difficulties raised in recent literature do not suffice for trusts the settlors or beneficiaries of which hold title in the trust assets, without also serving as trustees, to be estimated as definitely inferior to trusts on the traditional model. Nor do they suffice for similarly condemning the Chinese-Israeli shapeless trust model. Trusts are created for various purposes. Different trust models could suit different circumstances. Property held on revocable trusts, for example, is already seen by American law as if it was still held by its settlor, at least as regards

---

[113] See the text to n 26 above.

the rights of that settlor's spouse, relatives and creditors.[114] The step from such a presumption to facilitating settlors' actual retention of title in trust property does not appear to be impossible. It may be that holding the trust assets to be retained by the settlor would frustrate the purpose of trusts created in order to avoid probate or minimise the burden of estate taxation. That such trust designs defeat the purpose of *some* trusts does not imply that they would never be useful.

Indeed, shapeless trust regimes may also have some advantages over the traditional trust model. One is their making the duties that the law of trusts imposes on trustees and the effective remedies that it gives beneficiaries applicable in fiduciary situations involving non-owner asset managers, which are conventionally analysed as agency, nomineeship or, under civil law systems, mandate situations. The application to such asset managers of the trustee's duties, such as the duties of prudence, loyalty, impartiality, full and prompt accounting and reporting, and refraining from conflicts of interest and duty,[115] seems desirable, considering the significant risk of such managers succumbing to the temptation of preferring self-interest over their clients' interests. Such an application may not, however, bring about a significant transformation in the duties and liabilities to which such managers are in fact subject, since legislation has already in many jurisdictions applied similar duties to such managers, independently of their being subjected to trustees' duties, as such.[116] Further, insofar as some or all of these duties may be disapplied by contract or trust deed, and are so disapplied in practice by way of exemption clauses, their extension to additional classes of asset managers is likely to be even less consequential.

A further advantage, which is perhaps of more consequence, is that shapeless trusts may help to introduce the trust mechanism to potential settlors unaccustomed to it, who may be deterred by the prospect of giving away title in their property. Many property owners outside the traditional Anglo-Saxon sphere of trust practice would be very much deterred by such a prospect. Ho wrote that the Chinese Act's not requiring that trust assets vest in the trustee might be a result of its drafters' fear of such a deterrent effect,[117] and Kaplan has told me that such deterrence is very much a fact among potential Israeli and Jewish settlors.[118] The adaptation of imported legal institutions to local circumstances in the importing jurisdiction, such as the fears and expectations of potential users, has been shown to be an important condition for the imported institution being successfully received.[119] Offshore jurisdictions, purportedly adhering to the traditional common law trust model, have developed 'settlor-reserved powers' so as to successfully market trust services to potential settlors fearful of or uninterested in letting go of their property. Some such jurisdictions, while vesting title to the trust assets in the trustee, permit the settlor to retain a vast panoply of both administrative and dispositive powers, providing

---

[114] Restatement of Trusts, 3rd, §25(2) and cmt a.

[115] Ibid, §§77, 78, 79, 82, 83.

[116] See, eg, the Investment Advisers Act of 1940, 15 USC §80b-1 to 21 (US); An Act for the Regulation of Investment Advice, Marketing and Management, 5755-1995, 1539 *Statutes*, 10 August 1995, p 416, ss 11–27C (Israel).

[117] Ho, 'Trust Laws in China' (n 8) 201.

[118] Alon Kaplan, communication with the author, 22 May 2011.

[119] D Berkowitz, K Pistor and J-F Richard, 'The Transplant Effect' (2003) 51 *American Journal of Comparative Law* 163, 167–68.

explicitly by statute that such reservation shall not invalidate a trust.[120] The Chinese and Israeli 'shapeless trusts', by leaving actual power to administer and dispose of trust assets in the hands of trustees, stick rather closer, in functional terms, to the traditional trust model than do those offshore regimes. So long as adequate means are in place to ensure that settlors do not use their retained ownership to interfere in trustees' execution of their functions, the 'settlor title retention trust' can be seen as a relatively direct means of making trusts palatable for a wider circle of potential settlors, involving less real injury to the separation of enjoyment and control, one of the foundational ideas behind trusts, than do the alternative means developed, for the same purpose, by offshore jurisdictions.

To conclude, the schematic division of labour envisioned by the traditional trust model, with the settlor having nothing to do with the trust once constituted, the trustee serving as its exclusive manager and beneficiaries passively enjoying their entitlements, has for hundreds of years been and is now being challenged by both the real-life functioning of actual trusts and innovative trust regimes developed by various jurisdictions. Settlors can, if they wish, find ways to influence their trustees' conduct, whether that influence is formalised in the trust instrument or not, and whether or not it is in keeping with the trust's governing law or other relevant legal frameworks. Beneficiaries, similarly, sometimes try to influence trustees' decisions. Given the fundamentally facilitative nature of trust law and the increasing variety of trust regimes worldwide, many of which apply to populations unfamiliar with traditional Anglo-Saxon trust culture, it may be that there are few reasons to insist on the continuing exclusivity of the traditional trust paradigm, granting title in the trust assets to the trustees. Other models, including 'settlor title retention trusts', may have their uses. Though such models, contradicting the traditional common law trust paradigm, raise doctrinal challenges—how, for example, are trusts the beneficiaries of which own their assets to cope with the traditional doctrine of merger?[121]—it seems that the cautious, permissive Chinese and Israeli approach, 'shapeless' though it may be, could, if each of the trust models it permits is allowed to develop according to its internal logic, have some potential after all.

---

[120] See, eg, s 9A of the Trusts (Jersey) Law 1984, inserted by the Trusts (Amendment No 4) (Jersey) Law 2006, which provides, inter alia, that the reservation by a settlor of powers to revoke, vary or amend the trust, of powers to pay trust income or capital, or of powers to give the trustee binding directions regarding management of the trust assets, 'shall not affect the validity of the trust nor delay the trust taking effect'. Section 15(1) of the Trusts (Guernsey) Law 2007 improves on the Jersey model by providing that even should a settlor reserve powers of all those types, the trust shall not thereby be invalidated. See discussion in Panico (n 39) 63–77.

[121] See Restatement of Trusts, 3rd, §69.

6

Misplaced Trust: First Principles and the Conveyance of Legal Leases to Minors

LESLIE TURANO-TAYLOR[*]

I. INTRODUCTION

EVERY SO OFTEN a decision on what seems at first a minor and straight-forward point can nevertheless lead us to reassess long-held assumptions. The Court of Appeal handed down one such decision in *Hammersmith and Fulham LBC v Alexander-David* on the effect of the transfer of a legal estate to a minor.[1] Here, the local authority had granted a legal periodic tenancy to a home-less 16-year-old, but, as the purported grantee was a minor, the Court found that the transfer constituted an express declaration of a trust of land under Schedule 1, para 1 to the Trusts of Land and Appointment of Trustees Act (TLATA) 1996. There is nothing untoward in the Court's application of the statute: minors are pre-cluded from holding legal estates in land,[2] and the grant of a legal lease could not be construed as the grant of an equitable lease for its failure to vest the legal estate in the grantee; it could be only what it was expressly intended to be, the grant of a legal estate, which, because the grantee was a minor, took (unintended) effect as an express trust of land. The problem is that in these particular circumstances the land-lord becomes the trustee for the tenant and is bound by a trustee's obligations under the Act, which, it will be argued, are incompatible with the usual rights accorded to landlords. Moreover, the rule treats without distinction the assignment of an exist-ing interest and the creation of a new interest, contrary to the way in which trusts of land are normally constituted. Finally, the nature of the tenant's interest is not clear: she cannot hold an equitable lease, but neither can she have an interest in the only thing her trustee holds—the fee simple. The effect of the ruling is a departure from first principles, giving the defendant an unlimited interest in land which con-forms neither to the nature of a beneficial interest under a trust of land nor to the

---

[*] Lecturer in Law, King's College London. I am grateful to Emma Ford for her comments on an ear-lier draft and to the participants in the Modern Studies in Property Law Conference 2012. Any errors, misconceptions and inconsistencies, however, are mine.
[1] *Hammersmith and Fulham LBC v Alexander-David* [2009] EWCA Civ 259, [2010] 2 WLR 1126.
[2] Law of Property Act 1925, s 1(6).

categories of the *numerus clausus*. The anomaly results from the application of a rule to a problem which it was never intended to resolve—paragraph 1 of Schedule 1 to the TLATA 1996 is derived from section 27(1) of the Settled Land Act 1925—and so a provision that was conceived for the purpose of preserving dynastic wealth is nowadays used to govern the short-term social housing of vulnerable teenagers. The result is that a simple application of a statutory provision in unusual circumstances leads to both theoretical and practical difficulties which in turn raise fundamental questions about the way in which English property law attends to the fragmentation of ownership of land.

II. THE BACKGROUND

As is well known, the purpose of the Settled Land Act 1882 was to remove the 'evils' of strict settlements by giving the tenant for life wide powers of dealing, some of which were shortly thereafter extended to the trustee of a trust for sale for the benefit of a person with a life interest.[3] The Settled Land Act 1925 continued and extended the policy of the 1882 Act, but, in light of changes that would be made under the Law of Property Act 1925, addressed the position of minors. Since 1926, a minor cannot hold a legal estate in land, although there is nothing to prevent him from holding an equitable one.[4] The problem arising in settlements before 1997 was that if the life tenant were a minor, he would have the wide statutory powers of a legal owner. To avoid this, section 27(1) of the Settled Land Act 1925 provided that where a conveyance to a minor was made, it operated as a contract for value to make a settlement by vesting deed and trust instrument. Until that time, the party making the conveyance held the land on trust for the minor.[5] Thereafter, a conveyance of a legal estate to a minor created a settlement. Since part of the purpose of the TLATA 1996 was to eradicate the distinction between settlements and trusts of land, after January 1997, existing contracts to make a settlement have been converted into a declaration that the land is held on express trust of land, and any attempt to convey a legal estate to a minor now creates an express trust of land.[6]

In *Alexander-David*, the claimant local authority had used a standard form to grant a weekly periodic tenancy to the homeless defendant, to whom it owed a duty under section 193 of the Housing Act 1996 and who had a priority need. Fifteen months later, owing to the defendant's disruptive behaviour, it served notice to quit in accordance with clause 2 of the lease agreement. This was a standard clause allowing either party to determine the tenancy by giving four weeks' notice. Following possession proceedings (by which time the defendant was no longer a

---

[3] Settled Land Act 1882 s 6(1).

[4] Law of Property Act 1925, s 1(6); Settled Land Act 1925, s 26(6); *R v Tower Hamlets LBC, ex p Von Goetz* [1999] QB 1019 (CA); see Law Commission, *Minors' Contracts* (Law Com WP No 143, 1984) [5.16].

[5] Law of Property Act 1925, s 19(1); Settled Land Act 1925, s 27(i) (both now repealed); C Harpum, S Bridge and M Dixon (eds), *Megarry and Wade: The Law of Real Property*, 17th edn (London, Sweet & Maxwell, 2008) paras [36-005]–[26-006]. See also B English and J Saville, *Strict Settlement*, University of Hull Occasional Papers in Economic and Social History 10 (University of Hull, 1983) 17.

[6] TLATA 1996, s 2(6); sch 1, para 1(1) and (3).

minor), the district judge ordered the defendant to give up possession. She appealed against the order and the Court of Appeal accepted her two arguments: first, that, as she had been a minor when the lease was granted to her, the effect of paragraph 1(1) of Schedule 1 to the TLATA 1996 meant that she was a beneficiary under a trust of land; and, second, that the claimant's attempt to determine the tenancy amounted to a breach of trust.

III. THE CONCEPTUAL PROBLEM

Those who teach property law will be familiar with the problem of getting students to distinguish between equitable interests in general and equitable interests in a trust. Once students grasp the idea of the trust, they tend to see it every time an equitable interest appears. Perhaps because the institution of the trust looms large to claim most of the student's attention in any course on equity, he simply forgets that an equitable interest can exist outside of a trust. In land law in particular, the novice is inclined to think that a trust of land must arise every time there is a failure of formality or registration. The error results where one fails to distinguish between the transfer of an existing interest and the creation of a new one. Three examples illustrate this error in student reasoning. In the first example, if A purports to transfer the legal fee simple to B, fails for want of a deed,[7] but has entered into an enforceable contract, the doctrine in *Walsh v Lonsdale* enforces that contract in equity, and a trust of land arises, with A still holding the legal fee simple but now on trust for B, who has claim in equity to have the legal fee simple transferred to him.[8] In the second example, if the transfer is made by deed, but B fails to register the legal title, a trust of land also arises because, while A's title remains on the register, equity recognises that the transfer has taken place.[9] The same would occur where tenant A seeks to assign an existing legal lease to B. So, the novice reasons, where, in a third example, A holds the legal fee simple and purports to create a new legal lease in favour of B, but fails for want of formalities as in the examples above,[10] the

---

[7] Law of Property Act 1925, s 52; Law of Property (Miscellaneous Provisions) Act 1989, ss 1–2.

[8] *Walsh v Lonsdale* (1881) Ch D 9 (CA). See also *Lysaght v Edwards* (1875–76) LR 2 Ch D 499, 507 (Jessel MR): 'a valid contract actually changes the ownership in equity'; *Rose v Watson* (1864) X House of Lords Cases (Clark's) 672, 678 (Lord Westbury LC): 'When the owner of an estate contracts with a purchaser for the immediate sale of it, the ownership of the estate is, in equity, transferred by that contract'; *Wall v Bright* (1820) 1 JAC & W 494, 500; 37 ER 456, 458 (Sir Thomas Plumer): 'the contract to sell is a disposition of the estate, and by it the purchaser parts with his right and dominion over it. It is in equity no longer his'.

[9] This is a result of the combined effect of s 27(1) of the Land Registration Act 2002 and s 1(2)(a) of the TLATA 1996; the first denies legal effect of the transfer, thereby creating a bare trust of the estate, and the second expressly includes bare trusts as trusts of land. It should be noted that, strictly speaking, the *Walsh* doctrine does indeed give the interest contracted for in equity, but it has nothing to say about trusts. Where a fee simple or an existing lease is assigned but not by deed, the trust that ensues by operation of the doctrine does not contain an equitable version of the fee simple or lease, but rather an equity against the legal owner to have that interest conveyed. An equitable lease, like the one found in *Walsh* itself, is an altogether different thing.

[10] Assuming there is an enforceable agreement in accordance with s 2 of the Law of Property (Miscellaneous Provisions) Act 1989.

Walsh doctrine applies to give the lease in equity, with the result that A must be the trustee for B. This is to misunderstand the purpose of the trust of land.

The trust of land is primarily a vehicle for the co-ownership of estates in land. But it is important to distinguish between co-ownership in a broad sense and in a narrow one. It should be noted that the first two examples are examples of a bare trust and so are not instances of co-ownership in the narrow sense, as neither of the forms of co-ownership—the joint tenancy and the tenancy in common—exists. The estate lies in single hands both at law and in equity. Before 1997, there was some doubt as to whether such an arrangement was a trust for sale with the attendant overreaching mechanism, since the provisions creating such a trust were concerned only with co-ownership.[11] However, the TLATA 1996 expressly includes bare trusts under section 1(2)(a). In light of this, it is sensible to regard bare trusts as co-ownership in a broader sense, in that both the trustee and the beneficiary have interests in the *same estate*. But where Landlord A attempts to create a new legal estate, the lease, in favour of B, but the legal title fails to vest in B, it is not an instance of co-ownership, for what is co-owned? If it were, then all applications of the *Walsh* doctrine would result in trusts of land. The fee simple is not co-owned, nor is the lease, which would be the case where the conveyance purported to transfer the fee simple or an existing lease. The *Walsh* doctrine does indeed operate here, but what B gets is an equitable lease, not an interest behind a trust of land, for the simple reason that this, unlike the first two examples, is not a case of co-ownership. B owns the (equitable) lease in its entirety; A owns the entirety of the reversion.

Students often confuse co-ownership with fragmentation of ownership. The latter occurs when the various rights that together constitute ownership of land are distributed between the landlord and the tenant for the duration of the lease, but they are allotted in such a way that, where there was once a single, unencumbered fee simple, there are now two separate and smaller objects of ownership: the leasehold and the reversion.[12] Here, the fee-simple owner has broken off a piece, so to speak, of the sum of his ownership by giving his right to possession to the tenant—but he is not a co-owner of any rights granted to the tenant.

The lease is, like any other lesser property right, derived from and dependent on (or, as we often say, 'carved *out* of') the fee simple, but it is not a part of it; it is a separate, differentiated interest. The difference is that in the first two examples, where A has an existing interest and fails to transfer it to B in a way that is recognised at law, he keeps what he has (at law) but on trust for B, since equity will deem the interest to have passed to the grantee. By contrast, in the third example, A does not have, never has had and, it is argued here, *could* not have a legal lease, the benefit of which would accrue to B. In the third example, the absence of a trust is explained by the fact that the legal title to the new interest has never been in the hands of the grantor, so there is nothing for him to hold on trust; this is in fact what happened in *Walsh*. In that case, there was no trust since there was no attempt to transfer an existing interest, only to create a new one. Indeed, Jessel MR held the

---

[11] Law of Property Act 1925, ss 34 and 36.
[12] S Bright, *Landlord and Tenant Law in Context* (Oxford, Hart Publishing, 2007) 49.

existence of a legal lease to be incompatible with the equitable lease.[13] Where there is a trust of a lease, it is the legal lease which is held on trust for B, who has not an equitable lease but a right against A's legal lease. The same is true of an attempt to grant a legal charge. Where A fails to create a legal charge in favour of B so that B has a charge effective only in equity, there is no trust for the simple reason that A does not have a legal charge against which B has an equitable right. A's only asset is the fee simple. B's equitable right lies against A's fee simple, but not as a share in the ownership of A's asset under a trust of land. What the charge and the lease have in common is that they are encumbrances on the fee simple; they are rights against the owner of the fee simple and they are incompatible with the trust of land paradigm, because one cannot hold, on trust or otherwise, a right against oneself.[14] So, although the law of real property allows an owner of an estate to grant lesser proprietary interests, including estates, to others, it only recognises co-ownership (and hence a trust of land) where there is more than one owner of the same estate.

IV. THE PRACTICAL PROBLEM

So, then, how does one explain the effect of Schedule 1 to the TLATA 1996 when it is applied to the creation of a lease? Paragraph 1(1) of Schedule 1 states that a conveyance of a legal estate to a minor takes effect as a declaration of a trust of land. The statute accords with section 1(6) of the Law of Property Act 1925, which precludes minors from holding a legal estate in land.[15] But there is nothing to prevent the minor from holding an equitable estate, and, in fact, a contract to grant an interest in property is one of the few contracts which are enforceable against minors.[16] But legislation turns this into a statutory trust: the purported transferor becomes the trustee and the minor becomes the beneficiary. Legislation is needed to create a trust where there is a transfer of an existing legal estate to a minor, because equitable principles would not suffice to achieve the same end as in the case of a failed transfer to an adult. This is because there is no specific performance available to the minor and so no basis on which the *Walsh* doctrine can operate.[17] Thus, in the case

---

[13] *Walsh v Lonsdale* (n 8) 14. On equity's treatment of contracts for the sale of an interest in land, see Jessel MR in *Lysaght v Edwards* (n 8) 506: 'It is that the moment you have a valid contract for sale the vendor becomes in equity a trustee for the purchaser of the estate sold, and the beneficial ownership passes to the purchaser, the vendor having a right to the purchase-money, a charge or lien on the estate for the security of that purchase-money, and a right to retain possession of the estate until the purchase-money is paid'. However, it should be noted that it is not an ordinary trusteeship: Stamp LJ in *Berkley v Poulett* [1977] 1 EGLR 86 (CA) 93: 'He is said to be a trustee because of the duties which he has, and the duties do not arise because he is a trustee but because he has agreed to sell the land to the purchaser and the purchaser on tendering the price is entitled to have the contract specifically performed according to its terms. Nor does the relationship in the meantime have all the incidents of the relationship of trustee and *cestui qui trust*. That this is so is sufficiently illustrated by the fact that *prima facie* the vendor is until the date fixed for the completion entitled to receive and retain the rents and profits and that as from that date the purchaser is bound to pay interest.'

[14] Unless the estate owner also assumed a different legal personality, eg, as a member of a corporation.

[15] As noted in *Phillips v Peace* [2004] EWHC 1380 (Fam); [2005] 2 FLR 1212 [21].

[16] *Davies v Benyon-Harris* (1931) 47 TLR 424; Law Commission (n 4) [2.10]–[2.12].

[17] This argument is predicated on the view that the availability of specific performance determines whether there is an equitable interest: see dicta in *Austin v Sheldon* [1974] 2 NSWLR 661, 670

of a purported transfer of an *existing* legal estate, all paragraph 1(1) of Schedule 1 does is to give the same result as the principles of equity would give in the case of a failed transfer at law of an existing interest to an adult. But Schedule 1 does not expressly restrict the effect to conveyances of a fee simple or existing legal lease, and the term conveyance also includes the creation of a new interest.[18] As such, the Court of Appeal held in *Alexander-David* that the local authority claimant, in fulfilling its statutory duty to house a homeless 16-year-old, had, by operation of paragraph 1(1), become the latter's trustee by purporting to grant her a legal lease.[19] On such a conveyance, Schedule 1 operates to give the minor grantee an interest under a trust, just as it does where there is a purported conveyance of an existing interest. But, contrary to its operation in the first two examples, here Schedule 1 does not replicate the ordinary rules of equity; it creates a trust where there would be none if the transferee were an adult. In the case of an adult transferee, the *Walsh* doctrine would simply recognise the lease as a differentiated equitable estate, not as an interest under a trust.

If the purpose of the provision is to effect the same result as would ensue under equitable principles if the grantee were an adult, then it fails in two ways: first, on the attempted conveyance of an existing interest, it creates an *express* trust for the minor, whereas equitable principles might give a *constructive* trust (the practical difference is that the express trustee has far-reaching positive duties, unlike the constructive trustee, whose only duty may be to transfer the title to the beneficiary);[20] and, second, in the case of the creation of a new lease, it creates a very odd trust, one which does not sit comfortably within the trust paradigm. For one thing, it is not clear what the subject matter is. The only property held by the local authority—the claimant 'trustee'—is the fee simple, but it cannot be said that the local authority holds this on trust for the defendant. Conversely, the weekly periodic tenancy, which the defendant was said to enjoy in equity, is patently not in the hands of the trustee. If it were, then the claimant local authority would become its own legal tenant. So what is the claimant supposed to hold on trust? It is clear that the landlord's fee simple is not unencumbered—it is (or ought to be) subject to the lease in equity, but this does not raise a trust of land on ordinary principles. Of course, the short answer to why it does here is that Parliament has said it does.

On analysis, such a trust in these circumstances is unsatisfactory for three reasons. First, the imposition of a trust of land under Schedule 1 in *Alexander-David* gives the beneficiary something different from what had been intended by the parties, not just in form but in substance. Second, a trust under which the trustee is the beneficiary's landlord cannot conform to the way in which trusts of land operate generally.

(Mahoney J); *British Malayan Trustees Ltd v Sibdo Realty Pte Ltd (in liquidation) and others* [1999] 1 SLR 623 [79] (Karthigesu J); *Lowther v Kim* [2003] 1 NZLR 327 [23] (Randerson J). For an alternative view, see *Hewett v Court* (1982) 149 CLR 639, 666 (Deane J).

[18] Law of Property Act 1925, s 205(1)(ii).

[19] Housing Act 1996, s 193(2).

[20] PJ Millett, 'Restitution and Constructive Trusts' [1998] *LQR* 399, 402. See Lord Millett's objection (406) to ascribing the express trustee's ordinary fiduciary obligations to a constructive trustee: 'It should not be hard to accept that a constructive trust does not necessarily attract fiduciary obligations. It is well established that a contracting vendor of land holds the land on a constructive trust for the purchaser; yet no one thinks that he is under any fiduciary duty towards his purchaser.'

The interests of a trustee and beneficiary are aligned, whereas those of a landlord and tenant are often opposed. A weekly periodic tenancy is a relatively small interest in land: it is determinable by a week's notice and has no capital value.[21] The landlord and tenant have duties towards each other, but also enjoy rights to protect their own interests. But an interest under a trust of land is valuable to the beneficiary as it may give the beneficiary an interest in the share of any proceeds of sale by trustees of the legal interest. It imposes a strict obligation on the trustee generally to serve the beneficiary's interest, while the beneficiary has no duties towards the trustee. Third, such a *sui generis* trust creates serious problems for local authorities as there is no suggestion of how the trust can be brought to an end, since here the court found that an attempt to determine the tenancy by notice as provided for under clause 3 of the lease agreement constituted a breach of trust. It will be argued that the finding of a breach of trust is inconsistent not only with authority but also with the very idea of a trust in these circumstances. So why should Parliament have insisted that the creation of a legal lease in favour of a minor take the form of a trust?

V. SUBJECT MATTER OF THE TRUST I: EQUITABLE INTERESTS AND INTERESTS UNDER A TRUST OF LAND

Another common error is to assume that an interest under a trust of land is simply an equitable version of a legal interest when it is in fact a different kind of interest altogether. Proprietary interests in equity may be distinguished as, on the one hand, differentiated interests such as an equitable easement or the mortgagor's equitable right to redeem and, on the other hand, those under a trust of land.[22] The differentiated equitable interests are those which resemble legal interests (with the obvious exception of those interests which can exist only in equity, such as the benefit of a restrictive covenant or a right of pre-emption). The category is limited in number, as in the case of legal interests, by the *numerus clausus*, the closed list of permissible forms of proprietary entitlement.[23] In general, the purpose of the *numerus clausus* is to restrict the variety of rights that can affect third parties, thereby reducing the transaction costs that would otherwise attend the trading of unfamiliar or unorthodox packages of entitlement.[24] Equitable rights under a trust lie outside the *numerus clausus* as they are not intended to affect third parties—or perhaps it would better to say that equitable interests under a trust lie within the trustee's particular interest,

---

[21] This might be a justification, albeit a weak one, for the court's finding that to determine a tenancy held on trust would be a breach of that trust: for if the trustee/landlord cannot sell the trust asset for value, then the beneficiary's rights do indeed disappear on determination, because there are no proceeds of sale to substitute for the lost asset.

[22] *Westdeutsche Landesbank Girozentrale v Islington LBC* [1996] AC 669 (HL), 706–07 (Lord Browne-Wilkinson).

[23] The strict adherence to known interests in land is expressed in *Keppell v Bailey* (1834) 2 My & K 517, 535; 39 ER 1042, 1049 (Lord Brougham LC).

[24] K Gray and SF Gray, 'The Rhetoric of Realty' in J Getzler (ed), *Rationalising Property, Equity and Trusts: Essays in Honour of Edward Burn* (London, LexisNexis, 2003), 204, 210–11; RC Nolan, 'Equitable Property' (2006) 122 *LQR* 232, 260. An exception to this might be the 'inchoate equity', now protected by s 116 of the Land Registration Act 2002; see B McFarlane, 'Proprietary Estoppel and Third Parties after the Land Registration Act 2002' [2003] *CLJ* 661.

which is itself determined by the *numerus clausus*. On either view, where there is a trust of land, the beneficiary's interest is not in the form of a differentiated equitable interest recognisable as one of the permitted interests in land.[25] Rather, it is a right to make a claim against the trustee's interest, and it is the latter which *must* take form as one of the *numerus clausus* rights.[26] The extent of the beneficiary's interest under the trust is variable:[27] it may be as limited as a mere hope to receive some of the proceeds of sale under a discretionary trust or a right to occupy the premises for one's lifetime, or as extensive as the right to direct the trustee in the property's management as under a bare trust. The extent of the beneficial interest may be anything except larger than the trustee's.[28] But the trust of land does not comprise a legal estate and a separate 'shadow' estate in equity; it comprises a legal estate affected by equitable rights in that very estate. As such, co-ownership is only made possible by the trust of land.

The trust of land serves the purpose of the *numerus clausus* principle in two ways. First, the overreaching mechanism ensures that in most cases, the purchaser is not affected by amorphous or undefined rights, but only by recognised property rights that appear on the register (and in limited circumstances by discoverable rights not appearing on the register).[29] Second, where a purchaser takes subject to the beneficiary's interest, the scope of the beneficiary's right can be no greater than the defined proprietary right of the trustee, as it is contained within that recognised property right, whatever the latter may be. Equitable interests behind a trust of land may take any form, but are ultimately dependent on, and are indeed part of, a recognised, differentiated proprietary interest which may be held at law or, in the absence of a legal interest, in equity. Equitable interests not held in trust must take shape as one of the recognised interests in land, and they are antithetical to the same interests at law. An equitable lease can only exist if there is no legal lease present.[30] In *Walsh v Lonsdale*, Jessel MR explained that by reason of the fusion of law and equity, there cannot be two identical estates in the same land, one at law and one in equity,[31] and since equity prevailed, the claimant in that case had an equitable lease. There was certainly no trust of a lease.

---

[25] Hence it cannot be entered as a notice: Land Registration Act 2002, s 33.

[26] Nor can such rights be entered on the register positively as a notice (Land Registration Act 2002 s 33(a)(i)), but only negatively, as a restriction against dealing with the title (s 40).

[27] J Mowbray (ed), *Lewin on Trusts*, 18th edn (London, Sweet & Maxwell, 2011) paras [1.06]–[1.07]: the beneficiary has no equitable proprietary interest in the narrow sense, and of course no equitable ownership, if either his rights or the assets in which they are to be enjoyed are not sufficiently ascertained (eg, under a discretionary trust or where assets are in the course of administration), but beneficiaries are entitled to enforce due administration of the assets, and this gives them ownership in the wide sense. See also Nolan (n 24) 264: 'The unifying features of equitable property rights under a trust are, at root, negative: the core function of equitable property is to exclude non-beneficiaries from the trust assets.'

[28] See *Ayerst v CK (Construction) Ltd* [1976] AC 167 (HL) 177 (Lord Diplock) for the idea that a beneficial interest under a trust is ownership.

[29] Land Registration Act 2002, scheds 1 and 3.

[30] Unless it is a sub-lease, but in that case it is a different interest from the head-lease, in the same way that a head-lease is different from the reversion out of which it is carved.

[31] *Walsh v Lonsdale* (n 4) 14. This point is often missed: see, for example, Hale J in *Kingston upon Thames RLBC v Prince* [1999] 1 FLR 593 (CA) 802, where an adult lessee held a secure legal tenancy on trust for a minor: 'the relevant tenancy is the equitable tenancy held by [the minor]'.

So, to summarise, in order for a trust of land to exist, there must be an interest in the hands of the trustee against which the beneficiary can make a claim. This is often, although not necessarily, a legal interest. As such, a legal lessee may hold the legal lease on trust for a beneficiary, just as the owner of a legal fee simple may hold that interest on trust. Where such a legal interest is present, the equitable interest is not differentiated from the legal interest, because it is parasitic upon that interest. It is, in other words, an equitable interest *in* the legal fee simple or legal lease. The paradigm becomes clear by comparison with that *sine qua non* of all rights in land, the fee simple absolute in possession. Equity cannot recognise that estate as anything other than an interest in a trust of land. This is because it is the primary interest in land from which all other interests derive and so any claim of an equitable interest in land must rest on the existence of a legal fee simple. But lesser rights, such as a lease or charge, which of course derive from the legal fee simple, may, in a particular piece of land, have no legal counterpart themselves, and in this case there is no trust, only the recognition of these differentiated interests in equity. In other words, the owner of a differentiated equitable interest has a claim against the owner of the legal estate, but not a claim *in* the estate. However, under a trust of land, the beneficiary has a claim *in the very interest* in the hands of the trustee. What is more, the entirety of the trustee's interest is subject to the beneficiary's claim. Even where A holds an estate on trust for himself and B, or for B and C, it is not said that A holds part of the estate on trust for any of the beneficiaries. The entirety of A's estate is affected by the trust.

The different characteristics of interests under a trust of land as opposed to differentiated equitable interests also require different doctrinal approaches, hence the application of constructive trusts and proprietary estoppel. Although the two often overlap in cases where a claim is made to a share in an existing estate,[32] only proprietary estoppel is appropriate where the claimant asserts a new interest, one that the defendant does not hold. Proprietary estoppel may be used to show that the claimant has acquired an equitable interest under a (constructive) trust, that is, an equitable interest in the interest already held by the constructive trustee. But only proprietary estoppel can assist the claimant who asserts that a new, independent interest has been promised to him and that the circumstances are such that it would be inequitable for the defendant to deny. So, for example, in *Crabb v Arun DC*, it could not possibly be that the defendant held a legal or equitable easement against its own fee simple on trust for the claimant, but that the defendant's conscience was bound to grant the claimant an easement against the defendant's fee simple.[33] Certainly, there are cases in which a constructive trust is used to ensure the performance of an obligation arising under proprietary estoppel. But it is argued here that in some cases this is a misuse of the trust device. In *Kinane v Mackie-Konteh*,[34] an equitable charge was deemed to have been created and to be held on trust by

---

[32] That is, where the court remedies an estoppel claim by awarding an interest under a constructive trust, as in, for example, *Pascoe v Turner* [1979] 1 WLR 431 (CA).
[33] *Crabb v Arun DC* [1976] Ch 179 (CA). See also the recent decision in *Chaudhary v Yavuz* [2011] EWCA Civ 1314, in which the Court of Appeal recognised an easement by estoppel, but rejected the notion that it was held on constructive trust by the servient owner.
[34] *Kinane v Mackie-Konteh* [2005] EWCA Civ 45; [2005] WTLR 345.

the freeholder against his own title. The result followed the decision in *Yaxley v Gotts*,[35] but in that case a constructive trust was possible because the promise was to transfer freehold already in the hands of the constructive trustee. Writing extra-judicially, Lord Neuberger asserts that 'in order to give rise to a constructive trust, the property in question must have already been acquired by one party under an agreement with the other party, so that it can be said that equity is simply giving effect to that agreement'.[36] It must be that the 'property acquired' is the subject matter of the trust itself, not property against which the subject matter of the trust may lie. In both *Yaxley* and *Kinane*, the Court of Appeal addressed the question whether the defendant's unconscionable conduct permitted the claimant to enforce an otherwise unenforceable agreement; it did not attend to the nature of the trust imposed. However, it is certainly open to question why the Court in *Kinane* felt the need to award the remedy in the form of a constructive trust.[37] An equitable charge, after all, is an interest capable of protection against third parties in its own right. And the defendant is bound by the equitable obligation not because he is a trustee but because his conscience is affected.

However, in *Alexander-David*, the Court of Appeal has held that there is a trust of a lease, despite the absence of a lease in the hands of the trustee. It should be pointed out that this conundrum only arises in cases where Schedule 1 operates to impose a trust of land on the occasion of a creation of a legal lease in favour of a minor. It does not occur where there is a failure to create a legal lease in favour of an adult, because, as noted above, this will result in either an equitable lease, where there is an enforceable contract, or in nothing at all, where there is no enforceable agreement (and in the absence of any estoppel claim). The incidences of such a trust for minors may be few,[38] but this does not solve the problem that the statute has created. The rule was intended to give to a minor what she could not get under the ordinary rules of equity because of her minority status: the subject of the unenforceable contract. In other words, the purpose was to allow a minor to obtain a result that would be consistent with the application of first principles had she been an adult. But it would be odd if the purpose of the statute were to ensure that a trust arises in a situation where it would not ordinarily do so under first principles, as where the thing bargained for is not an assignment of an existing interest but the creation of a new interest such as a lease.

A. Trusts, Co-ownership and Value

One often distinguishes estates from other rights in land by regarding the former as 'ownership rights'.[39] Equitable interests under a trust must be included in this

---

[35] *Yaxley v Gotts* [2000] Ch 162 (CA).

[36] 'The Stuffing of Minerva's Owl? Taxonomy and Taxidermy in Equity' [2009] *CLJ* 537, 548.

[37] It was not deemed to be necessary in Lord Neuberger's obiter view at [46].

[38] Although see the claim of Hammersmith and Fulham LBC in *Alexander-David* that since the coming into force of the Order on 31 July 2002, there had been a significant increase amounting to 144 applications from 16- and 17-year-olds over 12 months: [2009] EWCA Civ 259 [11].

[39] A discussion of whether ownership of land is possible in English law is outside the scope of this chapter. The argument presented here assumes the view of JW Harris that English land law does employ

category; they are 'co-ownership' rights, whether successive or concurrent. What distinguishes rights under a trust of land from rights in land not so held is that the beneficiary has a right (or the hope of a right) to the market value, or a share of the market value, in the form of the proceeds of sale of the asset in the hands of the trustee. But, apart from an estate holder, the holder of a differentiated right in land, whether held on trust or not—and whether that right is equitable or legal—has no claim on the value of the estate over which the right lies. The right may have an independent market value, but it is not the same as having a right to the value of the burdened estate. So the holder of a legal or equitable lease has no right to the value of the freehold, nor would a beneficiary of a trust of a lease, in the same way that a mortgagee or owner of an easement has no such right.

However, it must be made clear whether one is talking about ownership of 'land' or ownership of rights. All rights in land can be owned, but not all rights in land are 'ownership' rights. In common parlance, 'land ownership' means ownership of one of the two estates. The significance of the difference is brought home by asking whether the rightholder can claim a percentage of the market value of the estate. Here, it is the potential for exploitation that Harris marks as defining a certain sense of ownership.[40] Joint tenants of the fee simple or leasehold estate have identical interests in the market value of the estate, and in both cases, the joint tenants assume both the risk of devaluation and the boon of appreciation of the trust asset. In a similar way, tenants in common of both estates have a stake in the market value of their respective interests, in the form of shares in the same equitable interest. By contrast, a mortgagee has a claim only to the value of the outstanding loan plus interest, regardless of the value of the land. The mortgagee's interest has a nominal value as a capital-certain asset, the worth of which is independent of the property market, whereas the worth of the estate owner's interest lies in the market value of the asset. This is also the case with equitable charges and equitable liens, options to purchase and other interests which are not ownership interests but rights to receive ownership interests in the future, as in a contract to sell.[41]

It might be said that all interests have their own market value, although in this respect, not all interests are equal. Easements only have a market value at the time of their creation, and this may be limited as the interest is not available generally, but only to those who own estates in land contiguous with the servient tenement. But the 'owner' of an easement over Blackacre is patently not an owner of Blackacre and has no claim to any of the value of Blackacre: the value of the easement rests in the use value to the owner/occupier of the dominant tenement (whether freeholder/ leaseholder) and also in any enhanced market value that such a right lends to the estate of the dominant tenement.

the concept of ownership of land: see JW Harris, 'Ownership of Land in English Law' in N MacCormick and P Birks (eds), *The Legal Mind* (Oxford, Oxford University Press, 1986) 143–61.

[40] Above n 39, at 160.

[41] FW Maitland, *Equity: A Course of Lectures* (J Brunyate (ed), Cambridge, Cambridge University Press, 1969) 106.

Easements also provide an example of the proposition that not all rights in land can be accommodated within the trust paradigm.[42] They are, of course, proprietary interests and as such are transferable, but unlike other interests, they are only transferable once, at the time of their creation. An easement cannot lie in gross; once created, it is inseparable from the dominant tenement. It cannot be transferred apart from the dominant tenement, so it is meaningless to speak of anyone 'owning' an easement or holding one on trust. Similarly, once the benefit of a restrictive covenant is annexed to the dominant tenement, it too becomes inseparable from it. The distinction between interests under a trust of land and commercial interests in land, such as easements, restrictive covenants, options to purchase and estate contracts, is that only interests under a trust of land can properly be represented as a financial asset. This is why such interests are overreacheable. The overreaching mechanism was intended to apply only to those interests for which it was possible to substitute an interest in the proceeds of sale, hence the exclusion of commercial interests from the overreaching mechanism.[43]

The trust of land's predecessor, the trust for sale, originated as a device to enhance the exchange value of land by facilitating its trade. The trust for sale was underpinned by the doctrine of conversion, which embodied the view that the point of a beneficial interest in land was its investment value.[44] It is well understood that this narrow view of the beneficiary's interest could result in hardship, and it was the principal reason for the demise of the trust for sale and its replacement by the trust of land.[45] From Lord Wilberforce's famous characterisation of the doctrine of conversion as 'a little unreal'[46] until its abolition by means of section 3 of the TLATA 1996, the increase in home ownership in the UK has led the courts and Parliament to acknowledge that by the late twentieth century, the value of a beneficiary's interest in residential premises will normally lie in its use as a home rather than in its exchange value.[47] Nevertheless, the 1996 Act was not intended to undo the conveyancing advances achieved by the 1925 legislation, and so interests behind trusts of land, even if protected by actual occupation, are still 'detached' from the land where overreaching occurs, whereupon they lie in the proceeds of sale.[48]

---

[42] See *Chaudhary v Yavuz* (n 33) for an example in which a claim that a right of way was held on constructive trust by the servient owner was rejected.

[43] Law of Property Act 1925, s 2(2)–(3); A Clarke and P Kohler, *Property Law: Commentary and Materials* (Cambridge, Cambridge University Press, 2005) 524.

[44] Law Commission, *Transfer of Land: Overreaching; Beneficiaries in Occupation* (Law Com No 188, 1989) [2.2] and [2.9].

[45] Ibid, [3.2]–[3.3].

[46] *William & Glyn's Bank Ltd v Boland* [1981] AC 487 (HL), 507.

[47] It is arguable, however, that since the first of the housing bubbles appeared in the mid-1980s, the modern trend is, on the contrary, to regard even one's own home as an investment. Despite periodic bursts of the bubbles, many home owners nowadays follow house prices as they would the stock market, and indeed the consensus has been that bricks and mortar are more profitable than shares and more secure than private pension funds. And although defaulting borrowers' resistance to possession by mortgagees may principally stem from their reluctance to leave their home, it may also arise from a reluctance to be forced to sell an asset at a loss.

[48] Law of Property Act 1925, ss 2(2), 27(1); and see *City of London Building Society v Flegg* [1988] AC 54 (HL).

B. Ownership of Land and the Nature of Trusts

The nature of the trust was not addressed in *Alexander-David* and so the opportunity was missed to consider whether Schedule 1 was ever intended to apply in cases like this. The omission itself is significant as it allows several odd assumptions to go unchallenged. First, it assumes that there is nothing strange about a fee-simple owner holding a lease of the same property on trust. Second, there appears to be a surprising assumption, perhaps deriving from the language of the statute, that the subject matter of the trust is the land itself. Of course, one need not be reminded that it is not really the land but the estate that is the subject matter of any trust of land, for that is the only thing that anyone can ever 'own' with regard to real property. And while we normally speak of the subject matter of the trust as the land rather than an estate in it, we also take care to point out to students that this common misusage is nothing more than a kind of shorthand and that lawyers mean something quite precise and different from what the layperson would understand by the phrase 'A owns Blackacre'. Often the point is dismissed as mere pedantry, but the decision in *Alexander-David* illustrates the danger of taking first principles for granted. Although it has been argued that ownership as a legal concept is not (nor should be) relevant to discussions about rights in land, it is still pervasive.[49] To compound the problem, we still talk of 'ownership' of *land*, as if reluctant to relinquish a concrete, visual, even Arcadian idea in favour of the drier, more abstract notion of estates and rights.[50] Moreover, the language of equity injects the notion of ownership into such discussions, with the description of the beneficiary as the 'true' owner, as does talk of 'concurrent ownership' and 'fragmentation of ownership'.[51] It is almost impossible to escape the idea that it is the land that we own; easements and restrictive covenants are annexed to the land, not to the estate.[52] Indeed, we talk of a trust of land and not a trust of the estate.

But despite the prevalence of the idea of ownership, it is notoriously evanescent; it is a common currency the value of which is unknown. Is ownership the sum of all its parts or the sum of a few parts which are more integral than others? We accept that one may give away various rights which in themselves constitute the incidents of ownership and yet remain recognisable as the owner of Blackacre.[53] If we separate the strands of proprietary entitlement, does ownership dissolve?[54] Yet, despite the absence of a definition of ownership, we seem to know intuitively when a right

---

[49] See AD Hargreaves, 'Review of *Modern Real Property*' (1956) 19 MLR 14.

[50] It has always been this way: see AD Hargreaves, *Introduction to the Principles of Land Law*, 4th edn (London, Sweet & Maxwell, 1963) 48: 'materialism is a phenomenon which pervades the whole of the medieval land law. Whenever it meets with a conception which we should not regard as a right, it tends to transform it into an almost concrete thing'. Cited in AW Brian Simpson, *A History of the Land Law*, 2nd edn (Oxford, Clarendon Press, 1986) 47.

[51] For an example, see Jessel MR's dictum in *Lysaght v Edwards* (n 8) 507 that a valid contract 'actually changes the ownership in equity'.

[52] Section 62 of the Law of Property Act 1925 enables such interests to pass to successors in title on 'conveyances of land'.

[53] See generally AM Honoré, 'Ownership' in *Making Laws Bind* (Oxford, Oxford University Press, 1987) 165.

[54] TC Grey, 'The Disintegration of Property' in *Nomos XII* (New York, New York University Press 1980) 69.

constitutes ownership of land. Ownership appears to reside only in the notion of the estate.[55] Even if one conceives of property in land as a collective bundle of rights, a trust does not arise simply because the owner alienates some of those rights: if A distributes so many rights from the bundle that it is difficult to say who, if anyone, owns the land, it is still not the case that A holds anything on trust for anyone else. A may have given the right to occupy the premises exclusively for a certain time to B, but that is not to say that he holds that right on trust for B—he does not hold it at all. If formalities have been complied with, then B has a legal lease; if not, then B may have an equitable lease, but at no time can it be said that A holds the right to occupy exclusively for a certain period on trust for B, for A holds no such right either at law or in equity. The right to occupy exclusively for a certain period, although dependent on the right of someone else to occupy the land exclusively *forever*, is not a sub-set of that right but a distinct right altogether.

Leases further complicate matters: nowhere else does discussion appear to slip confusingly between ownership of land and ownership of rights in land. We might agree that only estates confer rights amounting to ownership of land, but the problem does not end there, because we then treat equally a weekly tenancy and a long lease at a premium. If freeholder A grants a 99-year lease at a premium to B and so gives to B his right to exclusive possession for that term, A's ownership appears attenuated to the extreme, but we have no problem in regarding both A and B as simultaneous 'owners' of Blackacre (albeit not co-owners). But if one of the important attributes of property is its transferability so that, to paraphrase Rudden,[56] is not just a thing but *wealth*, then it is somewhat harder to conceive of a weekly tenant, who is unlikely to have significant powers of alienation, as the owner of anything, despite the interest having long been recognised as an estate in land.[57] Nevertheless, it can at least be said that in the case of both the long lease at a premium and the periodic tenancy, the interest-holder 'owns' an estate in land, but it cannot be meaningful to say that the short-term tenant 'owns the premises'.

However, the casual misidentification of property—of what is 'owned'—is what leads students to think that a landlord and tenant 'co-own' Blackacre. It is only when we explain that the landlord and tenant each own something entirely different that the concept of the trust of land becomes clear by contrast. So it is disheartening to find that paragraph 1(1)(b) of Schedule 1 to the TLATA 1996 states that a conveyance of a legal estate to a minor 'operates as a declaration that the *land* is held in trust' (emphasis added—would it have been too difficult to have substituted 'estate' for 'land'?). The Act is even unclear in its definition of what constitutes a trust of land: the definition at section 1 states that a 'trust of land' means 'any trust of property which consists of or includes land'. The unhelpful way in which the Court of Appeal expresses its second finding in *Alexander-David*—that the claimant

---

[55] See, eg, Local Government and Housing Act 1989, s 104: '"owner's interest" means an interest which ... is either an estate in fee simple absolute in possession or a term of years absolute ...' Cited in *R v Tower Hamlets LBC, ex p Von Goetz* (n 4) 1021. See also S Bright, 'Of Estates and Interests: A Tale of Ownership and Property Rights' in S Bright and J Dewar (eds), *Land Law: Themes and Perspectives* (Oxford, Oxford University Press, 1998) 529, 534.

[56] B Rudden, 'Things as Things and Things as Wealth' (1994) 14 *OJLS* 81.

[57] S Worthington, *Equity* (Oxford, Clarendon Press, 2003) 54; Bright (n 12) 50.

local authority could not determine the tenancy as long as it 'held the *premises* in trust' for the defendant (emphasis added)—does nothing to clarify the matter. It is incorrect to say that the premises are held in trust, since only the *numerus clausus* rights can be held on trust of land and 'premises' is not one of them. Real difficulties follow from this failure to specify precisely the subject matter of the trust. It is clear that Sullivan LJ understands the legal term of years to be the subject matter of the purported grant. His Lordship notes that 'the claimant is, in the absence of any other trustee, in the uncomfortable position of being both lessor and trustee',[58] but in fact a trust of a lease in these circumstances means that the trustee is in the impossible position of being both lessor and *lessee*, holding the lease against his own fee simple on trust for the beneficiary.[59]

It is axiomatic that in any trust of a lease, the trustee must hold either a legal lease or, in its absence, an equitable lease. This is what happened in the cases Sullivan LJ cites in the preceding paragraphs, *Hammersmith and Fulham LBC v Monk* and *Crawley BC v Ure*.[60] The trust of land in each of these cases is the ordinary one under which two or more people co-own a lease on trust for themselves as beneficiaries. In *Kingston upon Thames RLBC v Prince*,[61] the result could have resembled that in *Alexander-David*: a secure tenant had died, leaving his 13-year-old granddaughter resident in the flat. She could have succeeded to the secure legal tenancy but for the fact that she was a minor. The only adult on the premises was her mother, who was disqualified from taking the secure tenancy for herself. The Court applied paragraph (1)(1) of Schedule 1 to find that she could take it on trust for her daughter. So here again is a normal situation of a legal lease held by the lessee on trust for a minor.[62] The *Alexander-David* result was also avoided in *Newham LBC v Ria*.[63] Sir Martin Nourse noted that the notion of a landlord being a trustee of a tenancy of the demised premises for the benefit of the tenant was a very curious one, to which effect should not be given without express provision.[64] The legal lease was therefore awarded to the minor's adult relation, who, as in *Prince*, was precluded from taking the secure tenancy beneficially. But *Ria* was not cited by the Court in *Alexander-David*; and since *Monk* and *Ure* were cited only in support of the claimant's argument that the decision to terminate the tenancy could not amount to a breach of trust, the point about the nature of the trust itself was not put to the Court.

However, on the facts of *Alexander-David*, the imposition of a trust of the lease accomplishes the impossible by making the trustee-landlord his own tenant. In *Rye v Rye*,[65] Viscount Simonds noted: 'The question, then, can conveniently be

---

[58] *Alexander-David* (n 1) [35].

[59] Indicative of the circularity *ad absurdum* of the situation is the defence counsel's submission that the local authority had not properly served the notice to quit because it had delivered it only to the beneficiary and not to the trustee—ie, to itself: ibid [14].

[60] *Hammersmith and Fulham LBC v Monk* and *Crawley BC v Ure* [1992] 1 AC 478 (HL); [1996] QB 13 (CA), cited in *Alexander-David* (n 1) [32].

[61] *Kingston upon Thames RLBC v Prince* (n 31).

[62] Ibid, 602.

[63] *Newman LBC v Ria* [2004] EWCA Civ 41.

[64] Ibid [14].

[65] *Rye v Rye* [1962] AC 496 (HL).

examined by asking whether ... [section 72(3) of the Law of Property Act 1925] enables A to grant a lease to himself of land of which he is the owner, or, in other words, to carve out of his larger estate a lesser estate which creates (I know not how to put it otherwise) the relationship of landlord and tenant between himself and himself.'[66] The structure of English property law makes this impossible. Where the possession of leasehold premises falls into the hands of the reversioner, the estates merge and the lease is destroyed. In *Barrett v Morgan*, Lord Millett said: 'The destruction of the tenancy by surrender reflects the principle that a person cannot at the same time be both landlord and tenant of the same premises.'[67] A person could hold a lease against his own freehold if he were a member of a partnership so that the landlord and the tenant were different legal persons. But a trustee has no separate legal identity; even if he is a joint tenant of the freehold, his legal identity remains that of an individual, hence the result in *Rye* that one of the joint tenants of the freehold could not grant a lease to himself as an individual. So it is unfortunate that the fact which distinguishes the trust in *Alexander-David* from all other cases concerning paragraph 1 of Schedule 1 should not have been queried.

VI. SUBJECT MATTER OF THE TRUST II: THE INDETERMINABLE TENANCY

The difficulty with a trust in these circumstances is that by applying paragraph 1 of Schedule 1, the Court of Appeal in *Alexander-David* gave the defendant a much greater interest than she would have had under the lease agreement. If one interprets the Court's finding of a trust of the 'premises' as a trust of the lease, then it follows that the beneficiary's rights in relation to the premises do not exceed those given to her under the lease agreement. However, despite the fact that the local authority had intended to grant her only the briefest estate possible—the weekly periodic tenancy—the Court, through its second finding, effectively gave her an unlimited right to occupy. If the landlord's attempt to determine the tenancy according to the terms of the agreement results in a breach of its duties as trustee, then no determination is possible without the trustee incurring liability for breach.[68] Of course, it is always open for the tenant/beneficiary in such a situation to bring the lease to an end, but she is unlikely to want to do so. If we suppose there is a legal lease in the hands of the trustee, once the tenant/beneficiary reaches the age of majority, she could call for the legal title to be vested in her,[69] but it is not incumbent on her do so. In fact, it would be better for her to remain a beneficiary rather than become a legal periodic tenant, since, as long as the courts are willing to find that for the trustee

---

[66] Ibid, 505. See D Cavill et al (eds), *Ruoff & Roper: Registered Conveyancing* (London, Sweet & Maxwell, 2012), para [25.016]: 'Leases to oneself are not leases at all.'

[67] *Barrett v Morgan* [2000] 2 AC 264 (HL), 271. See also *Ingram v IRC* [2000] 1 AC 293 (HL), 300 (Lord Hoffmann).

[68] The judgment in *Alexander-David* omits the possibility that the trustee-landlord could commit a breach and thereafter remain personally liable; here he is deemed unable a priori to commit the breach. Discussion of whether this is correct is beyond the scope of this chapter.

[69] Under the rule in *Saunders v Vautier* (1841) 4 Beav 115; 41 ER 482 (see also *Newham LBC v Ria* (n 63) [9]). Section 6(2) of the TLATA 1996 gives the trustee the power to convey the land to the beneficiary even though the latter has not required the trustee to do so, but it is hard to imagine that the trustee could force the beneficiary to take the estate.

to determine the lease would be a breach of trust, she could remain on the premises indefinitely. Only once the local authority was released from its trustee obligations could it serve her notice to quit.[70]

Moreover, the ruling seems to indicate that the trustee is generally barred from determining the lease, even when the beneficiary has committed a breach of the tenancy agreement, as happened in *Alexander-David*. This is the effect of the unusual paradigm presented in this case. The normal paradigm of lessor A and lessee B (who is trustee for beneficiary C) allows the normal leasehold obligations to be performed outside of the context of the trust, since as far as the lessor and lessee are concerned, there is no trust, only the usual relation of privity of estate. This was the situation that obtained in *Monk*.[71] The terms of the tenancy were not affected by the fact that the lessees were also trustees.[72] But the *Alexander-David* paradigm of (lessor/trustee A and lessee/beneficiary B) places the lease relationship within the context of the trust, whereby, on this ruling, the principles of equity governing trusts displace the normal leasehold obligations. After this ruling, it must be queried whether such a beneficiary must comply with any of the terms of an agreement: for example, is she obliged to pay rent or has she effectively obtained exclusive possession of the premises indefinitely and free of charge?[73] After all, a beneficiary under an ordinary trust has no duties to perform and so cannot be deprived of the benefit through a failure to fulfil some obligation, unless the settlement imposed some condition. But in *Alexander-David*, the terms of the lease agreement were not deemed to be conditions of the trust; they became unenforceable by the lessor as they had been overtaken by the lessor/trustee's equitable obligations. The problem here is that the court has found that the defendant has something, but it is not clear what it is: a trust of a lease is necessarily framed by the terms of the lease agreement, and this is usually unproblematic because the *lessee*/trustee is obligated to the lessor, who normally stands outside the trust. Where the *Walsh* doctrine applies, the tenant holds under the same terms in equity as if a lease had been granted. Thus, he cannot complain if the landlord exercises the same rights as he would have had under a legal lease agreement.[74] The choice for the court in *Walsh* was between a periodic tenancy arising at law on the facts or the seven-year lease which the parties had intended. It might be said that the court in *Walsh* took a contractual approach to leases, applying equitable principles to give the parties what they had bargained for and not what the law said they had. But here we have a lessee/*beneficiary* whose obligations to abide by those terms the court has effectively excluded by disabling the lessor-trustee's power to enforce them.

---

[70] Emily Orme makes the point that such a position puts the public authority landlord in a conflict of interest between its trustee duty to the minor and its duty to the public to make the best use of the property, an obligation which may entail possessing the premises: 'Child Tenants—A Minor Problem' (2005) 155 *NLJ* 1522, 1522. One way around the problem would be for the landlord to appoint another trustee in its stead, thereby freeing itself to terminate the trustee's lease.

[71] *Hammersmith and Fulham LBC v Monk* (n 60).

[72] Ibid, 493 (Lord Browne-Wilkinson).

[73] The defendant in *Alexander-David* had violated almost every express term of the agreement, including the obligation to pay rent.

[74] *Walsh v Lonsdale* (n 8) 14 (Jessel MR).

The conundrum is that, if indeed the lease is held on trust, it is a lease for an indefinite term. It has been settled law since the fifteenth century that a lease for an indefinite term is not a lease.[75] But the imposition of a trust in this case puts a new spin on that old anomaly, the periodic tenancy. By Littleton's time, it was settled that a fixed duration was essential to a lease; a person who was let into possession of land by the freeholder but who was not granted any certain term was ranked as a tenant at will and his interest was wholly precarious.[76] Nowadays, of course, such possession can amount to a periodic tenancy, but there is some disagreement as to whether such a tenancy is a lease for a definite term. As Simpson points out:

> Such periodic or 'running' leases obviously pose a problem in legal analysis which is glossed over in modern textbooks, for in a sense they do not conform to the rule which requires a lease to be a fixed term—they are in effect leases for an uncertain duration, determinable by notice. They are not leases for a fixed term with an option to renew; such an analysis is quite unrealistic. In short they are anomalous, and when they first came before the courts at the end of the fifteenth and the beginning of the sixteenth centuries they provoked a great deal of controversy.[77]

The traditional view involves a 'doctrinal embarrassment', as the periodic tenancy is accepted as a term perpetually elongating itself by the automatic addition of a fresh period.[78] At times confusing efforts have been made to show that the periodic tenancy complies with the certainty requirement: Parke B in *Oxley v James* saw the yearly tenancy almost as a cancerous cell multiplying until stopped by some outside force: it was 'a lease for a year *certain*, with a growing interest during every year thereafter, springing out of the original contract, and parcel of it' (emphasis added).[79] Elsewhere, modern opinion tends towards the view that such tenancies are a succession of terms.[80] But, whatever the view, what is important is not how long the tenancy does in fact continue, but that the lessor be able to know at the outset when he may regain entry: that is the rationale underlying the certainty rule. So it is essential to a tenancy from year to year that both the landlord and the tenant be entitled to give notice determining the tenancy.[81] Any curtailment of this entitlement is repugnant.[82] Before 1926, a failure to set a term could give rise to a tenancy for

---

[75] For the modern statement, see *Lace v Chantler* [1944] KB 368 (CA); *Prudential Assurance Ltd v London Residuary Board* [1992] AC 386 (HL); and *Mexfield Housing Co-operative Ltd v Beresford* [2011] UKSC 52.

[76] Above n 50, at 252–53.

[77] Ibid. See *Jones v Chappell* (1875) LR 20 Eq 539, 544 (Sir George Jessel MR): '[a weekly tenancy] is not a holding for one week, but it is a holding from week to week'.

[78] K Gray and SF Gray, *Elements of Land Law*, 5th edn (Oxford, Oxford University Press, 2009) para [4.1.54].

[79] *Oxley v James* (1844) 13 M & W 209, 214; 153 ER 87, 89; see also *Gandy v Jubber* (1865) 5 B & S 15; 122 ER 911.

[80] Harpum, Bridge and Dixon (n 5) para [17-064]. See also B McFarlane, *The Structure of Property Law* (Oxford, Hart Publishing, 2008) 678.

[81] *Prudential Assurance Co Ltd v London Residuary Board* [1992] 2 AC 386 (HL), 392 (Lord Templeman).

[82] *Doe d Warner v Browne* (1807) 8 East 165, 167; 103 ER 105, 306, where it was declared repugnant to the nature of a tenancy from year to year that the right to determine should rest solely with the tenant, otherwise the interest would be an estate for life (Lord Ellenborough CJ); and *Centaploy Ltd v Matlodge Ltd* [1974] Ch 1, where a weekly tenancy agreement under which the landlord was never going to have the right to determine was said to be a contradiction in terms.

life, which since 1926 is converted into a lease for 90 years, as was recently seen in *Mexfield Housing Co-operative Ltd v Beresford*. But the lease agreement in *Alexander-David* did express a term; it was just that the landlord was precluded from enforcing it.[83] The result is that the application of Schedule 1 to the creation of a new lease effectively creates an interest that defies all known categories of proprietary entitlement—a right to exclusive possession of the land forever, but which is not a freehold.

The claimant local authority asserted that the court should look to the content of the agreement and that the conditions contained therein would determine the boundaries of the beneficiary's claim against the trustee. But the court looked selectively at the content of the agreement—it disregarded everything *but* the purported grant of the legal estate. However, in any case, a trust must be on some terms: if not the terms of the lease agreement, then what? The approach of the court in this instance goes against the recent tendency. Over the last 30 years, the English courts have tended to focus their attention on the contractual character of the lease.[84] A lease is more than the sum of its parts—it is not simply some separable incidents of ownership, some 'sticks from the bundle' cobbled together. A lease contains specific terms and attracts other rights and obligations implied by law which are not present in the fee simple. So is the nature of this trust one in which the landlord holds his right to exclusive possession of the flat on trust for the beneficiary for a term? It cannot be, because such a right is not recognised as a property right—other than as a lease—and it cannot be said that the landlord holds the lease. And if the landlord does indeed hold a right to exclusive possession on trust for the tenant-beneficiary, it must be for a term shorter than his freehold—otherwise he would hold the freehold on trust. But the court's decision has made the interest indeterminable, so that it is tantamount to a trust of the freehold.

VII. CONCLUSION

At first glance, the problem appears to be a small point in practice—these trusts may not be common and they are easily avoided if one heeds Sullivan LJ's advice to local housing authorities that they should in future take care expressly to grant only equitable leases to minors.[85] There is no restriction on minors holding equitable interests in land,[86] and such a grant would fall outside Schedule 1 to the TLATA 1996, thereby avoiding the imposition of a trust. However, these trusts can arise all too easily and they can have a deleterious effect on the ability of local housing authorities to manage their properties. Once established, it is not clear what happens to the trust once the minor reaches the age of majority. By the time *Alexander-David* was

---

[83] *Mexfield v Beresford* [2011] UKSC 52; Law of Property Act 1925, s 149(6).

[84] J Morgan, 'Leases: Property, Contract or More?' in M Dixon (ed), *Modern Studies in Property Law*, vol 5 (Oxford, Hart Publishing, 2009) 419, 423. See also *United Scientific Holdings Ltd v Burnley BC* [1978] AC 904 (HL); *National Carriers Ltd v Panalpina (Northern) Ltd* [1981] AC 1965 (HL); *Hussein v Mehlman* [1992] 2 EGLR. 87; *Hammersmith and Fulham LBC v Monk* (n 60); *Mexfield Housing Co-operative v Beresford* (n 75).

[85] *Alexander-David* (n 1) [29].

[86] *R v Tower Hamlets LBC, ex p Von Goetz* (n 4).

heard in the Court of Appeal, the defendant was 21, yet there was no indication that the trust had come to an end. And, of course, there was no trust instrument to impose any conditions.

There is nothing untoward in the workings of Schedule 1 in most cases. Its purpose is to ensure that a conveyance of a legal estate to a minor accords with the prohibition against minors holding legal estates and to enable the minor to receive the property which she was intended to receive. In the present case, the purpose may also be to ensure security of tenure for a vulnerable teenager. But in such a case, where the conveyance takes the form of the creation of a lease rather than the transfer of an existing estate, the imposition of a trust changes the normal lessor/lessee relationship in a way which poses problems both theoretical and practical. It is essential that minors have their interests protected, but it is submitted that a better way is to enact legislation aimed specifically at this problem that operates in accordance with, and not in contravention of, first principles.

7

The Community of Owners' Regulation of Common Property in Polish Condominium Schemes

MAGDALENA HABDAS*

I. INTRODUCTION

CONDOMINIUM SCHEMES IN Poland (the so-called unit ownership) have gained increased popularity after Poland's shift to a democratic system, a market economy and the subsequent introduction of the 1994 Law on Unit Ownership (LUO).[1] As an important alternative to cooperative flats, ownership of units is a very popular way of acquiring the ownership of a unit in newly built developments, but also in older buildings often previously owned by local authorities. Becoming an owner of a unit inevitably leads to the creation of a community, which must cooperate in matters concerning the use and enjoyment of common parts of the real estate in question (ie common parts of the building and the land it stands on) as well as of the separate units. Moreover, this community exists not only in a sociological sense but also in a legal sense.

The question that naturally arises concerns the legal status of such a community, its competencies and duties. The community of owners has legal instruments in the form of resolutions and house rules which are utilised to regulate matters necessary for the proper functioning of the community and the building it occupies. These regulations may, however, prove to be very intrusive from the point of view of individual unit owners, as some communities attempt to introduce penalties for untimely payment of fees (assessments), regulate the keeping of pets or assign exclusive use areas. Community regulations often directly influence the rights of unit ownership and may even bring about changes in their market value. Practice shows that many regulations introduced in various communities are simply an answer to the unit owners' changing needs and modes of living, which may not necessarily

---

* Associate Professor (Dr Hab MSc, Sheffield Hallam University, MA), University of Silesia in Katowice, Poland; Faculty of Law and Administration, Department of Civil and Private International Law, licensed Polish property valuer, member of the working team of the Polish Commission for the Codification of Civil Law (succession law), active participant in the Common Core of European Private Law project (time-limited interests in land and condominiums).

[1] (*Ustawa o własności lokali*); Act of 24 June 1994, Journal of Statutes 2000, no 80, item 903 with subsequent amendments.

be adequately catered for in legal provisions. Nevertheless, the community must be aware of the scope of its competencies and the unacceptability of violating individual unit ownership rights.

The purpose of this chapter is to analyse the competencies of the community of owners with respect to common parts and the extent to which they are binding on owners of units. In order to do this, it is necessary to elaborate on the highly debated legal status of the community of owners, as it determines its legal capacity and permissible activities. The concise provisions of the LUO have also led to divergent solutions being applied in practice by various communities of owners; however, their legal validity may often be questioned. Simultaneously, it is necessary to find legally sound solutions to the arrangements that the communities wish to implement, since most of these arrangements are not aimed at circumventing the law or violating public order, but are simply a reaction to the market needs of prospective and actual unit owners.

II. THE RESIDENTIAL COMMUNITY

Although in the introductory remarks above, the term 'community of owners' has been employed, the Polish legislator employs a different one to denote such a community. According to Article 6 of the LUO, owners of units form a 'residential community' (*wspólnota mieszkaniowa*), which comes into existence as soon as at least one unit has been isolated and subsequently transferred to a party other than the original owner of all the units[2] or, to be more precise, other than the original owner of the land and therefore of the building which stands on it (the *superficies solo cedit* principle—all that is on the land belongs to it). The residential community is formed by operation of law (ie automatically), regardless of the wishes or the awareness of unit owners,[3] and cannot be dissolved as long as separate owners of isolated units exist.[4]

The community is called a residential community because the legislator envisaged that ownership of units will concern mainly residential developments.[5] Consequently, the definition of a unit contained in Article 2, section 2 of the LUO stipulates that a 'unit' is a room or a set of rooms which is isolated from other parts of the building by permanent walls and is to be used, together with accessory chambers (utility rooms, pantries and so on), as a permanent residence for people in order to fulfil their residential needs. The provision also stipulates that it is to be applied to isolated units, used in accordance with their function, for purposes other than residential purposes. As a result of the above, the LUO is aimed at first and foremost satisfying residential needs and lacks specialised, legal instruments, which could prove necessary in schemes comprising only or mostly non-residential units. In practice, such schemes are still rare; however, mixed residential and retail schemes

[2] J Pisuliński, 'Własność lokali' in E Gniewek (ed), *System Prawa Prywatnego. Tom 4. Prawo rzeczowe* (Warsaw, CH Beck—PAN, 2007) 284.

[3] A Doliwa, *Prawo rzeczowe* (Warsaw, CH Beck, 2010) 116.

[4] G Bieniek, *Ustawa o własności lokali w praktyce* (Bydgoszcz, Branta, 2010) 97.

[5] J Ignatowicz, *Komentarz do ustawy o własności lokali* (Warsaw, Wydawnictwo Prawnicze, 1995) 22.

are very common, with ground-floor units often planned as retail or office units and the first floor and above as residential units. Such a community is thus, despite its name, not purely residential.

The residential community is not, according to Polish law, a legal person. The choice not to grant the residential community legal personality was, as Ignatowicz indicates, a conscious decision of the legislator, who noticed that such communities are usually small and by their very nature will lack the organisation, motivation and funds characteristic of a legal person. Therefore, they should be perceived as a community rather than a legal entity.[6] The legislator did, however, agree to equip the residential community with the basic instruments necessary for its recognition by third parties, namely the possibility of the residential community to acquire rights and create obligations and to be both claimant and defendant in litigation (Article 6 of the LUO). The residential community thus has a status of a defective legal person, as defined in Article 33[1] of the Polish Civil Code (PCC).[7] According to this provision, regulations on legal persons are to be applied accordingly (mutatis mutandis) to entities which are not legal persons, but which by virtue of statutory provisions have legal capacity (§ 1). The members of such an entity are liable for its debts only when the entity is unable to pay for its obligations (subsidiary liability of the members), unless special legal provisions introduce other rules of liability for obligations (§ 2).

Unfortunately, the above regulations do not ensure a uniform understanding of the residential community and its legal status. Although it is generally no longer disputed that the residential community is a defective legal person,[8] its legal capacity and the exact content of that capacity has been and remains an object of diverging opinions expressed by academics and the courts alike. There is no consent as to whether the residential community acquires rights for itself or only on behalf of the individual owners proportionate to their share in the common property. Accepting the former option would seem to follow directly from the wording of Article 6 of the LUO, in which it is clearly stated that the residential community may acquire rights and create obligations, as well as from Article 17 of the LUO, which provides that the residential community is liable for the obligations connected with common property without any limitation, whereas each unit owner is liable for those obligations only up to the value of his share in common property.[9] The Supreme Court has also on numerous occasions confirmed the ability of the residential community to

---

[6] Ibid, 43.

[7] (*Kodeks cywilny*); Act of 23 April 1964, Journal of Statutes 1964, no 16, item 93 with subsequent amendments.

[8] The introduction in the PCC of a third category of persons—the defective legal person (apart from physical persons and legal persons)—took place on 25 September 2003 (Act of 14 February 2003, Journal of Statutes 2003, no 49, item 408).

[9] J Ignatowicz and K Stefaniuk, *Prawo rzeczowe* (Warsaw, LexisNexis, 2009) 150; R Dziczek, *Własność Lokali. Komentarz. Wzory Pozwów i Wniosków Sądowych*, 5th edn (Warsaw, LexisNexis, 2010) 80; M Pazdan, 'Tytuł II. Osoby' in K Pietrzykowski (ed), *Kodeks cywilny. Tom I. Komentarz* (Warsaw, CH Beck, 2011) 188–91; K Dadańska, *Prawo rzeczowe* (Warsaw, CH Beck, 2010) 141–42; G. Jędrejek, 'Podejmowanie uchwał przez członków wspólnoty mieszkaniowej—zagadnienia wybrane' (2007) 4 *Studia Prawnicze KUL* 54–55. See also, very convincingly, G Gorczyński, 'Wspólnota mieszkaniowa jako jednostka organizacyjna w rozumieniu Article 33[1] k.c.' (2009) 3 *Rejent* 49–50.

acquire rights and have its own estate.[10] It is, however, important to remember that the residential community's legal capacity only comprises matters connected with the management of common property, like its repairs, maintenance and change of use.[11] The community is not a commercial entity which has the capacity to conduct a business. Consequently, the residential community may only, for example, acquire real estate if it is needed for the proper management of common property (eg the purchase of a unit for the janitor),[12] but would not be able to acquire land in order to convert it into a parking area and start operating business. The residential community may rent out units or utility rooms which are a part of common property. It may also set aside a part of the parking area not used by the owners of units and make it available for third parties, subject to a fee.[13]

The above views are not shared by authors, who do not accept that the residential community is an entity legally separate from unit owners.[14] In their opinion, the residential community acts only on behalf of the individual owners, does not possess legal capacity and cannot have its own estate. Anything purchased by the residential community is in fact purchased by and for unit owners, who acquire it in the shares they have in common property.[15] Such opinions, particularly in the light of Article 33[1] of the PCC and the now-prevalent line of judgment of the Supreme Court, are difficult to accept, particularly since authors who reject the legal capacity of the residential community simultaneously accept its capacity to be the claimant or defendant in litigation, although both kinds of capacity are mentioned side by side in Article 6 of the LUO.[16] Consistency requires that it is accepted that if the community may sue and be sued in its own name, then the acquisition of rights must also take place in the name of the community. As has already been mentioned, the community has legal capacity only with respect to the management of common parts of the scheme and is not entitled to undertake ultra vires activities such as investment or economic activity on the market. The latter may only be undertaken by individual unit owners, who are free to create commercial companies, foundations and other legal entities in order to pursue goals which may be beneficial to the residential community of which they are a part.

---

[10] Most notably, see the resolution of seven judges (which has the status of a legal principle), 21 December 2007, III CZP 65/07, OSNC 2008/7-8/69, in which the Supreme Court confirmed the existence of the community's own estate and its own legal capacity; see also Supreme Court judgment 10 December 2004, III CK 55/04, OSNC 2005/12/212; Supreme Court resolution 23 November 2004, III CZP 48/04, OSNC 2005/9/153; Supreme Court resolution 28 February 2006, III CZP 5/06, OSNC 2007/1/6.

[11] Supreme Court judgment 8 October 2008, V CSK 143/08, LEX no 485919.

[12] Bieniek (n 4) 98–99.

[13] WJ Katner, 'Podmiotowość prawna wspólnoty mieszkaniowej' (2009) 2 *Glosa* 37.

[14] A Doliwa, *Prawo mieszkaniowe. Komentarz* (Warsaw, CH Beck, 2003) 651–53; M. Nazar, 'Status cywilnoprawny wspólnoty mieszkaniowej' (2000) 4 *Rejent* 138 et seq; Pisuliński (n 2) 287–88; P Bielski 'Zdolność prawna wspólnoty mieszkaniowej—problem modelu regulacji prawnej' (2007) 3 *Rejent* 46; MJ Naworski, 'Status prawny wspólnoty mieszkaniowej' (2002) 13 *Monitor Prawniczy* 598.

[15] A Doliwa, *Prawo mieszkaniowe. Komentarz* (Warsaw, CH Beck, 2003) 651–53; M Nazar, 'Status cywilnoprawny wspólnoty mieszkaniowej' (2000) 4 *Rejent* 138 et seq; Pisuliński (n 2) 287–88; P Bielski 'Zdolność prawna wspólnoty mieszkaniowej—problem modelu regulacji prawnej' (2007) 3 *Rejent* 46; MJ Naworski, 'Status prawny wspólnoty mieszkaniowej' (2002) 13 *Monitor Prawniczy* 598.

[16] A Turlej, 'Art. 6. Wspólnota mieszkaniowa' in A Turlej and R Strzelczyk, *Własność Lokali. Komentarz* (Warsaw, CH Beck, 2010) 168, 172.

It must be noted that in the area of liability for debts, there is also considerable confusion. It is unclear whether the liability of unit owners for debts connected with the management of common real estate is subsidiary or joint and several in relation to the liability of the residential community. If the liability is subsidiary, the owners could only be called on to pay once the funds of the community have been exhausted (Article 17 of the LUO in connection with Article 33[1], § 2 of the PCC).[17] If the liability is joint and several, the creditor could simultaneously sue the residential community and each of the unit owners up to the value of his share (Article 17 of the LUO interpreted as *lex speciali* to Article 33[1], § 2 of the PCC, the former thus excluding the application of the latter).[18] In practice, both the residential community and each of its owners are sued, which would suggest that the second option has been accepted.[19]

The above doubts concerning the legal capacity and the liability of the residential community have been the effect of the legislator's conviction that such communities will be small and therefore will not resemble an organised and complex body, such as a legal person. Currently, in practice, the opposite is true. Condominium schemes often, if not predominantly, comprise large developments and residential communities must be well-organised entities with clear competencies in order to effectively manage the common parts of real estate and promote cooperation, responsibility and understanding among the unit owners. This must also take into account the fact that in an era of a worldwide recession, unit owners may have more restricted financial means than would usually be the case. They may thus be preoccupied mostly with their private interests without taking into account the interests of the community as such.

Although the residential community is not a legal person, it is a defective legal person, so provisions concerning such an entity should provide a minimum framework for it to operate and must clearly delimit its scope of legal capacity. It may be useful to point out that in Polish law, commercial partnerships are, apart from residential communities, the most important group of defective legal persons.[20] In order to create a commercial partnership, it is, however, necessary to conclude a contract. The legislator clearly indicates its subject matter and the amount of freedom the partners have to introduce their own regulations in the mentioned contract.[21] The latter thus functions as a constitution (bylaws) of the commercial partnership. With respect to residential communities, the legislator does not provide for a constitution to be adopted and consequently does not specify what matters should be resolved in such a document or what rules the voting procedure on a constitution must adhere

---

[17] J Kołacz, 'Glosa do postanowienia sądu apelacyjnego z dnia 19 kwietnia 2006r., I ACz 1172/06' (2007) 7–8 *Prawo Spółek* 81 et seq; Doliwa (n 14) 712–13; Katner (n 13) 39; compare CG van der Merwe and M Habdas, 'Polish Apartment Ownership Compared with South African Sectional Titles' (2006) 1 *Stellenbosh Law Review* 184.

[18] E Drozd, 'Prawa i obowiązki właścicieli lokali' (1995) 3 *Rejent* 17–18; A Turlej 'Art. 17. Odpowiedzialność' in Turlej and Strzelczyk (n 15) 661–63; Nazar (n 14) 135–36; compare Pisuliński (n 2) 291–92.

[19] See also E Bończak-Kucharczyk, *Własność lokali i wspólnota mieszkaniowa. Komentarz* (Warsaw, Wolters Kluwer, 2010) 2405.

[20] Polish Commercial Companies Code (*Kodeks spółek handlowych*); Act of 15 September 2000, Journal of Statutes 2000, no 94, item 1037 with subsequent amendments.

[21] See, eg, Polish Commercial Companies Code, arts 25, 25, 37.

to (eg *quorum* requirements). Instead, the LUO provides that the residential community may only pass resolutions concerning the management of common property and may establish house rules.

Practice has shown that this does not meet the needs of residential communities, which often pass resolutions entitled: the constitution (bylaws) of a residential community. Some commentaries on unit ownership even contain model constitutions of a residential community, although their authors fail to indicate the legal basis for adopting such constitutions, their legal relevance and the question of their binding force on future unit buyers.[22] Sometimes these authors suggest that such constitutions are the most important documents of a residential community, which make statutory requirements more specific and suited to the needs of a given residential community, or that these constitutions provide operating principles of the residential community if a contractual (and not the statutory) model of management is chosen.[23] The fact is that such documents are not a constitution of a residential community, but a simple resolution which can only be enforced if it concerns matters of common property management (this does not include modifying management rules—see below) and if it has been passed in accordance with the prescribed procedure.

Meanwhile, communities adopt constitutions in the belief that the latter are somehow more superior resolutions and are therefore the basis for making ordinary resolutions. Such constitutions usually contain a mixture of selected provisions copied from the PCC, the LUO and other statutes, with a few house rules thrown in to make the document more substantial, as well as some modifications of the statutory management model. The residential community is thus convinced that by adhering to its constitution, containing a random mixture of copied statutory provisions and usually a few home-made provisions which frustrate the purpose of the statutory provisions, it does not need to take into account the full content of statutory legislation pertaining to residential communities. This practice must be perceived as legally unacceptable, because the legislator did not confer any rights onto the residential community to adopt constitutions in order to self-regulate specified matters.[24]

The legislator has only provided that unit owners may waive the default statutory rules of common property management by introducing their own management model. An agreement concerning the above may be entered into either at the time of the subdivision of the building (Article 8, section 2 of the LUO) or at a later stage (Article 18, section 1 of the LUO). It must be executed in notarial form, bind successive owners and can only be modified by a resolution expressed in a notarial protocol entered into the land records for the scheme (Article 18, section 2 and 2a of the LUO). Since statutory management rules are default rules, the legislator clearly prefers management rules to be introduced by the unit owners themselves.[25] It must

---

[22] L Myczkowski, *Własność budynków i lokali oraz inne prawa rzeczowe w praktyce* (Warsaw, CH Beck, 2005) 229–35.

[23] M Tertelis, *Wspólnota mieszkaniowa w pytaniach i odpowiedziach* (Warsaw, CH Beck, 2004) 28, 107, 252.

[24] K Korzan, 'Niewypał legislacyjny czyli o odrębnej reglamentacji stosunku własności lokali' (1995) 7–8 *Rejent* 15–17.

[25] M Zięba, 'Ustawowy zarząd nieruchomością wspólną w dużych wspólnotach mieszkaniowych. Ocena istniejących rozwiązań na tle przyjętej przez polskiego ustawodawcę koncepcji ochrony właścicieli mniejszościowych. Sugestie *de lege ferenda*' (2011) 4 *Rejent* 99.

be emphasised that the introduction of management rules by the unit owners is an act in law concluded by all the unit owners and not by the residential community. The latter is not competent to change the default statutory management model (this particularly concerns attempts to modify the statutory management model by adopting a constitution), as this competence belongs to the unit owners, who must unanimously agree on a new model.[26] The agreed management model will specify how subsequent resolutions of the residential community are to be passed.

It is not clear how far the management model introduced by the unit owners may deviate from the default statutory rules. It seems that, as with any act in law, the management model may not violate the law, rules of social conduct or be aimed at circumventing the law (Article 58 of the PCC), but it is obvious that these restrictions are subject to an *in casu* interpretation. Residential communities often appoint audit committees or supervisory boards and specify the competencies of these bodies. It is, however, doubtful whether management issues which in the default statutory system are to be decided by the unit owners in a resolution may be decided by a few persons sitting on boards or committees. This would seem to frustrate the object of the LUO, which ensures the active participation of the unit owners in decision making concerning common property.[27]

In my opinion, the above lack of clarity demonstrates that the 1994 LUO legislation lags behind the needs of the property market and of the unit owners. The very fact that most residential communities adopt constitutions, create special bodies, like supervisory boards, and attempt to modify statutory management models in various ways and with varying legal results[28] proves that the residential community requires a more complex (which is not synonymous with a more complicated) regulation. Although the residential community is not a commercial entity and does not conduct a business, the number and complexity of issues it has to resolve bring it much closer to commercial partnerships than originally envisioned. Consequently, a more comprehensive and practice-based regulation is needed, as leaving matters to the assessment of courts and academics does not resolve practical problems. As has been shown in the remarks made above, almost every controversial LUO issue has a set of opposing views which causes the residential communities to choose incidental solutions

---

[26] Ignatowicz (n 5) 74; M Nazar, *Własność lokali. Podstawowe zagadnienia cywilnoprawne* (Lublin, Lubelskie Wydawnictwo Prawnicze, 1995) 75–76; A Doliwa and T Mróz, 'Wspólnoty mieszkaniowe. Podziały i łączenie' (2002) 9 *Monitor Prawniczy* 392; compare Bieniek (n 4) 150, who is of the opinion that in order to change an already-existing management model which had been previously introduced by unit owners, it is sufficient for the residential community to pass a majority vote resolution. The author does not explain if majority voting would apply only to large communities (more than seven units in a scheme) or also small communities (seven or fewer units in a scheme). The latter must have a unanimous vote on matters concerning extraordinary management issues and this would most definitely include the change of a management model.

[27] A Turlej 'Art. 18. Umowa o sposobie zarządu' in Turlej and Strzelczyk (n 15) 380–81; J Frąckowiak 'Charakter prawny wspólnoty mieszkaniowej' in E Drozd, A Oleszko and M Pazdan (eds), *Rozprawy z prawa prywatnego, prawa o notariacie i prawa europejskiego ofiarowane Panu Rejentowi Romualdowi Sztykowi* (Kluczbork, Kluczdruk, 2007) 93–94; compare R Dziczek, *Spółdzielnia mieszkaniowa i wspólnota mieszkaniowa jako zarządcy nieruchomości wielolokalowych* (Warsaw, LexisNexis, 2009) 94–97, who accepts the residential community's freedom to shape its management model in a detailed manner, together with the creation of various bodies with defined competencies assigned to them exclusively.

[28] These phenomena have been noted and described in academic writings that I refer to in nn 21–26 above.

that they happen to come across while searching for an answer in publications or court judgments.

The above comments compel one to conclude that introducing a regulation concerning the community's constitution, its admissible content and the procedure of its adoption would stimulate a much-needed uniformity in practice. It would also give unit owners more certainty as to what issues they may question or oppose and to what extent the interests of the residential community override the interests of an individual unit owner.

III. PROPERTY AND EXCLUSIVE USE AREAS

One of the few non-controversial matters within the LUO is the residential community's capacity and competence to pass resolutions on management issues concerning common property. The latter has been defined in Article 3, section 2 of the LUO as land and those parts of the building which do not serve the exclusive needs of individual owners. The legislator has thus provided an exclusive (as opposed to an inclusive) definition of common property.[29] It seems plausible to rephrase this definition by stipulating that land and all parts of the building which do not form a part of a unit and are therefore not subject to private ownership constitute common property, regardless of whether it is in actual fact used by all or selected unit owners.[30] To some extent, the scope of common property will be determined by parties who isolate units as objects of separate ownership and who decide whether, for example, the basement area will be common property or whether it will be divided into cubicles which will form constituent parts of the isolated units.[31] Needless to say, some parts of the building must always form common property and unit owners cannot decide otherwise.[32] These will include the roof, the outer walls, structural walls, most hallways and staircases, as well as installations such as water, gas, electricity and heating ducts.[33]

According to Article 12, section 1 of the LUO, each unit owner has the right to use the entire common property in accordance with its purpose and is obliged to do so in a manner which does not prejudice the corresponding rights of other unit owners (Article 13, section 1 of the LUO). The right to use common property includes all common land and common parts of the building; however, since unit owners are co-owners of common property, it would follow that they are entitled to introduce different rules concerning the usage of common property, which is, after all, subject to their right of ownership.[34] These new rules would inevitably denote assigning

---

[29] See further van der Merwe and Habdas (n 16) 171–72.

[30] Doliwa (n 14) 622–23; Supreme Court judgment, 2 December 1998, I CKN 903/97, OSNC 1999/6/113.

[31] Supreme Court resolution, 3 October 2003, III CZP 65/03, OSNC 2004/12/189.

[32] M Watarkiewicz, 'Nieruchomość wspólna według ustawy o własności lokali' (2002) 3 *Kwartalnik Prawa Prywatnego* 643–44.

[33] Bieniek (n 4) 56–57; Dziczek (n 26) 101; E Gniewek, *Prawo rzeczowe* (Warsaw, CH Beck, 2010) 156; E Gniewek, 'Aktualne problemy stosowania ustawy o własności lokali (część 1)' (2006) 10 *Rejent* 10, 22.

[34] Drozd (n 17) 12–13.

certain areas to the exclusive use of one or more specified unit owners.[35] It cannot be disputed that areas assigned to such use cannot constitute those parts of common property that are necessary in order to use and access the individual units.[36] Therefore, it would be inadmissible to establish a staircase as an exclusive use area when it must be used by other unit owners in order to gain access to their units. It would, however, be possible to designate a staircase as an exclusive use area if it only leads to one unit and not to any other units or common property.

It must also be determined who is competent to establish an exclusive use area and what the available legal instruments of doing so are. Establishing an exclusive use area clearly concerns the use of common property and, as has already been mentioned, the management of the latter is within the competence of the residential community. Nevertheless, it is not necessarily true that matters concerning the usage rights of common property are an element of common property management. If one concludes that, indeed, they are not, the residential community will not be able to establish exclusive use areas via a resolution, but a unanimous decision of all the co-owners of common property (ie the unit owners) will be necessary.

Questioning the residential community's competence to establish exclusive use areas is connected with Article 221 of the PCC. The latter may be applied to matters connected with unit ownership because issues not explicitly regulated in the LUO are to be resolved on the basis of the adequate PCC provisions (Article 1, section 2 of the LUO). In Article 221 of the PCC, it is stipulated that acts in law concluded by co-owners which concern matters of management and of the use of a common thing are binding on future co-owners (if specified conditions are met). This provision clearly separates matters of management from matters of use. Decisions on management are made by co-owners via resolutions, whereas decisions altering the statutory right of every co-owner to use the entire object (*res*) should not be subject to a majority vote. It seems improper that the majority could, against the will of another co-owner, exclude his statutory right to possess and use the common thing in a manner which does not prejudice the equivalent rights of other co-owners (Article 206 of the PCC). Modifications of Article 206 of the PCC (and its equivalent—Article 12, section 1 of the LUO) should be allowed only if all co-owners agree on how they wish to alter their right to use the entire thing.[37]

It is difficult to accept that rules on who possesses and uses a given part of common property are imposed by majority co-owners (who may by head count be fewer than the remaining co-owners) without the consent of other co-owners, the latter being forced to use the thing according to rules to which they do not agree. It should also be noted that establishing exclusive use areas by majority voting could easily lead to a quasi-expropriation of some co-owners, who will effectively be banned

---

[35] Compare A Turlej, 'Art. 12. Współkorzystanie.' in Turlej and Strzelczyk (n 15) 290–91, who does not accept the possibility of introducing exclusive use areas within common property on the basis of a division according to usage.

[36] E Gniewek, 'Wspólnota mieszkaniowa według ustawy o własności lokali' (1995) 1 *Rejent* 71.

[37] Compare E Drozd, 'Zarząd nieruchomością wspólną według ustawy o własności lokali' (1995) 4 *Rejent* 13–15, who considers whether decisions modifying the statutory right to use the entire thing by co-owners are matters of management or not, but does not arrive at a clear conclusion. Similar deliberations are conducted by Bończak-Kucharczyk (n 18) 352–54.

from areas which in theory they own and which induced the decision to buy a unit within a given development![38]

The above assessment of the possibility of altering Article 206 of the PCC, and consequently Article 12, section 1 of the LUO (which is a repetition of the PCC provision) only by a unanimous agreement of all co-owners is currently voiced by an increasing number of academics,[39] who point out that majority decisions cannot limit the protected right of ownership. There is, however, at least an equal number of scholars who accept that alterations of Article 206 of the PCC entitlements are a matter of management that usually qualifies as the so-called ordinary management, which even in small residential communities (seven or less units) requires only a majority vote under the statutory management model. This opinion can also be supported by several Supreme Court judgments and it is safe to state that in litigation, this is the view that most courts would currently take.[40]

It is difficult not to notice its practical merit. Particularly in the case of large residential communities (more than seven units), it will often be impossible to gain a unanimous agreement concerning new rules of using common property. This may not only result from the fact that it is next to impossible to convince everyone to agree but also from the fact that some unit owners may be simply unavailable. They may have bought the unit for investment purposes and may be renting it out to various tenants while they live abroad. They may not have a proxy who could take part in the voting. They may keep the unit unoccupied with only a family member collecting mail once every few weeks. Such situations are quite common and could completely remove the possibility of making decisions which require the unanimous consent of all unit owners.

IV. DIVISIONS OF COMMON PROPERTY ACCORDING TO USAGE (*QUOAD USUM* DIVISIONS)

Regardless of whether one requires the unanimous consent of co-owners or just a majority vote, it is not usually contested that exclusive use areas may be designated

---

[38] This is not an issue specific to Polish ownership of units. On the extent to which communities of owners may influence the lives of individual unit owners and alter their proprietary rights in the context of American and Australian condominium regulations, see further C Sherry, 'The Complexities of Multi-owned Property: Australian Strata and Community Title and the United States Condominiums and Homeowner Associations' in L Bennett Moses, B Edgeworth and C Sherry (eds), *Property and Security* (Sydney, Thomson Reuters, 2010) 263 et seq, particularly 267–70.

[39] See E Gniewek, 'Współwłasność' in T Dybowski (ed), *System Prawa Prywatnego. Tom 3. Prawo rzeczowe* (Warsaw, CH Beck, 2007) 466–67, who convincingly identifies differences between matters of management and matters of possession and use; J Biernat, 'Umowa określająca sposób korzystania przez współwłaścicieli z nieruchomości wspólnej' (2008) 11 *Monitor Prawniczy* 602; G Matusik, 'Wyodrębnienie i zbycie lokalu wraz z powierzchnią przynależną—uwagi de lege lata i de lege ferenda' (2011) 7–8 *Rejent* 95–96; E Drozd, 'Podział do korzystania nieruchomości wspólnej' in E Drozd, A Oleszko and M Pazdan (eds), *Rozprawy z prawa prywatnego, prawa o notariacie i prawa europejskiego ofiarowane Panu Rejentowi Romualdowi Sztykowi* (Kluczbork, Kluczdruk, 2007) 78–79; Bończak-Kucharczyk (n 18) 352.

[40] For an account of the mentioned opinions and judgments, see Biernat (n 38) 602–03; Matusik (n 38) 95–96.

within common property.[41] The Polish legislator does not provide for their creation expressly, nor does he employ the phrase 'exclusive use area'. Instead, such areas are created by a division according to usage on which the co-owners agree. In practice, agreements on divisions based on usage may concern allocating parking spaces outside the building or in an underground parking area (which forms a part of common property). Often the aim is to allocate gardens to ground floor units. Sometimes, such an arrangement could concern the use of an area outside a restaurant/bar for outside tables available to the clients. Introducing a division according to usage does not, in any way, extinguish co-ownership of common parts, but merely introduces special rules concerning their use.[42]

The problem of paramount importance, particularly for unit owners, is the stability of this division. Needless to say, an acquisition of a ground-floor flat may be desirable only on the condition that an adjoining garden is allocated as an exclusive use area. A possibility to easily change an arrangement according to usage could not only gravely disappoint the unit buyer, but also bring about a steep decrease in the value of his unit. In this context, it is desirable to view an agreement according to usage as a modification of Article 206 of the PCC and Article 12, section 1 of the LUO, and require a unanimous agreement of all unit owners, who simultaneously are co-owners of common parts. Again, it must be emphasised that this could be difficult to achieve in practice, particularly in large residential communities.[43] The adverse effect of this difficulty would be the virtual impossibility of altering previous arrangements according to usage which in the course of time and changes of unit owners may have become obsolete. It is important to note that a division according to usage is not intended to be a final, permanent arrangement,[44] although it may be expected to last a substantial amount of time.[45] On the other hand, accepting the opposing view, which requires only a majority resolution of the residential community, undermines the stability of the division according to usage. However, as has already been mentioned, in case of a dispute, the chances are that the courts will view this division as a matter of management and will not require unanimous consent to change it.

It should also be noted that in small residential communities, in the statutory management model, matters of management which concern extraordinary issues must be decided by the co-owners unanimously (Article 199 of the PCC). This does not apply to large residential communities in which matters of extraordinary

---

[41] See B Załęska-Świątkiewicz, 'Wspólnoty mieszkaniowe' (2011) 6 *Rejent* 142, who denies the legal possibility of creating exclusive use areas, but without providing arguments in favour of such an opinion.

[42] Gniewek (n 38) 468.

[43] This problem has also been noticed by Drozd (n 38) 83–84, who nevertheless prefers the requirement of a unanimous decision and recourse to court (through an extensive interpretation of PCC provisions on co-ownership) rather than accepting that the division according to usage is a matter of ordinary management.

[44] M Smolny, 'Charakterystyka podziału nieruchomości do korzystania (quoad usum)' (2007) 5 *Polish Construction Review* 17; Bończak-Kucharczyk (n 18) 355.

[45] Therefore, it is difficult to agree with R Strzelczyk, 'Glosa do postanowienia Sądu Najwyższego z 19 maja 2004, I CK 696/03' (2005) 5 *Orzecznictwo Sądów Polskich* 257, who perceives an agreement on a division according to usage as a means of granting a permanent right to exclusively use an allocated parking space.

management are made, according to the statutory management model, by a vote of the majority (usually calculated on the basis of share values—Article 22, section 2 and Article 23, section 2 of the LUO). In a judgment of 6 March 1997 (I CZ 7/97),[46] the Supreme Court concluded that a division according to usage is usually a matter of ordinary management,[47] which would denote that in small residential communities, only a majority vote is needed and in large communities, the division is performed without any consultation, independently by the management board or the hired manager (Article 22, section 1 of the LUO). This view has not been supported by academics, who argue that particularly in cases of real estate, a division according to usage, if it is to be qualified as a matter of management, is an issue of extraordinary management.[48] At the same time, it is also possible to argue that if physical characteristics of real estate are such that its use is in practice divided among co-owners, a division according to usage may indeed qualify as a matter of ordinary management.[49] In a more recent Supreme Court judgment, it has been observed that the court's intervention into a division according to usage is justified by both Articles 199 and 201 of the PCC, the former relating to matters of ordinary management and the latter relating to matters of extraordinary management.[50] Unfortunately, this only further obscures the picture, as neither small nor large residential communities can be sure whether their decisions as to divisions according to usage should adhere to procedures for matters of ordinary or extraordinary management.

The practical importance of determining clear rules for making divisions according to usage cannot be underestimated. This may be illustrated by a case which involved a real estate developer who began to sell separate ownership of units in his building. The first 17 units were sold by the developer with a right to the exclusive use of indicated parking spaces located in an underground garage, which comprised 44 parking spaces. The developer sold the next 25 units without the exclusive use clause. The final two units the developer kept for himself with a clause that allowed him to benefit from the exclusive use of the remaining 27 parking spaces. In effect, 15 unit owners were left with no possibility to park their cars, particularly since the developer did not complete an outside parking area, despite his contractual obligation do so. Since the underground garage constituted common property, the unit owners, who now formed a residential community, passed a resolution in which they determined a new manner of using the underground parking area.

The initial resolution provided that the developer's 27 parking spaces were not an exclusive use area and could be used on a first-come, first-served basis by all unit owners. This resolution was set aside in court. The judge noted that leaving the developer with not even a single parking space violated his interests and could be

---

[46] OSNC 8/97/111.

[47] This was established in a Supreme Court resolution of the Full Panel of the Civil Chamber, 28 September 1963, III CZP 33/62, OSNCP 1964/2/22.

[48] S Rudnicki and G Rudnicki, *Komentarz do kodeksu cywilnego. Księga druga. Własność i inne prawa rzeczowe* (Warsaw, LexisNexis, 2008) 309; Dziczek (n 9) 119.

[49] Rudnicki and Rudnicki (n 47) 313–14.

[50] Supreme Court resolution, 29 November 2007, III CZP 94/07, LEX no 319929; similarly, Supreme Court decision 26 May 2000, I CZ 66/00, LEX no 51345; Supreme Court decision 12 September 1973, III CRN 188/73, OSNC 1974/11/183.

opposed to on the basis of Article 25, section 1 of the LUO. The court also observed that the developer's wish to have 27 exclusive use parking spaces, when there were unit owners who were completely deprived of parking spaces, violated rules of orderly management and rules of social justice. Consequently, the residential community passed another resolution in which it was agreed that out of the 44 parking spaces, 17 exclusive use parking spaces were left unchanged in accordance with the original unit sale contracts, 12 were assigned to the exclusive use of the developer and the remaining 15 parking spaces were open to use by all unit owners. It was also decided that each exclusive use area should carry a charge of 25 PLN per month (approximately €6).

This resolution was contested in court by the developer, who claimed that his interests had been violated. Both the Court of Appeal and later the Supreme Court emphasised that a division according to usage is not definitive and since it relates to changing the use of common property, it is a matter that may be decided by the residential community as an issue of extraordinary management (Article 22, section 3, point 4 of the LUO). Furthermore, it was stated that a division according to usage cannot completely displace selected unit owners from using common property (ie the 15 unit owners who had nowhere to park) and that as an act in law, such a division cannot violate rules of social justice, as this amounts to an abuse of right (Article 5 of the PCC). The courts found no grounds for setting aside the contested resolution of the residential community, as there was no objective violation of the developer's interests, which must be balanced against the interests of other unit owners and the residential community as such.[51]

The above case illustrates that the division according to usage originally implemented by the developer was unfair and that changing it through a unanimous agreement of all the unit owners would be impossible, since the developer was not interested in giving up his exclusive use areas. The court was right to point out that implementing a division according to usage is an act in law which must conform with the rule of law, the rules of social justice and cannot be aimed at circumventing the law (Article 58 of the PCC).[52] Consequently, when deciding whether to set a resolution of the residential community aside, the court must consider the objective interests of the parties involved in the dispute. The court, however, did not consider if the division according to usage was in fact effectively implemented, since units were being sold by the developer successively.

It escaped the court's attention that when the developer sold the very first unit to a buyer and established an exclusive use area consisting of a parking space for that unit owner, a residential community was formed and common property began to exist. From that moment on, establishing new exclusive use areas within the common property would not only require the developer's consent (expressed in the sale contract of the next unit), but also that of the first unit buyer (who now co-owned common property where new exclusive use areas were to be created). Each consecutive unit buyer who wished to acquire an exclusive use area would not only have to obtain the developer's consent but also the consent of all unit owners already within

[51] Supreme Court judgment, 29 June 2010, III CSK 325/09, LEX no 602266.
[52] E Skowrońska-Bocian, 'Art. 206. Współposiadanie' in Pietrzykowski (n 9) 648.

the scheme, as they co-owned, together with the developer, the common property. The developer could require each consecutive unit buyer to appoint him as proxy, so that when selling the next unit, the developer in matters concerning common property would act on behalf of himself and the unit owners already within the scheme.[53] Alternatively, when the first unit was sold together with an exclusive use area, the developer and the first buyer should have agreed on all the remaining exclusive use areas.[54] Such an agreement may be entered in the land register and automatically become effective against third parties, but even without such an entry, it is effective against third parties if they knew or could have easily discovered its existence (Article 221 of the PCC).[55]

In practice, most developers, with the obligatory assistance of notaries, who draw up the necessary sale contracts, are unaware of these formal and technical requirements. As a result, sale contracts concluded with developers who sell units together with exclusive use areas are ineffective with respect to the latter.[56] These contracts also lack clauses determining possible additional fees for benefiting from an exclusive use area. This eventually results in court disputes very similar to the case described above. It is difficult not to agree with J Wszołek's assessment that provisions currently in force do not provide a basis for a transparent creation of exclusive use areas. Moreover, they do not offer any model rules or clear solutions concerning the allocation of common property maintenance costs among exclusive use area holders and the remaining unit owners.[57]

V. EASEMENTS OF UNIT OWNERS OVER COMMON PROPERTY

The lack of explicit regulations concerning various exclusive use areas and the above-mentioned difficulties that may be encountered with divisions according to usage have caused practitioners and academics to turn to easements in search of more effective solutions relating to exclusive use areas on common property. According to Article 285, § 1 of the PCC, an easement may be created over a servient immovable in order to benefit the owner of a dominant immovable. The purpose of establishing an easement is clearly indicated in Article 285, § 2 of the PCC. The legislator makes it possible to create easements only when they bring about an increase in the usefulness of the dominant immovable or its part, which is to be understood as an objective, economically substantiated increase in the use value of the dominant immovable. An easement cannot be purely aimed at satisfying the aesthetic needs of the owner.[58] Consequently, an easement will permanently

[53] J Wszołek, 'Sprzedaż miejsc parkingowych w umowach zawieranych z deweloperami' (2011) 4 *Rejent* 86–88.
[54] Matusik (n 38) 94–95; Bończak-Kucharczyk (n 18) 355.
[55] See further P Siciński, Prawo do miejsca postojowego, cz.II' (2002) 8 *Nieruchomości* 11–13.
[56] Wszołek (n 52) 83; R Strzelczyk, 'Art. 2. Lokal samodzielny; część składowa' in Turlej and Strzelczyk (n 15) 74; Bończak-Kucharczyk (n 18) 355.
[57] Wszołek (n 52) 77; Załęska-Świątkiewicz (n 40) 143.
[58] Ignatowicz and Stefaniuk (n 9) 228; J Pazdan, 'O zakresie i sposobie wykonywania służebności gruntowej' in J Gołaczyński and P Machnikowski (eds), *Współczesne problemy prawa prywatnego. Księga pamiątkowa ku czci Profesora Edwarda Gniewka* (Warsaw, CH Beck, 2010) 439.

benefit every consecutive owner of the dominant immovable (not just the owner who originally benefited from the easement) and that is precisely the legal purpose and objective of establishing this limited real right.[59]

Moreover, the creation of easements is admissible only when the owners of the servient and the dominant immovables are not the same person.[60] This requirement is derived from the fact that an easement is a right over another's thing (*ius in re aliena*). The Polish legislator did not retain the solution of the 1946 Decree on Real Rights[61] that an easement may be created as long as there are two different immovables, but not necessarily two different owners.[62] It is also possible to establish a personal easement, which benefits only an indicated physical person (there is only a servient immovable, but not a dominant one), but such an easement can only be exercised by that person and is not transferable. Therefore its application to ownership of units is virtually non-existent and will not be discussed in this chapter.

The attractiveness of establishing an easement over common property in favour of a unit owner doubtlessly results from the fact that the mentioned owner will acquire a real right, ie effective against everyone, which cannot be changed or altered by the unit owners or the residential community. The right is therefore permanent and may only be modified or completely extinguished by its holder or by a court in special situations provided for in Articles 291, 294 and 295 of the PCC.[63] It is also possible to establish an easement over a servient unit for the benefit of a dominant unit. One must, however, remember that established easements within condominium schemes cannot bring about the loss of isolation of a unit and cause its factual conversion into some sort of a common space.[64]

The first question that arises in relation to easements concerns the fact as to whether it is possible to create an easement for the benefit of a unit owner who is simultaneously a co-owner of common property, ie of the prospective servient immovable. The Supreme Court has accepted such a possibility, indicating that the owner of the dominant immovable cannot be equated with co-owners of the servient immovable. In other words, the parties involved on each side of the easement contract are not identical.[65]

The second question relates to the need of an objective increase in the usefulness of the dominant immovable. In other words, it is necessary to establish if the owner of the dominant immovable will, by creating an easement over the servient

---

[59] Doliwa (n 3) 171; Pazdan (n 57) 441.

[60] Rudnicki and Rudnicki (n 47) 543–44; K Zaradkiewicz, 'Art. 285. Treśćcel' in Pietrzykowski (n 9) 1003.

[61] Decree of 11 October 1946, Journal of Statutes 1946, no 57, item 319, see art 187.

[62] S Rudnicki, 'Służebności' in G Bieniek and S Rudnicki, *Nieruchomości. Problematyka prawna* (Warsaw, LexisNexis, 2009) 709.

[63] See further Pazdan (n 57) 441–44.

[64] See Supreme Court decision, 13 April 1999, II CKN 259/98, presented by Bieniek (n 4) 38–40, who notes that if easements of access and passing through the unit of another need to be created, then it is questionable whether the units were in fact separate, isolated units according to the requirements of the LUO. For this reason, creating easements over a unit for the benefit of another unit should be treated as absolutely exceptional.

[65] Supreme Court decision, 20 October 2005, IV CK 65/05, LEX no 176343; Supreme Court decision, 21 July 2010, III CSK 23/10; LEX no 677759; Supreme Court resolution, 29 October 2002, III CZP 47/02, OSNC 2003/7-8/93.

immovable, gain objective, additional benefits other than those he already has with respect to the servient immovable by virtue of his co-ownership.[66] It may be argued that as co-owner of the prospective servient immovable, the unit owner does not have a right to exclusively use a specified area of common property unless a division according to usage is implemented. The latter, however, is not a permanent arrangement (as has been explained above), whereas an easement confers a proprietary right that as a rule cannot be modified without the consent of the entitled party. Consequently, an easement does offer the co-owner a right which is qualitatively and quantitatively different from his entitlements derived from co-ownership.[67]

The final question concerns the admissible scope of using the servient immovable by the owner of the dominant immovable. The content of Article 285, § 1 of the PCC provides that the owner of the dominant immovable may use the servient immovable within a designated scope. This has not, as a rule, been interpreted as entailing the right to completely remove the owner of the servient immovable from using it alongside the owner of the dominant immovable. Instead, the owner of the servient immovable continues to use it as before, while the owner of the dominant immovable is allowed to also use the servient property within the designated scope. Allowing the owner of the dominant immovable to exclusively use even a part of the servient immovable would denote an unacceptable limitation of the right of ownership and remains outside the content of an easement.[68] Meanwhile, the Supreme Court has not been consistent in its evaluation of the above matter and has on some occasions agreed to easements which generate exclusive use areas, and on others did not allow for their creation.[69]

In relation to residential communities, easements are most commonly applied to allocate gardens to ground-floor flats, although they have also been employed to allocate parking spaces in underground garage areas. It is not difficult to imagine other purposes for which establishing exclusive use areas could be in the interest not only of the individual unit owners, but also of the residential community. The latter could undoubtedly benefit from fees paid by unit owners entitled to exclusive use areas. Establishing exclusive use areas, particularly with respect to gardens for ground-floor flats, has a visible opposition among academics,[70] while others argue that the institution of an easement and its legal scope as defined in Article 285 of the PCC does in fact allow for creating exclusive use areas.[71] In most recent Supreme Court decisions, it was held that creating easements over common property for the benefit of a unit owner, who may exclusively use an indicated area, does not limit the right of ownership of a servient immovable in an unacceptable manner. In

---

[66] Bieniek (n 4) 85.

[67] J Biernat, 'Glosa do postanowienia z dnia 20 października 2005, (IV CK 65/05)' (2008) 10 *Przegląd Sądowy* 140–41.

[68] S Rudnicki, 'Glosa do postanowienia z dnia 21 stycznia 2006, (III CSK 38/05)' (2006) 10 *Orzecznictwo Sądów Polskich* 530–31; Bieniek (n 4) 85–87; G Rudnicki, *Sąsiedztwo nieruchomości. Problematyka prawna* (Krakow, Zakamycze, 1998) 99–102.

[69] For an account of the opposing judgments, see B Janiszewska, 'O służebności gruntowej ogródka przydomowego na nieruchomości wspólnej' in J Gołaczyński and P Machnikowski (eds), *Współczesne problemy prawa prywatnego. Księga pamiątkowa ku czci Profesora Edwarda Gniewka* (Warsaw, CH Beck, 2010) 226–27.

[70] Janiszewska (n 68) 231–33; Bieniek (n 4) 85–87.

[71] Wszołek (n 52) 92; Matusik (n 38) 92; Biernat (n 66) 134 et seq.

particular, creating a servitude by which a ground-floor unit owner may exclusively use a garden area designated around the windows of his unit in no way deprives co-owners of common property of their ownership rights.[72]

This line of judgment is, in my opinion, justified and reasonable, particularly when the developer, from the very beginning, intends to grant a permanent right to exclusively use an area which directly benefits only one specified unit. It must be explained that according to the LUO, units may comprise, as their constituent parts, utility chambers, regardless of whether the latter are adjacent to the unit in question or are located somewhere else within the building or an outbuilding within the boundaries of the parcel of land (Article 2, section 4 of the LUO).[73] It is not unusual for this chamber to be a basement cubicle or a pantry, and unit owners expect that the ownership of such chambers will be 'tied' to the ownership of the unit. This expectation cannot be met with respect to areas which do not constitute a chamber (ie that are not isolated by walls). To a large extent, it will, however, be satisfied by the creation of an easement, which is a right tied to the ownership of the dominant immovable (ie a specified unit).

In practice, the mentioned easements are being created; however, once again, it is unclear who the parties to the contract should be, ie the unit owner and the residential community, or the unit owner and all the remaining co-owners. Moreover, technical difficulties, similar to those described with respect to divisions according to usage, arise when units are sold by the developer successively, over a substantial or even a long period of time (which is usually the case).[74] The Supreme Court has so far not offered a clear solution to this dilemma. In particular, it does not seem appropriate to apply the conclusions in a case concerning the rental of an outside wall by one of the unit owners for advertising purposes to cases concerning the creation of an easement for a unit owner. In the former case, the Supreme Court concluded that a residential community is entitled to conclude a rental contract with one of the unit owners, on the basis of which the unit owner will be able to hang an advertisement on an outside wall of the building. The court held that concluding such contracts is within the residential community's statutorily defined capacity to undertake actions of common property management.[75]

VI. HOUSE RULES

An important aspect of owning a unit within a building is the increased necessity to take into account the interests of other unit owners. The proximity of living denotes that most activities of one unit owner will to some extent influence the enjoyment by another owner of his unit,[76] and will have an impact on that owner's

---

[72] Supreme Court decision, 30 June 2011, III CSK 272/10, LEX no 1096041; Supreme Court decision, 30 June 2011, III CSK 271/10, LEX no 898253.
[73] Van der Merwe and Habdas (n 16) 170.
[74] Wszołek (n 52) 92–93; Matusik (n 38) 92–93.
[75] Supreme Court resolution 19 June 2007, III CZP 59/07, OSNC 2008/7-8/81; compare A Doliwa, 'Glosa do uchwały Sądu Najwyższego z dnia 19 czerwca 2007 (III CZP 59/07)' (2008) 7–8 *Rejent* 164 et seq.
[76] Dziczek (n 26) 106–07.

personal as well as proprietary rights.[77] Consequently, the legislator imposes duties on unit owners, who must, among other obligations, abide by the established house rules. The latter do not have a statutory definition, but it is understood that they pertain to activities both within a unit as well as on common property and contain principles of conduct.[78] They may take the form of a written document, ie a regulation on house rules, but may also function through custom.[79] In the latter case, it is difficult for potential unit buyers to ascertain what the exact contents of house rules are; however, these rules, as is discussed below, cannot be too restrictive. Most unit buyers will expect a period of silence to be observed as well as the existence of arrangements concerning the normal use of common parts and removing waste. Consequently, they do not normally consider these rules as something that may materially influence the transaction or the value of the unit in question.

It is interesting to note that the LUO does not expressly provide for adopting a set of house rules through a resolution of the residential community, but merely stipulates that unit owners should abide by house rules (Article 13, section 1 of the LUO). It seems that implementing a regulation on house rules is subject to general PCC provisions (Articles 384 et seq and 683 et seq of the PCC), follows from Article 13, section 1 of the LUO and must be viewed as a matter concerning, at least to some extent, the management of common parts. K Korzan emphasises that a regulation of house rules should only contain clauses necessary to ensure an orderly use of the land and building by its co-owners, but should not attempt to duplicate duties the owners are subjected to through general legal provisions.[80] The content of the regulation of house rules cannot attempt to modify mandatory legal provisions and cannot violate the right of unit ownership.[81] Although house rules introducing silence periods from, customarily, 10 pm to 7 am, prohibiting the collection of rubbish in hallways or the use of basement corridors for playing football, etc are fairly common and generally uncontested, the line between an acceptable and an unacceptable limitation of unit ownership is very fine. As has been mentioned above, the legislator has chosen not to provide any guidance in this matter.

The Supreme Court has held in a fairly recent judgment that resolutions of the residential community cannot interfere with the right of unit ownership.[82] The regulation of house rules which had been presented in the dispute included the following clauses:

1. the unit owner is liable for the behaviour of persons who, with his knowledge, use his unit;
2. the unit owner bears responsibility for ensuring that these persons abide by the regulation on house rules and is obliged to inform them of the content of these rules;

[77] Doliwa (n 14) 696.
[78] Pisuliński (n 2) 277; J Jezioro 'Art. 683. Prządek domowy' in E Gniewek (ed), *Kodeks Cywilny. Komentarz* (Warsaw, CH Beck, 2011) 1176–77.
[79] Jezioro (n 77) 1176; Bończak-Kucharczyk (n 18) 237.
[80] Korzan (n 23) 16–17.
[81] A Turlej, 'Art. 13. Utrzymanie lokalu i nieruchomości wspólnej' in Turlej and Strzelczyk (n 15) 319–20.
[82] Supreme Court judgment, 3 April 2009, II CSK 600/08, LEX no 500188.

3. the unit owner must inform the residential community's management board about renting his unit, any substantial changes concerning the unit, as well as the number of persons who live in/use the unit;
4. the unit owner may not conduct a business activity in a residential unit without the consent of the residential community;
5. the unit owner may not install electric sockets in basement cubicles or conduct a business activity (services, production, etc) without the consent of the residential community.

It is interesting to note that the court of first instance held that none of the above rules violates the law. In particular, the regulation on house rules does not establish the unit owner's increased liability for damage caused to the residential community by third parties and the requirement to obtain consent to change the use of a residential unit to a commercial one relates to Article 140 of the PCC, according to which the right of ownership is limited by the socioeconomic purpose of the owned thing (the unit was clearly of a residential nature) and thus does not violate the right of ownership.

The Court of Appeal took a completely different view and held that all of the above clauses are inadmissible as they interfere with proprietary rights (ie ownership) of the individual unit owners. This view was subsequently supported by the Supreme Court. Moreover, the Supreme Court also noted that the disputed clauses of the regulation on house rules had been adopted with a violation of the residential community's statutory competence, because they did not pertain exclusively to common property.

In the light of the above judgment, it is difficult to precisely ascertain what rules may be included in house rules. It is obvious that they should first and foremost concern rules of conduct and use of common property, although only to the extent that these are necessary to ensure an orderly functioning of the community. In my opinion, it would be questionable whether the residential community could implement a ban on children playing ball on the lawns if such activity did not damage the lawn, the nearby flowerbeds, parked cars or prevent other unit owners from using the common property around the building. If, however, playing ball by the children takes the form of a soccer match and the ball usually does hit cars, windows or outer walls of the building, then an adequate provision in the house rules would be acceptable.[83]

It also seems, and has been supported by custom, that some rules may relate to behaviour inside the unit. The most common rule relates to a time of silence, which is normally scheduled from 9–10 pm to 6–7 am. It is understood that during that time, unit owners should abstain from activities which generate excessive noise, such as performing repairs, renovations or playing musical instruments (eg children practising playing the violin or the piano). It would, however, be problematic as to whether this period of silence (of course, this does not denote absolute silence) could be extended to 24 hours a day on weekends. Extending it to Sundays only, which for most persons

---

[83] For example: 'It is forbidden to play ball in a way which may damage the lawn, the flowerbeds and be a hazard to persons or their belongings.' An outright ban on playing ball ('It is forbidden to play ball outside') would not be acceptable, but it would be possible to impose a ban on playing ball in the parking area. It seems that the acceptable clauses will largely depend on the size of the common property outside the building and its uses (parking lot, flowerbeds, empty lawns, playgrounds, etc).

is a day off work, would probably be acceptable. All clauses relating to the keeping of pets, allowing entry of guests, hanging washing to dry on balconies, etc should be viewed as unnecessary and unacceptable due to the infringement of unit ownership.

It is important to remember that all unit owners must abide by rules of neighbour law, particularly by rules established in Article 144 of the PCC.[84] According to this provision, it is forbidden to use an immovable in a manner that creates disturbances to other owners which extend beyond the ordinary level. This level is to be determined on the basis of the socioeconomic designation of the immovable and local custom. Therefore, instead of creating overly detailed house rules relating to acceptable behaviour within a unit and risking the infringement of the right of ownership, it would be wiser to simply remind unit owners, in a house rules clause, that the use of an immovable (ie the unit) must conform with Article 144 of the PCC. It is obvious that some house rules, which in certain respects may make the general formula of Article 144 of the PCC more specific,[85] will be useful, but they must not be aimed at comprehensively regulating the personal freedom of unit owners. Nevertheless, due to the very general nature of Article 144 of the PCC, house rules are an important instrument of specifying acceptable behaviour and consequently of making principles of conduct more 'tangible' to unit owners.[86]

The residential community cannot impose penalties on unit owners who violate house rules or other statutory duties because it is not a body with administrative or other public law powers. The residential community may, of course, always sue for damages, according to general civil law rules on liability (Articles 415 et seq of the PCC—tortious liability; Articles 471 et seq of the PCC—contractual liability) and demand the payment of interest on fees that had not been paid on time (Articles 359 PCC, 481–82 of the PCC). In a Court of Appeal case, it was held that the residential community may regulate in house rules the admissible use of basements, which formed common property (they were not assigned to units as constituent parts). The residential community adopted a resolution in which it was forbidden for unit owners to rent out basement cubicles to third parties. This was held to be a valid resolution; however, the court set aside a later resolution of the residential community in which a penalty fee was levied on a unit owner who rented out his basement cubicle in violation of the adopted house rules.[87]

At this point, it must be noted that the residential community has only one legal instrument that allows it to react when house rules are being violated. According to Article 16 of the LUO, when a unit owner does not pay his share of the maintenance costs for a prolonged period of time, when he flagrantly and persistently violates the accepted house rules of the scheme or when he, through his improper conduct, makes life intolerable for other owners, the community of owners can resolve to approach the court for an order that the unit be sold by the bailiff in execution proceedings. It is beyond the scope of this chapter to discuss whether this severe sanction is justified or not,[88] but it is difficult not to notice that there

---

[84] Bieniek (n 4) 137.
[85] Drozd (n 17) 19.
[86] Tertelis (n 22) 109–10.
[87] See Court of Appeal in Warsaw judgment, 8 September 2010, VI ACa 76/10, LEX no 785514.
[88] See further K Hryćków, 'Licytacyjna sprzedaż lokalu w trybie przepisu art. 16 ustawy z dnia 24 czerwca 1994 o własności lokali—uwagi krytyczne' (2000) 1 *Rejent* 140 et seq.

are no interim, legally defined measures that could be employed by the residential community.[89] The residential community may always enforce its claims in court (eg *actio negatoria* for nuisance), but regular court proceedings are lengthy, expensive and the judgments may be difficult to enforce in practice. It would therefore be most advisable for the Polish legislator to consider other mechanisms that the residential community could employ to motivate obstinate unit owners to fulfil their financial and social obligations towards the community.[90]

The Polish LUO does not indicate who is entitled to implement house rules. J Ignatowicz, one of the authors of the Law on Ownership of Units act, explained that this can be done either by all the unit owners or, in case they cannot agree, by a body which represents them, ie the management board of the residential community.[91] It is reasonable to accept that adopting house rules is a matter of extraordinary management and is therefore within the competence of the residential community. This means that in a statutory management model, a unanimous decision is required (small communities) or a majority vote is needed (large communities). This solution has generally been accepted by scholars who also indicate that the unit owner is responsible not only for his own actions, but also for the behaviour of persons who live with him, visit him or use his unit. Consequently, the sanction of Article 16 of the LUO may also be applied in cases where the person misbehaving is not a unit owner, but persons who use his unit with his permission or knowledge.[92]

In this context, it is surprising that the Supreme Court, in the case described above, held that house rules cannot contain clauses pertaining to the liability of a unit owner for persons who, with his knowledge, use the unit. It is obvious that house rules cannot create new grounds for civil liability or extend its scope (this also applies to penal liability); however, in the considered case, the wording of the first clause did not suggest such an objective. It was the court of first instance that correctly assessed this clause as informational (particularly in the context of Article 16 of the LUO) rather than aimed at circumventing the law. The second clause, however, obliging the unit owner to bear responsibility for ensuring that his other unit users abide by the regulation on house rules and to inform them of the content of these rules, did contain an inadmissible interference into the unit owner's legal interests.

VII. CONCLUSIONS

Residential communities have become an important part of the real estate market; however, their functioning and legal status is a source of numerous disputes (both in theory and in practice), despite the fact that the LUO has been in force for almost

---

[89] See further van der Merwe and Habdas (n 16) 182–83.

[90] For brief comparative remarks as to the possible measures, see van der Merwe and Habdas (n 16) 183 and further CG van der Merwe, 'Apartment Ownership. Ch 5 Vol 6 Property and Trust' in K Drobing and K Zweigert (eds), *International Encyclopedia of Comparative Law* (Tübingen, JCB Mohr, 1994) 258; L Muñiz-Argüelles and CG van der Merwe, 'Enforcement Of Financial Obligations in a Condominium or Apartment Ownership Scheme' (2006) 16 *Duke Journal of Comparative & International Law* 125 et seq.

[91] Ignatowicz (n 5) 64.

[92] Drozd (n 17) 20–22; Hryćków (n 87) 143–44; Doliwa (n 14) 696; Turlej (n 80) 320; Dziczek (n 26) 116–17.

20 years. The observations made in this chapter seem to point to the fact that confusion surrounding residential communities is a derivative of refusing to accept that they are defective legal persons and thus legal entities. Moreover, the reason for the existence of the residential community is to exclude the need for all unit owners to act jointly and unanimously in all matters concerning their real estate. This is particularly visible in large communities, where assuming that all unit owners will actually be present to unanimously agree on a matter of common property management is simply unrealistic and impractical.

Although, from a theoretical point of view, accepting that the residential community may through a resolution establish a division according to usage or create an easement could cause anxiety, in practical terms it is difficult to deny the sensibility of such an arrangement. After all, isn't this why residential communities come into existence? Aren't they supposed to regulate the use and enjoyment of common property through resolutions?

It is correct for the legislator to require that in small communities of seven or less units, the unit owners, as co-owners of common property, should be in complete agreement with respect to matters of extraordinary management (the requirement of unanimous resolutions). Such a requirement is not practical or constructive in large communities; therefore, in matters of extraordinary management, the legislator has substituted the agreement of all unit owners with a majority vote resolution of the residential community. It is difficult to argue with the fact that this was the legislator's intention and that it was a sensible one.

Simultaneously, it is imperative to note that the legislator has fallen short of providing further principles for an orderly operation of a residential community in the context of the need to protect the right of ownership of the individual unit owners. First, resolutions on divisions according to usage and on easements could greatly and often adversely affect unit owners. This does not mean that in large communities one should require a unanimous vote of, eg 100 unit owners. It should mean that resolutions on such matters must adhere to higher standards as regards the procedure of their adoption. Currently, it is not necessary for anyone to show up at a meeting where the pros and cons may be discussed and an expert can answer legal questions. It is enough for the manager/member of the management board to go around and collect signatures from unit owners (over an unspecified period of time) who may not be aware what the significance of a given resolution is. In this context, it is understandable that academics advocate for an agreement of all unit owners. If, however, such a resolution was to be adopted at a meeting where a quorum is required, the role of the residential community and its competence to 'decide' would be more justified and acceptable.

Second, the legislator has failed to notice that the notion of ancillary chambers as constituent parts of a unit[93] is too narrow to include parking spaces and gardens for ground-floor flats. Meanwhile, most unit owners are convinced that they may actually buy a unit with a parking space or with a garden and are unaware of the fact that, legally, this is not possible. To overcome this obstacle, divisions according

---

[93] An ancillary chamber which is a constituent part of a unit is treated as its integral part; it forms a part of the unit itself, even if it is not adjacent to it (eg basement cubicle, pantry).

to usage and easements are being created when from the very beginning it is obvious that the parties do not want these spaces to ever form a part of the common area. It has already been suggested in the literature that a vast amount of divisions according to usage and easements would be unnecessary if the legislator allowed for the creation of not only ancillary chambers but also ancillary spaces.[94] In this way, creating exclusive use areas would only be necessary for more unusual circumstances and more specialised needs. It would also be more obvious that such areas require a careful calculation of additional fees paid to the residential community.

Finally, the legislator has not given the residential community a true framework for efficient operation. Apart from the draconian Article 16 of the LUO measure and the access to regular court proceedings, the residential community has no mechanisms to more gently but surely motivate unit owners to comply with their financial and social obligations. Consequently, the communities attempt to self-regulate these issues in constitutions (for which there is no legal basis) and house rules, often violating the acceptable modes of operation and the right of unit ownership.

The above are a clear indication that the Polish legislator needs to reconsider the assumptions made in 1994 and modify them in a way that will be more consistent with current needs and practice. It is necessary to accept that particularly in large residential communities, these communities must make decisions for the unit owners. However, there must be mechanisms which ensure a proper decision-making process. It is justified to conclude that in order for majority voting to yield socially fair and convincing results, it should be subject to a quorum requirement if it relates to matters of extraordinary management. This could also motivate unit owners to be more involved in matters connected with the common parts. Such a requirement would need to have safeguards, such as recourse to court, if unit owners boycott meetings and legally effective resolutions cannot be taken. Moreover, it would be wise to resolve disagreements concerning common parts and their management as well the behaviour of unit owners through mandatory mediation procedures. This would require the further development of mediation practice in Poland as well as a comprehensive social campaign aimed at educating the society of the benefits of mediation, particularly in cases concerning communities of unit owners.

In the light of the current confusion over numerous legal issues concerning residential communities, it would be irrational to accept that the regulation in force adequately caters for the needs of the unit owners, the market and the legal system as such. The latter requires transparency and consistency of judgments in order to properly function and stimulate law-abiding attitudes among citizens. There is scope for improvement and the need to reflect the society's needs concerning unit ownership should not be neglected.

[94] See Matusik (n 38) 102–04.

8

Collective Property: Owning and Sharing Residential Space

SARAH BLANDY[*]

L ET US IMAGINE an island a couple of miles from the mainland where a modern Western society in all its complexity is thriving. Just over 10 years ago, 15 households came to live on the island, which until then had been uninhabited. The original islanders arrived with very definite ideas about a communal way of life, which they had already been discussing together for some time as an informal group. Their ideal was to have a private dwelling for each household, combined with space which all could share. Some had already lived in shared houses, while others had utopian dreams about communal living. This period of discussions proved too long and gruelling for some, and others left because the anticipated costs increased. However, enough members of the original group remained committed and new members joined. Their ideas were encapsulated at the time of the move to the island in a written document setting out the expectations of conduct and commitment of the island residents.

This group was not short of money; they raised loans to buy the island, employ an architect and pay a building company to put up a very well-designed village, which now has 30 houses. These range in size from two to five bedrooms, and each house is allocated a small area of garden. There is a green in the centre of the village. An unusual feature of the development is a large three-storey shared building. The ground floor accommodates indoor games; the first floor has a small kitchen and a large comfortable sitting area; and on the top floor is a dining area large enough to seat about 40 people and a well-equipped large kitchen.

The original group of islanders moved into the first dwellings to be built and then set about finding others to occupy the remaining houses. In the 10 years since the island has been inhabited, a way of life has evolved. Residents meet every two weeks to discuss any issues that have arisen, for example, how the shared building is to be used. Decisions are reached by consensus rather than voting and are recorded for future reference, thus changing the original written 'rules'. Communal meals are prepared every other evening in the shared building and every adult islander must take his or her turn on the cooking rota. Other sub-groups have formed, such as a gardening group, which any resident may join. Some of the boundaries between private and common space, and those between some of the private dwellings have been

[*] Professor of Law, University of Sheffield; s.blandy@sheffield.ac.uk.

renegotiated to reflect the way that space is used in practice rather than as depicted on the original architect's plan. None of the islanders would assume the right to enter another's house without invitation, although strong social bonds have developed between the residents. The green, the common building and pathways through the village are seen as 'ours': the collective responsibility of all the islanders.

Since the village on the island was first built, five houses have been sold. The newcomers buying into the island community were not 'vetted' by the other residents, but were invited to take part in communal meals and to observe meetings before purchasing their house. New islanders are self-selecting on the basis of these experiences and the information about expectations of conduct and commitment provided orally and in writing before purchasing. Islanders accept that no resident can be forced to leave, although considerable social pressure would be exerted on anyone who failed to comply with the expectations of conduct and commitment, such as taking part in the cooking rota. A complex disputes procedure has been established, although most disputes are resolved without recourse to it. No serious difficulties have threatened the community on the island, although a few disputes rumble on and some residents are less satisfied, or more vocal in their complaints than others.

I. INTRODUCTION

What has been described above is, apart from a few unimportant details,[1] a real housing site. Its residents call it a 'cohousing development', and I will adopt this description (which has no meaning in law). Its portrayal as an imaginary island is a device for analysing its property regime without reference to any specific legal jurisdiction. Harris, for example, invented societies to illustrate concepts and conceptualisations of property, concluding that the existence of trespassory rules and the right to exclude is 'analytically tied to the existence of private property in land'.[2] Examining the cohousing site as an imaginary island shows a clear institution of property as the division between private and common property is accepted and respected, even though in practice the boundaries may become blurred and open to negotiation. Trespassory rules and the right to exclude underpin the islanders' understanding of the distinction between 'ours' and 'mine'. If property rests ultimately on the ability to exclude and control, to exert sovereignty over land, this is exercised collectively by the residents in respect of the island as a whole.

The next part of the chapter sets out the actual property framework for the cohousing development, under the legal regime in twenty-first century England.

---

[1] Its offshore location is one of the invented details, in order to free it from any existing property regime. The material discussed in this chapter is drawn from a larger empirical research project funded by the British Academy into how residents of eight different sites (with different legal frameworks) share and manage their non-privately owned space, referred to as the 'common parts' in technical conveyancing terminology.

[2] JW Harris, *Property and Justice* (Oxford, Oxford University Press, 1996) 145. See also Scott Shapiro's example in *Legality* (Cambridge MA, Harvard University Press, 2011) of a legal system developed on an island by a group of people whose community originated in making meals collectively, although his view is that hierarchy is inevitable.

I then outline some of the pervasive theoretical and philosophical models of individual property and conclude that these models could support the non-individual version of property, as practised on the imaginary island (and in the cohousing development). The chapter next discusses how different categories of property: public, private and common are defined and discussed in the legal and common-pool resources (CPR) literatures. The latter has proved very informative in addressing the question of how property should be categorised in multi-owned housing sites, where individual property is subject to collective governance regimes but remains private. I suggest that the term 'collective' is the most appropriate for this type of property.

In the penultimate substantive section, extracts from interviews with residents are used to illustrate and build theory about the ways in which rights, governance and everyday practice in the cohousing site are intertwined to produce what I term collective property. This is followed by an exploration of how the legal recognition of collective property might develop over time, rejecting a positivist approach in which current law forms the basis for analysis of property doctrine. Various currently available legal frameworks for multi-housing sites are discussed, none of which adequately reflect the inter-related property and governance regime of the cohousing site.

The aim of this chapter is to examine through empirical research how property is constituted by those who live it. I suggest that this offers an alternative way of understanding property, different from the established philosophical and doctrinal approaches and better able to capture property as a lived process. My research approach was taken from legal anthropology, which shares the understanding of many legal scholars that property is concerned with relations between people,[3] and also informed by the work of Elinor Ostrom and other CPR scholars.[4] CPR analysts start with a detailed examination of what is happening on the ground as a foundation for theory. Their work points to the importance of 'operational details in the real world' to test theories of property: is the right to exclude the be-all and end-all; is alienability crucial?[5] This chapter, and the empirical research on which it is based, is intended to contribute to this emerging debate.

My research techniques were less immersive and time-consuming than the ethnographic studies conducted by anthropologists although I avoided a 'law-first' approach to focus on actual everyday property practices. My intention was to investigate the cohousing development as an example of what the eminent legal anthropologist Sally Falk Moore termed a 'semi-autonomous social field', generating its

---

[3] See, for example, CM Hann (ed), *Property Relations: Renewing the Anthropological Tradition* (Cambridge, Cambridge University Press, 1998). Similarly, property theorists have defined property as, for instance, 'relations among persons with respect to things' in R Munzer, *A Theory of Property* (Cambridge, Cambridge University Press, 1990) 17; and as 'a network of jural relationships between individuals in respect of valued resources' in K Gray and SF Gray, *Elements of Land Law*, 5th edn (Oxford, Oxford University Press, 2009) 6.

[4] See, primarily, E Ostrom, *Governing the Commons: The Evolution of Institutions for Collective Action* (Princeton, Princeton University Press, 1990); E Ostrom, *Understanding Institutional Diversity* (Oxford, Oxford University Press, 2005).

[5] LA Fennell, 'Ostrom's Law: Property Rights in the Commons' (2011) 5 *International Journal of the Commons* 9, 16.

own rules and decisions and means of enforcement, but also penetrated by the external legal system.[6] I visited and observed the cohousing development, sharing one of their communal meals, and interviewed five residents there. In these interviews I avoided any direct questioning about legal issues, allowing the respondents to raise these and to describe in their own words the way in which space is shared and how collective understanding or rules have developed. However, I also obtained and examined the relevant legal documents. This empirical research was designed to capture and explore the complex landscape of the inter-resident legal relationships, as well as the social norms which the cohousing residents have developed over time, and the more formal rules which they have deliberately created.

This approach suggested the idea of portraying the cohousing development as an imaginary island in order to analyse its property regime free of preconceptions. A legal anthropologist researching the island would be particularly interested in the social relations between the residents and the social norms which have developed over time to deal with the complex interaction between individual and collective property interests. This anthropological focus would reveal another aspect of property relations, demonstrating that use of the non-privately owned land is shaped by shared commitment and responsibility, while individual control over the private dwellings is subject to the established principle that each resident is part of the whole community. Decisions on matters applicable to individual houses, such as the colour of external paintwork, are taken collectively. There is a tiered dispute resolution system to address problems which cannot be settled informally between neighbours. The property regime on the island is therefore continuously constituted by the islanders' evolving practices in living and making decisions collectively.

My research is informed by social constructionist views that 'law is an aspect or field of social experience, not some mysteriously external force acting on it. They are mutually constituting'.[7] Thus, law 'shapes society from the inside out, by providing the principal categories that make social life seem natural, normal, cohesive and coherent'.[8] One of these principal categories is property. Some property theorists also consider law as a narrative which shapes how we see the world, a persuasive framework to be called upon when necessary.[9] The idea of an intuitive understanding of property has also been extensively discussed in the property literature, especially in relation to possession. Gray and Gray suggest that, at least in respect of land, the notion of property 'connotes, ultimately a deeply instinctive self-affirming sense of belonging and control'.[10] The right to control which is inseparably associated with property has a psychological importance as well.

---

[6] SF Moore, 'Law and Social Change: The Semi-Autonomous Social Field as an Appropriate Subject of Study' (1973) 7 *Law and Society Review* 719.

[7] R Cotterell, *Law, Culture and Society: Legal Ideas in the Mirror of Society* (Farnham, Ashgate, 2006) 25.

[8] A Sarat and TR Kearns, 'Beyond the Great Divide: Forms of Legal Scholarship and Everyday Life' in A Sarat and TR Kearns (eds), *Law in Everyday Life* (Ann Arbor, University of Michigan Press, 1993) 22.

[9] See CM Rose, *Property and Persuasion: Essays on the History, Theory and Rhetoric of Ownership* (Boulder, Westview Press, 1994).

[10] K Gray and SF Gray, 'The Idea of Property in Land' in S Bright (ed), *Land Law: Themes and Perspectives* (Oxford, Oxford University Press, 1998) 19.

This deep-seated nature of property understanding has recently been explored in relation to the informal property-based norms which govern on-street car parking[11] and to queues.[12] These self-governing mechanisms rely on property-based behaviour and norms such as trust, solidarity and cohesion to achieve a balance between self-interest and the collective normative order. Further, the empirical observations which underpin these observations and analyses emphasise that property is both an attitude of mind and a process based on continual enactment on the ground. This chapter extends the argument of Epstein and of Gray to assert that, in the cohousing development and indeed in other multi-owned housing sites, a property regime is being produced which should be legally recognised.

I argue that the lived experience of the cohousing residents who share common space does not accord with the prevailing idea that property relations are fixed at the time of a grant of property in land, accompanied by contractual rights and obligations. The theory that law and social life are mutually constitutive offers a way around this difficulty, while reflecting the view that property is both a continual and active process 'on the ground', and a set of subjective attitudes. My conclusion is that collective property is a legally distinct form of property and should be recognised as such.

II. PROPERTY IN REALITY

Returning to the island, mapping the property regime found there against the current legal framework applicable in England and Wales,[13] raises interesting questions. For example, would it be accurate to describe each household as having a freehold interest in their individual dwelling? If so, would an easement best describe the nature of residents' rights to the common parts? Or perhaps the individual dwellings are held on leases or licences granted by whoever owns the freehold of the whole island? If so, who is the freeholder? The technical details of property law in the real world provide answers. Freehold and leasehold are the only permissible estates in land at law,[14] and positive covenants cannot be enforced against subsequent freehold owners.[15] Thus, leasehold tenure is commonly used for the individual dwellings in this type of housing site to ensure that residents' obligations to pay for the maintenance and repair of the common parts remain enforceable. Multiple interests in common parts cannot take effect as co-owned private property.[16]

---

[11] R Epstein, 'The Allocation of the Commons: Parking on Public Roads' (2002) 31 *Journal of Legal Studies* S515.

[12] K Gray, 'Property in a Queue' in GS Alexander and EM Penalver (eds), *Property and Community* (Oxford, Oxford University Press, 2010).

[13] Broadly speaking, the structure of estates and interests established by the Law of Property Act 1925.

[14] Law of Property Act 1925, s 1.

[15] *Austerbery v Oldham Corporation* [1885] Ch D 750; *Rhone v Stevens* [1994] 2 All ER 65 (HL).

[16] Section 34 of the Law of Property Act 1925 provides that there can be no more than four legal co-owners of land. In other jurisdictions, multiple co-ownership is accepted; for example, Hong Kong (see NM Yip, 'Management Rights in Multi-owned Properties in Hong Kong' in S Blandy, A Dupuis and J Dixon (eds), *Multi-owned Housing: Law, Power and Practice* (Farnham, Ashgate, 2010) and Israel (see R Alterman, 'The Maintenance of Residential Towers in Condominium Tenure: A Comparative Analysis of Two Extremes—Israel and Florida' in S Blandy, A Dupuis and J Dixon (eds), *Multi-owned Housing: Law, Power and Practice* (Farnham, Ashgate, 2010)).

This is the legal framework in which the cohousing site exists. Property rights are established as a leasehold estate of 999 years in respect of each individual dwelling with leaseholders' rights and obligations in relation to the common parts created through the lease, a hybrid of property and contract. The parties to each lease are the lessee and the freeholder. The original freeholder was a company owned by one of the residents, who had been a member of the group from the outset and a driving force behind the development. Unlike in many similar developments, the parties to the lease do not include a residents' management company created to take on ownership of the freehold. However, some five years after the first occupation of the site, the freehold was transferred to a management company whose members are the leaseholders. Although the lease provides for a Residents' Association to be 'formed by the majority of the lessees from time to time' and includes a requirement that all occupiers be members of the Association, it is given no legal status or role.

The lease defines the common parts as 'those parts of the estate not exclusively enjoyed by lease, licence or otherwise by one of the occupiers, including pathways, common halls staircases and landings, and all other parts of the estate used in common with other lessees'. The freeholder covenants to maintain and repair these common parts, and in return for payment of a peppercorn ground rent and annual service charges, each lessee gains rights 'to use in common with others enjoying the same rights incidental to the occupation and enjoyment of the demised premises, the Common Parts, communal garden areas for quiet recreational purposes only, and the Communal House for quiet recreational purposes only'. Lessees are bound by mutual covenants to 'comply with the Principles of Co Housing'[17] and to refrain from causing nuisance, noise, obstruction of the Common Parts and having barbecues or bonfires. The property which is subject to the lease must first be offered to the freeholder when put up for sale, and any assignee of the lease must execute an identical Deed of Covenant. The lease further binds lessees to comply with 'other such regulations reasonably imposed from time to time by the Lessor or by the Residents Association with the prior consent of the Lessor'.

From the very detailed legal provisions of this lease, which runs to 28 pages and nine schedules, we now turn to the consideration of property at a more abstract level. How can theoretical models of property encompass this combination of the residents' leasehold rights which amount (almost) to full ownership in respect of their houses and more restricted property rights to use the common parts of the site in common with the other lessees?

III. MODELS AND CATEGORIES OF PROPERTY

In the liberal model of full individual ownership, 'cases of split ownership ... present baffling problems to one who is compelled to fix on one of those interested as *the* owner of the thing'.[18] This dominant concept of property in Anglo-American property

---

[17] Defined in the lease as the principles set out in K Macamant, *Cohousing: A Contemporary Approach to Housing Ourselves* (Berkeley, Ten Speed Press, 1989).

[18] T Honoré, 'Ownership' in AG Guest (ed), *Oxford Essays in Jurisprudence* (Oxford, Oxford University Press, 1961) 164 (emphasis in original).

scholarship is organised around the idea that each resource belongs to an individual; the name of the individual is attached to the resource in what Waldron has described as the name/object correlation, the essence of ownership.[19] If we accept that the 'law creates conceptual categories and determines their contents',[20] then individual ownership appears a very strong concept indeed. However, it remains resistant to precise analysis; theorists continue to debate whether property ownership is best categorised using the 'bundle of rights' model or can be reduced to one essential right, the right to exclude. Whichever of these models is adopted, property philosophers acknowledge that individual property ownership is tempered by the needs of wider society and the fact of coexistence with others.

It therefore seems that there may yet be room for a different, more inclusive and collective model of property. Even property theorists committed to the individual property model suggest that its strength relies on shared understandings with non-owners. For example, Penner argues that property resides in 'the right to determine the use or disposition' of a thing, which is concomitant with 'others excluding themselves from it'.[21] What Penner terms this duty of non-interference, protected by trespassory rules, is based on the general recognition that we should exclude ourselves from property that is not ours. Penner points out that although exclusion and control are not written into any conveyancing document or covenant, we understand them as an integral part of property.[22] The 'gut sense' which we all have of property is shared by owners and non-owners alike.[23] Carol Rose has described property as 'one of the most sociable institutions that human beings have created, depending as it does on mutual forbearance and on the recognition of and respect for the claims of others'.[24]

Another aspect of the individual notion of property is apparently supported by the Hegelian assertion that appropriation and ownership of property is required for self-fulfilled personhood. The contemporary property theorist most associated with this view, Margaret Radin, nonetheless suggests that the 'physical and social characteristics of a community [meaning the local neighbourhood] can become bound up over time with the personhood of individual residents *and with the group's existence as a community*' in a process she refers to as 'status creation'.[25] There are two strands to this argument: first, that property can engender community identity as well as individual personhood; and, second, that there is a temporal element involved in the concept of property.[26] Both of these aspects will be examined later in relation to property in practice at the cohousing development.

The classification of the common parts, and the rights in them, clearly present difficulties for theoretical models. The once satisfyingly neat division between private

---

[19] J Waldron, *The Right to Private Property* (Oxford, Clarendon Press, 1988).
[20] K Calavita, *Invitation to Law and Society* (Chicago, University of Chicago Press, 2010) 35.
[21] JE Penner, *The Idea of Property in Law* (Oxford, Clarendon Press, 1997) 152.
[22] Ibid.
[23] K Gray and SF Gray, *Land Law* (London, Butterworths, 1999) 45.
[24] Rose (n 9) 1019.
[25] MJ Radin, 'Time, Possession, and Alienation' (1986) 64 *Washington University Law Quarterly* 739, 757 (emphasis added).
[26] On the temporal element in property, see also A Clarke, 'Use, Time and Entitlement' in *Current Legal Problems* (Oxford, Oxford University Press, 2004); and Fennell (n 5).

and public property no longer provides an adequate analytic framework,[27] opening up new territory for discussion by property and CPR scholars. Precision is needed for this analysis yet despite pleas for a common multi-disciplinary vocabulary of property, both inconsistent use of the same terms and application of different terms to the same type of property are confusingly frequent.[28] For example, the oceans are referred to variously as 'non-property' and as 'open access commons'.[29] Terminology matters; in Hardin's hugely influential analysis of how property from which free riders cannot be excluded becomes over-used and ultimately degraded,[30] he used the term 'commons'. It is argued that this has led law and economics theorists to criticise all property rights held in common, although this 'communal property paradigm—the open access unregulated common—simply does not exist'.[31] Hardin therefore erroneously labelled 'an ungoverned open-access regime' as 'the commons'.[32] Fennell notes that property used by ubiquitous groups such as households or firms represents overlooked 'everyday examples of non-tragic commons'.[33] The point is that property held or used in common is always, in practice, subject to some regulation or governance, and rights to control or exclude may be exercised collectively.

For Michael Heller, the main distinction is now between private and commons property: resources held in common 'may be arranged along a continuum from open-access to limited-access'.[34] Analysis of the different property categories along that continuum is determined by rights. What Carol Rose describes as 'public property', such as fully accessible parks and highways held in trust for the public by the state which owns it,[35] can only be subject to 'imaginary proprietary control' exercised by individuals, which is usually effective in practice but lacking any legal power.[36] This argument is echoed by Clarke and Kohler in their discussion of 'tacitly accepted conventions about behaviour', for example, that the first person to reach a park bench has the right to sit there until he or she decides to leave. However, the terms used are confusingly different. Clarke and Kohler refer to this type of property not as 'public property', but as 'open-access communal property', which may not be provided or owned by the state, for example, public

---

[27] ET Freyfogle, 'Goodbye to the Public-Private Divide' (2006) 36 *Environmental Law* 7.

[28] See, eg, N Dolšak and E Ostrom, 'The Challenges of the Commons' in N Dolšak and E Ostrom (eds), *The Commons in the New Millennium: Challenges and Adaptation* (Cambridge MA, MIT Press, 2004) 7.

[29] E Ostrom and D Cole (eds), *Property in Land and Other Resources* (Washington, Lincoln Institute of Land Policy, 2011).

[30] G Hardin, 'The Tragedy of the Commons' (1968) 162 *Science* 124.

[31] A Clarke, 'Property Law: Re-establishing Diversity' in *Current Legal Problems* (Oxford, Oxford University Press, 1997) 135–36.

[32] Fennell (n 5) 12.

[33] Ibid, 13. Alastair Hudson, whose thought-provoking comments I very much appreciate, points out that industrial and provident societies are another example of jointly owned and controlled property in which no member has individual proprietary rights. See further, A Hudson, *Law and Investment Entities* (London, Sweet and Maxwell, 2000).

[34] MA Heller, 'The Boundaries of Private Property' (1999) 108 *Yale Law Journal* 1163, 1195.

[35] This term is also used by CPR scholars; see MA McKean, 'Success on the Commons—A Comparative Examination of Institutions for Common Property Resource Management' (1992) 4 *Journal of Theoretical Politics* 247; see also Ostrom and Cole (n 29).

[36] Rose (n 9) 290–94.

rights of way over private land. Rights not to be excluded from this type of open-access communal property, such as highways, are enshrined in law and cannot be withdrawn without some legal change taking place. This differentiates it from 'state property', such as a library, from which the state may unilaterally decide to withdraw public rights of access.[37]

Clarke and Kohler contend that communities can hold property rights in limited-access communal property where the community is defined in relation to a particular locality or by membership of a defined class.[38] These rights include the right not to be excluded and the right to exclude non-members, but not the right to transmit property interests.[39] Margaret McKean, a CPR theorist, considers that the rights of each group member in limited-access common property amount to private property.[40] She makes a further distinction between 'common or communal property', where the individual co-owners may only sell their shares simultaneously with all other co-owners, or only in accordance with very stringent rules laid down by the group, and 'jointly owned private property', where the individual co-owners may sell their shares at will.[41]

At this point we could conclude that the cohousing site's common parts are not public property, but might be categorised as limited-access common property, with accompanying individual and jointly owned private property rights. In the property literature, the crucial difference appears to depend on whether residents' rights or shares can be transmitted, either at all or without reference to other members of the community. The cohousing residents may transmit their rights to the common parts by selling their leasehold rights, subject only to the requirement to first offer the property to the freeholder when put up for sale and that the assignee must enter into identical covenants. However, to end our analysis here would be to ignore the most distinctive feature of the cohousing development—the collective governance arrangements through which the residents together continuously constitute their property relations in respect of both the individual dwellings and the collective spaces.

In 1999 Heller wrote that the 'dynamics of rules' governing this type of property rights 'are a relatively little-analysed, real-world problem'.[42] That may have been true then of property theorists, but not of CPR analysts.[43] CPR analysis has 'place[d] limited commons management on the table as an alternative to bureaucratic administration and individual private property [which] certainly made it easier to conceive of parallel issues in property theory'.[44] However, it is important to note that CPR scholars and property scholars are not concerned with the same issues. Charlotte Hess and Elinor Ostrom make a clear distinction

---

[37] A Clarke and P Kohler, *Property Law: Commentary and Materials* (Cambridge, Cambridge University Press, 2005) 39.

[38] Ibid, 35.

[39] Ibid, 39.

[40] McKean (n 35) 251.

[41] Ibid, 252.

[42] Heller (n 34) 1167.

[43] See Rose (n 9).

[44] CM Rose, 'Ostrom and the Lawyers: the Impact of *Governing the Commons* on the American Legal Academy' (2011) 5 *International Journal of the Commons* 28, 33.

between common-pool *resources* as 'types of economic goods, independent of particular property rights' and common *property* as 'a legal regime—a jointly owned legal set of rights'.[45] According to Ostrom, the task of CPR analysts is to refine the analytical tools to establish why some governance mechanisms succeed and others are ineffective.[46] CPR theorists are not primarily interested in property but in analysing the collective governance of common-pool resources. These resources are characterised by two essential features. First, they must contend with 'subtractability or rivalness', meaning that whatever one person takes from the resource subtracts from the ability of others (the rivals) to do the same. This leads to the second essential characteristic, which is that in all CPRs it is necessary to establish mechanisms of exclusion.[47] In other ways, CPRs are very varied in form.

Therefore, as Fennell points out, governance mechanisms are not determined solely by the fact that this is a CPR, but vary according to context. For example, Fennell emphasises the importance of scale; governance arrangements suited to the management of a small CPR cannot be assumed to transfer effectively to a much larger resource. Certainly, 'the attributes of the resource in question will influence how property rights develop', but that is a separate issue, as property rights 'are matters of human construction'.[48] Empirical CPR research has found that in practice the categories of public, private, individual and common property are combined in various ways. Property theorists have recently been criticised by Elinor Ostrom and Daniel Cole for failing to recognise and take into account the complexity of property systems.[49] CPR theorists are also critical of what has been termed the 'naïve theory of property rights', the law and economics analysis based on Demetz's work, which identifies and welcomes a one-way progression through history towards the full institution of private property.[50] Most CPR scholars argue against the privatisation of property rights in natural resources on the grounds that systems develop organically for managing these resources, which are efficient and adaptable.

Nevertheless, the CPR analytic approach has increasingly been applied to novel types of 'commons' property, in particular intellectual property.[51] Multi-owned housing sites such as the cohousing development have also been described as 'new de facto commons'.[52] The following section focuses more closely on this particular type of property, concluding that 'commons' is not the most apt description.

---

[45] C Hess and E Ostrom (eds), *Understanding Knowledge as a Commons: From Theory to Practice* (Cambridge MA, MIT Press, 2011) 5.

[46] Fennell (n 5) 9.

[47] Dolšak and Ostrom (n 28) 7.

[48] Ibid, 13.

[49] Ostrom and Cole (n 29).

[50] T Eggertsson, *Economic Behaviour and Institutions* (Cambridge, Cambridge University Press, 1990) 254.

[51] See, eg, JB Holder and T Flessas, 'Emerging Commons: Introduction to Special Issue' (2008) 17 *Social and Legal Studies* 299; Editors, 'Introduction to Special Issue on Community and Property' (2010) 1 *Theoretical Inquiries in Law* 1; Hess and Ostrom (n 45).

[52] A Clarke, 'Creating New Commons: Recognition of Communal Land Rights within a Private Property Framework' in *Current Legal Problems* (Oxford, Oxford University Press, 2007) 319.

IV. RIGHTS AND GOVERNANCE IN COLLECTIVE PROPERTY

The recent property law scholarship which is most relevant to this chapter addresses common interest developments (CIDs) in the US.[53] In terms of property category, CID owners would appear to enjoy private property rights, but these are 'subject to limits imposed by other private citizens—by a homeowners' association', suggesting a continuum between private and public control and use of the land.[54] Levahi has posited the model of a mixed property regime, a 'private-common-public property triangle' to replace the outdated public–private dichotomy. He terms CIDS a new 'hybrid' form of property, made up of the distinct but interrelated realms of rights allocation and governance.[55] CPR analysts also consider condominium developments (ie CIDs) as an example of mixed private and common property.[56] This interconnection between individual and group property rights in CIDs has led Heller to situate them 'at the crossroads of legal theory, between commons and anticommons along the axis of property law, between private and public on the axis of governance'.[57] Smith's analysis of property rights within the CID suggests that they 'fall on a spectrum between the poles of exclusion and governance', with rights to exclude equated with rules of access, and governance with rules of use.[58] In the CPR literature, 'governance' usually refers to the fine detail of common resource management, but Smith extends its meaning and application 'from contractual provisions, to norms of proper use, to nuisance law and public environmental regulation'.[59]

From his theoretical perspective, Heller considers that CIDs which provide homes for 'upwards of 40 million Americans' represent 'a stunning example of the power of law in action—of getting a liberal commons form right'.[60] However, empirical research suggests that this form of property benefits municipal government and developers more than it does many residents. McKenzie, for example, concludes that the law and economics analytic approach ignores both the 'many large and powerful institutions [which] are heavily invested in such housing' and the advantages which they derive from it.[61] Far from representing liberal ideals of free choice, McKenzie asserts that compulsory membership of homeowner associations has 'so little appeal to homeowners that it must be forced on them' as an integral part of their purchase package in one of the 300,000 CID developments.[62] McKenzie argues that rational choice theory cannot fully encompass or explain the

---

[53] In CIDs, resident-managed homeowners' associations are similar to a residents' management company or commonhold association in the English context, owning the freehold of the common parts.

[54] Freyfogle (n 27) 5.

[55] A Levahi, 'Mixing Property' (1998) 38 *Seton Hall Law Review* 137; A Lehavi, 'How Property Can Create, Maintain, or Destroy Community (2009) 10 *Theoretical Inquiries in Law* 43.

[56] Dolšak and Ostrom (n 28) 4.

[57] MA Heller, 'Common Interest Developments at the Crossroads of Legal Theory' (2005) 37 *Urban Lawyer* 329, 334.

[58] HE Smith, 'Exclusion versus Governance: Two Strategies for Delineating Property Rights' (2002) 31(S2) *Journal of Legal Studies* S453, S455.

[59] Ibid.

[60] Heller (n 57) 333.

[61] E McKenzie, *Beyond Privatopia: Rethinking Private Residential Government* (Washington DC, Urban Institute Press, 2011) 64.

[62] Ibid, 52.

complexities of collective action, social norms and social structure; analyses based on this theoretical approach are often driven by an underlying belief in 'the moral superiority of private, contractual, and voluntary living arrangements over those compelled by government authority'.[63]

Further, McKenzie's research found that CID internal rules are generally non-negotiable, having been set by the developer. The outcome is that many North American common interest developments are riven with dissent, disputes and difficulties between residents, officers of homeowner associations and their lawyers.[64] McKenzie has provided compelling evidence that Heller's depiction is not borne out in reality by setting out the regulatory provisions which have been introduced by many US states in an attempt to ensure protection for CID residents.[65] In the case of English multi-owned residential sites, it appears to be accepted by most commentators that 'the community cannot choose the form of governance appropriate to its circumstances ... [as this] is dictated by the legal form the underlying owner happens to take'.[66] This choice of legal framework usually depends on how the developer hopes to make a profit out of the site: either as a long-term investment with a continuing right to benefit from residents' service charges or from quick sales to individual owners.[67] If it is the latter, a residents' management company will be established and included as a third party to the lease to become the freehold owner of the whole site in a similar way to the US homeowner associations which own the common parts of the development, and often engendering similar (although perhaps less widespread and serious) difficulties for residents.[68] Evidence from the cohousing development indicates that residents need not *necessarily* be passive recipients of a legal structure adopted in advance to suit the interests of the developer, and nor are residents *necessarily* 'subject to the whim of their neighbours, just as feudal tenants were subject to the whim of their lords', as Singer puts it in relation to US CIDs.[69] As the detailed work of CPR analysts shows, the specific context of a particular site is extremely important.

Where the freehold estate is owned by a legal entity such as a residents' management company, residents' rights over the common parts are not 'rights over property belonging to another' in any meaningful sense, as all resident owners are members of the legal entity that owns the freehold. The type of property in the cohousing development is hard to align precisely with any of the categories discussed in the literature; in any event, 'public', 'private' and 'common or communal' property, together with 'the commons', are now overworked terms used differently

---

[63] Ibid, 45.

[64] See RK Lippert, 'Governing Condominiums and Renters with Legal Knowledge Flows and External Institutions' (2012) 34 *Law & Policy* 263.

[65] E McKenzie, 'Emerging Regulatory Trends, Power and Competing Interests in US Common Interest Developments' in Blandy, Dupuis and Dixon (n 16) 53.

[66] Clarke (n 52) 348.

[67] D Clarke, 'Long Residential Leases: Future Directions', in S Bright (ed), *Landlord and Tenant Law: Past, Present and Future* (Oxford, Hart Publishing, 2006).

[68] The unequal relationship between the developer/freeholder and the leaseholder/residents has been examined as an illustration of how power is exercised and materialised through law, in Blandy, Dupuis and Dixon (n 16).

[69] JW Singer, 'Democratic Estates: Property Law in a Free and Democratic Society (2008–09) 94 *Cornell Law Review* 1009, 1026.

by different authors. Perhaps the most appropriate term would be Lehavi's 'hybrid property',[70] but it hardly captures the way in which residents' property rights are inextricably associated with governance obligations, nor the way in which rights over the common parts cannot be legally or physically separated from the property rights in individual dwellings. In the cohousing site, for example, it is difficult to see how a resident's rights over the common parts could ever be 'not-purtenant' to their home.[71]

I therefore suggest that the term 'collective property' is the most apt expression for the property and self-governance rights and obligations in the cohousing site. Here, residents must develop collective rules and norms about the use and management of both individual and collective property, define their boundaries (legal and physical) and decide how to resolve any disputes that may arise. The following section makes use of data from observation and from interviews conducted with five residents to examine more closely how property and governance are practised in the routine life of the cohousing development.

V. PROPERTY AND GOVERNANCE IN THE COHOUSING DEVELOPMENT

The cohousing development is not strictly speaking a CPR; it is not a profit-making resource whose users must contend with subtractability or rivalness, and mechanisms of exclusion are therefore not the most important aspect of this site's property regime.[72] However, it demonstrates many features of successful self-governing CPR institutions, as identified by Ostrom.[73] The cohousing residents' collective commitment to self-governance has a profound effect on their understanding and practice of property in relation to both individual leasehold properties and the common parts. As discussed earlier, social life and (property) law are mutually constitutive; property is both a continual and active process 'on the ground', and a set of psycho-spatial attitudes with a subjective dimension. The ways in which property is thereby 'produced' at the cohousing site are illustrated here through the residents' own words.

The boundaries of the cohousing development are made clear physically through the distinctive style of the buildings and legally through the mechanism of the lease, meeting Ostrom's suggestion that it is essential for collective property to have defined boundaries. Residents understand the internal boundaries within the site, between the collective space and individual property: '*I feel that this house is my space and outside is the shared space ... space that I can use.*' So far as the shared space is concerned, residents' practice and explanations clearly reflect a proprietorial psycho-spatial attitude: '*there is a perception that we own the common spaces together*', together with

---

[70] Lehavi, 'Mixing Property' (n 55).

[71] This creates a very strong legal and spatial link between the two, echoing medieval grazing rights. However, the decision in *Bettison v Langton* [2001] UKHL 24 has converted most communal grazing rights into fully tradable rights which can be detached from the agricultural holding to which they were once appurtenant.

[72] These are the two essential characteristics of CPRs identified by Dolšak and Ostrom (n 28).

[73] Unless otherwise stated, this section of the chapter draws on the features of effective self-governing CPR organisations listed in Ostrom, *Understanding Institutional Diversity* (n 4) 88 onwards.

collective property as practice: '*There is a sort of collective responsibility ... people go and clear it up after the kids have dropped litter.*' Rules have developed; for example, there is a reservation system for using the middle floor of the communal house for private parties or meetings (with right of veto by other residents if they object to the type of use), but the village green cannot be 'booked'. This space is governed by informal norms, so that it is accepted that adult residents will intervene if, for example, a football game played by older children is preventing quiet use of the green by others. The principle of give and take is well understood by the cohousing residents: '*You can do whatever you want* [on the green] *as long as it doesn't interfere with anyone else. If you want to invite your mates over to have a game of rounders, but you've got little Johnny there playing with his cars in the middle* [of the green], *then it's better to go to the park* [outside the site] *and play your rounders there.*'

At the cohousing site there was a strange, at least to my eyes, disregard of legal property boundaries. The location of boundaries seemed determined more by a practical understanding of property relations: '*in fact the slope, I think, is common land ... it's just regarded as my garden; actually, I've put the plants in there*'. In this instance, Lockean appropriation had led to a recognition by others of that individual's property rights. Trading of individually owned property has also taken place, in the full awareness that: '*I mean, legally it was my garden, and she wanted to have that bit of land close to one of her windows. In the end a solution was reached ... she paid some money to me and I passed that on to someone else, and I got another bit of garden.*'

Interviews at the cohousing site demonstrated that the usual understanding of individual property rights was considerably compromised by the collective control that could be exercised over individual owners and their dwellings. Far from confidently exercising and expressing sovereign control, one resident said: '*I still feel* [the house] *is mine, but it's a new situation for me, having to negotiate.*' At the time that the research took place, a debate was under way over the rights of another resident who wished to paint the external wall of his house. He explained that: '*where I come from, you know, it's your house and you do what you want with it. So we had big long meetings ... and we've come to some sort of compromise.*' This solution was achieved through the constitution of a 'colour committee' made up of interested residents, which would recommend a range of acceptable paint colours for those who wanted to paint their external walls.

Thus, any resident could find his or her present or projected use of his or her property up for discussion and subject to collective decision making. The residents had, in effect, made 'a binding contract to commit themselves to a cooperative strategy that they themselves will work out' in a similar manner to many CPRs.[74] However, the clause in the cohousing leases referred to earlier—that each leaseholder covenants to 'comply with the Principles of CoHousing'—is likely to be unenforceable in law as it does not touch and concern the land.[75] Nonetheless, it is

---

[74] Ostrom, *Understanding Institutional Diversity* (n 4) 15.

[75] *Spencer's Case* [1583] 5 Co Rep 16a; it would be an interesting argument that this covenant affects the nature, quality and mode of use of the land, thus meeting the test set out in *P & A Swift Investments v Combined English Stores Group plc* [1988] UKHL 3 [1989] AC 632 (HL).

accepted as binding by the residents who have chosen to live at the cohousing site. This way of life demands much of their time. Unlike most sites of this size, there is no professional property manager employed; all tasks are taken on by the residents themselves. Each adult resident must join a team for cooking the communal meal at least once a month, through a highly organised rota system. The experience of working in a cooking team, just as much as the pleasurable experience of eating communally, was described to me as playing a key role in forging community ties.

Decision making is not delegated to the officers of a residents' management committee.[76] Fortnightly meetings of the Residents Committee are well attended and residents understand that their contributions to discussion about individual and common property are not based on '*whether we like it or want it personally, but as to whether it's good for* [name of the cohousing development]'. Consensus rather than majority voting is the basis of decision making, a process described as '*really, really good because nothing needs to happen quickly … which leads to strong decisions that everyone's agreed with*'. Other residents told me that they were sometimes frustrated at the time taken to reach consensus, but valued the process nonetheless. Robert Ellickson discusses the process of consensus decision making in his exploration of the household (which he defines widely to include cohousing) through the prism of transaction cost analysis.[77] His summary of the advantages and disadvantages misses an important point which was made by most of my interviewees. In the words of one of them, '*the whole process "makes" the community. The fact that we've had endless fraught meetings as well as nice meetings is the glue*'. As in the example of the colour committee mentioned earlier, alongside the formal fortnightly meeting for all residents, a structure of sub-groups has emerged over time: '*sub-committees* [for example, the one which organises the cooking rota] *form when somebody who's really interested in it will hold a meeting, and anybody who's also interested will go. It seems to be rather sort of ad hoc and informal but it works*'.

Ostrom's model of working rules[78] provides a helpful framework for analysing how property is constituted through the everyday practices which contribute to the social ordering of the site. She defines working rules as those which are actually used, monitored and enforced by those directly involved, and which are known about by most of the people affected by them. Ostrom distinguishes between rules, norms and shared strategies; these are all 'institutional statements', but the critical difference is that sanctions for breach, determined by collective decisions and action, only apply to rules.[79] There are multiple sources for these working rules, ranging from state legislation to the collective working out over time of how best to resolve frequently encountered practical problems.[80]

---

[76] This can lead to problematic divisions between residents, as in many US CIDs (see McKenzie (n 61) and as empirical research in England has found (see, for example, R Atkinson, S Blandy, J Flint and D Lister, *Gated Communities in England* (London, Office of the Deputy Prime Minister, 2003)).

[77] RC Ellickson, *The Household: Informal Order Around the Hearth* (Princeton, Princeton University Press, 2008) 97–100.

[78] Ostrom, *Understanding Institutional Diversity* (n 4).

[79] Ibid, 137, 149.

[80] Ibid, 19.

It was very evident from my interviews that working rules in the cohousing development are developed over time through a cooperative process; one resident summarised their approach as: '*let's get on with each other, make these rules and sort things out and see how best to make it work*'. Dolšak and Ostrom stress the importance of trust and connections between CPR members.[81] The population of cohousing residents has been reasonably stable; mutual trust is developed through the system of meetings, communal meals and use of the collective space. A relatively new resident said: '*I don't know them all very well but I trust them because I know that generally we're all going in the right, in the same direction ... everyone is in it for the long haul.*' The rules which are developed through these processes are context-specific, a feature noted by Ostrom as characterising successful CPRs. In the cohousing site, for instance, '*if you want to use this middle floor* [of the communal house] *for a party, you can't book it exclusively for yourself and your guests, you have to throw it open to the whole community*'.

Dolšak and Ostrom consider it crucial that resource users can design and implement new rules to ensure the 'best fit' for managing the particular resource.[82] There is wide participation amongst cohousing residents in clarifying and modifying their operational rules in response to new circumstances, for example, the debate over whether residents have the right to choose external paint colour. Compliance with the working rules is monitored by members, although the CPR parallel is somewhat strained in respect of the requirement for graduated sanctions for breach of the rules.[83] In the cohousing development, the management company ultimately has the power as the freeholder to bring forfeiture proceedings for persistent breach of the lease, subject to strict procedural requirements and the leaseholder's right to apply for relief from forfeiture.[84] Any such proceedings brought for breach of requirements to take part in collective cooking or to observe other principles of cohousing would test their legal enforceability. More effective is the considerable social pressure to conform to the collective norms: '*It's difficult to go against the group or go against your neighbour or go against your friend.*' These constraints are internalised by residents, with the effect that conflict is usually avoided: '*I didn't want to ostracise myself or do something which upsets people.*' However, acknowledged disagreements between residents have arisen; some have been satisfactorily resolved while others rumble on. Fairly formal mechanisms have been developed for conflict resolution as part of the working rules, something explained by one member of the disputes committee:

> We do have a disputes process. The idea is that you try and talk to each other. Each individual would have a buddy and try and reach agreement. And if that fails, it would then go to the disputes committee. It hasn't ever got as far as that. The disputes committee is like any sort of group, about four or five people volunteered to be on it. The people in dispute would have to agree to stick with what the committee decides, it's a voluntary process. Things can also go to the residents' committee and be talked about there.

---

[81] Dolšak and Ostrom (n 28) 17.
[82] Ibid, 21.
[83] Ibid, 22.
[84] Law of Property Act 1925, s 146.

As well as these working rules, other everyday practices have developed over time into accepted norms. This resident articulated rules and norms as distinct: '*I think as we live together longer and these things develop, you know what the rules are, what the unwritten rules are, what the conventions are.*' Residents also routinely used broadly legal procedural notions; for example, while the residents' committee meetings are minuted, there was reluctance to record some decisions for fear of '*setting a precedent*'. It was also striking how frequently formal law was invoked as a way of justifying the rules by which they live, as these extracts from interviews with different residents illustrate: '*You have to cook ... I think that is in the lease somewhere*'; '*legally, or in the lease, the communal house is supposed to be an extension of our own sitting rooms*'. Although the lease does not specifically include either of these points, they were reiterated by other residents I interviewed. The provision in the lease for the addition of further regulations 'reasonably imposed from time to time' may provide some basis for this belief. The lease seems to be frequently referred to in residents' meetings: '*Then we all have to get the lease out and trawl through it and come to an interpretation of the lease that everyone is happy with*'; '*There are a number of things in the lease that are talked about quite a lot*'; '*The lease provides a platform for someone to say "well, are you aware this is against the lease?"*', indicating that it is a legal document that is taken seriously.

However, at the same time, respondents acknowledged that: '*There are all sorts of minor violations of the lease going on, naturally.*' Just as with property boundaries, the provisions of the lease may be ignored when convenient by tacit mutual agreement. The same approach was found in relation to the freehold property interest. The original freeholder of the cohousing site was a company set up and run by one of the founding members of the community. Some years later, with no urgency, the freehold was transferred to a residents' management company that had been established for this purpose. The formal vertical legal relationship was irrelevant to most residents; those interviewed expressed the view that the freehold had always been owned by all residents collectively and that governance arrangements had always been conducted on that basis.

There is a strong argument here that parallel rules have been developed through consensus to match actual property practices at the cohousing site, illustrating Ostrom's reference to collective rules which 'assign de facto rights and duties that are contrary to the de jure rights and duties'.[85] As in the case of property boundaries, the working rules collectively constituted over time can depart from the formal rules, as one resident described: '*We sort of choose not to enforce some things* [that are set out in the lease]—*like no barbecues, or hanging out washing—because after a while we discovered what as a group we want to do.*' The phrase 'after a while' illustrates the temporal dimension of collective property; it is not static and cannot be captured in a once-and-for-all document.

Successful CPRs depend on the existence of an external (if minimal) recognition of the right to organise as a group.[86] The Residents Association recognised in the cohousing lease arguably meets this requirement. However, Dolšak and Ostrom

---

[85] Ostrom, *Understanding Institutional Diversity* (n 4) 51.
[86] Ibid.

expand the point by stating that either governance mechanisms must conform to requirements devised by the external legal environment or the external legal environment must legitimate users devising and implementing their own institutions.[87] On the basis of empirical evidence, it can be asserted that the 'real' property status in the cohousing development is constituted by the residents' everyday practices and their conscious decisions leading to parallel rules, most appropriately described as collective property and governance. However, in legal terms, property in the site consists of leasehold interests in the individual dwellings, rights of access amounting to an easement over the common parts, with a separate freehold interest in the whole site.

Collective property rights are currently not recognised in law, which in the positivist sense fatally undermines any claim that this is a particular type of property. The next part of the chapter examines the value and application of the suggestion that property is a concept broader than merely legally recognised rights: 'a claim which the individual can count on having enforced in his favour by society or the state, by custom or convention or law'.[88]

VI. TOWARDS THE LEGAL RECOGNITION OF COLLECTIVE PROPERTY?

If collective property is to be established as a form of property, we must break out of the 'horrible circularity' inherent in theories that property must be deduced from the law, so that only those rights that have become established as property rights can tell us what property is.[89] The most promising approach to conceptualising property, for my purposes, is 'a right ultimately validated by some social or collective judgement about the propriety of the claim involved'.[90] This both reflects the mutual constitution of law and the social, and holds the implication that over time social or collective judgments are capable of reflecting new realities. Grear links the notion of propriety, a concept which has a strong linguistic association with property, to a rights discourse which 'is naturally quite amenable to inclusive, community-oriented values'.[91] For Macpherson, the fundamental property right is *not to be excluded* from a resource rather than the right to exclude, based on his understanding that common property had been of great importance until comparatively recently.[92] Other authors[93] have also drawn attention to the long history of property rights held in common which were swept away by the 1925 legislation in order to simplify

---

[87] Dolšak and Ostrom (n 28) 20.

[88] CB Macpherson, 'Capitalism and the Changing Concept of Property' in E Kamenka and RS Neale (eds), *Feudalism, Capitalism and Beyond* (Canberra, Australian National University Press, 1975) 106.

[89] K Gray, 'Property in Thin Air' (1991) 50 *CLJ* 252, 293.

[90] Gray and Gray (n 23) 77.

[91] A Grear, 'A Tale of the Land, the Insider, the Outsider and Human Rights (an Exploration of some Problems and Possiblities in the Relationship between the English Common Law Property Concept, Human Rights Law, and Discourses of Exclusion and Inclusion)' (2003) 23 *Legal Studies* 33, 61 and 62.

[92] CB Macpherson (ed), *Property, Mainstream and Critical Positions* (Toronto, University of Toronto Press, 1978).

[93] See, for example, RW Gordon, 'Paradoxical Property' in J Brewer and S Staves (eds), *Early Modern Conceptions of Property* (London, Routledge, 1995); Clarke (n 31).

conveyancing and to make rights in land 'clearly defined, easily identifiable by third parties, and readily convertible into money'.[94]

Over the course of the transformation from feudalism to capitalism, legal principles of 'private property, free contract, and individual rights ... came to be seen as part of the natural order of things'.[95] It is arguable, however, that the type of collective property most often associated with the mediaeval open fields system never actually disappeared, meaning that 'the question of the commons is not and has never been archaic'.[96] Indeed, in the past few decades, the rights in common held over village greens have been specifically acknowledged and protected.[97] Courts are becoming more used to dealing with collective rights, holding, for example, that recreational easements and rights to use village greens registered under the Commons Acts are to be exercised collectively, on the basis of the common law principle of 'give and take'.[98]

Against the argument that 'the mid twentieth century template for a property interest—well established, clearly defined, and readily converted into money—is too rigid and simplistic',[99] other influential theorists have emphasised the need for clarity and stability in property rights.[100] The classic statement of what is required for a right or an interest to be included in the 'category of property, or of a right affecting property' is that it must be 'definable, identifiable by third parties, capable in its nature of assumption by third parties, and have some degree of permanence or stability'.[101] This presents difficulties for collective property rights, as illustrated by Susan Bright, who set out the principles that determine which rights should have a proprietary edge.[102] Citing *Thomson v Park*[103] as illustrative of the 'general principle' that a property right must be capable of practical enforcement, Bright concludes that 'rights requiring active cooperation and mutual trust and confidence between the right-holder and the landowner cannot be property rights'[104] within the system established by the Law of Property Act 1925. *Thomson* concerned a problematic licence agreement that one prep school would share another school's premises during wartime, and it was observed that 'the court cannot specifically enforce an agreement for two people to live peaceably under the same roof'.[105] However, those two 'people' in *Thomson* were a landlord and a lessee in a vertical

---

[94] Clarke (n 31) 120.

[95] Calavita (n 20) 18; see also Gordon (n 93).

[96] BJ McKay, 'Foreword' in N Dolšak and E Ostrom (eds) (n 28) xvi.

[97] Commons Registration Act 1965 and Commons Act 2006.

[98] *R (on the application of Lewis) v Redcar and Cleveland BC* [2010] UKSC 11; [2010] 2 AC 70 [48] (Walker JSC); and see the discussion in Adam Baker, 'Recreational Privileges as Easements: Law and Policy' [2012] *Conv* 37.

[99] Clarke (n 31) 121.

[100] See principally T Merrill and H Smith, 'Optimal Standardization in the Law of Property: The Numerus Clausus Principle' (2000) 110 *Yale Law Journal* 4, who argue that the alienability of property is central to property law.

[101] *National Provincial Bank Ltd v Ainsworth* [1965] AC 1175, 1278 (Wilberforce LJ).

[102] S Bright, 'Of Estates and Interests: A Tale of Ownership and Property Rights' in S Bright and J Dewar (eds), *Land Law: Themes and Perspectives* (Oxford, Oxford University Press, 1998).

[103] *Thomson v Park* [1944] KB 408.

[104] Bright (n 102) 541.

[105] *Thomson* (n 103) 409 (Lord Goddard).

relationship, whereas the collective property that is the subject of this chapter derives from the horizontal relationship between residents of equal status.

An alternative, functional conception of property which allows for change in the interests of the individual and of society has been put forward by scholars holding a range of different views about which rights are central to property.[106] Describing property as a rights paradigm, van der Walt argues that nonetheless interests that are not compatible with established property rights can be valued in the margins. He points to many examples of once marginal property interests joining the mainstream rights paradigm as a result of wider societal changes or of legal and political developments.[107] More specifically, in relation to the recognition of collective and individual rights, Fennell makes the point that 'as a human institution [property can] adapt dynamically to changing circumstances ... by moving the wall between common and private elements'.[108] The theory is that property practices established on the ground will be recognised at common law: 'the identification of 'property' in land is an earthily pragmatic affair',[109] which 'utilises a foundation of de facto control to generate a legal (hence normative) proprietary entitlement'.[110] There have indeed been some recent examples of this process at common law.[111] However, most recent new property rights have been introduced through legislation, which Bright describes as 'break[ing] the mould' for sound policy reasons, such as the spouse's statutory right of occupation in the matrimonial home.[112]

The history of the legislative reform of leasehold does not inspire confidence that collective property will soon achieve statutory recognition. Reflecting the power of vested interests, slow progress has been made in redressing the inherent imbalance of the vertical relationship between freeholder and leaseholder, involving almost 30 attempts over the past 100 years.[113] These include the Landlord and Tenant Acts 1985 and 1987, which enhanced the rights of individual leaseholders, and the Leasehold Reform, Housing and Urban Development Act 1993, which introduced collective enfranchisement for leaseholders of flats. Indicating the complexity achieved by these piecemeal reforms, a government-produced advice booklet for long leaseholders runs to just under 150 pages.[114] The long-awaited commonhold title, finally brought in by the Commonhold and Leasehold Reform Act 2002, has proved a failure, with less than 20 such developments registered to date.[115] Commonhold does not suit developers' interests and nor has it been adopted by groups wishing to establish intentional communities. The prescribed standard

---

[106] Eg, C Rotherham 'Conceptions of Property in Common Law Discourse' (1998) 18 *Legal Studies* 41.

[107] A van der Walt, *Property in the Margins* (Oxford, Hart Publishing, 2009).

[108] Fennell (n 5) 17.

[109] Gray and Gray (n 4) 104.

[110] Grear (n 91) 40.

[111] Instances include milk quotas: *Swift v Dairywise Farms Ltd* [2000] 1 WLR 1177; and carbon emission allowances, known as European Union Allowances: *Armstrong DLW GMBH v Winnington Networks Ltd* [2012] EWHC 10 (Ch).

[112] Bright (n 102) 545.

[113] S Blandy and D Robinson, 'Reforming Leasehold: Discursive Events and Outcomes, 1984–2000' (2001) 28 *Journal of Law and Society* 384.

[114] Communities and Local Government, *Residential Long Leaseholders: A Guide to Your Rights and Responsibilities* (London, Communities and Local Government, 2008).

[115] Personal communication to the author from the Land Registry, 17 February 2012.

documents for commonhold associations prevent the organic development of rules specific to each development, the company structure is onerous and does not reflect the true relationships between residents and there is no right to expel members, which some groups consider to be a necessary final sanction. Leasehold does, at least theoretically, offer the possibility of forfeiture for breach of covenant.

Other currently available legal structures include companies limited by shares or by guarantee, and trusts. In his discussion of the household from a law and economics theory perspective, Ellickson briefly considers these alternatives. He suggests rather unconvincingly that 'limited liability corporations with shares allocated in proportion to investments made' might be appropriate for cohousing, while a trust 'might serve occupants' interests, providing that the trustees were so instructed'.[116] Following her more thorough review of these options, Alison Clarke concludes that limited liability cannot reflect the commitment required from residents in collective property and that company formalities prevent the evolution of site-specific rules, whereas trusts are essentially an investment device not suited to self-governance.[117] The residents would be beneficiaries of the trust and, as such, would not be entitled to control and manage the trust property, as that is the role of the trustee. From the findings of my larger empirical study, it would seem that the trust structure can work well in sites where a small number of residents share collective property and wish to safeguard their shares acquired through monetary contributions to the property. However, for the reasons discussed by Clarke, the trust structure would not seem appropriate for larger sites such as the cohousing development. Fully mutual housing cooperatives offer an alternative structure for those committed to collective ownership and management[118] but as cooperative residents are tenants rather than owners, this legal framework is unlikely to have wide appeal. Further, a recent decision of the Supreme Court has highlighted deficiencies in the legal framework of housing cooperatives.[119]

VII. CONCLUSIONS

Returning for a final time to the imaginary island, we have seen that its property regime could be accommodated by contemporary property philosophy. By contrast, our actual property law framework is still centred on individual property ownership and does not recognise collective property. As Clarke points out, 'in real life we organise ourselves into communities for all sorts of purposes ... and we acquire and use resources in our group capacity. As long as we think only in private property terms, we have no satisfactory legal mechanisms for this group-holding of property'.[120] Cohousing is only one example among a range of different approaches

---

[116] Ellickson (n 77) 73.
[117] See Clarke (n 52) 349–56.
[118] Industrial and provident societies.
[119] *Berrisford v Mexfield Housing Co-operative Ltd* [2011] UKSC 52 found that a tenancy for life had been granted rather than a periodic tenancy. The Welsh government is committed to the introduction of a Housing Bill to resolve difficulties in the legal framework for housing cooperatives, but at the time of writing no parallel provision is envisaged for England.
[120] Clarke (n 31) 136.

to the management and ownership of common parts in multi-owned sites, which are becoming more common in England and around the world. Freyfogle accurately predicted the 'greater use of novel collective-management arrangements … that involve collaboration, cooperation and adaptive management'.[121] The empirical research on which this chapter is based indicates that a variety of such arrangements are already flourishing.

Investigating property 'from the bottom up' in sites such as in the cohousing development adds weight to the existing arguments that collective rights in property are in need of legal recognition, and provides an alternative to the legal positivist approach that can only produce normative property statements from existing statute and case law. This research was based on the premise that law and society are mutually constitutive. The literature on common-pool resources provides a valuable background for the examination of how self-governance mechanisms are continually developed by the residents, but cannot on its own tell us much about property relations or the relationship between state law and other forms of legal ordering. The critical question is whether the cohousing residents are engaged in legal ordering (in the form of property) or whether they are only creating 'order without law', to use Ellickson's term for describing how ranchers avoided law through the development and use of common-sense norms and informal rules.[122]

This research demonstrates that cohousing residents do more than social ordering. They exercise the rights to manage and control both their individual properties and the site's common parts collectively, and have developed complex mechanisms for self-governance through working rules which are capable of adaptation to suit new circumstances. Equally importantly, the cohousing residents have a sense of collective belonging and ownership. Their parallel rules, differing in material ways from formal law, constitute a different form of property incorporating collective self-governance which should now be legally recognised. The empirical methodological approach adopted here ensures that this conclusion is firmly based on property practices in real life, which should drive developments in the law.

---

[121] Freyfogle (n 27) 23.
[122] RC Ellickson, *Order Without Law: How Neighbors Settle Disputes* (Cambridge, MA, Harvard University Press, 1991).

9

Earth under the Nails: The Extraordinary Return to the Land

I. INTRODUCTION

P EOPLE ARE GOING back to the land. Not in the sense of returning to
farming or going back to the roots of their rural ancestors, but in the sense
of coming together to cultivate land and grow things. What is behind this
impetus to get dirt under the nails, how does it manifest itself, what is the enabling
legal framework, what, if any, land rights does it confer on those involved, and what
questions does this phenomenon raise for contemporary perceptions of property
and property law?

The growth of collective as opposed to individual interests in land can be
located against a wider social-cultural and legal background exemplified by twen-
ty-first-century changes to public access to the countryside and reforms to the law
relating to village and city greens and common ground.[1] Greater environmental
awareness and popular cultural concerns, such as the interest in organic food or
worries about vegetable air miles, are changing perceptions of land use and the
exploitation of natural resources, while the engagement of numerous interest
groups with land in which they may have no or very limited property rights has
shifted the boundaries of what is and is not within the domain of people's relationship with land. It is also clear that new partnerships between non-state players—
organisations and individuals—and public authorities are being forged, with land
forming a bridge between the two. This in turn is blurring the edges of what is
public land and what is private land, or the extent to which public interest is also
private interest. Increasingly mixed public/private land interests are emerging,
sometimes with uncertainty about the applicable legal regime.

The property law environment in which this shift is occurring is conservative and
grounded in early twentieth-century thinking about land. In order to facilitate land
transfers, a relatively limited range of rights and interests in land are recognised.

---

* Professor of Laws, University of Northumbria.
[1] Notably under the Commons Act 2006, the Countryside and Rights of Way Act 2000 and the
Land Reform (Scotland) Act 2003. Earlier legislation facilitating public access to land includes: s 193 of
the Law of Property Act 1925, the National Parks Access to the Countryside Act 1949, the Commons
Registration Act 1965 and certain procedural safeguards under s 123(2A) of the Local Government Act
1972, as amended.

Third party rights are also limited and often depend on the claimant having other land rights.[2] While considerations of 'public interest' may impinge on or support the exercise of the above (usually in the form of planning, environment or health and safety regulations), the use of 'public interest' to determine and create new rights is often constrained by statutory powers or requires new or amended legislation. Consequently, existing legal responses may be of limited use to a new breed of land interests, so that combinations of legal structures have to be utilised or non-legal arrangements made. At the same time, these new relationships of people with land challenge our understanding of what land as property means and the policies that underpin current land law.

This chapter starts by sketching the ways in which people are getting back to the land. It then considers the ways in which those involved are engaging with the legal framework or acting outside it. Recent developments in the law and their potential relevance to the various ways in which this return to the land manifests itself are also examined. Finally, the chapter reflects on the significance of this phenomenon as part of a broader shift in the relationship between people and things and the relevance this might have for defining and regulating our relationship with the land.

II. BACK TO THE LAND

Land and its association with social and political movements is nothing new. From the early days of feudalism, the enclosures of the late Tudor period and the Industrial Revolution[3] to garden cities and manifestations of the Victorian enthusiasm for the moral improvement of the labouring classes through the provision of green spaces in urban areas, land use has been a key to the age in which people live.

Despite an environment in which rural depopulation continues while urban populations increase,[4] greenbelts shrink[5] and the number of owner-occupiers has probably reached its peak,[6] the twenty-first century is witnessing an extraordinary return to the land. This is being evidenced in diverse forms: community gardens, orchards, woodlands and farms; city and school farms; land and crop sharing;

---

[2] Easements and 'neighbour rights' are typical examples, but early allotment rights and rights of common were generally appurtenant to other land rights. Exceptions are where these rights exist 'in gross'.

[3] Effected by private Acts of Parliament, enclosures continued until the mid-nineteenth century. In the period 1760–1800, some 3,554 private enclosure Acts were passed.

[4] During the twentieth century, the urban population of England increased from 77 per cent to 89 per cent. 'A Century of Change: Trends in UK Statistics since 1900', Research Paper 99/111, 21 December 1999, 13, http://www.parliament.uk/documents/commons/lib/research/rp99/rp99-111.pdf (21/03/2013). *The Guardian* suggests that this figure 'is set to rise to 92.2% by 2030': www.guardian.co.uk/news/datablog/2009/aug/18/percentage-population-living-cities. In 2010, the World Bank estimated that there were 56,059,103.66 urban residents in the UK, and the rural population represented just 10 per cent of the total population: www.tradingeconomics.com/united-kingdom/urban-population-wb-data.html.

[5] For recent greenbelt policy, see C Barclay, 'Greenbelt Standard Note', House of Commons SN/SC/934, 16 September 2011.

[6] The rate of owner-occupation increased from 10 per cent to 68 per cent between 1914 and 1999 (www.parliament.uk/documents/commons/lib/research/rp99/rp99-111.pdf, 12), peaking at 71 per cent in 2003, since when it has declined. The 2010 estimate was around 68 per cent according to the Royal Institute of Chartered Surveyors: S Dale 'Owner-occupier Rates Falling, Says RICS', www.mortgagestrategy.co.uk/economy/owner-occupier-rates-falling-says-rics/1023503.article.

escalating demands for allotments; claims for new commons and village greens and expanding pockets of guerrilla gardening. Some of these engagements with the land are transitory, while others are much more permanent.

The reasons for this return to the land are diverse, as is the identity of those involved,[7] but a number of themes emerge across the different forms that this engagement takes. Among these are notions of empowerment; building and nurturing community spirit; public engagement with physical space; concerns about sustainability and environmental responsibility; antipathy to waste, neglect and ugliness; physical and mental health enhancement; forging access to green spaces; and diverse educational imperatives. The twentieth century witnessed radical changes in land ownership. While the landed gentry lost land as a result of the impact of two world wars on male heirs, the burden of taxation and changes in agricultural policies and practices, and the collapse of industrialisation, other sectors of society acquired property as a result of the post-war social housing policy and the subsequent selling of much of this housing stock, the construction of new towns, the shift to high-rise urban construction, and latterly through promotion of the right to buy and owner-occupancy. The twenty-first century is arguably witnessing something different. Many people are landless (which is not synonymous with homeless) and live in high-density urban areas.[8] Even if they do not, increasingly people are becoming more environmentally aware, have more leisure time and are being encouraged, through various government initiatives, to pursue healthier lifestyles. There is also a dawning recognition that numerous aspects of local heritage are being lost, ranging from loss of biodiversity to loss of crafts and skills.

The present engagement of people with the land often originates in groups of private individuals, not public bodies, and is not necessarily linked to public policy goals but may indeed be a counteraction to the current policies and practices which inform land use and development. Some of the manifestations of the phenomenon remain outside or on the edges of the public domain, while others represent or become hybrid public/private relationships with land. Some find echoes in historical relations with land or are a continuation of these,[9] while others represent new departures.

III. FORMS OF ENGAGEMENT

People are getting back to the land in a variety of ways: through allotments; community farms, gardens, orchards and woodlands; and in schools, hospitals, housing developments and tenement blocks. Land in public or private ownership is

---

[7] Further research needs to be done to establish the demographic profile of those involved across the projects considered here, but information derived from the publicity material of various organisations suggests that there is demographic diversity.

[8] In the UK, for example, 69 per cent of the total land area is owned by 0.3 per cent of the population, and 89 per cent of people have an average 0.07 acres of living space each: R Reynolds, *On Guerrilla Gardening* (London, Bloomsbury, 2008) 41. Considerable areas of land are owned by the Crown (including the Duchy of Lancaster and Cornwall), the Church of England and bodies such as the National Trust and the Forestry Commission (and their Scottish equivalents). There are also still some very extensive private land-holdings.

[9] Eg, village greens and commons.

being used as well as land where ownership is unclear or disputed. Some forms of engagement have a long history of legal regulation; others do not or deliberately flout the law. Not all of these can be considered here, so the focus will be on a limited selection in order to give a sense of how this engagement manifests itself.

A. Allotments

Allotment gardening is probably the form of engagement with land with which people are most familiar. Allotment gardens date back to the period of enclosures of common land and the consolidation of scattered land-holdings by large estate owners. Originally, allotment holders were themselves land-holders (not usually landlords) or agricultural labourers, but today allotment holders may have no other land interests and may be individuals or small groups, cultivating land owned by others and dedicated for allotment gardening. The landlord may be a local authority, a trust—including large trusts such as the National Trust—a private landowner, a church[10] or a charity. Allotments holders may cultivate the land either under a lease or a contractual licence.

Early allotments were in rural areas or on the edge of villages or small towns and most were on private land and provided voluntarily, partly for philanthropic reasons but also to supplement poor agricultural wages,[11] but since the late nineteenth century, a statutory obligation was imposed on local authorities to provide allotment land where there was a need for or demand to provide such amenities for the labouring class.[12] The growth of private and public allotments in the pre-war years and during the two world wars declined with the advent of council housing, much of which had sizeable garden ground, so that the labouring classes could continue to cultivate vegetables, and gradually the availability of cheaper food. Many former allotments fell into neglect and from a high in 1943 of 1,750,000,[13] the number of allotments fell to 296,923 in 1996.[14] In 1997, the English Allotments Survey revealed that there were 43,000 untended, vacant plots and around 13,000 people registered on waiting lists for allotments.[15] However, the last decade has seen an upsurge in demand for allotments. Today there are about 330,000 allotments in use in the UK[16] and around 100,000 people are on waiting lists, which are getting

---

[10] Glebe land, owned by the church or parish, was frequently used for allotments to provide for the poor.

[11] See W Onslow (4th Earl of), *Landlords and Allotments: the History and Present Condition of the Allotment System* (1886, London, Longmans, Green and Co. Digital Reprint, Internet Archive, University of Toronto 2007).

[12] Under the Allotments Act 1887 and 1890. The socioeconomic status attached to allotments was only removed in 1919 by the Land Settlement (Facilities) Act.

[13] S Poole, *The Allotment Chronicles* (Kettering, Silverlink Publishing, 2006) appendix 1, 205.

[14] P Clayden, *The Law of Allotments* (Dartford, Shaw & Sons, 2002) 5. However, Poole ((n 13) 200) suggests that there were 400,000 allotments remaining in the 1990s.

[15] 'English Allotments Survey: Report of the Joint Survey of Allotments in England', National Society of Allotment and Leisure Gardeners Limited and Anglia Polytechnic University, November 1997, 7. See also a Survey of Allotments, Community Gardens and City Farms by the University of Derby, July 2006, Department of Communities and Local Government.

[16] Reynolds (n 8) 43.

longer, with some people having to wait over a year to get an allotment.[17] The traditional size of an allotment is 10 poles—which equates roughly to one-sixteenth of an acre.[18]

Although overall responsibility for government policy in respect of allotments lies with the central government in the Department for Communities and Local Government (DCLG) (except where devolved), responsibility for acquiring land for allotments—either by compulsory acquisition, from its land stock or by leasing— lies with the various local authorities.[19] Because of boundary changes, poor record-keeping and general neglect over the years, many local authorities are unaware or unable to indicate how much allotment land they have or where it is located.[20] The current demand for allotments has also encouraged some private landlords to diversify into leasing land for allotments under agreements which do not have any of the statutory protections afford to allotments in the public domain. Although there have been some attempts to map the current location and acreage of allotments, the extent of allotment land remains unclear.[21]

While allotment gardening is one of the areas of engagement with land which is regulated by statute, the legislative framework is incoherent and in need of rationalisation. There is a plurality of laws that govern different aspects of allotments, many of which reflect the original policy issues behind this form of land use.[22] There are therefore a number of areas of uncertainty which arise. Some of these concern the powers and obligations imposed on local authorities, for example, the interpretation of the mandatory duty under the Smallholdings and Allotments Act 1908 to provide a 'sufficient' number of allotments,[23] the requirements in section 146 of the Law of Property Act 1925 to give 'a reasonable opportunity' to a tenant to remedy a breach which provides grounds for terminating the tenancy, and whether the statutory twelve-month period for written notice to terminate can in any circumstances be shortened.[24]

---

[17] Department for Communities and Local Government, 'Survey of Allotments, Community Gardens and City Farms', No 23, 2006, Urban Research Summary, 3–4. See also Farida Vis and Yana Manyukhina, 'The English Allotment Lottery' (*The Guardian*, 10 November 2011), www.guardian. co.uk/news/datablog/2011/nov/10/allotments-rents-waiting-list.

[18] A pole was also referred to as a rod, perch or lug and measured about 5.5 yards (5.027 metres). The legislation is inconsistent on measurements, so it would seem that while the norm is not more than 40 poles, there is flexibility on this.

[19] In England, local authorities include parish councils, borough councils and district councils. If a district council proposes to get rid of allotment land, usually for development purposes, then the consent of the Secretary of State is required: Allotments Act 1925, s 8.

[20] This lack of basic data may explain why recommendations by two select committees on allotments and the applicable laws came to nothing. These were the Thorpe Committee of Inquiry into Allotments in 1969 (Cmnd 4166) and a Select Committee in 1998, the Environment, Transport and Regional Affairs—Fifth Report 1997–1998 'The Future of Allotments' House of Commons.

[21] This was being done using open access mapping: http://wiki.openstreetmap.org/wiki/Allotments_Project.

[22] Legislation includes: the Small Holdings and Allotments Act 1908, the Land Settlement (Facilities) Act 1919, the Allotments Act 1922, 1925 and 1950, the Small Holdings and Allotments Act 1926 and the Agricultural Land (Utilisation) Act 1931. Legislation governing planning and local authority powers is also relevant, eg the Local Government, Planning and Land Act 1980, the Town and Country Planning Act 1990, the Local Government Acts 1972 and 1992 and the Local Government (Wales) Act 1994.

[23] Small Holdings and Allotments Act 1908, s 23(1).

[24] Allotments Act 1922, s 1(1)(A) (amended by Allotments Act 1950, s 1).

From the point of view of the allotment holder, there are questions about rent reviews, compensation for crops or land improvement on the termination of the allotment lease, whether planning permission is required for greenhouses and sheds,[25] whether livestock can be kept on allotments as of right or only subject to permission of the local authority[26] and whether flowers as opposed to vegetables can be grown.[27] With the increasing demand for allotments, there is evidence to suggest that some public authorities are imposing quite considerable rent increases and imposing more restrictive conditions on allotment activity.[28] There is also evidence that some local authorities designate allotment sites as temporary and that this uncertain status can persist over several decades. While under statute the tenants of local authority allotments are secure for a maximum of 12 months, the designation of 'temporary' avoids some of the statutory protections afforded to tenants.[29] Although many allotment agreements will be in writing, with an implied renewal from year to year after the first year, some may not, and where an agreement is verbal, it will only operate as a tenancy at will until rent referable to a yearly tenancy is paid.[30] Most allotment agreements contain standard, non-negotiable terms restricting what can and cannot be done on allotments, and may include residential requirements for application eligibility. Rights of re-entry are also usually attached to allotment agreements and are exercisable in the case of non-payment of rent or breach of the terms—including non-cultivation. Allotment agreements may also be terminated by serving notices to quit and forfeiture followed by orders to recover possession.

B. Community Land Spaces

While allotments provide access to land for individual members of the community in which the allotments are situated, community land spaces are emerging as a distinctive category of land use. Community land spaces may be community orchards, gardens, farms, woodlands or green burial sites. The projects may involve other community or public organisations such as schools, hospitals, parish councils, local authorities or private individuals, for example, landowners or local businesses.

Advocates of community growing projects suggest that 'they promote access to a nutritious diet, physical activity and mental well-being while fostering a sense of social inclusion and community cohesion'.[31] While the nutritious diet will not always be relevant to community projects, certainly the success of community

---

[25] Different rules apply to previously agricultural land compared to land that was not previously agricultural: Town and Country Planning Act 1990.

[26] Section 12 of the Allotments Act 1950 suggests that chickens and rabbits can be kept 'as of right', while s 61 of the Small Holdings and Allotments Act 1908 suggests the same for bees.

[27] Fruit-growing raises further issues as many fruit trees and shrubs have to be in situ for several years before they yield good crops and are of course 'attached to the land'.

[28] See Vis and Manyukhina (n 17). The statutes do not state a rent, only that it should be what 'a tenant may reasonably be expected to pay': Allotments Act 1950, s 10.

[29] Allotments on private land may also escape various statutory protections.

[30] Clayden (n 14) 48.

[31] A O'Neill, 'Growing Projects; Harnessing the Opportunities', Edinburgh Community Backgreens Association, 2010, 2, www.ecba.org.uk/health.aspx.

land spaces depends on people coming together and collaborating in a common cause. Such projects may be a catalyst for better community relations, especially intergenerational relations, may create safe spaces in otherwise hostile environments and may be a vehicle for new or improved liaison with other organisations such as educational institutions, mental health services, local charities and NGOs, as well as public and private landowners.

i. Community Orchards

Orchards and their related biodiversity have been under threat for some time. It is estimated that since the 1950s, about 63 per cent of orchards have been lost,[32] with the percentage being much higher in some counties,[33] with a consequential loss of biodiversity in fruit trees and dependent flora and fauna. Some community orchards have been a rescue response to old orchards under threat,[34] while others have been established as new orchards. Landowners of orchards may be the Crown Commissioners, local authorities, private individuals, corporations[35] or members of the community themselves.

According to the organisation Common Ground, there are around 300 registered community orchards in the UK—with new orchards and revived old orchards being added every year with additional orchard activity marking special occasions such as the millennium and the Queen's Diamond Jubilee.[36] Orchards not only provide a green space but also the possibility of edible harvests and related products, such as jams and apple and pear cider. Consequently, while some community orchards will be essentially non-trading entities, others may combine trading activities with other activities such as education, the provision of leisure space, community gardening projects and so on. This in turn may influence the legal form or forms which are adopted.

ii. Community Gardens

There are estimated to be around 1,000 community gardens in the UK.[37] Like community orchards, community gardens are increasingly popular and may perform a number of functions. They may be established on existing cultivated land, such as school or hospital grounds, or on private or local authority derelict or neglected land,[38] either for a specific project, such as a memorial garden, or as social and therapeutic space, or to improve an eyesore.

---

[32] Natural England, quoted in the *Community Orchards Handbook* 2008,14.

[33] As much as 90 per cent in Kent and Devon, for example.

[34] Eg Cleeve Prior, Worcestershire and Carhampton Community Orchard, Somerset.

[35] In Birmingham, for example, a community orchard was established on land originally owned by British Rail.

[36] See for example, orchards such as that at Baslow to celebrate the Queen's Jubilee, which was opened in November 2012, http://www.baslow-orchard.org/, the Diamond Jubilee Community Orchard on the Game and Wildlife Conservation Trust's Allerton Project research farm at Loddington in Leicestershire and the Jubilee Community Orchard in Bourton-on-the-Water which formally opened in April 2012.

[37] Federation of City Farms and Community Gardens (FCFCG), www.farmgarden.org.uk.

[38] The FCFCG starter pack suggests: common land on a housing estate, allotment plots, hospital grounds, land owned by a charity for public benefit, land within existing parks and recreation grounds, old churchyards and cemeteries, school grounds, urban fringe agricultural land, waste ground and derelict sites.

For example, one of the most successful enterprises has taken place in Edinburgh, where over half of the city's residents live in high-rise tenement buildings which enclose backgreens.[39] Along with stairwells and roofs these are communal areas, but with a rapid turnover of tenants and often disinterested landlords, many were neglected. Initiatives to form Community Backgreen Associations started in the early 2000s, and have led to the development of 16 community gardens in backgreens to date, including, in some cases, the leasing of gardening space to non-residents of the tenement block where the backgreen is situated.

In the Edinburgh example, the community gardeners were already on site and had lawful access to the backgreens of the tenement buildings, although traditionally (except for ground-floor tenants) only for drying rights and not cultivation rights. Often, however, community gardens will be cultivated on land belonging to others, sometimes with permission, sometimes without—especially if the land is neglected or ownership is unclear.

iii. Community Farms and City Farms

Community farms bring together people who want to grow their own food but do not have access to sufficient land to do so individually. The structure of community farms may vary. For example, Loxley Community Farm, near Sheffield, established in 2009, is a not-for profit social enterprise set up as a company limited by guarantee. It is run as a cooperative, with all members paying an annual membership fee and purchasing individual or co-owned shares entitling them to pro-rata produce. Members are expected to contribute a minimum number of hours of labour and any profits are ploughed back into the project. Originally, the community rented a site from a private landlord, but has recently acquired land from the council through a partnership set up by members. The farm now pays rent to the partners, raising the money through membership fees.[40]

In Somerset, members of the Chew Valley Community Farm run a not-for-profit organic vegetable business on 22 acres of private farmland. The farm is run as a community-benefit society. Funds are raised by annual membership subscriptions and lifelong investor-share membership, under which investors are able to purchase shares in the farm. By 2011, enough money had been raised under two Community Share Offers to enable the Community Farm to take over the business of growing, boxing and selling organic produce from the landowners' company.

Farming is not just a rural pursuit. There are 59 city farms registered with the FCFCG. Emerging in the 1970s, city farms take a variety of forms, but usually share common features of being in urban areas and providing local educational and recreational facilities. Most are working farms, but may also have conservation areas, community gardens, play areas and leisure facilities. Some sell their surplus produce and a number now employ staff as well as using volunteers. Many offer opportunities of engagement with horticulture and livestock to disadvantage groups. Most city farms are now charities, although their origins are diverse.

---

[39] Edinburgh Community Backgreens Association, www.ecba.org.uk/home.aspx.
[40] Email communication with Loxley Community Farm, 2 March 2012.

In London, where the first city farms started, there is considerable diversity of structure and land interests. Surrey Docks Farm, for example, is a Provident Society, although it is also a charity, while Woodland Farm near Welling/Woolwich was originally a cooperative run by the Royal Arsenal Cooperative Society in the 1920s on existing farmland as a 'model' pig farm. The farm fell into disuse in the 1980s, but in 1997 the Woodlands Farm Alliance bought a 999-year lease from the Co-operative Wholesale Society, which then owned the land, and established a charitable trust. Hackney City Farm started in the derelict lorry parking lot of a haulage company on land that had formerly been private farm land, but in 1982 the City Farm was given a 100-year lease by Hackney Council. Formerly dependent on modest grants from the London Borough of Hackney, cutbacks have meant that it must supplement grant income with earned income, so it is now a combination of a community and a commercial enterprise. Stepney City Farm, which was also set up in the 1980s, is built on land owned and preserved for recreational use by the King George VI Playing Fields' Trust. The farm became a charity in 2009. Vauxhall City Farm started as a squat on an abandoned bomb site. The squatters started to cultivate the land and raise chickens, and in 1977 Lambeth Council recognised the squat. Today the land is leased from Lambeth Council.

Windmill Hill City Farm in Bristol was the first city farm outside London and was established in 1976 on urban wasteland. Today it is run as a registered charity and a company limited by guarantee. It has a board of trustees and its activities are determined by its articles of association and memorandum of understanding. It attracts funding from a range of sources[41] as well as generating income from its training courses and leisure facilities.

Some city farms are therefore taking the land back to its roots, while others are reclaiming a heritage contact with land for the benefit of present and future generations. Although it is not clear how much land is taken up with community projects, some statistics suggest that this movement is more than negligible. For example, it is claimed that community gardens and city farms provide approximately 2,500 annual training places for adults with learning disabilities, employ the equivalent of approximately 500 full-time paid staff and over 15,000 volunteers, and have a combined annual turnover of up to £40 million.[42]

iv. Guerrilla Gardening

Guerrilla gardening is 'illicit gardening on someone else's land'.[43] Most often it is gardening by those who are themselves landless, on land that may be private or public, and may be neglected or only partially cultivated, and the gardening takes place (at least initially) without permission. Thus, 'gardens' may be planted on roundabouts, neglected churchyards, unkempt municipal flowerbeds, roadside verges, empty industrial sites, rooftops or in the pavements around street trees. According to Richard Reynolds, guerrilla gardening is 'a battle for resources, a battle against

---

[41] Including the John Paul Getty Foundation, the Big Lottery Fund and the Nominet Trust.
[42] See www.farmgarden.org.uk/farms-gardens.
[43] Reynolds (n 8) 5.

scarcity of land, environmental abuse and wasted opportunities. It is also a fight for freedom of expression and for community cohesion'.[44] Although there are older similar movements,[45] the present movement is international, having first started in New York in the 1970s as part of the counter-culture movement of the time.[46] While it has political overtones as a form of protest, it is also a social and cultural phenomenon which brings people together either as individual members of the movement or as groups initiating community projects through guerrilla gardening. Gardens may be planted to provide food, to serve as memorials,[47] to draw attention, by comparison, to the ugliness of buildings, to provide an educative or leisure space, or to enrich the biodiversity of the urban landscape.

Although technically illegal, involving torts of trespass and nuisance, potential breaches of the criminal law,[48] and in some cases breaches of health and safety legislation or planning law, the prosecution of guerrilla gardeners in the UK seems very rare, although guerrilla gardens may be destroyed either by officials or vandals. The legal armoury of local authorities seeking to prosecute guerrilla gardeners is weak. While gardening on central reservations, roundabouts or railway sidings may raise health and safety issues, often it is the local authority that should be charged with health and safety offences for allowing the land to become a hazard—for example, because of the rubbish fly-tipped on it, the use to which it is put for drug-dealing and prostitution or because noxious weeds such as ragwort are allowed to take hold. The tort of trespass is available to these landlords, but the quantum of damages is likely to be negligible if the guerrilla gardeners have cleared the space of rubbish and enhanced it by planting. Similarly, the tort of nuisance is unlikely to successfully pursued, especially where the gardeners may have removed a number of the pre-existing potential nuisances.[49] It is also the case that urban development, the privatisation of formerly national assets such as railways, and the shifting demarcation of council and borough boundaries leaves land orphaned. There are pockets of land that lie unclaimed or the ownership of which is unclear. There is also land which has been purchased for development, often by non-resident investors (especially in London), which is left undeveloped. Thus, the issue arises as to who is to bring any legal claim, and it may be many years before the guerrilla gardening activity is challenged.

Guerrilla gardeners are therefore often doing local councils a favour.[50] Indeed, a number of projects which have started out as guerrilla gardens have subsequently been given official approval. Where community gardens are initially established

---

[44] Ibid.

[45] Eg that of the Diggers led by Gerrard Winstanly in 1649; see L Berens, *The Digger Movement in the Days of the Commonwealth* (London, Simpkin, Marshall, Hamilton, Kent and Co Ltd, 1906).

[46] 'Flower power' at its most literal. Reynolds claims that the term was coined by Liz Christy in New York: Reynolds (n 8) 75.

[47] There is, eg, a guerrilla project marking homophobic attacks by the planting of pansies throughout England and the US: ibid, 35.

[48] See R Ward and R Card, 'Access to the Countryside—The Impact of the Criminal Justice and Public Order Act 1994' (1996) *Journal of Planning and Environment Law* 447.

[49] See similarly criminal damage.

[50] The costs of watering, pruning and planting land and collecting litter are high and cash-strapped local authorities rarely have the resources, so effectively members of the public are performing a public service.

through guerrilla gardening, local councils may either adopt such gardens or provide alternative 'official' ground for community gardens, thereby incidentally terminating guerrilla status. Institutional recognition may be given in other ways; for example, Newcastle University has a guerrilla gardening group which operates openly under the Student Union Community Action programme and won an Orange award under its 'Do some good' initiative.[51] Ironically, improvements to the locality due to guerrilla gardening undertaken as a protest against private property or public authority neglect may enhance the value of property in the area, putting at risk any undeveloped land and further excluding those who have no land.

The categories indicated above are not closed and the boundaries between them are porous. For example, a bit of individual guerrilla gardening may attract a community following and become a community garden which may include or become a community orchard or may take over neglected allotment ground, or part of an allotment site may become a community garden.[52] The local authority may intervene to adopt the community project and provide assistance and support, or it may seek to remove it and offer in exchange other land or other sites for the activity. Alternatively, a private landowner may seek diversification and set aside some land for allotments or for a community orchard or woodland, or donate or lease land for a farm-share scheme. There are therefore a number of possible permutations and so legal structures need to be adaptable. However, as the next part of this chapter shows, the legal environment is a somewhat unkempt garden and could do with some attention.

IV. THE LEGAL ENVIRONMENT

Although there are a number of shared aspects to the motives behind the various projects which mark this return to the land, the legal framework is very fractured, and even within projects sharing similar aspects there is diversity. So, for example, of the 590 members of the Federation of City Farms and Community Gardens, 12 are charitable companies, 22 are charities, seven are companies, 16 are constituted associations, four fall into the public sector, two are trusts and five are unconstituted groups. One is an industrial and provident society.[53] In many cases, the legal status or constitution of the members is unknown or unrecorded, as is their legal relationship with the land.[54] For those communities or individuals keen to get 'earth under their nails', there are a number of organisations which offer advice and information, including legal advice and templates for documents such as constitutions and leases. Not all, however, point to the advantages and/or disadvantages of different legal models or the various alternatives that exist, and in practice there seems to be considerable diversity of legal forms applicable to this return to the land. In order

[51] SCAN, www.nusu.co.uk/scan.

[52] Eg near Newcastle, the Prudhoe Community Allotment which opened in 2006 to give access to disabled and elderly gardeners and non-gardeners is on part of an allotment site.

[53] Email communication from the FCFCG, 9 August 2011. Where allotment associations wish to own their allotment land, they are required to incorporate, for example, under the Industrial and Provident Societies Acts 1965 to 2002.

[54] Further research is in hand to try and address this.

to understand this, I have chosen to focus on just some of the legal structures which are being used and to consider their suitability for these forms of engagement.

As has been indicated, in the case of allotments, the relationship of people with the land is largely governed by legislation. The need to consolidate and review this has been highlighted in several government papers—without effect[55]—and in any case the legislation alone may not govern all aspects of allotment gardening. Importantly, the various applicable laws do not stipulate the legal arrangements between the allotment holders themselves, who may form local associations, site committees or affiliate individually, or as groups, with the allotment representative body at a local or national level. Although local authorities often devolve the management of allotments to these associations,[56] the legal status of these—and therefore the extent of liability of individual members—may be unclear or uncertain.

Therefore, in the case of allotments the applicable law will be a mix of specific legislation and the law relating to unincorporated associations or societies, leases and licences. Whether the allotments are on public or private land, various planning laws, health and safety regulations and local bylaws may also apply. In the case of allotments on private land, there may be covenants or easements binding on the allotment holders, and it may be unclear whether the land is or is not governed by laws regulating agricultural land, depending on the former status of such land.[57]

Community land initiatives may also use, or be bound by, many of the above, and may also come under the laws governing companies limited by guarantee, community interest companies, charitable trusts, co-ownership or cooperatives. Some of the limitations to these legal regimes are well known to property lawyers,[58] although gardening projects may raise particular issues. For example, in the case of unincorporated associations, there may be particular uncertainties relating to any movable or immovable property which may be acquired, what land laws they fall under—especially if the land is or was agricultural land—and what is to happen to that property in the event that the association ceases to operate.

It has been held, in a case concerning an allotment association, that during its existence, the assets of the association were held collectively under a species of co-ownership by current members subject to any contractual obligations under the rules of the association. On its dissolution, these assets were to be divided equally among the current members.[59] This 'contract-holding theory' has been recently endorsed[60] and seems to be the preferred way of approaching the property

---

[55] See n 19.

[56] Under the enabling provisions of the Local Government Act 1972.

[57] Eg under the Landlord and Tenant Act 1954, which offers security of tenure, farm business tenancies are excluded (s 43) so that they fall under the relatively insecure provisions of the Agricultural Tenancies Act 1995. See I Dawson, 'Farming and the Divide between the Landlord and Tenant Act 1954 and the Agricultural Tenancies Act 1995' (2000) *Journal of Business Law* 541.

[58] Regarding the uncertain status of unincorporated associations, see P Harris, 'Company, Person, Body of Persons, Entity: What's the Difference and Why?' (2011) *British Tax Review* 188.

[59] *Re St Andrews Allotment Association* [1969] 1 WLR 229.

[60] *Hanchett-Stamford v Attorney General* [2008] EWHC 330 (Ch).

holding of such groups.[61] While this approach overcomes problems associated with the receipt of gifts, insofar as it is presumed that the property is given to the trustees of the beneficial co-ownership rather than to individual members or to the association for its purposes, confusion as to the exact nature of this 'species' of co-ownership or joint tenancy remains. Much may also depend on the drafting of the constitution of the unincorporated association and any document transferring land or any other property to the association.

In the case of leases, where these are used for community projects, there are challenges to one of the fundamental principles of a lease: exclusive possession. The membership of the community and the purposes of the project will usually require access by many people most of the time and it is likely that the membership will be fluid. Leases are also for a determinable period of time, so that where long-term investment is made in the form of tree planting or landscaping, there may be questions about sustainability or compensation on the expiry of the lease. Inevitably, therefore, some of these projects may be short-lived, for example, where a local council grants a short-term lease over vacant land for a community project and then decides that it needs the land for development. Even where leases or periodic tenancies are renewable, they may not be renewed or rents may be increased to unaffordable levels.[62] Where leases are for longer periods, the question of enforceability of management agreements or tenancy agreements regarding how the land is to be used and what services are to be provided may arise in respect of successors in title, for example, where council boundaries alter or where the composition of the community group changes.

Where licences are used, the dangers inherent in the revocability of licences and the personal nature of these present potential problems, especially if the project is to continue over an extended period of time.[63]

Some legal forms may be better suited to this engagement with the land but may be more expensive to use or more complicated to understand. These include some recent and proposed innovations.

A. Charitable Incorporated Organisation

There have been proposals since 2007 to introduce a hybrid institution, similar to the unincorporated association but with the advantages of charitable status, which would make it possible to own land, although probably not to lease it. The scope to do so is found in the Charities Act 2006 (England and Wales) and the Charities and Trustee Investment (Scotland) Act 2005.[64] As Cross explains, recognition of the deficiencies of existing legal structures has prompted the design of a new legal form.

---

[61] See S Baughen, 'Performing Animals and the Dissolution of Unincorporated Associations: The "Contract Holding Theory" Vindicated' [2010] *Conv* 216.

[62] Often original leases are negotiated for 'peppercorn' rent or the payment of rent in kind, eg apples from community orchards. See also http://peppercornrent.co.uk/.

[63] Legal developments in law post-*Bruton v London Quadrant Housing Trust* [2000] AC 1 may be significant here, however, if there is a shift towards the personal contractual nature of land rights.

[64] See S Cross, 'New Legal Forms for Charities in the United Kingdom (2008) *Journal of Business Law* 662 for background.

The Charitable Incorporated Organisation (CIO) has a separate legal personality from its members, who are therefore safeguarded from any liabilities incurred by the organisation. Designed to provide the benefits of incorporation without the burdens of being a company, the CIO may provide a useful model for community land projects.[65] Provided that the purpose of the applicant body is charitable within the enlarged scope of the 2006 Charities Act or its Scottish equivalent, the CIO is available either to new charities or to existing charitable companies wishing to convert. An unincorporated charity wishing to become a CIO first has to create a CIO, then transfer assets and liabilities to it, and then wind up the unincorporated charity. This may be off-putting for unincorporated charities, but for those established as companies limited by guarantee, or new charities, the CIO has the attractions of only requiring one registration with the Charity Commission, not the current two with the Charity Commission and the Registrar of Companies, lower costs, and fewer annual returns and reports. However, there are concerns that the extent of the rights and duties of members is not always clear from the legislation and the fit with existing company law may need to be worked out in more detail.[66] It also seems likely that the CIO (or its Scottish equivalent, the SCIO) will operate alongside the various pre-existing forms of incorporation, so that community groups may be faced with a confusing choice of forms.

Unfortunately, while the Scottish CIO was launched in January 2012,[67] this has been delayed in England and Wales. Consequently, here, community projects seeking some form of corporate status still have to go down the company law route.

B. Community Interest Companies

Although some community land ventures may adopt the company limited by guarantee structure in order to limit the liability of members, a new alternative is now available. Emerging from various working groups in 2001,[68] Community Interest Companies (CICs) came on the scene in 2005. Defined as 'a business with primarily social objectives, whose surpluses are primarily reinvested in the business or community',[69] a CIC is registered initially either as a company limited by guarantee or a company limited by shares. It can then apply to the CIC Regulator to be registered as a CIC and change its name to reflect this. Approval depends on sufficient evidence of community interest and benefit. Directors are accountable both to Companies House and the CIC Regulator. In the context of community land projects, CICs may be useful because they include 'asset lock' mechanisms to protect land, other assets and any profits these generate, retaining these for the benefit of the community and also preventing demutualisation through the

---

[65] C Priestley, 'Charitable Incorporated Associations' (2009) *Private Client Business* 149.
[66] Cross (n 64) 687.
[67] Following provisions made for this in the Charities and Trustee Investment (Scotland) Act 2005.
[68] See Cross (n 64) and J Burchfield, 'Private Action, Public Benefit' (2003) 2 *Private Client Business* 110.
[69] Department for Business Innovation and Skills, 'Community Interest Companies', www.bis.gov.uk/cicregulator/about-us.

distribution of profits and assets to directors and/or members. However, the CIC is not charitable in status and so lacks the advantages accruing to charities, although for some purposes it seems it they may be treated similarly to incorporated charities.[70] Today there are over 5,000 registered CICs. The 5,000th CIC, which registered in April 2011, was Hogacre Common Eco Park in Oxfordshire, which acquired college playing fields to convert into a community woodland.[71]

C. Community Land Trusts

'A community land trust is a mechanism for the democratic ownership of land and housing by the local community. This model of tenure also potentially allows for the reinvestment of any land profits back into community interest.'[72] Although envisaged primarily as a way of generating affordable social housing, the definition of a community land trust is broad enough to include a number of community land projects provided a) the trust is a corporate body, b) which is established 'for the express purpose of furthering the social, economic and environmental interests of a local community by acquiring and managing land and other assets in order to benefit the community'.[73] As the community land trust can only manage the land in such a way as the members of the community believe to be beneficial, there is effectively an asset lock on the land. A further condition on the community land trust is that any profits made from the management of its assets are used to benefit the local community and that anyone in the specified area of locality has the right to become a member of the community land trust. It is the members who control the trust. No particular form of incorporation is specified, so community land trusts may be charities, companies limited by guarantee, industrial provident societies, community interest companies or cooperatives.[74]

D. Community Asset Transfer Arrangements

It is possible for local authorities to transfer land to communities under the initiative of community asset transfers. Although this is not a new power available to local councils, it has received recent impetus through the 2007 Quirk Review and

---

[70] I Dawson and J Adler, 'The Nature of the Proprietary Interest of a Charitable Company or a Community Interest Company in its Property' (2007) *Trust Law International* 3, 15.

[71] See www.bis.gov.uk/assets/bispartners/cicregulator/docs/quarterly-reports/11-p119c-community-interest-companies-operational-report-first-quarter-2011-2012.

[72] C Handy, 'Community Land Trusts' (2010) *Journal of Housing Law* 83. As the author points out, these are not an entirely novel concept. See the inception of Letchworth Garden City in 1910: 'From Garden City to Green City', Lambeth Garden Museum.

[73] Housing and Regeneration Act 2008, s 79(2).

[74] 'A co-operative is an autonomous association of persons united voluntarily to meet common economic, social and cultural objectives through a jointly owned and democratically controlled enterprise': (2008) *Company Lawyer* 306. Cooperatives may be registered under the Industrial and Provident Societies Act 1965 (and are registerable under the Co-operative and Community Benefit Societies and Credit Unions Act 2010 when it comes into force) or be a company, a partnership, unregistered unincorporated association or a limited liability partnership.

the establishment of the government-funded Asset Transfer Unit (ATU).[75] However, local authorities will rarely make outright transfers of ownership of land to communities and may prefer to lease or grant a licence to the community for its proposed project, or for the community to take over the management of an existing project, for example, a park, garden or memorial site. The arrangement can work well and can build good relationships between communities and councils,[76] but may also be challenging in terms of negotiating terms which are favourable to both sides and can be legally complicated because of the potential involvement of several local government departments.[77] Supporters of CATs argue that 'Managing these facilities helps to empower local communities and can bring opportunities for greater independence and financial sustainability. When done well, CAT can create lasting change in local neighbourhoods',[78] while sceptics suggest that this is a good way for local authorities to balance their books in the present climate of austerity without the problem of releasing capital.[79]

The above discussion indicates some of the legal forms which may be used by land projects. Some projects, however, appear to operate outside any legal formality and depend on 'gentlemen's agreements', goodwill or mutual trusts. Other more novel arrangements also emerge, for example, crop-shares and tree leases in community orchards, raised-bed leasing in the community backyards of tenement buildings, land-sharing,[80] community farm shares and local food coalitions.[81]

V. THE RELATIONSHIP BETWEEN PEOPLE AND LAND

This return to the land poses two challenges to orthodox land law. The first is that if property law is about rights in respect of property (real rights or rights in realty which are 'proper' to an individual or incorporated body), then in most of the above examples, it appears that quite nebulous property rights in the traditional sense are being acquired. If any rights are being acquired, they may be 'weak' rights, such as use rights rather than possession or ownership rights. What is replacing the language of rights in these situations is the language of obligations: people are engaging with the land as custodians or guardians for future generations and are seeing the land as valuable in a variety of social and cultural ways. Land in this way is perceived as heritage, not as in the past of the propertied elite, but of the 'common man', and not as communal or state property in a Platonic or Marxist sense. This growing sense of 'stewardship' of land (which is distinct from but perhaps related

---

[75] This is part of 'Locality', an organisation formed by the merger of the Development Trusts Association and the British Association of Settlements and Social Action Centres; see atu.org.uk.

[76] See, eg, S Salman, 'Making Community Asset Transfer Work' (*The Guardian*, 25 May 2011).

[77] There is a legal toolkit provided by ATU.

[78] Bristol City Council, www.bristol.gov.uk/page/community-asset-transfer-policy.

[79] D Alcock, 'Community Asset Transfer—Where Balancing the Books and "Big Society" Meet' (*The Guardian*, 8 December 2010).

[80] Described as a social network for the 'grow your own movement' to connect people who want to grow food with people who have land: www.landshare.net.

[81] See for example, Incredible Edible Todmorden, www.incredible-edible-todmorden.co.uk/history.

to the countryside stewardship scheme)[82] can concern land in the public or private domain, but the forms of engagement outlined above may be distinct from and not dependent on ownership.

The second challenge which flows from the above is whether the concept of property as a 'bundle of rights' needs to be reconsidered or reinterpreted. For example, do traditional understandings of ownership and possession need to change? Do these forms of engagement with the land mark a shift in the balance between the general interests of the community and the protection of the individual's fundamental property rights—for example, under Article 1, Protocol 1 of the European Convention on Human Rights?[83] Do the phenomena considered above mark 'a move away from individualisation and the atomised society to one there where is more co-operation and socialisation'[84] and, if so, how does this relate to property law?

The previous position in which there was 'no general legal recognition that there may be wider interests in the use of the countryside going beyond the rights of property owners'[85] and that 'the notion of a public right of recreation is not a traditionally recognised legal category'[86] has already changed with the Countryside and Rights of Way Act 2000, and is set to change further with the Marine and Coastal Access Act 2009.[87] Assessments of 'proportionality' in respect of private property rights may therefore be changing. Similarly, it has already been recognised that the absence of a specific property interest to which a right can attach may not be fatal,[88] and it may be that where the land is under the control of a public authority, claims of ownership rights may have to succumb to reasonableness principles, taking into account a wider understanding of public interest.[89] Support for this direction of legal development is implied in the consultation surrounding the 'Community right to challenge' and the 'Community right to buy', which took place in 2011.[90]

---

[82] Introduced in 1991 as a government initiative to encourage farmers to diversify their agricultural practices in an environmentally friendly way, this scheme is being phased out and existing projects will come to an end in 2014, to be replaced by an Environmental Stewardship Scheme.

[83] The requirement of economic value of property to bring it within the Convention right may be challengeable, and the infringement defence of 'public interest' might be enlarged.

[84] This is a question asked by Handy in respect of cooperative housing schemes: C Handy, 'Housing Co-operatives: Legal Issues' (2011) *Journal of Housing Law* 29.

[85] Ward and Card (n 48) 447.

[86] J Hill, 'Public Access to Land for the Purpose of Recreation' [1988] *Conv* 369.

[87] For comment, see B Mayfield, 'Troubled Waters: The Unifying Influence of Conservation and Public Health on the Access Provisions of the Marine and Coastal Access Act' (2009) 30 *Liverpool Law Review* 247. The new law is not without its critics, however. See T Appleby and P Jones, 'The Marine and Coastal Access Act—A Hornet's Nest?' (2012) 36 *Marine Policy* 73.

[88] *R v Doncaster MBC, ex p Braim* (1989) 57 P & CR 1. See also *Goodman v Mayor of Saltash* [1892] 7 App Cas 633 and comment by Hill (n 86).

[89] *R v Somerset CC, ex p Fewings* [1995] 3 All ER 20; *R v Wear Valley DC, ex p Binks* [1985] 2 All ER 699.

[90] S Smith, 'The UK Government's Consultation Paper on Proposals to Introduce a Community Right to Challenge' (2011) *Public Procurement Law Review* 14. The Community right to challenge is now found in pt 5 of the Localism Act 2011. Whether it will achieve a more democratic process is debatable: see W Le-Las and E Shirley, 'Does the Planning System Need a "Tea-Party"?' (2012) *Journal of Planning and Environmental Law* 239. Moreover, some cynics might see it as a way of offloading some responsibility (and costs) by local authorities.

VI. CONCLUSION

The examples chosen to illustrate the theme of this chapter, 'the extraordinary return to the land', may be regarded as a 'flash in the pan' or as optimistic as Port Sunlight,[91] or they may suggest new ways of looking at land and different ways of approaching the law of property.

Contemporary land law is driven by the liberal political economic viewpoint. While it is not entirely novel to suggest that Western property rights cannot be totally extricated from social, communal and historical factors,[92] conventionally in Western contexts, property is isolated from place,[93] and the law has provided a supportive context for the principle that 'property and land are alienable and tradable'.[94] Property law has in consequence become abstracted from the material-ity of the subject to which it applies. This 'dephysicalisation' and 'placelessness'[95] of property has, however, been challenged in recent decades by the emergence of environmental law, concerns about biodiversity and the sustainable management of natural resources.[96] These same concerns are being reflected in the different ways in which people, on a local and small-scale level, are physically engaging with land sometimes quite transiently, sometimes more permanently.

Social anthropologists refer to 'legalscape' or 'lawscape' to describe the inter-action between people, land and the law, in which legal forms and language are adopted, modified and adapted to reflect the changing relationship of people with land, especially in their dealings with external agencies, such as third parties or alien forums like courts. In developing societies, this process evolves, drawing on a range of legal resources including traditional land customs and laws and new forms of legal regulation. The examples used in this chapter suggest that this process need not be limited to developing societies, but is being experienced elsewhere, almost as a reverse process—a shift away from land as a commodity towards land as heritage, and a current source of physical, spiritual and social well-being.

As in developing countries, the legal background to these new relationships of people with land consists of a melange of different laws and legal concepts, as well as the use of non-legal mechanisms. In the contemporary 'legalscape', these are being combined and used for purposes for which they may not be best suited. This raises the question of whether the property law menu should be reviewed to determine if it is fit for purpose for non-commercial, non-residential land use or whether it is more appropriate to leave this engagement with the land outside a legal box because it is about so much more than legal rights and remedies. There

---

[91] Built by the industrialist and philanthropist William Lever (later Lord Leverhulme) in 1882, Port Sunlight was designed as a model Garden City: George McKay, *Radical Gardening: Politics, Idealism and Rebellion in the Garden* (London, Francis Lincoln, 2011) 26–41.

[92] Hepburn, for example, states that 'property is a social dynamic; mutable, mercurial and value laden': S Hepburn, *Principles of Property Law* (Sydney and London, Cavendish Publishing, 1998) 2.

[93] N Graham, *Lawscape: Property; Environment and Law* (Abingdon, Routledge, 2011) 7, with the consequence that these underpinning ideas were transplanted to the colonies. Compare, however, indig-enous perspectives of land found among Pacific Islanders, Maori, Aboriginal people and First Nations.

[94] Ibid, 10.

[95] Terms used by A Layard, 'Book Review: *Lawscape: Property; Environment and Law* by Nicole Graham' (2011) *Journal of Environmental Law* 160.

[96] The longer-established role of planning law might also be included.

is already evidence that political capital at a number of levels is being made out of community-based projects, even where there is little or no investment by the state or its representatives. For example, passive or active encouragement enables local and national authorities to demonstrate 'green' credentials, a concern for the preservation of biodiversity, the promotion of healthy lifestyles and empathy with local community concerns. Indeed, community projects may fit with local development or service delivery plans without the local authority having to undertake the work itself.[97] More recently, community engagement with land has been seized upon by the current government to endorse its 'Big Society' agenda,[98] even though many of these projects pre-date this latest political cry.[99] Greater legal formality, therefore, could lead to the disempowerment of those who have initiated these projects and facilitate reclamation of control and initiative by the 'official' public sector, thereby undermining the very reasons for getting back to the land in the first place.

It is recognised that more research needs to be done to establish what motivates people to get earth under their nails and what legal and non-legal forms are being most often used and why. The preliminary research reflected in this chapter suggests that while there may be some scope for improved legal frameworks, for example, as regards unincorporated associations or the rationalisation of legislation pertaining to allotments, the history of land law has been one in which people's relationship with land has been shaped by the instrumentality of the law, not the other way round. If the return to the land illustrated by the above examples marks a changing relationship with land, then perhaps it is time to reassess our perceptions of property law, to broaden our understanding of what 'land' means, to reassess the role that law is to play in responding to these shifts in value and perception and to realise that for many it is the land that is important, not some abstract 'bundle of rights'.

[97] Eg in 2010, the Sustainable Development Commission in its report 'Securing Food Supplies up to 2050: The Challenges Faced by the UK' recognises the role that community gardens and allotments have in helping to address the issue of food insecurity in the UK, while some local councils through non-intervention appear to endorse the aesthetic improvement of neglected public land areas by guerrilla gardeners.

[98] See Communities and Local Government, 'Building the Big Society', www.communities.gov.uk/communities/bigsociety.

[99] See, eg, N McInroy and S MacDonald, *From Community Garden to Westminster: Active Citizenship and the Role of Public Space* (Manchester, Centre for Local Economic Strategies, 2005).

Part III

Intersections between Private Property, the Public and the State

10

Towards an Understanding of Public Property

JOHN PAGE[*]

I. INTRODUCTION

PUBLIC PROPERTY IN land is remarkable for its unremarked ubiquity, obvious to identification, yet oblivious[1] to coherent understanding. While richly embroidering human landscapes, we remain pauperised by public property's theoretical under-development. As American scholars Sally Fairfax and Jon Souder observe: 'The flourishing literature concerning property ... is little reflected in the debate surrounding U.S. public resources. Discussions of public lands—our national parks, forests, wildlife refuges, and grazing districts—has been surprisingly unconcerned with theories of property, access and ownership'.[2] Leigh Raymond concurs, noting the surprising absence of property rights from the public lands 'conversation'.[3] Such lack of concern for 'property' in public land is one that resonates beyond America.[4] This chapter seeks to redress this imbalance, to canvass 'theories of [public] property, access, and ownership', and the contributions of jurists to its putative jurisprudence. From an antipodean vantage, it explores the public estate in comparative common law jurisdictions, with an emphasis on three 'settler' societies.[5]

Part II commences with a brief definition of public property in land. Part III then reviews the spectrum of public property type, from corporeal to incorporeal, and beyond to custom and illusion. Part IV aims to identify public property's vexed proprietorship. Part V scrutinises *inclusion*, its elusive, unconsummated relationship

---

[*] Senior Lecturer in Law, Southern Cross University.

[1] CM Rose, 'The Several Futures of Property: Of Cyberspace and Folk Tales, Emission Trades and Ecosystems' (1998–99) 83 *Minnesota Law Review* 129, 132.

[2] 'Our understanding of publicly owned property is largely restricted to principles of scientific management and multiple use': J Souder and S Fairfax, 'In Lands We Trusted: State Trust Lands as an Alternative Theory of Public Ownership' in C Geisler and G Daneker (eds), *Property and Values: Alternatives to Public and Private Ownership* (Washington DC, Island Press, 2000) 89.

[3] LS Raymond, 'Sovereignty without Property? Recent Books in Public Lands' (2003) 43 *Natural Resources Journal* 313, 315.

[4] 'There is little written about public property ... except in contradistinction to private property': JW Hamilton and N Bankes, 'Different Views of the Cathedral: The Literature on Property Law Theory' in A McHarg et al (eds), *Property and the Law in Energy and Natural Resources* (Oxford, Oxford University Press, 2010) 19–20.

[5] Australia, New Zealand and the US.

with access, analogies to use and enjoyment, and how it facilitates property as propriety. Part VI concludes with a call for greater sophistry in public property discourse.

As Fairfax and Raymond intimate, scrutiny of public property in land is overdue. To myopically overlook the public estate is to consign its values and meanings to the periphery. Conversely, to better 'see'[6] the public estate is to dispel the corrosive implication that it is at one extreme an oxymoron[7] or, at the other, a perverse variant of private ownership.[8] Its better understanding makes clearer sense of what is ours.

II. DEFINING PUBLIC PROPERTY

Public property in land is typically defined by what it is not: property that is *not* private property. Common property is arguably better understood.[9] The public estate suffers the paradoxical risk of being perceived as non-property, a passive res awaiting capture. As Margaret Davies argues, 'the private nature of property is naturalised and universalised, as though other forms are somehow less ethically defensible'.[10] Centuries of marginalisation of non-private property dating from the enclosure period[11] have obscured public property; its seeing dispersed and drowned out by private rhetoric.

To define public property is to jettison the familiar paradigms of exclusion and alienability, and embrace an expansive conception of property that is 'not a monolithic notion of standard content ... [but] the most comprehensive of all the terms which can be used ... indicative and descriptive ... of all or any of the very many different kinds of relationship between a person and a subject matter'.[12] Such a perspective accommodates the idea of public property in land as those 'interests in which the individual concerned has no greater claim than any other member of the public',[13] collective rights, enjoyed by individuals in common with others, and measured by their public sum.

This chapter expands on this preliminary definition by next identifying three indicators of public property in land: the diversity of its type; the conundrum of its ownership; and its right of inclusion. Each attribute amplifies further comprehension of the public estate; type expands recognition; ownership exposes the fault line

[6] CM Rose, *Property and Persuasion: Essays on the History, Theory and Rhetoric of Ownership* (Boulder, Westview Press, 1994).

[7] CM Rose, 'The Comedy of the Commons: Custom, Commerce, and Inherently Public Property' (1986) 53 *University of Chicago Law Review* 711.

[8] 'In the strict common law tradition even government-owned property is regarded, technically, as ... subject to private ownership': K Gray and SF Gray, 'Private Property and Public Propriety' in J McLean (ed), *Property and the Constitution* (Oxford, Hart Publishing, 1999) 13.

[9] E Ostrom, *Governing the Commons: The Evolution of Institutions for Collective Action* (New York, Cambridge University Press, 1990).

[10] M Davies, *Property: Meanings, Histories, Theories* (Abingdon, Routledge, 2007) 13.

[11] CM Rose, 'Romans, Roads and Romantic Creators: Traditions of Public Property in the Information Age' (2003) 66 *Law & Contemporary Problems* 89, 91.

[12] *Yanner v Eaton* (1999) 201 CLR 351 (HC).

[13] *Stow v Mineral Holdings (Australia) Pty Ltd* (1977) 51 ALJR 672, 679 (HC).

between property's collective and individual values; while inclusion represents the hope of a nascent touchstone right, presently ill formed and amorphous.

III. THE SPECTRUM OF TYPE

Public property in land takes a plethora of forms. This part seeks taxonomic order by adopting a blunt divide familiar to property lawyers: corporeal versus incorporeal. Corporeal public property refers to tangible, identifiable lands. Incorporeal public property comprises non-possessory, intangible, less than fee interests in land. The study of type then diverges to examining the sources of public property beyond statute and the common law, those of custom, even illusion.

Traditionally seen as government-owned land, the spectral breadth of public property type demonstrates both a surprising diversity and a refutation of any distinct public/private divide in property. Rather, public property occupies space across a broad continuum, where degrees of 'public-ness' are relative, not absolute, questions.

A. Corporeal Public Property

Public property is most recognisable in its corporeal form, typically alienated land held by the state or the Crown, state agencies, or public lands leased to long-term private rightholders.[14] Public land held by government agencies is primarily land dedicated[15] or reserved for public purposes. Its usage depends on its public function: conservation; resource exploitation; education; transport; health; defence; public administration; recreation; and so on. Then there are public lands with no present use; unalienated Crown lands or non-allocated public domain lands that have not been dedicated, reserved or otherwise dealt with. Interspersed is an inchoate miscellany, the like of permissive occupancies, travelling stock routes or 'paper' roads, ad hoc interests that reflected periodic policy imperatives.

The physical footprint of corporeal public property is impressive. In the US, one-third of the continental landmass comprises federally owned public lands.[16] In three of the 11 western states, the percentage exceeds 50 per cent.[17] In Australia, Crown land amounts to 50 per cent of the landmass of the populous state of New South Wales. In more sparsely settled Western Australia, it is 93 per cent. State-owned conservation land alone constitutes one-third of New Zealand's area. Yet despite its superlative acreage, public property lacks the legitimacy or normalcy of private property, a consequence of a binary liberal worldview that naturalises the primacy

---

[14] For example, lands leased or licensed to pastoral right holders under Land Acts in Australian states or New Zealand, or Taylor Grazing Act permittees in the US.

[15] *Randwick Municipal Council v Rutledge* (1959) 33 ALJR 367, 372–73 (HC).

[16] 'One Third of the Nation's Land', a report to the President and to the Congress by the Public Land Law Review Commission (1970).

[17] Nevada 82 per cent, Utah 64 per cent and California 61 per cent. S Lehmann, *Privatizing Public Lands* (New York, Oxford University Press, 1995) 4, 22–23.

of the private rights holder and views the state with deep suspicion.[18] Hence, public boundaries, both physical and metaphorical, are perpetually tested, while collective values are perceived as inferior to the individual values of the private estate. In the western US, 'sagebrush rebellions'[19] or 'storms over the rangelands'[20] are well-documented episodic revolts against the public property estate. Elsewhere, the unidirectional propensity of private rights to encroach into public space has been observed.[21]

The sheer size of the corporeal public estate seemingly fails to address such existential or normative shortcomings. That it may take incorporeal form unlocks potentialities for new, non-reactive ways to 'see' and understand public property in land.

B. Incorporeal Public Property

Less recognisable is public property's manifestation as an array of incorporeal property rights. As less than fee interests; they comprise a panoply of covenants, easements, servitudes and *sui generis* statutory rights, held by the state, state agencies, the public at large and even private entities that act in the public interest. Incorporeal rights subsist over both private lands, as public rights encumbering private title, and corporeal public land.[22]

Conceptualised as abstract, non-possessory sticks within the bundle metaphor, incorporeal public rights are separate and divisible from the physical land itself. For example, the right of recreational access to private property is a use and enjoyment 'stick' held by the general public. When enacted in England by the Countryside and Rights of Way Act 2000, the statutory right was described in bundle terms as a transfer or reallocation of 'a valuable property right from private landowners to the public'.[23]

Despite its inherently abstract nature, incorporeal public property plays a (surprisingly) key role in contextualising property right to place[24] and connecting otherwise fragmented land parcels. Examples include scenic easements that preserve natural

---

[18] GE Frug, 'The City as a Legal Concept' (1980) 93 *Harvard Law Review* 1057; N Blomley, *Law, Space, and the Geographies of Power* (New York, Guilford Press, 1994).

[19] RH Nelson, *Public Lands and Private Rights: The Failure of Scientific Management* (Lanham, Rowman & Littlefield, 1995).

[20] W Hage, *Storms over Rangelands Private Rights in Federal Lands* (Bellevue, Free Enterprise Press, 1989).

[21] A Brower et al, 'The Cowboy, the Southern Man, and the Man from Snowy River' (2009) 21 *Georgetown International Environmental Law Review* 455.

[22] Restrictions and positive covenants are imposed on Crown land under ss 77A and 77B of the Crown Lands Act 1989 (NSW).

[23] J Anderson, 'Countryside Access and Environmental Protection: An American View of Britain's Right to Roam' (2007) 9 *Environmental Law* 241, 246.

[24] It is surprising because of the historical tendency of private property since enclosure to decouple property right from context. The end result is what Nicole Graham calls 'lawscapes', landscapes where 'standardised, universal and measurable space was grafted over place so that physicality and particularity of places became irrelevant': N Graham, *Lawscape Property Environment Law* (Abingdon, Routledge, 2010) 66.

vistas,[25] public footpaths that link villages across privately owned farmland[26] or conservation covenants that form wildlife corridors across private habitat. Reinserting links between disparate property ownerships militates against Eric Freyfogle's 'tragedy of fragmentation', the private rights-dominated landscape where property holdings are island enclaves 'with no mechanisms to achieve landscape-scale goals'. Freyfogle prescribes as a remedy the reconceptualisation of private property and a need to 'reassert the public's varied interests in private lands'.[27]

The conservation easement exemplifies the connectivity potential of incorporeal public property. Ostensibly modelled on the common law easement,[28] conservation easements first appeared in the 1930s,[29] but their use did not become widespread until 50 years later, when taxation incentives encouraged the donation or sale of perpetual conservation easements to public agencies or land trusts.[30] By the beginning of the twenty-first century, conservation easements were 'the fastest-growing method for protecting land' in the US, preserving 1.2 million acres from development at growth rates over the preceding decade of 377 per cent.[31] Many conservation easements vest in or benefit land trusts, 'non-profit organizations that preserve or enhance environmental amenities ... on private land'.[32] Landscape resources protected by conservation easements include open space, wetlands, forests, scenic views, recreation and trails, greenways and coastlines.[33] The legal justification for conservation easements is said to be 'significant public benefit'.[34] Often, the public benefit is indirect, the provision of 'ecosystem services ... a nice view ... habitat for wildlife or protected farmland'.[35] Direct public goods manifest as walking trails linking national parks, or trails using disused railway corridors.[36]

In Australia, conservation agreements,[37] or positive covenants protecting environmental, cultural, heritage or natural resource values,[38] are analogous incorporeal

---

[25] W Hutton, 'Conservation Easements in the Ninth Federal Circuit' in JA Gustanski and RH Squires (eds), *Protecting the Land: Conservation Easements Past, Present and Future* (Washington DC, Island Press, 2000) 381; R Cunningham, 'Scenic Easements in the Highway Beautification Program' (1968) 45 *Denver Law Journal* 167.

[26] A Sydenham, 'The Countryside and Rights of Way Act 2000: Balancing Public Access and Environmental Protection?' (2002) 4 *Environmental Law* 87, 95–96.

[27] ET Freyfogle, *The Land We Share: Private Property and the Common Good* (Washington DC, Island Press, 2003) 177, 203.

[28] 'The conservation easement statute purposefully creates and defines a specific right or interest in property having ... its own set of rules': TD Mayo, 'A Holistic Examination of the Law of Conservation Easements' in Gustanski and Squires (n 25). Statutorily defined in § 1(1) of the Uniform Conservation Easement Act.

[29] Cunningham (n 25) 181–83; SK Fairfax et al, *Buying Nature* (Cambridge, MA, MIT Press, 2005) 122.

[30] R Brewer, *Conservancy: The Land Trust Movement in the United States* (Hanover, Dartmouth College Press, 2003) 148, 155.

[31] JA Gustanski, 'Protecting the Land: Conservation Easements, Voluntary Actions, and Private Lands' in Gustanski and Squires (n 25).

[32] D Parker, 'Land Trusts and the Choice to Conserve Land with Full Ownership or Conservation Easements' (2004) 44 *Natural Resources Journal* 483.

[33] Gustanski (n 31) 21.

[34] Brewer (n 30) 116.

[35] Ibid.

[36] JA Gustanski, 'Protecting the Land: Conservation Easements, Voluntary Actions and Private Lands' in Gustanski and Squires (n 25) 22.

[37] National Parks and Wildlife Act 1974 (NSW), s 69C(1)(a).

[38] Crown Lands Act 1989 (NSW), ss 88D and 88E; Conveyancing Act 1919 (NSW), s 77A.

public rights, the benefit vesting in the relevant land conservation agency. The American land trust is replicated by not-for-profit organisations such as the Nature Conservation Trust,[39] where voluntary landowner agreements and revolving fund arrangements protect natural and cultural heritage[40] and run with the land through registration.[41] In New Zealand, conservation[42] or open space[43] covenants fulfil similar functions to protect ecological or landscape values.[44]

The significance of incorporeal public rights is threefold. First, they broaden our understanding of public property to encompass a diversity of rights beyond fee simple state ownership. Second, they highlight the anachronism of any distinct public/private divide. Conservation easements exemplify that public rights subsist on private lands and condemn by their existence the notion of a distinct property duality as 'confusion elevated to principle'.[45] Third, they demonstrate public property's potential to invigorate connections across human landscapes, to link property with place and context, and obviate the risks of countless 'tragedies of fragmentation'.

C. Customary Public Property

The sources of public property type are not restricted to the mainstream. Property's commodification has masked an ancient alter ego, one with meaning for personhood, identity and community.[46] Customary public property evidences faint but 'surprising connections between informal usages and understandings' about public property and their binding effect amongst 'those who practice and share them'.[47]

Custom[48] is an awkward, anachronistic source of modern property law, particularly in settler societies lacking the social history from which customary rules arose. Nonetheless, customary norms find ways to percolate into the margins of property discourse. Robert Ellickson's 'order without law' in Shasta County, California observes the powerful, all-pervasive effect of custom in generating rights, including property rights, amongst tightly knit communities of ranchers.[49] Ellickson concludes that such informal rules arise 'through decentralized social processes, rather

---

[39] Nature Conservation Trust Act 2001 (NSW).
[40] Ibid, s 30(1).
[41] Nature Conservation Trust Act 2001 (NSW), s 37.
[42] Conservation Act 1987 (NZ) or Reserves Act 1977 (NZ).
[43] Queen Elizabeth the Second National Trust Act 1977 (NZ).
[44] D Donohue, 'The Law and Practice of Open Space Covenants' (2003) 7 *New Zealand Journal Environmental Law* 119.
[45] C Geisler, 'Property Pluralism' in Geisler and Daneker (n 2) 79.
[46] GS Alexander and EM Penalver (eds), *Property and Community* (New York, Oxford University Press, 2010); GS Alexander, *Commodity & Propriety: Competing Visions of Property in American Thought 1776–1970* (Chicago, University of Chicago Press, 1997).
[47] D Bederman, 'The Curious Resurrection of Custom: Beach Access and Judicial Takings' (1996) 96 *Columbia Law Review* 1375.
[48] Custom's traditional definition is 'ancient customs practiced by a definite community in a distinct geographical locale … recognized … to constitute a local common law'. A Loux, 'The Persistence of the Ancient Regime: Custom, Utility and the Common Law in the Nineteenth Century' (1993) 79 *Cornell Law Review* 183. A wider definition embraces informal practices that have community adherence.
[49] RC Ellickson, *Order Without Law: How Neighbors Settle Disputes* (Cambridge, MA, Harvard University Press, 1991).

than from the law'.[50] Similarly, Gregory Duhl studies food cart owners at Temple University and surmises that 'the ordering of lunch trucks and carts ... illustrates how, in the absence of private property ownership, communities adopt and follow customs and norms to create and order property rights'.[51]

Carol Rose escapes territorial constraints to explore the wider relationship between custom and public property, noting that 'custom provides powerful insights into the nature of 'inherently public property'.[52] Rose posits that the effective management of public property arises 'through the medium of the customs and habits of a civilized citizenry'.[53] Efficient albeit informal governance of public resources by the customary public averts a tragedy of the commons and instead enhances a 'comedy of the commons', where the greater the use of public property, the greater the resource's social value is maximised, and the 'solidarity and fellow-feeling of the whole community' is reinforced.[54]

The paradox of custom[55] and property is the normative strength of the former—or, as Leigh Raymond describes when the contest is determined informally, 'what is most striking about th[e] incongruity between law and custom, is how often custom wins'.[56] Even in the courts, custom as the basis of a public right occasionally prevails.[57] In Oregon, the celebrated case of *State ex rel Thornton v Hay*[58] established a statewide public easement over private dry sands on the basis of customary practice.[59]

D. Illusory Public Property

Type concludes with a foray into illusory public property. Carol Rose posits that people 'see' property in a variety of ways, even as false claims, 'the imaginative construction of property ... where the law recognizes none'.[60] Much of Rose's discussion centres on people claiming transient entitlements to public spaces as their imagined own, such as lunchtime 'rights' to park benches. Kevin Gray's study of the property norms of spatial order in queues is an analogous example.[61] Arguably, the modern

---

[50] Ibid, 139.

[51] GM Duhl, 'Property and Custom: Allocating Space in Public Spaces' (2006) 79 *Temple Law Review* 199, 207.

[52] Rose (n 7) 722.

[53] Ibid, 774.

[54] Ibid, 759.

[55] Custom in the US is based on 'communitarian norms ... a norm shared by all of the constituent groups within a community': Duhl (n 51) 238.

[56] LS Raymond, 'Viewpoint: Are Grazing Rights on Public Lands a Form of Private Property?' (1997) 50 *Journal of Range Management* 431. The migration of customary norm into law in the American West is studied in TL Anderson and PJ Hill, *The Not So Wild, Wild West* (Stanford, Stanford University Press, 2004).

[57] N Ubhi and B Denyer-Green, *Law of Commons and Town and Village Greens* (Bristol, Jordans, 2004) 135. In the US context, the judicial application of custom is discussed in S Eagle, 'Unitary Law of State Takings' 69(2) *Planning & Environmental Law* (2010) 6.

[58] *State ex rel Thornton v Hay*, 462 P 2d 671 (1969).

[59] S Bender, 'Castles in the Sand: Balancing Public Custom and Private Ownership Interests on Oregon Beaches' (1998) 77 *Oregon Law Review* 913, 917.

[60] Rose (n 6) 274.

[61] K Gray, 'Property in a Queue' in Alexander and Penalver (n 46) 165–95.

shopping mall best typifies illusory public property, 'private space masquerading as a public space'.[62] As 'open-access private properties'[63] or privately owned 'quasi-public property',[64] these hybrids foster illusory expectations of public rights of inclusion. The illusion is shattered when private owners enforce behaviour or dress codes, or restrain public assembly or political protest. In such circumstances, 'private proprietorial power [the right to exclude] intrudes into the public sphere'.[65] According to James Kunstler, 'the mall commercialized the public realm'.[66]

E. Type and Property Plurality

The diverse range of public property type is a reminder that public property is capable of being 'seen' in the most likely and unlikely of places. Incorporeal property in particular underscores that there is no bright line,[67] no distinct public/private divide. Rather, public property can be found across a continuum, where 'notions of "public" and "private" operate, not dichotomously, but continuously ... in which adjacent connotations shade easily into one another'[68] and 'finely intercalated distinctions or gradations'[69] segue from state-owned public lands through to customary public rights. In seeking to understand public property through the spectrum of type, it is the differing degrees of 'public-ness' in land, rather than the formal technicality of individual type, that may prove the most instructive.

Importantly, a wider 'seeing' of public property in land enlivens a pluralistic mosaic[70] of property rights and uses across human landscapes. Public property contributes to the mosaic by adding different tiles, both corporeal and incorporeal, to the private monotony. The more we 'see' a variety (and greater quantity) of different property types,[71] the less conditioned we become to a self-imposed straitjacket where property and private property are synonymous.[72] Also, by diluting the dominance of the abstract private right, the propensity for property to become relational to rather than divorced from its physical context is enhanced. The Hohfieldian analysis of (essentially private) property as relations between person and person, 'where land is not property, but the subject of property',[73] has narrowed and hardened how we

---

[62] JH Kunstler, *The Geography of Nowhere* (New York, Simon & Schuster, 1993) 119–20.

[63] C Geisler, 'Property and Pluralism' in Geisler and Daneker (n 2) 75.

[64] K Gray and SF Gray, 'Civil Rights, Civil Wrongs and Quasi-Public Space' (1999) *European Human Rights Law Review* 46.

[65] Davies (n 10) 11.

[66] Kuntsler (n 62) 119–20.

[67] Davies (n 10) 11.

[68] Gray and Gray (n 8) 11.

[69] Ibid, 18.

[70] Fairfax et al (n 29) 34.

[71] A Brower and J Page, 'Property Rights Across Sustainable Landscapes' in D Grinlinton and P Taylor (eds), *Property Rights and Sustainability* (Leiden, Martinus Nijhoff, 2011) 305.

[72] 'It is a genuine misconception, which affects the whole theoretical handling of the concept of property by many modern writers': CB Macpherson, 'The Meaning of Property' in *Property: Mainstream and Critical Positions* (Toronto, University of Toronto Press, 1999) 5–6.

[73] W Hohfield, 'Some Fundamental Legal Conceptions as Applied in Legal Reasoning' (1913) 23 *Yale Law Journal* 16, 22.

see land.[74] Optimistically, property plurality has the potential for human landscapes to become less like a universalised 'Blackacre'[75] and more representative of 'where we live'.[76]

Legal geographers such as Nicholas Blomley emphasise that property is best understood by context, 'by reference to its place in and relationship to social, economic, political and ecological systems'.[77] In so doing, they reject an idealised paradigm where the 'law's separateness ... [is] deaf to material, physical, spatial and cultural influences'.[78] Edward Relph argues that 'an authentic attitude to context is important ... because from such a relation, authentic places emerge, places which ... sustain the earth and those dwelling on it'. Relph believes the ability to make 'authentic relations with place' is rare, which he attributes to 'weakening symbolic qualities of modern places'.[79] Property matters in the pursuit of authenticity, 'both symbolically and literally'.[80] Eric Freyfogle's bleak description of Champaign County, Illinois, where the public owns less than one per cent of the county 'setting aside roadways and the remnants of a now-abandoned [and contaminated] air force base',[81] is a depressing symbolic and literal vision of property uniformity. To Freyfogle, public lands are the 'remedy for private irresponsibility'.[82] James Kunstler's *The Geography of Nowhere* is an equally grim visage of the decline of the American public realm, the 'landscape tissue that ties together the thousands of pieces of private property that make up a town, a suburb, a state'.[83]

While largely a descriptive exercise, the spectrum of type subverts the inevitability of Kunstler's thesis or the unremitting bleakness of Freyfogle's imagery. Its opportunities lie in expanding the definitional parameters of public property, a weakening of private ubiquity and the optimistic consequences this may pose for re-physicalising property rights to place. Its risk is to complicate a coherent account of public property, where type and form necessarily vary according to a particular context. On balance, its overarching worth is to demonstrate that we are not prospectively fated by Eduardo Penalver's 'land memory', 'the consequence of countless decisions made decades, even generations, ago',[84] about singular property patterns, and that there

---

[74] Hohfield's lasting legacy was not 'hocus-pocus' terminology, but his emphasis on property as relations between people, see S Banner, *American Property* (Cambridge, MA, Harvard University Press, 2011) 104.

[75] 'Blackacre' is a hypothetical parcel of land invoked in property law classes. Freyfogle charts the rise of Blackacre to a trend at Harvard Law School in 1870 to instil abstract scientific principles into the teaching of law: Freyfogle (n 27) 107–25.

[76] R Garbutt, *The Locals* (Bern, Peter Lang, 2011) 29–30.

[77] J Holder and C Harrison, 'Connecting Law and Geography' in J Holder and C Harrison (eds), *Law and Geography* (2003) 3.

[78] Ibid.

[79] E Relph, cited in Garbutt (n 76) 54–55.

[80] H Jacobs, 'Is an Answer Blowin' in the Wind?' (2010) 62(9) *Planning & Environmental Law* 8.

[81] ET Freyfogle, 'Private Rights in Nature: Two Paradigms' in P Burdon (ed), *Wild Law: The Philosophy of Earth Jurisprudence* (Adelaide, Wakefield Press, 2011) 271.

[82] ET Freyfogle, *Agrarianism and the Good Society: Land, Culture, Conflict and Hope* (Lexington, The University Press of Kentucky, 2007) 96.

[83] Kunstler (n 62).

[84] EM Penalver, 'Land Virtues' (2009) 94 *Cornell Law Review* 822, 830. The 'collective interdependence of individual land uses reinforces their inertial power. Once in place, land uses presuppose and reinforce one another in ways that make it difficult to undo one piece without affecting many others.

are alternatives to Champaign County-like uniformity. Seeing a wide diversity of public type may alter such restrictive path dependencies for the better.

IV. THE CONUNDRUM OF OWNERSHIP

Ownership is premised on the vesting of property rights in a recognisable entity in its capacity as owner,[85] a 'right to have and to dispose of possession and enjoyment of the subject matter'.[86] In the case of public property, the ownership entity is assumedly public: the state or an agency of the state.[87] But this assumption poses further questions: does the state or state agency own the land absolutely or pursuant to some trust for and on behalf of its citizens? And what of private organisations such as land trusts that hold stick rights in property that benefit the public? These questions suggest that the issue of ownership is likewise not a 'bright line'.[88]

Putative ownership by the public at large is a further muddying of the ownership waters. Carol Rose argues that rights in 'inherently public property' are controlled neither by government agencies nor by private entitles, but by society at large.[89] Rose calls this owner the 'unorganized public'.[90] In the US, ownership of inherently public property by the unorganised public is given effect by the doctrine of public trust. Originally concerned with core areas such as navigable waterways, 'inherently public property' has proven a 'resurgent concept',[91] bringing within its ambit new forms of contestable public property that recognise community or public values in diffuse resources.[92] This in turn expands the types of property capable of ownership by an amorphous public.

Joseph Sax frames ownership from a values perspective, in the process identifying a fault line common to the cultural divide between property as a private commodity and property's ancient social or personhood meanings.[93] Sax states that: 'The debate over ownership of the public lands is basically part of a much larger controversy over the legitimacy of collective versus individualistic values'.[94] Courts tend to prefer individualistic values: 'The common law tradition is not entirely friendly to group

---

The interplay of these physical, psychological and social components of land's memory yields a pervasive path-dependence in land use' (830–31).

[85] Waldron defines property type by owner: J Waldron, *The Right to Private Property* (New York, Oxford University Press, 1988) 47.
[86] *Yanner v Eaton* (1999) 201 CLR 351.
[87] Rose (n 7) 719.
[88] Davies (n 10) 10.
[89] Rose (n 7) 720.
[90] Ibid, 722.
[91] JL Sax, 'Some Thoughts on the Decline of Private Property' (1982) 58 *Washington Law Review* 481, 482.
[92] CM Rose, 'Joseph Sax and the Idea of the Public Trust' (1998) 25 *Ecology Law Quarterly* 351, 355.
[93] Alexander (n 46).
[94] JL Sax, 'The Claim for Retention of the Public Lands' in S Brubacker (ed), *Rethinking the Federal Lands*, (Washington DC, RFF Press,1984) 130. 'Property may be better understood, both historically and legally, as the result of a balance struck between competing individual and collective goals, the private and the public interest': Gray and Gray (n 8) 15.

rights.'[95] In Australia, the High Court held that members of the public generally do not acquire a proprietary interest in public land.[96] However, its judgment was framed from the perspective of the private paradigm, where 'right ... does not in its context mean a public right; it means an individual right of a proprietary nature', and 'interest' means 'interests held by persons in their individual capacity'.[97] Yet the court did touch on what public ownership may entail:

> It [the statute] does not embrace interests in which the individual concerned has no greater claim than any other member of the public. All members of the public have a right to pass freely along and across public highways but none have in their capacity as members of the public any estate or interest in such land. Likewise members of the public may be entitled pursuant to particular statutes to use specified areas of Crown lands for the purpose of recreation ... All members of the public may have the right to go upon such land [to] freely walk thereon ... and may resist attempts by the Crown or anyone else to eject them from such land.

Ownership of public property demands context, informed through the lens of property's collective values rather than its sense of individual entitlement.

A. Entity or No Entity?

Unlike private property,[98] the involvement of a distinct ownership entity may not be a theoretical necessity for public property. Rose's 'unorganized public' exemplifies that 'inherently public property' may be owned by the collective public at large.[99] The prima facie answer to this question suggests that there is no limitation on who owns public property. The state, a state agency, the public at large and even (in the case of conservation easements) private owners may 'own' public interests in land.

Direct ownership by the state or a state agency is a paradigm framed within (private) property's individualistic values and rhetoric of exclusion.[100] It also has perverse consequences. Richard Barnes observes that ownership of collective property by the 'individual' state is a variation of private ownership that precludes it generating 'a specific normative meaning'.[101] Margaret Davies agrees in part. In articulating a 'taxonomy of owners', Davies lists five possible classes of owner: private individuals, companies, governments, a limited community or the public at large. Davies argues that individual and corporate ownerships are 'private', while 'government ownership of resources such as office buildings [is also] essentially private'.[102] On the other hand, ownership by limited communities or the public at large are 'dispersed'. But government ownership of 'public infrastructure and environmental

---

[95] CM Rose, 'Property and Language, or the Ghost of the Fifth Panel' (2006) 18 *Yale Journal of Law and the Humanities* 1, 13.

[96] *Stow v Mineral Holdings (Australia) Pty Ltd* (1977) 51 ALJR 672.

[97] Ibid, 679.

[98] Jeremy Waldron, 'What is Private Property?' (1985) 5 *OJLS* 313, 327.

[99] Rose (n 7).

[100] T Merrill, 'Property and the Right to Exclude' (1998) 77 *Nebraska Law Review* 730; S Balganesh, 'Demystifying the Right to Exclude' (2008) 31 *Harvard Journal of Law & Public Policy* 593.

[101] R Barnes, *Property Rights and Natural Resources* (Oxford, Hart Publishing, 2009) 154.

[102] Davies (n 10) 63–64.

resources such as parks and beaches on trust for the public'[103] are neither private nor public, an unsatisfactory lacuna. Crawford Macpherson describes 'state property' as 'corporate private property', where a 'smaller body of persons authorized to command its citizens' exercise a corporate right to exclude.[104] It is as if explicit state ownership taints public property's 'public-ness' and relegates the ownership of key public places (such as Davies' parks and beaches) to an uncertain no-man's land.

By contrast, 'public domain goods' are in Davies' terms 'fundamental to a flourishing community; they provide us with the basic ability to move about, to undertake trade and commerce, to engage in recreation, to situate ourselves historically, culturally, or even spiritually, to communicate and express ourselves'.[105] As Rose argues, they vest in an unorganised public. Macpherson also writes of an 'unorganized public', a mass of individuals with individual rights in analogous 'common property'.[106] He argues that rights in such property are 'the most unadulterated kind of property, a right of each natural person not to be excluded from the property's use and benefit'.[107]

Thus, ownership by the public at large, whether Rose's amorphous mass or Macpherson's mass of individuals, may be preferable since it avoids unfavourable analogy with private ownership and sidesteps the implications of exclusion. And by invoking property's collective values, it may prove the sanguine catalyst for greater normative meaning for public property in land.

B. In Trust for the Public?

References to public property in land regularly invoke the concept of trust. To borrow from trust terminology, the trust may be express (such as charitable trusts)[108] or implied or resulting (where the term is used in a non-technical sense). Private land trusts also conform, signifying that the public stick they hold over private land is impressed by obligations in favour of local communities, the wider public or the public interest.

Souder and Fairfax use the educational state land trust as a platform for arguing that 'trust principles ought to occupy a more prominent place in our understanding of publicly owned land than they do'.[109] As 'arguably the oldest of all federal programs and ... the most durable national approach to public resource ownership',[110] the state land trust provides an existing template. Raising its profile presents an opportunity for a 'new but not untested route to thinking about public ownership'.[111]

---

[103] Ibid, 64.

[104] Macpherson (n 72) 5–6. 'In the strict common law tradition, even government-owned property is regarded, technically, as ... subject to private ownership': Gray and Gray (n 8) 13.

[105] Davies (n 10) 65–66.

[106] Macpherson cites 'public parks, city streets, highways' as 'common use' property: Macpherson (n 72) 4.

[107] Ibid, 6.

[108] A Bradbrook et al, *Australian Real Property Law*, 5th edn (Sydney, Lawbook Co, 2011) 357.

[109] Souder and Fairfax (n 2) 87, 89.

[110] Souder and Fairfax (n 2).

[111] Ibid.

By contrast, the public trust doctrine enjoys a high profile and is the subject of a rich literature. Its contemporary resurrection since the 1970s is attributed to Joseph Sax,[112] although its history can be traced back to the *jus publicum* of Roman law, and the English common law before its reception in the US.[113] It origins lie in the nature of property in rivers, lakes, submerged lands and foreshores adjoining water bodies as inherently public property, or 'at least subject to a kind of inherent easement for certain public purposes'.[114] While private ownership of foreshores was possible, the incorporeal public property inherent in those lands (such as rights to navigable waters) was itself inalienable.[115]

The doctrine was neglected until growing environmental awareness in the late 1960s reawakened its potential, 'liberating it from its historical shackles',[116] to protect public rights in a diverse range of public resources.[117] These include access rights over the dry sands of beaches, limits on the appropriation of water to serve public trust values[118] and even 'property' in surfing waves.[119] This expansion has relied on a lateral interpretation of its founding shackles, a creative linking of new public resources with the common denominators of navigable waters or foreshores below the high-water mark.[120] These newer forms of public trust property have been described as possessing a 'natural suitability for common use' and a tendency towards 'scarcity',[121] or qualities essential for communication, travel and sociability.[122] Despite its critics,[123] the public trust is 'a recognition of important public property rights'[124] premised on the fragmentation of ownership between bare legal title and beneficial property subject to public trust. In the case of private lands, the grantee holds a naked fee subject to public trust rights.[125] In the case of public lands, there is no merger that extinguishes the public trust.

Trust relationships in public property also arise through the gift or transfer of private land to public authorities for specified purposes,[126] as conditions of planning consent[127] or by operation of statute. For example, in New South Wales, the Crown

---

[112] JL Sax, 'The Public Trust Doctrine in Natural Resource Law: Effective Judicial Intervention' (1969–70) 68 *Michigan Law Review* 471.

[113] Higgins, 'Public Access to the Shore: Public rights and Private Property' in DM Whitelaw and GR Visgilio (eds), *America's Changing Coasts: Private Rights and Public Trust* (Cheltenham, Edward Elgar, 2005) 183–84.

[114] Rose (n 92) 355.

[115] HC Dunning, 'The Public Trust: A Fundamental Doctrine of American Property Law' (1988–89) 19 *Environmental Law* 515, 516.

[116] JL Sax, 'Liberating the Public Trust Doctrine from its Historical Shackles' (1980) 14 *UC Davis Law Review* 185.

[117] C Rechtschaffen and D Antolini, *Creative Common Law Strategies for Protecting the Environment* (Washington DC, Environmental Law Institute, 2007).

[118] *National Audubon Society v Superior Court*, 33 Cal. 3d 419, 658 P 2d 3.

[119] D Nazer, 'The Tragicomedy of the Surfers' Commons' (2004) 9 *Deakin Law Review* 655, 677.

[120] In Mono Lake, the link was the navigability of waters in the lake.

[121] Dunning (n 115) 523.

[122] Rose (n 7).

[123] S Jawetz, 'The Public Trust Totem in Public Land Law: Ineffective and Undesirable Judicial Intervention' (1982) 10 *Ecology Law Quarterly* 455.

[124] Dunning (n 115) 516.

[125] J Stevens, 'The Public Trust: A Sovereign's Ancient Prerogative Becomes the People's Environmental Right' (1980) 14 *UC Davis Law Review* 195, 215–16.

[126] *Brisbane City Council v Attorney-General (Qld)* [1978] 3 Qd R 299.

[127] Bradbrook et al (n 108) 357.

reserve trust is a statutory creature under the Crown Lands Act 1989 (NSW).[128] The New Zealand Reserves Act 1977 establishes a similar regime. This Act applies to Crown land classified according to its primary purpose, including recreation,[129] historic[130] or scenic[131] reserves. Title is vested under sections 26 and 26A, such that 'all land so vested shall be held in trust for the purpose or purposes for which the reserve is classified'. In a High Court judgment dealing with conflicting private uses on Crown land,[132] section 26A was scrutinised, the court concluding that 'the general public of New Zealand must be regarded as its beneficiaries'.[133] The Reserves Act 'confer[s] legal ownership ... in the Crown while making it clear that the land is held on trust for all New Zealanders'.[134]

Nor is the language of trust necessarily restrained by a lack of an equitable or statutory basis for the beneficial relationship claimed. Narratives surrounding the public estate often describe lands being held 'in trust for' or 'on behalf of' citizens. This beneficial claim is substantiated by broad-brush references to the nature of democratic governance or the people's common legacy in important natural resources. On the fiftieth anniversary of the US National Park Act in 1966, *National Geographic* magazine quoted first director Stephen Mather claiming that the park system belonged 'to everyone—now and always'.[135] The landmark Report of the Public Land Law Review Commission in 1970 repeated this common legacy view: 'These lands are a natural heritage and national asset that belong to us all.'[136]

An implied trust seemingly results from state ownership, which is accentuated where the lands are iconic or under threat of loss.[137] While the nominal owner may be the state, its title is a threadbare one. The true beneficial owner, illusory or otherwise, is the people. Margaret Davies' description of 'parks and beaches being held in trust for the public'[138] is a previously traversed exemplar of this narrative. Carol Rose speaks similarly of 'the public ... as a kind of beneficial owner of diffuse resource rights'.[139]

The concept of trust permeates public property, its doctrines, statutes and rhetoric. Its redolence suggests an inclination for public property to vest in the collective 'sum of us'. But where does that leave the individualistic state?

---

[128] Crown reserve trusts are 'legal bod[ies] which cares for a Crown reserve on behalf of the people of NSW': http://www.lpma.nsw.gov.au/trusts/trusts2.

[129] Reserves Act 1977 (NZ), s 17.

[130] Ibid, s 18.

[131] Ibid, s 19.

[132] *Gibbs v The New Plymouth District Council* [2006] NZHC 231.

[133] Ibid, [16]–[17].

[134] Ibid, [14].

[135] (1966) 130(1) *National Geographic* 2.

[136] 'One Third of the Nation's Land' (n 16) 20.

[137] 'The loss of New Zealander's "birthrights" to access public lands': M Philp, 'The No-Go Zones' (*North & South*, August 2008) 44.

[138] Davies (n 10) 64.

[139] CM Rose, 'A Dozen Propositions' (1996) 53 *Washington & Lee Law Review* 265, 276; H Scheiber, 'Public Rights and the Rule of Law in American Legal History' (1984) 72 *California Law Review* 217, 223.

C. Ownership or Management Rights?

Eric Freyfogle believes that the 'biggest difference between public and private lands has to do with management power over the land'.[140] Yet again, there is no bright line: 'Decisions about public lands are mostly made by public decision-makers, but not completely so. Public decision-makers are often influenced by private parties who want to use the lands.'[141]

Freyfogle's emphasis on state management rather than ownership may be apt if one adopts the concept of underlying beneficial ownership by the public at large. Where the state is a bare trustee, its role is reduced to management of trust assets for the exclusive benefit of the true beneficial owners, who retain the bulk of the key bundle rights. The state's residual right is essentially a right to manage constrained by trust obligations. Shorn of most of the hallmark property rights, it may be unrealistic to describe the state's dearth of bundle rights in public property as proprietorial.[142]

Indeed, from the state's perspective, is ownership per se the prime objective? As Sally Fairfax and her colleagues observe:

> Ownership does not ensure control. The relevant myth here suggests that if you own land, you can protect it. The reality ... is that formal ownership frequently provides little control or resource protection at all.[143]

The state as bare owner may be better employed devoting its energies to the effective control of the public land that it manages on behalf of its citizens. Good state management may reinforce the integrity of public property and silence its critics.[144]

Ownership of public property is a vexed issue. Its inexactitude suggests that it is not the defining characteristic of public property that it should be. Who owns public property and in what capacity are complex questions lacking ready answers. Part of this struggle may be attributed to a values paradigm of dominant individualism. Its end result leaves us less equipped to meaningfully understand the ownership of public property in land.

D. Ownership and Diffusion

One clearer way to explain the conundrum of ownership is the idea of diffusion, Rose's 'the more the merrier'.[145] Simply, the more dispersed a sense of 'ownership' by individual members of the public of the vast public estate, the more self-interested we become in its management, use and welfare. Diffusion rests on an

---

[140] Freyfogle (n 27) 93.

[141] Ibid.

[142] 'Property rights may contain so few traditional sticks in the bundle as to defy continued description by the term *property*': LS Raymond, *Private Rights in Public Resources* (Washington DC, Resources for the Future, 2003) 18 (emphasis in original).

[143] Fairfax et al (n 29) 257.

[144] Brower et al (n 21).

[145] Rose, above n 7.

instinctive imperative that citizens should conceive of public property as their own, no matter how thin the 'ownership'.

Such a disaggregation of property ownership amongst the public at large decentralises property 'rights' and spreads relative degrees of 'ownership' amongst a wide class of persons.[146] Joseph Singer describes similar ideas of dispersal as inherent to his 'nuisance model' of property: 'The effect is to identify multiple persons who have legally protected interests in the same piece of property and therefore have something to say about how it is used.'[147] That the law will act to protect public property rights,[148] sometimes at the behest of the state, but often at the instigation of informal community or representative groups, the spontaneous 'friends of public space' movements, is a tangible manifestation of the diffusion of public ownership of land.

Diffusion is deeply conceptual and problematic in practice. How can scattered public 'ownership' rights be regulated and enforced? What can prevent a motivated, self-interested few capturing the public estate to the detriment of an apathetic many? The American experience of the public trust suggests a role for the judiciary as guardians of the public interest in public property. This chapter does not purport to provide ready answers to such prosaic matters. Yet, fundamentally, developing a sense of public propriety requires paradigmatic change. Articulating what a right of inclusion may encompass is one step in beginning such an incremental shift.

V. THE RIGHT TO INCLUDE

If exclusion is the hallmark right of modern private property,[149] logically inclusion should be public property's inverse gatekeeper.[150] As a guiding principle, what is meant by a right to include? Does its foil define it, such that it is a right *not* to exclude? Or does it have an independent, positive meaning?

Carol Rose warns that:

> It is a serious mistake to think of property only in metaphors of exclusion, boundaries, and disengagement. These are metaphors drawn chiefly from land, but human[s] have devised ways to allocate property in many other things ... We have created not only individual property, but also partnership property, common property and public property. Human interactions make property into a thoroughly malleable institution, and one that adjusts to a vast variety of subjects.[151]

Rose's advice intimates that exclusion is a flawed place to start. Nor is Rose alone in observing that property is a 'thoroughly malleable institution' that moulds to its

---

[146] J Page, 'Towards a Sustainable Paradigm for Property' (2011) 1 *Property Law Journal* 86.

[147] JW Singer, *Entitlement: The Paradoxes of Property* (New Haven, Yale University Press, 2000) 88. His 'environmental or good neighbor' model is a later refinement. JW Singer, 'Property Norms Construct the Externalities of Ownership' in Alexander and Penalver (n 46) 57, 60.

[148] Rose (n 7).

[149] Merrill (n 100).

[150] Hamilton and Bankes (n 4) 19, 26.

[151] CM Rose, 'Rhetoric and Romance: A Comment on Spouses and Strangers' (1992–93) 82 *Georgetown Law Journal* 2409, 2420.

context.[152] To define inclusion by what it is not is counter-contextual and affirms that exclusion is the sine qua non of property.[153] Inclusion merits a stand-alone definition.

Language is one starting point. *Roget's Thesaurus* lists numerous synonyms for 'inclusion'—participation, membership, affiliation, eligibility, admission—terms that embody shared or common use of space.[154] The links between language and property are intimate and powerful; Carol Rose calls them 'a central project of her legal scholarship'.[155] Language is not only words in a thesaurus but, in a broader sense, a means of persuasive communication. In the case of property, it is its symbols, visual cues or collective narratives.[156] Rose proffers a number of images as the 'expressive endeavor' or 'symbolic presentation'[157] of public property: streetscapes, parks, highways and, most evocatively, a fresco of a medieval street scene, a 'good life' where 'people stop to chat with one another and with the street vendors ... laugh at a pet monkey's antics, drop into a shop and buy something, or have a seat and watch the other passers-by'.[158] The democratic sharing of a public space is an uncomplicated way to 'see' public property in land, an image that captures the diverse language of inclusion. It is the antithesis of private property's 'expressive endeavor', the fence, gate and keep-out sign.

A. Inclusion and Access

Access ought to be the epitome of inclusion. It lies at the heart of Rose's street scene. Yet the right of access is far from clear-cut. Some public lands are openly accessible, others have conditions attached to their intrusion (such as the payment of entrance fees in popular national parks), while in other cases, there is no access at all (military land, or dedicated wilderness or wildlife preservation areas).[159] In other cases, legislation may give an occupier of prescribed public lands the discretion to eject intruders, provided that a prior demand to leave is made, deeming the recalcitrant intruder a trespasser.[160] Such legislation places the emphasis on the right to exclude, at times confusing Barnes' 'needs of society as a whole' with the 'self-serving interest' of the particular occupier.[161] In sum, access as a proposition is a mélange of unqualified, qualified or denied entitlement.

---

[152] See, eg, Singer, *Entitlement* (n 147); JL Sax, 'Property Rights and the Economy of Nature' (1992) 45 *Stanford Law Review* 1433, 1446.

[153] Merrill (n 100).

[154] *Roget's Thesaurus of English Words and Phrases* (Hammondsworth, Penguin, 1962) 755.

[155] Rose (n 95) 2.

[156] CM Rose, 'Property as Storytelling: Perspectives from Game Theory, Narrative Theory, Feminist Theory' (1990) 2 *Yale Journal of Law & the Humanities* 37.

[157] Ibid.

[158] Rose (n 95) 18.

[159] Public access is denied to Codfish Island in New Zealand, home to a Department of Conservation breeding programme for the endangered flightless Kakapo parrot.

[160] See, eg, Inclosed Lands Protection Land Act 1901 (NSW) or Trespass Act 1980 (NZ).

[161] Proceedings of the Federated Mountain Clubs Backcountry Recreation 2000 Conference, *Ruling and Regulating or Freedom of the Hills*, St Arnaud, Nelson Lakes, 27–29 September 1991.

Even where access appears unfettered, externalities may in practice restrict freedom of entry. A surrounding land-holder may effectively capture the public lands by impeding the most feasible points of access. A consequence of effective capture is their de facto privatisation. Private capture of public lands in New Zealand's iconic high country is the subject of separate academic scrutiny.[162] Equally, contested access through private land to beach and coastal foreshore attracts vocal, high-profile attention.[163] In June 2010, *Stop the Beach Renourishment v Florida Department of Environmental Protection*[164] was 'the [US Supreme Court's] case of the year for planners and land use practitioners',[165] a curious dispute about property rights, accretion and littoral access. Beaches are much-loved public places.[166] Access to them engages the *many* as well as the *few*[167] in both theory and practice. Yet, despite their revered status, access to wet sands can be perplexing.[168] In the US, piecemeal[169] public rights depend on the vagaries of jurisdiction, limited by the low tide in some states, extending to the mean high-tide mark in others, and in Texas protected by public rolling easements to the first vegetation line.[170] Access is an underdeveloped discourse in the common law,[171] too often dependent on agency whim rather than espoused as a universal right qualified only on principle.[172] Its uncertainties deny it default status as a benchmark for public property rights in land.

B. Inclusion and Use and Enjoyment

It is imperative therefore that inclusion embraces wider meanings than ingress and egress. Can public property be *used and enjoyed* without physical access? As previously traversed, the incorporeal conservation easement serves a multitude of uses and purposes. These include the provision of ecosystem services,[173] 'viewsheds',[174]

---

[162] A Brower, *Who Owns the High Country?* (Nelson, Craig Potton, 2008); J Page and A Brower, *Property Law in the South Island High Country—Statutory Not Common Law Leases* (2007) 15 *Waikato Law Review* 48.

[163] At the Sea Ranch in northern California, 'developers and other private littoral owners have either unknowingly or intentionally, blocked existing means of public access': D Dyer, 'California Beach Access: The Mexican Law and the Public Trust' (1972) 2 *Ecology Law Quarterly* 571, 573.

[164] *Stop the Beach Renourishment v Florida Department of Environmental Protection*, 130 S Ct 2592, 17 June 2010.

[165] L Lucero, 'Stop the Beach Renourishment—Six Perspectives' (2010) 3 *Planning & Environmental Law* 62–69.

[166] Bederman (n 47).

[167] M Olson, *The Logic of Collective Action: Public Goods and the Theory of Groups* (Cambridge, MA, Harvard University Press, 1968).

[168] Stevens (n 125) 230.

[169] Bender (n 59) 914.

[170] T Eichenberg et al, 'Climate Change and the Public Trust Doctrine: Using an Ancient Doctrine to Adapt to Rising Sea Levels in San Francisco Bay' (2010) 3 *Golden Gate University Environmental Law Journal* 243, 248–49; M Peloso and M Caldwell, 'Dynamic Property Rights: The Public Trust Doctrine and Takings in a Changing Climate' (2011) 30 *Stanford Environmental Law Journal* 51, 57–85.

[171] *Cf* Scandinavia's allemansratten: Anderson (n 23) 404.

[172] R Boast, *Foreshore and Seabed* (Auckland, LexisNexis, 2005) 6.

[173] Examples include lands set aside for carbon sequestration.

[174] S McKee, 'Conservation Easements to Protect Historic Viewsheds' in Gustanski and Squires (n 25).

open space[175] or wildlife corridors.[176] Inherent to each is an intangible and indirect public *enjoyment* absent access.

The right of use and enjoyment is described as hierarchically lower, 'less compelling'[177] than other significant property rights, in particular the right to exclude. While the private right is dominated by the descriptor of active *use*, its public equivalent may have a different conjunctive emphasis, one where physical use is ancillary to a primary enjoyment. Where physical access is permitted, the public right may encompass both limbs—use and enjoyment—but where other indirect public benefits ensue minus access, the right falls away to one of enjoyment *simpliciter*. The umbrella right of inclusion is analogous to a diffuse public enjoyment of land, in which individuals derive a public good, but where individual enjoyment of that good is no greater than any other member's enjoyment. Pointedly, access is a non-essential component.

However, the public good is a malleable, circumstantial concept. Eric Freyfogle advocates the need for private property to serve the 'public good'.[178] Jeremy Waldron observes the primacy of a 'collective social interest' in defining collective property.[179] Richard Barnes agrees: 'The organizing idea of collective property is that the needs of society as a whole take precedence over those of individuals.'[180] What overarching societal need explains public enjoyment? Why should the public enjoy a general right to be included? *Propriety* offers the beginnings of at least one answer to this question.

C. Inclusion and Propriety

To Gregory Alexander, the commodity view of property is only one-half of the dialectic of modern property. The missing half, 'property as propriety', provides the 'material foundation for creating and maintaining the proper social order', a civic conception of a 'properly ordered society'.[181] Propriety enables the 'well-lived life',[182] in which individual interaction and reciprocity of social obligation within community constitutes 'human flourishing in a very deep sense'.[183] Human flourishing speaks to property's marginalised communitarian values:

> Flourishing is an unavoidably cooperative endeavor rather than an individual pursuit or purely personal project. Our ability to flourish requires certain basic material goods and a

---

[175] Brewer (n 30) 155; Donohue (n 44) 119; S Silverstone, 'Open Space Preservation through Conservation Easements' (1974) 12 *Osgoode Hall Law Journal* 105.

[176] K Ewing, 'Conservation Covenants and Community Conservation Groups' (2009) *New Zealand Journal Environmental Law* 316.

[177] L Underkuffler, *The Idea of Property: Its Meaning and Power* (Oxford, Oxford University Press, 2003) 25.

[178] ET Freyfogle, *On Private Property: Finding Common Ground on the Ownership of Land* (Boston, Beacon Press, 2007).

[179] Waldron (n 85) 328.

[180] Barnes (n 101) 154.

[181] Alexander (n 46) 2–3; Barnes (n 101) 112.

[182] GS Alexander, 'The Social-Obligation Norm in North American Property Law' (2009) 94 *Cornell Law Review* 745, 763.

[183] Ibid, 761.

communal infrastructure ... However much we value our personal independence, it is quite literally impossible for a person to flourish without others.[184]

Public property in land is an important component in the propitious, well-ordered community. It is the 'communal infrastructure', the physical and metaphorical common ground, where shared activities 'socialize, democratize and educate society'.[185] In its corporeal form, it provides space for egalitarian recreation.[186] In its incorporeal form, it may minimise the tragic risk of fragmentation[187] or engender what Kevin Gray terms 'pedestrian democracy', a 'flourishing of the civil and ecological communities of which we humans are a part'[188] that heightens 'civic responsibility and ... participation in an integrative society of equals'.[189] By contrast, modern private property marginalises propriety. Its commoditisation leaves scant scope for alternative paradigms, the likes of stewardship[190] or economies of nature,[191] to take root. Its abstraction decouples property right from place, preferring anonymous cartographic space to the lived sociable experience of community.[192]

James Kunstler's study of the decline of America's cities highlights the importance of public property to properly ordered communities. Kunstler writes of growing up in a soulless suburbia whose 'motive force [was] the exaltation of privacy and the elimination of the public realm'.[193] By contrast, summer camp visits to Lebanon, New Hampshire, with its 'town square, band shells, elm street trees, and various civic buildings',[194] highlighted the lost dignity and substance of public space. Nicholas Blomley likewise draws the link between property diversity and community, arguing that the private-centric 'ownership model'[195] is inadequate to describe a 'diversity of property on the ground'.[196] Modern global cities are 'intensely propertied places', *terra populi*,[197] where communities are given form and normative meaning by their collective claims to public space.

Public property is critical to the social and communal fabric. It fills the void vacated by a commoditised private property, such that Alexander's theory is optimally *public* property as propriety. Rather than a false dawn for access, the right to include may be better understood as a universal entitlement to flourish in well-ordered

---

[184] GS Alexander and EM Penalver, *An Introduction to Property Theory* (New York, Cambridge University Press, 2012) 87.

[185] Rose (n 7) 779, 781.

[186] J Laitos and T Carr, 'The Transformation on Public Lands' (1999) 26 *Ecology Law Quarterly* 178.

[187] ET Freyfogle, *Agrarianism and the Good Society* (Lexington, University Press of Kentucky, 2007) 9–24.

[188] K Gray, 'Pedestrian Democracy and the Geography of Hope' (2010) 1 *Journal of Human Rights and the Environment* 45, 52, writing of the right to roam.

[189] Ibid, 54.

[190] W Lucy and C Mitchell, 'Replacing Private Property: The Case for Stewardship' (1996) 55 *CLJ* 566.

[191] JL Sax, *Ownership, Property and Sustainability* (Salt Lake City, University of Utah Press, 2011) 14; Sax (n 152) 1446.

[192] C Meine, *Correction Lines: Essays on Land, Leopold, and Conservation* (Washington DC, Island Press, 2004); N Blomley, *Unsettling the City: Urban Land and the Politics of Property* (New York, Routledge, 2004) 91.

[193] Kuntsler (n 62) 189.

[194] Ibid, 13.

[195] Singer, 'Property Norms' (n 147).

[196] Blomley (n 192) 15.

[197] Blomley (n 192) 93.

communities, places symbolised by Rose's deeply expressive streetscape. Public property enables well-lived lives by acting as an 'entrance to community',[198] the vehicle through which public inclusion imposes and legitimises the idea of public property rights in land.

VI. CONCLUSION

It has been an explicit objective of this chapter to highlight the 'property' in the public property equation. In so doing, diverse interests in public land have been explored, vexed issues of ownership canvassed and aspects of inclusion laid open to initial scrutiny.

In the common law, modern public property remains a work in progress, an underdeveloped institution deficient in the ways identified in this chapter's introduction. But immaturity need not be its evolutionary end.[199] Structure, sophistry and coherence should be our ambitions for public property in land. At the heart of any resurgent public property lies the right to include. Inclusion speaks to property's collective values, representing what we can peaceably enjoy in common beyond individual allocation and exploitation. Properly formed and defined, inclusion is the perfect foil to exclusion. It renders a harmonious balance between, on the one hand, property's social and communitarian traditions, and, on the other, its private and individualistic instincts.

---

[198] EM Penalver, 'Property as Entrance' (2005) 91 *Virginia Law Review* 1889.

[199] *Cf* public property in Roman or Spanish American law: D Coquillette, 'Mosses from an Old Manse: Another Look at Some Historic Property Cases about the Environment' (1979) 64 *Cornell Law Review* 761, 802–03; Dyer (n 163) 573.

11

The Sale of Items in Museum Collections

JANET ULPH[*]

I. INTRODUCTION

FOR MANY YEARS, museums have been used as repositories for items donated by benevolent people either during their lifetime or by will. Curators and managers once unquestioningly accepted these donations. Many museums amassed large collections in this manner. It was not simply a case of museums not asking about the history of an item or how the donor had come to acquire it: at times, insufficient consideration was given to the cultural value of the item and whether it would be of interest to either researchers or the viewing public, and what it might cost to store. Little thought was given as to what the future might hold.

The process of management of museum collections has changed in recent years and senior officers in the museum sector have become cautious in relation to accepting items and formally accessioning them into their permanent collections.[1] In particular, officers have become increasingly aware of the danger of accidentally acquiring illicit material that has been looted and exported from overseas. Reviews of collections have become regular and more thorough. It has become apparent that, at least in some cases, irresponsible accessioning of items has created a financial dilemma for the museum concerned. Furthermore, there is greater awareness that storage of museum items can be a costly business. Some items, such as those made with animal or vegetable fibres, are vulnerable to decay due to changes in temperature and attacks by pests. Collections may be expensive to preserve. For example, in 1996, the Director of the National Maritime Museum declared that it cost £20,000 per year to care for 3,000 flags in its collection.[2] Large items stored outside may begin to deteriorate in wet weather. The costs of storage have become a matter of acute concern in the face of government financial cutbacks. Unless a museum is independently wealthy, it is vulnerable in a recession: cuts in financial support from central or local government may mean unambitious displays, staff redundancies, shorter opening hours or even closure.

---

[*] AHRC Fellow with the Museums Association 2011–12, School of Law, University of Leicester.
[1] Guidance is provided by pt 5 of the Code of Ethics of the Museums Association; and the Department for Culture Media and Sport, *Combating Illicit Trade: Due Diligence Guidelines for Museums, Libraries and Archives on Collecting and Borrowing Cultural Material* (2005).
[2] C Milner, 'Greenwich Sell-off Triggers Art Row' *Sunday Telegraph* (29 October 1996).

In certain circumstances, an item can be removed from a museum collection. It will be done by a process of deaccession and, if the removal is intended to be permanent, this removal will be described as 'disposal'. However, the phrase 'disposal' does not tell us what will happen to that object: it may be transferred to another museum, sold, destroyed or repatriated to its source country. The transfer of an item to another museum, or its repatriation to a community, can be welcomed because it will normally be done in order to increase public engagement. In contrast, if an item from a museum collection is sold to a private collector, it may be lost forever to the viewing public. Consequently, a sale can be controversial. If only a few restrictions exist, there is a risk that these items will be viewed purely in financial terms: members of its governing body may see their sale as a simple way to raise money for other causes. Even where the decision to remove items has been taken as part of a review of the collection by the museum curators and staff, without a desire to obtain cash as a primary motive, mistakes can be made.

The sustainability of museums does not simply have a financial dimension. The items in museum collections have a cultural value and the museums exist to serve the long-term public benefit. Museums must therefore be sustainable in the sense of being relevant to people today, whilst caring for collections for the benefit of generations to come. There is thus a tension between two different schools of thought. On the one hand, some people consider that all items in museum collections need to be preserved for future generations, while, on the other hand, there is a concern that museums should enjoy sufficient flexibility to evolve in response to social and economic changes.[3] These issues have been the focus of debate.[4] However, I would suggest that the more fundamental question is the extent to which the law, as opposed to ethical principles, does and should provide guidance in relation to the care and disposal of cultural objects forming part of museum collections.

This chapter concentrates on transfers and sales to other museums and auction sales to the highest bidder. It explores the application of the law and ethical principles to the disposal of unwanted items. It demonstrates that the law provides museums with guidance which is currently inadequate by itself. But it maintains that this gap should be filled by ethical principles, which have a vital role to play in assisting museums in deciding what they should and should not do in order to fulfil their role of engaging with current members of the public whilst acting as stewards of their collections for the benefit of future generations.

II. CULTURAL VALUE

Cultural objects enjoy a special status because of their intrinsic cultural value.[5] They are a source of information relating to our past, assisting us in understanding how the

---

[3] Museums might therefore be expected to act as moral activists in relation to issues such as social inclusion and human rights: R Sandell, 'On Ethics, Activism and Human Rights' in J Marstine (ed), *The Routledge Companion to Museum Ethics* (London and New York, Routledge, 2011) 129.

[4] For a collection of essays on this debate, see P Davies (ed), *Museums and the Disposal Debate* (Edinburgh, MuseumsEtc Publishing, 2011).

[5] S Guest, 'The Value of Art' (2002) VII(4) *Art Antiquity and Law* 305.

world and our nation have evolved. They help to define us as human beings. Elsen observes that: 'Art tells us who we are and where we came from.'[6] Merryman has commented that: 'A cultural object embodies or expresses or evokes some aspect of the culture of its time and place.'[7] It is precisely these attributes which prompt members of the public to go to museums to admire these objects and to learn more about them.

Cultural objects are therefore complex because of their dual nature: they will have a financial value in the marketplace and yet will also possess cultural value in terms of creativity and information. To an extent, their financial value will be linked to their cultural value. For example, over the centuries, archaeologists have gathered information about the past, which formed the archaeological record. This information eventually became absorbed into national stories of development and civilisation.[8] Objects of antiquity which were integral to these stories attracted great interest. Some of these objects were acquired by museums, but others were purchased by private collectors. Increasingly, as these types of items were amassed in collections, whether public or private, their financial value soared.

Everyday items normally have a relatively short life and are regularly bought and sold without any detailed consideration of their history. However, cultural items deserve special protection, so that they can be safeguarded for the benefit of mankind in the long term. Increasingly from the eighteenth century onwards, international conventions and agreements have recognised the special status of cultural property.[9] In 2002, the UK government acceded to the United Nations Convention on the Means of Prohibiting and Preventing the Illicit Import, Export and Transfer of Ownership of Cultural Property 1970.[10] This Convention requires Contracting States to take steps to protect their own cultural items and to prevent the illicit movement or transfer of cultural objects which have been stolen or illegally exported. Article 5(e) calls for the establishment of ethical codes for curators, collectors and dealers in order to encourage compliance with its principles. Museums in the UK follow guidance in the Code of Ethics, which has been produced and revised by the Museums Association (which is an independent association representing museums and galleries in the UK). The Code of Ethics provides a set of general ethical principles. It requires museums to take care in acquiring cultural objects and to refuse any object with a dubious provenance.[11] It is therefore not unreasonable to expect

---

[6] A Elsen, 'Why Do We Care about Art?' 27 *Hastings Law Journal* 951, 952. For further discussion of the notion that art is special and is a mirror of culture, see PM Bator, 'An Essay on the International Trade in Art' (1982) 34 *Stanford Law Review* 275, 304–06. See also D Watkins, 'The Value of Art or the Art We Value?' (2006) XI(3) *Art Antiquity and Law* 251, 258.

[7] JH Merryman, 'Counterfeit Art' (1992) 1 *International Journal of Cultural Property* 27, reproduced in JH Merryman, *Thinking About the Elgin Marbles* (The Netherlands, Kluwer Law International, 2009), 468.

[8] See Y Hamilakis, 'From Ethics to Politics' in Y Hamilakis and PH Duke (eds), *Archaeology and Capitalism: from Ethics to Politics* (Walnut Creek, CA, Left Coast Press) 15, 17.

[9] For example, the idea that cultural property must be protected because it is the heritage of all mankind is emphasised in the Preamble to the Convention for the Protection of Cultural Property in the Event of Armed Conflict, 14 May 1954, 249 UNTS 216, 240. See further K Chamberlain, *War and Cultural Heritage* (Leicester, Institute of Art and Law, 2004) 7-8.

[10] 14 November 1970 (1971) 823 UNTS 231, 10 ILM 289.

[11] See pt 5 of the Museums Association's Code of Ethics 2008; DCMS guidance, *Combating Illicit Trade: Due Diligence Guidelines for Museums, Libraries and Archives on Collecting and Borrowing Cultural Material* (2005).

museums to exercise the same high level of diligence when they are considering the deaccessioning and disposal of cultural items.

It might be assumed that the law is adequate to govern the disposal of items from museum collections. The law can regulate situations where people consent to hold property for the benefit of others rather than themselves. The mechanism is a trust, and trustees will be under a legal obligation to take reasonable care of trust property. If trustees fail to insure trust property or if they transfer such property to a person who is not entitled to it, they will be in breach of trust. But is trusts law sufficient in this context? It can be argued that what the law can provide works well in a situation which is concerned with legal entitlement and business-like conduct. The law offers a framework to regulate dealings in any type of property, where a person has the legal estate (the trustee) and holds it for a beneficiary or for a charitable purpose. Yet applying principles of private law alone to dealings with cultural property may not necessarily be appropriate, particularly where one needs to consider how the acquisition, care and disposal of cultural items may benefit future generations. This is because these items will usually be significant in terms of human relationships, such as an individual's family ties, or spiritual beliefs, or sense of belonging within a local community. This is where the law may be at the edge of its frontier and where ethical principles may be needed to provide guidance.

III. STEWARDSHIP

Ethical principles will normally be irrelevant where the governing body of a museum decides to dispose of commonplace items, such as unwanted office furniture or equipment. However, in the case of cultural items, the position is different. Cultural items may assist in creating a sense of cultural identity, establishing common bonds and bringing communities together. It is because of these qualities that they attract ethical duties. Once one recognises, for example, that cultural items may be used to support a sense of group identity, it then becomes a natural (and ethical) step to assume that one should consult local communities when it is proposed to dispose of them.

In response to increasing professionalism, ethical principles have been articulated in a formal manner in codes within the museum sector,[12] followed by the archaeological sector. These codes, which often combine both legal and ethical considerations, usually provide that professionals are 'stewards' or guardians of cultural property in their care. The notion of stewardship suggests that there will be responsibility for the care of cultural property over a substantial period of time. Like trustees in law, stewards are expected to avoid any conflict of interest and should not purchase any items for which they have responsibility. However, the role of a steward should be distinguished from that of a trustee. First, trustees do not necessarily have any expertise in relation to the property in their care: they may be chosen by the testator or donor due to a family relationship or friendship, for example; even charity trustees (including museum trustees) may be selected for their business acumen and their

---

[12] See, eg the Museums Association's Code of Ethics 2008 and the International Council of Museums (ICOM) Code of Ethics 2004. The American Association of Museums (AAM) introduced its first statement of ethical principles in 1925.

potential for establishing partnerships with corporate sponsors rather than on the basis of their knowledge of the property held by the charity. In contrast, the concept of stewardship (or guardianship) is normally associated not only with professional care,[13] but also with intimate knowledge and appreciation of the cultural value of the property in question.[14]

Various common threads emerge in considering how ethical considerations apply to cultural property. An understanding of cultural value will mean that the steward will be sensitive to the relationship between communities and their heritage.[15] Thus, it is increasingly recognised by archaeologists in this country and elsewhere that their discipline is not the exclusive preserve of trained professionals and that the public are stakeholders in their heritage and deserve to be consulted where appropriate.[16] For museums, this may mean reflecting on new ways to share the rights and responsibilities of heritage objects. In both sectors, there is intense concern to avoid commodifying cultural property. Consequently, in the archaeological sector, ethical considerations may dictate that professionals should not offer expert advice to people such as dealers and collectors. The rationale is that assisting such people merely helps to fuel the illicit trade in archaeological artefacts by increasing the interest of collectors in certain types of object. There is concern that, from an ethical perspective, archaeologists should not put themselves in a position where they seem to be encouraging others to buy and sell antiquities in the market, thereby encouraging an environment where the cultural dimension of objects is viewed as subsidiary to the price that they may realise.

Sustainability is also part of stewardship. In the UK, this point is reflected in the Code of Ethics of the Museums Association.[17] It is also recognised by the Institute for Archaeologists, who observe in their professional guidance that:

> Protection and enhancement is part of stewardship for the global environment. By managing change, stewardship sustains valued assets so that they can meet the needs of today's communities and remain available for the benefit of future generations. Stewardship reflects the public value of the historic environment by encouraging active involvement in its management and prompting community awareness.[18]

In the archaeological sector, stewardship is linked to the archaeological record. The emphasis is upon stewardship of information, as the objects themselves eventually

---

[13] See, eg the By-Laws, *Code of Conduct* (2009), of the Institute for Archaeologists which, in its Introduction, stated that: 'Archaeology is the study and care for the physical evidence of the human past.'

[14] *Standard and Guidance for Stewardship of the Historic Environment* (2009) of the Institute for Archaeologists, para [1.5].

[15] A Pantazatos, 'Does Diaspora Test the Limits of Stewardship? Stewardship and the Ethics of Care' (2010) 62 *Museum International* 96, 99.

[16] As regards the US, see Principle 1 of the Code of Ethics of the Society for American Archaeology (SAA), which was first adopted in 1996: 'Stewards are both caretakers of and advocates for the archaeological record for the benefit of all people; as they investigate and interpret the record, they should use the specialized knowledge they gain to promote public understanding and support for its long-term preservation.' In relation to 'collaborative stewardship', see A Wylie, 'The Promise and the Perils of an Ethic of Stewardship' in L Meskell and P Pells (eds), *Embedding Ethics* (Oxford and New York, Berg Press) 47, 65.

[17] Code of Ethics, para [6.0].

[18] *Standard and Guidance for Stewardship of the Historic Environment* (2009) of the Institute for Archaeologists, para [1.4].

may be handed over to the local landowner or a museum.[19] In the museum sector, ethical principles have a longer history and are more complex because they are concerned with the acquisition of the objects themselves and their preservation in the long term.

The Museums Association's Code of Ethics has evolved over a period of more than 35 years. It has been revised at times after consultation with the museum sector, enabling it to have sufficient flexibility to deal with new problems which have emerged. In its current form, the Code of Ethics opens by stating that: 'Museums behave as ethical guardians as well as owners of collections. They never relinquish the trust invested in them, without public consent.'[20] The Code goes on to provide further general principles, such as the proposition that museum officers should never view items in collections as their personal property.[21] They are expected to recognise the public purpose of museums and to put the public interest before other interests.[22] The Code emphasises that museums must hold the items in their care for the benefit of the public and should encourage people to explore the collections for inspiration, learning and enjoyment. Museums are expected to consult stakeholders, such as donors, and also the public at large. Museums must be sustainable and must manage their collections in a responsible manner.

The Code of Ethics is valuable because it provides a form of guiding principles to regulate the ethical conduct of the museum sector. The Code's general principles have been supplemented by a booklet entitled the 'Disposals Toolkit', which supplies further principles. The Ethics Committee of the Museums Association holds regular meetings at which it considers confidential applications from individual museums seeking further guidance in relation to the application of these principles. The Code of Ethics permits the governing bodies of museums to take responsibility for their conduct, whilst encouraging them to seek advice from various sources.

The Code of Ethics is not merely an aspirational set of principles: members of the Museums Association expect their colleagues to adhere to them. There is an ultimate sanction: those who flagrantly break the rules can be thrown out of the Museums Association, and they may then be unable to apply for government grants. This approach, whereby the Code does more than merely encourage members to act in an ethical manner, has the potential to act as a brake on change; even so, the Code is kept under review by the Museums Association and the museum sector is regularly consulted on topical issues.

---

[19] See the By-Laws, *Code of Conduct*, of the Institute for Archaeologists, para [3.5]: 'A member shall ensure that the record, including artefacts and specimens and experimental results, is maintained in good condition while in his/her charge and shall seek to ensure that it is eventually deposited where it is likely to receive adequate curatorial care.'

[20] Museums Association, Code of Ethics, para [1.0]. The International Council of Museums (ICOM) has a Code of Ethics which suggest, at [2.0], that inherent in the nature of public trust is the notion of stewardship. The ICOM's principles have been generally accepted within the international museum community.

[21] Ibid, para [1.3].

[22] Ibid, para [2.1].

IV. NATIONAL MUSEUMS

Statutory principles exist to regulate disposals of items from national museum collections in the UK. For example, the British Museum Act 1963 provides that trustees of the British Museum and the Natural History Museum have a statutory duty to keep items in their collections.[23] The emphasis is upon accessibility by the public. Consequently, the trustees may decide to keep part of their collection in storage, but, even so, they must make items available for inspection by members of the public, such as researchers, upon request.[24] The trustees may decide to lend items for public exhibitions (and, in the case of the Natural History Museum, for the purposes of research), taking account of such matters as the rarity of the item, its physical condition and any risks to which it is likely to be exposed.[25] The 1963 Act does allow the trustees of the British Museum and the Natural History Museum to sell, exchange or give away an item from their collections if it is a duplicate, if it is a print made after 1850 where a copy is available or if the item is unfit to be retained in the collection and its removal would not be to the detriment of researchers.[26] There is also a statutory power to transfer items between specified national museums.[27] Apart from these limited exceptions, the trustees are prohibited from transferring or selling items.

The main statute governing other national museums is the Museums and Galleries Act 1992.[28] Its provisions affect museums as diverse as the British Library, the Imperial War Museum, the National Portrait Gallery, the Science Museum, the Tate Gallery and the Victoria and Albert Museum.[29] In addition, there are a number of other statutes which relate to particular museums. The museums have different missions: the Victoria and Albert Museum promotes the aesthetic world, for example, while the National Portrait Gallery is concerned, unsurprisingly, with portraits. It might therefore be assumed that the relevant statutes would vary greatly one from another. In fact, this is not the case. All of the statutes, including the British Museum Act 1963 and the Museums and Galleries Act 1992, have common threads. They all emphasise that trustees must take care of items in their collections. They focus on public benefit and direct the trustees to ensure that items from the collections are exhibited to the public or are readily available to researchers. In order to broaden

---

[23] British Museum Act 1963, s 3(4). The two museums can transfer items from one to the other: ibid, s 9(1), as amended by the Museums and Galleries Act 1992.

[24] Ibid, ss 3, 8.

[25] Ibid ss 4, 8(3), as amended by Museums and Galleries Act 1992, s 11(2), sch 8.

[26] British Museums Act 1963, ss 5(1), 8(3), as amended by the Museums and Galleries Act 1992, s 11(2), sch 8, para 1.

[27] British Museums Act 1963, s 9, as amended by the Museums and Galleries Act 1992, s 11(3), sch 9. The statutory power to transfer to other museums is provided by s 6 of the Museums and Galleries Act 1992.

[28] The 1992 Act amended the British Museum Act 1963, thereby affecting the powers and responsibilities of the trustees of the British Museum and the Natural History Museum.

[29] See Museums and Galleries Act 1992, sch 5, pt I (amended by SI 2000/2955). The statute also extends to the Armouries, the Wallace Collection, the Museum of London, the National Gallery, the National Maritime Museum, the National Museums and Galleries of Merseyside, the Historic Buildings and Monuments Commissions for England, the National Library of Scotland, the National Museums of Scotland and the National Galleries of Scotland. As regards Welsh museums, see the Government of Wales Act 2006, sch 11, para 30.

public engagement, they provide that museums can make loans of items from their collections, but must have regard to the purposes for which a loan was requested (such as a public exhibition), the interests of stakeholders, the physical condition of the item and any risks to which it might be exposed.[30]

The Museums and Galleries Act 1992 permits museums to transfer items to other national museums.[31] However, the Act more generally imposes restrictions on sale, exchange or gift which are similar to the British Museum Act 1963.[32] The 1992 Act and other relevant statutes permit certain museums to dispose of items which are duplicates, or which are items which are unsuitable to be retained in the collection and where their removal would not be to the detriment of researchers and other members of the public.[33] The restrictions vary according to the mission of the museum. For example, an additional ground for disposal is given to the National Portrait Gallery: it is permitted to sell a portrait where the trustees are satisfied the identification of the person in the portrait which was originally provided has been discredited. Yet, as the main purpose of the National Portrait Gallery is to maintain a collection of portraits of the most eminent persons in British history, this additional power of disposal fits with the mission of the museum. In contrast, the Wallace Collection Board has a duty to maintain the collection of objects known as the 'Wallace Collection' intact; the Board therefore cannot either add or remove any items from the collection.[34]

At first glance, these statutory provisions appear to severely restrict the powers of museums to dispose of items. Thus, for example, even if museum trustees would like to return items in order to satisfy a moral obligation, such as by repatriating an item to a source country, they may not be able to do so if their governing statute prohibits it.[35] It is only where the statute is silent or ambiguous that the trustees may seek authorisation from the Charity Commissioners or the courts to sanction a scheme which involves a change of purpose but which does not conflict with the statute.[36] The rigid statutory prohibition on the deaccessioning and disposal of items, apart from in narrowly confined circumstances, has caused problems. For example, the UK government established a Spoliation Advisory Panel in 2000 to make recommendations when there was a request for the return of cultural items from those who had been stripped of their possessions during the Holocaust period. However, some museums did not have the legal power to

---

[30] Museums and Galleries Act 1992, s 5(1), (2). In relation to other statutes applying to designated museums, see the National Maritime Museum Act 1934, s 2(3); the Museum of London Act 1965, s 6; the National Heritage Act 1983, ss 7, 15, 19, 28; the Imperial War Museum Act 1920, s 2(1), as amended by the Museums and Galleries Act 1992, s 11, sch 8, para 9, sch 9.

[31] Museums and Galleries Act 1992, ss 4(4), 6.

[32] Ibid, s 6.

[33] Ibid, s 4(4), (5). See further the Imperial War Museum Act 1920, s 2; the Museum of London Act 1965, s 5(2); the National Heritage Act 1963, ss 6(3), 14(3), 20(3), 27(2); the British Library Act 1972, sch para 11(4). However, the National Gallery is not provided with this statutory power of disposal: the Museums and Galleries Act 1992, s 4(3).

[34] Museums and Galleries Act 1992, s 4(6).

[35] *Attorney General v Trustees of the British Museum (Commission for Looted Art in Europe intervening)* [2005] EWHC 1089, [2005] Ch 397, 412.

[36] Ibid, 408–09. See further *Re Shipwrecked Fishermen and Mariners' Royal Benevolent Society* [1959] Ch 220; *Re Royal Society's Charitable Trusts* [1956] Ch 87.

return the item because they were governed by legislation which prevented them from doing so. Parliament was forced to intervene and the Holocaust (Return of Cultural Objects) Act 2009 permitted museums to comply with the Spoliation Advisory Panel's recommendations.[37]

However, further examination of the legislation governing national museums reveals that the curators and their governing bodies have considerable discretion in relation to the disposal of items despite the restrictions imposed upon them. For example, there is considerable discretion permitted in relation to the destruction of a cultural item: museums are entitled to destroy an item where it has become useless for the museums' purposes by reason of damage, physical deterioration or infestation with destructive organisms.[38] It is no doubt expected that curators will attempt to save and repair such items where they can. Yet the decision to destroy may be made in relation to items which are not damaged at all. For example, in the 1950s and 1960s, some museums destroyed plaster copies of sculptures because they were mere copies. The National Museums Directors' Council noted that:

> The contempt then felt for all kinds of copies even resulted in the destruction of Richard Evans' copies of Raphael's frescoes for the Vatican Loggia. These had been acquired by the V&A ... with a Treasury grant of £310 (approximately £50,000 today) and had occupied a prominent and influential place in its displays from 1843 onwards.[39]

The limited guidance provided by legislation in relation to destruction means that items in collections have been at risk where they have fallen out of fashion and where no one seemed to want them.

These statutes also provide curators and their governing bodies with a broad discretion to dispose of items by way of transfer or sale where they are unsuitable to be retained in the collection and where their removal would not be to the detriment of researchers. Serious blunders have been made by museums over the years. For example, in 1949, the Victoria and Albert Museum sold some chairs at auction; it was later discovered that the chairs were of great cultural value, having been part of a set of chairs commissioned in the eighteenth century by Doge Paolo Renier of Venice. In the meantime, the purchaser of the chairs had turned them into stools and mirror frames.[40] There have been a number of sales between the 1950s and the 1970s which followed the same pattern: museums selling at a low price and learning subsequently that the items were far more valuable in both cultural and financial terms than was appreciated at the time. It is evident that curators and their governing bodies sometimes exercised poor judgment not only in relation to acquisitions during this period, but also in relation to sales. Gradually, the tide began to change. The public outcry when the Tate Gallery sold one of its paintings led to the Cottesloe Report on the

---

[37] *Official Report*, 8 May 2000, col 349, c 491. The Spoliation Advisory Panel has received only a small number of claims and has generally been successful in resolving them. See generally NE Palmer, *Museums and the Holocaust* (Leicester, Institute of Art and Law, 2000).

[38] British Museum Act 1963, ss 5(2), 8, as amended. In relation to other museums, see the Museums and Galleries Act 1992, s 4(4), (5). See also, eg the National Heritage Act 1983, ss 6(3), 14(3), 20(3), 27(2).

[39] National Museums Directors' Council, *Too Much Stuff? Disposal from Museums*, 27 October 2003.

[40] Ibid.

Sale of Works of Art in 1964,[41] which emphasised that even where museums had the legal power to dispose of items in their collections, they should only do so where it could be demonstrated that the disposal was in the public interest.

But is it a criticism of these statutes that a more detailed scheme relating to disposal was not laid down in order to restrain the excesses of idiosyncratic curators and their governing bodies? I suggest not. In this field, where cultural value can be subjective and open to review, and where museums differ so widely in their purposes, it might well have been impossible to have created detailed rules which could be applied uniformly to all museums. Furthermore, the consideration which should dominate whenever a museum acquires or disposes of an item is whether it is acting in the public interest in doing so. This issue is complex and it can be argued that the law should be supplemented by ethical principles which are more flexible and which can focus more effectively upon the public interest.

V. DISPOSALS BY OTHER MUSEUMS: ETHICAL CONCERNS

There is no special legislation governing museums other than the national museums.[42] However, the Museums Association's Code of Ethics provides principles which apply uniformly to all museums in the UK, regardless of their purpose or size. Until 2007, the principles in the Code which related to disposals of items from museum collections largely reflected the legislation which applied to national museums. Museums were expected to dispose only where there were good curatorial reasons and where it was in the public interest to do so. The original set of ethical principles drafted in 1977[43] established a strong presumption against transfer or sale outside of the museum sector, encouraging disposal of superfluous items to other museums instead. The 1994 revision baldly stated that: 'Decisions to dispose should never be taken as a means of raising money.' This prohibition on what is known as 'financially motivated' disposal stayed in place until 2007. Unfortunately, these ethical principles had an obvious drawback: they relied upon consensus amongst the members of the Museums Association and there were no legal mechanisms which could be called into play to prevent irresponsible sales.

The lack of legal control over sales of items from the collections of museums other than national museums came to the public notice after a number of instances where local authorities sold items in order to meet a budget deficit. For example, in 1991, Derbyshire County Council sold items from the collection in the Buxton Museum and Art Gallery in order to plug a shortfall in its finances: as this contravened the ethical guidelines, it was expelled from the Museums Association.[44] However, the most

---

[41] *Report of the Committee of Enquiry into the Sale of Works of Art by Public Bodies* (1964). See N Merriman, 'Museum Collections and Sustainability' (2005) *MLA: Research and Evaluation* 7.

[42] Although s 12 of the Public Libraries and Museums Act 1964 empowers local authorities to maintain museums, they may establish an art fund to be used for the purchase of objects for exhibition: ibid, s 15, sch 2.

[43] Code of Practice for Museum Authorities.

[44] See T Jenkins, 'Just Say No: You Cannot Be Too Careful in Embracing Disposal' in Davies (n 4) 72; S Heal, 'The Great Giveaway' (2006) 106(10) *Museums Journal* 32–35. More generally, see I Robertson, 'Infamous De-accessions' in A Fahy (ed), *Collections Management* (London, Routledge, 1995), 168, 170.

notorious case involved Bury Metropolitan Borough Council, which, in 2006, sold a painting, 'A Riverbank' by LS Lowry, from its collection at Bury Museum and Art Gallery. Bury Metropolitan Borough Council had purchased the painting from the artist for £175 in 1951. It was sold for £1.4 million and this money was not applied for the benefit of the remaining collection, but was used instead to pay for social services. Representatives from Bury Metropolitan Borough Council suggested that the painting was not central to the museum's collection, which was primarily concerned with nineteenth-century and contemporary works of art. Even so, the decision to sell on the open market was made without any attempt to see if another museum might wish to buy it. Moreover, the decision was not made by the curator but by the local authority. The Museums Association observed that: 'Treating a museum's collection as a financial asset is absolutely contrary to the Council's obligations to safeguard the museum collections in its stewardship for current visitors and future generations.'[45] The Disciplinary Committee of the Museums Association severely reprimanded Bury Museum and Art Gallery which resigned from the Association.

A large number of museums and galleries have registered under the Accreditation Scheme, which is now administered by the Arts Council of England (ACE), but which was formerly the responsibility of the Museums, Archives and Libraries Association (MLA). The Scheme sets out nationally agreed standards in relation to the management of collections. It follows the principles to be found in the Museums Association's Code of Ethics, particularly as regards serving the long-term public interest by safeguarding museum collections and respecting the interests of stakeholders. As a consequence of the local authority's actions, the MLA removed the accredited status of Bury Museum and Art Gallery, thereby making it ineligible to apply for government grants.

In 2007, the Culture, Media and Sport Committee interviewed a large number of witnesses to obtain evidence relating to the general health and vitality of museums across the country. Despite the conduct of Bury Metropolitan Borough Council in relation to the Lowry painting, the Museums Association took a balanced view. It was supportive of responsible disposals of items from collections, stating that:

> Museums collect for the long term. But that does not mean that their collections are set in stone. They should grow and develop in response to changing needs and priorities. That needs to include the possibility of disposing of objects that no longer fulfil a need and are not appropriate to a museum's mission, especially those that would be more accessible to the public elsewhere.[46]

Other witnesses to the Culture, Media and Sport Committee confirmed that there was a growing recognition that there were items in collections across the country which should not have been acquired and which were costly to store and take care of.[47] But there was a fear that any encouragement of disposal of unwanted '1970s ephemera' would put 'a light bulb on in the councils' minds that perhaps they could sell off their pre-Raphaelites'.[48]

---

[45] Sixth Report, *Caring for Our Collections*, para [3.11], HC 176-II, published on 27 June 2007.
[46] Ibid, [3.8].
[47] Ibid, Ev 7, Q9 (Dr Maurice Davies, Deputy Director, Museums Association).
[48] Ibid, Ev 7, Q9 (Ms Helen Wilkinson, Policy Officer, Museums Association).

The Committee discussed the question of whether legislation was needed in order to protect collections from being sold off in a reckless manner. However, it was suggested that it might be difficult to draft legislation which was sufficiently flexible.[49] A different concern related to whether the legislation should encourage disposal or not. As the issues were so complex, it was decided not to press for legislative action.

VI. TOO MUCH STUFF?

At one time, the generally held view appeared to be that museums must keep items in their collections forever. This approach was challenged in 2003 by a document entitled *Too Much Stuff?* which was published by the National Museums Directors' Council (NMDC). The document noted that in a number of instances, museums could not afford to preserve items, which had gradually fallen into decay before being destroyed. It was argued that it would be better to rationalise collections and to sell, transfer or lend items, as appropriate, in order to ensure that the items were preserved and used. This strategy would mean that resources could be released and directed to other items in the collection.[50]

The NMDC observed that various museums have far more items than they can display. For example, the Natural History Museum has 70 million specimens. However, items not on display should not necessarily be removed from the collection because they may be needed by researchers. On the other hand, museums have items in their collections which either should never have been become part of the collection in the first place or which could be more popular if located elsewhere. For example, in 2000, the British Museum transferred its photograph collection to the national collection of photography at the Victoria and Albert Museum in order to increase public access and engagement.[51] Similarly, the National Museum of Antiquities of Scotland transferred Irish archaeological material to the National Museum of Ireland. There is no public benefit in merely hoarding items.

More controversially, the NMDC discussed whether British museums should be able to trade up without censure, as their American counterparts can do, selling items from their collections to raise finance to purchase a more interesting and higher-quality item in the same field.[52] Yet, there are obvious dangers if museum curators and their governing bodies were to regularly engage in buying and selling. One risk is that there would be a temptation to sell items which were out of fashion—and such items will not realise high prices. An associated risk is that if items were sold and then these sales were viewed (with the benefit of hindsight) as

---

[49] Ibid, Ex 7 Q11 (Rosemary McKenna, MP, Member of the Culture, Media and Sport Committee).
[50] National Museums Directors' Council (n 39) 13.
[51] Ibid, 7.
[52] See further D Fincham, 'Deacccession of Art from the Public Trust' (2011) XVI *Art Antiquity and Law* 93, 99.

a major mistake, the museum might not be able to afford to reacquire them. The NMDC concluded that:

> There is a place for both museums which improve and refine their collections through purposeful disposal and for those which retain the evidence of other generations' tastes and attitudes, and provide opportunity for re-evaluation and rediscovery of a particular works as taste changes.[53]

This conclusion might not seem particularly helpful at first sight. How would you be able to determine whether the governing body had acted improperly in selling an item? But it must be recalled that every museum is different and each has its own mission statement. The answer then becomes clear. If a museum is dedicated to contemporary art, it may well be that it *should* be permitted to sell and purchase in order to satisfy its mission. At the other end of the spectrum, a museum which is dedicated to preserving the items which catalogue the life of one family should not ordinarily sell any of those items because its mission will be to preserve the current collection. Be that as it may, in the period leading up to 2007, the Code of Ethics banned museums from selling on the open market to buy a 'better' item.

VII. FINANCIALLY MOTIVATED DISPOSALS: SELLING TO RAISE MONEY

In 2005, the Museums Association published a report, *Collections for the Future*, which suggested that museums needed to consider how to make the most of their collections. It accepted that this might involve disposals in cases where the items could be better used elsewhere. The report signalled a cautious reappraisal of the ethical restraints upon disposal in response to concerns that they might simply encourage stagnation. Following the publication of the report, the Museums Association engaged in extensive consultation and received over 90 individual submissions from museums and other organisations. There appeared to be a consensus that sales for financial reasons to raise money would be tolerated in the museum sector in certain limited circumstances. As a result, the Code of Ethics was revised in 2007 and the current version was published in 2010.

The principles relating to disposals of items from collections can be found in Part 6 of the Code, which divides disposals into those which are 'curatorially motivated' and those which are 'financially motivated'. The distinction is important because financially motivated disposals are hedged round with severe restrictions to be found in paragraph 6.14, which is set out below. However, perhaps surprisingly, no definition is offered of a financially motivated disposal.

The Code of Ethics states that museums should:

> **6.13** Refuse to undertake disposal principally for financial reasons, except in exceptional circumstances, as defined in 6.14.

> Financially motivated disposal risks damaging public confidence in museums and the principle that collections should not normally be regarded as financially negotiable assets.

---

[53] National Museums Directors' Council (n 39).

6.14 Consider financially motivated disposal only in exceptional circumstances and when it can be demonstrated that:

— It will significantly improve the long-term public benefit derived from the remaining collection;
— It is not to generate short-term revenue (for example to meet a budget deficit);
— It is as a last resort after other sources of funding have been thoroughly explored;
— Extensive prior consultation with sector bodies has been undertaken;
— The item under consideration lies outside the museum's established core collection as defined in the collections policy.

Paragraph 6.15 adds a final touch to the list of restrictions with arguably the most important point of all: the proceeds of sale must be ring-fenced 'solely and directly for the benefit of the museum's collection'.

Although this change was made in 2007, there have been relatively few applications to the Museums Association's Ethics Committee until very recently. As more applications are anticipated in the future, however, this distinction between curatorially motivated and financially motivated disposal called out for fresh scrutiny. The Code does not provide a definition of a financially motivated disposal and does not specify whose motivation matters. Even so, it would appear that it is the motivation of the governing body, rather than the motivation of the curator, which is significant. It is the governing body which has the power to arrive at a decision to dispose.[54] For example, in the case of the sale of the Lowry painting by Bury Metropolitan Borough Council, it appeared that the decision to sell was being made by local authority councillors. There was no evidence that a curator had made a decision beforehand on the issue or had even been consulted. It can be objected that it is artificial to place so much emphasis upon the intention of the governing body, as it may be difficult to pin down people's knowledge and motives.[55] For example, shortly before the Code of Ethics was revised in 2007, the Watts Gallery decided to sell two paintings to pay for construction work. Although this was presented as a curatorially motivated disposal and received approval from the Museums Association, it could more readily have been interpreted as a financially motivated disposal.[56] There was a risk that a disposal would be classified as a financially motivated disposal only if the governing body of a museum was brazen enough to acknowledge it, as in the case of Bury Metropolitan Borough Council.

In the absence of any definition, a reference to motivation did not appear to be satisfactory as a trigger for the series of restraints set out in paragraphs 6.13 and 6.14 of the Code of Ethics. Yet creating a definition for the first time has proved difficult because there was no consensus amongst museums who responded to a consultation exercise carried out between May and July 2012. It is important to

---

[54] Some local authorities have adopted a Cabinet system, whereby decision-making powers are devolved upon particular individuals (Cabinet portfolio holders) who are executive Cabinet members; see Egeria and Farrer & Co, 'Moving to Museum Trusts' produced for the MLA in 2006, at 23.

[55] In the civil law, the common law torts such as conversion are simple to apply because there is no need to bring forward proof of the recipient's state of mind; in contrast, the position in equity in relation to 'unconscionable' receipt poses more difficulties: *BCCI v Akindele* [2001] Ch 437 (CA); *Starglade Properties Ltd v Nash* [2009] EWHC 148; *Law Society v Isaac & Isaac International* [2010] EWHC 1670.

[56] For critical discussion, see D Rykner, 'UK Deaccessioning' *The Art Tribune* (2008) 1 March.

create a definition which does not alienate a large section of the museum sector; any definition also needs to be sufficiently flexible to apply in an appropriate manner to a wide variety of fact situations. A compromise was reached and can be found in the draft Due Diligence Guidelines Relating to Sale of Items from Museum Collections, which provide detailed guidance to all museums in relation to transfers and sales. The Due Diligence Guidelines state that a sale will be financially motivated if a primary reason for disposing is to raise funds.[57]

The definition of financially motivated disposal, which was newly created in the draft Due Diligence Guidelines, had to satisfy one fundamental test. The definition needed to mesh with other guiding principles on disposal which are clustered together in Part 6 of the Code of Ethics. Frequent reference is made to the need to safeguard collections for future generations. Although it might seem strange to place so many restraints on disposals which are financially motivated, this approach is more readily comprehensible once one appreciates that the overarching theme of the Code of Ethics is the necessity of serving the long-term public interest. The new definition of a financially motivated disposal reflects the concern to protect the public interest: where the primary reason for sale is to raise funds, special checks are necessary because the decision to sell an item presents a risk that an item of great cultural value may be lost to the public forever.

VIII. THE ROLE OF LAW

The law has an essential role to play in determining entitlement to property. Any museum will need to ensure that it has legal title to an item before it can consider disposing of it. If items have been lent to a museum,[58] it will have a possessory title but not a legal title and should not sell; if it does so without disclosing the nature of its title, it will be liable to a purchaser for breach of contract.[59] Equally, some museums have been established as charities with property provided on trust as a 'permanent endowment'. The governing body of the museum will not be able to deal freely with such property because of the restrictions imposed by the trust.[60] Statutes governing national museums acknowledge this point and state that a museum may not be able to dispose of an item if it is subject to a trust or condition.[61] Equally, codes of ethics will make reference, either implicitly or expressly,[62] to the issue of ownership.

---

[57] These draft Due Diligence Guidelines were drawn up by the author, working with Maurice Davies and Sally Colvin of the Museums Association, liaising as appropriate with Isabel Wilson and Sam Rowlands at the Arts Council of England and representatives from its regional counterparts.

[58] It may also be provided that, if the museum is a charity and has ceased to display the item donated, an automatic gift over to another charity will take effect.

[59] Sale of Goods Act 1979, s 12.

[60] Charities Act 2011, ss 273, 274,. As regards applications to the Charity Commissioners to vary the terms of the trust, see the Charity Commission's webpages: Spending Permanent Endowment http://www .charitycommission.gov.uk/Manage_your_charity/spend_permanent_endowment.aspx.

[61] Even if a transfer is possible, that museum will hold the item subject to the trust or condition: the British Museums Act 1963, ss 5(1), 8(3); the Museums and Galleries Act 1992, s 6.

[62] Paragraph [6.8] of the Museums Association's Code of Ethics states vaguely that governing bodies must take into account 'all legal and other attendant circumstances'; para [2.0] of the ICOM's Code of Ethics is somewhat more legalistic in tone, referring to 'rightful ownership' and documentation.

There are also certain general principles relating to good governance which apply across the museum sector. For example, trustees and directors will owe fiduciary duties to the museum, which will include avoiding any undisclosed conflicts of interest.[63] Equally, senior employees who have responsibility for the collections may owe fiduciary duties too.[64] Part 2 of the Museums Association's Code of Ethics reflects the law by stating that members of governing bodies and employees of museums must put the public interest first and must 'avoid any private activity or pursuit of a personal interest that may conflict or be perceived to conflict with the public interest'.

Beyond issues of entitlement to property, and fiduciary duties and duties of care, the law operates in a piecemeal way. Governance structures vary. Local authority museums make up approximately 40 per cent of the museums in the UK.[65] In the past, they have been owned and run by local authorities as part of their civic responsibilities. Some local authorities have adopted a Cabinet system, whereby decision-making powers are devolved upon particular individuals who are executive Cabinet members.[66] An alternative is scrutiny committees which will oversee the management of the museum. Other museums are regulated by the law of trusts and others have registered as a company limited by guarantee. Some museums are registered as charities and must therefore comply with charity law.[67] However, a large number are not charitable. For example, a museum's collection may be held for purposes which benefit a company as well as the public so that it is not exclusively charitable.[68] Furthermore, the collections held by local authorities are not usually held on charitable trusts, but are treated as belonging to the local authority and are held for its statutory purposes.[69]

A drawback in creating a legal framework to govern the process of deaccessioning and disposal is the complexity of the task. Apart from the different legal forms of governance which may have been adopted, the items which museums hold for the benefit of the public can vary greatly, from fine art, to machines, to the flora and fauna of the natural world. Furthermore, although the main purpose of all museums is to act for the long-term public benefit, they may have very different missions.

---

[63] Eg, *Keech v Sandford* (1726) Cas temp King 61, [1558–1774] All ER Rep 230, Lord Chancellor's Court; *Boardman v Phipps* [1967] 2 AC 46 (HL); *Bishopsgate Investment Management Ltd v Maxwell (No 2)* [1994] 1 All ER 261 (CA).

[64] *Brinks v Abu-Saleh (No 3)* [1996] CLC 133, where Rimer J held that a security guard was a fiduciary.

[65] I Lawley, 'Local Authority Museums and the Modernizing Government Agenda in England' (2003) 1 *Museum and Society* 75.

[66] Egeria and Farrer & Co (n 53) 23.

[67] For specific guidance provided for charitable trustees, see *The Essential Trustee*, htttp://www.charitycommission.gov.uk/Publications/cc3.aspx.

[68] There is a risk to the collection if the collection is not held for charitable purposes and the company becomes insolvent: see *In the Matter of Wedgwood Museum Trust Ltd (in administration)* [2011] EWHC 3782 [8]–[10].

[69] Museums run by local authorities are regulated by the Public Libraries and Museums Act 1964. It is possible for local authorities to transfer their collections into separate charitable trusts, but this is unusual. Instead, some local authorities have created charitable trusts relating to the management of the museum in order to gain fiscal advantages. In this situation, the museum's collections will be retained by the local authority and will be lent to the charitable management trust. See Lawley (n 64); Egeria and Farrer & Co (n 53).

The difficulties are demonstrated by the hypothetical example of a museum which discovers that it has a forgery in its collection. Many curators would wish to dispose of any forgeries which have been discovered. Yet, if a museum's key concern was aesthetics, such as the Victoria and Albert Museum, it might be decided to retain a known forgery on aesthetic grounds. Thus, given the particular mission of the museum and the specialist nature of a curator's work, it may be difficult if not impossible for an outside observer to determine whether an item is unsuitable for a particular collection and whether the governing body has acted properly in deciding to dispose of it.

The law can respond to such a complex situation by providing simple statements. One of the great strengths of the Trustee Act 2000 is the fact that its principles relating to trustees' duty of investment and their use of agents can be easily applied to all trusts, big and small. Similarly, the Sale of Goods Act 1979 applies to all types of sales, whether it concerns large-scale international contracts for oil or consumer purchases of low-cost items. However, as the Museums Association's Code of Ethics provides general principles and a system of self-regulation of the profession, it is difficult to see what legislation dealing with disposal would add, beyond offering legal sanctions in cases of non-compliance.

Nevertheless, the UK government's decision to reduce its financial support for museums has prompted further discussion as to whether further regulation was needed to ensure that museums acted responsibly.[70] For example, there have been calls for the government to establish a special advisory panel on deaccessioning, with a range of experts who can help to prevent mistakes being made, where items of great cultural value are sold cheaply and disappear into obscurity.[71] This call for reform may well be appropriate in relation to fine art. However, it would be problematic to establish a panel which can pronounce on every type of item which a museum may choose to dispose of. Even if such a panel is established, it is unlikely to offer general guidance to curators and their governing bodies in relation to taking care over the management of the disposal process.

There is also a danger that any calls for law reform will overlook the most obvious and fundamental point: that museums exist to benefit the public in the long term. How can legislation concretise such an abstract concept? It is here that I would maintain that the law fails museums and why ethical principles have become so valuable. Marstine has argued as follows:

> But the most significance difference between law and ethics is that the former is characterised by constraints—what one cannot do—while the latter concerns ever-shifting opportunities—what one can do—for the common good.[72]

Marstine's argument rings true in relation to disposals. Apart from entitlement, museums will need to ensure that there is a system of good governance, regardless

---

[70] See E Manisty and J Smith, 'The Deaccessioning of Objects from Public Institutions: Legal and Related Considerations' (2010) XV *Art Antiquity and Law* 1. See further D Fincham, 'Deacccession of Art from the Public Trust' (2011) XVI *Art Antiquity and Law* 93; Davies (n 4).

[71] See P Mould, 'In the Basement' *Art History News* (9 May 2011).

[72] J Marstine, 'The Contingent Nature of the New Museum Ethics' in Marstine (n 3) 3, 7.

of whether they are charities or not. Yet, as will be demonstrated below, the law has relatively little to say on what museums *should* do for the common good.

IX. LONG-TERM PUBLIC BENEFIT

Museums can apply for registration as charities because their main purpose is to advance education in general or, in particular, the arts, culture, heritage or science.[73] In order to assist the governing bodies of museums, including those seeking charitable status, the Charity Commissioners published a research report in August 2002, entitled *Museums and Art Galleries*, which provides guidance in relation to the qualities expected of museums which make them deserving of charitable status.[74] Paragraphs 7–9 of the report explain that the collections and exhibits must have an educational value. The report repeatedly emphasises that the collection must have merit.[75] This principle rests on decided cases. Thus, in *Re Pinion*,[76] the testator had provided in his will that his studio and its contents should be kept intact as a museum. Harman LJ noted that most of the items were utterly worthless and concluded that the gift 'has neither public utility nor educative value'.[77] A particular difficulty with the testator's gift was that he had directed that the items should be exhibited as a whole; as Davies LJ observed, although there were some chairs which had some educative value, 'they would be smothered by the intolerable deal of rubbish'.[78] The Charity Commissioners' report reflects established law, but its insistence upon merit would appear to add pressure upon museums to dispose of any item which is viewed by experts as of poor educative value.[79]

The other key concern in the report was public access and it therefore encouraged museums to lend objects to further public engagement.[80] The report does not expressly discuss sale, but states that:

> There is no objection to storage of exhibits for good reasons but there comes a point where 'storage' becomes hoarding if there is no reasonable expectation that they can or will be exhibited. Where a museum or art gallery runs into this sort of difficulty we would expect the trustees to consider whether their holding of such collections is for the public benefit if access to the public, or interested sections of it, is in practice negligible or non-existent.[81]

---

[73] Charities Act 2006, s 2(b)(f). See further *Re Holburne* (1885) 53 LT 212; *Re Spense* [1938] Ch 96; *Royal Choral Society v Inland Revenue Commissioners* [1943] 2 All ER 101 (CA); *Re Delius* [1957] Ch 299. Membership of the Museums Association gives rise to a presumption that the collection has merit: RR10 (Version 08/02) para [10], Annex [A.7].

[74] RR10 (Version 08/02). See http://www.charity.commission.gov.uk/Library/guidance/rr10text.pdf.

[75] Ibid, paras [7]–[11], [14], Annex [A.1–18], [B.15–16].

[76] *Re Pinion* [1965] Ch 85 (CA).

[77] Ibid, 106,

[78] Ibid, 108. The same objection caused the trust to fail as a charity in the Scottish case of *Sutherland's Trustee v Verschoyle* 1967 SLT 106, Court of Session.

[79] See RR10 (Version 08/02), Annex A: 'In the case of a museum not concerned with art, for example a science museum, we need to be satisfied that the collection(s) and the use made of it/them educate the visitor, or is/are capable of doing so.'

[80] Ibid, [A.25].

[81] Ibid, [A.27].

This statement can be interpreted as also encouraging disposal of items where there is no sound reason to retain them in the collection. However, no further guidance is offered to assist museums in this regard.

Why does the law have nothing positive to say which will provide further guidance on how museums may serve the long-term public benefit? It is submitted that one reason why there is silence is because of how the law has developed. After the end of the Second World War, money had to be found to support the birth of the welfare state. Private trusts were subjected to heavy taxation. The fiscal benefits which charities enjoyed prompted fresh scrutiny of their stated purposes and whether they were essentially public or private in character. There has been particular attention paid to the question of whether trusts deserved their charitable status rather than upon what should or should not be done for the common good.

The strength of the Code of Ethics is that its principles rest squarely on the premise that every museum, in fulfilling its purpose, must act for the benefit of current members of the public and of future generations. It therefore reminds museums of their obligations to care for their collections and to protect them from any risk of damage or theft. Museums are expected to transfer items to other museums or, failing that, to other public institutions.[82] The principle of ring-fencing the proceeds of sale to be spent on the collection, which can be found in legislation governing national museums,[83] seems rational in the light of public benefit considerations. However, there are other significant principles, most notably that there should be transparent procedures.[84] Museums must also seek the views of stakeholders.[85] It can be argued that if governing bodies comply with the requirement that there must be transparency in the decision-making process, this will encourage consultation, reflection and accountability.

Once an understanding of long-term benefit is absorbed, it assists the museum in grappling with unexpected ethical dilemmas not dealt with in the Code of Ethics itself. For example, suppose a museum offers to transfer an item to other museums. It is possible that more than one museum may offer a home for the object. In this situation, a museum may well choose between the museums by selecting the one which offers the most convincing evidence that there will be active public engagement with the object.

A consciousness that public benefit considerations should always underpin dealings with collections may also assist in determining how legal principles may apply in this area. For example, where an agent is selling property on behalf of another, he will normally owe a duty to obtain the best price.[86] This is because the object of the transaction is solely a commercial one: to bargain for the best financial return. Yet, in the context of the sale of items from collections, the duties of museum directors

---

[82] Code of Ethics, para [6.10].

[83] British Museum Act 1963, s 5(3) and Museums and Galleries Act 1992, s 6(7). As regards local authorities, sch 2 to the Public Libraries and Museums Act 1964 provides that if any item is sold from a museum or gallery maintained by the local authority, the proceeds of sale may be paid into the art fund.

[84] Code of Ethics, para [6.11].

[85] Ibid, para [6.12].

[86] See, in the context of estate agents, *Keppel v Wheeler* [1927] 1 KB 577 (CA).

and trustees are affected by public benefit considerations. They must maintain the reputation of the museum and ensure that further donations are made; they must ensure that the museum continues to enjoy the public's support and that they continue to visit and engage with the collection. In *Harries v Church Commissioners*, the court accepted that trustees are entitled to take account of the objects of the trust in exercising their duty of care.[87] Trustees and directors also owe fiduciary duties to act loyally and in good faith. However, fiduciary duties can be tailored to specific situations.[88] Governing bodies of museums must act within the trusts and powers conferred by their governing document. They must consider the mission of the museum, its reputation and the long-term public benefit in deciding to transfer or sell a deaccessioned item. Where a sale is contemplated, governing bodies may therefore decide to sell a deaccessioned item for less than its estimated financial worth to another museum rather than to put it up for auction and risk selling it to a private collector, with the result that it disappears from public view. A sale at less than full value can be agreed where it furthers the museum's purposes or is otherwise in its interests.[89] For example, a sale at an undervalue is justified where it maintains or enhances the reputation of the selling museum and where it also benefits the public, both now and in the future, because the item is being transferred to another museum to be enjoyed there.

X. DUE DILIGENCE GUIDELINES RELATING TO SALE OF ITEMS FROM MUSEUM COLLECTIONS 2013

A. Collections Review

The Due Diligence Guidelines have been drawn up to provide museums with more detailed advice in relation to the transfer and sale of items from collections. They refer to the law and ethics, providing a framework for what a museum should do based upon the mission of the museum and long-term public benefit.[90] The Guidelines refer to the Collections Review which is carried out by the curator and other museum professionals in their capacity as stewards of the collection. Collections Reviews vary in detail from one museum to another. To ensure that museums possess adequate information as they begin the process of disposal, the Guidelines require that certain information should be documented. This information will include: the historical legacy of collecting, including dates when reviews of the collection have been undertaken and any outcomes from such reviews; the number and nature of items selected for transfer to another museum or sale; the impact of the disposal of each item on the remainder of the collection; whether the item

---

[87] *Harries v Church Commissioners* [1992] 1 WLR 1241.

[88] See, eg, *Item Software (UK) Ltd v Fassihi* [2004] EWCA Civ 1244, [2005] 2 BCLC 91; see further R Lee, 'Rethinking the Content of the Fiduciary Obligation' [2009] *Conv* 236.

[89] This view has been confirmed by the Charity Commission in correspondence with the author. The principle of selling at less than market value to another museum or gallery has been included in the draft Due Diligence Guidelines Relating to Sale of Items from Museum Collections.

[90] These Guidelines were drawn up by the author of this chapter, working with the Museums Association and liaising as appropriate with the Arts Council of England.

would fit better and be more widely used and more accessible in another museum's collection; how the particular items selected for disposal were selected; and why other items were not selected instead. The aim of these questions is to provide a permanent record in relation to a particular disposal and to ensure that, at the initial stage of selection, the process of disposal is being carried out with due care.[91]

The Collections Review is important in another respect. The stated mission of a museum will act as a constraint on disposal. There is an absolute ethical bar on disposing of any item from the 'core' collection of a museum and this prohibition is repeated in the draft Guidelines.[92] Part of the process of any Collections Review should be its scrutiny of items and their link to the mission of the museum, so that it is clear why an item earmarked for deaccession and disposal does not fall within the 'core' collection. However, although the mission of some museums may remain the same over the centuries, the mission of other museums may change and evolve. The Guidelines require information about the history of collecting in order to illuminate whether the decision to deaccession an item is being made on sound curatorially based grounds rather than primarily to raise money. There are also further supplementary matters that are dealt with in the Guidelines. For example, a decision to sell high-value items (such as fine art) relative to the collection as a whole may require a more detailed explanation of how this decision was arrived at in order to ensure that items are not being selected because they are easier to sell than a much larger group of less valuable items.

B. Acting with Reasonable Care in Taking Advice and Consulting Others

All disposals need to be carried out with proper care, regardless of whether they are curatorially motivated or financially motivated.[93] Although the current Code of Ethics encourages museums to take care and obtain advice from others in the sector, it is vague. The draft Due Diligence Guidelines spell out that advice must be obtained not only in relation to an item's financial value but also its cultural value. It is vital that cultural items are not seen only in terms of their financial worth.

The Guidelines attempt to develop ethical principles relating to seeking advice and consulting stakeholders. Consequently, museums are expected to seek advice within the museums sector and also from more than one source in the commercial sector, such as auction houses, dealers and other experts. The importance of transparency is also brought to the fore so that, in relation to consultation with either the public or stakeholders, such as researchers and, where appropriate, the donor or creator, there are minimum periods of consultation provided. This process of

---

[91] There are additional provisions designed to ensure that a museum does not sell a national treasure which falls within the Waverley criteria and which will be subject to export controls: see DCMS Guidance, *Export Controls on Objects of Cultural Interest* (November 2005). See further J Ulph and I Smith, *The Illicit Trade in Art and Antiquities: International Recovery and Criminal and Civil Liability* (Oxford, Hart Publishing, 2012) para [3.56].

[92] Code of Ethics, para [6.14]; Acquisition and Disposal Policy, para [12.b].

[93] As regards trustees, the standard of care is an objective standard, but one which also takes account of the experience and special expertise of those concerned: Trustee Act 2000, s 1, sch 1.

consultation is valuable not only because it reflects the fact that the museums serve the public interest by considering all views, but also because the possibility exists that new information will emerge during this process in relation to the items earmarked for disposal.

Having set out certain general principles relating to transfers and sales, such as the fact that responsible disposals are part of good collection management, the Guidelines provide a step-by-step process for curatorially motivated disposals and financially motivated disposals in turn. The process is intended to ensure that there are opportunities to pause and reflect. As regards financially motivated disposals in particular, the emphasis placed by the Guidelines on garnering information is intended to guarantee that if advice is sought from the Ethics Committee of the Museums Association, the Arts Council or others in relation to the ethical position, there is sufficient factual material which can be used by its members to make a judgement.

The Guidelines direct museums to take further advice and carry out more research where an item lacks a detailed history of ownership. For example, a museum should carry out checks to ensure that an item has not been stolen or illegally exported from another country some years ago. If this research is not carried out and a foreign government makes a claim to a cultural object which has been put up for auction, it will tarnish the museum's image and may even give the impression that it is indifferent to the plunder of heritage objects from vulnerable countries. Even so, the Guidelines can only suggest that 'reasonable efforts' should be made to investigate the provenance of the item. What is reasonable will depend upon the context. For example, it is known that some countries are more at risk than others, and some of these are identified on the Red List published by the ICOM.[94] Objects derived from countries under military occupation should also excite suspicion. If an item appears to be from a country where it is known that looting has occurred on a significant scale, every effort should be made to discover more about the provenance of an object. Practical measures can include making searches of relevant electronic databases.

If an item is being disposed of because it is suspected of being a forgery, more research should be undertaken in relation to its authenticity. This extra work may reveal that the item is genuine and therefore highly valuable.[95] If, after further enquiry, doubts persist over the authenticity of an item, a museum will need to disclose this to a purchaser in order to avoid liability for breach of contract.[96] However, more worryingly, if a forgery is sold, there is a risk that a purchaser will later dishonestly present it as genuine to buyers.[97] In order to avoid a situation

---

[94] The ICOM publishes on its website a 'red list' of certain cultural objects at risk from Africa (2000), Latin America (2003), Iraq (2003), Afghanistan (2006), Peru (2007), Central America and Mexico (2009) and Egypt (2012).

[95] See, eg, G Evans, 'Doubts over Welsh Museum's Turner Painting Finally Vanish into the Mist' *Western Mail* (1 August 2011), discussing a Turner painting, 'Off Margate', held by the Museum of Wales.

[96] For an extensive discussion of potential liability under the Sale of Goods Act 1979 for breaches of ss 12, 13 and 14, see J Ulph, 'Markets and Responsibilities: Forgeries and the Sale of Goods Act 1979' (2011) 3 *Journal of Business Law* 261.

[97] Ibid, 265.

where a disposal of an item from a museum collection becomes a catalyst for later fraud, it has now been arranged that any museum can register a forgery without charge at the Art Loss Register. This Register is an international electronic database which catalogues lost and stolen works of art, antiques and other cultural items. It was created in 1991 by a private consortium of auction houses, insurers, art trade associations and the International Foundation for Art Research. It is essentially a commercial concern and charges are normally levied if an object is registered, or a search is made, which help to meet its running costs. As it is not possible to search the database before registering, this significantly reduces the risk of thieves and accessories accessing it. The Guidelines encourage museums to register items where there is doubt over their authenticity on the basis that it helps the museum community and the public in general: registration of items aids the detection of other forgeries and should also eliminate the risk of those items being presented as genuine in the future.

The Guidelines also direct museums to investigate further where the origins of an object are obscure. These are known in the art trade as 'sleepers'.[98] There is a possibility that further research might reveal that the item has a far greater financial or cultural value than was originally appreciated. For example, the National Gallery discovered a Botticelli in its reserve collection in 2007.[99] If insufficient efforts are made regarding an item's provenance, the museum could lose a great deal of money. It will be forced to adopt a cautious approach to describing the item when it is consigned for auction in order to avoid any potential liability to the purchaser. However, due to a lack of knowledge of its history and also because it will appear unwanted by the museum which is disposing of it, the item is unlikely to fetch a high price. If the item later turns out to be worth hundreds of thousands of pounds, this is money lost which could have been spent on the rest of the collection. Obviously, not all items will be hidden masterpieces and everything will depend upon the context. Research efforts should therefore be proportionate to the apparent cultural value of the item.

C. Financially Motivated Disposal

A sale is defined in the Due Diligence Guidelines as financially motivated if a primary reason for disposing is to raise funds. The Guidelines provide that, in this situation, further checks will be needed at each stage of the process so that it can be demonstrated that the sale will be in the public interest. In order to do this, more information needs to be obtained in relation to whether other museums wish to acquire the items in question and whether the items would be displayed if they were transferred to other museums. If, for example, other museums already have similar items in their collections, it would be easier to justify a sale because it may

---

[98] See Mould (n 70).
[99] See J Fenton, 'Things That Have Interested Me' *The Guardian* (29 September 2007), who comments that it is unlikely that the Botticelli would have survived 'an aggressive clear-out of the reserve collection'.

be evident that there is no particular advantage to the public, either now or in the future, in retaining the items in the public domain.[100] Museums are expected to consult extensively with the public and with museums and experts in the art trade. They are expected to contact the Museums Association informally and to seek formal advice from its Ethics Committee at a later stage (and, if the museum is accredited, the Arts Council), providing these bodies with sufficient information to allow them to respond efficiently to requests for guidance. This regulation of the dialogue which must be carried out with all stakeholders is designed to ensure that a sale is carried out in a responsible and open manner.

XI. CONCLUSIONS

In various countries, there has been debate between those who view sales of items from collections as a necessary part of sound economic management[101] and those who believe that every item in a museum collection should remain in the public sector forever. The differing attitudes which exist have their roots to some extent in societal attitudes towards the role of museums and the support which they obtain from public funds. Thus, sales of items from museum collections to the highest bidder are not uncommon in the US, where a large number of the museums are private and independent non-profit organisations.[102]

Although a precise figure of items in museum collections is not available, it was estimated in 1999 that UK museums had 149 million objects in their possession.[103] The cost of storing certain objects which may have little educational value has been the impetus for reviewing this area. There is increasing recognition that continuous growth of museum collections is not financially sustainable in the long term and that if museums are to continue to bring new items into their collections, there should also be a regular review of collections so that unsuitable items may be removed.

One of the arguments put forward in this chapter is that the process of disposal should be carried out in a responsible and transparent manner because museums act as stewards of the items in their care. This means that curators and governing bodies must not view these items as if they were their own property. The decision by Bury Metropolitan Borough Council to sell the Lowry painting was objectionable because the councillors seemed to consider that they had the right to make a decision to sell according to their own ethical views. Yet the items in a museum collection are not private property and therefore members of a governing body should not apply their own personal sense of ethics.

---

[100] Code of Ethics, paras [6.9], [6.14.i]; Acquisition and Disposal Policy, para [12f].

[101] See P Ainslie, 'Deaccessioning as a Collections Management Tool', in S Knell (ed), *Museums and the Future of Collecting* (Aldershot, Ashgate, 2004) 235.

[102] See MS Brown, 'Disposal as an Essential Collections Management Tool: The Legal, Ethical and Practical Case for Deaccessioning in the United States' in Davies (n 4) 105, 106. In contrast, in France, the vast majority of collections are state property, which is inalienable under a 2002 law: the only possibility is to apply to a special scientific committee to change their status.

[103] S Matty (ed), *Overview of Data in the Museums, Libraries and Archives Sector* (London, Museums, Libraries and Archives Council, 2004) 44, referring to the DOMUS survey in 1998 (S Carter, B Hurst, RH Kerr, E Taylor and P Winsor, *Museum Focus. Facts and Figures on Museums in the UK*, Issue 2 (London, MGC, 1999).

I have sought to demonstrate that a fluid notion of public benefit lies at the core of what a museum should or should not do. Each museum's mission will differ from that of another museum, but will serve this notion of public benefit. Those museums which have highly flexible missions, such as those concerned with local history and its evolution up to the present day, will need to carry out their roles in a more dynamic manner because they must engage with issues such as social well-being. This ability to evolve in line with their mission makes museums sustainable in a broader sense.

As acting in a dynamic manner may well involve uncertainties, it is desirable to have some guidelines in place to manage and minimise the risks involved in relation to the sale of a cultural object by a museum. UK law currently provides guidance in relation to entitlement to property and governance issues involving administrative and fiduciary duties. It acts to provide some restraint upon those who act irresponsibly in seeking the most money in the fastest and easiest way. Should the law play a greater role in the management of collections? This chapter has sought to explain why further ethical guidelines relating to sales of items from museum collections are seen by the museum sector as a better option. Admittedly, ethical codes and guidelines suffer from a lack of strong enforcement measures, relying as they do upon group pressure. However, the strength of the new draft Due Diligence Guidelines is that they can mesh with the law but are better able to articulate ethical principles which stem from the notion of long-term public benefit, such as shared guardianship of heritage items and transparency and consultation with stakeholders. They can be revised so that they continue to reflect the views of professionals working within the museums sector. As this chapter has demonstrated, where cultural objects and issues of public benefit are concerned, ethical principles are necessary to give museums a better understanding of their mission and what they should do for the public good.

12

Property as a Human Right: Another Casualty of the 'War on Terror'?

FRANKIE McCARTHY[*]

I. INTRODUCTION

ARE TERRORISTS ENTITLED to peaceful enjoyment of their possessions? Anti-threat financing measures, designed to prevent terror groups obtaining the funds necessary to carry out acts of violence,[1] raise difficult questions in respect of the right to property enshrined in Article 1 of the First Protocol to the European Convention on Human Rights (hereinafter 'A1-P1'). A party designated as a possible funder of terrorism can find their entire patrimony frozen without limit of time. Much academic and political focus surrounding these measures has necessarily been placed on the due process concerns arising from the procedure by which parties are added to 'terror lists', but the A1-P1 implications of such a radical incursion of state power into private life also require examination. At its heart, the issue is whether the right to property is a human right in the fullest sense of the term.

Anti-terrorist financing techniques have history tracing to the beginning of the twentieth century in the Global North.[2] The events of 11 September 2001 and the subsequent 'War on Terror' precipitated an unprecedented expansion of state powers to freeze and seize property, giving rise in their turn to human rights concerns of a new magnitude. This chapter begins with an overview of the legal framework on which state action is founded, from the UN Security Council, through the EU and on to UK-specific provision, incorporating the key case law at each level. To what extent do these regimes represent a challenge to compliance with A1-P1? An analysis of European and domestic jurisprudence is used to answer this question as a matter of current practice, predicting how the courts *would* deal with an action centred on the property concerns. The chapter concludes with an exploration of the underlying question of principle: taking into account the political and practical motivations for including protection of property in a human rights convention, *should* the courts find anti-terrorist financing measures to be in contravention of A1-P1?

---

[*] Lecturer in Private Law, University of Glasgow.

[1] A detailed examination of the historical origins and the impact of anti-terrorist financing measures can be found in M Levi, 'Combating the Financing of Terrorism: A History and Assessment of the Control of "Threat Finance"' (2010) *British Journal of Criminolgy* 650.

[2] LK Donohue, 'Anti-Terrorist Finance in the United Kingdom and the United States' (2006) 27 *Michigan Journal of International Law* 303.

II. ANTI-THREAT FINANCING: THE LEGAL FRAMEWORK

A. 1267: The UN Regime

UN Security Council Resolution 1267 recognises that the actions of Osama bin Laden, al-Qaeda and the Taliban represent a threat to peace globally, and sets out various measures designed to dismantle sources of funding for that threat. States are obliged to freeze financial resources which could benefit the Taliban. More controversially, assets of parties listed as 'associated with' the Taliban are also to be frozen.[3] The task of designating parties to the list is assigned to the 1267 Committee, which is comprised of all current Security Council members. States bring forward names to the Committee for consideration. The basis on which the Committee is meant to accept or reject such names remains unclear, despite numerous modifications to the regime.[4] Parties have no opportunity to dispute the decision to place them on the list, or even the right to know why they have been listed. Initially, there was no process by which a party could have their name removed from the list, and although a procedure was subsequently introduced,[5] the requirements are onerous and the decision to delist is subject to a veto by any Security Council member. It is perhaps unsurprising that the compliance of the regime with the rights of listed persons to due process has been repeatedly called into question.[6]

1267 has been reaffirmed and modified by several subsequent resolutions, most notably UNSCR 1373, which expanded the scope of the obligation to cover financial assets of all entities who commit or attempt to commit terrorist acts, or participate in or facilitate terrorism. States are required to take whatever action is required domestically to achieve the aims set out by the 1267 regime.

B. 881/2002: The European Regime

The EU employed a number of measures to give direct effect to the 1267 regime at the European level. Most significantly, Council Regulation (EC) 881/2002 imposed an asset freeze on parties listed by the 1267 Committee, whilst Council Regulation (EC) 2580/2001 enabled the Council's Sanctions Committee to draw up its own list of parties associated with terrorism who would be subject, within the EU, to the same penalties as those on the 1267 list.

Due process concerns, protected in the European context by Article 6 of the Convention, were once again to the fore. A successful challenge was mounted to the legitimacy of Regulation 2580/2001 in *Organisation de Modjahedines du Peuple*

---

[3] The effects of an asset freeze are set out in detail in the discussion on proportionality below.

[4] In particular UNSCR 1526 (2004) and UNSCR 1617 (2005).

[5] See UNSCR 1730 (2006).

[6] A Hudson, 'Not a Great Asset: the UN Security Council's Counter-Terrorism Regime: Violating Human Rights' (2007) 25 *Berkeley Journal of International Law* 204; J Almqvist, 'A Human Rights Critique of European Judicial Review: Counter-Terrorism Sanctions' (2008) 57 *ICLQ* 303; S Yankson, 'Starving Terrorists of their Financial Oxygen: At All Costs?' (2010) *Journal of Money Laundering Control* 202.

d'Iran (OMPI) v Council of the European Union,[7] in which the Council Decision[8] placing the applicant on the list was annulled insofar as it related to the applicant. The Court of First Instance found that it was impossible for the OMPI to exercise its right of action since it had not, at any stage, been advised of why it had been placed on the list.

The potential A1-P1 issue raised by the regime, which was not mentioned in *OMPI,* did form part of the challenge to Regulation 881/2002 contained in the joined cases of *Kadi v Council of the European Union* and *Al Barakaat International Foundation v Council Of the European Union.*[9] Both applicants had been listed under 881/2002 in consequence of their presence on the 1267 list, and the Court of Justice, sitting as a Grand Chamber, was accordingly required to wrestle with the question of whether the obligations imposed by the UN under the 1267 regime could override the protection of fundamental rights enshrined in the EC Treaty on which 881/2002 was based. In a decision which has rightfully been the subject of much academic commentary,[10] the court found that compliance with 1267 did not justify compromising European constitutional guarantees, including the human rights principles which had clearly been violated by the asset freeze.

The nature of these rights violations has not attracted the same level of comment as the European constitutional concerns, but from an A1-P1 perspective, the analysis offered by the court here is helpful. Although due process was the focus of the human rights argument, the court also gave careful consideration to the impact of listing on the applicants' property rights. It was noted that, although a temporary measure, the very broad scope of the asset freeze combined with the fact that it had been in place for several years represented a considerable restriction on the exercise of the applicants' rights. Reference was made to *Bosphorus Hava Yollari Turizm ve Ticaret Anonim Sirketi v Ireland,*[11] in which the impoundment of the applicant airline company's plane for three years on the basis of EC sanctions against the former Federal Republic of Yugoslavia was not found to infringe the company's A1-P1 rights. The court was satisfied that even substantial negative consequences for 'innocent' parties could be justified where the aim sought by the restriction on their rights was sufficiently important. Given the profound importance of the fight against

[7] *Organisation de Modjahedines du Peuple d'Iran (OMPI) v Council of the European Union* (Case T-228/02) [2007] All ER (EC) 447.

[8] Decision 2005/930.

[9] Joined cases *Kadi v Council of the European Union* (Case C/402/05) and *Al Barakaat International Foundation v Council Of the European Union* (Case C/415-05 P) [2009] 1 AC 1225.

[10] See, eg, S Griller, 'International Law, Human Rights and the European Community's Autonomous Legal Order: Notes on the European Court of Justice Decision in Kadi' (2008) 4(3) *European Constitutional Law Review* 528; G De Búrca, 'The ECJ and the International Legal Order after Kadi' (2009) 51 *Harvard International Law Journal* 1; J D'Aspremont and F Dopagne, 'Kadi: The ECJ's Reminder of the Elementary Divide between Legal Orders' (2009) 5 *International Organizations Law Review* 371; PJ Cardwell, D French and N White, 'Kadi v Council of the European Union' (2009) 58 *ICLQ* 229; KS Ziegler, 'Strengthening the Rule of Law, but Fragmenting International Law: The Kadi Decision of the ECJ from the Perspective of Human Rights' (2009) 9 *Human Rights Law Review* 288; S Chesterman, '"I'll take Manhattan": The International Rule of Law and the United Nations Security Council' (2009) 1 *Hague Journal on the Rule of Law* 67; A Johnston, 'Frozen in Time? The ECJ Finally Rules on the Kadi Appeal' (2009) 68 *CLJ* 1; D Halberstam and E Stein, 'The United Nations, The European Union and the King of Sweden: Economic Sanctions and Individual Rights in a Plural World Order' (2009) *Common Market Law Review* 13.

[11] *Bosphorus Hava Yollari Turizm ve Ticaret Anonim Sirketi v Ireland* (2006) 42 EHRR 1.

terrorism, an asset freeze could not be considered disproportionate per se. This conclusion was reinforced by the possibility of exceptions to the freeze to release funds for basic living expenses, medical costs and so on, in addition to the fact that the 1267 regime allowed for periodic review of the listing of the applicants.

The restrictive measures could therefore, in principle, be justified. However, the fact that the applicants had had no opportunity to exercise their rights of action in a situation where the impact on their property rights was significant was enough in itself to amount to a breach of A1-P1.

The court emphasised that the decision had no further import in respect of the property rights issues:

> In so far as it follows from this judgment that the contested Regulation must be annulled so far as concerns the applicants, by reason of breach of principles applicable in the proce-dure followed when the restrictive measures introduced by that Regulation were adopted, it cannot be excluded that, on the merits of the case, the imposition of those measures on the applicants may for all that prove to be justified.[12]

In consequence, the Council was given time to remedy the defects in process, during which the restrictions were to remain in place. The *Kadi* approach was followed in subsequent cases dealing with other individuals listed under the auspices of 881/2002, including the joined cases of *Hassan v Council of the European Union* and *Ayadi v Council of the European Union*[13] and an application originating in the UK, *Othman v Council of the European Union*.[14]

However, it could be suggested that the position of the ECJ has shifted since the conclusion of the first *Kadi* application. The Council subsequently introduced Regulation 1190/2008, with various modifications to the listing procedure intended to address the problems identified in that judgment. The Regulation maintained Kadi's name on the list, and again he challenged the legality of the measure on the basis, inter alia, of its failure to comply with human rights.[15] In examining the prop-erty aspect of the case, the court suggested that it might be time to call into question the earlier finding that an asset freeze was a temporary, albeit significant, restriction on the applicant's rights:

> Such measures are particularly draconian for those who are subject to them. All the applicant's funds and other assets have been indefinitely frozen for nearly 10 years now and he cannot gain access to them without first obtaining an exemption from the Sanctions Committee ... In the scale of a human life, 10 years in fact represent a sub-stantial period of time and the question of the classification of the measures in question as preventative or punitive, protective or confiscatory, civil or criminal seems now to be an open one.[16]

In support of this assertion, the court paraphrased the finding of the UK Supreme Court in *A v HM Treasury*[17] to the effect that listed individuals are effectively

---

[12] *Kadi* [2009] 1 AC 1225 [374].
[13] Joined cases *Hassan v Council of the European Union* (Case C-399/06 P) and *Ayadi v Council of the European Union* (Case C-403/06 P) [2010] 2 CMLR 18.
[14] *Othman v Council of the European Union* (Case T-318/01) [2009] All ER (EC) 873.
[15] *Kadi v European Commission* (Case T-85/09) [2011] All ER (EC) 165.
[16] Ibid, [149] and [150].
[17] *A v HM Treasury* [2010] 2 AC 534, discussed further below.

'prisoners' of the state as a result of the asset freeze and reiterated concerns expressed by the 1267 Committee's Sanctions Monitoring Team[18] and the United Nations High Commissioner for Human Rights[19] as to the compliance of the regime with property rights. A focus was placed on the length of time the sanctions had been, and could continue to be, in place. Although beyond the scope of the application as pleaded, the court suggested that a 'full and rigorous judicial review' of the measures would be justified in light of the 'marked and long-lasting effects' on the fundamental rights of listed persons.[20]

At present, then, the compliance of the European measures with A1-P1 would appear to be in real doubt.

C. The Anti-terrorism, Crime and Security Act 2001: The UK legislation

The anti-terrorist financing regime currently in operation in the UK has its roots in the Prevention of Terrorism Act 1989, which was introduced in response to the activities of the IRA. As elsewhere, the events of 9/11 were the catalyst for the significant augmentation of state powers. In October 2001, Gordon Brown, then Chancellor of the Exchequer, stated that:

> Those who finance terror are as guilty as those who commit it. So our response to the funding of terrorist acts must be every bit as clear, as unequivocal and as united as our response to the terrorist acts themselves.[21]

The UK framework is constructed from a number of overlapping pieces of legislation. In the first place, the UNSCRs have been directly implemented through the Al-Qaida and Taliban (United Nations Measures) Order 2006, which gives effect to the 1267 regime as it relates specifically to the Taliban, and the Terrorism (United Nations Measures) Order 2006, which gives effect to the wider counter-terrorism scheme envisaged by Resolution 1373. In addition, the UK has introduced domestic powers which allow state action beyond freezing assets in the hands of the listed party, primarily through the Anti-terrorism, Crime and Security Act 2001 (ATCSA).

The ATCSA builds on the financial offences created by the Terrorism Act 2000 (essentially fundraising, using and possessing funds, arranging finance or laundering funds for the purposes of terrorism) to set out a variety of methods by which funding of terrorism can be intercepted or dismantled. Section 1 provides for the forfeiture of 'terrorist cash', defined as cash intended for use for the purposes of terrorism, cash which forms part of the resources of a proscribed organisation and cash which is or represents property obtained through terrorism. Sections 4 and 5 confer on the Treasury the power to make a freezing order, which prohibits the

---

[18] Ninth Report of the Analytical Support and Sanctions Monitoring Team, established pursuant to Resolution 1526 (2004) (Document S/2009/245), para [34].

[19] Report of the UN High Commissioner on the protection of human rights and fundamental freedoms while countering terrorism (Document A/HRC/12/22) at point 42.

[20] *Kadi* (n 15) [151].

[21] 'Action Against Financing of Terrorism—Statement of the Chancellor of the Exchequer', 16 October 2001.

person on whom the order is served from making financial assets and economic benefits of any kind available *to* specified persons. Failure to comply with the order is a criminal offence. Schedule 2 enhances the powers of seizure and forfeiture of terrorist cash and property set out in Part 3 of the 2000 Act.[22]

The Treasury's powers were augmented by the Counter-Terrorism Act 2008. Section 62 of and Schedule 7 to this Act set out a scheme in which the Treasury may give a direction imposing certain requirements on any credit or financial institution operating in the UK. Such a direction can only be given where certain conditions are fulfilled, primarily where the Financial Action Task Force[23] has advised a risk of terrorist financing or the Treasury 'reasonably believe' there is a risk of terrorist financing being carried out in a specific country, by that country's government or by persons in the country. A direction can include a variety of requirements. Most pertinent for the purposes of A1-P1 is the requirement to limit or cease business set out in paragraphs 9 and 13 of the schedule, which prohibits entering into or continuing specific transactions, all transactions of a specified type or all transactions with particular persons. Again, non-compliance with the terms of a direction will result in penalties, in this case both civil and criminal.[24]

The focus of these measures is not on the party providing funds, but on individuals or institutions which might facilitate the passing of funds from supportive parties to terrorist organisations.

As with the European measures, the UK legislation has been subject to a number of legal challenges in terms of its compatibility with human rights. The legality of the statutory instruments giving effect to the UN regime formed the subject matter of *A v HM Treasury*,[25] where it was contended that the Orders went beyond the powers conferred on the Executive by section 1 of the United Nations Act 1946 and were also contrary to the Human Rights Act 1998. The Terrorism (United Nations Measures) Order 2006 was found to be ultra vires, since it required only reasonable suspicion of terrorist activity for an asset-freezing order, when no such attenuated standard of proof was found in 1267. Section 3(1)(b) of the Al-Qaida and Taliban (United Nations Measures) Order 2006, was also ultra vires as a result of the same due process concerns that had underscored discussion of the listing process in other judicial contexts. The Supreme Court was not prepared to make a finding that the Human Rights Act had been breached, since it was not clear that the European Convention on Human Rights could take precedence over the United Nations Charter. Nevertheless, it touched briefly on the impact on applicants' property rights, with Lord Mance commenting that an asset freeze had 'radical consequences

---

[22] A more detailed account of the new powers introduced by the 2000 Act can be found in P Binning, 'In Safe Hands? Striking the Balance between Privacy and Security—Anti-Terrorist Financing Measures' (2002) *European Human Rights Law Review* 737.

[23] Established by the G-7 Summit in Paris 1989, the FATF is an intergovernmental body whose purpose is the development and promotion of national and international policies to combat money laundering and terrorist financing. Detailed information on its role and remit can be found at its website, www. fatf-gafi.org.

[24] For more details on the extensive powers set out in sch 7, see G Rees and T Moloney, 'The Latest Efforts to Interrupt Terrorist Supply Lines: Schedule to the Counter-Terrorism Act 2008' (2010) *Criminal Law Review* 127.

[25] Also reported as *HM Treasury v Ahmed* [2010] 2 AC 534.

for personal and family life'[26] and Lord Hope noting that the 'case is not simply about the making of executive orders which freeze individuals' assets to a point where they are effectively prisoners of the state'.[27]

Although it should be emphasised that A1-P1 was not considered relevant to the issues before the court, it is nevertheless interesting to note the comment of Lord Phillips of Worth Matravers that:

> The common law rights of [the applicants] to the enjoyment of their property, to privacy and to family life are very severely invaded by the [Al-Qaida and Taliban (United Nations Measures)] Order [2006] ... If, however, they have justifiably been placed on the consolidated list on the ground that they have been supporting the activities of Al-Qaida, Usama Bin Laden or the Taliban they can reasonably expect serious interferences with those rights.[28]

The recognition of the extent of interference with the applicants' property rights here, coupled with the assertion that this can be 'reasonably expected' if terrorism is supported, is a connection to which we will return below in the discussion of the lawfulness of the asset-freezing regime. It should be kept in mind that this decision was taken prior to the more critical views of the ECJ presented in *Kadi II*.[29]

The Executive responded to the decision in *A v HM Treasury* with the Terrorist Asset-Freezing (Temporary Provisions) Act 2010, which was replaced on its expiry in December of that year by the permanent framework of the Terrorist Asset-Freezing Act 2010 (which was intended to deal with the broad terrorism regime under UNSCR 1373) and the Al-Qaida and Taliban (Asset-Freezing) Regulations 2010 (for the Taliban-specific regime under 1267). The new legislation aimed to deal with the due process concerns by changing the test of 'reasonable suspicion' to one of 'reasonable belief' and including provision for quarterly reviews by the government and annual reviews by an independent observer. JUSTICE, in response to the consultation on the bill which became the 2010 Act, expressed concerns about whether the legislation would be able to meet the required human rights standards in terms not only of the right to a fair trial, but also as regards A1-P1, and the right to private and family life under Article 8 of the European Convention.[30] No challenge has yet been made to the new legislation.[31]

A different challenge was made to the provisions of the Counter-Terrorism Act 2008 in *Bank Mellat v HM Treasury*.[32] Under Schedule 7 to the 2008 Act, the Treasury had introduced the Financial Restrictions (Iran) Order 2009, which prevented UK financial institutions from transacting with the applicant, who had been involved in making financial arrangements in respect of Iran's nuclear proliferation efforts. The bank was essentially excluded from the UK financial market. It challenged the order on the basis, inter alia, that it breached its rights under A1-P1.

---

[26] *A v HM Treasury* (n 17) [249].
[27] Ibid, [125].
[28] Ibid, [145].
[29] *Kadi* (n 15).
[30] JUSTICE response to HM Treasury Consultation CM 7852 (June 2010), available at www.justice.org.uk/data/files/resources/12/Terrorist-Asset-Freezing-Bill-JUSTICE-response-HM-Treasury-consultation.pdf.
[31] Written statement by Mark Hoban, Financial Secretary, HM Treasury: HC Deb, 4 May 2011, c19WS, confirming the position as at May 2011. The author is not aware of any more recent challenge.
[32] *Bank Mellat v HM Treasury* [2010] Lloyd's Rep FC 504 (QB), [2011] HRLR 13 (CA).

This argument did not find favour, with Mitting J at first instance summarising the position as follows:

> In my opinion, the risk of very great harm to vital national interests justifies the imposition of a severe and costly inhibition on the business of the bank which will entail long-term damage to its goodwill in the United Kingdom. However the test is phrased—fair balance, reasonable relationship of proportionality, justified or not manifestly unreasonable—I am satisfied that it is fulfilled … [T]here really is no other reasonably practicable means of ensuring reliably that the facilities of an Iranian bank with international reach will not be used for the purpose of facilitating the development of nuclear weapons by Iran.[33]

This approach was confirmed by the Court of Appeal, which noted that, although the regime was intrusive (the word 'draconian' was again employed), such an approach was justified given the very high value of the legitimate aim, namely protecting national interests.[34]

Overall, then, despite recognition of the extent of the interference posed by anti-threat financing measures, the UK courts have yet to go as far as the ECJ in *Kadi II*[35] in questioning their compliance with the right to property. As previously noted, it should be borne in mind that the Supreme Court decision in *A v HM Treasury* pre-dates *Kadi II*.

III. WOULD THE COURTS FIND A VIOLATION OF A1-P1?

The challenges to the legal measures implementing the anti-terrorist financing regime at all levels have focused largely on the very real due process concerns that arise in respect of the listing process by which assets are frozen. Although property rights in general and A1-P1 in particular have been invoked regularly in the discussion, their application has generally been connected to the question of rights of action. Under A1-P1, property rights can be compromised, but such an interference cannot be justified where the interference is disproportionate. The absence of an effective right to dispute the listing process renders the asset-freezing regime disproportionate in terms of its impact on the enjoyment of property. This argument is quite correct.

However, if the assumption is made that the due process concerns can be addressed, further A1-P1 questions remain. The extent and unlimited duration of asset-freezing measures create a heavy burden on individual parties. That this might be enough to contravene A1-P1 seems to have been in the contemplation of the ECJ in *Kadi II*[36] when it suggested the need for 'full and rigorous judicial review' of the provisions. This section of the chapter will use the existing jurisprudence of the Strasbourg and domestic courts to examine the likely judicial treatment of a challenge to anti-terrorist financing measures based purely on the property right.

The Strasbourg court has established a series of questions that must be addressed in every A1-P1 application. The first issue is whether the applicant holds a possession

---

[33] *Bank Mellat v HM Treasury* [2010] Lloyd's Rep FC 504 (QB) [20].
[34] *Bank Mellat v HM Treasury* [2011] HRLR 13 (CA) [47].
[35] *Kadi* (n 15).
[36] Ibid, [151].

which could be subject to interference. Asset-freezing measures impact across the entire patrimony of a listed party, so no potential difficulty arises in this regard. The court will then determine which of three categories of interference state action might represent—a deprivation, a control of use or a more general interference with the peaceful enjoyment of possessions[37]—before asking whether state action is lawful, pursues a legitimate aim in the public interest and strikes a fair balance between the needs of the state and the burden placed on the individual.[38] Each of these issues will be addressed in turn.

A. The Nature of the Interference

On its face, a seizure of assets is a straightforward control of the use of possessions. Listed parties under the various regimes do not lose ownership of their assets. An argument can be made that the extent and duration of an asset freeze carried out under the anti-terrorist legislation is so great that the listed party *does* lose owner-ship in everything other than the most technical sense of legal title. The Strasbourg jurisprudence offers clear authority that de facto deprivation of possessions should be treated in the same way as de jure deprivation.[39] It is submitted, however, that even if de facto deprivation can be established based on the evidence, the interfer-ence caused by an anti-terrorist asset freeze will nevertheless be categorised by the Strasbourg court as a control of the use of possessions.

This assertion is based on the existing cases on confiscation and forfeiture. Even in situations where property has been destroyed by the state—arguably the clearest possible example of deprivation of possessions—so long as that destruction has fol-lowed on seizure or confiscation provisions, the court has deemed the interference to be a control of use. As the Strasbourg court explains in *Allgemeine Gold- und Silberscheideanstalt v United Kingdom*,[40] the deprivation of property resulting from forfeiture is merely a constituent element of the procedure for the control of use of assets where seizure provisions are in place.[41]

This seems to be the case regardless of whether the confiscation is designed with a purely preventative effect in mind—as with applications resulting from the seizure and slaughter of animals to prevent the spread of infectious diseases such as foot-and-mouth[42]—or whether it is intended to perform a punitive function either solely or in combination with a preventative effect. The proceeds of crime legislation is perhaps the best example of this combined approach, where benefit received from earlier crimes is recovered from convicted offenders in order to prevent its use in the

---

[37] *Sporrong and Lonnroth v Sweden* (1983) 5 EHRR 35; *Allgemeine Gold- und Silberscheideanstalt v United Kingdom* (1986) 9 EHRR 1.

[38] For a detailed discussion of this framework with full reference to authority, see T Allen, *Property and the Human Rights Act 1998* (Oxford, Hart Publishing, 2005).

[39] *Sporrong and Lonnroth v Sweden* (n 37).

[40] *Allgemeine Gold- und Silberscheideanstalt v United Kingdom* (n 37).

[41] Ibid, [51]. See also *Riela v Italy* 52439/99 (4 September 2001).

[42] *Westerhall Farms v Scottish Ministers* (Court of Session, 25 April 2001); *Christopher Shepherd v Scottish Ministers* (Court of Session, 1 May 2001); *Booker Aquaculture v Secretary of State for Scotland* (Case C20-00) [2003] 3 CMLR 6—all are discussed further in relation to proportionality below.

commission of further criminal activity in addition to deterring potential offenders in the broader sense.[43]

Lord Bingham of Cornhill summarised the position in the context of confiscation under the proceeds of crime legislation when delivering the opinion of the committee in the House of Lords in *R v May*:

> Although 'confiscation' is the name ordinarily given to this process, it is not confiscation in the sense in which schoolchildren and others understand it. A criminal caught in possession of criminally-acquired assets will, it is true, suffer their seizure by the state. Where, however, a criminal has benefited financially from crime but no longer possesses the specific fruits of his crime, he will be deprived of assets of equivalent value if he has them. The object is to deprive him, directly or indirectly, of what he has gained. 'Confiscation' is, as Lord Hobhouse of Woodborough observed in *In Re Norris* [2001] WLR 1388, para 12, a misnomer.[44]

Accordingly, an asset freeze will be a control of use. This may have implications for proportionality, which is discussed further below.

B. The Lawfulness Requirement

Three criteria are essential to the concept of lawfulness in the Convention sense: state action must have a clear basis in domestic law, which must be freely accessible to the public and which must produce a foreseeable result both in terms of the action taken by the state and the consequences for the applicant.[45] Examples of a violation on the basis of an absence of lawfulness are thin on the ground in the A1-P1 jurisprudence,[46] and given the limited nature of the expectations which seem to arise from this requirement of the right, the potential for a successful challenge to anti-terrorist financing measures under this heading must be doubtful. However, two potential lines of argument do emerge here in light of the pre-existing jurisprudence.

The shorter point concerns the existing findings of both the ECJ and the UK courts to the effect that the asset-freezing measures introduced in implementation of the 1267 regime are in breach of the right to a fair trial. Recent case law of the Strasbourg court indicates that, where the legal provisions underlying an interference with property are in contravention of any article of the Convention, they must accordingly fail the test of lawfulness as required by A1-P1. *Družstevní Záložna Pria v Czech Republic*[47] and *Russian Conservative Party of Entrepreneurs v Russia*[48] dealt with applications where Article 6 had been breached by the legal provisions underlying the state action which engaged A1-P1. Both cases accordingly found a

---

[43] See the discussion on proportionality below.

[44] *R v May* [2008] 1 AC 1028 [151].

[45] *James v United Kingdom* (1984) 6 EHRR CD 475 (Commission decision) and (1986) 8 EHRR 123 (Court judgment).

[46] Some examples include *Vasilescu v Romania* (1999) 28 EHRR 241; *Iatridis v Greece* (2000) 30 EHRR 97; *Islamic Republic of Iran Shipping Lines v Turkey* (2008) 47 EHRR 24 (all concerning a lack of a clear basis in domestic law); and *Hentrich v France* (1994) 18 EHRR 440 (lack of foreseeability).

[47] *Družstevní Záložna Pria v Czech Republic*, 24 July 2008 (72034/01).

[48] *Russian Conservative Party of Entrepreneurs v Russia* (2008) 46 EHRR 39.

violation of A1-P1, since any purported basis for state action which contravened human rights norms could not be lawful. By this token, the ongoing contravention of due process rights by the asset-freezing regimes has the result that A1-P1 is also violated, not simply because it is disproportionate as discussed in the authorities but also because the freeze is without a legal basis.

Significant though this point may be, the bigger question under consideration in this chapter is whether the property right will have any impact should the due process issues be rectified. Of more relevance, then, may be the second potential issue with lawfulness. In its response to the bill which became the Terrorist Asset-Freezing Act 2010, JUSTICE expressed serious concerns about the complex and fragmented nature of the UK law on anti-threat financing:

> Rather than continue to add to the current 'patchwork', we think it better that the entire law on terrorist financing should be addressed as part of a comprehensive overhaul of counter-terrorism legislation. Amongst other things, this would enable Parliament to consider such questions as the implementation of UN obligations, national security and the protection of human rights in the round—ie by reference to the full range of measures, rather than in a piecemeal fashion.[49]

It could be argued that the complexity of current legal provision is such as to render the law inaccessible to persons who may be affected by its terms, or at least to render its consequences unforeseeable. This argument was strongly made in respect of one particularly high-profile use of the counter-terrorism legislation by the UK government following the entry into receivership of Icelandic financial institution Landsbanki in 2008. In order to protect UK depositors in Landsbanki subsidiary Icesave, many of whom were public bodies,[50] the government passed the Landsbanki Freezing Order 2008 under section 4 of the ATCSA. The Order prohibited funds being made available to Landsbanki, the Central Bank of Iceland, the Icelandic Financial Services Authority, the Landsbanki receivership committee and the government of Iceland.[51]

Commentators identified a disconnect between the perceived legislative aim of tackling terrorism—a perception supported not least by the name of the statute—and the circumstances in which it had been employed. In Iceland, there was a clear sense that the use of the legislation had been unjust.[52] Landsbanki indicated an intention to seek recourse from the Strasbourg court.[53] In a critical appraisal of the situation, Lennon and Walker noted that:

> The Government adopted an almost flippant response to inquiries about the legal basis of the order, disclosing that 'it happened to be in the Anti-Terrorism, Crime and Security Act.'[54]

---

[49] JUSTICE response (n 30) [7].
[50] 'Icelandic Government Seizes Control of Landsbanki' (*The Guardian*, 7 October 2008).
[51] Landsbanki Freezing Order 2008, arts 2–4.
[52] AJ Turner, 'Anti-Terrorism or Breeding Resentment?' (2010) 174(11) *Criminal Law & Justice* 146.
[53] 'Iceland May Take UK to European Court over Freezing of Bank Assets' (*The Guardian*, 6 January 2009). It seems that no application has actually been made.
[54] G Lennon and C Walker, 'Hot Money in a Cold Climate' [2009] *Public Law* 37.

However, the wording of the ATCSA makes it quite clear that the state may take action in response to an economic threat of any kind. There is no requirement that it arise from terrorism. Moreover, at the debate stage in the House of Lords, a proposed amendment creating an express link to terrorism was withdrawn following a clear indication from the government that no such link was intended.[55]

The concerns expressed by JUSTICE and the criticisms made of the Landsbanki Freezing Order relate back to the same issue of foreseeability. Where the letter of the law empowers the state to carry out certain actions, does it matter that the presentation of the law operates to obfuscate that power from parties who may be subject to it? A key principle of Convention interpretation is that it should provide real and effective protection of rights. Strict adherence to this principle would surely argue for a finding of arbitrariness in respect of the anti-terrorist financing legislation in the UK. However, there is little in the jurisprudence to suggest that the courts would, in fact, adopt this approach. The A1-P1 cases in particular indicate a standard that is far from exacting, with a requirement only that experts be able to make sense of legal provision[56] and concern generally focusing on the exercise of discretion rather than the comprehensibility of the law itself.[57]

No matter how robust an argument might be constructed under this head, it must be conceded that the test applied by the courts in the existing jurisprudence is unlikely to be met by the problematic aspects of the anti-terrorist financing legislation. The issues may, however, come into play in respect of proportionality, which is discussed below.

C. A Legitimate Aim in the Public Interest

Little need be said under this heading. It is impossible to imagine any argument to the effect that dismantling the financial infrastructure of terrorism is not a legitimate aim in the public interest. The motivation for the interference with property rights will clearly be justified from a Strasbourg standpoint.

D. Proportionality

To determine whether a fair balance has been struck between the impact of an asset freeze on the listed party and the public interest served by the regime, it is first necessary to give an account of the wide-ranging effects of being placed on the list. Hudson summarises the position as follows:

> An individual on the list faces grave consequences. Not only is this individual stigmatized by being labelled a terrorist, but all of his or her formal means of employment and ability to derive income are removed.[58]

---

[55] For the discussion, see generally HL Deb 28 November 2001, col 629, cols 347–58.
[56] *Spacek v Czech Republic* (2000) 30 EHRR 1010.
[57] The paradigm example is *Hentrich v France* (1994) 18 EHRR 440.
[58] Hudson (n 6) 206.

The measures to be imposed on listed persons are set out in paragraph 2 of UNSCR 1390 (2002), which obliges states to freeze 'without delay ... funds and other financial assets or economic resources ... including funds derived from property' belonging to the party, and to prevent any other funds, financial assets or economic resources being made available to them, whether directly or indirectly. The definitions of 'funds' and 'economic resources' set out in Article 1 of 881/2002 are too lengthy to bear repeating here, but are expansive in their interpretation of what can be caught by the asset freeze. Limited exceptions for humanitarian purposes were introduced by UNSCR 1452 (2002), providing that funds did not have to be frozen where they were determined by the relevant state to be 'necessary for basic expenses'. These are reflected in Article 2a of 881/2002,[59] which allows funds or resources to escape the freeze where it is:

1(a) (i) necessary to cover basic expenses, including payments for foodstuffs, rent or mortgage, medicines and medical treatment, taxes, insurance premiums, and public utility charges;
   (ii) intended exclusively for payment of reasonable professional fees and reimbursement of incurred expenses associated with the provision of legal services;
   (iii) intended exclusively for payment of fees or service charges for the routine holding or maintenance of frozen funds or frozen economic resources; or
   (iv) necessary for extraordinary expenses.

A listed person wishing to benefit from such an exception must apply to the relevant state authority in writing justifying the request, on which the state will then rule.

The provisions have been strictly applied, as in the case of *Mollendorf*,[60] where the applicant had contracted to sell land and buildings to three buyers, one of whom was listed under 881/2002. The Regulation had not come into force until partway through the transaction, when the only remaining step to be undertaken was registration of the title in the Land Registry.[61] Notwithstanding that the sale price had already been paid, the ECJ considered that registration of title would amount to the property being 'made available' to the listed party and was therefore prohibited by the Regulation.

There are common-sense exceptions, however. The UK Treasury had determined that payment of welfare benefits to the spouses of listed individuals was prohibited by 881/2002, since where the money was spent on basic household needs, the listed person would be in receipt of a benefit in kind. In determining the challenge to this decision brought by affected spouses in *R (on the application of M) v HM Treasury*,[62] the ECJ observed that the purpose of the Regulation was to prevent funds being made available for terrorist purposes, and that receipt of a benefit in kind through spending on household needs could hardly compromise that objective, so there was no need to restrict benefit payments on that basis.

Notwithstanding the limited exceptions for basic needs, it is clear that the impact on listed persons is extremely severe, as encapsulated in Lord Hope's comment in

---

[59] Inserted by Regulation 561/2003.
[60] *Mollendorf* (Case C-117-06) [2008] 1 CMLR 11.
[61] Under German law, which governed the transaction, registration of title is necessary before ownership can transfer to the buyer.
[62] *R (on the application of M) v HM Treasury* (Case C-340/08) [2010] 3 CMLR 31.

A v HM Treasury[63] to the effect that listed persons are prisoners of the state. He noted that the effect can also be devastating for the families of targeted individuals.[64] The impact of an asset freeze on a listed party could scarcely be greater not only in its scope, covering the entire patrimony of the designated person, and its effect, which prevents the exercise of every right normally associated with ownership, but also as regards its seemingly unlimited duration. Parties placed on the list at the inception of the 1267 regime have now been subject to these constraints for over a decade, which is considered by the ECJ to be a substantial period of time in the scale of a human life.[65]

Could such an extensive interference with property rights ever be considered proportionate? In the first place, the jurisprudence illustrates that even permanent deprivation of assets can be in keeping with A1-P1 where the needs of the public are sufficiently pressing. Health and safety concerns resulting in the slaughter of herds of cattle based on potential exposure to foot-and-mouth disease were considered by the Court of Session to be a proportionate interference with the property rights of their owners in *Westerhall Farms v Scottish Ministers*[66] and *Christopher Shepherd v Scottish Ministers*.[67] The ECJ reached the same conclusion in respect of the destruction of fish stocks to prevent the potential spread of piscine disease in *Booker Aquaculture Ltd v Secretary of State for Scotland*,[68] notwithstanding that the applicant in this case had not even the benefit of the limited compensation that formed part of the foot-and-mouth regime.

An alternative example is *Butler v United Kingdom*,[69] in which £240,000 in cash found during a random car search was subject to a forfeiture order, based on the belief that it had resulted from, or was intended to be used in, drug trafficking. The applicant had claimed the cash was to fund the purchase of a holiday house in Spain. Neither he nor the owner of the car had ever been convicted of a drug-related offence, and no allegation of wrongdoing was made against them.

In these cases, the significance of the harm that the state action was designed to prevent was of considerable importance to the question of proportionality. Evidently, the aim of preventing terrorism would weigh just as heavily in favour of state action, if not more so. The applicants in these cases were also permanently deprived of their possessions, which is not obviously the case for parties on terrorist lists. However, in each example cited, the applicant was subjected to a one-off interference with their property rights. Although the impact might have been significant in economic terms, it was limited in both extent and duration. The sprawling scope of the asset-freezing regime seems to present quite a different challenge to listed parties; this is no discrete piece of state action, but an extensive, blanket constraint which could endure for decades. Its severity is of a different magnitude.

---

[63] *A v HM Treasury* (n 17).
[64] Ibid, [125].
[65] *Kadi* (n 15) [150].
[66] *Westerhall Farms* (n 42).
[67] *Christopher Shepherd* (n 42).
[68] *Booker Aquaculture Ltd* (n 42).
[69] *Butler v United Kingsom*, 41661/98, 27 June 2002.

Taking this into account, a closer comparator may be legislative measures allowing for the confiscation of the proceeds of crime. In the UK, such powers have been available to the state since the introduction of the Criminal Justice Act 1988, followed by the Drug Trafficking Act 1994. The present regime is contained primarily within the Proceeds of Crime Act 2002.

As with anti-terrorist financing, the powers available to the state here are broad-ranging. The 2002 Act establishes two routes by which cash or assets may come to be categorised as the proceeds of crime (or 'benefit', in the terminology of the Act)[70] and thus liable to confiscation. In the more straightforward case of 'particular criminal conduct', benefit is essentially the proceeds of the particular offence(s) of which the party has been convicted.[71] However, the alternate basis of 'general criminal conduct'[72] provides a more useful point of comparison for the asset-freezing regime. This comes into play where the party's conviction is for certain key offences (primarily drug trafficking and fraud) or fits a defined pattern of recidivism, in which case he will be considered to have a 'criminal lifestyle'.[73] The effect is that all property obtained by the party during the six years prior to the criminal proceedings is *assumed* to be benefit unless he is able to prove that it has a legitimate source.[74] The word 'obtained' has been very broadly defined to include, essentially, any asset over which the party had control, even where it may simply have been passing through his hands.[75] A large proportion of the defendant's patrimony could accordingly be covered by these assumptions.

Benefit is recovered through the mechanism of a confiscation order, which obliges the party to pay a sum of money.[76] The figure to be paid (the 'recoverable amount') will be the total benefit received[77] or, where the defendant does not have sufficient resources to repay that value, the 'available amount' comprising all free property currently held by the defendant minus certain preferential debts.[78] The court is empowered to appoint a receiver to manage the defendant's property prior to conviction and to realise the property in satisfaction of a confiscation order should one subsequently be made,[79] much as a receiver in an insolvency procedure might realise assets for the satisfaction of creditors.

A defendant subject to a confiscation order based on their 'criminal lifestyle' and a listed person under the asset-freezing regime are not in a precisely similar situation. One significant difference from an A1-P1 perspective is that a defendant may face de jure transfer of possessions out of their patrimony at the hands of a receiver, whereas the listed party under the anti-terrorist financing regime will maintain title to their property at least in name. However, the broad picture in each case is the same: state action impacting significantly on the major part of the person's

---

[70] Proceeds of Crime Act 2002, s 76(4)–(7).
[71] Ibid, s 76(3).
[72] Ibid, s 76(2).
[73] Ibid, s 75 and sch 2.
[74] Ibid, s 10.
[75] *Jennings v Crown Prosecution Service* [2008] 1 AC 1046 (HL).
[76] Proceeds of Crime Act 2002, ss 6, 7 and 11.
[77] Ibid, s 7.
[78] Ibid, s 9.
[79] Ibid, ss 48–51.

patrimony, even where no connection has been proved between the property and any wrongdoing. On that basis, the jurisprudence on proportionality in respect of the proceeds of crime regime may give some insight into the likely judicial treatment of an anti-threat financing case.

In both cases, state measures are designed to deal with a complex problem which can impact profoundly on society as a whole. In *HMA v McSalley*, Lady Cosgrove referred to 'the evils and dangers of illegal drugs whose effects are pervasive and which cause untold human misery'.[80] In *Kadi I*, the ECJ referred to the 'fight by all means ... against the threats to international peace and security posed by acts of terrorism' as 'fundamental to the international community'.[81] The networks implicated both in the drugs trade and in terrorist activity employ sophisticated economic infrastructures, operating both within and outside the law across many jurisdictions. The seriousness of these problems, in combination with their intractability, means that an uncommonly high level of intervention on the part of the state may be required to tackle them effectively. (Whether state measures are actually achieving this aim as a matter of fact is a separate question.)[82]

The motivations underlying the proceeds of crime regime can be summarised, albeit contentiously, as punitive, preventative or deterrent, and reparative. That confiscation is intended to be a punishment is contested in the recent jurisprudence,[83] arguably because the 2002 Act regime does not meet the due process standards required of a criminal trial, with no need for a direct link between the conviction and the assets seized and issues surrounding the so-called 'reverse burden of proof' of legitimacy of the source of assets. However, the older authorities accept the punitive aspect of confiscating proceeds of crime[84] and, in respect of A1-P1, the Strasbourg court has consistently held that this form of interference is correctly characterised as a 'penalty'. The preventative or deterrent effect operates both in the specific sense that the assets confiscated cannot be used in the commission of future crimes and in the broader sense of deterring potential criminals by illustrating that 'crime does not pay'.

The reparative function of the proceeds of crime regime, given primary emphasis by the UK government,[85] consists in restoring ill-gotten gains to their rightful owners. As Ulph notes, 'few would object if criminals were deprived of their net profits: this would merely restore the status quo, removing assets to which they were never entitled'.[86] A similar point is made in *HMA v McSalley*, which emphasises that legislative measures designed to tackle drug trafficking can only be effective

---

[80] *HM Advocate v McSalley* [2000] JC 485, 495.

[81] *Kadi* (n 12) [363].

[82] Donohue (n 2); N Ridley and D Alexander; 'Combating Terrorist Financing in the First Decade of the Twenty-First Century' [2012] *Journal of Money Laundering Control* 38. However, a more positive analysis is presented in PA Sproat, 'Counter-Terrorist Finance in the UK: A Quantitative and Qualitative Commentary Based on Open Source Materials' [2010] *Journal of Money Laundering Control* 315.

[83] *R (on the application of Assets Recovery Agency) v Ashton*, *Belton v Assets Recovery Agency* [2005] NIQB 58; *R v Jia Jin He* 2004 WL 3089191.

[84] *Phillips v United Kingdom* (41087/98), 5 July 2001 [49].

[85] *Welch v United Kingdom* (1995) 20 EHRR 247; *R v Benjafield* [2003] 1 AC 1099; *R v Rezvi* [2003] 1 AC 1099; *McIntosh v Lord Advocate* [2003] 1 AC 1078.

[86] J Ulph, 'Confiscation Orders, Human Rights and Penal Measures' (2010) 126 *LQR* 251, 251.

where the drug trafficker is stripped of the net profits of their crime.[87] In *CPS v D*, it is suggested that there is a need for confiscation orders where it is shown that a criminal 'retains the benefit of his crime'.[88] The reparative justification evidently only operates to a limited extent, given the breadth of the current regime, where the entire benefit obtained by an applicant as the result of crime will be liable to confiscation, not simply the profits. The wide definition of 'obtains' even allows for recovery of the same 'benefit' from several different offenders where assets may have passed along a chain, which sets the regime some way adrift of purely reparative intentions.[89] Nevertheless, the reparative function of the regime plays an important role.

This interweaving series of motivations for the proceeds of crime legislation do not easily find counterparts in the context of anti-terrorist asset-freezing. It is not necessary to state that the preventative elements of state action are mirrored both in terms of denying the use of assets in potential future acts and in the sense of deterring future perpetrators. However, no punitive justification can be offered in respect of the listing process, given that no underlying offence is required, and no such offence existed in the majority of the litigated cases to date. There also seems no role for reparation in justifying an asset freeze. The measures are aimed at a listed party's assets not because the acquisition of such assets renders them unmeritorious of the protection of A1-P1; rather, it is the potential intended use of the assets in future which gives rise to the interference on the part of the state.

The breadth of the proceeds of crime regime can also be justified by further considerations that do not find a corollary in the asset-freezing context. In particular, the sweeping assumption that every asset obtained by the defendant in the six years prior to conviction is the result of crime may be considered reasonable because the source of assets is peculiarly within the defendant's knowledge.[90] It would be almost impossible for the state to provide proof of the origins of much of the defendant's patrimony. However, it should be straightforward in the majority of cases for the defendant to bring proof of a legitimate source, should one exist. A listed party under the anti-terrorist regime is in almost exactly the opposite position: how is it possible to demonstrate that they did not and do not intend to make use of the assets for terrorist purposes in the future?

Perhaps most critically, the proceeds of crime regime incorporates safeguards to help ensure the burden placed on the criminal defendant remains reasonable. Beyond the initial requirement for a criminal conviction and the opportunity for the defendant to rebut the statutory assumptions as to the source of assets before a judge, the benefit figure cannot outweigh the defendant's realisable assets, and the judge has discretion to consider the overall hardship which the confiscation order might cause to ensure that it is not oppressive.[91] Aside from the extremely limited provision for basic humanitarian needs which has now been included within the

---

[87] *HM Advocate v McSalley* (n 80) 495.
[88] *CPS v D* [2006] EWHC 2738 (Admin) [20].
[89] *R v May (Raymond George)* [2008] 1 AC 1028 (HL).
[90] See, eg, the discussion in *McIntosh v Lord Advocate* (n 85) [33]–[35].
[91] *R v Shabir* [2009] 1 Cr App R(S) 84.

1267 regime, there seems no such concern for the overall hardship visited on a listed party for an indefinite period of time as a result of the blanket freezing of assets.

Looked at in the round, it seems far from clear that the interference with A1-P1 resulting from an asset freeze would meet the requirement of proportionality. The proceeds of crime regime, which provides the closest comparator in terms of extent of interference, is justified by a number of significant motivations that are not mirrored in the counter-terrorist context. Taken together with the arguments on lawfulness set out above, there is at least a stateable case that, even without the due process concerns that have animated the debate to date, the asset-freezing regime is in violation of the property rights of listed parties.

This argument is important. However, the jurisprudence of the Strasbourg court in respect of A1-P1 is not marked by a strong political flavour. The margin of appreciation afforded to states is exceptionally wide and, given the political significance of counter-terrorism measures, it may not be sensible to assume that a challenge to A1-P1 would ultimately be resolved by reference to previous jurisprudence in exactly the manner set out above. If the jurisprudential approach cannot provide an answer in which it is possible to have faith, perhaps an alternative question of principle can be posed: *should* the Strasbourg court find the asset-freezing regime in violation of A1-P1, based on the principles underlying the inclusion of that right in the Convention in the first place?

IV. SHOULD THE COURTS FIND A VIOLATION OF A1-P1?

Before an attempt is made to respond to this normative question, it is useful to distil the issue at hand down to its essential elements. As discussed above, the effect of an asset freeze put in place as part of the anti-terrorist financing regime can be extensive in its scope and unlimited in its duration. There is at least an argument that, after a sufficient period of time, the applicant has been effectively deprived of virtually the entirety of their patrimony. If the due process concerns in relation to the regime are addressed—if it is assumed, for example, that the party subject to the asset freeze has been found by a criminal court to have participated in funding terrorist activity—is it justifiable to compromise their rights under A1-P1 to this extent? In other words, is a person convicted of terrorist funding no longer entitled to protection of possessions?

At the heart of this enquiry is the issue of why protection of property was considered appropriate for inclusion in a human rights treaty in the first place. It is clear that protection of ownership against arbitrary interference by the state has long been an organising concept of private law in both the Scots and Anglo-Welsh traditions. In his analysis of *Burmah Oil v Lord Advocate*[92] and the subsequent War Damage Act 1965, both of which concerned appropriate levels of compensation in respect of property deliberately destroyed by British forces during the Second World War, Allen notes that the government's careful arguments on the constitutionality of providing limited compensation might imply that an expectation of full

---

[92] *Burmah Oil v Lord Advocate* [1965] AC 75.

compensation formed part of fundamental law.[93] The UN Declaration of Human Rights, on which the Convention was modelled, included a right to own property backed up by a freedom from arbitrary deprivation at the hands of the state.[94] There seemed to have been an expectation from the beginning that protection of property would form part of any European rights charter.

However, examination of the *travaux préparatoires* on the Convention reveals little consensus over what the extent or function of such a protection should be. The absence of any shared ideology on this point amongst state delegates contributed significantly to the difficulty in framing the terms of the property right. The struggle to reach agreement resulted in the protection being pushed back into the First Protocol rather than forming part of the Convention itself, and required such significant compromise on all sides that the wording eventually settled upon is ambiguous almost to the point of incomprehensibility. Pierre-Henri Teitgen, in his report to the Consultative Assembly on the findings of the committee on legal and administrative questions following initial discussion of a bill of rights, summarised the position neatly:

> When it is a question of freedom of assembly, of association, of the press, of thought, of individual security, these are easy to control, because in the laws of all civilised countries there are common principles which the judge could easily discern, formulate and expound.

> When, on the contrary, it is a question of nationalisation, of the financial system, of the right of succession, it is much more difficult at the present time to discover the general principles of law recognised by civilised nations and who, in the different national laws, are the persons to resolve this problem.[95]

The vigorous debate surrounding the property right throughout the drafting process spans a range of viewpoints influenced at least partly by nationality, diverging largely along traditional political lines. At one extreme, there was a sense that the right to property was essentially economic in character and accordingly had no place in a convention designed to uphold civil and political freedoms.[96] This view was largely tempered by the experiences in particular of states subject to occupation during the Second World War, who recognised that expropriation was a powerful tool in the hands of a totalitarian regime looking to exert pressure on nationals in order to quell dissent.[97] Delegates adhering to broadly social democratic principles, including those from the UK government who were perhaps the most vocal opponents of mandatory compensation for deprivation, expressed concern that strong property rights would prevent states from undertaking programmes of nationalisation such as those planned in austere post-war Britain.[98]

Despite the marked disagreement on the nature of the property protection, there did appear to be an acceptance on the whole that ownership of property

---

[93] Allen (n 38) 10–12.
[94] Universal Declaration of Human Rights, art 17.
[95] Council of Europe, Directorate of Human Rights, *Collected Edition of the 'Travaux Préparatoires' on the European Convention on Human Rights* (The Hague, Martinus Nijhoff, 1975) vol 2, 126.
[96] Eg Roberts at ibid, vol 6, 88.
[97] See the report to the Consultative Assembly by the Committee of Experts at ibid, vol 4, 18–21.
[98] Eg Labour Party delegate Nally at ibid, vol 2, 80.

was something more than a matter of economics or a purely social right. Eamon de Valera, leader at the time of the Irish Republican party Fianna Fáil, expressed the point simply: 'I believe that it is a fundamental right necessary for the full development of the human being that he should have the right to own property.'[99] A more emotive interpretation was offered by French delegate Bastid, speaking to the Assembly:

> Property is an extension of the man, and man cannot feel safe if he is exposed to arbitrary dispossession ... I do not know if there is any right more ancient or more firmly established than the right to own property.[100]

David Maxwell-Fyfe, chair of the drafting committee, emphasised the importance of property rights in ensuring the practical enjoyment of the personal and political freedoms contained elsewhere in the Convention.[101] At its most fundamental level, it seems fair to assert that the drafters of the Convention accepted the right to property as an essential aspect of humanity or human dignity—a civil right rather than simply an economic interest.

If this interpretation is correct, the protection of peaceful enjoyment of possessions is no less essential than the other rights contained within the Convention. However, the unparalleled powers now available to states to freeze and seize assets in response to suspected terrorist funding amount to a quasi-deprivation of possessions that could be argued to eclipse the property right entirely, at least in terms of the 'real and effective' protection it is designed to offer. It is recognised that the threat posed by terrorist activity, and the potential consequences where such activity is not tackled, merit a high level of state intervention in property ownership. However, even where a legitimate finding of terrorist funding has been made, can the severity of this threat justify de facto removal of the funder's rights under A1-P1? In the normal course of events, offenders are not stripped of their human rights. On the contrary, it is trite to suggest that parties on the margins of law and society are most in need of the guarantees that human rights can offer. The profound complexity and intense political sensitivity of the 'War on Terror' provide particularly compelling grounds to argue that human rights standards must continue to be applied in this context.

In *McIntosh v Lord Advocate*, Lord Bingham of Cornhill noted that 'the general interest of the community in suppressing crime, however important, will not justify a state in riding roughshod over the rights of a criminal defendant'.[102] The same principle must be true of the general interest of the community in tackling terrorism. The full and rigorous judicial review of anti-threat financing regimes called for by the ECJ in *Kadi II*,[103] together with a thorough examination of the normative role of property as a human right, must now be undertaken to ensure that the state is not riding roughshod over the A1-P1 rights of parties designated to a 'terror list'.

---

[99] Ibid, vol 2, 104.
[100] Ibid, vol 6, 120.
[101] Ibid, vol 5, 224.
[102] *McIntosh v Lord Advocate* (n 85) [31].
[103] *Kadi* (n 15) [151].

13

The Evolving Relationship between Property and Participation in English Planning Law

RACHAEL WALSH[*]

I. INTRODUCTION

R EGULATORY CONTROL OF the use and ownership of private property is pervasive and deep in modern society. As Richard Stewart and Cass Sunstein note, 'individual welfare is shaped less and less by common law rules, more and more by legislative and administrative action'.[1] Rights of ownership are no longer generally understood to entail rights to possess and control the use of private property, subject only to the limits set by the common law. Rather, ownership rights are affected by a diffuse regulatory power exercised by the state to acquire private property and to control how it is used. As a result, the meaning of ownership is shaped by regulation and is contingent in many cases upon administrative decision-making processes that employ participation rights as a key means of ensuring fairness in balancing public and private interests in land use.

In this chapter, I identify and analyse a two-stage shift over time in the English regulatory response to this conflict between private rights of ownership and collective interests in the use of land by exploring trends in the protection of control of use and possession in planning law. As a long-standing, pervasive system of public control of private land use, English planning law provides an apt point of focus for considering the evolving relationship between property and participation. Its introduction marked the first major regulatory attempt to delimit the use of private land by reference to public concerns.[2] Largely through a combination of restrictions on private user and public appropriations, planning law seeks to optimise the utility

[*] Assistant Professor in Law, Trinity College Dublin. The author wishes to thank all of the participants at the Modern Studies in Property Law Conference 2012 for their helpful comments, especially Professor Kevin Gray, who provided useful references. In addition, thanks are due to my former colleagues at King's College London (where I worked on an early draft of this chapter), Dr Eloise Scotford and Professor Tanya Aplin, both of whom also commented on the chapter. Finally, the comments of the anonymous reviewer for *Modern Studies in Property Law* are gratefully acknowledged.

[1] Richard B Stewart and Cass R Sunstein, 'Public Programs and Private Rights' (1982) 95 *Harvard Law Review* 1193, 1204.

[2] As Victor Moore notes, the Housing, Town Planning, etc Act 1909 was the first legislative attempt to deal with general land use problems. V Moore, *A Practical Approach to Planning Law* (Oxford, Oxford University Press, 2010) 1.

of land use in the public interest. The common law understanding of the effect of these interferences with private ownership is that legislative measures regulating the use of private property do not require compensation, whereas measures involving compulsory purchase do require compensation.[3] Nonetheless, owners in England were initially protected against the adverse consequences of planning decisions controlling the use of their property through statutory liability rules entitling them to compensation from the state. However, these liability rules have now been largely abrogated. Instead, owners must rely on participation rules in the planning framework to defend their interests. These rules aim to capture and consider the interests of non-owners as well as owners in relation to private land use. In addition, participation rules have helped to legitimise the controversial move from property rule to liability rule protection that is involved in compulsory purchase by giving an owner a voice within the acquisition process.

Through exploring these trends in English planning law, I attempt in this chapter to shed further light on the relationship between property and participation. I argue that the major role accorded to participation rules in modern English planning law is evidence of the increasing 'democratisation of property'.[4] The functions that participation rights perform suggest that the connection between property and participation has come full circle from an historical understanding of property as constitutive *of* democracy to a contemporary understanding of property as an institution constituted *through* democracy. At the same time, the institution of property that is enforced at any moment in time and in any given context has systemic effects. Consequently, a symbiotic relationship exists between property and participation, as participation contributes to the definition of the meaning and scope of property rights, but in turn is affected by the resulting individual entitlements. Such impacts create the need for development of the institution of private ownership over time through further participation, so that participation and property are intricately and inevitably linked in a cycle of reciprocal influence.

In Part II, I consider some major milestones in our understanding of the relationship between property and participation. This has changed over time from an initial civic-republican view of property as constitutive of democracy to a modern regulatory approach in planning law that substitutes participation rights for use rights and employs participation rights to help to justify expropriations. In Part III, I explore in detail the existing statutory participation provisions in English planning law in order to illustrate the centrality of participation in the planning framework, as well as the extent to which the participation involved increasingly attempts to capture the interests and views of non-owners as well as owners. I focus on participation in development planning and control, and in compulsory purchase for planning

---

[3] See, eg, *France Fenwick and Co Ltd v The King* [1927] 1 KB 458, 576; *Belfast Corporation v OD Cars Ltd* [1960] AC 490, 517–18; and *Grape Bay Ltd v Attorney General of Bermuda* [2000] 1 WLR 574, 583B–C. See also K Gray, 'Can Environmental Regulation Constitute a Taking of Property at Common Law?' (2007) 24 *Environmental and Planning Law Journal* 161, 165–66.
[4] The phrase 'democratisation of property' is borrowed from K Gray, 'Pedestrian Democracy and the Geography of Home' (2010) 1 *Journal of Human Rights and the Environment* 45, 48; see also K Gray, 'Regulatory Property and the Jurisprudence of the Quasi-Public Trust' (2010) 32 *Sydney Law Review* 221, 222.

purposes, as these contexts capture the classic distinction drawn by the common law between regulations of the use of private property and deprivations of property. In Part IV, I consider what the two key trends identified in Parts II and III—the increased reliance on participation rules to protect property rights in English planning law and the ever-widening range of voices that are afforded participation rights—mean. I argue that they are evidence of the 'democratisation of property' in practice. I consider the potential problems raised by these trends and I suggest that participation rules may provide a useful starting point for judges called upon to address the impact of planning restrictions on property rights on constitutional grounds.

II.   TRENDS IN THE RELATIONSHIP BETWEEN PARTICIPATION AND PROPERTY

A. Private Property as a Pillar of Democracy

Private ownership's relationship with participation was once understood to be primarily facilitative. Property rights were regarded as clearly defined entitlements that were knowable and predictable, and operated to secure robust participation in the political system.[5] As Patrick McAuslan notes: 'Until well into the nineteenth century, the lawful exercise of political power and the possession and ownership of land were intimately related, so protection of private property was also a defence of the constitutional order.'[6] Taking the view that independent and robust civic engagement was not possible without private property, governments made the right to vote conditional on private ownership. For example, property restrictions on suffrage existed in the UK until 1928.[7]

The relationship between property and participation at the heart of such civic-republican thinking on private ownership had two main aspects. First, owning private property was understood to be a key mechanism for avoiding dependence upon one's rulers for material well-being, which was thought to prevent fully free and engaged civic participation.[8] According to this view, some (undefined) level of secure private possession of property and freedom of use is a vital ingredient in developing

---

[5] See JGA Pocock, *The Machiavellian Moment: Florentine Political Thought and the Atlantic Republican Tradition* (Princeton, Princeton University Press, 2003).

[6] P McAuslan, *The Ideologies of Planning Law* (Oxford, Pergamon Press, 1980) 3.

[7] The Representation of the People Act 1928 removed property restrictions that previously applied to women's suffrage.

[8] See, eg, K Green, 'Citizens and Squatters: Under the Surfaces of Land Law' in S Bright and J Dewar (eds), *Land Law: Themes and Perspectives* (Oxford, Oxford University Press, 1998) 229, 252; J Raven, 'Defending Conduct and Property—The London Press and the Luxury Debate' in J Brewar and S Staves (eds), *Early Modern Conceptions of Property* (London, Routledge, 1995) 301, 305; C Sunstein, *Designing Democracy—What Constitutions Do* (Oxford, Oxford University Press, 2001), 223; C Sunstein, 'On Property and Constitutionalism' (1992) 14 *Cardozo Law Review* 907; JW Harris, *Property and Justice* (Oxford, Oxford University Press, 1996) 303; FI Michelman, 'Property as a Constitutional Right' (1981) 38 *Washington and Lee Law Review* 1097, 1102; DR McCoy, *The Elusive Republic: Political Economy in Jeffersonian America* (Chapel Hill, University of North Carolina Press, 1980) 68.

a society of free-thinking and acting individuals within which a democratic system can flourish.

Second, private ownership, particularly ownership of land, was understood to give an owner a tangible stake and interest in the collective well-being. By becoming an owner, an individual was rooted in the community and was thereafter directly affected by the flourishing or decline of the society as a whole.[9] In this vein, Thomas Jefferson wrote that: 'Cultivators of the earth are the most valuable citizens. They are the most vigorous, the most independent, the most virtuous, and they are tied to their country and wedded to its liberty and interests by the most lasting bands.'[10] Modern research supports some of these assumptions, insofar as it indicates that the permanence of home ownership binds an individual closely to a particular community.[11] Indeed, these assumptions have underpinned much government policy on housing in the UK.[12]

In summary, according to civic-republican thinking, property was not protected to secure a private sphere for individuals, but rather to ensure that they were sufficiently independent, engaged and concerned with the public interest, to be effective actors in the political system.[13] These connections drawn by civic-republicans between property, independence and the enhancement of democracy find an echo in theories of 'property as propriety', which conceive of property as a means of preserving proper social order. In particular, Carol Rose has developed this line of thought, according to which the purpose of property is 'to accord to each person or entity what is "proper" or "appropriate" to him or her ... And what is "proper" or appropriate, on this vision of property, is that which is needed to keep good order in the commonwealth or body politic'.[14] From this perspective, property is constitutive of the social and political structure of a state.

However, I contend throughout this chapter that the relationship that has developed in English planning law between property rights and participation is quite different to the civic-republican understanding. Whereas property rights used to be understood as primarily enabling participation in the democratic system through ensuring independence, participation rights now tend to replace ownership rights in planning provisions designed to resolve conflict between public and private interests

---

[9] See, eg, LE Klein, 'Property and Politeness in the Early Eighteenth-Century Whig Moralists—The Case of the *Spectator*' in J Brewar and S Staves (eds), *Early Modern Conceptions of Property* (London, Routledge, 1995) 221, 223; and McCoy (n 8).

[10] Letter from Thomas Jefferson to John Jay, 23 August 1785, in (1953) 8 *Jefferson Papers* 426–28, noted by SN Katz, 'Thomas Jefferson and the Right to Property in Revolutionary America' (1976) 19 *Journal of Law and Economics* 467, 474. See also L Fox, *Conceptualising Home: Theories, Laws and Practice* (Oxford, Hart Publishing, 2007) 194–95.

[11] E Peñalver, 'Property as Entrance' (2005) 91 *Virginia Law Review* 1889, 1950. See also TC Blum and PW Kingston, 'Homeownership and Social Attachment' (1984) 27 *Sociological Perspectives* 159, 173–74. See Fox (n 10) 198–99; and LJ Lundqvist, 'Property Owning and Democracy—Do the Twain Ever Meet?' (1998) 13 *Housing Studies* 217 for more sceptical readings of the empirical support for the connection between good citizenship and home ownership.

[12] See Fox (n 10) 193–94, 199. Similar trends are identifiable in US policy: see Blum and Kingston (n 11) 160.

[13] GS Alexander, 'Time and Property in the American Republican Legal Culture' (1991) 66 *New York University Law Review* 273, 284, 287; W Treanor, 'The Origins and Original Significance of the Just Compensation Clause of the Fifth Amendment' (1985) 94 *Yale Law Journal* 694, 699; FI Michelman, 'Possession vs Distribution in the Constitutional Idea of Property' (1987) 72 *Iowa Law Review* 1319, 1329.

[14] CM Rose, *Property and Persuasion* (Boulder, Westview Press, 1994) 58.

in the use of land. Property rights have become dependent on participation rights for their assertion and definition, thereby tying individuals to their communities through dependence, rather than through conferring independence on owners.

B. Protecting Property Rights—Distinguishing Property Rules and Liability Rules

During the early stages of the development of English planning law, property rights were protected against interference by the state either by giving owners the right to oppose and prevent restrictions or by guaranteeing compensation for any loss suffered as a result of the interference.[15] In this regard, in 1972, Douglas Melamed and Guido Calabresi famously developed a typology that identified and explained the significance of three broad categories of rules employed in the protection of property rights. First, protection could be through property rules, which allowed bargains in relation to entitlements to be privately ordered, giving the entitlement holder a veto over transfer, sale or other loss of entitlement. Under a property rule, an owner could not be deprived of an entitlement by the state or anyone else without her consent.[16] Second, liability rules allowed for the deprivation of property rights against the wishes of the entitlement holder, in return for payment of an objectively determined value (not necessarily the market value). Accordingly, they entitled an owner to monetary compensation for loss of entitlement, but not to a veto over such loss.[17] Finally, inalienability rules prevented any transfer of entitlement occurring, even in accordance with the owner's wishes.[18]

Calabresi and Melamed's typology of rules has been the basis for the further development and expansion of our understanding of the means by which property rights are protected. For instance, Abraham Bell and Gideon Parchomovsky advocate the use of 'pliability rules' combining the strengths and weaknesses of property and liability rules.[19] They contend that private entitlements are best protected by dynamic rules that may change depending on the occurrence of particular events. Such rules contain at least three elements: 'a first stage rule (either property or liability), a triggering event causing a shift between stages, and a second stage rule'.[20] For instance, they suggest affording property rule protection to an entitlement until a compulsory acquisition, which would trigger the temporary imposition of a liability rule to enable an acquisition for an objectively determined value. The cycle would then continue by affording the new owner property rule protection for her entitlement until the occurrence of another relevant triggering event.[21]

---

[15] See, eg the Housing, Town, Planning, etc Act 1909 and the Town and Country Planning Act 1932.

[16] Henry Smith has connected such rules to what he characterises as the core right of owners to exclude others from their property: HE Smith, 'Exclusion and Property Rules in the Law of Nuisance' (2004) 90 *Virginia Law Review* 965, 980.

[17] Smith identifies such rules with a 'governance' approach, whereby competing uses are balanced and adjudicated upon by judges: ibid.

[18] G Calabresi and AD Melamed, 'Property Rules, Liability Rules, and Inalienability: One View of the Cathedral' (1972) 85 *Harvard Law Review* 1089, 1092.

[19] A Bell and G Parchomovsky, 'Pliability Rules' (2002) 101 *Michigan Law Review* 1, 7.

[20] Ibid, 65.

[21] Ibid, 60.

In a further development, Christopher Rodgers has highlighted the use of property management rules as a method of regulating the imposition of burdens on the interests of property owners.[22] These rules reflect an understanding of an owner as a steward of public resources, bound by a social obligation to utilise and develop the resource in question in line with the public interest. As Rodgers notes, they 'dictate that the state decides not by whom a resource such as land is used—but rather how, when and in what manner that resource is used', meaning that the property remains private but subject to public-regarding obligations concerning its use.[23]

C. The Shift in Protection from Liability Rules to Participation Rules in English Planning Law

A further category of rules protecting property rights, additional to those identified by Calabresi and Melamed and by those who have built upon their theories, plays an increasingly central role in striking a balance between private and collective interests in planning law, namely participation rules. Modern English planning law has at its centre statutory rules that give owners, as well as other interested parties, a voice in the administrative decision-making processes that affect private rights of use and possession. Such rules provide a further source of protection for property rights. While participation has always been an element of the English planning framework, the abrogation of owners' compensation entitlements has heightened the importance of participation rules for owners.[24] In the context of control of use, participation rules give owners an opportunity to object to a proposed restriction. However, they strengthen the argument that a restriction, once imposed, does not have to be compensated. Therefore, a substitution of participation rules for liability rules occurs. As will be seen in Part III, in cases of compulsory acquisition, participation rules supplement the protection provided by liability rules and justify the acquisition of private property against an owner's wishes. In both contexts, participation rules are regarded as crucial to the legitimacy of planning law's impact on property rights, since they give an owner an opportunity to oppose a proposed interference with her possession and/or enjoyment of private property.

Private land use in England was subjected to comprehensive public control beginning with the adoption of the Housing, Town Planning, etc Act 1909. The introduction of public control over land use, resulting not from the application of long-standing common law principles governing private disputes, such as the law of nuisance and trespass, but from the enforcement of a democratically determined

---

[22] C Rodgers, 'Nature's Place? Property Rights, Property Rules and Environmental Stewardship' (2009) 68 *Cambridge Law Journal* 550, 565.

[23] Ibid, 573.

[24] See M Lee and C Abbot, 'Public Participation under the Aarhus Convention' (2003) 66 *MLR* 80, 97. Heather Campbell and Robert Marshall trace public participation in planning back at least as far as 1968, although they emphasise the greater emphasis and prominence that the concept has had since the mid-1990s. H Campbell and R Marshall, 'Public Involvement and Planning—Looking Beyond the One to the Many' (2000) 5 *International Planning Studies* 321, 322. P McAuslan goes back further, identifying *The Report of the Committee on Administrative Tribunals and Enquiries* (the Franks Report), Cmnd 218 (1957) as a key catalyst for public participation in planning: McAuslan (n 6) 6.

public interest concerning local planning and development, was initially treated by the legislature and the courts in England as a restriction of private ownership.[25] As McAuslan notes, the burdens imposed on owners through planning control were understood to be 'not part of the normal or natural bundle of rights of the land-owner', meaning that they had to be controlled in the interests of owners.[26] Consequently, until 1947 at least, English planning legislation afforded owners a general entitlement to compensation for adverse planning decisions.[27] Applying Calabresi and Melamed's typology, planning control was understood by the legislature to require a move from property rule protection of freedom of use to liability rule protection. An owner was guaranteed security of value in respect of her property, but not security of control.[28]

This early understanding of the effect of planning control arguably reflected an understanding of ownership that Margaret Jane Radin calls 'conceptual severance', according to which all of the incidents of ownership receive discrete protection.[29] As a result, restrictions on the use of private property are understood to require compensation. The conception of ownership driving this approach to analysing interferences with ownership rights reflects what James Harris termed 'full-blooded ownership', understood to confer 'unlimited privileges of use or abuse' over the thing owned as well as presumptively unlimited powers of control and transmission.[30]

Such an understanding of the meaning of ownership, and in particular of the strength of the entitlement of an owner to exclusively determine the use of private property, was in fact at odds with the judicial approach to this issue. As noted in the introduction, the common law position is that compensation is generally required for deprivations of private property, not for regulations of use.[31] English judges from an early stage regarded uncompensated restrictions on the use, as opposed to the possession, of private property as consistent with the common law. For example, Wright J said in *France Fenwick and Co Ltd v The King*: 'A mere negative prohibition, though it involves interference with an owner's enjoyment of property, does not, I think, merely because it is obeyed, carry with it at common law any right to compensation.'[32] English judges tended to focus their efforts to protect property rights in the context of land-use regulation on protecting owners' procedural rights.[33] As McAuslan notes, 'where statutes were silent, as they often were, rules of

---

[25] See, eg, *Buxton v Minister of Housing* [1961] 1 QB 278, 283.

[26] McAuslan (n 6) 4.

[27] R Duxbury, *Telling and Duxbury's Planning Law and Procedure*, 14th edn (Oxford, Oxford University Press) 584.

[28] Even at this stage, the guarantee of security of value was not absolute. Both the Housing, Town Planning, etc Act 1909 and the Town and Country Plannng Act 1932 contained limited exceptions to the general right to compensation for injurious affection due to planning decisions.

[29] MJ Radin, *Reinterpreting Property* (Chicago, University of Chicago Press, 1993) 129.

[30] Harris (n 8) 30.

[31] See, eg, *Belfast Corporation* (n 3) 517–18; and *Grape Bay Ltd* (n 3) 583B–C. See also Gray (n 3) 165–66 for a detailed exploration of these two common law rules.

[32] *France Fenwick* (n 3) 476.

[33] See, eg, *Cooper v Wandsworth Board of Works* (1863) 14 CB (NS) 180; *Re Ellis and the Ruislip-Northwood Urban Council* [1920] 1 KB 343. See also McAuslan (n 6) 83–93; D Millichap, 'Real Property and its Regulation: The Community-Rights Rationale for Town Planning' in Bright and Dewar (n 8) 428.

procedure were imposed on public officials which gave land-owners an opportunity to put their case before action was taken against them'.[34]

A change in legislative approach was signalled in the final report of the Expert Committee on Compensation and Betterment (known as the Uthwatt Report), which was published in 1943. The Committee said:

> Ownership of land does not carry with it an unqualified right of user. Therefore restrictions based on the duties of neighbourliness may be imposed without involving the conception that the landowner is being deprived of any property or interest. Therefore such restrictions can be imposed without liability to pay compensation.[35]

However, it cautioned that restrictions could in some cases go so far as to be tantamount to a deprivation, prompting a need for compensation.[36]

The Town and Country Planning Act 1947 removed the general entitlement to compensation for the adverse consequences of planning decisions.[37] The denial of compensation for adverse planning decisions was subsequently upheld against challenge in *Belfast Corporation v OD Cars Ltd*.[38] Viscount Simonds expressly rejected conceptual severance as the appropriate method for analysing legislative controls on ownership, holding that the right to control the use of property was 'not itself property' such that any interference with it would constitute an expropriation.[39]

The Planning and Compensation Act 1991 marked the culmination of the work begun in the 1947 Act to abolish compensation for adverse consequences of planning decisions, as it abrogated most of the remaining exceptions to the general presumption against compensation.[40] Consequently, an owner was no longer entitled to use her property in a manner inconsistent with the public interest, or to receive compensation in the event of a coercive exercise of public power to prevent such use. Rather, she was simply entitled to participate, along with others, in the democratic decision-making process that determined land-use rights. This process was established through planning law, which conferred participation rights on affected

---

[34] McAuslan (n 6) 3.

[35] *Final Report of the Expert Committee on Compensation and Betterment* (HMSO, 1943) 20–21. The Committee argued that: 'Ownership of land involves duties to the community as well as rights in the individual owner.' ibid, 19.

[36] Ibid.

[37] In *Westminster Bank Ltd v Minister of Housing and Local Government* [1971] AC 508, 529, Lord Reid could confidently state that: 'It is quite clear that when planning permission is refused the general rule is that the unsuccessful applicant does not receive any compensation.' See also *Canterbury City Council v Colley* [1993] AC 401, 407.

[38] *Belfast Corporation* (n 3). The challenge was against an application under s 10(2) of the Planning and Housing Act (Northern Ireland) 1931, the effect of which was to deny the owner compensation for adverse consequences flowing from a particular planning decision. The challenge was based on s 5(1) of the Government of Ireland Act 1920, which prohibited any taking of property without compensation.

[39] *Belfast Corporation* (n 3) 516. See also *Grape Bay Ltd* (n 3) 582–83; *Government of Mauritius v Union Flacq Sugar Estates Co Ltd* [1992] 1 WLR 903, 909–10; *La Compagnie Sucrière de Bel Ombre Ltd v Government of Mauritius* (Privy Council, 13 December 1995).

[40] The Planning and Compensation Act 1991 repealed most of the earlier statutory provisions for compensation for adverse planning decisions. However, compensation remains payable in a very narrow category of cases, discussed by Duxbury (n 27) 592. Compensation also remains payable in situations where a statute applies to appropriate physical rights over private land, for example, the Electricity Act 1989, sch 4, para 7; the Telecommunications Act 1984, sch 2, paras 4 and 7; and the Highways Act 1980, s 28(1).

owners. Whereas property rules afforded an owner a veto, and liability rules gave her control of value, participation rules simply gave her a voice in the debate over the scope of her rights.

This change in English planning policy, and the consequent reliance on participation rules to protect property rights, is arguably explicable by the gradual normalisation of planning control over time. As planning control became a familiar and well-understood aspect of the regulatory backdrop to private ownership, its key tools (control of use and compulsory purchase powers) came to be regarded as permissible, run-of-the-mill burdens on private ownership. This shift in understanding prompted a shift in the applicable statutory rules away from property and liability rules towards participation rules.

Alongside this development, there was an expansion in the planning framework of the range of interests to be considered in regulatory decision making concerning the use of private property. As will be seen in Part III, wide-ranging provisions were introduced to both expand the range of stakeholders entitled to participate in the planning process and to facilitate deliberative participation at the community level in planning. Broadly speaking, deliberative participation aims to engage a wide range of individuals and groups in a reasoned, value-driven decision-making process that is not focused on reconciling competing private interests.[41] This marks a change from the historical understanding of planning control as a closed process concerning only the decision maker and the affected owner.[42] The distinction between stakeholder and deliberative participation is blurred in practice, since rights conferred with the aim of facilitating broad-based, value-driven input can be employed to advance individual or group interests, and in fact are often triggered by the existence of a perceived interest in the relevant decision.[43] Moreover, the meaning of deliberation is contested, and detailed consideration of the various views on what it entails is beyond the scope of this chapter.[44] It suffices to note that a legislative trend towards encouraging broad-based participation, including by individuals and groups who might not be directly affected by a decision, is discernible in modern English planning law. This is particularly clear following the adoption of the Localism Act 2011,

---

[41] For more on the meaning of deliberative participation in planning and environmental regulation, see Lee and Abbot (n 24) 85–86; the Royal Commission on Environmental Pollution's 21st report, *Setting Environmental Standards*, Cm 4053 (1998), 101–02; Jenny Steele, 'Participation and Deliberation in Environmental Law: Exploring a Problem-Solving Approach' (2001) 21 *OJLS* 415, 421, 428; Campbell and Marshall (n 24) 327; P Healy, *Collaborative Planning—Shaping Places in Fragmented Societies*, 2nd edn (Basingstoke, Palgrave Macmillan, 2006). For early examples of judicial decisions apparently taking a broad view of the range of voices entitled to be heard in land-use decision making, see, eg, *Wilson v Secretary of State for the Environment* [1973] 1 WLR 1083 and *Turner v Secretary of State for the Environment* (1973) 28 P & CR 123.

[42] Steele (n 41) 418.

[43] See, eg the decision in *Ashton v Secretary of State for Communities and Local Government* [2010] EWCA Civ 600, discussed at n 57 below.

[44] For discussion of the meaning of deliberation and its relationship with participation, see, eg, C Pateman, *Participation and Democratic Theory* (Cambridge, Cambridge University Press, 1970); J Dryzek, *Deliberative Democracy and Beyond: Liberals, Critics, Contestations* (Oxford, Oxford University Press, 2000); J Rossi, 'Participation Run Amok: The Costs of Mass Participation for Deliberative Agency Decisionmaking' (1997) 92 *Northwestern University Law Review* 173.

which gives legal effect to neighbourhood deliberative processes in planning decision making.[45]

Consequently, the planning process has become a tri-partite participatory regime involving affected owners, the regulator and other members of the public, either individually or through representative groups. The ideology identified by McAuslan as 'public participation' has developed as a strong strand of the structure of English planning law. This ideology reflects the view that:

> [A]ll who are likely to be affected by or who have, for whatever reason, an interest or concern in a proposed development of land or change in the environment should have the right of participation in the decision on that proposal just because they might be affected or are interested.[46]

It is instantiated in the extensive statutory provision that has been made for participation by non-owners in the planning regime. Examples of such statutory provisions are examined in the following part, along with participation provisions that protect property rights. These examples demonstrate that participation rights take different forms depending on the objectives that they are intended to attain.[47]

III. ILLUSTRATING PARTICIPATION RULES IN PRACTICE

A. Control of Use in Planning—Development Planning and Consent Procedures

In its procedures for formulating and adopting development plans, and for determining applications for planning consent, the English planning framework makes extensive use of participation rules as a substitute for liability rules protecting owners' control of use, and as a means of ensuring an inclusive debate about the appropriate balance between public and private interests in land use. English planning law provides for both stakeholder and deliberative participation in its rules in order to achieve these goals, with the interests of affected property owners and occupiers (such as applicants and neighbours) receiving slightly more protection than those of the wider community. However, the dominant trend evidenced in recent developments in English planning law is towards enhanced and expanded deliberative participation rights that give legal effect to community claims to have their interests heard and considered in the determination of the scope of private land-use rights. Consequently, modern English planning law reflects what Stewart and Sunstein refer to as a 'public values' conception of regulation. They argue:

> Rules governing private activity both shape and express societal norms. The goal of the public values conception is to ensure that choices among such norms are made through democratic processes, rather than through a private law system in which important social decisions are made by judges and private rightholders.[48]

---

[45] See Lee and Abbot (n 24) 94 for discussion of the general trend in government policy to promote public participation in environmental law.
[46] McAuslan (n 6) 5.
[47] Campbell and Marshall (n 24) 340–41.
[48] Stewart and Sunstein (n 1) 1200.

Consistently with this conception, participation rules have replaced liability rules as the core means of protecting private owners' freedom of use in a way that gives owners a voice in the planning process that is only marginally privileged over the voices of other interested parties.

Existing owners have some special participation rights in the English planning system. They, as well as those interested in acquiring an interest in the relevant property, may apply for planning permission for a proposed development of land.[49] The Localism Act 2011 has given an expanded range of stakeholders an entitlement to contribute to the actual shape of a planning application. Under section 61W of the Town and Country Planning Act 1990 (TCPA), in advance of submitting any application for planning permission, an applicant must consult neighbouring occupants. Their representations must be taken into account in drawing up the final application. This may reflect the fact that neighbours often have property rights that are affected by planning decisions in their local vicinity. However, the right to be consulted is not contingent upon ownership of neighbouring property—mere occupation is sufficient.

Once an application is lodged with the local planning authority, owners (along with anyone else who complies with the prescribed procedure) are entitled to make representations to the decision maker concerning the application, which must be taken into account pursuant to Regulation 28 of the Town and Country Planning (Development Management Procedure) Order 2010. Post-decision, section 78 of the TCPA allows applicants to challenge a refusal of planning permission, or its grant subject to conditions. The right to initiate such challenges is not given to third parties and, as such, it affords owners and prospective owners a distinctive opportunity to defend their right to control the use of their land. The right of appeal in part substitutes for individual control of use by giving an owner a voice in the decision-making process that determines the scope of her entitlements. In addition, an applicant can challenge a planning decision of the Secretary of State through section 288 of the TCPA on the grounds of ultra vires action or non-compliance with procedural requirements, or through judicial review. Where enforcement action is taken for breaches of planning law, anyone with an interest in or occupying the relevant property may be entitled to challenge the action pursuant to section 174 of the TCPA.

While applicants, owners and occupants receive special rights of defence in relation to planning applications and enforcement proceedings, individuals and groups are increasingly entitled to participate in local development planning regardless of whether they have a direct stake in the decision. Deliberative participation in the control of land use is facilitated through statutory rules from the outset of the development planning process. The local planning authority is required to publish a statement of community involvement and to consult the community concerning the terms of a proposed plan.[50] In *R (on the application of Majed) v Camden LBC*, community members were held to have legitimate expectations entitling them to

---

[49] A proprietary interest in the relevant land is not a prerequisite for initiating a planning application. The applicant must simply demonstrate an intention to acquire an interest in the land in order to carry out the proposed development. *Hanily v Minister for Local Government* [1952] 2 QB 444, 451.

[50] See the Planning and Compulsory Purchase Act 2004, ss 18 and 20.

demand compliance with such statements.[51] Arden LJ stated that: 'The statement of community involvement is intended to promote a culture of open and participatory decision-making.'[52] Under section 113 of the Planning and Compulsory Purchase Act 2004, any person aggrieved by an adopted plan can challenge it in the High Court on the grounds that the document was not adopted within the scope of the authority's statutory powers or on the grounds of non-compliance with the required procedure.

Once a planning application is lodged, third parties can make representations to the decision maker concerning its merits or demerits, which must be taken into account in the same way as representations by applicants. The right of third parties to make such submissions is secured in practice by imposing a duty on the local planning authority to publicise the application.[53] In particular, neighbouring owners and occupants who might be adversely affected by a grant of planning permission are afforded the right to notice, which is strongly defended by the courts, albeit subject to the need to maintain certainty in respect of planning decisions.[54]

Where an applicant appeals a planning decision under section 78 of the TCPA, third parties are entitled to participate in the resulting process, although not necessarily by making oral representations.[55] However, *R (Adlard) v Secretary of State for the Environment* confirms that judicial review challenges can be brought by third parties in order to argue that their interests have been unreasonably disregarded in an appeal process.[56] In addition, aggrieved non-applicants can often bring appeals against decisions of the Secretary of State under section 288 of the TCPA, provided that they participated in the planning proceedings prior to the appeal. In *Ashton v Secretary of State for Communities and Local Government*, the Court of Appeal identified the nature and weight of the applicant's substantive interest in the decision, the public interest in the implementation of projects and the delay involved in judicial proceedings as relevant factors in deciding on standing under section 288.[57]

Building on the provision for non-owner participation already present in the planning framework, the Localism Act 2011 adds a range of important new deliberative participation rights for interested groups.[58] Most fundamentally, it affords local communities collective rights of initiation in the planning context, both as regards development planning and development consent applications. Accordingly, the Localism Act 2011 further affirms the central importance of McAuslan's 'public

---

[51] *R (on the application of Majed) v Camden LBC* [2009] EWCA Civ 1029. See also *The Queen (on the application of Kelly) v Hounslow LBC* [2010] EWHC 1256 (Admin).

[52] *R (on the application of Majed) v Camden LBC* [2009] EWCA Civ 1029 [36].

[53] Town and Country Planning (Development Management Procedure) (England) Order 2010, reg 13.

[54] *R (on the application of Gavin) v Harnigey LBC* [2004] 1 PLR 61.

[55] *R (on the application of Vetterlein) v Hampshire County Council* [2001] EWHC 560 (Admin) [68].

[56] *R (Adlard) v Secretary of State for the Environment* [2002] EWCA Civ 735 [32], [2002] 1 WLR 2515, 2529.

[57] *Ashton* (n 43) [53].

[58] For full discussion of the changes introduced by the Localism Act, see, eg, A Layard, 'The Localism Act 2011: What is "Local" and How Do We (Legally) Construct it?' (2012) 14 *Environmental Law Review* 134; and A Layard, 'Law and Localism: The Case of Multiple Occupancy Housing', (2012) 32, *Legal Studies* 551.

participation ideology' in English planning law. It confirms that the community as a whole is regarded as having a relevant voice in land-use decision making.

First, under section 38A of the Planning and Compulsory Purchase Act 2004 (as amended) (PCPA), any 'qualifying body' can propose the adoption of a 'neighbourhood development plan'. Qualifying bodies are parish councils and organisations designated as neighbourhood forums for a particular neighbourhood area.[59] Neighbourhood areas are designated following application by a parish council or other neighbourhood forum pursuant to section 61G of the TCPA. A neighbourhood development plan is defined in section 38A(2) of the PCPA as 'a plan which sets out policies (however expressed) in relation to the development and use of land in the whole or any part of a particular neighbourhood area specified in the plan'. Such plans must be consistent with local plans.[60]

Second, any 'qualifying body' can seek a neighbourhood development order under the new section 61E of the TCPA. Such orders can permit development in relation to all or part of a neighbourhood area, removing the need for individual planning applications. Like neighbourhood development plans, neighbourhood development orders must be consistent with the strategic policies set out in local plans.[61] Schedule 4B to the TCPA establishes the procedure for the adoption of neighbourhood development orders. There must be an independent examination of the proposal, with the possibility for a hearing or for examination by written representations.[62] Thereafter, the examiner must submit a report recommending one of three options: that the proposal should be submitted to referendum as is; that the proposal should be modified in one or more of the ways specified in the schedule and then submitted; or that the application should be refused.[63] The adoption of both plans and orders by a local planning authority is generally required if the proposal is approved by more than half of the voters in a local referendum.[64] Schedule 4C applies broadly the same procedure to the making of 'community right to build orders', which allow 'community organisations' to carry out particular developments in their neighbourhood.[65]

Third, communities, through parish councils or other community groups, can protect their enjoyment of 'assets of community value', which they can nominate

---

[59] Town and Country Planning Act 1990, s 61E(6). Section 61F(5) sets out the procedure for designation as neighbourhood forums.

[60] National Planning Policy Framework (Department for Communities and Local Government, March 2012, available at http://www.communities.gov.uk/publications/planningandbuilding/nppf) paras [16], [184].

[61] Ibid.

[62] Town and Country Planning Act, sch 4B, paras 7 and 9, as inserted by the Localism Act 2011, sch 9.

[63] Town and Country Planning Act 1990, sch 4B, para 10(2).

[64] However, if the relevant area is a designated business area, two referenda must be held, according to the Town and Country Planning Act 1990, sch 4B, para 15. If a majority endorses the proposal in one, but not both, referenda, the council has the discretion as to whether to adopt it (TCPA s 61E(5))

[65] The key differences in procedure are that if the examiner's report recommends that the draft community right to build order is refused, the authority must refuse the proposal, and the examiner is only free to suggest a more limited range of modifications prior to submission to referendum than is the case with neighbourhood development orders generally. 'Community organisations' are defined in s 3 as those 'established for the express purpose of furthering the social, economic and environmental well-being of individuals living, or wanting to live, in a particular area', subject to the prescription of further criteria by regulation.

to a local authority under section 89 of the Localism Act. An asset is of community value if it is currently, and is likely in the future to be, used to further the social well-being or interests of the community, or if it was so used in the recent past and is likely to be so used again within the next five years.[66] Section 91 requires that notice of the listing of a property as an asset of community value is served on the owners and occupiers of the relevant property to give them an opportunity to seek a review of the listing. However, if the listing is maintained, an owner must inform the council of any proposed disposal of the land. For six weeks after such notification, community groups can apply requesting to be considered as bidders for the property. An owner cannot dispose of the property until that period has passed without an application or, if an application is made, until six months have passed since the date of notification of the proposed disposal.[67]

These measures further widen the range of voices that are heard and afforded weight in planning law by giving legal effect to community claims over private property through deliberative processes. By facilitating neighbourhood participation and control in determining the 'common good' by reference to which local land-use decisions should be taken, the provisions introduced in the Localism Act echo the core ideas of civic-republicanism about the connection between property and participation, which was discussed in Part II.[68] At the same time, they subject private property rights to further local community control. Consequently, such rights reinforce the growing strength of McAuslan's 'public participation' ideology in English planning law and confirm that it reflects a 'public values' model of regulation. The property rights of both owners directly affected by development planning decisions, and the wider community, are balanced administratively through rights of participation in the planning framework.[69] By exercising those rights, owners can attempt to ensure that account is taken of their interests in the decision-making process, and members of the public can assert a voice in land-use regulation.

B. Illustrating Participation Rules in Practice—Compulsory Purchase in Planning

In the compulsory purchase context in planning law, participation rules perform a different function than they do in respect of control of use.[70] Instead of substituting for liability rules and facilitating broad-based participation, they justify the use of

---

[66] Localism Act 2011, s 88.

[67] Ibid, s 95. Interestingly, s 99 provides for the introduction of regulations to provide compensation for owners adversely affected by these restrictions on alienation.

[68] See also J Poisner, 'A Civic Republican Perspective on the National Environmental Policy Act's Process for Citizen Participation' (1996) 26 *Environmental Law* 53, 58.

[69] In *Lough v First Secretary of State* [2004] EWCA Civ 905, the Court of Appeal stressed the need to balance the rights of owners and the community at large in planning law.

[70] Other potential functions for participation rules in both contexts, not discussed in detail in this chapter, include enhancing the quality of decisions, enhancing the acceptability of decisions to affected parties, inspiring public confidence in the regulatory system, educating the public on environmental issues and enabling the transformation of individual interests through collective deliberation. See S Herbert, 'The Trapdoor of Community' (2005) 95 *Annals of the Association of American Geographers* 850, 854; MA Melo and G Baiocchi, 'Deliberative Democracy and Local Governance: Towards a New Agenda' (2006) *International Journal of Urban and Regional Research* 587, 590; D Shaw and A Lord, 'From

liability rules rather than property rules to protect property rights by allowing an owner to participate in the process that will ultimately result in the coercive acquisition of her property. Such rules provide an opportunity for owners to defend their interests in the continued possession of private property, as opposed to its exchange value. They do so by giving an owner an opportunity to object to an acquisition, for example, on the basis of the purpose of the acquisition, the statutory powers employed or the procedure followed by the decision maker. This in turn supports the legitimacy of compulsory purchase powers by suggesting that a fair balance has been struck between the relevant public and private interests through the operation of the acquisition process itself.

This justificatory function for participation rules in compulsory purchase contexts means that the regulatory model that is employed is different from the 'public values' conception identified as relevant in the procedures for development planning and consent applications. Overall, the role of participation rules in the compulsory purchase context fits what Stewart and Sunstein describe as an 'entitlement conception' of regulation, which aims to protect personal rights.[71] The participation rules involved are predominantly stakeholder-oriented and their function is to supplement liability rule protection for property rights. In doing so, they justify coercive deprivation of private property in the public interest by ensuring the proportionality of an expropriatory measure. Owners are guaranteed a voice and an entitlement to compensation, but are denied continued possession of their property.

This role for participation rules is well illustrated by the statutory framework for compulsory acquisition of private property for planning purposes by local authorities, pursuant to section 226 of the TCPA. The procedure followed for such acquisitions is the general procedure for compulsory purchase orders set out in the Acquisition of Land Act 1981. It provides for publicity and notification to those with a proprietary interest in the property before a compulsory purchase order is confirmed.[72] If no relevant objections are made and maintained, the order can be confirmed under section 13. However, if objections are maintained, section 14 provides for further participation by qualifying persons, including owners. This may be either through a written representations procedure (where the objectors consent to this approach) or through a public inquiry or other means of affording qualifying persons an opportunity to put their case to an independent party. Once the chosen procedure has taken place, the acquisition order can be confirmed. Upon confirmation, section 15 requires a copy of the order and a confirmation notice to be served on owners, occupants, tenants and those with an interest in the property, as well as being affixed at the property. In addition, another newspaper notice must be published. An appeal under section 23 to the High Court is then possible on the

---

Land-Use to "Spatial Planning": Reflections on the Reform of the English Planning System' (2009) 5 *Town Planning Review* 415, 419; Rossi (n 44).

[71] Stewart and Sunstein (n 1) 1200.

[72] Section 11 requires newspaper notices to be published, which must be addressed to persons occupying or having an interest in the relevant property. Section 12 requires notice to be served on owners, lessees, occupants and those having an interest in the property, or the power to sell or release it. These notices must explain the nature and content of the compulsory purchase order and outline where and when objections can be made to its proposed confirmation.

grounds that the acquisition order was not issued on the basis of proper statutory authority or that the required procedure was not followed, resulting in substantial prejudice. As Sullivan J (as he then was) said in *Powell and others v Secretary of State for Communities and Local Government*, an appeal under section 23 'is not an opportunity to rerun the merits of the Compulsory Purchase Order, it is simply an opportunity to see whether there is any procedural or legal error in the process of confirmation'.[73] Section 24 empowers the High Court upon such an application to quash the acquisition order, but section 25 rules out any alternative form of legal challenge.

Despite the narrow scope for challenge under section 23, the courts have always been astute to supervise carefully the exercise of compulsory acquisition powers.[74] They have generally interpreted statutory provisions allowing for compulsory purchase restrictively.[75] This strict approach has been applied by the courts in reviewing the exercise of compulsory purchase powers. For example, in *De Rothschild and another v Secretary of State for Transport*, Slade LJ suggested that given the 'draconian nature' of compulsory purchase orders, they were more vulnerable to being invalidated on grounds of unreasonableness.[76] The Court of Appeal accepted that it would be unreasonable to compulsorily acquire land where other land being offered by the relevant owner was equally suitable for the intended use. Slade LJ stressed the importance of identifying a justification for a compulsory purchase order, saying:

> Given the obvious importance and value to land owners of their property rights, the abrogation of those rights in the exercise of his discretionary power to confirm a compulsory purchase order would, in the absence of what he perceived to be a sufficient justification on the merits, be a course which surely no reasonable Secretary of State would take.[77]

Considered against the backdrop of this judicial approach, the rights to participate in the compulsory purchase process and to challenge decisions through judicial review provide key opportunities for owners to challenge the justification of proposed acquisitions, thereby defending their security of possession.[78] For example,

---

[73] *Powell and others v Secretary of State for Communities and Local Government* [2007] EWHC 2051 (Admin) [3].

[74] For example, McAuslan traces an early tendency on the part of the courts to use procedural arguments to quash compulsory purchase orders issued for clearance purposes in order to protect the interests of private property owners: McAuslan (n 6) 84–89. See especially *Fairmount Investments v Secretary of State for the Environment* [1976] 2 All ER 865.

[75] See, eg, *Sovmots Investments Ltd v Secretary of State for the Environment* [1979] AC 144, 183, where Lord Keith of Kinkel said that: 'Compulsory purchase enactments are to be strictly construed, and a particular power of compulsory acquisition, which is not expressly conferred, can be conferred by implication only where the statutory provisions would otherwise lack sensible content.' See also *The Western Counties Railway Company v The Windsor and Annapolis Railway Company* (1881–82) LR 7 App Cas 178, 188; *Inglewood Pulp and Paper Company v New Brunswick Electric Power Commission* [1928] AC 492, 499; *Regina (Lord Chancellor) v Chief Land Registrar* [2005] EWHC 1706 (Admin) [37], [2006] QB 795, 805; *London and North Western Railway Company v Evans* [1893] 1 Ch 16, 28.

[76] *De Rothschild and another v Secretary of State for Transport* (1989) 57 P & CR 330, 336. See also *Prest v Secretary of State for Wales* (1982) 81 LGR 193.

[77] *De Rothschild* (n 76) 337.

[78] In *Bushell v Secretary of State* [1986] AC 75, 94, Lord Diplock noted that public inquiries into compulsory purchase orders helped to ensure that ministers 'weighed the harm to local interests and private persons who may be adversely affected by the scheme against the public benefit which the scheme is likely to achieve'.

in *Coleen Properties v Minister for Housing and Local Government*, a compulsory purchase order was quashed because of insufficient evidence showing that the acquisition was reasonably necessary for clearance purposes.[79] More recently, the courts have expressly accepted that a heightened *Wednesbury* standard of unreasonableness applies in the context of judicial review of decisions concerning the compulsory acquisition of private property because of the interference with property rights involved in such orders.[80]

The range of arguments that can be raised under the participation rules in the compulsory purchase process has been further widened by the incorporation of the European Convention on Human Rights into English law through the Human Rights Act 1998. Most significantly, owners can now invoke Article 1 of Protocol 1, and Articles 6 and 8 of the Convention in such challenges, or indeed in pre-confirmation objections.[81] For example, in *The Queen on the Application of Mortell v Secretary of State for Community and Local Government*, owners used their opportunity to object to the confirmation of compulsory purchase orders to invoke Article 8 and Article 1 of Protocol 1.[82] They contended that given the likely impact on their Convention rights in light of their various personal circumstances, their homes should not be compulsorily acquired for regeneration purposes.[83] Sullivan LJ accepted the relevance of such arguments in principle, noting that the

[79] *Coleen Properties v Minister for Housing and Local Government* [1971] 1 All ER 1049.

[80] *Chesterfield Properties plc v Secretary of State for the Environment* (1997) 76 P & CR 117, 130–31. See also *London Borough of Bexley v Secretary of State for the Environment, Sainsbury's Supermarkets Limited v Secretary of State for the Environment* [2001] EWHC 323 (Admin) [46], which held that there must be shown to be a substantial public interest outweighing the interests of a landowner in order to justify compulsory acquisition.

[81] Article 6 provides: '1. In the determination of his civil rights and obligations or of any criminal charge against him, everyone is entitled to a fair and public hearing within a reasonable time by an independent and impartial tribunal established by law.'

Article 8 provides: '1. Everyone has the right to respect for his private and family life, his home and his correspondence. 2. There shall be no interference by a public authority with the exercise of this right except such as is in accordance with the law and is necessary in a democratic society in the interests of national security, public safety or the economic well-being of the country, for the prevention of disorder or crime, for the protection of health or morals, or for the protection of the rights and freedoms of others.'

Article 1 of the Protocol 1 provides: '1. Every natural or legal person is entitled to the peaceful enjoyment of his possessions. No one shall be deprived of his possessions except in the public interest and subject to the conditions provided for by law and by the general principles of international law. 2. The preceding provisions shall not, however, in any way impair the right of a State to enforce such laws as it deems necessary to control the use of property in accordance with the general interest or to secure the payment of taxes or other contributions or penalties.'

For planning challenges based on these Convention rights, see, eg, *R (on the application of Vetterlein) v Hampshire County Council* (n 55) (a judicial review challenge raising arts 6 and 8); *Friends Provident Life and Pensions Ltd v Secretary of State for the Environment* [2001] EWHC 820 (Admin) (judicial review raising art 6); *R (on the application of Rose Malster) v Ipswich Borough Council* [2001] EWHC 711 (Admin) (judicial review raising arts 6 and 8); *R (Cummins) v Camden LBC* [2001] EWHC 116 (judicial review raising arts 6 and 8); *London Borough of Bexley* (n 80) (appeal under s 23 raising art 1 of Protocol 1); *Peart v Secretary of State for Transport, Local Government and the Regions* [2003] EWCA Civ 295 (raising both art 1 of Protocol 1 and art 8 in challenging a compulsory purchase order); *Davies v Crawley Borough Council* [2001] EWHC 854 (Admin) (judicial review raising art 1 of Protocol 1).

[82] *The Queen on the Application of Mortell v Secretary of State for Community and Local Government* [2009] EWCA Civ 1274.

[83] For a similar challenge, see *Pascoe v Secretary of State for Communities and Local Government* [2006] EWHC 2356 (Admin), [2007] 1 WLR 885.

fact of ownership of particular property in a family for many generations, a long life lived by an elderly person in a given property or the presence of neighbours and relatives nearby could all be relevant to the determination of the proportionality of a compulsory purchase order, even where compensation was paid.[84]

However, the human rights challenge in *Mortell* failed on the facts. Indeed, arguments challenging the balance struck in regulatory decisions controlling possession or use of private property, either on traditional judicial review grounds or in reliance on Convention rights, often fail.[85] This trend is explicable at least in part by the existence of participation rules in English land-use control systems that help to justify the protection of the relevant property rights through liability rules, or not at all.[86] Such rules augur in favour of a conclusion that an impugned interference with the enjoyment of property rights through the administration of planning law is proportionate.[87] As Beatson J noted in *R (on the Application of Burnley Borough Council) v The First Secretary of State and Others*:

> The courts in this country ... have held that, as a general rule, domestic planning law and regulatory procedures, including provisions for inquiries and decision-making following such an inquiry by a minister, constitute the balancing exercise required by the Convention in weighing the rights of private individuals in connection with their property and the interests of the broader community. Those procedures are generally themselves compliant in principle with the Convention.[88]

The balancing process required to establish proportionality is understood to be achieved through the participation of owners in the planning process rather than through ex post judicial balancing. Consequently, the participation rules designed to protect property rights have the effect of justifying the restriction that the owners suffer as a result of the relevant administrative decision.

Therefore, in the context of compulsory purchase, participation rules guarantee owners an opportunity to defend their right to continued possession of their property on various grounds, in line with an 'entitlement' conception of regulation. However, successful challenges are rare, particularly where the objection is not based on procedural non-compliance. Where procedures for participation are in place in the relevant statutory framework and are followed, the shift from property rule to liability rule protection involved in a compulsory purchase order tends to be regarded as a fair and proportionate interference with private ownership in the public interest.

---

[84] See also *Elliott v London Borough of Southwark* [1976] 1 WLR 499, 503.

[85] See, eg the decisions cited at n 81, where all of the Convention arguments raised in challenge to planning decisions failed.

[86] Also relevant is the fact that a planning decision, whether in relation to control of use or compulsory acquisition, does not have to be shown to be the least intrusive alternative from a human rights perspective in order to be proportionate: *Lough v First Secretary of State* [2004] EWCA Civ 905 [49], [55]; *R (Clays Lane Housing Co-operative Ltd) v The Housing Corporation* [2004] EWCA Civ 1658 [25], [2005] 1 WLR 2229, 2240–42.

[87] For example, in *Davies v Crawley Borough Council* (n 81) [103], Mr Justice Goldring referred to the comprehensive consultation process involved in the adoption of a street trading scheme when he refused to quash it on the grounds, inter alia, of interference with property rights without compensation.

[88] *R (on the application of Burnley Borough Council) v First Secretary of State and others* [2006] EWHC 798 (Admin) [8].

IV. UNDERSTANDING THE SHIFT TO PARTICIPATION RULE PROTECTION
OF PROPERTY RIGHTS IN ENGLISH PLANNING LAW

A. Prioritising Voice over Value

The shift over time from property rule protection of ownership rights to liability rule protection and now to participation rule protection has affected the degree to which different rights of ownership are secured to individuals. The impact of Calabresi and Melamed's typology of rules, and of the move to liability rule protection of possession, and initially control of use, in English planning law was to concentrate debates concerning the protection of property rights on their exchange value as opposed to their possessory value.[89] Liability rules are concerned with guaranteeing an objectively determined economic value of affected property rights, whereas property rules protect their possessory value. Consequently, the move from property rule to liability rule protection of property rights limited security of possession and use of private property. Property rights tended to be understood as rights to compensation in the event of interference, and their non-economic function in owners' lives was largely disregarded.[90]

The increased reliance on participation rules as a means of protecting property rights could potentially facilitate a resurgence in protection for the possessory values previously secured by property rules. While participation rules do not give owners a veto over public control of their use and/or possession of their property, they do give owners a guaranteed role in the decision-making process. By focusing on voice as the core protection for freedom of use of private property and as a vital aspect of the justification for compulsory acquisition powers, the current regulatory approach provides owners with an opportunity to direct the attention of regulators to the importance of private possession and control of property. Rather than defaulting to questions of compensation, as was commonly the case when rights to possess and use private property were protected by liability rules, owners and decision makers are now forced to reflect on the merits of competing claims in relation to land use. Thus participation rules give owners a chance to persuade a regulator that private use would best promote the public interest.[91]

Such an opportunity may become an increasingly useful weapon for owners in defending their entitlement to control the use of their property, as national

---

[89] Bell and Parchomovsky note that 'the focus on transacting has reduced the status of property rights from near-absolute rights that denote individual autonomy and security to fungible bargaining chips': Bell and Parchomovsky (n 19) 23. See also N Graham, *Lawscape: Property, Environment, Law* (Oxford, Routledge, 2011) 7; Fox (n 10) 250–55.

[90] See, eg in the US context, the decision of the majority of the US Supreme Court in *Lucas v South Carolina Coastal Council*, 505 US 1003 (1992). See also P Manus, 'The Blackbird Whistling—The Silence Just After: Evaluating the Environmental Legacy of Justice Blackmun' (2000) 85 *Iowa Law Review* 429, 486–92, and in the context of compulsory purchase, R Walsh, '"The Principles of Social Justice" and the Compulsory Acquisition of Private Property for Redevelopment in the United States and Ireland' (2010) 32 *Dublin University Law Journal* 1, 13–15.

[91] Cooke J in *Stringer v Ministry of Housing and Local Government* [1970] 1 WLR 1281, 1295 rejected the contention that local planning authorities and the Minister on appeal were restricted to considering public interests, not private interests, noting: 'The protection of the interests of individual occupiers is one aspect and an important one of the public interest as a whole.'

planning policy in England has taken an apparently pro-development turn with the introduction of a presumption in favour of sustainable development as a material consideration in planning decisions.[92] As Lee and Abbot point out, 'a commitment to participation is embedded in the rhetoric of sustainable development, where objective criteria by which to make decisions are elusive, and indeed the very meaning of the term is contentious'.[93] By exercising their voices in the administrative debate over the meaning of sustainable development in the planning context, owners and other interested parties may find a fruitful new channel for defending their various interests, including property rights.

Therefore, while rights-based challenges to planning decisions may have limited success in the courts, as seen above, participation rights may prove to be a useful means of protecting property rights to possession and use, as opposed to value, at the administrative level. Consequently, an impact of the increasing regulatory reliance on participation rights as a means of protecting property rights may be to elevate what Radin refers to as property's 'personal value'—its importance to the individual for use and possession—alongside its 'fungible value'—its value in exchange.[94] This would re-balance what has become an increasingly narrow debate around private ownership as a limited right to security of investment, rather than a right that has functional importance in peoples' everyday lives in its held form, as distinct from its exchange value.

B. Participation Trends in English Planning Law—The 'Democratisation of Property' in Practice

The two modern trends in the relationship between property rights and participation rights in English planning law identified in this chapter—on the one hand, the increased use of participation rules as a substitute for, or supplement to, liability rules in land-use regulation contexts and, on the other hand, the expanded range of interests that are considered in decisions concerning the exercise of property rights—are practical examples of an increasing level of democratic control being asserted over the scope of property rights.

These trends demonstrate that what Joseph Singer has termed a 'democratic model' of property is applied in practice in English planning law insofar as it regulates the possession and control of private property.[95] The distinctive essence of the democratic model of property articulated by Singer is that it 'focuses our attention on the need to make normative judgments about the appropriate contours of property relationships in a free and democratic society'.[96] Choices must be made, through democratic processes, about the meaning of private ownership, bearing in mind that the scope of protection afforded to private property rights *through*

---

[92]   National Planning Policy Framework (n 60) para [14].
[93]   Lee and Abbot (n 24) 83.
[94]   Radin (n 29) 37.
[95]   J Singer, 'Democratic Estates: Property Law in a Free and Democratic Society' (2009) 94 *Cornell Law Review* 1009.
[96]   Ibid, 1057.

democratic decisions in turn impacts *on* democracy.[97] Consequently, property rights are not defined by a once-in-time construction generating fixed entitlements, but rather are the product of an ongoing dialectic between affected private interests, the interests advanced by legislators and regulators, and the interests of other affected members of the public. In this regard, Laura Underkuffler describes a conception of 'property as an individual right, *fluid* in time, *established and re-established*' in accordance with changing circumstances.[98] This understanding of the meaning and nature of private property rights as democratically constituted and evolving is reflected in, and helps to explain, both of the changes in the relationship between property and participation in planning law identified in this chapter.

First, the use of participation rules as a substitute for, or supplement to, liability rules in English planning law acknowledges that an owner is entitled to a voice in the decision-making process that defines the meaning and scope of ownership in a particular context, but no more than that. Moreover, the owner's voice may only be one amongst many relevant voices to be heard and considered by the decision maker, and may be only slightly privileged above other voices. By using participation rules to protect property rights, the planning framework operates on the basis that property rights are not fixed, but rather are defined and redefined contextually, in part through regulatory processes that delimit property rights in light of debate amongst stakeholders, regulators and the public at large. Viewed in this light, the evolution away from property and liability rule protection for control of use in English planning law arguably reflects what Frank Michelman refers to as an understanding of property law as 'a jurisprudence of adaptive and evolving principles including expansive principles of public trust and social responsibility', according to which the entitlements of owners are shaped by social, cultural and economic developments on an ongoing basis.[99]

Furthermore, the participation rules employed in English planning law demonstrate that in this context, property rights are regarded as appropriately protected by what Carol Rose refers to as 'mud doctrine' rather than 'crystal rules'.[100] Whereas property rules and liability rules are crystalline in nature, presupposing a fixed entitlement on the part of an owner, albeit one that is fungible in nature, participation rules do not presuppose that any entitlement exists in a particular case concerning the use or possession of private property. Rather, they regard the scope of such rights as context-dependent, requiring case-by-case deliberation on the appropriate balance to be struck between the interests of the regulated owner, other owners, and society as a whole. Following this approach, property rights are treated in English planning law as something that we 'collectively construct'.[101] The use of participation rules rather than property or liability rules as the main means of protecting

---

[97] Ibid, 1059.

[98] LS Underkuffler, *The Idea of Property: its Meaning and Power* (Oxford, Oxford University Press, 2003) 50 (emphasis in original).

[99] FI Michelman, 'Property, Federalism and Jurisprudence: A Comment on *Lucas* and Judicial Conservatism' (1993) 35 *William and Mary Law Review* 201, 317. See also FS Philbrick, 'Changing Conceptions of Property in Law' (1938) 86 *University of Pennsylvania Law Review* 691, 696.

[100] CM Rose, 'Crystals and Mud in Property Law' (1988) 40 *Stanford Law Review* 577, 578–79.

[101] JW Singer, *Entitlement: The Paradoxes of Property* (New Haven, Yale University Press, 2000), 215.

property rights in planning law marks a statutory recognition of the fact that private interests have a place in that construction, but alongside a variety of other relevant considerations to be taken into account in a broadly based process.

The extension of participation rights within the planning framework to a wide variety of interests facilitates an inclusive and democratic debate about the meaning of property. It recognises that the scope of private property rights is not predetermined, but rather is worked out through a continuous deliberative process involving individuals, the state and other community interests. The participation tools employed in English planning law fit the democratic model of property articulated by Singer, since broad-based engagement in regulatory processes controlling land use helps to ensure that private ownership remains responsive to changing collective concerns. The participation rules employed reflect the fact that the collective understanding of property is dynamic and evolving, meaning that regulators need an effective means of 'reading the temperature' of that understanding on a continuing basis, so that they can adjust the freedom afforded to owners in relation to land use as appropriate.[102]

The increasingly significant role of participation rules in English planning law, and the expansion in the non-owner participation rights that it recognises, can also be understood as practical illustrations of the recent emphasis placed by Eduardo Peñalver on the right of entrance as a core facet of private ownership.[103] According to this approach, property rights are understood to play a key role in allowing owners to engage with, and develop, local communities. As a result, 'the individual's acquisition of property is not so much seen as facilitating acts of defiant exit, but as reinforcing his bonds to the community in which that property is situated'.[104] Using participation rules as the key means of protecting property rights in planning law gives clear effect to this binding function for property ownership, because it means that property rights can only be asserted and defined through participation in regulatory processes. Where participation rules are employed in this way, ownership ties an individual into a process of collective deliberation on the meaning of property. Accordingly, English planning law secures the engagement between owner and community envisaged by Peñalver, and also in the civic-republican theory considered in Part II, by making the assertion of property rights dependent upon participation in collective deliberation on the appropriate use of land.

C. Controlling the 'Democratisation of Property' in English Planning Law

The trends identified and explored in this chapter suggest that in practice, English planning law increasingly treats property as a concept that is subject to contextual definition through regulation. The 'democratisation of property' is presupposed

---

[102] As Rose notes, one of the criticisms made of crystal rules is that they presume 'that human beings have no memories or new ideas that influence later choices, no ability to persuade each other—in short, no changes of consciousness over time that will cause them to redefine their views about "entitlements," just as they redefine other aspects of their thought': Rose (n 100) 606.

[103] Peñalver (n 11).

[104] Ibid, 1894.

by, and implemented through, the key features of the current English planning framework. Consequently, the question arises as to what problems such a planning framework may generate, and how, if at all, its effects can be controlled. While a complete answer to this question cannot be attempted here due to space constraints, I wish to briefly identify some of the potential pitfalls of the central role afforded to participation rules in modern English planning law. I also wish to suggest how judges might assert control over such 'democratisation of property' while at the same time respecting the democratically determined allocation of decision-making power in the planning system.[105]

First, the English planning process has the proven ability to exclude and alienate those affected by its decisions, notwithstanding the inclusion of participation rights of various kinds in its framework since at least 1969.[106] As Allen and Crookes put it, 'place shaping contains a symbolic power to exclude'.[107] For example, urban regeneration schemes implemented through compulsory purchase programmes have had well-documented adverse effects on local communities.[108] Indeed, the human rights challenge in *Mortell*, considered in the previous part of this chapter, concerned just such a situation.[109] In that case, elderly residents challenged the compulsory acquisition of their properties for regeneration purposes, objecting to being required to move from their homes within settled communities to more expensive housing elsewhere. The experience of such schemes in England demonstrates that practical outcomes of planning decisions can differ from those envisaged and intended by decision makers, and indeed by participants in the planning process more generally.[110] Notwithstanding extensive provision for public participation in such schemes, they can have serious adverse effects on local communities.[111]

In fact, there is a risk that participation rights may entrench the power of already-engaged actors rather than bringing disenfranchised parties into the collective discussion on land use.[112] Consequently, as Abbot and Lee rightly argue, 'a move to participation needs to be informed by an awareness of the existing distribution of power and how participation will affect that power'.[113] In this regard, the expansion of statutory provision for participation, most significantly through the Localism Act

---

[105] See Lord Hoffmann's comments on the democratic nature of the planning system in *R (Alconbury) v Secretary of State for the Environment* [2001] UKHL 23 [69], [2003] 2 AC 295, 325.

[106] See discussion from Campbell and Marshall (n 24) and McAuslan (n 6).

[107] C Allen and L Crookes, 'Fables of the Reconstruction: A Phenomenology of "Place Shaping" in the North of England' (2009) 80 *Town Planning Review* 455, 469.

[108] See C Allen, *Housing Market Renewal and Social Class* (London, Routledge, 2008); G Macleod and C Johnstone, 'Stretching Urban Renaissance: Privatizing Space, Civilizing Place, Summoning "Community"' (2012) 36 *International Journal of Urban and Regional Research* 1; B Nevin, 'Housing Market Renewal in Liverpool: Locating the Gentrification Debate in History, Context and Evidence' (2010) 25 *Housing Studies* 715.

[109] See also *Secretary of State for Communities and Local Government v Pascoe* [2006] EWHC 2356 (Admin).

[110] See Nevin (n 108) 731 and Macleod and Johnston (n 108) 22.

[111] See, eg, Allen (n 108) 180-90.

[112] Shaw and Lord suggest that: 'There is evidence to suggest that in some contexts early consultation has occurred and that some hard-to-reach groups are becoming more involved in planning, although this is far from a widespread experience.' Shaw and Lord (n 70) 427. See also AR Davies, 'Hidden or Hiding?' (2001) 72 *Town Planning Review* 193, 194; Abbot and Lee (n 24) 108.

[113] Abbot and Lee (n 24) 107.

2011, may in fact exacerbate the exclusionary risks inherent in the English planning process. The increased empowerment of local communities raises the possibility that the powers conferred will be exercised to exclude those perceived as outsiders.[114] In addition, there are legitimate questions to be asked about the accountability and representativeness of groups such as neighbourhood forums.[115] As Paul Brest notes, deliberation 'among people who ... represent a relatively narrow spectrum of perspectives may create or reinforce a distorted but strongly held consensus'.[116]

Second, and related to the first problem, participation rights that on paper appear to strongly vindicate the interests of affected parties can prove much less meaningful in practice, depending on the manner in which they are implemented by decision makers. As Sherry Arnstein notes: 'There is a critical difference between going through the empty ritual of participation and having the real power needed to affect the outcome of the process.'[117] Participation rights must be given practical effect, including serious consideration of submissions made to decision makers, if they are to afford affected parties a significant voice in the planning process.[118] Where such rights replace liability rule protection for property rights, the legitimacy of such substitution should be treated as contingent upon the *quality* of the opportunity for participation that is in reality afforded to affected owners, rather than the mere *existence* of that opportunity. Kevin Gray correctly argues that 'to be recognised as having authority to "speak for" an asset—to have a dispositive voice or strategic vote in determining its mode of utilisation—is, in itself, to command an intensely significant component of "property" in the resource'.[119] However, the value of such authority is contingent on the nature of the participatory process in which an owner, or indeed any other interested party, is permitted to engage, and particularly on the extent to which one's voice can in fact be meaningfully heard by decision makers. The participation structure that has been established within the English planning framework to ensure fairness, as well as meaningful deliberation at a local level as to the common good of a community, may in fact subvert those goals if all voices are not in practice heard and considered through its processes. The experience of participation in housing market renewal programmes in England suggests that in reality, participatory processes in the planning context are not always administered in a way that effectively captures and considers all relevant interests.[120]

A third, related challenge is preventing minority oppression through the contextual definition of the scope of ownership rights in the administration of planning regulation. As was discussed in the previous part of this chapter, judicial review actions and Human Rights Act challenges are two related avenues of potential redress for those

---

[114] Herbert (n 70) 856–58.

[115] Layard, 'Law and Localism' (n 58) 557.

[116] P Brest, 'Constitutional Citizenship' (1986) 34 *Cleveland State Law Review* 175, 196. See also M Galston, 'Taking Aristotle Seriously: Republican-Oriented Legal Theory and the Moral Foundation of Deliberative Democracy' (1994) 82 *California Law Review* 329, 359 on the importance of marginal perspectives in deliberative democracy.

[117] SR Arnstein, 'A Ladder of Citizen Participation' (1969) 35 *Journal of American Planners* 216.

[118] See P Somerville, 'Empowerment through Residence' (1998) 13 *Housing Studies* 233, 234–35.

[119] K Gray, 'Equitable Property' (1994) 47 *Current Legal Problems* 157, 193.

[120] Allen (n 108) 180–90. Allen concluded that housing market renewal was being imposed on the community in Kensington, Liverpool, regardless of their wishes (at 194).

who regard themselves as unfairly burdened by planning decisions. The protection of property rights achieved through the incorporation of the right to peaceful enjoyment of possessions in Article 1 of Protocol 1 of the European Convention on Human Rights into English law via the Human Rights Act 1998 suggests that owners should be protected against disproportionate interferences with their property rights in the public interest. The problem that has plagued this area of law has been how to identify when an interference is disproportionate, a difficulty that is heightened where the scope of property rights in a particular context is defined contextually through regulatory processes.[121] However, the participation rules at the heart of English planning law may in fact be a useful starting point for judges called upon to engage with this seemingly intractable problem, whether through Human Rights Act challenges or through traditional judicial review actions.

Hanoch Dagan identifies a risk that the imposition of uncompensated restrictions on ownership in the public interest could result in disproportionate burdening of politically weak groups in society.[122] Accordingly, he suggests that in extreme cases, it should be open to an affected owner 'to insist on a heightened scrutiny of proportionality where she is either poor or belongs to a politically weak segment of society'.[123] Applying Dagan's analysis to English planning law suggests that a judicial approach that is 'participation-oriented' and 'representation-reinforcing', to borrow from John Hart Ely, may be a useful tool in attempting to ensure that the 'democratisation of property' through planning regulation does not unfairly burden individuals or discrete groups in society.[124] Ely argued that judicial intervention was appropriate where the 'channels of political change' might be closed to some individuals or groups in society.[125] He contended that by focusing on protecting participation, the courts could stay true to the underpinning premises of the democratic system and to their core skills as process experts, while at the same time preventing minority oppression.[126] Similarly, William Treanor argued that in 'takings' cases brought under the Fifth Amendment of the US Constitution alleging an entitlement to compensation for regulatory control of private ownership, the courts

---

[121] See Gray (n 3) 175.

[122] H Dagan, *Property—Values and Institutions* (New York, Oxford University Press, 2011) 107, 143.

[123] Ibid, 111.

[124] JH Ely, *Democracy and Distrust—A Theory of Judicial Review* (Cambridge, MA, Harvard University Press, 1980), 87. Margaret Jane Radin and Frank Michelman have both similarly stressed the need for judges to attend to political empowerment in property law: Radin (n 29) 143–44, 159; F Michelman, 'Tutelary Jurisprudence and Constitutional Property' in Ellen Frankel Paul and Howard Dickman (eds), *Liberty, Property, and the Future of Constitutional Development* (New York, State University New York Press, 1990) 127, 138. A different approach to addressing majority tyranny in the planning system is suggested by Millichap, who argues for an approach focused on the *administrative decision maker's* duty to consider 'community rights', both local, disparate and future, in land-use decision making: Millichap (n 33) 449–51.

[125] The Takings Clause provides 'nor shall private property be taken for public use, without just compensation'. Ely characterises this clause as providing 'yet another protection of the few against the many': Ely (n 124) 97.

[126] Ibid, 88.

should focus on identifying and resolving instances of process failure, such as where 'discrete and insular minorities' are exploited in the public interest.[127]

Applying this approach to the protection of property rights in the English planning context, judicial intervention to protect individual owners adversely affected by planning decisions is arguably particularly warranted where the individual or group targeted by a restriction is socially and politically weak and would not be able to defend its interests through the political system.[128] A cycle may emerge if such an approach is not adopted whereby the property rights of politically weak groups are diminished through regulatory control, thereby further reducing their influence within the political process and exposing their property rights to yet more restriction in the interests of the majority. Participation rules are apparently the core means now used in English planning legislation to avoid such an outcome by ensuring broad-based engagement in a land-use decision-making process that is designed to be transparent and fair. Accordingly, judges must police the quality of participation in the planning process in order to ensure that the fairness that is supposed to be achieved through the processes set up by the planning framework is in fact realised. Furthermore, where judges are called upon to adjudicate constitutional property challenges to planning decisions, it may be useful for them in the first instance to focus on the application of statutory participation rules in the particular case. Weak participation by affected parties, whether as a result of disenfranchisement or administrative failure, could signal the need for heightened review of the proportionality of the impugned interference with property rights.

By attending to the quality of a particular category of owners' voices in the decision-making process affecting their ownership rights, and to the attention paid to their views by decision makers, the courts may be able to protect the rights of

---

[127] Treanor argues that: 'Compensation is due when a governmental action affects only the property interests of an individual or a small group of people and when, in the absence of compensation, there would be a lack of horizontal equity (ie when compensation is the norm in similar circumstances).' W Treanor, 'The Original Understanding of the Takings Clause and the Political Process' (1995) 95 *Columbia Law Review* 782, 872. See also P Boudreaux, 'Eminent Domain, Property Rights, and the Solution of Representation Reinforcement' (2005) 83 *Denver University Law Review* 1, 43–53 for an application of a representation reinforcement approach to eminent domain under the Takings Clause of the Fifth Amendment. The phrase 'discrete and insular minorities' comes from Justice Stone's footnote 4 in the Supreme Court's decision in *United States v Carolene Products*, where he stated: 'It is unnecessary to consider now whether legislation which restricts those political processes which can ordinarily be expected to bring about repeal of undesirable legislation, is to be subjected to more exacting judicial scrutiny under the general prohibitions of the Fourteenth Amendment than are most other types of legislation ... Nor need we enquire whether similar considerations enter into the review of statutes directed at particular religious ... or national ... or racial minorities ...; whether prejudice against discrete and insular minorities may be a special condition, which tends seriously to curtail the operation of those political processes ordinarily to be relied upon to protect minorities, and which may call for a correspondingly more searching judicial inquiry.'
United States v Carolene Products Co (1938) 304 US 144, 152–53 (citations omitted). Ely characterises both of these paragraphs as concerned with participation in the political processes by which competing values in society are accommodated: Ely (n 124) 77.
[128] Ely describes how political processes can fail minority groups as follows: 'Malfunction occurs when the *process* is undeserving of trust, when (1) the ins are choking off the channels of political change to ensure that they will stay in and the outs will stay out, or (2) though no one is actually denied a voice or a vote, representatives beholden to an effective majority are systematically disadvantaging some minority out of simple hostility or a prejudiced refusal to recognize commonalities of interest, and thereby denying that minority the protection afforded other groups by a representative system.' Ely (n 124) 103.

owners and other affected rightholders while at the same time respecting the clear tendency of English planning law to treat the meaning and scope of ownership rights as democratically defined. Indeed, English judges have naturally assumed such a role in adjudicating upon disputes arising out of the planning process, preferring to protect property rights in land-use regulation contexts by enforcing procedural rights rather than by substantively reviewing the merits of planning decisions.[129] They have instinctively defended the process whereby property is democratised, rather than property itself. However, if participation is to be relied upon as the key mediator of fairness in the contextual definition of ownership rights through planning regulation, legislators, regulators and judges alike must be cognisant of the planning system's capacity to exclude and oppress affected parties while appearing to be inclusive.

V. CONCLUSIONS

It seems that we have come full circle from the civic-republican relationship between participation rights and property rights in common law jurisdictions. Whereas property was formerly seen as constitutive of democracy, now property itself is constituted on an ongoing basis through the application of participation rules in English planning law. Property ownership binds individuals to their communities and to the democratic system, not by giving them independence as civic-republicans thought, but instead by requiring democratic engagement for the definition of the scope of their land-use rights.[130] Participation rules provide a key mechanism for asserting the right to possess and control private property in the context of pervasive planning control and, as such, they force individuals to engage in the collective construction of the meaning of ownership. The resulting relational structures in turn affect the broader social and economic structure of society.

Accordingly, it appears that property now has a symbiotic relationship with participation. On the one hand, property is defined through a dynamic participatory process, but on the other hand, the definition that is applied at any point in time in a particular context has effects on the democratic system. Thus, whereas property was once regarded as dominant in its relationship with participation, since it was a requirement for the *capacity and right* to engage in the democratic system, now participation is dominant, as it defines and controls the meaning and scope of property rights in the planning law context, thereby *demanding* political engagement by owners who wish to assert their rights. Moreover, the voices of non-owners are increasingly heard in the democratic processes that set the parameters within which ownership rights can be asserted. While decisions on the scope of owners' freedom in relation to land-use have systemic effects, they are always subject to revision

---

[129] See the discussion in Part I, at n 32. See also Lord Nolan's statement in *Alconbury* that 'a review of the merits of the *decision-making process* is fundamental to the courts' jurisdiction': [2001] UKHL 23 [61], [2003] 2 AC 295, 322.

[130] As Peñalver notes, 'in contrast to the analysis of civic republicans, it appears to be the greater vulnerability and responsibility of property owners, and not their financial self-sufficiency, that enhance their involvement in community life': Peñalver (n 11) 1950.

through further democratic deliberation, meaning that property in this context is a product of participation, not a prerequisite for it. As a result, policing the enforcement of participation rules, and reviewing the impact of participation on planning decisions, is arguably of central importance for judges attempting to supervise the 'democratisation of property' through the application of English planning law.

14

The Rise of Property Rights: Implications for Urban Planning, Environmental Protection and Biodiversity Conservation in Australia

PETER WILLIAMS*

I. INTRODUCTION

T HIS CHAPTER EXAMINES the rise of property and development rights in Australia in recent years, and its significant implications for various aspects of urban planning policy and law. It argues that there has been a substantial shift in landowner, developer and, in some cases, administrative and judicial perceptions and interpretations of rights pertaining to property. This has been a key factor that has prompted a major re-adjustment of policy and legislative approaches on the part of government in relation to a range of planning, environmental and natural resource issues. Fundamentally, a trend may be detected away from traditional 'command and control' regulatory tools such as zoning towards a wider array of market-based incentives and statutory and common law mechanisms. The focus of the discussion in this chapter is thus the intersection of property rights, urban planning, environmental protection and biodiversity conservation. Sydney and its attendant state of New South Wales (NSW) provide much of the context of this analysis.

The chapter is divided into five parts. Part I outlines the structure of the chapter and introduces the topic by providing a brief overview of Australian planning systems and the concepts of 'command and control' regulation and 'smart' regulation. Part II presents a closer examination of command regulation, particularly in the face of enhanced perceptions of property rights, including claims for compensation for diminution of these rights. Some of the contemporary problems confronting planning in Australia, in terms of limitations of command and control regulation in the face of property rights, are illustrated in Part III through a series of case studies. Spanning three areas of concern, these case studies relate to first, urban planning (affordable housing), second, environmental protection (compulsory acquisition required for injurious affection in environment protection zones) and, third, natural

* Director, Planning and Urban Development Program, Faculty of the Built Environment, University of New South Wales, Sydney, Australia.

resource conservation (biodiversity protection through proposed green zones). Part IV examines one solution in the form of 'smart' regulation, which is a hybrid of command and control and other—particularly market-based—mechanisms that operate within the context of property rights. Considered here are examples such as voluntary planning agreements, transferable development rights, green offsets, conservation covenants, statutory conservation agreements and stewardship payments. A conclusion to the chapter in Part V provides comment on the future of these approaches.

Fundamental to the discussion in this chapter is the notion of 'development rights'. In Australia there is no inherent right to develop land; rather, development rights are regulated by planning legislation,[1] with the permissibility of different types of development on a particular parcel of land determined by the relevant statutory planning controls (such as the zoning) that apply to that land. Thus, development may be permissible without the need for planning consent (that is, 'as of right'); or a property owner may have the right to seek development consent, after the granting of which, development for the specific purpose approved can legally commence; or development may be prohibited. Nevertheless, in practice, the Australian experience is that a landowner may have certain development expectations based on the applicable statutory planning controls. Implicit in the controls is a perceived probability of gaining approval for a certain type and quantity of development.[2]

Australia has a federal system of government under which jurisdictional responsibility for urban and regional planning, environmental protection and natural resource management generally resides with its constituent states and territories, rather than the Commonwealth (ie national) government.[3] Planning in Australia has predominantly relied on 'command and control' regulatory approaches with their origins in traditional British town and country planning.[4] Australian planning systems are statutory-based in that they are prescribed by various state and territory legislation, including a dominant *planning act*. In NSW, for example, this is the Environmental Planning and Assessment Act 1979. Such statutes in turn impose a series of controls or regulation through a system of land use zoning, development standards, building regulations, subdivision controls, heritage provisions, etc. The dominant source of government planning regulatory power is thus statutory law in the form of overriding planning legislation and subsequent delegated or subordinate legislation such as planning instruments, ordinances and regulations. Planning—and more specifically development control—in Australia therefore operates within the framework of what can be described as a *regulatory-based statutory planning system*.

---

[1] See P Ryan, 'Freedom of Property—An Urban Planning Perspective' (1988) 11 *University of New South Wales Law Journal* 48.

[2] J Bindon, 'Transferable Development Rights: A Review' (1992) 30 *Australian Planner* 136.

[3] D Farrier and P Stein, *The Environmental Law Handbook*, 4th edn (Redfern, Redfern Legal Centre Publishing, 2006) 12.

[4] JG Starke, *The Law of Town and Country Planning in New South Wales* (Sydney, Butterworths, 1966) 39; B Gleeson and N Low, *Australian Urban Planning: New Challenges, New Agendas* (St Leonards, NSW, Allen & Unwin, 2000) 145.

Although the statutory and regulatory emphases pertain in Australia—particularly reliance on land use zoning—more recently planning approaches influenced by US systems of financial and planning incentives have emerged to complement this traditional 'command and control' regulation hegemony. Part of a self-styled 'smart' regulation package, these seek to give Australian planning systems greater flexibility through the use of market-based mechanisms and financial incentives.[5] One particular benefit of using this approach is that it can help decide *how land is managed*—something which command and control regulation usually cannot do, as it merely determines whether land is developed or not. This is particularly important from the perspective of ensuring that the ongoing management of land—from the perspective of environmental protection and sustaining long-term productive capacity and natural ecosystems—is financially attractive (or at least not burdensome) to private landowners. Tools utilised here include planning bonuses, stewardship payments, green offsets and the acquisition of development 'rights' related to land. Often these also involve the utilisation of traditional common law mechanisms such as covenants and easements. One sphere of application of this hybrid mix of planning approaches and tools is the protection of biodiversity and other natural resource values such as agricultural lands in areas subject to urbanisation. Further fields of application of hybrid regulatory and market-based mechanisms include heritage conservation and landscape protection.

II. COMMAND AND CONTROL REGULATION AND PROPERTY RIGHTS

A. Command and Control Regulation in Urban Planning

'The most common form of public control of land use is restriction of private use by regulation'.[6] The defining character of 'command' regulation[7] is its obligatory nature—it involves an authoritative relationship between the individuals or groups being regulated and the government.[8] Regulation over the use and development of land has a long history that has established it as a normal 'incident' in the exercise of government power. Town and country planning as a function of government evolved initially in Britain as a response to the Industrial Revolution. Planning regulation was manifested, in historical sequence, in the public health codes dating from the mid-nineteenth century, the housing codes from the late nineteenth century and the planning codes of the early twentieth century.[9]

Underpinning the regulatory approach to planning is reliance on traditional 'command and control' regulation. Historically, regulation has been the most common approach adopted for the implementation of planning and environmental objectives. Regulation has taken many forms. Initially in the narrower sense of 'town

---

[5] N Gunningham and P Grabosky, *Smart Regulation: Designing Environmental Policy* (Oxford, Oxford University Press, 1998).

[6] J Harte, *Landscape, Land Use and the Law* (London, E & FN Spon, 1985) 49.

[7] 'Regulation' is increasingly used in a much broader way to include any attempt by government to influence behaviour. Here regulation is being used in a narrower way to mean 'command regulation'.

[8] A Stone, *Regulation and Its Alternatives* (Washington DC, Congressional Quarterly Press, 1982).

[9] D Heap, *An Outline of Planning Law*, 9th edn (London, Sweet & Maxwell, 1987).

planning', it involved the exercise of public control over matters such as building, subdivision and land use through the use of zoning and other statutory-based controls. Specifically, building regulation was exercised through a range of controls including building height, density, materials and setbacks. Subdivision regulation was manifested in the form of controls such as minimum allotment sizes, density of subdivision and building erection, and minimum site frontages. The regulation of land use still remains at the core of environmental and planning law.[10] Land use has been regulated primarily through land use zoning and planning standards. With the expansion of 'planning' into the broader fields of environmental planning and protection and natural resource management, these traditional tools have been extended, augmented and refashioned, but the characteristic 'regulatory' approach largely remains.

The core of the planning—and more particularly development control—system is land use zoning, 'the device responsible for the "spatial allocation of land uses": the selective placement of possible uses in some areas and not in others across a municipality or regional area'.[11] In Australia, zoning has long been (and remains) the basis of land use control. The system of planning law in this country based on the production of zoning schemes containing legal ordinances or instruments and zoning maps is essentially derived from the British Town and Country Planning Act 1932, and before that the Acts of 1925, 1919 and 1909. Zoning and other forms of planning regulation such as statutory-based development or planning standards form the cornerstone for the implementation of most urban planning systems. In this sense, Australia is arguably fortunate to have retained a strong zoning tradition, based on the pre-Second World War British statutory planning control heritage. Nonetheless, the Australian experience of this adaptation of statutory planning has been very different from the British one, caused by obvious dissimilarities in geography, sociopolitical culture and history.[12]

Regulation through statutory planning continues to have its advocates for both philosophical and practical reasons. From a conceptual perspective, regulation of development—'development control'—is seen as fundamental to planning;[13] at the same time, from a practical viewpoint, it is argued that regulation and prescriptive planning controls promote greater certainty and consistency in decision making.[14]

B. Regulation, Injurious Affection and Property Rights

Although the inviolability of property still remains an important value in Western legal systems, significant inroads have been made into this principle. For example,

---

[10] Farrier and Stein (n 3) 7.

[11] L Stein, *Principles of Planning Law* (Melbourne, Oxford University Press, 2008) 9.

[12] The differences include, for example: geography (focus on urban coastal development clustering around cities in Australia): sociopolitical culture (different assumptions about the role of the state, with the historical development of the welfare state, including its manifestation in planning, something arguably not as strong in Australia): and historical (the British experience of Victorian industrialisation and bombing during the Second World War).

[13] J Dawkins, 'In Praise of Regulation' (1996) 33 *Australian Planner* 10.

[14] J Walton, 'In Praise of Certainty' (1997) 34 *Australian Planner* 12.

the control by planning legislation of the uses to which land and buildings can be put, and powers of compulsory acquisition enabling authorities to acquire land from private owners without their consent, are accepted today as essential features of the state machinery for promoting the welfare of the community. Fundamental belief in the recognition of private property continues to the present day, however, in the notion that property should not be arbitrarily acquired from private persons without adequate compensation.[15] Yet, the situation with regard to possible compensation for diminished property rights as a consequence of planning regulations—injurious affection or regulatory takings—is less clear-cut. Differences exist across countries generated by a diverse 'culture' of property rights: aspects of the distinct Australian experience are discussed below.

Reduction in the value of land—injurious affection—may be caused either by reservation or down-zoning. A 'reserve' is created when land is designated in a statutory planning instrument as being able to be used only for a 'public purpose' such as a road, recreation or conservation. 'It is a declaration that the land should be set aside for the community even though it remains in private ownership'[16] until actually acquired by government for that purpose. If a planning instrument permits uses in a reserve, they must be ones that that are compatible with its future public purpose. In NSW, for example, the reservation of land for a public purpose in a planning instrument is deemed to be a compulsory acquisition of the land and compensation must be paid.[17] Because planning authorities generally seek to avoid paying compensation because of the financial burden, it is common practice to 'down-zone' land to a use where development of a limited type is permitted, rather than reserve the land. This has the effect of avoiding acquisition and compensation, yet restricting the use of the land, a distinction recognised in *Bingham's* case, the first claim for compensation for down-zoning under the planning provisions of the NSW Local Government Act 1919.[18] However, recent evidence in relation to down-zoning of land to environmental protection zones in NSW, discussed in more detail below, indicates a reversal of this position.

In Australia, section 51(xxxi) of the Commonwealth Constitution provides that any 'acquisition' of property by instrumentalities of the Commonwealth must be

---

[15] D Lloyd, *The Idea of Law* (Harmondsworth, Penguin, 1981) 146.

[16] Stein (n 11) 52.

[17] M Wilcox, *The Law of Land Development in New South Wales* (Sydney, Law Book Co, 1967) 277–97.

[18] *Bingham v Cumberland County Council* (1954) 20 LGR 1. Here the NSW Valuation Court considered a claim for compensation under planning provisions introduced in 1945 as pt XIIA of the Local Government Act 1919 (NSW). The Act contained a provision (s 342AC(1)) that landholders were entitled to compensation for injurious affection caused by planning schemes. But Sugerman J recognised that 'whereas legislation authorising government to acquire land typically provided that its former owner should be compensated in full, legislation which imposed restrictions on the use of land in the public interest contained no such provision' (at 26; see also *Baker v Cumberland County Council* (1956) 1 LGRA 321, 333). Consistent with this distinction, Sugerman J found that the Local Government Act's general declaration of a right to compensation was subject to so many qualifications that it represented more of an exception than the rule. As in other jurisdictions, landowners had little prospect of successfully claiming compensation unless their land was reserved for a public purpose (T Bonyhady, 'Property Rights' in T Bonyhady (ed), *Environmental Protection and Legal Change* (Leichhardt, NSW, Federation Press, 1992) 49).

made on just terms.[19] The constitutional position in Australia is that compensation is not payable for planning incidents such as 'takings' or 'injurious affection',[20] but only for the 'acquisition' of property on just terms'.[21] Thus, there is no constitutional guarantee of compensation for *restrictions* on land use, subject to the findings regarding 'acquisition' by the High Court in the *Tasmanian Dam* and *Newcrest Mining* cases.[22] These decisions of the High Court appear to be consistent with the situation at common law in both Australia and Britain, where 'there is no right to compensation for the injurious effects of legislative restrictions upon land use imposed in the general interest, as distinct from acquisitions of property'.[23] Any right to compensation—including for injurious affection—must therefore be entirely the creature of statute.[24] On the basis of this distinction between the actual taking of property and a mere affectation of it, the 'general practice, under both common law and statute, has been to allow many people no compensation but a few people some'.[25] Nonetheless, it has been a common political assumption that *substantial restrictions* on land use (for example, a significant down-zoning of land) must not be imposed without compensation for any diminution in value produced by these restrictions.[26]

---

[19] The Commonwealth of Australia Constitution Act 1900 (Imp) states:
'Section 51—Concurrent legislative powers of the Federal Parliament.
The Parliament shall, subject to this Constitution, have power to make laws for the peace, order, and good government of the Commonwealth with respect to:-
(xxxi) The acquisition of property on just terms from any State or person in respect of which the Parliament has power to make laws.'

[20] Stein (n 11) 53.

[21] A view supported by the findings of two Commonwealth inquiries—the Commission of Inquiry into Land Tenures, *Final Report* (Canberra, AGPS, 1976); and the Australian Law Reform Commission, *Lands Acquisition and Compensation* (ALRC 14, Canberra, AGPS, 1980).

[22] In the *Tasmanian Dam* case (*Commonwealth v Tasmania* (1983) 158 CLR 1), the High Court held that even the severe restrictions on land use imposed under the World Heritage Properties Conservation Act 1983 (Cth) did not constitute an 'acquisition' requiring the payment of compensation. This was because the Commonwealth had not acquired a proprietary interest in the land in question, even though in terms of its potential use, the property was sterilised in the same way as a dedicated national park (at 145–46 (Mason J)). The point at which regulation imposed on land by Commonwealth environmental laws amounts to an acquisition of property and thus attracts the just terms compensation provision of the Constitution was realised in the *Newcrest Mining* case (*Newcrest Mining (WA) Ltd v Commonwealth* (1997) 147 ALR 42), which involved mining leases acquired at Coronation Hill, adjacent to Kakadu National Park. Proclamations were made under the National Parks and Wildlife Conservation Act 1975 (Cth) incorporating the Coronation Hill area into the park. The Act prohibited mining in the park and, although the mining leases themselves were not extinguished, Newcrest was unable to exercise its rights over them and so the benefits the company might have derived from its leases were effectively sterilised. The High Court found that this amounted to an acquisition of property under s 51(xxxi), as the effect of the proclamations and the prohibition of mining was not merely to impair the bundle of rights that existed under the mining leases. The Court held that Newcrest had, 'as a legal and practical' matter, been denied the exercise of its rights under the leases (at 130 (Gummow J). See K Sperling, 'Going Down the Takings Path: Private Rights and Public Interest in Land Use Decision Making' (1997) 14 *Environmental and Planning Law Journal* 427.

[23] Starke (n 4) 148. In the case of Britain, this view was reinforced by the findings of the Uthwatt Report in 1942: United Kingdom, *Final Report of the Expert Committee on Compensation and Betterment* (the Uthwatt Committee, United Kingdom, Cmd 6386, 1942).

[24] *Baker v Cumberland County Council* (1956) 1 LGRA 321, 333.

[25] P Ryan, *Urban Development Law and Policy* (Sydney, Law Book Co, 1988) 276.

[26] Ibid.

Further, because there is no equivalent provision in the *State* Constitutions to section 51(xxxi) of the Commonwealth Constitution, the High Court has held that the Australian States 'may acquire on any terms which they may choose to provide in a statute, even though the terms are unjust' and that 'however hard or unjust it may be considered, there is nothing in section 51(xxxi) to restrain the power of the State'.[27] Indeed, 'there is nothing in the NSW Constitution that guarantees private property rights or provides for the payment of compensation if the government regulates land use, so the government is quite at liberty to regulate the use of privately owned land without paying compensation'.[28] Pertinently, planning, environmental and natural resources legislation bearing on private land emanates primarily from the states and territories, yet their constitutions do not provide for compensation for landowners, even in situations in which state action results in the loss of all economic use of, or they are excluded from, their land. At the state and territory level, the payment of compensation where land is resumed for public purposes or subject to planning restrictions is purely a matter of convention under the legislation. In NSW, the relevant legislation covering public acquisition of land is the Land Acquisition (Just Terms Compensation) Act 1991, which is discussed in more detail below.

Any diminution of the right to develop land or determine its use through regulation imposed by planning statutes needs to be qualified. The first qualification is based on the nexus between property and politics, and the role—indeed, the power—which property ownership possesses in influencing the direction of public policy decisions that might otherwise place restrictions on the use of private property. Evidence of the political and policy influence of property rights in the context of planning decisions in NSW is provided below. The second qualification relates to the legal convention (under the Commonwealth Constitution) and statutory requirement (in NSW under the Land Acquisition (Just Terms Compensation) Act 1991) that deprivation or acquisition of property can only be executed by government subject to 'just compensation'. A problem arises here, however, as to what constitutes a deprivation of the use of property and hence attracts compensation.[29] This is a vexing contemporary planning problem for the urban growth management of Sydney in terms of the potential for compensation arising from the *down-zoning* of land for environmental protection purposes,[30] an issue of particular significance which is also discussed later in this chapter. Clearly, the resumption of land through compulsory acquisition constitutes the deprivation of the use of property. But at what point does the imposition of planning restrictions—the taking of one or more sticks out of the bundle of sticks of property rights—diminish the *economic* use of land to a point where compensation is payable?

---

[27] *PG Magennis Pty Ltd v Commonwealth* (1949) 80 CLR 382, 397–98, 412. See also *Commonwealth v New South Wales* (1915) 20 CLR 54, 77.

[28] Farrier and Stein (n 3) 9.

[29] Stein (n 11) 13–15.

[30] 'Down-zoning' is the term used to describe the rezoning of land to a zone that imposes greater planning restriction. Typically the new zone reduces the range of permissible uses on the land, and thus the land's development potential and value.

Britain provided one answer to this question based on the recommendations of the Uthwatt Report in 1942, which made the following points:

— Ownership of land does not carry with it an unqualified right of use (even under the common law).
— Restrictions based on the duties of neighbourliness may be imposed without involving the conception that the landowner is being deprived of any property or interest.
— Therefore, such restrictions can be imposed without liability to pay compensation.
— But the point may be reached when the restrictions imposed extend beyond the obligations of neighbourliness.
— At this stage, the restrictions become equivalent to an expropriation of a proprietary right or interest and therefore (arguably) should carry a right to compensation.[31]

The converse of injurious affection or regulatory takings and claims for compensation is the situation where landowners benefit from favourable planning decisions, with calls to tax the windfall gains or 'unearned increment' accruing to landowners from this betterment. Central to the rationale of government attempting to recover, via a levy or tax, the betterment private landowners have gained was the widely held feeling in Australia and Britain that landowners have no moral right to the 'unearned increment': that is, to increases in land values that are not due to any effort of their own but merely to factors such as the growth of the city around them, rezoning and to public investment in roads, services, etc.

In Australia, the Commission of Inquiry into Land Tenures considered the 'unearned increments' resulting from changes in use associated with the retention by private landowners of development or urbanisation rights, which it described as the rights to convert land from rural to urban use or from one urban use to another of greater intensity. The Commission of Inquiry referred to these rights accruing from the unearned increment of land use change or rezoning as 'development rights' and took a similar view to the British one:

> We have argued that because development rights ensue from government action, it is the community generally and not individual landowners who should reap the benefits accruing from such rights. We therefore propose that all development rights be reserved to the Crown and that all future increments in development value be appropriated by public authorities for the benefit of the whole community.[32]

In defending its recommendation of government adopting the device of acquiring or reserving future development rights, the Chair of the Commission of Inquiry, the Hon Rae Else-Mitchell, pointed out that the suggestion was not novel. It was referred to in the Scotts Reports of 1918 and 1942 in Britain and was advocated by the Barlow and Uthwatt Reports in 1940 and 1942. It was observed that 'even in the USA the need has been recognised for a separation of development rights from use rights, the development rights being transferable and capable of being dealt

---

[31] The Uthwatt Committee (n 23).
[32] Commission of Inquiry into Land Tenures. *Final Report* (AGPS, Canberra, February 1976) 40.

with apart from the land itself, so as to enable better control of development and the preservation of existing uses'.[33] Acknowledgement of the distinction between development rights and use rights was instrumental to the formulation of transfer and purchase of development rights schemes as planning tools in that country. In Australia, the adoption of mechanisms based on the assignment and acquisition and transfer of development rights or the appropriation of those rights by government has not been widespread, and even when implemented not always successful.[34] A further discussion of transfer of development rights schemes in Australia is provided below.

C. Regaining Public Control Over Land—Partial Interests

Inherent in the concept of command and control regulation is the notion of government seeking to re-establish public control over land use. In urban areas in particular in Australia, much of this control had been lost by the granting of freehold title over formerly Crown land. Public control over land use can be established by regulatory means—such as town planning legislation—or by the other traditional mechanism of acquisition freehold land through normal market purchase or, where necessary, through reliance on the power of compulsory acquisition or resumption.[35]

Significantly, however, acquisition of fee simple title is not the only acquisition option open to government seeking public control over land use. Acquisition of specific rights or partial interests can be a less costly means of establishing land use control. Utilising the well-known analogy of likening property rights to a 'bundle of sticks',[36] the rights inherent in the ownership of fee simple absolute title to land can be separated and transferred individually to other people. Arising from the concept of likening property rights to a 'bundle of sticks' comes the notion that one or more of these rights may be acquired by government or individuals:[37] for example, the acquisition of 'partial interests' in the land in the form of its development potential

---

[33] Hon R Else-Mitchell, *Adelaide Conference on Land Tenures: Proceedings of a Conference on the First Report of the Commission of Inquiry into Land Tenures.* Convened by the Urban and Regional Planning Research Unit, University of Adelaide, 9 August 1974 (AGPS, Canberra, 1974), 9.

[34] In Australia the question of the unearned increment and betterment has a long, difficult and unsatisfying history. For example, the Local Government Act 1919 (NSW) empowered local councils to levy betterment charges where a prescribed planning scheme expressly provided. This charge was directed at the recovery of any increase in the value of land attributable to the operation of the prescribed scheme. However, the provision proved to be of little practical importance since only a handful of schemes under the Act provided for recovery of betterment, as councils were reluctant to claim betterment charges due to its electoral unpopularity. A later attempt in NSW to introduce a betterment tax—the Land Development Contribution Management Act 1970—operated briefly between 1970 and 1973, but was abandoned due to developer resistance. Currently in Australia, the power to claim a betterment levy operates only in the Australian Capital Territory, via a change-of-use-charge under the Land (Planning and Environment) Act 1991.

[35] Ryan (n 25) 276.

[36] JH Goldstein and WD Watson, 'Property Rights, Regulatory Taking, and Compensation: Implications for Environmental Protection' (1997) 15 *Contemporary Economic Policy* 32, 33; TL Daniels and D Bowers, *Holding Our Ground: Protecting America's Farms and Farmland* (Washington DC, Island Press, 1997) 32; G Torres, 'Taking and Giving: Police Power, Public Value, and Private Right' (1996) 26 *Environmental Law* 1, 14.

[37] Daniels and Bowers (n 36); Stein (n 11) 6–7.

or 'rights'. Partial interests—the individual sticks in the complex bundle of rights that constitutes land ownership—can be identified and traded separately, providing a mechanism for recognising the range of claimants on a resource even within a system of formalised land tenure. In this sense, the acquisition or transfer of partial interests or rights represents a return to a more traditional understanding of tenure and land use systems, which differentiated rights such as rights to draw water, graze livestock, produce crops or build houses.[38]

Within the modern system of formalised land tenure, however, the bundle of rights that constitute land ownership are often consolidated in the hands of a single 'owner'. As a consequence, many of the subtleties that historically allowed other rightholders to access, use or influence the disposition of land have been lost. It has been argued that this process of simplifying tenure arrangements to individual ownership, and then influencing behaviour by imposing regulations, is not necessarily optimal or even necessary.[39] More refined and flexible approaches include a focus on partial interests in land. By allowing voluntary acquisition and conveyance of specific rights for specific uses, partial interests offer this more refined alternative to a strictly regulatory approach or trading full ownership rights.[40]

Development rights have been viewed as one of a number of rights embodied in the ownership interest in property. These development rights have been classified as a real property interest, which entitles the owner of a fee simple interest to deal with the land as the owner wishes, subject only to government regulation, principally through zoning.[41] However, the right to transfer development rights is not ordinarily part of the bundle of rights that comes with land ownership, because in Australia at least (as discussed above), there is no right to develop land except within the terms of statutory planning controls or instruments. Government may therefore need to enact specific legislation to legalise the sending of a building right from one parcel to another.[42] Once legislatively sanctioned, an owner may separate and transfer one of the rights incidental to ownership whilst retaining the other rights.[43]

In the US, the acquisition and conveyance of partial interests to land have proven to be popular, flexible and effective tools for land use and conservation policy. Schemes such as the purchase or transfer of these interests or rights have allowed public agencies and private non-profit conservation groups to influence the use of public and private land without incurring the political costs of land regulation or the full financial costs of outright land acquisition.[44]

Generally in Australia, however, short of compulsory acquisition or widespread use of acquisition of partial interests in land to replace the Crown's loss of direct proprietary interest in land, it has been necessary to re-establish public control by means of statute and regulation. Thus, environmental planning legislation, for

---

[38] KD Wiebe, KD and R Meinzen-Dick, 'Property Rights as Policy Tools for Sustainable Development' (1998) 15 *Land Use Policy* 203.

[39] Ibid.

[40] Ibid, 204.

[41] C Arnold, 'Transferable Development Rights—A Planning Tool for the Preservation of Heritage Buildings' (1992) 9 *Environmental and Planning Law Journal* 459, 470.

[42] Daniels and Bowers (n 36) 172.

[43] Arnold (n 41) 470.

[44] Wiebe and Meinzen-Dick (n 38) 205.

example, can be seen as having the effect of transferring certain sticks out of the bundle belonging to individual landowners and into the hands of government or the community. As a result, typically when statutory planning controls are introduced, the right of landowners to do anything with the land that they desire (subject to the common law restriction that the ensuing activity is not a nuisance to adjoining landowners) is diminished:[45] 'planning is a direct interference with these rights'.[46]

III. PROPERTY RIGHTS CASE STUDIES

In the context of planning and urban growth management in Sydney, the question of compensation and acquisition as a consequence of planning restriction has been, and continues to remain, extremely problematic. Recently, it has been responsible for the invalidation of affordable housing schemes, the decision to abandon the proposed green zones in Sydney's growth areas, and presently is affecting environmental protection zonings in NSW.[47] Each of these situations is discussed in turn below.

A. Urban Planning and Property Rights

The growing importance of property rights in Australia has found expression in judicial review proceedings into the validity of planning decisions. In NSW, this was evident in the decision of the Land and Environment Court in *Meriton Apartments Pty Ltd v Minister for Urban Affairs and Planning & Or*,[48] where a developer successfully challenged a condition of development consent imposed under the provisions of a local planning instrument requiring that a contribution be made for affordable housing for low-income households. One of the grounds of challenge related to unlawful interference with property rights. Here the Court found for the applicant on two counts. First, in applying the legal maxim that property must not be taken away without the payment of compensation, it was held that the Environmental Planning and Assessment Act 1979 (hereinafter 'the EP&A Act') did not contain express provisions permitting the acquisition of property without compensation as envisaged by the challenged provisions. The Court concluded that it did 'not think that the New South Wales Parliament intended that well established principles relating to the limitation of powers of a local authority and to discrete issues of fundamental proprietary rights which have been enshrined in

---

[45] G Bates, *Environmental Law in Australia*, 5th edn (Chatswood, NSW, Butterworths, 2002) 39

[46] Stein (n 11) 6.

[47] Sydney is a sprawling city and, although in recent decades an 'urban consolidation' policy has been in place, still has low residential densities compared with many other world cities. The two growth centres are located on the fringes of Sydney and have been designated as areas for future urban expansion. Sydney also has some attractive undeveloped land in and around its borders. While much of this land is in public ownership, significant portions are in private ownership. To protect both these public and private lands from inappropriate development, various categories of environmental protection zonings are utilised under local government statutory planning schemes (or instruments as they are called in NSW).

[48] *Meriton Apartments Pty Ltd v Minister for Urban Affairs and Planning & Or* (2000) 107 LGERA 363.

the common law were to be discarded by the operation of the Act'.[49] Second, any condition imposed in reliance on those provisions was manifestly unreasonable in the *Wednesbury*[50] sense, since such conditions would represent an 'oppressive' or 'gratuitous' interference with property rights.

Although this case was simply a question of statutory interpretation, and there is no constitutional restriction on the power to devise land use controls in NSW, the EP&A Act nonetheless required amendment to mandate the imposition of affordable housing contributions on development consents under *existing* affordable housing schemes.[51] Further, it has been argued that the interpretation of Parliament's intention used in this case had 'the effect that planning ideologies and goals expressed in planning schemes must be strictly construed or read literally so as not to deprive a landowner of rights'.[52] Thus, as a matter of statutory interpretation and policy, it became apparent that planners in NSW had to take care in devising land use controls and be cognisant of 'how far' or 'how much' they could regulate before running afoul of property rights claims. Revolving around the question of when does a 'taking' or injurious affection constitute an 'acquisition' of property and thus attract compensation, the NSW government evaded confronting this question by deciding not to introduce further similar affordable housing schemes.[53]

B. Environment Protection Zones and Down-zoning

In 2005, the NSW government commenced major reforms of the planning process in NSW with the enactment of the Environmental Planning and Assessment (Infrastructure and Other Planning Reform) Act 2005. Amongst the suite of reforms contained in the 2005 amendments to the EP&A Act was the creation of a ministerial power to standardise statutory-based environmental planning instruments. This permitted the Minister for Planning to prescribe—via the Standard Instrument (Local Environmental Plans) Order 2006—the specific form and content that local councils are to adopt in their principal statutory planning instruments, known as local environmental plans (LEPs).[54] This LEP 'template' uses standard zones (including standard zone objectives and mandated permitted and prohibited uses), definitions, clauses and formatting. All local councils in NSW had to create new LEPs, compliant with the new mandated zones and zoning provisions, within a two-to-five-year period.

Four 'environment protection zones' are provided for under the Standard Instrument. Guidance to local councils in the form of a Practice Note, was provided by the NSW Department of Planning (DoP) on the environment protection

---

[49] Ibid, 381.

[50] *Associated Provincial Picture House Ltd v Wednesbury Corporation Ltd* [1948] 1 KB 233.

[51] Environmental Planning and Assessment Amendment Act 1999 (NSW), No 72; Environmental Planning and Assessment Amendment (Affordable Housing) Act 2000 (NSW), No 29.

[52] Stein (n 11) 7.

[53] P Williams, 'Statutory Planning and Affordable and Social Housing Provision: A Comparison of Recent Irish and Australian Experience' (2005) 27 *Dublin University Law Journal* 284–302.

[54] The precise form of the standard LEP template was subsequently prescribed by the Minister in the Standard Instrument (Local Environmental Plans) Order 2006.

zones and how they should be applied in the preparation of LEPs.[55] One of the environment protection zones—E1 National Parks and Nature Reserves—only applies to land reserved under the National Parks and Wildlife Act 1974 or areas identified as proposed for national park or nature reserves agreed by the NSW government. Environment protection zones E2 (Environmental Conservation), E3 (Environmental Management) and E4 (Environmental Living) are meant to be applied where the protection of the environmental significance of the land is the primary consideration. However, the DoP advised in relation to these zones that 'their importance for visitation, tourism and job creation should also be carefully considered'[56]—due to the potential to attract compensation through compulsory acquisition for injurious affection through down-zoning.

In relation to the designation of land under the environment protection zones, the potential to attract compensation through compulsory acquisition for down-zoning or 'back zoning' (ie imposition of a significant restriction on permissible land uses) has been a major issue of concern amongst local councils in NSW, and indeed was the primary reason for the issuance of a Practice Note.[57] Earlier informal advice from both the DoP and the Parliamentary Counsel's Office had indicated that if a significant down-zoning occurred as a consequence of rezoning land to an environment protection zone, compensation (through compulsory acquisition of the land under the Land Acquisition (Just Terms Compensation) Act 1991 (hereinafter 'the LAJTC Act') may be required. Subsequently, in the Practice Note, the Department provided the following advice in relation to the designation of permissible land uses in environment protection zones:

> The range of uses proposed to be permitted in the E zones is a consideration for council in consultation with the Department of Planning. In determining uses, council should be aware that the range of uses should not be drawn too restrictively as they may, depending on circumstances, invoke the Land Acquisition (Just Terms Compensation) Act 1991 and the need for the Minister to designate a relevant acquiring authority.

> Unless a relevant acquisition authority has been nominated and that authority has agreed to the proposed acquisition, council should ensure, wherever possible, that the range of proposed land uses assists in retaining the land in private ownership.[58]

This general advice in relation to the environment protection zones appears to be specifically targeted to proposed E2 and E3 zones.[59] However, this guidance is clearly contrary to the compulsory acquisition provisions of the LAJTC Act,[60] the land reservation and acquisition provisions of the EP&A Act[61] and the general position at law in NSW that compensation is not payable for mere injurious affection.[62] It envisages a situation where the economic use of private land has been

---

[55] Department of Planning, 'Environment Protection Zones', *LEP Practice Note PN 09-002*, issued 30 April 2009, www.planning.nsw.gov.au/planningsystem/pdf/pn09_002_envt_protection_zones.pdf.

[56] Ibid, 1.

[57] Ibid.

[58] Ibid, 2.

[59] Ibid, 6 and 8.

[60] Land Acquisition (Just Terms Compensation) Act 1991 (NSW), pt 2, Division 3.

[61] Environmental Planning and Assessment Act 1979 (NSW), ss 26(1)(c) and 27.

[62] Ryan (n 25).

significantly restricted (ie 'down-zoned') so that compulsory acquisition and hence compensation may be payable. This represents a major extension of the policy presumption and legal requirement that compensation is only payable in situations where land is identified in an environmental (ie statutory) planning instrument and is reserved for a future public purpose.

Thus, whether resumption is required and compensation is payable as a consequence of perceived down-zoning to an environmental conservation or environmental management zone under the standard LEP is ultimately a matter of the extent of diminution of development potential after rezoning, and not of law. This advice patently appears to be erroneous and should be rectified. In the meantime, the resolution of this question appears to rest on crafting a finely balanced zoning that achieves conservation objectives, but does not trigger compensation. The clear message from this situation is that 'property rights' appear to have been acknowledged (rightly or wrongly) by the NSW DoP. Yet, as will be seen below in the context of resisting the introduction of a formal transferable development rights (TDR) scheme in NSW, the DoP has reversed its policy position on property rights—in this case opposing a TDR scheme on the basis that it creates a system of rights that the Department argues landowners do not actually have.

C. Natural Resource Conservation—Sydney's Proposed 'Green Zones'

On 3 November 2005, a media release issued by the office of the NSW Minister for Planning announced the scrapping of two proposed 'green zones' in the south-west and north-west urban growth centres (that is, new urban release areas) of Sydney.[63] This 'green overlay', designed to preserve existing non-urban land for aesthetic, biodiversity conservation, recreation and agricultural purposes, covered 8,400 hectares in the land release areas and a further 14,000 hectares outside the growth centres boundary. The decision to abandon these green zones or areas—formally described as the Landscape and Rural Lifestyle Zone (LRLZ) under the prevailing Sydney Metropolitan Strategy[64]—was taken, stated the media release, 'following widespread public consultation'. Reasons given for the decision were basically twofold. First, the DoP had received more than 3,000 submissions on the growth centre plans over a four-month exhibition period. It was clear, stated the Minister, that 'the proposed LRLZ caused widespread concern and confusion, with nine in ten written submissions objecting to the new zone, which affected more than 7,000 properties'.[65] Many landowners complained about a perceived loss of property values and development rights.[66] Second, it was argued that the environmental benefits

---

[63] The Hon Frank Sartor MP, 'New Ground Rules for Green Space in Growth Centres' (Media Release, 3 November 2005).

[64] NSW Department of Planning, *City of Cities—A Plan for Sydney's Future* (Sydney, DoP, 2005), www.metrostrategy.nsw.gov.au/dev/uploads/paper/governance/index.html.

[65] Ibid.

[66] Department of Planning, *New Ground Rules for the North-West and South-West Land Release Areas, Fact Sheet* (NSW Department of Planning, Sydney, 2005), www.metrostrategy.nsw.gov.au/dev/digitalAssets/1350_1130983357783_051103%20fact%20sheet%201.pdf, viewed 11 August 2009.

were limited, because 45 per cent of the land identified for the LRLZ had already been cleared.[67]

Putting aside the issue of the poor quality of departmental mapping and the lack of 'ground-truthing' resulting in the misidentification of appropriate quality green space, the clear message was that public objection to the green zones was the primary reason for their demise, as both cleared and uncleared green areas were abandoned. This public objection rested on the expectation (whether reasonable or otherwise) that landowners' land—whose current zoning was not residential—in and around the south-west and north-west growth centres would be urbanised, with the windfall gain accruing to the property owners that this land use conversion process would entail. As described in the news media at the time, the 'dumping' of the green zone on Sydney's fringe occurred after 'a backlash from landowners angry [that] their properties would not be considered for housing subdivisions',[68] with fears that 'land values in some areas will plummet as a result'.[69]

One clear message from this episode is the role played by property 'rights' and concomitant development expectations or 'rights' in opposing—and ultimately determining—public policy designed to protect the environmental and natural resource values of the fringes of Sydney. This role was admitted by the Minister in an earlier media release (9 September 2005) when he announced a review of the LRLZ and stated that 'the green zones were never intended to change people's existing land use rights'.[70] It should be pointed out, however, that the green zone landowners were expecting more than their existing use rights. Rather, they wanted a right to develop or use their land in a way in which they were not presently entitled, that is, for residential purposes. This has two significant implications. First, this 'right' that was perceived to pertain to non-urban land does not exist even in land already zoned residential, since development consent is first required before residential subdivision and development can proceed. Second, landowner insistence on and State government accedence to such 'rights' can only lead to speculation in areas in and around the growth areas *not* zoned residential. Recognition of these implications was acknowledged in the *Sydney Morning Herald* the next day when it reported:

> Developers and groups representing thousands of aggrieved landholders yesterday applauded the State Government's decision to walk away from a green zoning proposal that had denied property owners the right to cash in on future housing estates.[71]

Planning implementation of the growth centres component of the Sydney Metropolitan Strategy was deferred to the making of a specific statutory plan in the form of a state environmental planning policy (SEPP), which finalised the release

---

[67] Sartor (n 63).

[68] D Goodsir, 'Angry Landowners Winning the War on Green Zone' (*Sydney Morning Herald* (Sydney), 9 September 2005, 3).

[69] D Goodsir, 'Landholders Rush Zoning Help Line' (*Sydney Morning Herald* (Sydney), 6 September 2005, 9).

[70] Department of Planning, 'Statement on Landscape and Rural Lifestyle Zone' (Media Release, 9 September 2005).

[71] D Goodsir, 'Owners' Joy as State Dumps Green Zone Plan' (*Sydney Morning Herald* (Sydney), 10 September 2005, 11).

area boundaries and the constituent land zones and controls. Work on a draft of this SEPP progressed throughout 2005, and major changes were made to its envisaged land use zones following the State government's decision to abandon the proposed green zones. A 'final' version of the draft SEPP—minus the moribund green zones—was released in January 2006 for public exhibition and comment. Subsequently, on 28 July 2006, the Minister for Planning gazetted the State Environmental Planning Policy (Sydney Region Growth Centres) 2006. However, further amendments had occurred in the interim, with the SEPP as gazetted modified from the version placed on public exhibition following 750 submissions from members of the public, industry and State government agencies, in which property rights issues again dominated.[72]

A further aspect of the State government's decision in regard to the abandoned green zones was the announcement that it would attempt to retain some environmental aspirations by focusing on protecting the best sections of vegetation and waterways in the two growth centres. This new approach, developed in consultation with the Department of Environment and Conservation, created four new zones into which land would be classified: flood-prone, urban-capable, urban edge and conservation. Significantly, the approach relied in part on a new environmental offsets or 'biobanking' scheme (discussed further below), under which developers would contribute financially to the conservation areas of bushland.[73]

IV. 'SMART' REGULATION AND MARKET-BASED MECHANISMS

The problems discussed above—which in some measure are due to a heavy reliance on 'command' regulation tools such as zoning and reservations, and the policy, legal and political practicalities of the operation of property rights—remain problematic. The increasing invasiveness and perceived affects of these regulations on the economic value and use of land has generated 'a backlash from landholders who see these controls as an attack on their livelihoods and property rights'.[74] One solution lies in the option of looking beyond the traditional regulatory planning approach, augmenting 'command' regulation by adopting tools which seek to work with the challenges presented by property rights and development expectations. Included here are programs that use the market to redistribute the costs and benefits of planning actions.[75] In the context of planning and managing urban growth, this means adopting a strategy that utilises tools which aim for natural resource conservation and environmental protection, but which also recognises the reality of property rights (that is, the *expectation of development* arising from land ownership) and continuing demand for housing and other urban uses.

---

[72] Department of Planning, *Managing Sydney's Growth Centres Fact Sheet—New State Environmental Planning Policy (Sydney Region Growth Centres) 2006* (Sydney, Department of Planning, 2006).
[73] Utilising provisions of the Threatened Species Legislation Amendment Act 2004 (NSW) and the Threatened Species Conservation Amendment (Biodiversity Banking) Act 2006 (NSW).
[74] S Ryan, 'Conservation through Development: The Potential for Transferable Development Rights in Queensland' (paper presented at the *2004 QELA Conference—Carrot, Sticks and Toolkits*, Cairns, 12–14 May 2004) 1.
[75] Ibid.

This approach to urban planning involves a number of market-based and economic tools linking both the public and private sectors. Mechanisms used here may either provide for compulsory action by government or rely on voluntary private sector participation in market-based schemes, including fiscal and planning incentives. Engagement by each sector in the range of market-based and economic tools includes the following:

— The public sector, which involves a combination of compulsory and voluntary fiscal measures. It includes acquisition—of either freehold title or development 'rights' through purchase (ie purchase of development rights), fiscal incentives, compensation and taxation.
— The private sector, which usually relies on voluntary market-based mechanisms (often mandated by government regulation) and includes transferable development rights, green offsets and planning incentives.

The concept of property rights is integral to many market-based and economic schemes. It is in this context that creative ideas and mechanisms such as transfer of development rights, purchase of development rights, and the facilitation of non-profit, public interest land trusts, have come to the fore in the US.[76] Often, a number of these schemes will also entail the imposition of traditional common law restrictions on the user in the form of covenants and easements, which may be mandated by statutory enactment governing a particular market-based or fiscal tool. They may also imply the offer of various financial or stewardship payments, and planning incentives or bonuses which involve the relaxation of regulatory controls which might otherwise apply to development. Explicit consideration of some of the Australian experience with these schemes is presented below.

A. 'Smart' Regulation

Potentially, town planning has an enormous influence because it operates by *controlling the use of land* upon which all human activities are ultimately based. It does this by restricting private property rights through statutory intervention, seeking a balance between the right of the private landowner to develop or use land or other resources and the safeguarding of the broader public interest in the protection of the environment and amenity.[77] Rights to develop land—to subdivide and build upon land or to change its use—are now generally controlled by planning legislation,[78] as are rights to extract natural resources both from private and public land; however, the right to decide how to *manage* the land is still largely unfettered. 'Yet the management of land is crucial to its ability to sustain long-term productive activity and natural ecosystems.'[79] Planning approaches which encourage the

---

[76] HM Jacobs, 'Fighting Over Land: America's Legacy ... America's Future?' (1999) 65 *Journal of the American Planning Association* 141, 147.
[77] See J Sax, 'Some Thoughts on the Decline of Private Property' (1983) 58 *Washington Law Review* 481.
[78] See Ryan (n 1).
[79] Bates (n 45) 40.

beneficial management of private land from a public interest in the maintenance of environmental quality are therefore necessary. However, regulating the use to which land can be put may have a major bearing on its value[80] and in any event may be ineffectual in influencing the management of private land. It is here that approaches that make environmental protection financially attractive (or at least not burdensome) to private landowners can play a role. In this context, market-based instruments and planning incentives and other forms of 'smart' regulation are pre-eminent. Inherent in this approach is the utilisation of market incentives—'incentive-based regulation'—involving the application of instruments that will facilitate positive management as an important part of the policy mix to achieve environmental and resource management goals.[81] To illustrate this point, providing incentives such as stewardship payments to encourage positive management of land and biodiversity by private landholders, for example, has been advocated so as to make the *voluntary* abandonment of existing incompatible uses a viable proposition.[82] Further, the attractiveness of such a scheme is that the burden of the costs of biodiversity conservation does not only fall on affected property owners, but is spread throughout the wider community.[83]

B. Economic—Fiscal and Market-Based—Mechanisms

Economic or market-based approaches may take a variety of forms,[84] but can be categorised by their impact as being either positive (eg payments or compensation) or negative (eg taxes). Either way, economic mechanisms can be perceived as an incentive-based approach, which 'involve either the handing out (incentives) or taking away (disincentives) of monetary and non-monetary material resources in order to change behaviour. The distinguishing characteristic of incentive-based approaches is that no one is obligated to take a particular course of action'.[85]

Increasingly, a hybrid approach of regulatory and policy-based economic instruments is being used in the areas of environmental protection and natural resource

---

[80] P Day, *Land: The Elusive Quest for Social Justice, Taxation Reform and a Sustainable Planetary Environment* (Brisbane, Australian Academic Press, 1995), 13.

[81] E Goodstein, *Economics and the Environment* (Englewood Cliffs, Prentice Hall, 1995) 267. In particular, Goodstein identifies pollution taxes (or effluent or emission charges) and marketable permit systems as two significant examples of incentive-based regulation within the field of environmental protection and pollution control.

[82] D Farrier, 'Conserving Biodiversity on Private Land: Incentives for Management or Compensation for Lost Expectations?' (1995) 19 *Harvard Environmental Law Review* 303.

[83] See, eg, C Rodgers, 'Nature's Place? Property Rights, Property Rules and Environmental Stewardship' (2009) 68 *CLJ* 550.

[84] Economic or market-based instruments may incorporate the following elements: property rights; market creation (that is, the creation of a market by government where none previously existed—for example of tradeable pollution or resource rights, individually transferable property-right mechanisms and certain offset arrangements); covenants and easements; leasing and licensing; fiscal instruments and charge systems; financial instruments; performance bonds; and deposit refund systems. See Gunningham and Grabosky (n 5).

[85] D Bengston, J Fletcher and K Nelson, 'Public Policies for Managing Urban Growth and Protecting Open Space: Policy Instruments and Lessons Learned in the United States' (2004) 69 *Landscape and Urban Planning* 271, 274.

management in Australia.[86] These economic instruments have mainly included trading mechanisms such as tradeable offsets, which can take several specific applications such as carbon (greenhouse gas) trading, salinity and native vegetation protection and regeneration. Offsets schemes, in terms of their characteristics and NSW examples, are discussed in more detail below.

A further related suite of economic mechanisms considered below are tools involving the voluntary acquisition of the development potential or 'rights' pertaining to land. These development rights-focused tools comprise situations where such rights may be acquired either through purchase by a public agency (that is, purchase of development rights—PDR), purchase by a private developer and transferred to another parcel of land (that is, transfer of development rights—TDR) or by donation by the landowner to a public agency (that is, 'donated' development rights,[87] also generally referred to as conservation covenants in Australia or conservation easements in the US).[88]

While TDR and PDR and conservation covenants are broadly similar in that they are voluntary, incentive-based urban planning tools, there are some key differences between them. Primarily, there is a technical difference—a conservation easement restricts the right to develop on a piece of property, while a development right is the right to build on a property.[89] Nonetheless, TDR and PDR schemes will normally involve the imposition of a land use restriction, in the form of a conservation covenant or easement, on land in which the development potential has been purchased or transferred. Conversely, conservation easement schemes can operate outside the PDR/TDR framework, usually with landowners voluntarily donating (ie no compensation is involved) certain development rights or potential pertaining to land to an authorised government agency or non-profit organisation, which is enforced by means of easements over such parcels. Under a donated conservation covenant scheme, there is no sale or transfer of any development rights, and to be effective, the covenants are intended as a perpetual restriction on the development of the land.[90] The perpetuity of land use restrictions via a covenant is the desired outcome of all three schemes (TDR, PDR and donated development rights).

---

[86] P Williams, 'Use of Transferable Development Rights as a Growth Management Tool' (2004) 21 *Environmental and Planning Law Journal* 105, 108.

[87] JB Wright, 'Conservation Easements: An Analysis of Donated Development Rights' (1993) 59 *Journal of the American Planning Association* 487.

[88] Gunningham and Grabosky (n 5) 318. Perhaps the best-established example of the use of this mechanism in Australia are conservation covenants derived from the Victorian Conservation Trust Act 1972 and operated by the Victorian Trust for Nature. For a general discussion of conservation covenants and easements in Australia, see Industry Commission, *Inquiry into Ecologically Sustainable Land Management* (Commonwealth of Australia, Belconnen ACT, Report No 60, 27 January 1998).

[89] LJ Maynard, TW Kelsey, SM Lembeck and JC Becker, 'Early Experience in Pennsylvania's Agricultural Conservation Easement Program' (1998) 53 *Journal of Soil and Water Conservation* 106.

[90] BW Ohm, 'The Purchase of Scenic Easements and Wisconsin's Great River Road: A Progress Report on Perpetuity' (2000) 66 *Journal of the American Planning Association* 177.

C. Transferable Development Rights

TDR involves the purchase and transfer of development rights to another site by developers. It is this aspect of private as opposed to public funding which defines one of the advantages of a TDR scheme over a PDR scheme. Where public funds are limited, TDR offers a land management and preservation technique which is not draining on the public purse.[91] Originally, the TDR concept derived from the English Town and Country Planning Act 1947, which allowed the separating of use rights from the underlying real estate.[92] However, its more contemporary foundation comes from its application in the US in the 1960s and 1970s.[93]

In essence, TDR is one type of planning tool that seeks to compensate landowners whose development rights have been restricted by regulation. Compensation is achieved by allocating to those owners an amount of development that may be transferred from the restricted site to another site.[94] Fundamentally, under this government-created program, development rights are severed from a parcel designated for protection (the 'sending area') and the severed rights are transferred to a parcel in an area where additional development is permitted (the 'receiving area').[95] The scheme thus allows more development on the receiving parcel while reducing or preventing development on the donor parcel. Under such a program, the development rights of the sending parcel may be either sold by that owner to the owner of the recipient parcel or transferred directly from the donor to the receiving site if they are under common ownership. The number of development rights that can be transferred depends on how many development-rights 'credits' a planning authority allocates and how much it allows in areas designated for growth.[96]

A TDR scheme offers a means of removing inappropriate development rights without unilaterally extinguishing them. This tool provides a means of reducing development potential in areas identified for protection without the costs of compensation to the local or state authority. Herein lies the driving rationale of a TDR scheme—owners of conserved land are compensated by developers who are able to profit from higher densities while securing significant areas for the benefit of the community at minimal cost to government.[97] However, the protection of property rights should be seen only as a partial justification for implementing a TDR program.

As a consequence, the fundamental principles behind the US model have been recognised and adopted by several local councils in Australia that have established TDR systems. These include schemes for the conservation of heritage buildings in

---

[91] KS Hanna, 'Regulation and Land-Use Conservation: A Case Study of the British Columbia Agricultural Land Reserve' (1997) 52 *Journal of Soil and Water Conservation* 166.

[92] Ryan (n 74).

[93] P Pizor P, 'Making TDR Work: A Study of Program Implementation' (1986) 52 *Journal of the American Planning Association* 203.

[94] Bindon (n 2).

[95] RA Johnston and ME Madison, 'From Landmarks to Landscapes: A Review of Current Practices in the Transfer of Development Rights' (1997) 63 *Journal of the American Planning Association* 365.

[96] TL Daniels, *When City and Country Collide: Managing Growth in the Metropolitan Fringe* (Washington DC, Island Press, 1999) 224.

[97] R Pruetz, 'Putting Growth in its Place with Transfer of Development Rights' (1998) 31 *Planning Commissioners Journal* 15.

inner Sydney, Adelaide, Melbourne and Brisbane,[98] the protection of the Mount Lofty Ranges near Adelaide, the provision of open space and conservation reserves in Gosford (NSW), urban growth management in Wellington (rural NSW) and the protection of the Illawarra Escarpment near Wollongong (NSW).[99] Thus, the method has been utilised in a variety of urban, peri-urban and rural contexts.

Despite a number of past and current examples of TDR schemes in Australia, the apparent reluctance to use TDR more widely as a planning tool persists in NSW. This is despite TDR being identified as a tool worthy of consideration, for example, in NSW proposed planning system reforms a decade ago.[100] Three reasons can be advanced to explain this situation. First, the utilisation of market-based tools is still relatively recent in Australia. There has been a tradition of reliance on 'command and control' regulation in Australia, which is quite different from the history of market-based tools in the US and bargaining for planning gain/negotiated planning agreements in Britain. Regulation generally, and zoning specifically, still lies at the heart of the Australian statutory planning systems. Second, there is a lack of understanding of the TDR mechanism by planning decision makers (both politicians and planners). For example, NSW State ministers have baulked at a consideration of a TDR scheme in Sydney in the mistaken belief that this would involve the public acquisition of land (which is costly in Sydney) rather than, correctly, merely requiring the acquisition of development rights over land by developers (which is cheaper and involves no cost to government). Third, there is ongoing legal uncertainty and impediments surrounding TDR. Evidence of the present legal impediments to the more widespread adoption of a TDR scheme in NSW includes expressions of doubt by the NSW Land Environment Court about the legality of TDR schemes (see, for example, *Leighton Properties Pty Limited v North Sydney Council*[101]), concerns raised by a Commission of Inquiry regarding the transparency of Wollongong City Council's TDR scheme for the protection of the Illawarra Escarpment[102] and the ongoing reluctance of the NSW Parliamentary Counsels Office to support draft statutory plans produced by local councils that seek to include TDR provisions.

D. Green Offsets and 'Biobanking'

Under an offset arrangement, industries or resource users are given the choice of either offsetting the damage they cause or paying an authority to do it on their behalf. The provision of an offset is a mandatory requirement or condition of the granting of approval to undertake development with potentially adverse environmental impacts. The arrangements operate partly through regulatory mechanisms such as permits or approvals and partly through a market-based system, which

---

[98] Ryan (n 74).

[99] Williams (n 86).

[100] Department of Urban Affairs and Planning, *PlanFirst: Review of Plan Making in New South Wales* (Sydney, DUAP, 2001).

[101] [1998] NSWLEC 39.

[102] Commission of Inquiry, *The Long Term Planning and Management of the Illawarra Escarpment, Wollongong Local Government Area* (Sydney, Office of the Commissioners of Inquiry for Environment and Planning, 1999).

allows one property owner who undertakes some form of environmental restoration to sell offset credits to another owner or industry seeking approval to undertake development.

Offset schemes are gaining prominence in Australia. For example, the potential to rely on offsets for dealing with salinity and native vegetation management has existed in NSW for several years.[103] Offsets are increasingly promoted as a tool for facilitating biodiversity outcomes from development proposals, being used to 'enable impacts on biodiversity to be counter-balanced by action taken elsewhere'.[104] The *NSW Biodiversity Banking and Offset Scheme* was established in 2008 following amendments to the Threatened Species Conservation Act 1995.[105] Known as 'BioBanking', this biodiversity offsets and banking scheme is site- or project-specific and is linked to the development approval process under the EP&A Act.

The NSW BioBanking Scheme seeks to address the loss of biodiversity by enabling landowners to establish biobank sites to secure conservation outcomes and offset impacts on biodiversity caused by development. Conceptually, this is achieved through the use of an 'improve or maintain' test for biodiversity values, which means avoiding significant biodiversity conservation areas and offsetting impacts in other areas.[106] The offsets are measured in terms of credits, using the published *BioBanking Assessment Methodology*,[107] and developers participating in the scheme are required to meet this improve and maintain test based on the impact of their proposed project. Under the scheme, biobank sites may be established by means of biobanking agreements entered into between the minister and the owner(s) of the land concerned.

The BioBanking Scheme has four key components.[108] First is the establishment of biobank sites on land through biobanking agreements between the Minister for Environment and Heritage and participating landowners. A biobanking agreement is similar to a covenant and is attached to the land title. It runs with the land and generally will have effect in perpetuity so as to offset the impacts of development on biodiversity values. The second component is the creation of biodiversity credits for management actions that are carried out, or are proposed to be carried out, to improve or maintain biodiversity values on biobank sites. The *Biobanking Assessment Methodology* is the tool used to determine the number of biodiversity credits that may be created for these management actions. The third component is the trading of credits, once they are created and registered. The final component is enabling the credits to be used to offset the impact of development on biodiversity values.

---

[103] NSW Department of Land and Water Conservation, *Offsets, Salinity and Native Vegetation: Discussion Paper* (Sydney, DLWC, July 2001).

[104] Department of Environment and Climate Change, *Working Draft Guidelines for Biodiversity Certification of Environmental Planning Instruments* (Parramatta, DECC, 2007) 5.

[105] Threatened Species Conservation Amendment (Biodiversity Banking) Act 2006 (NSW).

[106] NSW Department of Environment and Climate Change, *BioBanking. Biodiversity Banking and Offsets Scheme. Scheme Overview.* (Sydney, DECC, 2007) 4, www.environment.nsw.gov.au/resources/biobanking/biobankingoverview07528.pdf.

[107] NSW Department of Environment and Climate Change (n 105).

[108] Ibid.

Biobanking in NSW is still in its infancy—indeed, at the time of writing, only six biobanking agreements are listed publicly,[109] although several have been shortlisted as either potential biobank sites, development sites or joint biobank/development sites. One reason for the reluctance to take up biobanking is the complexity of this mechanism and the ability to achieve the same outcomes through less prescriptive voluntary planning agreements (VPAs) under the EP&A Act.[110] VPAs permit planning authorities (local councils and the Planning Minister) to negotiate planning benefit or gain with developers as a consequence of granting development consent or approving a rezoning application.

E. Conservation Covenants and Statutory Conservation Agreements

Conservation covenants or easements may either be imposed as part of TDR and PDR schemes or independently of such schemes, the latter generally as donated or voluntary mechanisms. This second variant is discussed here.

Voluntary statutory covenants, under which agencies have been given legislative powers to enter into covenants with landowners, are seen as the most applicable to the conservation of land in situations where the resources available to voluntary schemes are limited and thus preclude compensation payments. In Australia, although covenants and easements had historically not been used extensively for conservation purposes,[111] they have been used in some instances, such as voluntary Heritage Agreements between the South Australian government and landowners to protect land covered by native vegetation,[112] and permanent conservation covenants involving the Victorian Trust for Nature.[113] In NSW, conservation agreements are available under the National Parks and Wildlife Act 1974 as a voluntary option for landholders with land of high conservation value.[114] The conservation agreement is a joint agreement between landholders and the Minister for Environment which provides permanent protection for special features of land: the area under the agreement is registered on the title of the land, ensuring that, if the land is sold, the agreement and management requirements remain in place.[115]

A further scheme, which involves both the acquisition of land and the imposition of conservation covenants, is administered under the Revolving Fund of the

---

[109] Office of Environment and Heritage, *Full List of Biobanking Agreements* (2011), www.environment. nsw.gov.au/bimsprapp/Printing.aspx?type=5.

[110] Utilising the provisions of s 93F of the Environmental Planning and Assessment Act 1979 (NSW).

[111] Industry Commission (n 88) 497.

[112] Ibid, 498 and 505.

[113] Section 3 of the Victorian Conservation Trust Act 1972 (Vic) empowers the Victoria Conservation Trust (now the Trust for Nature) to negotiate 'negative' and 'positive' permanent conservation covenants for the conservation of the State's natural resources: specifically the preservation of areas which are ecologically significant, or of natural interest or beauty, or of historical interest, as well as the preservation of wildlife and natural plants and the preservation and conservation of areas for scientific study. For further discussion, see D Jones, 'The Role of the Victorian Conservation Trust and the Value of Covenants' (1989) 17 *Urban Policy and Research* 15.

[114] National Parks and Wildlife Act 1974 (NSW), pt 4, Division 4—Conservation Agreements.

[115] Office of Environment and Heritage, *Conservation Agreements* (Sydney, OEH, 2011), www.environment. nsw.gov.au/cpp/ConservationAgreements.htm.

NSW Nature Conservation Trust.[116] The Trust was established under the Nature Conservation Trust Act 2001 and commenced operations early in 2002. It was set up in response to efforts by government and conservation groups to establish in the marketplace a non-governmental organisation (NGO) that would facilitate nature conservation on private lands. The Trust is a hybrid organisation—it is government-supported, but as a not-for-profit NGO is less tied to government. There are other examples of this type of organisation, such as the Australian Bush Heritage Fund and the Private Land Conservation Program in Tasmania.[117] In particular, Tasmania's Private Land Conservation Program appears to have very effective, with 600 covenants covering 75,634 hectares of private land in place as at 1 November 2010.[118]

The NSW Nature Conservation Trust actively promotes the long-term protection of land by registering conservation agreements (also called Trust agreements) on the titles of properties with high conservation values. A conservation agreement is a form of protective covenant that is a legally binding agreement between a landowner and the Nature Conservation Trust to protect the environmental integrity and biodiversity of a property.[119] The conservation agreement is registered on the property title, which ensures that the land is protected in perpetuity. The Trust is able to enter into these agreements under the Nature Conservation Trust Act 2001.[120] A significant function of the Trust is to operate the *Revolving Fund Scheme*,[121] and in exercising this and other functions, it has the power 'to buy, sell, hold, lease or otherwise deal with land'.[122] The Revolving Fund Scheme is a scheme under which the Trust:

(a) buys or otherwise acquires land that is significant for the conservation of natural heritage (and any cultural heritage associated with natural heritage), and
(b) arranges for a protective covenant to be registered on the title to the land, and
(c) sells or leases the land subject to that protective covenant, and
(d) uses the proceeds of the sale or lease for the acquisition of further land referred to in paragraph (a) for the purposes of dealing with that land in accordance with paragraphs (b) and (c) and using the proceeds of the sale or lease as set out in this paragraph.[123]

The funds are thus used to purchase properties with high conservation values. The Trust then manages each property to maintain and improve its conservation and agricultural assets and then sells it to a supportive new owner with a conservation agreement attached. A management plan is prepared for each property to assist the new owner in meeting the Trust agreement requirements, and once the agreement

---

[116] Nature Conservation Trust Act 2001 (NSW).
[117] Interview with Tom Grosskopf, Board Member, Nature Conservation Trust of NSW (Parramatta, 28 February 2007).
[118] Department of Primary Industries, Parks, Water and Environment, *The Private Land Conservation Program* (2011), www.dpipwe.tas.gov.au/inter.nsf/WebPages/DRAR-7TR9ZR?open.
[119] Nature Conservation Trust of NSW, *Annual Report 2011–12* (2012), http://nct.org.au/media/files/pdf/NCT%20Annual%20Report%202011-12-web.pdf, viewed 25 March 2013.
[120] Nature Conservation Trust Act 2001 (NSW), s 30.
[121] Ibid, s 11(2)(a).
[122] Ibid, s 12(2)(a).
[123] Ibid, s 7(1)(a)–(d).

is registered, the new owner is supported by the Trust through its Stewardship Program.[124] All proceeds from the sale of a property are returned to the Revolving Fund for future acquisitions, so that a greater conservation return accrues from the initial investment. In 2003, the Trust received $2 million from the Australian and NSW governments, enabling it to establish its Revolving Fund. By 2011, the Trust's Revolving Fund totalled $25 million to be used for future acquisitions of conservational significance.[125]

V. CONCLUSION

The case studies and schemes discussed in this chapter reveal a number of key factors that must be taken into consideration in contemporary planning, particularly on the rural–urban fringe of Australian cities. First is the deficiency, on their own, of traditional command and control mechanisms such as land use zoning and planning restrictions to guarantee the protection of non-urban land. Second is the role—rightly or wrongly—that claims to property rights play in land use planning and development decisions. Third is the reluctance of government to rely on the public purse to protect non-urban land (for example, through land acquisition for the provision of green infrastructure). The fourth factor—argued here to be an inevitable conclusion given the previous three considerations—is the role that newer alternative mechanisms such as smart regulation and market-based instruments that operate within the context of property rights can play, particularly in the context of seeking to ensure that natural resource and environmental values are protected in the face of the pressure and expectations of continued urban expansion.

As property rights arguments gain greater policy traction in Australia, planning approaches and tools that recognise the reality of property rights are increasingly necessary. Although not part of the legal, political and planning tradition in Australia, recent NSW planning examples point to the challenge that property rights now pose. Evidence of this is seen in the political victory of affected property owners that culminated in the abandonment of the proposed green zones in the south-west and north-west growth centres of Sydney and the contemporary problem of down-zoning in the environment protection zones under the standard LEP. The clear message raised by this is the need for the adoption of a broader suite of planning mechanisms, justified in part from the perspective of addressing property rights expectations, to achieve planning, environmental and natural resource objectives. Faced with the rising influence of the property rights movement, the challenge to land use managers and planners has been to devise planning mechanisms which respect the integrity of private property on the one hand and yet still achieve planning policy objectives on the other. It is in this context that more creative mechanisms such as TDR, biobanking and conservation covenants need to be considered as planning and urban growth management tools.

---

[124] Nature Conservation Trust of NSW, *Stewardship* (2011), http://nct.org.au/protecting-private-land/stewardship.html, viewed 11 April 2011.

[125] Nature Conservation Trust of NSW, *About Revolving Funds* (2011), http://nct.org.au/properties-for-sale/about-revolving-funds.html, viewed 10 April 2011.

In the case of TDR, the issue of the lack of understanding of this mechanism by decision makers (including planners) and the present legal uncertainty surrounding its application must be resolved—the latter by legislative action. Several NSW State and local government organisations have considered the use of TDR as a planning tool, but any initial enthusiasm was generally extinguished by the discouragement of its use by the DoP and the problems presented by the EP&A Act. Here, the argument rests on the fact that the Act does not presume a development 'right'—instead, all that the Act permits is possibly the right to seek development consent. The NSW Office and Environment and Heritage has for some time tried to persuade the DoP and others to adopt a TDR scheme for biodiversity conservation.[126] This was opposed by the DoP on the basis that it creates a system of rights that landowners do not actually have. TDRs have therefore, unfortunately, not been embraced at a State government level in NSW. Yet successful examples exist in Australia—mainly dealing with heritage building conservation schemes implemented by local councils. The standard DoP mantra of resisting the broader introduction of a TDR scheme on the basis that the EP&A Act does not presume a development 'right' appears contradictory and is undermined when one considers that the Department's argument for the insertion of acquisition clauses in environment protection zones is to protect landowners' development rights!

Turning to offsets, the Office of Environment and Heritage diffidently perseveres with biobanking as it provides one of the few genuine alternatives available for biodiversity conservation in the face of continuing NSW Treasury funding restrictions for both the outright purchase and recurrent funding for the ongoing maintenance of high conservation lands. The benefit of biobanking is that tied up with the purchase by a developer of biobanking credits from a landowner are two financial components—a lump-sum payment to the landowner and a portion which goes into a management trust, known as the Biobanking Trust Fund, which is effectively a 'conservancy payments scheme'. This means that in addition to an upfront payment, private landowners also bear the responsibility of ongoing management of biobank sites through moneys paid out of the Biobanking Trust Fund, thus relieving government of this recurring financial burden. Thus, biobanking effectively obliges developers to contribute to the cost of such protection, as a normal, traditional incident of the rights and obligations arising from development approval.

Conservation covenants (and associated schemes such as stewardship payments) are gradually becoming more commonly accepted across many planning jurisdictions and need to be more widely embraced across NSW as an urban growth management tool focusing particularly on biodiversity conservation. Greater use should be made of the temporary acquisition and resale of land with protective covenants attached, as exists in NSW in the form of the Revolving Fund Scheme of the Nature Conservation Trust.

Perseverance with market-based instruments such as TDR, offsets and voluntary conservation covenant schemes is desirable in order to provide a range of tools so as

---

[126] M Fallding, A Kelly, P Bateson and I Donovan, *Biodiversity Planning Guide for NSW Local Government* (Hurstville NSW, National Parks and Wildlife Service, 2001). www.environment.gov.au/archive/biodiversity/toolbox/templates/pubs/nsw-bio-plan-guide.pdf.

to successfully implement planning objectives. Such perseverance is also warranted on the strength of the beneficial aspects and goals of several existing market-based schemes. The distillation of the successful elements of such schemes can provide the necessary ingredients to be replicated and extended to other applications of market-based instruments. The legal obstacles to such schemes are not insurmountable and statutory amendment, if necessary, is easily achievable. Indeed, schemes such as the City of Sydney's heritage floor space scheme have operated under the umbrella of the EP&A Act for many years. If not based in statute, however, TDR schemes can be adopted as government policy. In the case of offsets, whilst recent statutory amendment has created the BioBanking Scheme, the notion of developers and planning authorities negotiating and implementing similar outcomes through voluntary planning agreements pre-dates this legislation. The inference is that while legislation might be desirable, it is not essential. As is the case with TDR, it is policy intent and commitment—not necessarily legislation—that is the crucial ingredient to the success of these schemes.

Part IV

The Nature, Content and Acquisition of Property

15

'Persistent Rights' Appraised

SIMON GARDNER*

P ROFESSOR BEN McFARLANE, partly in collaboration with Professor
Robert Stevens, has in recent years drawn attention to, and enthusiastically
elaborated and urged, the theory of what he calls 'persistent rights', or 'rights
against rights'. This chapter reviews this project.

What follows draws upon the project's three principal statements,[1] as well as private communications I am fortunate enough to have had with Professor McFarlane.
It attempts to describe the project's features faithfully, but does not hesitate to
paraphrase them.

I. THE INQUIRY

A. McFarlane's Position

McFarlane asks us to distinguish especially two classes of right: rights in rem,[2]
which sound familiar, and persistent rights, which do not. What needs to be said
about these classes, and especially about persistent rights, can be stated as follows,
around four foci.[3]

First, their behaviour.

The rights that McFarlane calls rights in rem and persistent rights have in common that, by contrast with rights in personam, they are capable of binding others

* Hanbury Fellow, Lincoln College, Oxford; Professor of Law, Faculty of Law, University of Oxford.
I am indebted to the anonymous referee, to Roderick Bagshaw, Mindy Chen-Wishart (and her connections in the Obligations Discussion Group), Joshua Getzler, Amy Goymour, Emily MacKenzie, Mike
Macnair, Jenny Payne, Bill Swadling, and especially to Ben McFarlane, for their interest and assistance.

[1] B McFarlane, *The Structure of Property Law* (Oxford, Hart Publishing, 2008) 21–39; B McFarlane
and R Stevens, 'The Nature of Equitable Property' (2010) 4 *Journal of Equity* 1; B McFarlane, 'The
Numerus Clausus Principle and Covenants Relating to Land' in S Bright (ed), *Modern Studies in Property
Law, Volume 6* (Oxford, Hart Publishing, 2011) ch 15. Hereafter I shall refer to these as '(2008)',
'(2010)' and '(2011)', respectively. For other discussion of especially (2008), see in particular P Jaffey,
'The "Persistent Right" and the Remedial Part' (2011) 2(1) *Jurisprudence* 181; L Katz, 'The Concept
of Ownership and the Relativity of Title' (2011) 2(1) *Jurisprudence* 191; C Webb, 'The Double Lives
of Property' (2011) 2(1) *Jurisprudence* 205; *cf*, in response, B McFarlane, 'Reply: Property Law and its
Structure' (2011) 2(1) *Jurisprudence* 217.

[2] McFarlane as often calls them 'property rights'. I would be quite happy to follow suit here too, but
have chosen the expression 'rights in rem' as (perhaps) presenting a more striking contrast with 'persistent rights'. At any rate, as used here, there is no difference in significance between the two.

[3] See especially (2010) 1–2, 3–8, 10–15.

besides the person against whom they originate. Persistent rights are capable of binding disponees of the asset to which they relate. That is, they obtain against (whoever holds) a right in the asset that derives from the right held by the person against whom they originated. Rights in rem are capable of binding such disponees too, but also of binding third parties (ie persons other than the person against whom the right originated) who are not disponees.

Say X owns a house, and gives you a right to enjoy the house in some way. Consider two scenarios: (i) X transfers the house to Y, who wishes to terminate your enjoyment; (ii) the house is tortiously set on fire by Z, with results which spoil your enjoyment. If your right is in personam, you have no recourse against either Y or Z, only (if at all) against X. If your right is persistent, you have recourse against both X and Y, but not against Z. If your right is in rem, you have recourse against X, Y, and Z.

Second, the inherent natures of the different classes of right.

The account given so far describes the ways in which the two classes of right behave. McFarlane's position also offers a rationalisation or justification of that behaviour, drawn from his vision of the nature—conceptual source—of each class of right.

McFarlane tells us that a persistent right must be a right relating to (or to, or against, or in) a 'claim-right' or a 'power' belonging to X. An example of a right relating to a claim-right would be a right under a trust. X is the trustee, who, as common law owner of the asset (trust property) in question, has all the claim-rights (ie rights that others have a duty to respect) that the common law bestows via its idea of 'ownership'.[4] But being a trustee, she is obliged to hold all these for you, her beneficiary. The beneficiary's right is thus a right to the trustee's claim-rights.[5] An example of a right relating to a power would be an equitable lease. X is the landlord, who, as common law owner of the asset (freehold land) in question, has a power to create leases over it. If she obliges herself to exercise this power in your favour (ie contracts with you to grant you a lease), you thus acquire a right against her power.

So, to reiterate: for McFarlane, a persistent right must be a right relating to a claim-right or power belonging to X. Now, and this is the present point, he presents this as telling us *why* a persistent right operates in the way it does, binding a person (Y) to whom X transfers the relevant claim-right or power—ie a disponee of the latter—but

---

[4] It is X's *ownership* that is her claim-right, and so the subject of your persistent right. It is irrelevant whether the subject matter of her ownership, the asset she owns, is itself a physical thing, eg some land, or a claim-right itself, eg a credit, such as a bank account.

[5] I am not sure that I am completely comfortable talking, as I think McFarlane does, of the trustee's claim-*rights* in this way. The use of the plural suggests that we can, and for these purposes should, view the trustee's ownership as comprising a number of discrete such rights (on the lines of the familiar 'bundle of rights' vision of ownership—this of course being no accident, as Hohfeld, the proponent of 'claim-rights', was also a devotee of that vision). It may be more accurate/illuminating to see 'ownership' in a way that better captures its 'thingness' (M Heller, 'The Boundaries of Private Property' (1999) 108 *Yale Law Journal* 1163, 1191–94); as a unitary, essentially open-ended, idea, varying in substantive content between one instantiation and another (J Harris, 'Reason or Mumbo-Jumbo: The Common Law's Approach to Property' (2001) 117 *Proceedings of the British Academy* 445, 463–68). (See also J Penner, 'The "Bundle of Rights" Picture of Property' (1996) 43 *UCLA Law Review* 711.) But I do not think anything turns on the point in the present context.

not a person who does not fit that description, such as Z. It has no effect against Z precisely because Z does not have the claim-right or power to which it relates.

Contrast rights in rem, alias 'rights against things'. (It should be noted that for McFarlane, a 'thing' can only be a physical thing, such as a piece of land, not an abstraction such as a credit. So, in his eyes, a credit-right can only be the subject of a persistent right.) This description too is presented as capturing and explaining the behaviour of rights in rem, which (remember) obtain against anyone who comes into contact with the asset: not only Y, a disponee from X, but also Z, who for example sets fire to it. For McFarlane, symmetrically with what has been said about persistent rights, the reason *why* a right in rem behaves in this way is that it is a right relating to (or to, or against, or in) the thing—the very asset—in question. It has effect against (not only Y but also) Z precisely because (not only Y but also) Z does have, or otherwise comes into contact with, the thing to which it relates.

Third, the place of these classes of right in the law.

It seems possible to imagine in the abstract that the law might categorise rights on the lines that McFarlane terms persistent, and in rem. (Though of course, these categories are not exhaustive. To cover the whole ground, they need to be supplemented by rights in personam, and also by a set of further rights still, having yet other characteristics. McFarlane groups such further rights together and refers to them as 'background rights'.[6] But they are diffuse in nature,[7] and may best be divided in turn. One class of them, occasionally relevant to the present discussion, is what I shall call 'pure tort rights'. I have in mind the kind of right in which you have recourse against Z, but not against Y or, indeed, sometimes, even X—for there will be no X. Examples might be the right to bodily integrity, protected by the torts of negligence and trespass to the person, and the right to reputation, protected by the torts of slander and libel.)

But McFarlane goes beyond the abstract. He tells us that—and indeed where— his categories of rights in rem and persistent rights are to be found, concretely, in English law. Specifically, he maintains that, of all the rights in English law that are capable of binding not only X (as rights in personam do) but others too, those originating in the common law are in rem, ie can bind both Y and Z, whilst those originating in equity are persistent, ie can bind Y, but not Z.

For McFarlane, then, if the right that X confers on you is a contractual licence, it is a right in personam, giving you recourse only against X, not against Y or Z. If it is a (legal) lease, it is a right in rem, giving you recourse against not only X, but Y and Z too. While if it is a beneficial interest under a trust, it is[8] a persistent right, giving you recourse against X and Y, but not against Z.

Fourth, the role of the *numerus clausus* principle.

---

[6] (2008) 133–36.

[7] McFarlane gives as particular instances intellectual property rights ((2008) 133–36), and rights arising between landlord and tenant and binding their successors as such (ibid, 682). Both are capable of binding third parties, but for particular reasons, not pursued or tested here, are placed outside his categories of persistent rights and rights in rem.

[8] Or more accurately, contains: McFarlane accepts that only some elements of a beneficial interest are capable of binding a disponee (Y), the remainder binding only someone appointed trustee (X): (2008) 554–55. See n 19 below.

As is well known, and McFarlane accepts, the category of rights in rem is limited by the *numerus clausus* principle, whereby a right can exist and operate in rem only if its doing so is warranted, by reference to the right's substantive content. For practical purposes, then, X can generate a right in rem only if (inter alia) she so intends,[9] and the right in question corresponds, in its content, to an established, recognised, type of right in rem, such as a lease, or easement, or mortgage.

But according to McFarlane, the *numerus clausus* principle does not apply to persistent rights (equitable interests). Thus, so long as a right meets what McFarlane calls the 'conceptual test' of being such a right at all—ie being correctly describable as a right against a claim-right or a power, rather than against a physical thing—X can generate it as a persistent right whenever she so intends; regardless of whether, in its content, it corresponds to a previously recognised kind of persistent right. That is to say, a persistent right (equitable interest) simply *is* a right against a right, and vice versa.

B. The Review Agenda

Such, I hope, is McFarlane's position. The question is whether we should accept it.

In what follows, I shall inquire, in Part II whether McFarlane's account presents an accurate picture of the positive law; in Part III, when we find that it does not, whether it *must* do so—that is, whether the ways in which the positive law departs from it must be regarded as 'wrong'; and in Part IV, when we find that this is not the case, whether it *should* do so—that is, whether the ways in which the positive law departs from it should be regarded, not as 'wrong', but as making for practically inferior law.

When I refer to the rights that McFarlane calls rights in rem and persistent rights collectively, I shall do so as 'interests', to capture the point that, whatever else may be the case, both are envisaged to be effective against disponees.[10]

C. A Clarification

Before going any further, however, a final preliminary point—which may be important.

A concise but I think essentially comprehensive statement of McFarlane's thesis would read something like this:

(1) An equitable interest is necessarily a right against a right, that is, a right relating to a claim-right or power, and can bind only disponees of that claim-right or power—thus being

---

[9] According to *Street v Mountford* [1985] AC 809 (HL), this first condition need not be satisfied (or is automatically taken as satisfied) if the right in question is a lease, but there is authority for the position as stated in the text at least in the case of easements: *IDC Group Ltd v Clark* (1992) 65 P & CR 179 (CA). See generally J Hill, 'Intention and the Creation of Property Rights: Are Leases Different?' (1996) 16 *Legal Studies* 200.

[10] Note that this usage of 'interests' is a little narrower than the common one. In particular, it excludes intellectual property rights and landlord-and-tenant rights, both of which are capable of binding disponees but which behave in ways different from McFarlane's 'persistent' rights and rights 'in rem': see n 7 above. To reiterate, then: for present purposes, 'interests' means those rights which *both* (a) are capable of binding disponees *and* (b) are, in McFarlane's terms, either 'persistent' or 'in rem'.

a persistent right. (2) A common law interest is necessarily a right against a thing, that is, a right relating to a given asset, and can bind all who come into contact with that asset, whether or not disponees of rights in it—thus being a right in rem.

Now it would be possible for McFarlane simply to stipulate that this statement is true. Consider proposition (1). He might say that an interest will be an authentic equitable interest if, but only if, it relates to a claim-right or power (where 'relates to' means whatever he says it means) and binds only disponees of that claim-right or power, ie is (what he calls) persistent. And that an interest will be persistent, ie bind only disponees of that claim-right or power, if, but only if, it is equitable and relates to a claim-right or a power (where 'relates to' means whatever he says it means). And that an interest will relate to a claim-right or a power (where 'relate to' means whatever he says it means) if, but only if, it is equitable and binds only disponees of that claim-right or power, ie is (what he calls) persistent. In other words, the various terms of proposition (1) are, by McFarlane's stipulation, by definition synonymous; so if we have one, we necessarily have them all. And likewise with proposition (2).

I am not certain whether McFarlane has in fact ever argued in this way, at any rate advisedly and comprehensively. (Though in a moment we shall notice a particular instance of his pretty clearly doing so.) The important point is that, for the purposes of the present exercise, such an argument will not be entertained: for it is quite uninteresting. The reason is that, if the argument is put in this way, it has nothing to say to the rest of us, who live outside the stipulation, in a world where its terms mean what they actually do mean. Specifically, we have no means of testing its truth. Consider the statement 'Grass is red'. If its author stipulates that something *cannot by definition be* 'grass' unless it is 'red', and that something *cannot by definition be* 'red' unless it is the colour of 'grass', the statement will certainly be true, but this will be of interest only to its author. If the rest of us are to engage with the statement, we must recast its argument in a different style, assuming instead that its key components are used in a (probably, their usual) independent, external, sense. That is, we can know whether something is 'grass' because (to go no deeper) we know 'grass' when we see it. And we can know whether something is 'red' because (to go no deeper) we know 'red' when we see it. And we know what 'is' means because (to go no deeper) we just do. Then, using these pieces of external knowledge, we can test the statement—and find it to be (usually?) false. Which is an interesting, useful, thing to be able to do, at least in principle.

Reverting to McFarlane's argument, then, we must insist on reading it *not* in the stipulative style considered a moment ago, but rather in a style whereby its key terms are used in the (or at least a) sense in which they are used *externally to the argument*. Thus, we must treat an interest as authentically 'equitable' if it is a product of the Court of Chancery.[11] And we must treat an interest as 'persistent' if, according to the extant law, it can bind only disponees, but as 'in rem' if it can bind other third parties too.

---

[11] One might debate whether, in these terms, a right can be described as 'equitable'—or for that matter, 'legal'—if its first recognition occurred after the merger of the old separate courts by the Judicature Acts 1873–75. That might or might not be interesting. For present purposes, I am happy to rest with the statement in the text.

We shall take the same approach to the terms 'right relating to (or to, or in, or against) a right (ie a claim-right or power)' and 'right relating to (or to, or in, or against) a thing'—albeit that words such as 'relating to' appear to have no generally recognised legal meaning, so we shall have to rely simply on their ordinary usage. But here we encounter a difficulty. It is fairly clear that McFarlane himself uses these terms, and their components, in a stylised way. There are two facets.

First, remember that McFarlane posits a dichotomy between 'rights' and 'things'. There is no overlap between these; a 'thing' means a physical thing; an abstraction, such as a credit, is a 'right' *and is not* a 'thing'. This clearly departs from ordinary legal usage; as witnessed, to look no further, by the expression used to describe a *right* such as a credit, namely 'chose', ie *thing*, 'in action'. That is, in ordinary legal usage, a 'right' can quite decidedly be simultaneously a 'thing'.

And then secondly, regarding the words 'relating to' (or 'to', or 'in', or 'against'). As explained in section A above (the second focus), I think that for McFarlane, a right 'relating to' a physical thing necessarily, ie because of the very meaning of the words 'relating to' (etc), operates against both a disponee, Y, and one such as a tortfeasor, Z; whilst a right properly describable as 'relating to' (etc) a second right, such as a credit, necessarily, ie because of the very meaning of the words 'relating to' (etc), operates only against Y, and cannot operate against Z. But surely this involves changing the meaning of the words 'relating to' as we move between the two contexts.

Take a right 'relating to' a physical thing. Apparently the words 'relating to' are meant to justify the right's binding both Y and Z; both are bound *because* the right 'relates to' the thing. Then take a right 'relating to', say, a credit right. Here, the words 'relating to' are meant to justify the right's binding Y, while not binding Z; Y is bound, while Z is not, *because* the right 'relates to' the credit right. It seems to me impossible to say that this divergence follows as a matter of ordinary language. It makes perfectly good sense to say that a right 'relating to' a physical thing can be enforced against one who is not a disponee of it but nonetheless comes into contact with it, and reduces its value. It makes equally good sense to say that a right 'relating to', for example, a credit right can be enforced against who is not a disponee of it but nonetheless comes into contact with it, and reduces its value. The words 'relating to' can produce, or capture, the divergent results McFarlane has in mind only if he gives them his own meaning—or rather, two radically different meanings, the choice between these depending on their predicate.

Taking these points together, we find that it is therefore crucial to their role in justifying his theory that McFarlane uses the expressions 'right'/'thing' and 'relating to' (etc) in the particular stylised ways he does. But then, they cease to provide any real-world justification for it after all. All we are left with is a circular argument, whereby 'a right relating to a thing' and 'a right relating to a right' behave in the way that McFarlane says they do precisely, and only, because he defines the words in these expressions in such a way that the two kinds of rights must so behave. That is, he defines the words stipulatively; which, as already said, leaves an argument founded upon them empty of any interest.

Since, as noted, this part of McFarlane's thesis seems actually to provide the justification for the rest of it, one could therefore defensibly declare it necessarily devoid of justification, and examine it no further. Instead, however, I shall pass the point by.

Even if there is not—because there thus cannot be—a justification of McFarlane's thesis in the place he thinks to locate it, the observations contained in the thesis might nonetheless accord with the positive law, and/or might be in some sense supportable in principle. These are the questions we shall go on to examine—but, to reiterate, with an insistence that the examination be conducted in an externally referenced manner.[12]

Finally, we must remember also to take an externally referenced approach to terms such as 'is'. As applied to putative descriptions of the law, such as we are concerned with here, 'is' conventionally means either something like 'is, according to the direct authorities',[13] or 'is, as presenting the best fit with surrounding doctrine'.[14] It being acknowledged that neither meaning will necessarily have a clean 'yes/no' quality. And that the two meanings are not necessarily congruent; sometimes a proposition will be—at least arguably or apparently—true in terms of the one, while false in terms of the other. They are nonetheless both valid and significant; there is no reason to suppress one for the sake of the other; any such divergence between them will be a matter of interest, if however also of concern. Moreover, although our initial inquiries (in Parts II and III below) will be in terms of 'is', for the reason that that is the cast of McFarlane's thesis, it is also legitimate to think in terms of 'ought to be': that is, to consider (as we shall in Part IV), regardless of whether the law 'is' as McFarlane asserts, whether it 'ought to be' so.

So consider again proposition (1) of the concise statement of McFarlane's thesis essayed earlier. Imagine I challenged the proposition, saying *(a)* that restrictive covenants are equitable interests, but *(b)* that they do not relate to a claim-right or power, and *(c)* that they can bind not only disponees but also at least some other third parties. If, hypothetically, McFarlane were to adopt the stipulative style of argument discussed above, he could quite legitimately dismiss my challenge, correctly observing that if my *(a)* is true, my *(b)* and *(c) must* be false; or that if my *(b)* and/or *(c)* is true, my *(a) must* be false. But we have decided to reject that style of argument, in favour of one that gives externally referenced meanings to the statement's terms. This is in fact the style of argument that I use in making my challenge. My assertion *(a)* that 'restrictive covenants are equitable interests' thus claims that restrictive covenants originated in the Chancery. My assertion *(b)* that 'they do not relate to a claim-right or power' claims to track the (Hohfeldian) external meanings of 'claim-right' and 'power', and, implicitly, to invoke a meaning of 'relate to' concocted from ordinary usage. And my assertion *(c)* that 'they can bind not only disponees but also at least some other third parties' claims to treat 'can' in the way that a moment ago we treated 'is', and, therefore, to allege support in (for this purpose) the local and/or wider case law. Read thus, my challenge—and more importantly, its opposite, McFarlane's thesis—can be tested by asking whether it is

[12] In what follows, then, I shall be happy to use the expressions 'persistent right' and 'right in rem' to mean rights that operate in the way that McFarlane tells us they should, regardless of (ie leaving the question aside) whether such operation can be rooted in the justification that McFarlane himself advances, just discussed. In other words, I shall *not*, as some might insist, reserve the two expressions for rights that can be rooted in that justification; for, as explained in the text, that justification is in reality no justification at all, so to follow this path would leave us with nothing further to talk about.

[13] This will be the focus of Part II.

[14] This will be the focus of Part III.

in fact faithful to these sources. Such testing, together with a further inquiry as to whether McFarlane's thesis, read in the same way, *ought to be* right, occupies the remainder of this chapter.

II. *IS* McFARLANE RIGHT?

In this part of the chapter I shall ask whether McFarlane's thesis is true, in the sense that it fits with the positive law declared by the local—ie directly relevant—statutes and case law.

I shall approach this inquiry via the questions whether, in this sense, his two classes of interest—rights in rem and, our especial concern, persistent rights—are indeed known to English law; whether equitable interests do indeed always operate persistently (and legal ones in rem); and whether it is indeed the case that equitable interests, alias persistent rights, on the one hand have to conform to McFarlane's 'conceptual test' of 'relating to' a claim-right or power, but on the other are exempt from the *numerus clausus* principle.

A. Are Rights Behaving as 'Persistent Rights' and 'Rights in Rem' Both Known to English Law?

This question is quickly answered, and in the affirmative.

Say X grants you a lease of her house, then transfers the house to Y: your lease is capable of binding Y. And say Z commits a tort in respect of the house, for example by setting fire to it: you can sue Z. That is the current law; meaning that a lease behaves in the way that McFarlane refers to as in rem.

But earlier conceptions of leases had them operating in other ways. The rule making your lease effective against Y dates from the 1230s,[15] while the origins of that giving it effect against Z are a little later, probably some time between 1250 and 1275.[16] Originally, therefore—before the early thirteenth century—leases were in personam. For a period in the middle of that century, they were persistent. Eventually, by the end of that century, they had attained the in rem impact that they have today.[17]

---

[15] It entered the law in the shape of the writ *quare eiecit infra terminum*, which A Simpson, *A History of the Land Law* (Oxford, Oxford University Press, 1986) 74–75 dates to 1236.

[16] The root here is the writ *eiectione firmae*, giving you recourse at any rate against a trespasser: see generally ibid, 75. For the dating, see S Milsom, 'Trespass from Henry III to Edward III—Part I: General Writs' (1958) 74 *LQR* 195, 198–99.

[17] While specific relief—the physical reinstallation of a dispossessed lessee—had been available right from the introduction of *quare eiecit infra terminum* against Y, it seems not to have been firmly available against Z until *Gernes v Smyth* (1499–1500) CP 40/948 m 303: before that, *eiectione firmae* gave only damages. It is commonly said, therefore, that only in 1499–1500 did leases become 'full property interests'. One can see the point. For our purposes, however, the development does not matter in the same way. In terms of McFarlane's position, the characteristic quality of a right in rem—its effectiveness against a non-disponee third party such as a tortfeasor; the text instances an arsonist—will often be appropriately expressed by the award of damages.

Without needing to go any further, we thus have the means to say that rights behaving as both persistent rights and as rights in rem, in the senses that McFarlane uses those terms, are—or at any rate have been at some time—known to English law.

B. The Common Law/Equity Quadration

Then, is McFarlane is right to view rights operating in these two ways as respectively the creatures of equity and of the common law? The quick answer is no.

I do not propose to try to find rock-solid authority positively proving or disproving McFarlane's vision in respect of every single kind of common law and equitable interest.[18] In the nature of things, there are likely to be gaps in the data, leaving the matter *pro tanto* unresolvable either way. Rather, I shall draw attention to a few instances where there certainly is extant evidence that accords with McFarlane's vision … but also others, where there is evidence against it.

A common law interest according with McFarlane's vision is the lease. As just explained, since the end of the thirteenth century, this common law right has certainly operated in rem. Equally, there is authority to the effect that a beneficial interest under a trust—an equitable interest—is, or is sometimes or in part,[19] a persistent right. If X declares a trust of her house in your favour, then (illicitly[20]) transfers the house to Y, Y can be bound by your right;[21] but if Z commits a tort in respect of the house, as by setting fire to it, you cannot sue Z.[22]

Now some contrary evidence. First, on the common law side. As we saw above, for a time in the mid-thirteenth century, leases—which were and are common law interests—operated in the manner which McFarlane terms persistent, rather than

---

[18] Even assuming it is possible to enumerate these. In the case of equitable interests, McFarlane, with his assertion (considered below) that these are exempt from the *numerus clausus* principle, would presumably consider that the exercise could not be carried out at all.

[19] In truth, it seems likely that only the core elements of a beneficial interest (something like, the rights that the trustee shall treat the property as not her own and shall safeguard it pending its ultimate transfer to the beneficiary) are persistent in this way; that the remaining elements (the rights to the performance of the trustee's other duties) are in personam. If this were not the case—for example, if an appointed trustee illicitly transferred trust property or became insolvent—the transferee or the trustee in bankruptcy would incur her duties to exercise discretions: duties whose proper performance depends heavily on her individual personality, so cannot satisfactorily affect disponees in this way. (See R Nolan, 'Equitable Property' (2006) 122 *LQR* 232; S Gardner, *An Introduction to the Law of Trusts*, 3rd edn (Oxford, Oxford University Press, 2011) 214–15.) So far as I am concerned, therefore, all subsequent references to the nature of a beneficial interest under a trust should be read as qualified in this way. McFarlane concurs in this position: (2008) 31, 554–55.

[20] That is to say, in circumstances where she is not authorised to do so, whether by the terms of the trust or the general law.

[21] This rule is ancient, probably pre-dating the time when Chancery decisions began to be reported. It is visible in modern authority as having been assumed in, eg, *Polly Peck International plc v Nadir (No 2)* [1992] 4 All ER 769 (CA) (in point of 'the tracing claim') and *Attorney General for Hong Kong v Reid* [1994] 1 AC 324 (PC) (where the claimant argued that the bribe was caught by a constructive trust so as to reclaim houses bought with it from the defendant's wife and his solicitor, to whom he had conveyed them).

[22] See eg *Leigh & Sillavan Ltd v Aliakmon Shipping Co Ltd (The Aliakmon)* [1986] AC 785, 812 (HL), concerning negligence; *MCC Proceeds Inc v Lehman Bros International (Europe)* [1998] 4 All ER 675 (CA), concerning conversion.

in rem. Second, in equity. Restrictive covenants—equitable interests—bind not only disponees,[23] but also certain non-disponee third parties.[24]

So we have identified one set of interests (modern leases, and trust rights) in respect of which the evidence accords with McFarlane's vision, and another set (old leases and restrictive covenants) where the evidence goes against it. Given the cast of the proposition—that legal interests *always* operate in rem, while equitable interests *always* operate persistently—the existence of the latter set, even if there be no further interests of like structure, is enough to negate it, as a description of the positive law.

C. Equitable Interests, Persistent Rights, and the *Numerus Clausus* Principle

As will be recalled, McFarlane maintains that an equitable interest can exist only if it meets his 'conceptual test', ie if it relates to a claim-right or a power enjoyed by (originally) X; but that, on the other hand, equitable interests are not subject, as common law interests are, to the *numerus clausus* principle. And of course—since he, albeit as we have seen wrongly, identifies equitable interests with persistent rights—that persistent rights must behave likewise. In this section I shall consider whether equitable interests and persistent rights are indeed exempt from the *numerus clausus* principle; in section D, whether they do indeed have to meet his 'conceptual test'.

As regards the issue of the *numerus clausus* principle, we encounter an initial problem: we need to decide just what we mean by 'the *numerus clausus* principle'. Given one possible meaning, the principle does not apply even in respect of common law interests. If the principle requires the set of such interests to be immutably fixed, the reference already made to the history of leases—their progression during the thirteenth century from rights in personam to persistent rights and then to rights in rem—would immediately reveal it as inoperative. So to adopt this sense of the principle would doubtless be to set the bar too high. At the other extreme, given another possible meaning, the principle is so loose as to be more or less illusory. Take easements. To be an easement, a right has to fit the template set out in *Re Ellenborough Park*,[25] and it might be said that this represents the local application of the *numerus clausus* principle. Yet that template is not at all prescriptive as to the content of the right: except in one or two details having no very obvious theme,[26] it allows most rights to be cast as easements so long as they are taken not for the grantee's personal

---

[23] Given the decision's precise reasoning, this proposition may not have been established by *Tulk v Moxhay* (1848) 2 Ph 774 (Ch) itself, but it certainly became the conventional understanding after *London & South Western Railway Co v Gomm* (1882) 20 Ch D 562, 583 (CA).

[24] *Re Nisbet and Potts' Contract* [1905] 1 Ch 391 (Ch D), [1906] 1 Ch 386 (CA). McFarlane himself has much to say on the matter, of course; see n 38 below.

[25] *Re Ellenborough Park* [1956] Ch 131 (CA).

[26] Notably the rule limiting the possible kinds of negative easements (see *Phipps v Pears* [1965] 1 QB 76 (CA)); and that (of less than clear content itself) establishing what is possible in the way of occupation by the dominant owner of the servient land (see *Batchelor v Marlow* [2001] EWCA Civ 1051, [2003] 1 WLR 764 (CA); *Moncrieff v Jamieson* [2007] UKHL 42, [2007] 1 WLR 2620 (HL); *Virdi v Chana* [2008] EWHC 2901 (Ch D); *Polo Woods Foundation v Shelton-Agar* [2009] EWHC 1361 (Ch), [2010] 1 All ER 539 (Ch D)).

benefit, but by way of advantage connected to her land. So to fix the meaning of the principle by reference to this experience would be to set the bar too low. Steering between these two extremes, then, most would see the *numerus clausus* principle as asserting, albeit in a way that cannot be formulated very precisely, that there is indeed some sort of not-ultimately-rigid-but-nonetheless-reasonably-solid constraint, revolving around the right's content, on the law's preparedness to recognise a right as an interest.

It is McFarlane's contention that, while the principle (let us say, so conceived) certainly constrains the law's preparedness to recognise a right as common law interest, it has no such application to equitable interests. This seems to be incorrect. Consider the decisions in *Keppell v Bailey*[27] and *Haywood v Brunswick Permanent Benefit Building Society*.[28] In these, the courts refused to treat the parties, who had purported to create a new form of interest, as having effectively done so. The purported novel interest was in each decision considered both as a potentially legal one and as a potentially equitable one, and rejected on both footings. Significantly, too, one gains no impression, from reading the reports, that those involved saw the question as being a different one, in the way McFarlane suggests, depending on whether it was approached in terms of the common law or of equity.[29] We should therefore conclude that equitable interests are as much subject to the *numerus clausus* principle as common law interests are.[30]

Does McFarlane fare better if, instead of thus asking whether equitable rights are subject to the *numerus clausus* principle, we ask whether persistent rights are? I suggest not; that *Keppell v Bailey*[31] and *Haywood v Brunswick Permanent Benefit Building Society*[32] are once again to the contrary. There is a snag, however.

The interest being argued for in *Keppell v Bailey*[33] was a restrictive covenant, which, as we saw in section B, was eventually accepted into the law and, in its

---

[27] *Keppell v Bailey* (1834) 2 My & K 517 (Ch).

[28] *Haywood v Brunswick Permanent Benefit Building Society* (1881) 8 QBD 403 (CA).

[29] There is however one respect in which McFarlane is certainly right to differentiate between the treatment of legal and equitable interests as regards the *numerus clausus*. No new legal interest appears to have been established for several centuries (on at any rate a simple view, the most recent being the lease, already discussed); such innovative activity as has taken place has been on the equity side. One thinks of restrictive covenants and, for a time, contractual licences, as well as rights arising by proprietary estoppel. (But for a late flare on the common law side, see Law Commission, *Making Land Work: Easements, Covenants and Profits à Prendre*, Law Com No 327 (London, 2011) pt 6, proposing that the work of restrictive covenants—and indeed positive ones—should in future be done by a new legal interest known as a land obligation. This reform would, however, be effected by statute, which may be important.) But this observation does not amount to an affirmation that, while legal interests are absolutely subject to the *numerus clausus* principle, equitable interests are absolutely exempt from it.

[30] There may be a further difficulty. While McFarlane claims that the *numerus clausus* principle does not apply to equitable interests, he accepts that some other limiting rules, also based on substantive content, do; notably, the rule against perpetuities. But *quaere* whether the rule against perpetuities should be separated from the *numerus clausus* principle in this way. Why not view it as an aspect of the latter, establishing that an interest whose content includes an element of futurity of vesting can be created only if that element fits a certain pattern? In which case, it becomes impossible for this reason as well to say that the *numerus clausus* principle does not apply to equitable interests. (For an explicit yoking of the *numerus clausus* principle and the rule against perpetuities, see M Heller, 'The Boundaries of Private Property'. (1999) 108 *Yale Law Journal* 1163, 1176–81.)

[31] *Keppell* (n 27).

[32] *Haywood* (n 28).

[33] *Keppell* (n 27).

developed form, is—while certainly equitable—not a persistent right at all, but a right in rem. So one might regard the decision as providing no evidence that the *numerus clausus* principle applies to *persistent* rights. Perhaps *Haywood v Brunswick Permanent Benefit Building Society*[34] should be viewed in the same way. The interest being argued for there was a positive covenant. This has not been accepted by the law,[35] whether as a right in rem or as a persistent right. But one might say that if it had been accepted, it would, by analogy with the restrictive covenant, have been as a right in rem. In which case, the case again provides no evidence that the *numerus clausus* principle applies to *persistent* rights.

This treatment of the two decisions seems tortured, however. In both, the result unsuccessfully sought on the facts was that the right in question should bind a disponee (Y). To achieve this, the right need not have been accepted as a right in rem (so as to bind also Z); only as a persistent right. According to the hypothesis under consideration, the right's acceptance as a persistent right (as opposed to a right in rem) would not have involved consideration of the *numerus clausus* principle. If this were right, then in referring to the *numerus clausus* principle—as they assuredly did—the courts in the two decisions overlooked the claimant's best point. It is not very plausible. Those arguing and adjudicating the cases in question included a considerable number of very eminent lawyers indeed. And they quite clearly all considered that the interest contended for had to comply with the *numerus clausus* principle, *even so as to bind only a disponee*, ie to be persistent.

D. Equitable Interests, Persistent Rights, and the 'Conceptual Test'

So much for the question whether equitable interests and persistent rights are exempt from the *numerus clausus* principle. Now we come to the question whether, as McFarlane contends, an equitable interest or a persistent right may exist as such if, but only if, it complies with his 'conceptual test', ie only if it 'relates to' a right (a claim-right or a power) enjoyed by X, its originator—not if it 'relates to' a (physical) thing, this being the characteristic of a common law interest or right in rem.

Remember our insistence, as discussed in section C of Part I, on reading the words forming these contentions in an externally referenced way—even though McFarlane himself seems not to do so, but rather to use them stipulatively, ie in such a way as to leave the contentions circular, and so necessarily, but quite uninterestingly, correct.

So is it the law that equitable interests, and persistent rights, are always 'rights relating to rights', and never 'rights relating to things' (that being the mark of a common law interest, a right in rem)? It seems to me impossible to say so. One and the same right can perfectly well be both a 'right relating to a right' and a 'right relating to a thing'. As discussed in section C of Part I, this is both because the law's use of the word 'thing' overlaps with its use of the word 'right' (as in 'chose in action'), and because to say that a right 'relates to' some asset (whether a physical thing or an abstraction) is to say nothing determinative about whether the right

---

[34] *Haywood* (n 28).
[35] Its rejection was confirmed in *Rhone v Stephens* [1994] 2 AC 310 (HL).

does or should operate fully in rem or only persistently. In other words, McFarlane's contentions under discussion, read in an externally referenced way, simply lack the precision needed to be able to say that they follow the contours of the extant law. By the same token, one may not be able to say for certain that they do not; but if we think about concrete applications, we find their rendition of the extant law a peculiar one. I should find it baffling to be told, for example, that while a common law easement relates to its grantor's land, an equitable easement relates to its grantor's right.[36] Or that, when leases switched from persistent rights to rights in rem in the late thirteenth century, this accompanied a change whereby, in the real world, they no longer related (as they previously had) to the landlord's right, and instead related to her land. Or that a right relating to a credit can by definition not protect against injuries wrought by a non-disponee, whilst a right relating to say a vase can (indeed must). At the same time, coming at the matter from another direction, it seems to have been recently decided that an EU carbon emission allowance—obviously a purely abstract right, with no physical thing in sight—may be a common law interest, which according to McFarlane ought to be an impossibility.[37]

We must conclude, therefore, that the law does not see an equitable interest or persistent right as one that 'relates to' its originator's right, or vice versa; nor a common law interest or right in rem as one that 'relates to' her physical thing, or vice versa. And so, ultimately, that McFarlane is wrong, as a matter of positive law, to say that rights are to be allocated to these various classes by reference to his 'conceptual test'.

III. *MUST* McFARLANE BE RIGHT?

The previous part of this chapter tests McFarlane's claims against the positive law most directly applicable to them. It reveals in particular that, while he is correct to assert that two classes of interest—persistent and in rem, effective respectively against Y alone, and both Y and Z—are known to English law, he is incorrect to assert that persistent rights straightforwardly quadrate with equitable interests (and rights in rem with legal interests); and that his 'conceptual test' does, but the *numerus clausus* principle does not, govern such interests, whether focused as equitable interests or as persistent rights.

It might however be suggested that the features of the positive law yielding this conclusion are wrong. (Many of them coincide in restrictive covenants; so the suggestion might consist in, or include, the proposition that restrictive covenants cannot properly exist in the form they currently do.[38]) Now this is a suggestion that may make no sense whatsoever. One might say that if the law does operate these

---

[36] Similarly, I am simply bemused by McFarlane's suggestion ((2010) 14) that restrictive covenants, which he finds unacceptable as equitable interests, would be perfectly acceptable as common law interests.

[37] See *Armstrong DLW GmbH v Winnington Networks Ltd* [2012] EWHC 10 (Ch), [2012] 3 All ER 425 (Ch D).

[38] For McFarlane's own writings on this key difficulty for his view, see (2008) 893–94; (2010) 13–14; (2011) 322–25; and also 'Tulk v Moxhay (1848)' in C Mitchell and P Mitchell (eds), *Landmark Cases in Equity* (Oxford, Hart Publishing, 2012).

features without the sky in fact falling in (and the sky does not appear to have fallen in), it is futile, absurd, to say that it *cannot* do so, is *wrong* to do so. That would be an entirely sane position, to which we shall return at the end of this Part, in section F. But the suggestion can be given sense if we take 'wrong' to mean, specifically, that such features affront prior givens: other things we know about the law, which for some reason—most obviously, greater authority or historical antecedence—should take precedence.

A. The 'Conceptual Test' and the *Numerus Clausus* Principle

In fact McFarlane's proposition that equitable interests, *alias* persistent rights, are controlled by his 'conceptual test', but are not subject to the *numerus clausus* principle, cannot well be tested in this way, for lack, in its case, of such 'other things that we know about the law'.

English law appears to contain no canonical statement of the *numerus clausus* principle at all, nor data from which its precise reach can be gathered, even by inference or deduction. For what it is worth, the most explicit and worked-out judicial treatment of the principle appears to be the judgment in *Keppell v Bailey*,[39] referred to in Part II: and, as noted there, this is overtly inconsistent with McFarlane's proposition, whether we express the latter in terms of equitable interests or persistent rights. There appears no reason, therefore, to say that McFarlane's proposition about the *numerus clausus* principle *must* be right, in the manner under consideration.

Likewise, or all the more so, with the notion that equitable interests, alias persistent rights, are controlled by McFarlane's 'conceptual test', equating them with rights 'relating to' (or 'to', or 'in', or 'against') 'rights' rather than 'things'. Given, remember, an insistence on using the words 'relating to' (etc), 'rights' and 'things' in an externally referenced way, the notion seems without support. I may of course be overlooking something—as with all of us, my ignorance of the law is infinitely greater than my knowledge—but as things stand, quite simply, I know of nothing at all in the more distantly surrounding law to indicate the converse.

B. 'Equitable Interests are Persistent': The Traditional Law of Common Injunctions

It is otherwise, however, regarding McFarlane's proposition that equitable interests operate persistently rather than in rem. In other words, that equitable interests can be enforced against disponees of the asset to which they refer (Y), but not against non-disponees whose behaviour impinges on the asset, such as tortfeasors (Z). There is indeed evidence that equity cannot reach the latter.[40] If this evidence goes

---

[39] *Keppell* (n 27).

[40] Distinguish, of course, evidence that equity *sometimes does not* reach the latter. For example, McFarlane points out ((2010) 3) that if you have a beneficial interest in X's contractual debt, your right is necessarily persistent, rather than in rem: for while it will obtain against Y, a disponee of the debt, it

uncontradicted, it might be argued that this aspect of McFarlane's thesis must, in the sense under discussion, be correct. This evidence consists in the traditional jurisprudence regarding common injunctions.[41]

Common injunctions are the tool whereby the Court of Chancery used to override the common law courts when it chose to. Say A and B contracted, but A made an innocent misrepresentation in the process; then B failed to perform. If A sued B in a common law court, A would have judgment and an award of damages for the loss in question: at common law, innocent misrepresentations (as opposed to fraudulent ones) did not vitiate. In equity, however, an innocent misrepresentation rendered a contract voidable. Assuming B had done whatever it took to avoid the contract, therefore, according to equity she was not in breach, as there was no contract to be in breach of. From this point of view, then, A had no right to relief against her. Since equity took precedence over the common law, this ought to have been the ultimate outcome. B was able to secure it by taking, from the Chancery, an order—a 'common injunction'—restraining A from pursuing or enforcing her common law right.

The foregoing paragraph describes the traditional picture. During the nineteenth century, reforms—culminating in the Judicature Acts 1873–75—meant that B did not have to go to Chancery and obtain a real injunction so as to block A's common law right, but could instead achieve the same result simply by pointing to the equitable position in what eventually became, and remains today, a single court. In consequence, no one today bothers to remember that contracts are not vitiated by innocent misrepresentations at common law, as opposed to equity. There is simply the one rule (which happens to be, as a matter of history, one of equitable derivation): an innocent misrepresentation leaves a contract voidable. But analysing matters in terms of the common injunction is important for our present purposes, as it reveals the operation of, specifically, equity.

But—traditionally again—common injunctions could, roughly speaking, be used to suppress common law answers in favour of equitable ones in this way only in one type of case. This was the case where, as in the illustration just given, the common law gave relief against someone (B) who, in the judgment of the Chancery, should not suffer it. Common injunctions were not generally available in the converse case. Say C and D entered into a contract, the terms of which required performance by a certain date. So far as the common law was concerned, if D failed to perform her obligations in time, C could obtain an award of damages, and also treat the contract as at an end, ie legitimately refuse to perform her own obligations. In equity, however, stipulations as to time were, with some exceptions, disregarded—time was

---

cannot obtain against Z, a non-disponee whose behaviour affects the value of the debt ... because it is 'not meaningful' to think of tort rights in respect of debts, so that not even X can have such rights. Now this example is probably not watertight in itself. (On appropriate facts, X can surely sue Z for interference with his contractual relations with the debtor? Cf B McFarlane, 'Equity, Obligations and Third Parties' [2008] *Singapore Journal of Legal Studies* 1. And also for conversion, according to the minority in *OBG Ltd v Allan* [2007] UKHL 21, [2008] 1 AC 1 (HL), discussed by A Goymour in S Bright (ed), *Modern Studies in Property Law, Volume 6* (Oxford, Hart Publishing, 2011) ch 16.) But even if the example were watertight, it would prove only that a beneficial right under a trust *of this type of subject matter* would have to be persistent, not that all beneficial rights, let alone all equitable interests, are persistent.

[41] This chapter's treatment of common injunctions draws heavily on S Gardner, 'Equity, Estate Contracts and the Judicature Acts: *Walsh v Lonsdale* Revisited' (1987) 7 *OJLS* 60, 81–91.

regarded as 'not of the essence'. So if C were to go to common law for an award of damages, D could have a common injunction to block it, in the manner just described. By the same token, if C were to fail to perform her own obligations under the contract, equity treated her as having no legitimate basis on which to do so, and saw D as entitled to treat C's failure as a breach. D was thus able to claim specific performance against C, if the case was of a type that attracted this remedy. *But D could not have common law damages against C.* One might have expected D to be able to sue for such damages in a common law court, simultaneously obtaining a common injunction from the Chancery restraining C from defending the common law action by pointing to the stipulation as to time. Without which defence, the common law too would have found C in breach, and so liable to D. But this was not the traditional position. D's only positive relief was specific performance; damages were unavailable.[42,43]

In short, common injunctions were traditionally available, roughly speaking, to allow litigants supported by equity but not by the common law to *defend* themselves against common law relief, but not to allow them to *recruit* such relief.

This is important for the question whether equitable interests are persistent, rather than in rem, as follows. Recall our initial instance, in which X owns a house, but you have an equitable interest over it. Say the house is tortiously set on fire by Z, and you wish to sue Z for damages. An appropriate action for doing so might have been trespass.[44] This was a common law action. If you had attempted to bring it, Z could have met you with the defence that it was available only to persons (recognised by the common law as) having possession of the land; your equitable interest as such did not qualify you. If you had sought a common injunction to prevent Z from raising that defence, on the ground that equity saw matters differently, you would have failed. Even if, in equity's eyes, your right might in principle have been sufficient basis for the extraction of a remedy, we have seen that the Chancery did not generally issue common injunctions so as to allow a person with an equitable right to obtain common law relief in vindication of it. To that extent, therefore, you could not enforce your right against Z: that is, your right emerged as persistent rather than in rem.

And generalising beyond the example: since the majority of English law's torts are historically common law institutions, one would conclude that someone having only an equitable interest over the affected asset could not invoke them; that an equitable interest cannot, therefore, be enforced against the majority of tortfeasors; and that such a right is, therefore, to at least this extent persistent rather than in rem.

---

[42] *Stickney v Keeble* [1915] AC 386, 415–16. (By the Supreme Court of Judicature Act 1873 s 25(7), later replaced by the virtually identical Law of Property Act 1925 s 41, the equity rule was made to apply at law too. For the exact meaning of this, see *Rightside Properties Ltd v Gray* [1975] Ch 72 (Ch D).)

[43] Similarly if C and D contracted for the transfer of C's land to D, failing to comply with the requirement (originating in the Statute of Frauds 1677 s 4) that such a contract be made in writing. Until the Law of Property (Miscellaneous Provisions) Act 1989 s 2, if D had 'part performed' the contract, equity regarded it as good after all. But this meant only that D could have specific performance; not that he could, by seeking a common injunction to block C's defence at law, elicit common law damages. See *Britain v Rossiter* (1879) 11 QBD 123 (CA); *McManus v Cooke* (1887) 35 Ch D 681, 697 (Ch D); *Lavery v Pursell* (1888) 39 Ch D 508, 518 (Ch D).

[44] Another possibility is negligence: in which case, compare the discussion of that tort in section C of Part III below.

This is, however, not the whole story. We can in fact identify three (there may be more) ways in which you could—and can—after all enforce an equitable right against a non-disponee third party such as Z. These, and their significance, are the subject of sections C–E below.

C. 'Equitable Interests are Persistent': The Protection of Equitable Rights by Common Law Relief Per Se

The first of the three is this. Sometimes, a person having an equitable interest will find that interest protected against non-disponee third parties by a common law rule, simply because the rule is defined in such a way that its protection extends to her.

Consider the tort of negligence. Lord Atkin's defining 'neighbour' principle reads:

> The rule that you are to love your neighbour becomes in law, you must not injure your neighbour; and the lawyer's question, Who is my neighbour? receives a restricted reply. You must take reasonable care to avoid acts or omissions which you can reasonably foresee would be likely to injure your neighbour. Who, then, in law is my neighbour? The answer seems to be—persons who are so closely and directly affected by my act that I ought reasonably to have them in contemplation as being so affected when I am directing my mind to the acts or omissions which are called in question.[45]

This formula is, of course, accepted as covering one who has a common law interest in an affected asset: such as the owner of a negligently damaged car. It also covers those having interests not independently recognised by the law at all: such as one whose leg is negligently broken. Purely in terms of its wording, there is no reason why it should not cover one who holds an equitable interest too, such as perhaps a chargee of a negligently damaged aircraft (the chargor remains liable for the debt, but the tortfeasor has damaged the value of the security, to the chargee's detriment).

As the authorities stand, however, it cannot straightforwardly be said that the holder of an equitable interest will certainly be protected in this way. At any rate a beneficiary under a trust cannot sue one who negligently damages the trust property:[46] this step can only be taken—and indeed will be taken—by the trustee, who has a duty to do so on the beneficiary's behalf. But the resultant damages, which the trustee must hold for the beneficiary, will be fixed by reference to the beneficiary's loss.[47] This is rationalised by the proposition that the tortfeasor owes a duty of care to the beneficiary,[48] while the requirement of process via the trustee is rationalised as required in order to ensure that the defendant is not exposed to double recovery.[49] This may seem to come very close to a denial of the proposition

---

[45] *Donoghue v Stevenson* [1932] AC 562, 580 (HL).
[46] *The Aliakmon* (n 22).
[47] See *Shell UK Ltd v Total UK Ltd* [2010] EWCA Civ 180, [2011] QB 86 [137]–[144] (CA).
[48] Ibid [142].
[49] Ibid [141].

that the beneficiary has no right of action in her own name, but in that vestigial form the proposition stands.

Quaere whether the same is true where the loss is to the holder of any other kind of equitable interest, such as a charge. In such a case, it seems in principle unlikely that some other person, such as the chargor, has any duty to sue the tortfeasor on the chargee's behalf, as unlike a trustee vis-à-vis her beneficiary, she does not hold her right for the benefit of the chargee. So if the more complex position in the trust case rests on the presence and role of the trustee—as it appears to—then it surely follows that, in the case of some other type of equitable interest, the tortfeasor's duty to the holder of the interest should predicate direct actionability by the latter. This conclusion may require revision of the hitherto dominant judicial statement on the subject, but the latter may be too widely expressed;[50] the point under discussion seems never to have been properly considered.

So much for negligence. Consider also the claim for possession of land. It used to be the rule that this claim availed only one having a common law title to the land in question. This appears no longer to be the case. Instead, the claim can be brought 'by anyone entitled to use and control, effectively amounting to possession, of the land in question'.[51] Moreover, it appears that this qualification is not to be read technically. It embraces someone having a contractual licence over the land,[52] despite the fact that, by definition, she does *not* have possession in the full sense.[53] It is hard to see why it should not also embrace someone having a suitable equitable right, such as perhaps a beneficial interest giving her a 'right to occupy' under section 12 of the Trusts of Land and Appointment of Trustees Act 1996.[54]

Sometimes the equitable right (arguably) protected in such ways against a non-disponee third party (Z) will also be effective against a disponee (Y). Then, to the

---

[50] It is the following dictum of Lord Brandon in *The Aliakmon* (n 22): 'in order to enable a person to claim in negligence for loss caused to him by reason of loss of or damage to property, he must have had either the legal ownership of or a possessory title to the property concerned'. This would exclude a charge, as well as a trust interest. But Lord Brandon continues with the much narrower words (emphasis added): 'it is not enough for him to have *only* had *contractual* rights in relation to such property which have been adversely affected by the loss of or damage to it'. To allow a claim to the holder of a charge or a trust interest would infringe the first statement of the rule, but not the second. It is true that the possibility of actionability by a trust beneficiary was expressly rejected in *The Aliakmon* (at 812), but this was at least partly because no such interest had arisen there; on the facts as found, there was only a contractual right, so the decision against actionability required only the second statement. (Likewise the decisions in the original case on this matter, *Cattle v Stockton Waterworks Co* (1875) 10 QB 453 (QB), and various other cases since the latter.) According to *Shell UK Ltd* (n 47) [134]–[136], then, *The Aliakmon* should be read as authority for nothing wider than the second statement. There is however a very considerable body of secondary literature on the subject, predominantly supportive of something like the first statement. But for a recent critique of the latter, see R Bagshaw, 'The Edges of Tort Law's Rights' in D Nolan and A Robertson (eds), *Rights and Private Law* (Oxford, Hart Publishing, 2011) ch 14.

[51] *Mayor of London v Hall* [2010] EWCA Civ 817, [2011] 1 WLR 504, [27] (CA), Lord Neuberger MR; founding upon *Manchester Airport plc v Dutton* [2000] QB 133 (CA) and *Secretary of State for the Environment, Food and Rural Affairs v Meier* [2009] UKSC 11, [2009] 1 WLR 2780 (SC).

[52] *Manchester Airport plc v Dutton* [2000] QB 133 (CA).

[53] *Street v Mountford* (n 9).

[54] Lest anyone should discount this example as contaminated by statutory bastardisation, note that a similar right could be found before 1996: *Bull v Bull* [1955] 1 QB 234 (CA) (*cf Barclay v Barclay* [1970] 2 QB 677 (CA)).

extent of the protection under discussion, it will be what McFarlane calls a right in rem. This appears to go for both the kinds of right just discussed: charges and (at least some) trust interests.

D. 'Equitable Interests are Persistent': The Protection of Equitable Rights by Common Law Relief, Accessed by Common Injunction

Now the second way in which an equitable interest might be enforceable against a non-disponee third party such as Z.

Remember the account of common injunctions given in section B, explaining that 'traditionally', and 'roughly speaking' or 'generally', someone with an equitable right could not have a common injunction to block a common law defence and thereby elicit a common law remedy. As the words in quotation marks hint, this account is not the complete picture.

There was always an exception. Common injunctions of this latter kind could be had to achieve broadly procedural ends, 'to remove impediments to a fair decision of a question in other courts':[55] that is, so as to remove technical common law defences that stood in the way of a trial of the real issue.[56]

However, the size, shape and nature of this exception were never authoritatively defined, and the suggestion was made that it might in fact be broader, allowing common injunctions of this kind to be had 'where the courts of ordinary jurisdiction are made instruments of injustice',[57] ie to achieve ends that could more appropriately be described as substantive.[58] A number of later cases show its acceptance and exploitation. Probably significantly, they date from after the enactment of the Judicature Acts 1873–75, upon which, the courts of common law and equity being merged so

---

[55] J Mitford, *A Treatise on the Pleadings in Suits in the Court of Chancery by English Bill*, 2nd edn (London, W Owen, 1787) 104, developed at 121–22.

[56] See, eg *Dormer v Fortescue* (1741) 2 Atk 282 (Ch); *Pulteney v Warren* (1801) 6 Ves 73 (Ch); *Bond v Hopkins* (1802) 1 Sch & Lef 413 (Irish Ch); *Pemberton v Pemberton* (1805) 13 Ves 290, 298 (Ch); *Jones v Jones* (1817) 3 Mer 161 (Ch); *Armitage v Wadsworth* (1815) 1 Madd 189 (VC); *Crow v Tyrrell* (1818) 3 Madd 179 (VC); *Beer v Ward* (1821) Jac 194 (Ch); *Sirdefield v Price* (1827) 2 Y & J 73 (Ex); *Strickland v Strickland* (1842) 6 Beav 77 (Rolls). The jurisdiction is described in, eg, G Jeremy, *A Treatise on the Equity Jurisdiction of the High Court of Chancery* (London, J & WT Clarke, 1828) Book 2, ch 3 and 296, 308; C Drewry, *A Treatise on the Law and Practice of Injunctions* (London, S Sweet, 1841) pt II, ch 10; W Kerr, *A Treatise on the Law and Practice of Injunctions in Equity* (London, W Maxwell & Son, 1867) ch 27.

[57] Mitford (n 55) 103, developed at 116–20. See too *Bond v Hopkins* (n 56), especially at 430–34, where the same author—by this time Lord Redesdale LC—considers the area judicially. At 430, he puts the matter thus: 'One acknowledged principle on which courts of equity give relief, is to prevent an advantage gained at law from being used against conscience. There are two modes by which the court gives relief in such cases; one direct, the other indirect: in the first mode, it acts by giving of itself full relief [eg by granting specific performance]; in the second, by enabling the party to try his title at law, without the impediments which may against conscience be opposed at law to his proceedings [ie by giving a common injunction] ... Whether this court will interfere to take from one in favour of another that which would be a defence at law, depends on what is called good conscience.'

[58] The immediate catalyst for this suggestion seems to have been the decision in *Pincke v Thornycroft* (1785) 4 Bro PC 92 (HL). Notice the date, there thus being an interval of only two years before the publication of the second edition of Mitford's *Treatise* (n 55), in which the case is given prominence at 118. (Gardner (n 41) is in error in giving the later publication date of 1795: this was the publication date of a reprint of the same edition in Dublin.)

that all aspects of a case were triable together, common injunctions ceased to be used ... and the jurisprudence associated with them perhaps began to be forgotten or ignored.

An example of this development is *Industrial Properties (Barton Hill) Ltd v Associated Electrical Industries Ltd.*[59] A landlord sued its tenant for damages for breach of a repairing covenant in the lease—historically a common law proceeding. The decision has two strands, one treating the lease as legal, the other as equitable. If the lease was equitable, however, the tenant should have had the defence at common law that there was no lease, so the tenant owed no such obligation to the landlord. But the court, overlooking this problem, found for the landlord. In the terms of a common injunction analysis, it was as if the tenant was enjoined from raising the common law defence, so as to allow the landlord to vindicate its equitable interest via a legal remedy.

Similarly, persons having equitable rights were enabled to sue via a common law tort—in the terms of a common injunction analysis, the defendant was enjoined from raising the common law defence that she owed no duty to the claimant, allowing the latter to vindicate her equitable right via a legal remedy. Decisions on these lines include *Coatsworth v Johnson*[60] (involving an equitable lease) and *Hurst v Picture Theatres Ltd*[61] (involving a contractual licence).

So the apparatus exists—by at least one century ago, maybe two, had come to exist—whereby a common law tort can be deployed in protection of an equitable right, despite the tort's restriction at law to the protection of a legal right. To this extent too, then, equitable rights can be enforced against third parties other than disponees, such as tortfeasors (Z). Obviously, some equitable rights may also be enforceable against disponees (Y); of the rights just discussed, equitable leases are of this kind, though contractual licences are not. Cumulating the two axes of enforcement, such rights emerge as *pro tanto* (not persistent but) in rem.

E. 'Equitable Interests are Persistent': Equitable Relief against Non-disponee Third Parties

We now come to the third way in which equitable interests can be operated against non-disponee third parties (Z), and so be in rem. This way involves no engagement with the common law: we are dealing with equity alone. It is this: equitable relief (say, an injunction) is sometimes granted against defendants who are behaving, or

---

[59] *Industrial Properties (Barton Hill) Ltd v Associated Electrical Industries Ltd* [1977] QB 580 (CA).

[60] *Coatsworth v Johnson* (1886) 54 LT 520 (CA). An equitable tenant, suffering an incursion by his landlord, sued the latter for trespass—a common law tort. The landlord's possible defence, that at common law the tenant had no right *not* to suffer the incursion, was overlooked. Though on the facts, the tenant failed, as his equitable interest had lapsed. Similarly *Delaney v TP Smith Ltd* [1946] KB 393 (CA), though here too the tenant failed, as his supposed equitable interest turned out to be illusory.

[61] *Hurst v Picture Theatres Ltd* [1915] 1 KB 1 (CA). A contractual licensee, suffering forcible eviction from the land by the licensor, sued the latter for assault. The court treated the licensee as, whether or not having a common law right to be on the land, nonetheless having an equitable right to be there. The licensee's action succeeded. The licensor's possible defence, that the want of a common law right to be on the land meant that the licensee had no right *not* to be physically evicted, was overlooked.

proposing to behave, in ways to which equity alone takes exception. Indeed, in such instances, the availability of such relief may be the only reason we have to assert that there exists an equitable right at all.

One example is the jurisdiction to injunct one who breaches confidentiality. There are various difficult questions about this jurisdiction,[62] but it is clear that at least one form of it is historically rooted purely in equity, independently of contract or the common law of tort or, now, Article 8 of the European Convention on Human Rights, the right to privacy. It probably dates back to some nineteenth-century decisions,[63] but it is certainly to be seen in *Saltman Engineering Co Ltd v Campbell Engineering Co Ltd*,[64] *Duchess of Argyll v Duke of Argyll*,[65] *Seager v Copydex Ltd*[66] and *Coco v AN Clark (Engineers) Ltd*.[67] As it developed, it picked up the ability to yield relief in damages, to the point where Megarry J in the last of these decisions found himself saying, at any rate of commercial cases, 'the essence of the duty seems more likely to be that of not using without paying, rather than of not using at all'.[68] It is unclear how, technically, this development occurred—whether by pure equity still.[69] But given the late emergence of the damages dimension, we are here looking at a rule which for at least part of its history was undoubtedly a purely equitable one.

Another example is to be found in, or adjacent to, the tort of passing off.[70] As with breach of confidentiality, the modern law allows a claimant to recover damages no less widely than she can obtain an injunction: in particular, even if the defendant's misrepresentation was innocent.[71] But, originally, damages could be recovered—in a common law tort action—only where the activity in question was fraudulent; injunctive relief alone being available where it was innocent.[72] To that

---

[62] For a general treatment, see A Dugdale and M Jones (eds), *Clerk & Lindsell on Torts*, 20th edn (London, Sweet & Maxwell, 2010) ch 27. For a treatment especially attentive to the doctrine's equitable roots, see R Meagher, D Heydon and M Leeming, *Meagher, Gummow & Lehane's Equity Doctrines and Remedies*, 4th edn (Chatswood NSW, LexisNexis Butterworths, 2002) ch 41.

[63] *Abernethy v Hutchinson* (1825) 1 H & Tw 28 (Ch); *Prince Albert v Strange* (1849) 1 Mac & G 25 (Ch); *Morison v Moat* (1851) 9 Hare 241 (VC) (affirmed (1852) 21 LJ Ch 248 (CA in Ch)).

[64] *Saltman Engineering Co Ltd v Campbell Engineering Co Ltd* (1948) 65 RPC 203 (CA).

[65] *Duchess of Argyll v Duke of Argyll* [1967] Ch 302 (Ch D).

[66] *Seager v Copydex Ltd* [1967] 1 WLR 923 (CA).

[67] *Coco v AN Clark (Engineers) Ltd* [1968] FSR 415 (Ch D).

[68] Ibid, 423.

[69] Its genesis seems to have been *Seager v Copydex Ltd* (n 66), where the relief given was monetary rather than injunctive, but no real explanation was given for this. One possibility could be via Lord Cairns' Act (see *Attorney General v Observer Ltd* [1990] 1 AC 109, 286 (HL)). Another might be a fiduciary's duty to account (see perhaps *Peter Pan Manufacturing Corp v Corsets Silhouette Ltd* [1964] 1 WLR 96 (Ch D); cf *Attorney General v Blake* [2001] 1 AC 268, 287, 291–92 (HL)). A third is that, after the Judicature Acts 1873–75—though some would see this as an instance of 'fusion fallacy'—there is simply no reason why a doctrine originating in equity should not yield damages (see perhaps *Seager v Copydex Ltd (No 2)* [1969] 1 WLR 809, 813 (CA)).

[70] See generally Dugdale and Jones (n 62) ch 26; and, with an eye especially to the equity issues, Meagher, Heydon and Leeming (n 62) ch 42.

[71] See *Gillette UK Ltd v Edenwest Ltd* [1994] RPC 279, 289–93 (Ch D), basing itself especially upon *AG Spalding v AW Gamage Ltd* (1915) 32 RPC 273 (HL).

[72] See especially *Crawshay v Thompson* (1842) 4 Man & G 357 (CP); *Burgess v Burgess* (1853) 3 De GM & G 896 (Ch); *Millington v Fox* (1838) 3 My & Cr 338 (Ch); *The 'Singer' Machine Manufacturers v Wilson* (1877) 3 App Cas 376, 391–92, 396 (HL); *The Singer Manufacturing Co v Hermann Loog* (1882) 8 App Cas 15, 30–32 (HL). The widening of the availability of damages has

extent, therefore, equity, again operating purely via its own mechanisms, was once more enforcing against non-disponee third parties.

Rights of the kind under discussion should of course be contrasted with rights founded upon consent, notably contract rights. The former bind all whose conduct may affect the claimant in the manner in question. This is the point of saying that they obtain against (non-disponee) 'third parties' (Z). They are examples of the further category that we noticed earlier, pure tort rights.

To use McFarlane's language: if effectiveness against non-disponee third parties (Z) is combined with effectiveness against disponees (Y), ie persistence, the rights in question emerge as rights in rem. On occasion, the interests protected by breach of confidentiality and passing off—confidential information[73] and 'goodwill'[74] respectively—have been at least spoken of as forms of property. If this vision of them had had the particular import that is relevant to the present discussion and had stuck, it would have signified that the obligations under discussion bound disponees (Y) as well. Then, cumulating this with their effectiveness against non-disponee third parties (Z), we should have found ourselves looking here at two kinds of right in rem. But this is not the case: we are indeed looking at pure tort rights. The point is, however, that under appropriate circumstances, such cumulation is perfectly possible. In other words, that if equity is capable of creating rights that bind disponees (Y) alone and rights that bind non-disponee third parties (Z) alone, it is also capable of creating rights that bind both, ie are in rem—or at any rate, it is difficult to discern any reason why it should not be so capable.

Albeit perhaps artificial, this may be a way in which to view what we know of restrictive covenants. As we have seen, these are effective against disponees (Y), and also, by the equitable remedy of injunction, against certain non-disponee third parties whose behaviour may injure the interest they protect (Z).[75] And also in which to view beneficial interests under trusts. These are effective against disponees (Y),[76] and the liabilities of dishonest assistance and (probably also) de facto trusteeship show such interests to be additionally protected by equity (in point of its remedy of account) against certain non-disponee third parties whose behaviour may injure them (Z). Seen thus, there appears to be no reason not to regard these two equitable rights as *pro tanto*—though, should it matter, only *pro tanto*—(not persistent but) in rem.

---

been ascribed, convincingly or otherwise, to the effect of the Judicature Acts 1973–75: *Gillette UK Ltd v Edenwest Ltd* (n 71).

[73] See *Boardman v Phipps* [1967] 2 AC 46 (HL). See further J Harris, 'Reason or Mumbo Jumbo: The Common Law's Approach to Property' (Maccabaean Lecture in Jurisprudence) (2002) 117 *Proceedings of the British Academy* 445, 469.

[74] See *Star Industrial Co Ltd v Yap Kwee Kor* [1976] FSR 256 (PC). See further J Harris, *Property and Justice* (Oxford, Oxford University Press, 1996) 51–52.

[75] *London & South Western Railway Co v Gomm* (n 23) 583; *Re Nisbet* (n 24); see at nn 23 and 24 above.

[76] See at n 19 above.

F. A Caveat

Part II of this chapter showed that McFarlane's thesis is, at certain points, inconsistent with the directly relevant positive law. Part III has shown, further, that these inconsistencies are not to be judged 'wrong', in the sense that they are at odds with the positive law which, although not so directly relevant, might nonetheless might be seen as apt to influence the matter.

Note, however, that if we had reached the opposite conclusion in this part, it would have been necessary to introduce the following caveat. It is probably intelligible to inquire into a proposition's fit with not only the directly relevant, but also the somewhat less directly relevant, positive law. But we should not assume that, in such an inquiry, the latter should trump the former: that is, that a fit with the former should be rendered of no account by a non-fit with the latter. For it may very well be thought that the law—including 'equity'—can say anything, however gangly, that its creators make it say; even outright contradiction being seen as an infelicity, or some stronger word of that kind, rather than as a case of invalidity. Some might limit this statement in respect of rules, or 'rules', that infringe basic values (though others might regard such values rather as constraints on what the law *should* be),[77] but there seems nothing of this kind at stake in the present context. Here, we are at liberty to assert that if the law does in fact treat one or more equitable interests as operating in rem rather than persistently, or as untouched by McFarlane's 'conceptual test' and/or as subject to the *numerus clausus* principle—as Part II of this chapter revealed to be the case—that is simply that: in terms of doctrine, McFarlane's view is incorrect, and cannot be argued to be otherwise.

All this is however academic, as the message of this part is in fact supportive, rather than contradictory, of the conclusions reached in Part II.

IV. *SHOULD* McFARLANE BE RIGHT?

Parts II and III have shown that McFarlane's thesis is not right in the sense of capturing the positive law, however the latter be understood. We now come to our final inquiry: whether McFarlane's thesis *should* be right. That is: admitting that there is in principle a choice to be made about the shape of the law—whether *or not* equitable interests are to be persistent rather than in rem, subject to McFarlane's 'conceptual test', and exempt from the *numerus clausus* principle—should we regard the choice made by McFarlane's thesis as the better one?

I shall look first at the question of whether equitable interests had better be persistent rather than in rem, ie effective against only disponees (Y), not non-disponee third parties (Z). Then at whether equitable interests/persistent rights had better be subject to the 'conceptual test' and exempt from the *numerus clausus* principle.

---

[77] Easily the best treatment of this kind of issue, to my mind, is that of J Finnis, *Natural Law and Natural Rights*, 2nd edn (Oxford, Oxford University Press, 2011) 363–66.

In answering these questions, I adopt a functional perspective—that is, I ask whether adoption of McFarlane's thesis would make for a better law in terms of its substantive content. In these terms, I conclude that the thesis would not make for better law. One might of course challenge this conclusion by adopting a different perspective.[78] On the other hand, I cannot see how the functional perspective can be excluded altogether. So if a rival analysis were advanced, it would lead us to a contrary overall conclusion only if, *as well as* establishing the advantage of McFarlane's thesis in its own terms, it *also* showed that this advantage should outweigh the functional case which I demonstrate. I believe this to be quite an unlikely possibility.

A. Effectiveness against Non-disponees

As we saw in the previous part, the doctrinal equipment exists for giving equitable interests in rem effect, binding non-disponee third parties (Z) as well as disponees (Y). But there is nothing to say that the equipment has to be used in this way.

A holder of an equitable interest will be protected against a non-disponee third party (Z) by a common law rule as such (section C of Part III) only if the rule is so configured. She will, in old-fashioned terms, have access to a common law rule via a common injunction (section D of Part III) only if equity sees her as meriting such access, and so affords her such an injunction. And she will be protected by a purely equitable doctrine (section E of Part III) only, again, if that doctrine is so configured. From first principles, there is no reason to suppose that these things will always, let alone necessarily must, be the case.

Rather, we must seriously entertain the possibility that while equitable interests can thus operate in rem, they should not always, or ever, do so, but should sometimes, or always, operate only persistently. And, even where, or if, they do operate in rem, we must also consider the question of *which* non-disponee third parties (Z) they should bind, for as we saw earlier, this can be a matter of degree, rather than necessarily all or none. We must also contemplate that the position will, or might, differ from one such interest to another. In other words, everything depends, or at any rate should depend, on just what reach it is desired, as a matter of design, that any given equitable interests should have.[79]

---

[78] Insofar as McFarlane himself adopts a perspective, it seems to me (see (2010) 2, 8–9, 28) one of romantic conceptual dogmatism. He takes it—and, I think, wants, almost aesthetically, to take it—that when we label some interests 'common law' and others 'equitable', particular (and distinct) substantive upshots must ineluctably follow. Thus, he presents his analysis as one which 'recognises and celebrates the conceptual distinctiveness of equity in inventing the concept of a right against a right' ((2010) 9); such rights are thus to be credited to 'the genius of equity' (ibid, 2). I certainly reject this perspective. I do so neither from a distaste for aesthetics nor from a view that concepts can never signify per se, but out of a sense that conceptual sounding terms can properly be, and commonly are, used in legal discourse to a variety of ends, and with a variety of kinds of significance (including the rhetorical kind). In particular, I regard it as entirely, and validly, possible for the common law/equity distinction to be a purely historical matter, of no current functional significance. For further reflection on McFarlane's normative perspective, or lack thereof, see C Webb, 'The Double Lives of Property' (2011) 2(1) *Jurisprudence* 205.

[79] The argument here can usefully be read in parallel with that in Gardner (n 41) 99–103.

We can probably group together, as meriting the same treatment in this respect, equitable copies of common law interests: estate contracts (ie equitable freeholds), equitable leases, equitable easements, and so on. As equitable copies of common law rights,[80] these should track the design of their common law counterparts. Given that, nowadays, the latter operate in rem—that is, against non-disponee third parties (Z) as well as disponees (Y)—we should therefore want their equitable copies to do likewise.[81] We would thus conclude, for example, that an equitable tenant should be able to sue in trespass just as much as a legal tenant can; and that the holder of an equitable easement should be able to protect it in nuisance as much as the holder of a legal easement can.[82]

Equitable interests which do not copy legal interests are more interesting. For them, there can be no such presumptive off-the-peg answer. We need to decide exactly how they should operate, on their individual merits. We might want one to affect only disponees (Y), ie to be persistent; another to affect not only disponees but also some, but a limited class, of non-disponees (Z), ie to be in rem, but on only a smallish scale; a third to affect not only disponees but also some, and this time a wider class, of non-disponees (Z), ie to be in rem, on a larger scale. (For a right's impact on non-disponees has almost inevitably to be a matter of degree. It is possible to imagine, in the abstract, a right binding on absolutely everyone whose conduct may injure it, in any way whatsoever: but in practice, this would surely be found grotesquely oppressive.)

Consider restrictive covenants. These are equitable interests with no legal counterparts.[83] Depending on just what work we want them to do, they could be

---

[80] A traditionalist might object that many such equitable interests are, properly speaking, *not* equitable copies of the various common law interests; that the labels ('equitable leases', etc), suggesting otherwise, are in fact misleading shorthand. The objection would be rooted in the idea that where the alleged equitable interest arises via the conversion of a contract to grant the respective legal interest, the equitable interest can be claimed only by one who is entitled to have an order for specific performance of that contract at the time in question. (The *locus classicus* is perhaps *Swain v Ayres* (1888) 21 QBD 289, 295 (CA), Lindley LJ.) But this was never an inevitable position, nor indeed taken literally, nor particularly reflected in the extended expression of conversion, 'equity looks upon that as done which ought to be done'. Nowadays it is much more usual to overlook it, and treat such interests as indeed straightforward equitable copies of their legal counterparts. See Gardner (n 41).

[81] In which case, the only significant difference between the legal and equitable versions rests in the degree of formality required in the transaction giving rise to them: broadly, the legal version needing a grant by deed, and in many cases now also registration, while the equitable version needs only writing. One might well ask why the law should maintain two formality rules in this way, but it certainly could not sensibly be argued that its doing so should be justified by configuring the one type of interest as in rem, the other as only persistent: the formality difference has no functional implication in these terms. The real answer is probably that the law should *not* maintain two formality rules in this way; that instead, it should decide which (if either) it wants, and go with that, thus producing only one type of interest (which would presumably be in rem—there is no reason why that should alter as a result of this exercise). The (England and Wales) Land Registry's 'electronic conveyancing' project can be seen as making this move, if it ever comes about. See further S Gardner with E MacKenzie, *An Introduction to Land Law*, 3rd edn (Oxford, Hart Publishing, 2012) 111–13.

[82] For the current law's restriction of *locus standi* in nuisance to common law proprietors, see *Hunter v Canary Wharf Ltd* [1997] AC 655 (HL).

[83] Though of course they bear certain similarities to legal interests; in *London & Southern Railway Co v Gomm* (n 23) 582, Jessel MR remarked that they could be seen as 'either an extension in equity of the doctrine of *Spencer's Case* [(1583) 5 Co Rep 16a (QB)] to another line of cases, or else an extension in equity of the doctrine of negative easements'.

configured so as to bind disponees (Y) only, or some numbers of non-disponees (Z) as well. The current law tells us that they bind both disponees[84] and those who acquire title to the burdened land by adverse possession:[85] in other words, that they are in rem, to the extent of the latter rule. If that is the limit of their effect on non-disponee third parties, however, their operation in rem is not on a large scale. Indeed, the gist of it may be simply that, although in theory adverse possession extinguishes the previous title and establishes a new one in its place, in reality one who acquires title by adverse possession deserves to be treated in the same way as one who acquires it by disposition. In other words, it may in reality be less a matter of treating restrictive covenants as binding on non-disponees (Z), and more a substantively slight, and perfectly sensible, broadening of the idea of a 'disponee' (Y). The question remains—and indeed the positive law seems to offer no authority either way—whether these interests should operate against other kinds of non-disponees, ie persons whom we might naturally refer to as tortfeasors. Say X creates a covenant in your (adjacent land's) favour, to the effect that a row of trees on her land, which acts as a windblock protecting your crops, shall not be removed or destroyed. There seems no reason to doubt that this covenant will and should bind Y, a disponee from X, or indeed Z_1, who acquires the land by adverse possession in displacement of X or Y. The question is whether it should additionally bind Z_2, an outsider, who destroys the trees by setting fire to them: that is, whether you should be able to sue Z_2 for the damage to your interest, effectively in tort (trespass or negligence).

There is certainly no outright absurdity in the proposition that Z_2 should be bound. On the other hand, there is an argument that she should not. Z_2 will not be surprised that she is liable to the current owner of the land on which the trees were growing (X, or her successor). But she may be surprised to find (if it be the case) that she is additionally liable to you, the adjacent landowner—for quite an unexpected reason, and for quite an unexpected kind of loss. It is arguable that her liability should not have this unexpected dimension. The argument is not self-evidently compulsive; it may well prove too much, for a version of it is surely applicable to the case where Z_2 damages something to whose integrity you are entitled by way of easement, whether equitable or indeed legal (as where you have an easement of support from a building on X/Y's land, and Z_2 tortiously destroys that building); but it is certainly arguable. If we do accept the argument, one way of securing the result it indicates is to design restrictive covenants, as a concept, so that they do not give a right to damages—that is, are persistent rights only—*so far as concerns any impact on a non-disponee of the external tortfeasor variety* (ie on one such as Z_2). But we might not want to limit them in this way *so far as concerns one who acquires the servient land itself by adverse possession* (ie one such as Z_1): she may well be thought of as deserving of damages liability as a true disponee (Y). To that extent, we should want them to operate in rem. And the same may well be true so far as concerns their ability to generate injunctions, *against both an adverse possessor (Z_1) and a tortfeasor (Z_2*—say,

---

[84] *London & South Western Railway Co v Gomm* (n 23) 583.
[85] *Re Nisbet* (n 24).

another neighbour of the servient land, given to lighting bonfires in the vicinity of the trees). Moreover, even to the extent that we may wish to see a non-disponee spared liability—notably, a tortfeasor spared liability in damages—we might regard that end as more elegantly, subtly, achieved not by a blanket rule denying such liability in toto, but by attending to the remoteness (etc) rules of the tort in question, so that Z_2 could be liable to X or her successor, while not to you. If the latter strategy were adopted, there is no reason why restrictive covenants should not, nominally, be fully in rem.

Now consider, as a final case, beneficial interests under trusts. Of the areas we are looking at, these possess the greatest complexity, and so interest.

The heart of the problem is that there exist two rival visions of trusts, having diametrically opposite implications in terms of the issue under discussion. One vision is commonly referred to as the 'obligational' theory.[86] According to this, a trust is (disregarding some matters not presently relevant) a situation in which the asset in question is held by a trustee, but she can or must use it in the way indicated by a set of duties that she owes to the beneficiary (or other, non-personal, object). The other vision is commonly referred to as the 'proprietary' theory.[87] Here, while the asset is nominally vested in the trustee, it is in practical terms owned by the beneficiary (and not this time by a non-personal object, for then it could not be so owned); that is to say, the beneficiary is the equitable owner of the asset, and the trustee's duties are the predicate of this. This last point is the seat of the contrast with the obligational theory. The latter locates the essence of trusts not in the beneficiary's equitable ownership of the asset, but in the trustee's duties to the object. To be sure, where the object is a person, ie a beneficiary, these duties will entail rights on the beneficiary's part. Indeed, it is arguable that where such rights are sufficiently comprehensive, as in a bare trust, they will add up to equitable ownership—though it is also arguable that the vision's very thrust, its focus on the trustee's duties, rules out our regarding a beneficiary as ever having ownership in this way. But, in contrast to the proprietary theory, which as we have seen has a beneficiary's ownership of the asset at its core, the obligational theory claims it to be (at most) inessential to the idea of a trust that either of these things is the case.

The implications of these rival visions for our present purposes are as follows.

If we see the beneficiary as necessarily the *owner* of the trust asset, we must surely treat her interest as in rem rather than merely persistent: ie as effective not only against a disponee of the trust asset (Y), but also against a non-disponee third party such as someone who sets fire to it (Z). This is because effectiveness against

---

[86] Its icons include *Re Denley's Trust Deed* [1969] 1 Ch 373 (Ch D); *Barclays Bank Ltd v Quistclose Investments Ltd* [1970] AC 567 (HL); *McPhail v Doulton* [1971] AC 424 (HL) (note these decisions' interesting proximity in time), as well as the very idea that express trusts exist to effectuate a settlor's wishes.

[87] Its icons include the statutes 1 Ric III c 1 and 27 Hen VIII c 10 (Statute of Uses); *Hopkins v Hopkins* (1739) West temp Hard 606, 619 (Ch); *Burgess v Wheate* (1759) 1 Eden 177, 223 (Ch); *Saunders v Vautier* (1841) Cr & Ph 240 (Ch), together with the Variation of Trusts Act 1958; *Lambe v Eames* (1871) 6 Ch App 597 (CA in Ch); the Settled Land Acts 1882 and 1925; *Re Bowes* [1896] 1 Ch 507 (Ch D); *Re Astor's Settlement Trusts* [1952] Ch 534 (Ch D); *Twinsectra Ltd v Yardley* [2002] UKHL 12, [2002] 2 AC 164, [90]–[91] (HL).

not only the former but also the latter kind of third party is a key part of the very meaning of 'ownership'. To be sure, we are dealing here with *equitable* ownership, but it cannot be that the introduction of 'equitable' should properly make such a radical difference to the import of 'ownership' as would be involved in stripping the latter of this aspect of its meaning. The whole point of the proprietary vision of trusts seems to be an effort to adduce the ordinary—ie common law—meaning of 'ownership'.

By contrast, it would be no surprise if an obligationally envisioned beneficial interest were persistent rather than in rem. That is, if it were effective against Y, but not against Z. Within the universe of equitable interests, the beneficial interest, envisioned thus, is especially well adapted to this possibility. This is because, if the beneficiary has no claim of her own against Z, the trustee—as the legal owner of the asset—nevertheless does, and moreover holds this claim for the beneficiary, so can be required by the beneficiary to honour it and to make over any resultant compensation, or at any rate hold this on trust.[88] At the same time, however, it is not impossible to argue for in rem status after all. This might well be a sensible position where the duties owed to the beneficiary by the trustee do predicate such a comprehensive set of rights as to be appropriately labelled ownership, if this is conceivable at all (*cf* above). It is also a conceivable position even if ownership is not part of the equation, on the basis that it is unsatisfactory to leave protection against Z to the trustee. This could be the case on account of a number of deficiencies in the latter approach. One might be its gratuitous complexity: what is the advantage in requiring the beneficiary to deal with the Z problem via his trustee, rather than directly? Another, its possible technical insufficiency: if protection against Z did take the form of an action by the trustee, by what calculus would the damage to the beneficiary's interests, rather than merely the trustee's own, come into the picture at all?[89]

In my view it would be quite wrong to take sides, as some (including this chapter's anonymous referee) urge, between the two visions of trusts. While certainly incompatible, they nonetheless coexist as authentic expressions of the express trust

---

[88] Indeed, we might see the obligational vision as positively pointing away from status in rem, on the ground that it portrays the beneficiary as less having an interest (such as could be in rem) than being the object of the trustee's duties. But this argument may take us too far, as it could imply that the beneficial right should not even be persistent, which everyone agrees it is. This difficulty with the vision probably merits further reflection.

[89] The answer offered in *Shell UK Ltd* (n 47) [142] (CA) is that so far as concerns the tort of negligence, Z owes a duty of care directly to the beneficiary. Such an attempt to justify the recovery of the beneficiary's loss is something of a novelty. Certainly, it has long been the law that one in breach of a contract with a trustee has to pay the trustee damages calculated by reference not merely to the trustee's personal loss, but to the loss suffered by his beneficiary: see *Lloyd's v Harper* (1880) 16 Ch D 290 (CA); *Woodar Investment Development Ltd v Wimpey Construction UK Ltd* [1980] 1 WLR 277, 283 (HL); *Pan Atlantic Insurance Co Ltd v Pine Top Insurance Co Ltd* [1988] 2 Lloyd's Rep 505 (QBD), affirmed [1989] 1 Lloyd's Rep 568 (CA) (introducing, however, what appears to be a plausible remoteness control); *Darlington Borough Council v Wiltshier Northern Ltd* [1995] 1 WLR 68, 73 (CA); *Chappell v Somers & Blake* [2003] EWHC 1644 (Ch), [2004] Ch 19 (Ch D); *Malkins Nominees Ltd v Société Financière Mirelis SA* [2004] EWHC 2631 (Ch) [43]–[59]. And the *Darlington* and *Malkins* decisions clearly envisaged the same rule as obtaining not only in contract but also, analogously, in tort (negligence). None of these earlier treatments, however, offered a satisfactory justificatory analysis for the rule, in either context. (In the contractual context, the possibility of the beneficiary proceeding via the Contracts (Rights of Third Parties) Act 1999 has refocused, but not obviously solved, the problem.)

project. Both have considerable support in the sources and, above all, are indicated by serious considerations of principle.[90] As might therefore be expected, the law's handling of the question whether beneficial interests are persistent or in rem is equivocal. As observed earlier, the headline account is to the effect that they are persistent only, in that the beneficiary—as opposed to the trustee—cannot enforce against Z;[91] a position which, as we have just seen, appears to make sense only if one adopts the obligational vision. But that is not the whole story. Other pieces of information suggest a perspective in which the beneficiary comes at least close to being able to proceed against Z directly—in fact probably as close as could be, without reversing the headline rule altogether. Unsurprisingly, these pieces of information prominently include rules addressing the two inadequacies of the obligational/persistent vision identified a moment ago. One of these is the rule whereby, if a beneficiary wishes to see Z sued, but her trustee is reluctant to do so, she does not literally have to obtain an order against her trustee requiring the latter to oblige; she can simply proceed against Z in her own name, joining her reluctant trustee as co-defendant.[92] Alongside this is a rule whereby, when Z is sued, the loss recoverable from her is definitely that suffered by the beneficiary, not simply that suffered by the trustee personally.[93] These rules certainly tend in the direction of according beneficial interests in rem effect. As noted earlier, it may be possible to reconcile such a position with the obligational theory of trusts, but it is certainly predicted and indeed required by the proprietary theory. Given the undoubted power (whether or not dominance) of the latter, it is very far from unexpected that beneficial interests should have at least quasi-in rem status in this way.

To summarise. In Parts II and III of this chapter we saw that equitable rights are sometimes effective against a non-disponee third party (Z), whether or not against a disponee (Y) as well, and that there exists the technical capacity for this to be so (if indeed this be a meaningful or significant additional remark). Now we have seen, as regards a selection of equitable rights, that there exists at least a plausible case, in functional terms, for wishing to see such effect. Thus far, then, we have assembled what appears to be a convincing enough set of reasons to claim that equitable interests ought to be able to exist in rem.

But not that they should always do so. It is an important message of the foregoing that the nature of equitable interests (and indeed of common law interests: remember

---

[90] For more, see Gardner (n 19) 216–29.

[91] *The Aliakmon* (n 22) (negligence); *MCC Proceeds Inc* (n 22) (conversion).

[92] *Vandepitte v Preferred Accident Insurance Corporation of New York* [1933] AC 70, 79 (PC).

[93] At any rate where Z is liable in negligence: *Shell UK Ltd* (n 47); likewise where a trustee contracts with a third party, who breaches, and is sued for damages, as shown by the decisions cited in n 89. (It is as well to address a complication regarding this issue. Sometimes the trustee will be liable to the beneficiary for the loss, in that its occurrence through the actions of Z involves a breach of the trustee's own trust duties. For example, if a trustee of a valuable painting takes insufficient care of it, and it is negligently damaged by Z, the trustee will be liable to the beneficiary for the loss caused by Z's act. Under circumstances like these, the trustee's personal loss—reckoned by reference to her potential liability to the beneficiary—will be the same as the beneficiary's loss. And then, saying that Z is liable for the trustee's personal loss will be no different from saying that she is liable for the beneficiary's loss. But not all cases are like this. Say Z negligently damages the painting despite the trustee having taken proper care of it. Then, the trustee will not be liable to the beneficiary for the loss, so the latter's loss will not count in the trustee's personal loss. Here, therefore, we return to the issue canvassed in the text, of the choice to be made between redressing the trustee's personal loss and—this now being different—that suffered by the beneficiary.)

leases, discussed in section A of Part II) in this respect is not pre-ordained, but has to be decided by reference to what is most appropriate for the job they are put in place to do. And, further, that deciding that they should be 'persistent' or 'in rem' does not take us the whole way. If 'in rem', there is the further question of just which non-disponee third parties (Z)—persons whose behaviour may impinge on them—are to be bound by them. Likewise, indeed, if they are to be 'persistent', there is the further question of just which disponees (Y) they are to catch. (Where their subject matter is personalty, the answer to that question, so far as equitable interests are concerned, lies theoretically in the doctrine of 'notice', which however has such latitude as to be little of a practical answer at all—further specification is provided by thinking about what is appropriate to the kind of interest at issue, as well as contextual considerations.[94] Where the subject matter is land of registered title, the answer is supplied by the rules of the Land Registration Act 2002, which, though apparently more formulaic, none-theless contain a degree of latitude of their own.[95])

In truth, it might therefore be better not to see the category of 'interests' (ie rights capable of binding at least disponees) as simply divided into two classes, 'rights in rem' and 'persistent rights'. It is more subtly accurate, and quite possibly more illu-minating, to see it rather as involving independent continua along the two axes of 'operation against disponees (Y)' and 'operation against non-disponee third parties (Z)' ... with the added quirk that while those acquiring title by adverse possession officially count as among the latter, there is every temptation to treat them as among the former.[96]

B. The 'Conceptual Test'/*Numerus Clausus* Issue

As will be remembered, it is an element of McFarlane's thesis that while equitable interests/persistent rights must comply with his 'conceptual test', ie must 'relate to' a right (claim-right or power) originally enjoyed by X, they are not subject to the *numerus clausus* principle. (While the converse is true of common law interests/rights in rem, which must 'relate to' a physical thing.) We have seen that the positive law, whether viewed narrowly or more widely, does not reflect these claims. The question now is whether it should do so.

McFarlane regards 'equitable interests' and 'persistent rights' as coterminous, so his treatment brackets these categories together, but we have seen this to be incor-rect. Equitable interests can operate persistently or they can operate in rem. Equally, rights that operate persistently can be equitable or they can be legal. So in conducting the present inquiry, we have to think separately about persistent rights as opposed to rights in rem, and about equitable interests as opposed to legal interests.

First, the 'conceptual test' aspect of the question, ie the demand that a right behaving persistently or an equitable interest should 'relate to' a 'right' and not to a

---

[94] See, eg, S Gardner, 'Knowing Assistance and Knowing Receipt: Taking Stock' (1996) 112 *LQR* 56, 60–64; and more recently *Armstrong DLW GmbH* (n 37) [111]–[123].

[95] See eg, N Jackson, 'Title by Registration and Concealed Overriding Interests: The Cause and Effect of Antipathy to Documentary Proof' (2003) 119 *LQR* 660.

[96] See the text following n 85 above.

'thing'. Remember (see section C of Part I and section D of Part II) that McFarlane himself uses these key terms in special, and ultimately unsatisfactory, ways. We shall approach the matter by instead giving them externally referenced meanings. Doing so: to put it no higher, I cannot see why, as a matter of good legal design, McFarlane should be right. I cannot for example see why, in the real world, a right sensibly describable as 'relating to' a physical thing should be capable of binding Y *so long as it binds other third parties (Z) too* (ie should be capable of operating in rem), but incapable of binding Y *alone* (ie should be incapable of operating persistently). Nor why it should be fine for a right sensibly describable as 'relating to' an abstract asset, such as a credit, to be capable of binding Y, but unacceptable for it to bind Z as well (ie why it can only be persistent, and cannot possibly be in rem). I am even less able to see why, as a matter of good legal design, an equitable interest should necessarily need to operate persistently, a common law interest fully in rem. So, while I may be wrong, I am certainly inclined to conclude that (therefore) these positions of McFarlane's cannot be sustained.

Then the *numerus clausus* aspect of the question. The way into this ought to be to establish the point of the *numerus clausus* principle, then see whether that point is or is not relevant to persistent rights/equitable interests. But, to put it shortly, nobody knows the point of the *numerus clausus* principle.[97] Of course, the various writings about it mostly[98] claim that they do. But they dispute the matter among themselves, and it seems fair to say that none has landed the knock-out punch; so far as any idea of 'victory' goes, all we have is the chronological sequence, whereby one of them necessarily has the last (for the moment) word. For the purposes of the present inquiry, however, this is unimportant. What is important is that at least the best known of them generally consider, or at least assume, that the principle operates, sensibly or otherwise,[99] to regulate the class of interests effective against *disponees* (Y)[100]—whether or not those effective against non-disponee third parties (Z) as

---

[97] Which raises an intriguing possibility. Whenever a person is deprived of her home, ECHR Art 8 is engaged. If the deprivation is the result of applying some rule of domestic law, it will be defensible only if the rule is a proportionate means of achieving a legitimate end. So if a rule results in such a deprivation because it makes the person's right one in personam only, it will be defensible only if that is a proportionate means of achieving a legitimate end. If it makes the person's right one in personam only because the right does not feature in the *numerus clausus*, it will be defensible only if the *numerus clausus* principle is a proportionate means of achieving a legitimate end. And if we do not know the point of the *numerus clausus* principle, that cannot be shown. The result would be that rights in personam to one's home are logically impossible.

[98] The notable exception being B Rudden, 'Economic Theory v. Property Law: The *Numerus Clausus* Problem' in J Eekelaar and J Bell (eds), *Oxford Essays in Jurisprudence, Third Series* (Oxford, Oxford University Press, 1987) ch 11. B Akkermans, *The Principle of Numerus Clausus in European Property Law* (Antwerp and Oxford, Intersentia, 2008) offers no suggestion either, but does not set out to do so.

[99] Least convinced of its operational good sense are perhaps Rudden (n 98) and R Epstein, 'Notice and Freedom of Contract in the Law of Servitudes' (1981–82) 55 *Southern California Law Review* 1353.

[100] Unusual in this respect is H Dagan, 'The Craft of Property' (2003) 91 *California Law Review* 1517, which (at 1565–71) treats the principle as principally controlling the repertoire of property institutions *as they arise between the original parties* (in my terms, X and you). There is also more than a trace of the same perspective—albeit (it appears) unwittingly adopted—in J Singer, 'Democratic Estates: Property Law in a Free and Democratic Society' (2009) 94 *Cornell Law Review* 1009.

well.[101,102] That is to say, in terms of the present exercise, they treat the principle as aimed at persistent rights as well as at rights in rem.[103]

If these writings' understanding of the point of the *numerus clausus* principle is sustainable, McFarlane is wrong to see the principle as not appropriately to be applied to persistent rights. And I know of no reason to think that it is not sustainable.

McFarlane himself comes at the question via the assertion[104] that 'the basic principle underlying the *numerus clausus* [is] that a new duty or liability should not be imposed on [a third party][105] simply because of the conduct of others', these others being the creator(s) of the putative duty or liability, ie X and perhaps also you. The concern expressed by this 'basic principle', then, is relevant both to rights in rem and to persistent rights. McFarlane sees a divergence between the two kinds of interests, however, in point of the means by which the concern is to be addressed, so as to allow the imposition of a duty or liability on a third party in some cases after all. In the case of rights in rem, he sees the concern as to be addressed in a consequentialist way, as represented by the *numerus clausus* principle. In the case of persistent rights, however, he sees it as to be addressed rather in a conceptual way: that is, by reference to such rights' very conceptual make-up, viz the fact that they relate to a claim-right or power enjoyed by X in respect of some asset.[106] In other words (I think), he views the concern under discussion as automatically overcome in the

---

[101] This group includes the following distinguished efforts: Epstein (n 99); (I think, implicitly) M Heller, 'The Boundaries of Private Property' (1999) 108 *Yale Law Journal* 1163; T Merrill and H Smith, 'Optimal Standardization in the Law of Property: The *Numerus Clausus* Principle' (2000) 110 *Yale Law Journal* 1; H Hansmann and R Kraakman, 'Property, Contract, and Verification: The *Numerus Clausus* Problem and the Divisibility of Rights' (2002) 31 *Journal of Legal Studies* S373; B Edgeworth, 'The *Numerus Clausus* Principle in Contemporary Australian Property Law' (2006) 32 *Monash University Law Review* 387; N Davidson, 'Standardization and Pluralism in Property Law' (2008) 61 *Vanderbilt Law Review* 1597; Singer (n 100); A Dorfman, 'Property and Collective Undertaking: The Principle of *Numerus Clausus*' (2011) 61 *University of Toronto Law Journal* 467.

[102] Hansmann and Kraakman (n 101) S409–S411 undertake a rare explicit inquiry into the question whether the principles aims to protect Z, as opposed to Y. (As a matter of interest—it does not affect the present argument—they conclude not, at any rate where Z is a tortfeasor. They do so because the liability which Z would incur under a right in rem adds nothing to the liability to which she is exposed anyway. For example, her burning down the trees on X's land is a tort against X, and so is something not to be done, regardless of whether it is additionally a tort against you, by virtue of your—hypothetically in rem—restrictive covenant. This seems incorrect, however. Any liability Z owes to you does add something to the liability she owes X. It is not sufficient simply to say that she should not be burning down the trees in the first place. It is right, required by Rule of Law precepts, that the consequences of her doing so should be reasonably predictable.)

[103] The great majority regard the principle as aimed wholly or partly at preventing such functional damage as might ensue if rights binding upon disponees could be created *ad libidem*. Of these, some focus purely on economic damage: Rudden (n 98); Epstein (n 99); Merrill and Smith (n 101); and Hansmann and Kraakman (n 101). Others emphasise the likely importance of other considerations: especially Edgeworth (n 101); Davidson (n 101); and Singer (n 100), pointing, in a neo-republican manner, to the (excessive/improper) restriction of the disponee's freedom regarding the use of the asset in question. (See too Harris (n 73) 470–74.) A different slant is however taken by Dorfman (n 101), who views the principle as aimed not at preventing bad functional consequences, but at ensuring that rights can generate obligations on third parties only where acceptance by a democratic legislature gives them the political licence to do so.

[104] (2011) 326. For other statements to similar effect, see 315 and 330.

[105] In the original, 'X'. My translation of 'X' as 'a third party' suggests that 'X' can be either a disponee (my Y) or a non-disponee third party (my Z). This reading is supported by McFarlane's text (2011) 315 and 324, and it is confirmed by private communication between us.

[106] (2011) especially 319–20.

case of any right relating to X's claim-right or power regarding an asset, on the strength of the right's very characteristic as such.

The question for us is whether this vision would make for better law than the existing position, whereby, as regards both rights in rem and persistent rights, the concern is addressed by the *numerus clausus* principle. For myself, the short answer is that I can see no reason why it should do so.

Certainly, if calling the one device 'consequentialist' and the other 'conceptual' is intended to represent an argument in support of the vision (I am not sure if it is), it seems to me to fall short of doing so. In particular, if 'consequentialist' is good enough for rights in rem (ie those effective against both Y and Z), I cannot see why it should not be so for persistent rights (those effective against Y alone) too.

McFarlane may offer another suggestion, unless it is another way of putting the same suggestion. He seems to claim[107] that his approach to persistent rights permits greater 'flexibility' as to their possible content than would be the case if the *numerus clausus* principle were applied to them. Presumably because, receiving no attention from the *numerus clausus* principle, a persistent right can have any content the person(s) creating it (X and perhaps you) may desire, just so long as it relates to a claim-right or a power originally enjoyed by X. But, assuming that this is a correct reading of McFarlane's position, the question for our purposes is: should we regard this 'flexibility' as a good thing; as more desirable than the less 'flexible' position that would prevail if the *numerus clausus* principle applied?

I suppose by way of suggesting an affirmative answer to this question, McFarlane points us to the trust.[108] He avers that trusts (ie trustees' duties, beneficiaries' rights) can be configured in quite an *ad libidem* sort of way, and that the trust device is 'widely admired' in consequence. In particular, he instances the way that land ownership (the fee simple absolute in possession) cannot be fragmented at law, thanks to the *numerus clausus*; but in effect can be under a trust. But this seems to me an unfortunate example, for three reasons.[109]

First, because the reasons why legal fragmentation is no longer (as it once was) tolerated—notably the damage to the market (note the focus on disponees, Y, rather than non-disponee third parties, Z)—would as a matter of principle apply just as much to equitable fragmentation, if the equitable fragments were indeed seriously persistent rights. The point, and so the reason that equitable fragmentation is tolerated, is that they are actually *not* seriously persistent rights. By virtue both of overreaching, and of a number of other rules combining to make it really quite unlikely that a disponee will end up bound, equitable fragments are quite a long way from being seriously persistent.[110] Second, because the idea that trust rights can be configured *ad libidem* is very much aligned with the 'obligational' vision of trusts (see section A of Part IV), as opposed to the rival 'proprietary' vision, under which the only shape they can take is 'ownership' (albeit that there may be some unclarity as to the meaning of the latter in this context, and thus some latitude as to what this 'only shape' may involve).

---

[107] (2011) 320.

[108] Ibid.

[109] There is also the curiosity that, using my nomenclature, the person originally subject to the duty in question, X, is not—as she generally is (eg the landlord, in the case of a lease)—the most obvious candidate for its creator: for she is the trustee, rather than the settlor. But I am not sure that this matters.

[110] Gardner with MacKenzie (n 81) 359–77.

To put it at its lowest, the 'proprietary' vision is not to be neglected in this way. And third, because the bulk of the ways in which a trustee can be subjected to individually configured duties do not yield persistent rights anyway. It is well known, and agreed by McFarlane, that only a trustee's 'core' duties (something like, the duties not to treat the property as her own, and to safeguard it) can bind a disponee.[111] Such 'flexibility' as the trust device possesses is a function mainly of the remaining duties, which are effective only against a properly appointed trustee.

These three points show McFarlane's sponsorship of 'flexibility' in persistent rights not to be well supported by reference to the trust device, at any rate as the latter currently obtains: even if it is 'widely admired', it is not especially 'flexible', at any rate in a way germane to the present discussion. I am not sure that there is any other type of persistent right to which one could point in the trust's place, as an icon of widely admired 'flexibility'. All the other types (eg—if indeed these are merely persistent—equitable leases, equitable easements) copy rights in rem, and as such conform to the *numerus clausus*.

Lacking such an icon, we are left to make an abstract assessment of the proposition that, while rights in rem should be subject to the *numerus clausus* principle, persistent rights ought to be allowed 'flexibility' in their content. I cannot think of any reason why our assessment should be favourable. Quite simply, in terms of the mischief(s) against which the *numerus clausus* principle is commonly regarded as aimed, as explored above, 'flexibility' sounds like another name for the problem, not its solution.

The discussion thus far has focused on the relevance of the *numerus clausus* principle to persistent rights. McFarlane regards persistent rights as coterminous with equitable interests, but since, as noted, we find ourselves having to separate the two, we must finally consider any arguments that might arise against the exposure to the *numerus clausus* principle of *equitable* interests. I have failed to think of any such arguments. Remember that the principle seems to be aimed at regulating the impact that rights have on persons other than their creators. Given all the preceding discussion, to classify a right as equitable rather than legal gives us no help at all in deciding what, if any, such impact we should want it to have. So the classification should be irrelevant to the question of the principle's applicability.

V. MCFARLANE'S ERROR

We should therefore regard McFarlane's thesis as being marked by error, on all the three planes addressed in Parts II–IV. Though in the nature of things, it is of course easier to say this firmly in respect of the first plane than of the second, and of the second than of the third; the element of opinion grows as one proceeds through the series.

The following remarks expand upon this statement.

A. The Identity, and (Un)Importance, of the Key Error

We have seen (in Part II) that equity (and for that matter also the common law) has in its repertoire both the classes of interest in which McFarlane deals: not only

---

[111] See n 19 above.

persistent rights but also, contrary to his thesis, rights in rem. Again contrary to his thesis, we have also seen (in Part III) that there is no technical reason, and (in Part IV) no reason of principle, why it should not do so. Further, and once more contrary to McFarlane's thesis, we have seen (in Parts II and III) that persistent rights are subject to the *numerus clausus* principle, just as rights in rem are; and (in Part IV) that no reason of principle appears as to why this should be the case.

It would however be wrong to rush to conclude that McFarlane's thesis is, therefore, quite devoid of merit. Aside from its eccentric position on the *numerus clausus* issue—and one cannot ultimately accuse it of worse than eccentricity, as, to repeat, nobody really knows exactly what to make of that issue—it has only one serious weakness: its quadration of persistent rights with equitable interests, and rights in rem with common law interests. If we remove this common law/equity axis, nothing that remains is fundamentally problematic. There may be odd further infelicities, but nothing irreparable; and none of us can claim to do better than that.

Of course it might be objected that, if we remove the common law/equity axis, nothing remains of great value either: that it is hardly momentous to conclude that some interests are and ought to be (what McFarlane calls) persistent, others (what he calls) in rem, at any rate so long as we are prepared to regard these categories as continua rather than simple points, as explained at the end of section A of Part IV. This would be a smug rejoinder, however. McFarlane has done a great service in bringing the contrast between persistent rights and rights in rem into focus; indeed, in drawing attention to the possibility, and existence, of persistent rights at all—the material preceding his writings almost entirely overlooked them, as a discrete idea if not as a matter of fact. It is most welcome to have been prompted in this way to notice and, in consequence, examine them, as part of the law's repertoire.

B. The Nature of the Error

At the same time as pinning down its key error in this way, it is useful to reflect more abstractly on the manner in which McFarlane went astray. Other perspectives may be equally possible, but here is one.

McFarlane's analysis can be viewed as rooting into a realist, nominally Hohfeldian, vision, whereby 'property' is to be seen as a 'bundle of sticks'. Put more prosaically and exactly, 'property' is to be seen as a set of rights and other jural relations—this is key: the 'sticks' are all forms of interpersonal legal relations—that can be disaggregated, and moreover configured, and deployed, individually.[112] As can readily be appreciated, this vision provides a sympathetic matrix for the insight that 'interests' do not have to operate uniformly in rem, ie be potentially effective against all kinds of third parties (Y and Z), but can instead be persistent, ie be potentially effective against disponees (Y), but not other third parties (Z). So far, so good.

Where McFarlane goes wrong is (it seems to me) in using the realist toolbox in a formalist way. Ultimately, he appears to present the incidence of the different classes of interest as determined not by real-world reasons, as canvassed in Part IV

---

[112] For a fuller exegesis, with further references, see Dagan (n 100) 1531–32.

of this chapter,[113] but by the conceptual-dogmatic determinant of whether they were devised by a court of common law or of equity.[114] This is the same error as Professor Dagan perceives in the reasoning of the majority of the US Supreme Court in *United States v Craft*[115] and against which he writes as follows:

> Property theorists usually invoke the bundle of sticks understanding in an effort to examine critically the existing content of property rights and thus liberate property law from the confines of sheer form. The bundle metaphor captures the truism that property is an artifact, a human creation that can be, and has been, modified in accordance with human needs and values. There is neither an a priori list of entitlements that the owner of a given resource inevitably enjoys nor an exhaustive list of resources that enjoy the status of property. Property can take different configurations, which are not necessarily all manifested in the existing doctrine. Therefore, we cannot resolve legal debates by sheer reference to property's existing forms. As legal realists argue, legal decision makers have no choice but to shape the particular configuration of property for the issue at hand, thus making inevitable the application of normative judgment. Rather than resorting to internal deductive reasoning, decision makers must ask whether it is justified that a certain category of people (i.e., owners) will enjoy a particular right, privilege, power, or immunity over a category of resources (land, chattels, copyrights, patents, and so on) as against another category of people (spouses, neighbors, strangers, community members, and so on) ... [U]nderstanding property as bundles can and should liberate us from the imaginary methodology of deduction from frozen forms. But it cannot substitute for normative analysis. The whole point of the bundle metaphor, after all, is to trigger such an analysis.[116]

C. The Aetiology of the Error

So much for the identity, (un)importance and nature of McFarlane's error. Would it be presumptuous to reflect also on its aetiology? At the risk of that, let me venture that it is an instance of hubris[117] ... and commend it as such. Without hubris, we

---

[113] But also as canvassed in Part III, namely the legal-institutional fit between the proposed incidence of the different classes of interest and surrounding legal rules. It seems to me likely that a thoughtful and sophisticated realist such as Dagan would recognise such fit as entering into the normative reckoning required to fix the shape of a particular institution.

[114] See at n 78 above.

[115] *United States v Craft*, 535 US 274 (2002).

[116] Dagan (n 100) 1552–54 (original footnotes omitted).

[117] Though more mundanely, it seems also aimed at making at any rate trusts fit for export to civil law jurisdictions ((2010) 3, 9, 28)—in aspiring to show that, as merely persistent rights, they require no abandonment of these systems' insistence that the class of rights in rem should be closed (the *numerus clausus* principle). The delivery of this project would require solutions to two principal problems. (1) As we have seen, there is no reason to think that persistent rights are exempt from the *numerus clausus* principle (section C of Part II, section A of Part III), or indeed that they should be (section B of Part IV). This difficulty might be overcome by noticing that the discussion here has been about the *numerus clausus* principle *in the common law*, and speculating that the principle may play differently— without reference to persistent rights—*in the civil law*. I offer no assessment of the prospects of this argument. (2) As we have also seen (see section A of Part IV), English trust interests are at best only uneasily persistent. The solution here might be to produce an export (as it were, left-hand-drive) model of the 'trust': one whose interests are definitely persistent rather than in rem. (Such a move may be discernible in the ideas of 'trusts' adopted in the *Hague Convention on the Law Applicable to Trusts and on their Recognition*, and in the *Principles, Definition and Model Rules of European Private Law: Draft Common Frame of Reference*. These certainly privilege the 'obligational' perspective. As section A of Part IV explains, although this perspective does not entail that the resultant interests must be persistent rather

should be much the worse off. Icarus displayed it, or a form of it, when, having covered his arms with feathers bedded in wax, he flew; but, approaching the sun so closely as to melt the wax, lost his feathers and fell. He of course ended up dead. But so do we all in the end. What distinguishes us is the manner of our living and dying. Icarus strikes us as special in, perhaps inter alia, having epitomised the aspiration to fly—more generally, in the words of one of the foremost poets of Victorian Britain (and where would one sooner seek hubris?), the idea that 'a man's reach should exceed his grasp'.[118] Special enough, indeed, to be memorialised in a poem by one of the greatest writers of Augustine Rome[119] and in a painting attributed to one of the greatest painters of the Flemish renaissance[120] (though it is fair, but intriguing, to note that neither exactly invites us to celebrate Icarus's daring[121]). McFarlane can count himself in impressive, if mythical, company.

But the vision which I nonetheless prefer—and so am happy to discern in the material under discussion—is not without a greatness of its own; a greatness that seeks, and perhaps receives, less attention, but is nonetheless perceptible. I know of no better expression and celebration of it than this:

> Glory be to God for dappled things—
>   For skies of couple-colour as a brinded cow;
>   For rose-moles all in stipple upon trout that swim;
> Fresh-firecoal chestnut-falls; finches' wings;
>   Landscape plotted and pieced—fold, fallow, and plough;
>   And áll trádes, their gear and tackle and trim.
>
> All things counter, original, spare, strange;
>   Whatever is fickle, freckled (who knows how?)
>   With swift, slow; sweet, sour; adazzle, dim;
> He fathers-forth whose beauty is past change:
>   Praise him.[122]

than in rem, it is a necessary precondition to that position.) Notice, however, that this solution can be had on an entirely pragmatic basis, requiring no invocation of the (as we have seen, corrupt) proposal of principle that, as equitable concepts, trusts necessarily, intrinsically, operate persistently. But perhaps there is a marketing issue here....

[118] 'Ah, but a man's reach should exceed his grasp,/Or what's a heaven for?' Robert Browning, 'Andrea del Sarto' in *Men and Women* (London, Chapman & Hall, 1855) lines 97–98.

[119] Publius Ouidius Naso *Metamorphoses* viii 183–285: http://etext.virginia.edu/latin/ovid/trans/Ovhome.htm.

[120] ? Peter Bruegel the Elder [*Landscape with the Fall of Icarus*] ? 1569, Musée des Beaux-Arts, Brussels: http://www.fine-arts-museum.be/fabritiusweb/FullBBBody.csp?SearchMethod=Find_1&Profile=Default&OpacLanguage=fre&RequestId=26132_4&RecordNumber=1.

[121] See further the two fine poems inspired by ? Bruegel's painting (n 110 above); WH Auden, 'Musée des Beaux Arts' in *Another Time* (London and New York, 1940), http://english.emory.edu/classes/paintings&poems/auden.html; William Carlos Williams, 'Landscape with the Fall of Icarus' in *Pictures from Brueghel and Other Poems* (Norfolk, CT, J Laughlin, 1962), http://english.emory.edu/classes/paintings&poems/williams.html. With their individual voices and nuances, these seem to me to invite us to attend to hubris's aftermath, the fall that follows the pride; to notice its ordinariness, the ease with which it takes its place in the general run of things; and to feel all right, even good, about this. And so, most interestingly, to connect to or resonate with the perception suggested in the following paragraph of the text.

[122] Gerard Manley Hopkins Hopkins, 'Pied Beauty' (1877) in R Bridges (ed), *Poems of Gerard Manley Hopkins* (London, Humphrey Milford, 1918) # 13. I myself especially love the turn, in the penultimate line, which seems to me both to point up the nobility of what goes before, and to hint that even its contingency is itself contingent.

16

The Content of a Freehold:
A 'Right to Use' Land?

SIMON DOUGLAS[*]

I. INTRODUCTION

A 'FREEHOLD', OR 'fee simple absolute in possession', is the best type of right that one can have in respect of land. A freeholder, in colloquial terms, is an 'owner' of the land.[1] Despite the importance of this right, surprisingly little is written about its content. Whilst most textbooks give a detailed account of the rules governing the conveyance of this right, the methods of protecting it and how a freeholder can create lesser interests (such as leases) from it, very little is said about what the freeholder is actually entitled to do in respect of his land.[2] This is quite striking when one considers how much is written about the content of lesser rights: what the holder of an easement, restrictive covenant or security interest, for example, is entitled to do is set out in full in most textbooks. The absence of a detailed account of the content of the freehold right may result from the fact that we have a strong intuitive grasp of what it means to own land, and it may be difficult to express this in legal terminology. However, whilst it may be difficult for the law to cognise the full extent of this right, it is by no means impossible. The general aim of this piece, therefore, is to say something about the content of the freehold right.

The more specific question that this chapter aims to answer is whether it is correct to say that a freeholder has a 'right to use' his land. Many accounts of the concept of 'ownership' or 'property' have argued that an owner's right consists, solely or primarily, of a 'right to exclude' others from his thing. Writing in this tradition, Cohen argued: 'Private property may or may not involve a right to use something for oneself … but whatever else it involves, it must at least involve a right to exclude others.'[3] This 'exclusion' thesis has been extremely influential in attempts to describe the content of property rights.[4] However, there is an alternative line of argument that

---

[*] Peter Clarke Fellow and Tutor in Law, Jesus College, University of Oxford. I am very grateful to John Murphy, Roderick Bagshaw, Donal Nolan and the anonymous referee for their helpful comments on this chapter.

[1] See J Harris, 'Ownership of Land in English Law' in N McCormick and P Birks (eds), *The Legal Mind-Essays for Tony Honoré* (Oxford, Oxford University Press, 1986).

[2] The point made here is in relation to doctrinal accounts of the freehold right. Jurisprudential accounts of the more abstract concept of 'ownership' are ubiquitous.

[3] F Cohen, 'Dialogue on Private Property' (1954) 9 *Rutgers Law Review* 357, 371.

[4] See, for example, T Merrill, 'Property and the Right to Exclude' (1998) 77 *Nebraska Law Review* 730; and J Penner, *The Idea of Property in Law* (Oxford, Clarendon Press, 1997).

has sought to emphasise not the owner's ability to exclude others from his thing, but his ability to use his thing himself. For example, Clarke has written:

> To say that the defining characteristic of my ownership of a book is my right to exclude you from it is an extraordinarily negative, and potentially misleading, way of putting it. On the whole, the importance to me of book-owning is that it gives me free use of the book— I can read it whenever I want, or put it on the shelf to admire it.[5]

Honoré similarly argued that the 'right to use' is 'a cardinal feature of ownership' in his seminal article on the topic.[6] The purpose of this chapter is to ask whether this purported right, the 'right to use', has any legal content in the context of the freehold: is it correct to say that a freeholder (A) has a legal relationship with the rest of the world (B, C, D, etc) which can accurately be described as a 'right to use'?

The difficulty in answering this question is the ambiguity latent in the word 'right'. This word is frequently used to describe completely different types of legal relationships. When a freeholder, A, asserts that he has a 'right to use' his land against the rest of the world, it is not clear what type of legal relationship A is actually asserting against B, C, D, etc. The second part of this chapter will address this issue by introducing a Hohfeldian account of the different types of legal relationship that A could be asserting. We will see that there are two possibilities: first, A may be asserting that he has 'liberties' to use his land; second, he may be asserting that B, C, D, etc are under a 'duty' not to impair A's ability to use his land. 'Liberties' and 'duties' are very different types of legal relationships, so it is important to distinguish between them from the outset. The third and fourth parts of this chapter will then consider the evidence for each type of legal relationship.

II. DEFINING A 'RIGHT TO USE'

The word 'right' is frequently used to describe completely different types of legal relationships. Hohfeld saw this indiscriminate usage as a peril to clear thought and, in his famous account of rights,[7] he sought to distinguish these different legal relationships. First, he noted that one common way in which the word 'right' is used is to describe a legal duty owed by another. For example, if A is in a contractual relationship with B, under which B is bound to pay A £100, A's contractual 'right' is actually a shorthand description of a legal duty owed by B: it describes B's legal duty to pay A £100. Hohfeld suggested that this type of right be labelled a 'claim-right'.[8] This means is that if A asserts that he has a 'right' against B, this right is a claim-right if A is actually asserting that B owes A a legal 'duty' to behave in a certain way. A claim-right can therefore be described using the following formula:

A has a 'right' against B = B owes A a legal 'duty' to behave in a certain way.

---

[5] A Clarke, 'Use, Time and Entitlement' (2004) 57 *Current Legal Problems* 239, 241–2.
[6] A Honoré, 'Ownership' in A Guest (ed), *Oxford Essays in Jurisprudence* (Oxford, Clarendon Press, 1961) 116. See also J Harris, *Property and Justice* (Oxford, Oxford University Press, 1996) 30.
[7] W Hohfeld, 'Some Fundamental Legal Conceptions as Applied in Judicial Reasoning' (1913–14) 23 *Yale Law Journal* 16.
[8] Ibid, 32.

This usage of the word 'right' is extremely common. To give just one recent example, in *Campbell v MGN Ltd*,[9] the defendant had published information which gave details of therapy that the claimant, a celebrity, had received at a drug addiction group. The claimant repeatedly asserted that she had a '*right* to respect for private and family life'.[10] What the claimant was actually asserting when she claimed such a 'right' was that the defendant was under a legal 'duty' to the claimant to behave in a certain way, ie a duty to refrain from disclosing private information. This is clear from the fact that this 'right' asserted by the claimant was frequently translated into a 'duty of confidentiality' on the defendant.[11] The claimant's 'right' therefore denoted the defendant's 'duty' to behave in a certain way.

A second way in which the word 'right' is sometimes used is to describe the fact that the right-holder himself is permitted to behave in a certain way. An example of this would be the oft-repeated 'right to silence'. If A, suspected of committing a crime, is arrested by B, it is commonly said that A has a 'right to silence'. A's 'right' in this example is not a claim-right because it does not describe a legal duty owed by B. Rather, A is asserting that he himself is under no legal duty to B to behave in a certain way, ie he is under no duty to B to incriminate himself. The absence of this duty means that A is permitted to behave how he likes, in that he can choose to incriminate himself or not. A's 'right' in this example, therefore, is not the asser-tion that B must behave in a certain way; rather, it is the assertion that A himself is permitted to behave in a certain way. This type of right is commonly labelled a 'privilege' or 'liberty',[12] and the 'right to silence' is better described as the 'privilege against self-incrimination'.[13] This type of 'right' is represented in the following formula:

A has a 'right' against B = A is 'permitted', as against B, to behave in a certain way.

There is some scepticism over whether the term 'right' should be used to describe a permission to behave in a certain way or do a specific act. Kocourek, for exam-ple, criticised Hohfeld on the ground that the word 'right' should only be used to describe a legal constraint upon another's conduct, ie it should only be used to denote a legal duty upon another.[14] A permission to behave in a certain way, the opposite of a legal constraint, is simply not something that the law needs to cognise, Kocourek argued. We may concede to Kocourek that it is sometimes odd to describe a permission to behave in a certain way as a 'right'. Whilst I am free to scratch my head, for example, there seems to be no point in me asserting that

---

[9] *Campbell v MGN Ltd* [2004] 2 AC 457.

[10] Ibid, 459 (counsel's argument) (emphasis added).

[11] Ibid.

[12] Hohfeld (n 7) 38.

[13] Section 14 of the Civil Evidence Act 1968 labels this a 'privilege' against self-incrimination, but subsequently slips back into labelling it a 'right' when the sections defines it: 'The *right* of a person in any legal proceedings other than criminal proceedings to refuse to answer any question or produce any document' (emphasis added).

[14] A Kocourek, 'Various Definitions of Jural Relations' (1920) 20 *Columbia Law Review* 394, 412. See also J Singer, 'The Legal Rights Debate in Analytical Jurisprudence from Bentham to Hohfeld' [1982] *Wisconsin Law Review* 975, 991.

I have a 'right to scratch my head'.[15] However, the fact that this statement sounds odd does not mean that there is a conceptual bar to describing a permission to do an act as a 'right'. As Hohfeld said: 'A rule of law that *permits* is just as real as a rule of law that *forbids*.'[16] Further, as a matter of legal discourse, permissions have frequently been described as 'rights'. This typically happens when the legality of one's behaviour is called into question.[17] An example can be found in the case of *Lyon v Daily Telegraph Ltd*,[18] where the defendant had published criticism of the claimant's broadcast entertainment. In response to a claim in defamation, the defendant successfully argued that it had a 'right to free speech' and this allowed it to make fair comment on the claimant's broadcast.[19] This 'right' asserted by the defendant did not denote a duty upon the other party; rather, it was the assertion that the defendant itself was under no duty to the claimant not to publish the criticism and, consequently, its behaviour (publishing the criticism) was permitted. So it is possible to describe a permission to do an act or behave in a certain way as a 'right'. However, in order to distinguish this type of right from one that denotes a duty upon another, it is helpful to call it a 'liberty' or 'privilege'.

To summarise this section, we have seen that the word 'right' has at least two different meanings.[20] First, when A claims that he has a 'right' against B, he may be asserting that B has a legal 'duty' to behave in a certain way. Second, when A claims that he has a 'right' against B, he may be asserting he himself (A) is under no duty to B and, consequently, A is permitted to behave in a certain way or do a specific act. When describing this latter right, the better word is 'liberty' or 'privilege'. Returning to the question posed in this chapter of whether a freeholder has a 'right to use' his land, it should be apparent that his 'right' can denote different things: it can denote a legal 'duty' on others not to impair use or it can describe the freeholder's own 'liberties' to use. The next section will begin by considering the evidence for the latter interpretation: that of a 'liberties to use' land.

III. LIBERTIES TO USE LAND

When a freeholder claims that he has a 'right to use' his land, he may not be asserting that others owe him a legal duty to behave in a certain way; rather, he may be asserting that he himself is permitted to behave in a certain way, ie he is permitted to use his land. Put a little differently, when a freeholder, A, claims that he has a 'right to use' his land, he may be asserting that he is under no legal duty to B, C, D, etc not to use his land and, in the absence of such a duty, his use is permitted. Such a 'right to use' is better described as 'liberty to use'.

---

[15] See J Penner, 'Hohfeldian Use-Rights in Property' in J Harris (ed), *Property Problems: From Genes to Pension Funds* (London, Kluwer, 1997).

[16] Hohfeld (n 7) 42 at n 59.

[17] G Williams, 'The Concept of a Legal Liberty' (1956) 56 *Columbia Law Review* 1129.

[18] *Lyon v Daily Telegraph Ltd* [1943] KB 746.

[19] Ibid, 753.

[20] Hohfeld went on to identify two further meanings which he labelled 'powers' and 'immunities'. However, it is 'claim-rights' and 'liberties' that are important for the present analysis.

It should be immediately apparent that a freeholder holds such 'liberties'. This can be readily observed from everyday life. A freeholder, A, is free to walk in his garden, cook in his kitchen, read in his living room, sleep in his bedroom, etc. He does not owe a duty to B, C, D, etc not to do these things and, in the absence of such a duty, these uses are permitted. We can find judicial statements to this effect, typically in cases where someone has challenged a freeholder's particular use of his land. An example is the case of *Tapling v Jones*,[21] where the defendant had built on his land so as to obstruct the passage of light onto the claimant's land. Lord Cranworth expressly stated that the defendant was free to build on his land:

> His right is a right to use his own land by building on it as he thinks most to his interest; and if by so doing he obstructs the access of light to the new windows, he is doing that which affords no ground of complaint. He has a right to build, and if thereby he obstructs the new lights, he is not committing a wrong.[22]

The defendant's 'right' to build on his land discussed in this passage is quite clearly a 'liberty' because it does not describe a legal duty on the claimant to behave in a certain way. Rather, the 'right' denotes the fact that the defendant himself was under no legal duty to the claimant (or anyone else) not to build on his land and, in the absence of such a duty, that specific use was permitted. A similar case is *Bradford v Pickles*,[23] where the defendant, who acquired title to a parcel of land overlooking the city of Bradford, proceeded to sink a borehole into a natural reservoir under his land. The claimants sought an injunction to prevent the defendant taking water from this reservoir as it would have the effect of drying up natural springs used by the city. The House of Lords, rejecting the claim, held that the claimants could not challenge the defendant's use of his land, Lord Halsbury saying: 'If it was a lawful act, however ill the motive might be, [the defendant] had a right to do it.'[24] Again, this 'right' to take water from the land is actually a 'liberty'. It denotes the fact that the defendant was under no duty to the claimant not to take water from his land and, in the absence of such a duty, this specific use was permitted. Both cases are clear authority for the view that a freeholder, A, is under no legal duty to others, B, C, D, etc, not to use his land and, in the absence of such a duty, A is permitted to use his land. It is correct to say, therefore, that A has 'liberties to use' his land. Two further issues must be considered in relation to liberties. First, it must be asked whether ubiquitous public restrictions on the use of land undermine the conclusions drawn here. Second, the limitations of liberties must be considered.

A. Public Restrictions on Use of Land

Tapling v Jones was decided in 1865. Had the defendant been building on his land in modern times, he would have been met with a very different type of complaint

---

[21] *Tapling v Jones* (1865) 11 HLC 290, 11 ER 1344.
[22] Ibid, 311–12, 1353.
[23] *Bradford v Pickles* [1895] AC 587 (HL).
[24] Ibid, 594–95. For the historical context of this case and its relevance to the 'abuse of rights' doctrine, see J Getzler, *A History of Water Rights at Common Law* (Oxford, Oxford University Press, 2004) 315–16.

related to the need to seek planning permission. Under the Town and Country Planning Act 1990 and a raft of other environmental legislation,[25] any freeholder who wishes to carry out building, engineering, mining or other operations in, on, under or over his land must first apply to the relevant local authority for planning permission.[26] Further, a freeholder cannot materially change the use of his land, such as from residential to agricultural use, without obtaining permission.[27] This is a huge restriction on a freeholder's freedom to use his land. He is not, for example, free to build a house upon his land; if there is already a house upon his land, he is not free to build an extension to it, carry out a loft conversion, create more floor space, etc without obtaining permission. As Gray and Gray remark: 'The local authority planning officer can make or break a homeowner's aspirations for an extension or granny annex in his back garden.'[28] These public restrictions may cast doubt on the claim that a freeholder has 'liberties to use' his land. Indeed, the restrictions are so extensive that Lucy and Mitchell, for example, have argued that a freehold is no longer a type of property right, but merely a form of 'stewardship' over land.[29] So is it correct to say that public regulation of land has deprived the freeholder of his 'liberties to use' his land? It is suggested that it has not. There are two reasons for this. The first relates to the scope of the restrictions, while the second relates to the issue of exigibility.

The first reason stems from the fact that a freeholder's liberties to use his land have the characteristic of 'open-endedness'. What this means is that in the absence of a general duty not to use his land, there is no limit to the number of different ways in which the freeholder is able to use his land. Harris gives examples of the more esoteric uses in this lively passage:

> Granted that one has [freehold], what rights, privileges, powers and immunities relating to the land does one have? Keep out the world and live as a recluse; admit what visitors one wishes; create tenancies or sub-tenancies; grow mushrooms in the cellar; sing bawdy songs in the bath; paint the front door luminous green; sunbathe in the nude ...[30]

It would be impossible to compile a comprehensive list of all of the different acts that a freeholder could do on his land, so we say that his potential uses are 'open-ended'. Planning restrictions, seen in this context, do no more than deprive a freeholder of one specific use, namely his ability to 'build on' or 'develop' his land. Whilst this is no doubt an important use that a freeholder has been deprived of, the planning restrictions have in no way destroyed the 'open-endedness' of a freeholder's liberties as a whole. If a freeholder, for example, is denied planning permission to build a conservatory, then although he has lost an important freedom, nothing follows from this which suggests that he is unable to cook in his kitchen, eat in his dining room, read a book in his lounge, etc. There are still an unlimited number of other things that a freeholder can do. Planning restrictions do not undermine the open-endedness of the freeholder's liberties to use.

---

[25] See generally K Gray, 'Land Law and Human Rights' in L Tee (ed), *Land Law: Issues, Debate, Policy* (Cullompton, Willan, 2002).
[26] Town and Country Planning Act 1990, s 57.
[27] Ibid, s 55.
[28] K Gray and S Gray, *Elements of Land Law*, 5th edn (Oxford, Oxford University Press, 2009) 1378.
[29] W Lucy and C Mitchell, 'Replacing Private Property: The Case for Stewardship' [1996] *CLJ* 566, 567.
[30] Harris (n 1) 152.

The second objection to the view that public regulation has deprived a freeholder of his 'liberties to use' his land relates to the exigibility of his liberty. Because freehold is a type of property right, the right is 'exigible', or 'enforeceable', against the world (as opposed to personal rights, which are exigible against an individual).[31] If a freeholder, A, has 'liberties to use' his land, then this means that it is not just a specific individual, B, that A does not owe a duty not to use his land to, but to all persons (B, C, D, etc). The absence of such duties means that A is free as against all persons (B, C, D, etc) to use his land. The public restrictions on A's use of his land do not legally affect this relationship that A has with persons generally; rather, it just means that there is one party, the state, against whom A does not have a liberty to build on his land. A still has a liberty against everyone else to build on his land. The position seems to be comparable, as a matter of law, to that of a freeholder whose land is subject to a restrictive convenant. If A is a freeholder and B, his neighbour, holds a restrictive covenant over A's land prohibiting A from building on his land, then this just means that A does not have a liberty *as against* B to build on his land. He still has a liberty against all others (C, D, E, etc) to build on his land. Therefore, if A does build on his land, he breaches no duty to C, D, E, etc. It is still true to say that A's relationship with persons generally consists of a liberty to build on his land. The same is true of planning permission. If A has freehold of land, then there is a single party, the state (B), against whom A does not have a liberty to build on his land. If A does build on his land without planning permission, then although he breaches a duty to B and will incur some form of liability, he does not breach a duty to C, D, E, etc. As such, it is still true to say that A has a liberty against persons generally to build on his land.

This is not to say that there are not important practical differences between a freeholder being subject to a restrictive covenant and being subject to public planning controls. With the former, each individual freeholder only becomes subject to such a restriction if he consents to grant a neighbour a covenant (or is the successor in title to someone who consented). With public planning control, however, the restriction is imposed automatically on every freeholder in the country. The result is that planning controls have a far greater effect on what freeholders actually do with their land. Whilst this has important consequences for cultural and social notions of land ownership, the point being made in the present section is that they do not doctrinally affect the content of a freehold. It is still true to say that a freeholder has liberties against persons generally to use his land.

B. Limits of Liberties

A freeholder's liberties to use his land are extremely important. If he did not hold such liberties and was under a duty to others not to use his land, then he would not be able to do those basic things on his land that all freeholders do every day. Without 'liberties to use', there would be little point in owning land. Yet, despite their importance, liberties, on their own, count for very little. The reason for this is that if one has a 'liberty' to do a specific act, then although this means that one is

---

[31] See B McFarlane, *The Structure of Property Law* (Oxford, Hart Publishing, 2008) 132.

permitted to do the act, it does not mean that the law protects one's ability to do the act. To give an example, if A spots the last chicken sandwich on the shelf in his favourite sandwich shop, A has a 'liberty' to pick it up, take it to the counter and purchase it (these are all permitted acts). If B also spots the sandwich and, being quicker than A, is first to pick it up and purchase it, B has deprived A of his opportunity to exercise his liberty in this example, but B does not commit a tort against A in so doing because B is under no legal duty to A not to behave in this way. A's 'liberty to purchase the sandwich' merely denotes that A is permitted to purchase it; it does not mean that the law protects his ability to do so.[32]

The fact that a liberty offers no protection is key to understanding why legal liability for causing economic loss is so limited. Let us say that a worker, A, has a 'liberty' to offer his services and work for a particular employer, X. B, a union representative, threatens to call a strike if X goes ahead and employs A. As a result of this, X refuses to employ A. This is a simplified version of *Allen v Flood*,[33] which held that B commits no legal wrong against A in such circumstances, even though he has deprived A of his opportunity to exercise his liberty (A's liberty to work for X). The reason for this is that A's 'liberty to work' merely denotes that A was permitted to work; it does not mean that the law protects A's opportunity to work. Such protection would only be achieved by the imposition of a legal duty upon B not to behave in the way that he did, ie a duty not to impair A's opportunity to work. Whether or not the law should impose such a duty is essentially a question of policy:[34] for example, is A's liberty deserving of protection in these circumstances?; would the imposition of a duty on B be too restrictive on B's freedom? The majority of the House of Lords, in considering these issues, decided that there was not a good enough reason to impose a legal duty upon B. The consequence of this was that A's liberty to work was not protected.

Whilst the merits of the decision in *Allen v Flood* have been debated ever since,[35] the case is an important illustration of the fact that so far as one has a mere liberty to do an act, one has no security against interference.[36] The only way in which security can be achieved is if the law were to impose duties upon others. In context of freehold of land, whilst it is clear that a freeholder, A, has 'liberties to use' his land, A's ability to exercise these liberties will only be protected if the law were to impose legal duties on B, C, D, etc not to impair A's ability to use his land. If the law does not impose any duties on B, C, D, etc, then A's liberties to use his land, just like claimant's liberty to work in *Allen v Flood*, are potentially worthless.

IV. DUTIES NOT TO IMPAIR USE

It was explained above that if a freeholder, A, claimed that he had a 'right to use' his land, he could be asserting two very different types of legal relationships with

---

[32] Hohfeld (n 7) 34–35.
[33] *Allen v Flood* [1898] AC 1.
[34] Hohfeld (n 7) 36.
[35] The most recent case in the ongoing controversy is *OBG Ltd v Allen* [2007] UKHL 21.
[36] See generally Williams (n 17).

others. First, A could be asserting that *he himself* is permitted to behave in a certain way, ie that he is permitted to use his land. This type of 'right' is best described as a 'liberty' and so far we have seen that A does hold such liberties. Second, when A claims that he has a 'right to use' his land, he may be asserting that *others* (B, C, D, etc) must behave in a certain way. Used in this sense, A's 'right' is just a shorthand description of a legal duty imposed upon others (B, C, D, etc) not to impair A's ability to use his land. This type of 'right' is best described as a 'claim-right', and the purpose of this section is to determine whether a freeholder holds such a right. This requires us to ask the following question: are B, C, D, etc under a legal duty to A not to impair A's ability to use his land? This is an important question because, as we saw in the last section, A's liberties to use his land may have very little value unless they are protected by the imposition of such a duty upon others. Before looking at the evidence for the recognition of such a duty, however, this part will begin by considering the standard duty owed to a freeholder not to interfere physically with his land. This duty is universally accepted to exist, and it will first be asked whether it affords any protection to A's liberties to use his land.

A. The General Duty Owed to a Freeholder

A freeholder, A, is clearly owed a legal duty by all others (B, C, D, etc) not to interfere physically with A's land. This legal duty (a 'duty of non-interference' for short) can readily be inferred from tort law. A tort, which is a type of civil wrong, involves the breach of a legal duty.[37] This means that if a third party, let us say B, is held to have committed a tort by physically interfering with A's land, we can infer from B's liability in tort law that he (and all other third parties: C, D, E, etc) is under a legal duty to A not to interfere physically with A's land. It is the law of torts, therefore, which recognises that freeholders are owed a duty of non-interference.

The principal torts protecting a freeholder's right are trespass, negligence and nuisance, and we can see in each of these torts a clear recognition of this duty of non-interference. Beginning with trespass, a simple illustration of this duty can be found in *Ellis v Loftus*,[38] where the defendant's horse had bitten the claimant's horse through the railings that divided their properties. The bite was held to be proof of a trespass to land as the defendant's horse must have crossed the claimant's boundary, albeit by a very short distance. Lord Coleridge, emphasising that any physical crossing of the boundary can be a trespass, said:

> [I]f the defendant place a part of his foot on the plaintiff's land unlawfully, it is in law as much a trespass as if he had walked half a mile on it ... It seems to me sufficiently clear that some portion of the defendants' horse's body must have been over the boundary. That may be a very small trespass, but it is a trespass in law.[39]

---

[37] P Birks, 'Concept of a Civil Wrong' in D Owen (ed), *Philosophical Foundations of Tort Law* (Oxford, Clarendon Press, 1995).

[38] *Ellis v Loftus* (1874) LR 10 CP 10.

[39] Ibid, 12. See also *Lawrence v Obee* (1815) 1 Sta 22, 171 ER 389; *Gregory v Piper* (1829) 9 Bar & Cress 591, 109 ER 220; and *Kynoch v Rowlands* [1912] 1 Ch 527.

The defendant's liability in this case demonstrates that he was under a clear duty to the freeholder not to interfere physically with the land. A similar duty can be inferred from the tort of negligence. Take, for instance, the early case of *Vaughan v Menlove*,[40] where the defendant had negligently constructed a hay-rick close to the boundary with the claimant's land. He was warned of the danger of it catching fire, but did nothing about it. When it did ignite, the fire spread to the claimant's land and burnt down the claimant's house. The defendant was held liable, Vaughan J saying that 'every one takes upon himself the duty of so dealing with his own property as not to injure the property of others'.[41] The defendant was responsible for an interference with the claimant's land, in the form of fire crossing the boundary and the causing of physical damage to the land.[42] Again, the defendant's liability demonstrates that he was under a duty of non-interference to the claimant.

As to what counts as an interference with land, the focus is on the notion of boundary crossing. This results from the *ad coelum* principle which holds that a freeholder's right does not just relate to the surface of his land, but also to a vertical column extending both upwards and downwards. This effectively means that there is an invisible boundary demarcating the freeholder's land, and an 'interference' with the land can take the form of a physical crossing of this boundary. Take, for instance, *Anchor Brewhouse Developments Ltd v Berkley House (Docklands Developments) Ltd*,[43] where the top of the defendant's crane, elevated at a great height, oversailed the claimant's land and this was held to be sufficient for liability in trespass. The physical interference consisted of the defendant's crossing of the claimant's boundary. A similar case is *Star Energy Weald Ltd v Bocardo SA*,[44] where the defendant had bored a hole under its land in order to extract oil from a reservoir. At a great depth, this borehole crossed the boundary of the claimant's land. In finding the defendant liable, Lord Hope said that 'trespass occurs when there is an unjustified intrusion by one party upon land which is in the possession of another'.[45] The defendant was under a duty of non-interference, meaning that it had to refrain from any form of boundary crossing.

Turning to the tort of nuisance, the basis of liability in this tort is still much debated.[46] It is suggested that the tort, for the most part, establishes the same duty of non-interference as that established in trespass and negligence.[47] Nuisance typically involves the emanation of something such as smells[48], fumes[49] or noise[50] onto the

---

[40] *Vaughan v Menlove* (1837) 3 Bing NC 468, 132 ER 490.

[41] Ibid, 477, 494.

[42] The house is considered part of the land due to the doctrine of accession.

[43] *Anchor Brewhouse Developments Ltd v Berkley House (Docklands Developments) Ltd* [1987] 2 EGLR 1973.

[44] *Star Energy Weald Ltd v Bocardo SA* [2011] 1 AC 380.

[45] Ibid, 391.

[46] See C Gearty, 'The Place of Private Nuisance in the Modern Law of Torts' [1989] *CLJ* 214; D Nolan, 'A Tort Against Land: Private Nuisance as a Property Tort' and R Bagshaw, 'The Edges of Tort Law's Rights' in D Nolan and A Robertson (eds), *Rights and Private Law* (Oxford, Hart Publishing, 2012).

[47] Two forms of nuisance, encroachment and physical damage, clearly involve physical interferences.

[48] Eg, *Rapier v London Tramway Corp* [1893] 2 Ch 588 (CA).

[49] Eg, *St Helen's Smelting Co v Tipping* (1865) 11 HL Cas 642, 11 ER 1483.

[50] Eg, *Halsey v Esso Petroleum Co Ltd* [1961] 1 WLR 683.

claimant's land so as to interfere with the claimant's use and enjoyment of his land.[51] The relationship between this cause of action and other torts, particularly trespass, is a matter of some controversy. Nolan has recently argued that the historical division between trespass and actions on the case still governs the boundary between trespass to land and nuisance.[52] This would mean that if an interference is 'direct', then it should be litigated in trespass, whereas if it is 'indirect', it should be litigated in nuisance.[53] However, the direct/indirect division, which was once the organising principle in tort law generally, has been abandoned in other areas,[54] due, in large part, to the impossibility of defining what amounts to a 'direct' and an 'indirect' interference. This is equally true in nuisance: it is not clear in what sense smells or fumes coming onto a claimant's land are an 'indirect' rather than a 'direct' interference.[55] It is suggested, therefore, that this direct/indirect division is also obsolete in relation to nuisance. The better distinction between trespass and nuisance is that suggested by Merrill: whereas trespass typically involves 'gross invasions by tangible objects',[56] nuisance involves less tangible things, such as smoke, smells and the like crossing the claimant's boundary. Merrill calls this the 'dimensional' test:

> If the defendant blasts rocks onto the plantiff's land, or fires a shotgun across the plaintiff's land, this would constitute a trespass under the dimensional test: rocks and shotgun pellets are particles which, at least once they have come to rest, are visible to the naked eye ... However, smoke, noise, odors, shining light, aesthetic blight, funeral homes, halfway houses, and so forth would be actionable only as nuisances, because they do not involve the invasion of particles which are visible to the naked eye.[57]

Under this analysis, liability in nuisance is based upon the same physical boundary crossing as that found in trespass and negligence. All that nuisance has done is establish that the thing crossing the boundary need not have the same 'gross' and 'tangible' nature as normally found in trespass cases. If this analysis is correct (and we will return to this question below), then nuisance, like trespass and negligence, only establishes that a freeholder is owed a duty of non-interference.

B. Non-correlativity

The three torts of trespass, negligence and nuisance establish that a freeholder, A, is owed a duty of non-interference by all others (B, C, D, etc). The important question is how this duty relates to A's liberties to use his land: does the duty of non-

---

[51] Nolan (n 46) 463.

[52] Ibid. See also P Winfield, 'Nuisance as a Tort' (1930–32) 4 *CLJ* 189, 202–03.

[53] *Reynolds v Clarke* (1724) 1 Str 634, 93 ER 747.

[54] In the case of *Williams v Holland* (1833) 10 Bing 112, 131 ER 848.

[55] T Merrill, 'Trespass, Nuisance and the Costs of Determining Property Rights' (1985) 14 *Journal of Legal Studies* 13, 28.

[56] Ibid, 28. For an exceptional trespass case, see *Martin v Reynolds Metals Co*, 221 Or 86, 342 P2d 790 (1959).

[57] Ibid, 28–29. See also Bagshaw (n 46) 418–19. If trespass does involve 'gross invasions by tangible' objects, whereas nuisance involves invasions by more intangible things, then this lends support to Nolan's persuasive argument that liability in *Rylands v Fletcher*, which involves a tangible object (water) crossing the claimant's boundary, is more closely related to trespass than nuisance. See D Nolan, 'The Distinctiveness of *Rylands v Fletcher*' (2005) 121 *LQR* 421.

interference imposed on B, C, D, etc protect A's liberties to use his land? The answer is clearly 'yes'. Let us say that A wished to erect a building on his land. If he was not owed a duty of non-interference by B, C, D, etc, then A would find it very difficult to build on his land: B, C, D, etc could walk across or occupy A's land with impunity, thus frustrating A's plans. So the fact that A is owed a duty of non-interference, meaning that B, C, D, etc must keep off A's land, leaves A free to build upon his land. In this sense, A's ability to exercise his liberty is protected by the imposition of the duty of non-interference on others.

It would be a mistake to conclude from this, however, that the duty of non-interference imposed on B, C, D, etc correlates with A's liberties to use his land.[58] This is evident from the fact that it is possible for B, C, D, etc to deprive A of his opportunity to exercise his liberties to use his land without breaching the duty of non-interference. A good example of such a case is *Perre v Apand*.[59] The defendant had carelessly caused the outbreak of a crop disease, bacterial wilt, on its farm. Whilst this disease did not reach the claimant's nearby farm, a quarantine zone (which arose under environmental legislation) was imposed on a large area which included the claimant's farm. The effect of this was that the claimant could not properly exercise its liberty to use its land as a commercial farm (as it could no longer use its farm to produce potatoes for the export market). Yet the defendant, in depriving the claimant of this opportunity, did not in any way breach its duty of non-interference: at no point did the defendant cause anything physically to cross the claimant's boundary. This demonstrates that the content of the defendant's duty (its duty of non-interference) did not correlate with the claimant's liberty (its liberty to use). The claimant could be deprived of the latter without the defendant breaching the former.

In a case like *Perre v Apand*, the way in which the freeholder's liberty could be protected would be by the imposition of an additional duty on the defendant, the content of which would correlate with the freeholder's liberties. This would consist of a duty not to impair the freeholder's ability to use his land (a 'duty of non-impairment of use' for short). One could breach such a duty without physically interfering with the freeholder's land; all that would need to be shown would be that the defendant had performed some act which prevented the freeholder from making some use of his land. Had the defendant been under such a duty in *Perre v Apand*, then it is clear that it would have been in breach.[60]

To summarise this section, what cases such as *Perre v Apand* demonstrate is that the freeholder's liberties to use his land do not correlate with the general duty of non-interference that he is owed by others. The duty of non-interference only offers indirect or oblique protection to his liberties. The important question, therefore, is whether there is any evidence for the recognition of an additional duty that does correlate with the freeholder's liberties. In other words, is a freeholder owed a 'duty of non-impairment of use'? It is this question that the next section will attempt to answer.

---

[58] A case which makes this mistake, Hohfeld argued, is *Quinn v Leathem* [1901] AC 495. See Hohfeld (n 7) 42.

[59] *Perre v Apand* [1999] HCA 36, (1999) 198 CLR 180.

[60] The defendant was found liable in the case, but the claim was analysed as one of economic loss. Unfortunately, this meant that the court did not deal with the issue of the freeholder's property rights.

C. Evidence for a Duty of Non-impairment of Use

As was the case when we considered the general duty of non-interference, any evidence for the existence of a 'duty of non-impairment of use' will be found in the law of tort. A tort, as explained above, involves the breach of a legal duty. This means that if a defendant has been found liable in tort law for impairing a freeholder's ability to use his land, we can infer from this that the defendant was under a 'duty of non-impairment of use'.

Litigants have occasionally sought, unsuccessfully, to establish a duty of non-impairment of use in the torts of trespass and negligence. An example in trespass is the case of *Perera v Vandiyar*,[61] where the defendant sought to evict the claimant from the claimant's land.[62] The defendant did not physically come onto the claimant's land and dispossess him; rather, he sought to make the claimant's land uninhabitable by cutting off all of the gas and electricity supplies to the land. The tactic worked and the claimant eventually had to seek temporary accommodation elsewhere. This was a clear impairment of the claimant's ability to use his land as he was unable to do basic things like wash himself or cook a meal. However, the court held that this was not sufficient for liability in trespass, as the tort required some form of physical interference. Romer LJ said:

> That the defendant's action was deliberate is plain, and that it was malicious is, I think, reasonably plain, but I cannot for myself see that it amounted to a tort. It did not constitute an interference with any part of the demised premises and, therefore, could not be regarded as a trespass.[63]

This tells us that whilst trespass clearly establishes a duty of non-interference, it does not establish a duty of non-impairment of use. A similar picture can be seen in relation to negligence. In the recent case of *D Pride & Partners (a firm) v Institute for Animal Health*[64] (which bears a number of similarities to *Perre v Apand*), the defendant carelessly caused an outbreak of foot and mouth disease close to the claimant's land. Whilst this did not physically affect the claimant's land, in the sense that none of the livestock on his land was infected, the claimant's land was effectively sterilised by the imposition of a quarantine zone. Animals could not be moved on or off the claimant's land, thus impairing his commercial farming business. Yet, despite the defendant being responsible for this substantial impairment of use, it had not physically interfered with the claimant's land in any way as it had not caused anything physically to cross the claimant's boundary. Tugendhat J held that this was fatal to a claim in negligence, saying: 'No case was cited to me in which the concept of "damage" analogous to "physical damage" has been applied by an English court

---

[61] *Perera v Vandiyar* [1953] 1 WLR 672 (CA).
[62] The claimant was a tenant of the defendant. However, a tenancy, or 'leasehold', is identical in its content to a freehold, save for the fact that it does not last forever, but for a finite period. It is often called 'ownership for the time being'. As such, it makes no difference for the present purposes whether the claimant was a freeholder or a leaseholder.
[63] *Perera v Vandiyar* (n 63) 676.
[64] *D Pride & Partners (a firm) v Institute for Animal Health* [2009] EWHC 685 (QB).

in allowing a claim for damages.'[65] Negligence, like trespass, recognises a duty of non-interference, but it does not recognise a duty of non-impairment of use.

The cause of action where freeholders have had far more success in trying to establish that they are owed a duty of non-impairment of use is nuisance. As was explained above, the typical nuisance case involves fumes, smells or noise emanating onto the freeholder's land. Often the primary result of these emanations is that the freeholder suffers severe personal discomfort, such as where fumes from the nearby factory cause the freeholder to 'cough and splutter'.[66] This has sometimes led to the view that what nuisance protects is not the freeholder's property right, but his health and well-being.[67] However, as Nolan has recently demonstrated, nuisance can only be understood as a 'tort against land', in the sense that it creates duties in relation to a freeholder's land rather than his person.[68] The strongest evidence for this is that the only person with standing to sue in nuisance is the person with freehold or leasehold title;[69] if it was an action protecting one's health and well-being, any occupier would be able to sue in the tort. As to which aspect of the freeholder's right is being protected by nuisance, Nolan suggests that it is the freeholder's interest in the utility of his land:

> [T]he property tort analysis holds with equal force for all types of private nuisance, once it is appreciated that in cases involving noise, smells and so on the gist of the action is not the discomfort of those affected, but the diminished utility of the land on which they live.[70]

Similarly, in Murphy's recent book on the tort of nuisance, the author suggests that the origins of the tort, and even its very name, means that the focus is on 'use and enjoyment':

> [T]he word nuisance derives from the Latin, *nocumentum*, and (in turn) the old English, *noysaunce*, both of which terms connote purely the annoyance value of the wrong complained of. As such, judicial orthodoxy would seem to suggest that an action in private nuisance ought properly to be confined to interferences with the use or enjoyment of land.[71]

By focusing on the utility of the freeholder's land when describing the gist of nuisance, it is possible to interpret these passages as suggesting that nuisance establishes some sort of duty of non-impairment of use. Such an argument is not without its problems. It will be recalled that in the standard nuisance case, such as those involving fumes, smoke, noise, smells, etc, it is possible to say that there is something emanating onto—and hence crossing the physical boundary of—the claimant's land. The only difference between these forms of boundary crossings and those encountered in trespass is that in the nuisance cases the thing crossing the claimant's boundary does not normally have 'gross physical dimensions'.[72] It is suggested that

---

[65] Ibid [83].
[66] See FH Newark, 'The Boundaries of Nuisance' (1949) 65 *LQR* 480, 489.
[67] P Cane comes close to arguing this in 'What a Nuisance!' (1997) 113 *LQR* 515.
[68] Nolan (n 46) 460.
[69] Ibid, 473–75.
[70] Ibid, 461.
[71] J Murphy, *The Law of Nuisance* (Oxford, Oxford University Press, 2010) 61. However, as Murphy goes on to explain, a defendant can be liable in nuisance for causing physical damage. See Murphy at 61–63.
[72] Merrill (n 55).

the gist of liability in nuisance is not the impairment of the utility of the freeholder's land, but the physical interference with it. If this is the correct interpretation of the tort, then it would mean that nuisance is doing no more than reinforcing the duty of non-interference already established in trespass and negligence. Whilst it is suggested that this analysis is correct for the most part, there is one line of cases that does offer unequivocal support for the view put forward by Nolan and Murphy. These are the non-emanation nuisance cases.

There are a small number of claims successfully litigated in nuisance where there is no physical thing which can be said to have emanated onto the claimant's land. As such, the defendants in these cases cannot be said to be in breach of their duty of non-interference; rather, they seem to have been held to be in breach of a duty not to impair the utility of the freeholder's land. A good example is *Guppys (Bridport) Ltd v Brookling*,[73] where the defendant attempted to evict the claimant from the claimant's room in a block of flats. The defendant owned the rest of the building and was planning to redevelop it. At no point during this period did the defendant physically interfere with the claimant's land; rather, he sought to make it uninhabitable by cutting off the water and electricity, removing the external sanitary facilities and making access difficult. The claimant was unable to do basic things on his land such as wash or cook and he eventually moved out. Stephens LJ, finding for the claimant, said:

> If [the defendant] uses his own property—it may be lawfully—in a way which unduly interferes with the enjoyment of [the claimant's] property, it seems to me that he falls fairly and squarely within the category of wrongdoers who commit the tort of nuisance.[74]

The case is very similar to that of *Perera v Vandiyar* considered above, where the defendant had made the claimant's land uninhabitable by cutting off its utilities. It will be recalled that in *Perera* the claim in trespass was unsuccessful due to the absence of any form of physical interference with the claimant's land. In this later case the claim was litigated in nuisance and was successful. This supports the view that impairing a freeholder's ability to use his land, unaccompanied by any form of physical interference, can be sufficient for liability in nuisance.

A more recent case which also lends support to this view is *Birmingham Development Company Ltd v Tyler*,[75] where the claimant halted a redevelopment project on its land due to the fear of a poorly constructed building on the defendant's land collapsing. The claim did not succeed on the facts, as it was found that the claimant's fears were unfounded, the defendant's structure posing no danger of collapsing. However, the Court of Appeal held that if there had been a real danger of collapse, then that danger in itself could constitute a nuisance. This is important in the present context because the presence of such a danger does not (until it materialises) involve any form of physical interference with the claimant's land. The only effect it has is that it impairs the freeholder's ability to use his land (in this case the

---

[73] *Guppys (Bridport) Ltd v Brookling* (1984) 14 HLR 1.
[74] Ibid, 31.
[75] *Birmingham Development Company Ltd v Tyler* [2008] EWCA Civ 859.

claimant's ability to build on its land). Rimer LJ said that such an impairment of use could form the basis of a claim in nuisance:

> For the claimant to live in the shadow of such a danger will obviously be to interfere with his enjoyment of his property. It may prevent him from using part of it for fear of what will happen if there is a collapse. It may require him to vacate it altogether.[76]

The impossibility of alleging any form of physical interference with the land in these cases means that Rimer LJ may have considered impairments of use to be sufficient for liability in nuisance. This strongly suggests that the defendants in these cases, in addition to being under their standard duty of non-interference to the freeholder, were also under a duty of non-impairment of use.

Whilst *Guppys* and *Birmingham Development Council* support this interpretation of nuisance, other cases have insisted on the need for a physical interference with the freeholder's land. An example is the case considered above of *D Pride & Partners (a firm) v Institute for Animal Health*.[77] It will be recalled that when the defendant carelessly caused the outbreak of foot and mouth disease, the claimant's ability to use his land was significantly impaired by the imposition of a quarantine zone. Whilst a claim in negligence failed, the court also held that the facts did not constitute a nuisance, Tugendhat J saying that: 'If there had been any interference with the [claimant's] enjoyment of their land it has not been directly caused by anything emanating from the defendant's land.'[78]

The absence of a physical interference with the claimant's land in the form of a substance emanating onto the land and physically crossing its boundary meant that there was no claim in nuisance. A similar case is *Anglian Water Services v Crawshaw Robbins & Co*,[79] where the court had to decide whether the defendant committed the tort of nuisance when, during maintenance works, it cut through the wrong pipes and deprived a number of nearby houses of gas and water. The affected freeholders were in a similar position (although less serious) to that of the claimant in *Guppys*, who was also deprived of utilities. However, in *Anglian Water*, the court held that a mere impairment of use was not sufficient for liability and that there had to be some form of emanation onto the claimant's land. As to cases where a claim in nuisance had succeeded in the absence of an emanation, these were described as 'exceptional', Burton J saying:

> My conclusion is that the negligent interruption of a supply of gas by a third party is not actionable as a private nuisance. It does not involve an invasion of any substance or form of energy on to the claimant's land. It is not one of the exceptional cases of liability in nuisance without such an invasion. A home owner or tenant does not have a property right in the supply of gas.[80]

---

[76] Ibid [52]. Bagshaw correctly points out that the court did not consider whether this was an application for an injunction *quia timet*, in which case it may not be authority for the view that there can be a nuisance without an emanation. See Bagshaw (n 46) 420.

[77] *D Pride & Partners* (n 64).

[78] Ibid [133].

[79] *Anglian Water Services v Crawshaw Robbins & Co* [2001] BLR 173. See also *Tapling v Jones* (1865) 11 HLC 290, 11 ER 1344.

[80] Ibid, 54.

The most important modern case that seems to cast doubt on the view that merely impairing the freeholder's ability to use his land can be sufficient for liability in nuisance is *Hunter v Canary Wharf*.[81] The defendant, in building the Canary Wharf tower, had blocked television signals from a transmitter from reaching the claimant's land. This is obviously an impairment of use, as the freeholders were no longer at liberty to watch and enjoy television in their homes. Further, the House of Lords, reversing a previous decision,[82] held that being deprived of this liberty is a substantial impairment of use, potentially actionable in nuisance. Despite this, the claim failed. Although the House of Lords gave various reasons for rejecting the claim, the main problem, as in *Anglian Water*, was the absence of any form of physical interference with the claimant's land. The defendant had not caused anything physically to cross the claimant's boundary; rather, it had blocked something (television signals) from reaching the claimant's land. Lord Goff, whilst accepting that the courts had 'occasionally' held that a defendant could commit a nuisance without causing anything to emanate onto the claimant's land,[83] argued that an emanation was still a general requirement in the tort:

> [F]or an action in private nuisance to lie in respect of interference with the plaintiff's enjoyment of his land, it will generally arise from something emanating from the defendant's land. Such an emanation may take many forms—noise, dirt, fumes, a noxious smell, vibrations, and suchlike.[84]

As can be seen, the case law is in a state of some confusion. Cases such as *Guppys* and *Birmingham Development Company* clearly hold that mere impairments of use, unaccompanied by any form of physical interference, can constitute a nuisance. As Nolan correctly states, these cases cannot be forced into a 'trespass-type straightjacket'.[85] As such, they support the view that a freeholder, in addition to being owed the standard duty of non-interference by others, is also owed a duty of non-impairment of use. However, other cases, such as *D Pride*, *Anglian Water Services* and *Hunter* have held that mere impairments of use are not sufficient. Therefore, it is simply not clear whether a freeholder is owed a duty of non-impairment of use.

D. Should the Law Recognise a Duty of Non-impairment of Use?

Whilst it is not clear whether a freeholder is owed a duty of non-impairment of use, it is still important to ask whether, as a matter of policy, he should be owed such a duty. There seems to be two arguments against the recognition of such a duty.

---

[81] *Hunter v Canary Wharf* [1997] AC 655.
[82] *Bridlington Relay v Yorkshire Electricity Board* [1965] Ch 436.
[83] *Hunter v Canary Wharf* (n 83) 686.
[84] Ibid.
[85] Nolan (n 46) 467. See also Murphy (n 71) 36. The other non-emanation cases typically cited are *Thompson-Schwab v Costaki* [1956] 1 WLR 335 and *Laws v Florinplace Ltd* [1981] 1 All ER 659, where it was held that the defendants had caused a nuisance to the claimants by opening a nearby brothel and sex shop respectively. These cases are not strictly relevant to the present analysis as neither involved any form of impairment of use. As Nolan notes, they get very close to suggesting that merely causing diminution in value can constitute a nuisance: Nolan (n 46) 465.

The first argument is that such a duty may prove very onerous on others. If we consider the normal duty of non-interference owed to a freeholder, this duty is one that is relatively easy to discharge. If A has freehold title to land, and B, C, D, etc are under a duty of non-interference to A, this means that there is just one thing that B, C, D, etc must refrain from doing: they must refrain from causing something physically to cross A's boundary. This is a simple duty for B, C, D, etc to understand and comply with. If, however, B, C, D, etc were under a further duty to A, a duty of non-impairment of use, this potentially means that they would come under a duty to refrain from doing *any act* that could prevent A from making a specific use of his land. This means that there could be a much larger number of activities that B, C, D, etc must refrain from doing. Let us say that A, who plans to erect a building on his land, has attempted to purchase building materials. However, B has purchased the last of the available building materials for himself. By doing so, B has deprived A of his ability to use his land in a specific way as A cannot start his building works. If B were under a strict duty of non-impairment of use, then we would have to say that he was under a duty to refrain from doing this act (his buying of building materials). Let us say that A is subsequently able to order a delivery of the building materials from elsewhere. However, the van carrying the building materials cannot reach A's land because C, a careless driver, has caused a traffic jam on a nearby road. C's act prevents A from making a specific use of his land because A cannot start his building works at his planned time. Again, if C were under a strict duty of non-impairment of use, then we would have to say that C was under a duty to refrain from this act (the causing of a traffic jam). The purpose of these examples is to show that there are a large number of ways in which B, C, D, etc can prevent A from making a specific use of his land. Consequently, the imposition of a duty of non-impairment of use would mean that there are a large number of activities that B, C, D, etc must refrain from doing. This is arguably too extensive a restriction on their freedom.

The second argument against the recognition of a duty of non-impairment of use is that if the freeholder loses a specific liberty to use his land, he will not, in the normal course of things, be overly prejudiced. It was noted above that a freeholder's liberties to use his land have the characteristic of open-endedness. This means that it is impossible to list all of the different acts that a freeholder is permitted to do in relation to his land. It will be recalled that Harris illustrated the point by noting some of the more esoteric uses that a freeholder can make of his land: 'grow mushrooms in the cellar; sing bawdy songs in the bath; paint the front door luminous green; sunbathe in the nude …'.[86] The open-endedness of the freeholder's liberties means that if a defendant deprives the freeholder of the ability to make a specific use of his land, there are still an unlimited number of other ways in which he can use his land. Take, for instance, the case of *D Pride & Partners (a firm) v Institute for Animal Health*, where the defendant had effectively deprived the claimant of his ability to use his land as a livestock farm. This impairment of use, although seriously detrimental to the claimant, did not exclude the possibility of him making any one of a number of other uses of the land. Most obviously, he would have been able to switch the use of his farm to producing things not covered by the movement

---

[86] Harris (n 1) 152.

restrictions. He could have leased out his farm or he could have changed the use altogether to a non-farming business. The loss of a specific use does not exclude the possibility of other uses. An interesting parallel can be drawn with the conversion case of *England v Cowley*,[87] where the defendant had not physically interfered with the claimant's furniture, but had merely impaired the claimant's ability to make a specific use of the furniture (he had prevented the claimant from moving the furniture from a specific house). Bramwell B rejected the claim in conversion, saying that it is not a conversion to prevent a claimant from 'using [a chattel] in a particular way'.[88] In explaining the reason for his decision, he used the following example:

> I meet a man on horseback going in a particular direction, and say to him, 'You shall not go that way, you must turn back'; and make him comply. Who could say that I had been guilty of a conversion of the horse?[89]

Like the claimant in *D Pride*, the man on horseback is deprived of the opportunity to exercise a specific liberty because he cannot use his horse to go in a certain direction. However, this does not mean that he is not free to take his horse in any other direction. The open-endedness of an owner's liberties to use means that there will normally be an unlimited number of other ways in which he can use his property.

Despite these arguments, there may still be room for a very limited duty of non-impairment of use. In some extreme cases, the impaired utility of the freeholder's land is so great that there is no alternative use that can be made by him. An example may be the *Guppys (Bridport) Ltd v Brookling* case, discussed above, where the defendant had removed utilities and external sanitary facilities from a building which contained the claimant's flat. The defendant even went so far as to remove a staircase from the building, making it almost impossible for the claimant to reach his flat. The claimant was not deprived of the ability to make a specific use of his land; rather, the impairment was total, in the sense that there was no residual use that the claimant could practically make of his land. It may be that in such extreme cases, defendants should come under a duty of non-impairment of use. Further, such a limited duty would not prove too onerous on defendants because they would only be in breach where they had succeeded in the (quite difficult) task of completely controlling and sterilising another's land. Whilst the law has not settled the question of whether a freeholder is owed a duty of non-impairment of use, there may be an argument for the recognition of an extremely limited duty of this kind.

V. CONCLUSION

The question this chapter sought to answer is whether it is ever correct to say that a freeholder has a 'right to use' his land. It was seen that it is certainly true to say that

---

[87] *England v Cowley* (1872–73) LR 8 Ex 126 (Exch). See also *Club Cruise Entertainment and Travelling Services Europe BV v Department for Transport* [2008] EWHC 2794 (Comm Ct). These cases are discussed in Bagshaw (n 46) 421–27; and S Douglas, 'The Future of Actionable Interferences in the Chattel Torts' in J Edelman, S Degling and J Goudkamp (eds), *Torts and Commercial Law* (London, Thomson, 2012).
[88] Ibid, 129.
[89] Ibid.

a freeholder has such a right in the sense that he has 'liberties to use' his land. These liberties are important to a freeholder as they mean that he is permitted to make use of his land. However, it was also seen that these liberties, whilst expressing the freeholder's permission to use his land, do not actually protect his ability to use his land. The only way in which such protection can be achieved is by the imposition of duties on others. The important question, therefore, is whether the freeholder's 'right to use', in addition denoting his 'liberties to use' his land, also denotes a legal duty upon others. The answer to this question is not clear. Although the freeholder is owed a general 'duty of non-interference' with his land, this duty only offers indirect or oblique protection for his liberties. In order for the freeholder's liberties to be protected directly, the law must impose a correlative duty on the defendant, ie a 'duty of non-impairment of use'. Whilst there is some evidence that the tort of nuisance has recognised such a duty, it is at best an extremely limited duty, applicable only in cases where there has been a complete or substantial impairment of use.

17

Property and Alienation: Rights, Obligations, Restraints

SCOTT GRATTAN*

I. INTRODUCTION

IF I HAVE 'property' in a thing, what rights do I have in regard to it? And, conversely, if I have rights in respect of a thing, when do I have 'property' in it? These are questions that have fascinated property law scholars for a long time, at least since the seventeenth century.[1] This chapter seeks to tap into this enquiry in a specific context: the relationship between the concept of property and the right to alienate—that is, transfer by way of gift or sale—the object of a property right.

It has been said that the desire to restrict the alienability of property is 'deeply ingrained in human nature'.[2] Historically, this desire reflected a wish by the conveyor either to provide for the continuing maintenance of the immediate conveyee or to keep the property within the conveyor's family so as to preserve its material and social status for as many generations as possible.[3] Responding to this human desire, however, is the well-known legal principle, expounded by the highest courts in England and Australia, that the law favours the free alienability of resources, particularly land.[4] Scholars have supported the practice of striking down conditions imposed to restrict the alienability of property chiefly because such restraints obstruct commerce and productivity by militating against the improvement of property by the current owner or its transfer to another.[5]

This chapter will locate the significance of the right of alienation within various competing property models and will consider various property contexts where the right to alienate is missing *ab initio* or has been purportedly removed through contractual restraint. It will do so by taking the following course. Part II will describe

---

* Senior Lecturer, Sydney Law School.
[1] See A Mossoff, 'What is Property? Putting the Pieces Back Together' (2003) 45 *Arizona Law Review* 371, 376–91.

[2] C Sweet, 'Restraints on Alienation' (1917) 33 *LQR* 236, 237.

[3] M Schnebly, 'Restraints upon the Alienation of Legal Interests: I' (1935) 44 *Yale Law Journal* 961, 965.

[4] *Hall v Busst* (1960) 104 CLR 206, 218 (Dixon CJ); *National Provincial Bank Ltd v Ainsworth* [1965] AC 1175, 1233 (Lord Upjohn); *Linden Gardens Trust Ltd v Lenestra Sludge Disposals Ltd* [1994] 1 AC 85, 107 (Lord Browne-Wilkinson).

[5] See H Bernhard, 'The Minority Doctrine Concerning Direct Restraints on Alienation' (1959) 77 *Michigan Law Review* 1173, 1179–81.

two approaches to understanding the concept of property, namely the 'essentialist' approach and the 'bundle of rights' approach. Part III will outline two versions of the essentialist understanding of property: the economic conception of property and James Penner's theory of property. The role played by alienability in each theory will be examined. Part IV considers two areas of Australian law—native title and the constitutional provision dealing with the acquisition of property—in which the courts have recognised forms of property that are fundamentally inalienable. The significance of this for the essentialist and bundle of rights models will be discussed. In Part V English and Australian cases dealing with the validity of contractual restraints will be considered and analysed.

It will be demonstrated that 'alienability' plays a nuanced role in the economic conception of property, and for the most part this conception provides a very good explanation as to why the law gives alienability the contours it has. However, it will also be shown that despite Penner's criticism of it, the bundle of rights model plays an indispensable role in giving an account of the function of alienability—and, at times, the lack of it—in a range of challenging property contexts where economic factors alone do not hold sway.

II. COMPETING PROPERTY MODELS

Thomas Merrill asserts that there are two competing understandings of property: 'essentialism' and 'nominalism'.[6] A model is essentialist if it asserts the existence of 'the critical element or elements that make up the irreducible core of property in all its manifestations',[7] such as one or more of the rights of use, exclusion or alienation. Alternatively, one might see property as having no universally fixed content, but rather as a linguistic term that can be applied to a range of differently constituted aggregations of separate rights.[8] Under this nominalist perspective, the rights that make up property in a particular context have been '"bundled" together for ease of reference'.[9] This is why this understanding of property is known as the 'bundle of rights' model.

An essentialist view of property that holds that there is a single defining right that is synonymous with property is termed 'single-variable essentialism'.[10] Merrill is a self-identified single-variable essentialist because he believes that the right to exclude others from the benefit of a thing is the unique right that is both necessary and sufficient to give property in that thing. He asserts that other rights that exist in respect of the thing, such as rights of use and alienation, can be logically deduced from the right to exclude.[11]

For the multiple-variable essentialist, the stable core of the concept of property comes from not one, but rather several key ingredients. For example, Mossoff in his

---

[6] T Merrill, 'Property and the Right to Exclude' (1998) 77 *Nebraska Law Review* 730.
[7] Ibid, 734.
[8] Ibid, 737.
[9] Mossoff (n 1) 372.
[10] Merrill (n 6) 734–35.
[11] Ibid, 740–45.

'integrated theory' of property asserts that the ability to acquire, use and dispose of some thing forms a conceptual unity that gives a full account of the concept of property.[12] The right to exclude is also incorporated as a corollary of these rights, as the formal means by which these substantive rights are enjoyed.[13]

It is sometimes difficult to place a theorist who proclaims the essentialist foundations of property squarely within either the single- or multi-variable camp. For example, James Penner, whose comprehensive analysis of the concept of property in an influential article[14] and book[15] will be considered in Part III below, sees the right of *exclusive use* as the defining feature of the concept of property, but with the emphasis being on the ability to exclude. What is important for our purposes, however, is his downplaying of the importance for its own sake of alienability within the property framework. By contrast, the law and economics conception of property, advocated by Posner and others, is unreservedly multi-variable essentialist in nature. This conception of property holds that the role of property law is to move resources to their most highly valued (that is, efficient) uses, and for this to occur, property rights must be exclusive and alienable.[16] The importance given to the right of alienability by this theoretical perspective will be considered in detail when we look at it, alongside Penner's, in Part III.

The bundle of rights conception of property stands in stark contrast to these essentialist models. It has its intellectual pedigree in the Hohfeldian idea that a property right that is supposed to exist in respect of a thing (a right in rem) is, in reality, a set of variable jural relationships that exist between the owner and every individual non-owner.[17] The chief exponent of the bundle of rights model of property in more recent times is Tony Honoré.[18] Honoré claims that the attributes of ownership can be broken down into a number of incidents, which include:

> [T]he right to possess, the right to use, the right to manage, the right to the income of the thing, the right to the capital [the power to alienate, and the liberty to consume, waste, modify or destroy it], the right to security, the right or incidents of transmissibility [on death]; and the absence of term.[19]

Where a person has complete ownership of something, styled by Honoré as 'full' or 'liberal' ownership, all of these incidents are present. However, not all of these incidents must be present in order for someone to be the 'owner' of the thing.[20] I continue to own a house (or goods) that I have leased (or bailed) to another even though I lack the right of present possession and use.[21] And certainly it is possible

---

[12] Mossoff (n 1) 376.

[13] Ibid, 390–97.

[14] J Penner, 'The "Bundle of Rights" Picture of Property' (1996) 43 *UCLA Law Review* 711.

[15] J Penner, *The Idea of Property in Law* (Oxford, Clarendon Press, 1997).

[16] R Posner, *Economic Analysis of Law*, 7th edn (New York, Aspen Publishers, 2007) 33.

[17] W Hohfeld, 'Fundamental Legal Conceptions as Applied in Judicial Reasoning' (1917) 26 *Yale Law Journal* 710. See Penner (n 14) 724–31; Merrill (n 6) 737–38; Mossoff (n 1) 372–73.

[18] See Penner (n 14) 731–33, 737–38, 754–65.

[19] AM Honoré, 'Ownership' in AG Guest (ed), *Oxford Essays in Jurisprudence* (Oxford, Oxford University Press, 1961), 113.

[20] Ibid, 112–13.

[21] Ibid, 125.

for someone to have a 'lesser', but undoubtedly proprietary, right—such as a lease, easement or bailment—with only some of the incidents of ownership.[22]

Because Honoré's model gives the concept of 'property' an indeterminate content in terms of the rights that are included in the bundle in any particular situation, essentialists refer to it as 'nominalist'. We know something is property because that is the term we attach to it, rather than because it contains a definite essence. Penner condemns the use of the bundle of rights conception on the basis that it is a slogan rather than an explanatory model. He claims that although the term 'bundle of rights' may be rhetorically appealing, it does not provide a clear methodology for dealing with novel property issues (such as whether the news or excised body parts can be owned). Nor, Penner asserts, does it provide a useful framework in which to think about the role that property plays in our legal and moral landscape. Instead, the concept of a bundle of rights is so loose and malleable that it gives licence to a court to move quickly from an examination of the nature of property to broad policy considerations about whether the protection of property rights should be afforded in the case before it.[23]

In the Australian context, the bundle of rights model of property has been used in the native title jurisprudence, particularly in regard to the issue of extinguishment. As will be seen in Part IV, native title consists of rights and interests held by groups of Australia's Indigenous Peoples by virtue of their continuing normative connection with particular lands and waters. However, such native title can be extinguished where the Crown has granted an interest to a third party. One approach to deciding whether native title rights, such as the right to hunt, gather, fish or conduct traditional ceremonies, have been extinguished would be to hold that the grant to a third party of any proprietary interest (such as a pastoral lease) by the Crown extinguishes native title. An alternative approach would be to hold that only where the actual use made by the third party under the grant is incompatible with the rights of the Indigenous group would native title be extinguished.[24] The High Court of Australia has taken a middle course. It has held that native title rights are extinguished to the extent that they are inconsistent with the rights that have been granted to the third party by the Crown. So, where the Crown grant confers a right of exclusive possession, all native title rights are extinguished.[25] However, where the grant confers rights of use for a particular purpose, such as 'pastoral' activities, rather than exclusive possession, the native title rights are extinguished only to the extent that they conflict with those of the grant.[26] This enterprise requires an identification of, and

---

[22] Ibid, 124–26.

[23] See Penner (n 14) 714–15, 721–22.

[24] This approach was explained and rejected by Brennan CJ in *Wik Peoples v Queensland* (1996) 187 CLR 1, 87 and in *Western Australia v Ward* (2002) 213 CLR 1. See also *Yanner v Eaton* (1999) 201 CLR 351, 370, where a Queensland statute which vested property in native fauna in the Crown was held not to extinguish a native title right of an Indigenous claimant to hunt crocodiles. This was because the 'property' that was vested was not beneficial ownership, but rather limited rights of control to take and possess fauna and to receive a royalty payment for fauna taken by others.

[25] For example, a fee simple interest (*Fejo v Commonwealth* (1999) 195 CLR 96) or an interest under a statutory lease where, like its common law analogue, exclusive possession is granted (*Wilson v Anderson* (2002) 213 CLR 401).

[26] Examples of this partial extinguishment are found in *Wik* (n 24) and *Ward* (n 24).

comparison between, the precise legal nature and incidents of the native title rights and those of the third party grantee.[27]

This approach is essentially an application of the bundle of rights model.[28] Neither the interest granted to the third party nor the subsisting native title is monolithic. Each consists of distinct rights and when they conflict, the affected individual strands that comprise native title, but not the title itself, are extinguished. Although Penner might see this as the application of an unprincipled conception of property, it does align with the overarching purpose that underpins the Australian common law's recognition of native title—the potential coexistence between native title and interests granted by the Crown—but with the latter having priority over the former. Those holding grants from the Crown have security of tenure, as the rights conferred by those grants can be enjoyed irrespective of the existence of native title. On the other hand, the holders of native title are given some common law protection in the sense that their rights are not susceptible to being swept away completely by the granting of an interest that does not confer exclusive possession.[29]

We conclude this part by noting that in the bundle of rights understanding of property, the absence of the right to alienate is potentially of little consequence. This is because 'property' can quite comfortably exist without this, or any other, single right being present in the constitutive bundle.

III. TWO ESSENTIALIST PROPERTY MODELS

Having broadly contrasted the essentialist and nominalist views of property, we now turn to analyse in some detail two differing versions of the essentialist school: the economic view of property (clearly a multi-variable version of essentialism) and Penner's exclusive-use model (which we have classified as a single-variable version of essentialism). In both cases we are concerned about the role the right to alienate plays in the model.

A. The Economic View of Property

Under this view, the function of property is to promote the most efficient use of resources. A resource is allocated efficiently if it is put to its highest valued use,

---

[27] *Ward* (n 24) 208, [468].

[28] Ibid, 89, [76], 95, [95]. For an examination of the courts' use of the bundle of rights metaphor in the adjudication of the recognition and extinguishment of native title, see L Strelein, 'Conceptualising Native Title' (2001) 23 *Sydney Law* Review 95; and K Howden, 'The Common Law Doctrine of Extinguishment—More than a Pragmatic Compromise' (2001) 8 *Australian Property Law Journal* 1, 10–13.

[29] It should be obvious, however, that there are those who are unhappy with the bundle of rights model being used to allow extinguishment of native title piece by piece in this manner. See, for example, K Barnett, 'One Step Forward and Two Steps Back: Native Title and the Bundle of Rights Analysis' (2000) 24 *Melbourne Law Review* 462, who argues that native title should be seen as an indivisible whole, which must give way to interests granted by the Crown, but which will revive to its full vigour when the granted interest ceases.

which requires it to be held by the person who values it most.[30] Property must possess twin attributes in order to meet this end. First, property rights must allow the owner to use the resource and *exclude* others from the resource. This is necessary so that there is an incentive for the owner to invest the time and capital required to develop the resource so that it will be most productive. This incentive will not be present if a third party is able to capture the benefit of the owner's expenditure before the owner can. Second, the resource must be *alienable* so that it can be transferred if someone else values it more than the current owner. This transfer is effected by means of a mutually beneficial, voluntary exchange. The exchange is mutually beneficial because the seller values the sale price more than she values the resource (otherwise she would not sell) and the buyer values the resource more than he values the purchase price (otherwise he would not buy).[31] Because the wealth of society is increased where both parties to the transaction are left better off,[32] as many resources as possible (the *universality* criterion) should possess the *exclusivity* and *alienability* criteria.

The right to alienate is thus an essential component of property rights under this aspect of the efficiency-based model. If a resource cannot be transferred, it might be frozen in the hands of an owner who values it less than another who could use it more productively. But, in addition to this reason, there is clearly another justification for the right of alienation: individual freedom. An owner of a resource should be able to use it as he or she wishes, including selling it or even giving it away.[33] However, this coincidence of autonomy and efficiency only goes so far because, as we will see, there are circumstances in which the economic theory of property approves the involuntary expropriation of another's interest in a valuable resource. In such circumstances this right of expropriation from an owner can be seen as the *obligation* of an owner to alienate. Of course, this phenomenon would not sit well with a party who approves of the *right* to alienate as a manifestation of personal autonomy.

Economic theory concerns itself not only with the allocation of entitlements, but also with how they are protected. In a seminal article, Calabresi and Melamed describe two alternate remedial responses that may be applied when an entitlement has been infringed by another: (1) a *property rule* response (where relief *in specie*, such as an injunction, is granted); and (2) a *liability rule* response (the payment of monetary compensation in the form of damages).[34] The difference between the two can be illustrated by a simple example. Assume that you and I own adjacent parcels of land. I wish to develop my land by constructing a building on it. If I am able to encroach into the airspace above your land with a crane or scaffolding used in the construction process, I will be able to construct a larger building than I otherwise might, or at least I will save a substantial sum of money that I would otherwise have had to pay if I were to use a non-encroaching construction method. I ask for your

---

[30]   Posner (n 16) 9.

[31]   Ibid, 32–33.

[32]   R Posner, *The Economics of Justice* (Cambridge, MA, Harvard University Press, 1981) 61.

[33]   R Epstein, 'Why Restrain Alienation?' (1985) 85 *Columbia Law Review* 970, 971.

[34]   G Calabresi and D Melamed, 'Property Rules, Liability Rules and Inalienability: One View of the Cathedral' (1972) 85 *Harvard Law Review* 1089.

permission to encroach into your airspace, offering to pay you for the right to do so. However, you refuse, even though you have no current use for that portion of airspace and you would suffer only minor inconvenience if I were to use it. Despite your refusal, I go ahead and encroach into your airspace, and you sue me. It is clear that I have trespassed on your land,[35] but what remedy will the court award you? Will it grant you an injunction, forcing me to remove the encroachment and prohibiting me from encroaching in the future without your consent (a property rule)? Or will the court award you damages, perhaps for past and even future loss, so that I have to pay you compensation, but I am not compelled to stop my encroachment (a liability rule)?[36]

Where an entitlement is protected by a property rule, the holder has the right to sell or not to sell the entitlement as he or she thinks fit: it cannot be compulsorily expropriated by another. By contrast, where an entitlement is protected by a liability rule, another party who desires to can, in effect, acquire the entitlement by infringing it and paying damages.[37] From an economic perspective, the choice as to which of these two remedial responses is applicable is determined by which is the more likely to result in an efficient allocation of the entitlement.

If the context in which the dispute occurs is such that it is likely that the entitlement holder and the would-be acquirer of the entitlement can bargain between themselves as to its allocation, then a property rule is the appropriate response. If the would-be acquirer values the entitlement more than its current holder, the parties should be able to bargain successfully so that a sale of the entitlement can take place. If the current holder of the entitlement values it more than the would-be acquirer does, the entitlement is already efficiently allocated and the parties would not be able to agree on a mutually beneficial price for its transfer. If the would-be enquirer tries to take the entitlement, he or she can be stopped by an injunction. However, if the obstacles to bargaining are high, so that it is unlikely that a sale of the entitlement would be negotiated even where the party who wishes to acquire the entitlement values it more than does its current holder, then a liability rule is the correct remedial response. The party wishing to acquire the entitlement can force a transfer of it by infringing and paying damages. If the infringer does in fact value the entitlement more than its current holder, then the damages paid, reflecting the value of the entitlement to the holder, would be less than the benefit the infringer achieves from acquiring the entitlement.[38]

The point I am making here is that under the economic model of property rights, the right to alienate is simply a means to the end of an efficient allocation of resources. Where efficiency demands it, the right to alienate might be replaced by an obligation to alienate. The instrumentalist view that the economic theory takes of the phenomenon of alienation is also reflected in the existence of *inalienability* rules, which exist alongside of, but are less common than, property and liability rules. Inalienability rules prohibit or at least limit the ability of the holder of an

---

[35] *Anchor Brewhouse Developments Ltd v Jury's Hotel Management (UK) Ltd* (2001) 82 P & CR 286; *LJP Investments Pty Ltd v Howard Chia Investments Pty Ltd* (1989) 24 NSWLR 490.
[36] See, eg, *Jaggard v Sawyer* [1995] 2 All ER 189; *Jones v Ruth* [2011] EWCA Civ 804, [36]–[41].
[37] Calabresi and Melamed (n 34) 1106–10, 1115–20.
[38] Ibid, 1092.

entitlement to transfer that entitlement to another.[39] The rationale for the existence of inalienability rules is that it is sometimes necessary to restrict the transferability of entitlements in order to prevent negative externalities, or harmful spillover effects, being imposed on people who are not parties to the transfer.[40] Because they are not privy to the bargaining process, the bargaining parties do not take into account the potential detrimental effect of the transaction upon their welfare.[41] The mutual benefits of the transaction to the parties may be offset by costs imposed on third parties, meaning that the transaction is not efficient. In some contexts, limiting the alienability of the entitlement may be a more effective way of preventing these negative consequences from arising than simply relying of the availability of civil law sanctions once the harm has occurred.[42]

There are a number of goods whose transfer is highly regulated because of the potential negative externalities that could arise from their free alienability. For example, if guns, alcohol and narcotics were freely saleable, this would have an adverse effect upon members of society who might be physically injured by the aggressive conduct of those buying these commodities.[43] Also, if people were permitted to sell rather than donate blood, this might encourage the wrong type of person providing blood. Where no compensation is given for the provision of blood, it is likely that the donor will be motivated by altruistic concerns. In wishing to help others, it is unlikely that a person would donate blood knowing that it was contaminated with something like the hepatitis virus. On the other hand, if a 'donor' were paid for providing blood, this might attract people driven by commercial rather than altruistic motives and create an incentive to sell blood, even though it might be contaminated. This would create an additional risk of harm to the ultimate recipient.[44]

The economic perspective of property therefore takes a nuanced approach to the transferability of entitlements. Some entitlements are protected by a property rule and thus cannot be taken without the holder's consent. Others, protected by liability rules, can be taken without the owner's consent, provided that judicially determined compensation is paid. Finally, a few entitlements attract an inalienability rule, which means that their transfer is restricted, even where the holder desires it. But the overarching goal in the selection of which of these rules is appropriate in a given context is the quest for efficiency.[45]

B. Penner's Idea of Property

James Penner has articulated a detailed and sophisticated theory about the nature of property. In Part II we noted Penner's condemnation of the bundle of rights theory of property, but it should be recognised that Penner's project is also motivated by

---

[39] Ibid, 1092–93.
[40] Ibid, 1111.
[41] S Rose-Ackerman, 'Inalienability and the Theory of Property Rights' (1985) 85 *Columbia Law Review* 932, 938.
[42] Ibid, 938–39.
[43] Epstein (n 33) 97–98.
[44] See Rose-Ackerman (n 41) 945–46.
[45] L A Fennell, 'Adjusting Alienability' (2009) 122 *Harvard Law Review* 1404, 1404–07, 1411.

the desire to free property from what he sees as the pernicious influence of the economic model.[46] As we will see, Penner's complaint is twofold. First, economists see property as encompassing any sort of valuable entitlement,[47] whereas it should attach only to impersonal entitlements. Second, economists see sale, rather than gift, as the paradigmatic way of transferring property, and thus blur the distinction between contractual and proprietary norms.[48]

We now set out the main features of Penner's conception of property, paying particular attention to the role that alienability plays in his model.

The starting point for Penner's thesis is the proposition that individuals have *interests*, which are manifestations of various components of our well-being. These include an interest in bodily security, an interest in honouring promises (so that we may commit ourselves to others and particular courses of action) and an interest in exclusively using things in the external world (so as to access the necessities of life and to live in a culturally satisfying way). Society regards these interests as sufficiently important to protect them through the recognition of certain legal rights and duties that give effect to them.[49]

Various branches of the law can be 'individuated' on the basis of the fundamental interests they advance.[50] Tort law performs the function of protecting bodily security through the imposition of a duty to avoid inflicting harm.[51] Contract law deals with an individual's interest 'in forming co-operative relationships by making bargain agreements ... in which each party provides a quid pro quo ... for the benefit he [or she] is to receive under the contract'.[52] Property law is concerned with an individual's interest in 'exclusively determining the use of things'.[53]

For Penner, the idea of exclusion is central to a proper understanding of property. Although property carries with it a right of use, this right is a form of negative liberty: the right to be free from interference by others in regard to the thing owned. It does not carry with it the right to compel others to assist positively in the owner's enjoyment of the thing. If I own a piano, I can prevent you from playing it, but I cannot force you to teach me to play it simply because I have a right to use it.[54] Because of the primacy of exclusion over use—which he refers to as his 'exclusion thesis'[55]—Penner states that the concept of property is best understood as imposing on every individual a general duty to exclude themselves from things owned by others, which is logically prior to, and defines the contours of, the general right of the owner to use the thing free from interference by others. You have a duty to stay out of my garden, but not to refrain from looking at it as you walk by it on the street. It is the content of your duty that defines the content of my rights of use.[56]

---

[46] See Penner (n 15) 1.
[47] Such as the right to vote: see Rose-Ackerman (n 41) 962–63; Epstein (n 33) 987–88.
[48] Penner (n 15) 63–64.
[49] Ibid, 10–11, 14, 49.
[50] Ibid, 37–38, 48, 55.
[51] Penner (n 14) 740.
[52] Penner (n 15) 51.
[53] Ibid, 50, 71, 73.
[54] Ibid, 50.
[55] Ibid, 71.
[56] Ibid, 71–74.

Another important aspect of Penner's concept of property is that it is impersonal in at least two respects. First, property's general duty to exclude oneself and the general right to have the benefit of that exclusion are not dependent upon the identity of the relevant parties. My duty (and everyone else's) to refrain from interfering with an object that is owned by someone does not depend upon who the owner is.[57] As I walk through a car park, I know that I have a duty to refrain from interfering with each and every car that is there, irrespective of whether those cars are owned by the same or different persons. And the content of my duty in respect to a particular car does not vary upon whether the owner has owned the car for five minutes or five years, or whether the car was driven there by someone other than the owner.[58] In this way, property rights and duties operate in rem as they exist with respect to a res. The physical thing that is owned mediates between holders of the relevant rights and duties, 'blocking any content which has to do with the specific individuality of particular persons from entering into the right-duty relation'.[59] This is to be contrasted with relations between a specific owner and a specific non-owner in regard to a specific thing that is owned, such as when you lend me your car. In this situation our respective rights and duties subsist in personam. Your identity and my identity are crucial to the relationship, and that relationship is *about* the car rather than being mediated through it.[60]

The second way in which property is impersonal for Penner is set out in his 'separability thesis'. Only things that we see as being separate from ourselves and our 'personality rich' relationships with others can be the subject of property rights.[61] So, 'objects, space, ideas and even particular concretely specified relations between people, such as debts' can be objects of property,[62] but things such as 'our talents, our personalities, our eyesight, or our friendships cannot', even though they may be of value to us and even though we can protect them through an indirect form of exclusion.[63] Another way of thinking about the requirement of separability is to say that things can only be property if we can comfortably conceive of them as being contingently, and not inherently, ours. We must be easily able to envisage them as belonging to another and that other having a relationship with the thing that is fundamentally similar to that which exists between the thing and its current 'owner'.[64] For example,[65] my wedding ring is my property and I am very emotionally attached to it, but the fact that it is mine is somewhat a matter of chance; it might have been initially purchased by someone other than my wife, or she might have chosen to give it to someone else, or it might be used by someone else after my death or if it were stolen from me. Contrast this with my marriage, which is not my property. My marriage is so fundamentally connected to me that it does not make sense to say that

---

[57] Ibid, 26–27.
[58] Ibid, 75.
[59] Ibid, 29.
[60] Ibid, 26–27.
[61] Ibid, ch 5.
[62] Ibid, 105.
[63] Ibid, 111.
[64] Ibid, 111–12.
[65] See ibid, 126–27.

my marriage might just as easily have been someone else's. My marriage cannot be your marriage in the same way that my ring might have been your ring.

Having outlined Penner's conception of property, we now turn to what he has to say about the ability to alienate one's own property. His thoughts in this regard are derived from what he sees as the fundamental element of property: the right of exclusive use. What the right involves is the power of the owner to determine the disposition of the thing, and not a requirement to use it as one's own.[66] He explains:

> One of the traps that an analyst of property can fall into is to mistake the nature of this exclusivity. The right to property is like a gate, not a wall. The right to property permits the owner not only to make solitary use of his property, by excluding all others, but also permits him [sic] to make a social use of his property, by selectively excluding others, which is to say by selectively allowing some to enter. The exclusivity that attends the ownership of property is variable by the owner. By varying this exclusivity the owner can actually confer rights on others, by licensing them to use his property.[67]

For Penner, inherent in the power to determine the use of property is the right to share it (through a licence), or voluntarily terminate one's ownership of it, through abandonment or gift. However, most controversially, Penner asserts that the right to sell or contract to sell one's property is not inherent in the concept of property as exclusive use, although the power to do so is granted by an area of the law distinct from property: contract.[68]

Penner argues that either the right of abandonment or the right to share/licence provides the logical basis for the right to transfer the property by way of gift. In terms of the former, a gift can be seen as a form of 'directional abandonment'. The act of gift from me to you can be broken down into an abandonment by me, communication of that fact to you, and then you being the first person to take possession of the unowned object.[69] In terms of the latter, a gift is in effect the grant by the donor of an indefinite and exclusive licence by which he or she relaxes his or her own right to exclude and adopts the donee's future use of the object as the donor's, as well as the donee's, own.[70] Thus, a gift 'constitutes the ultimate expression of the social element of property because it transfers the totality of a right of exclusive use'.[71]

Whereas a right to gift property is a manifestation of the right of exclusive use, the right to sell or contract for the sale of property is not. With a gift, according to Penner, the donor—motivated by a desire to use the object by sharing it—adopts the donee's use as the donor's own. In contrast to the 'social' use of property involved with a gift, a sale requires the vendor to abandon his or her right to control the future use of the property; the vendor is not adopting the buyer's future use as his or her own. The receipt of consideration for the transfer takes the transaction outside the realm of property (and the interest of determining use) and into the domain of

---

[66] Ibid, 75.
[67] Ibid, 74–75.
[68] Ibid, 75.
[69] Ibid, 84.
[70] Ibid, 85.
[71] Ibid, 89.

contract, which is concerned with making binding agreements with others for one's own self-interest. Although there is nothing in the concept of property that renders its sale inappropriate, it is a mistake to see this ability as inherent in the concept.[72] Penner claims that he stands apart in the property-theorising world[73] in thinking that:

> [T]he right to exchange property rights is not entailed by the right of exclusive use. It arises because we have both property rights *and* a generally unlimited right to make contracts. These are different rights, however, protecting very different interests ... the former concerns the protection of our interests in exclusively determining the disposition of things ... the latter protects our ability to enter into a particular kind of voluntary relationship by which people can, for consideration, act co-operatively and consensually exploit each other's advantages of whatever kind.[74]

IV. INHERENTLY INALIENABLE PROPERTY

We now examine two contexts in which rights are characterised as proprietary even though the ability to transfer them is absent. Both of these were expounded by Justice (later Chief Justice) Gerard Brennan of the High Court of Australia in the early 1990s. The first relates to native title held by Australian Aboriginal and Torres Strait Islander Peoples, and the second, in the context of a constitutional protection, to the right of a Commonwealth of Australia employee to sue the Commonwealth in the tort of negligence.

A. Native Title

The landmark case of *Mabo v Queensland (No 2)*[75] established that the acquisition of sovereignty by the British Crown over the parts of the territory that was to become Australia did not, of itself, extinguish the rights and interests that Indigenous groups held over those lands and waters by virtue of their laws, customs and traditions. Provided that the normative connection between the Indigenous group and the relevant land or waters remains unbroken from the time of the acquisition of sovereignty, the radical title of the Crown is burdened by native title.[76]

Native title gives the relevant Indigenous group a communal title, being the right to carry out uses of land and waters in accordance with their traditional laws and customs, such as hunting, gathering, fishing and conducting ceremonies. Because native title is given its content by the laws and customs of the Indigenous group, and because it is not a creature of the common law, it is not alienable under the

---

[72] Ibid, 87, 90–91.
[73] Ibid, 5.
[74] Ibid, 92 (emphasis in original).
[75] *Mabo v Queensland (No 2)* (1992) 175 CLR 1.
[76] Ibid, 48–49, 50–52, 58–62 (Brennan J; Mason CJ and McHugh J agreeing). Section 223 of the Native Title Act 1993 (Cth) adopts the common law conception of native title in this respect.

common law: it cannot be transferred to a person who is not a member of the relevant Indigenous group.[77]

Deane and Gaudron JJ, implicitly adopting an essentialist view of property in land, stated that native title is a personal and not a proprietary right because it lacks the necessary characteristics of being alienable and being derived from an actual or presumed Crown grant.[78] Toohey J expressed the view that the question of whether native title is personal or proprietary is 'fruitless and unnecessarily complex' and is not determinative of the Crown's power to extinguish native title.[79] By contrast, Brennan J (with whom Mason CJ and McHugh J agreed) was at pains to classify native title as proprietary, despite its inalienability. This is because in order to estab-lish the existence of native title, the Indigenous group must demonstrate its exclusive occupation of the territory. Such a group will, by definition, be the owner of the territory as there is no other owner.[80] At least two consequences flow from the fact that native title is proprietary: it survives the acquisition of sovereignty (in case it is thought that personal rights do not); and proprietary remedies may be invoked to protect it.[81]

It is clear that this conception of native title is antithetical to the economic view of what property comprises. Instead of being an individual and alienable interest that allows a full range of intensive and productive uses, native title is communal, inalienable and only allows low-intensity, traditional uses of the land.[82] In con-structing native title in this way, the courts have clearly not set out to achieve the most efficient use of resources. Instead, the reformulation of the Australian com-mon law to recognise native title is motivated by a desire to ensure the equality of all Australians before the law by rejecting the discriminatory notion that Australia's Indigenous people were 'too low in the scale of social organisation to be acknowl-edged as possessing rights and interests in land'.[83] The recognition of native title removes the former distinction drawn by the English common law between colonies which were acquired through settlement (where no existing property rights were held to exist) and those acquired through conquest (where pre-existing property rights continued until expressly extinguished).[84]

It is not certain how Penner would view the recognition of native title. In one respect, native title involves the existence of a social disposition of property through sharing among members of the relevant Indigenous group. Obviously, the absence of the right to sell native title rights would not contradict Penner's idea of property. However, native title is based upon a profound cultural and spiritual connection

---

[77] *Mabo* (n 75) 59, 60.

[78] Ibid, 88–90.

[79] Ibid, 195.

[80] Ibid, 51.

[81] Ibid, 51, 61–62.

[82] It is not inevitable that native title rights be limited in such a manner. In *Delgamuukw v British Columbia* [1997] 3 SCR 1010, 1050–51, in delivering the majority decision for the Supreme Court of Canada, Lamer CJ stated that although Canadian Aboriginal title was inalienable, it permits the land to be used in non-traditional ways (such as mining), provided that such uses are not irreconcilable with the connection between the claimant group and their land. See S Grattan and L McNamara, 'The Common Law Construct of Native Title' (1998) 8 *Griffith Law Review* 50, 65–72.

[83] *Mabo* (n 75) 58.

[84] Ibid.

between Indigenous Peoples and their land, as evidenced though the continued observance of traditional laws and customs which pre-date the acquisition of sovereignty by the Crown. The connection is unique rather than fungible and is not one that would contemplate the possibility of voluntary abandonment, although of course it was susceptible to extinction where an Indigenous group has been forcibly dispossessed in the course of the 'tide of history'.[85] In this respect, native title infringes Penner's 'separability thesis', which as we have seen holds that for an object to be property, it *must not* be intimately related to persons or their relationships, and it *must* be susceptible to be thought of as being owned by someone other than the present owner.

The bundle of rights thesis, by contrast, does provide a good account of the contours of native title, with its limited range of permitted uses and lack of alienability. And we are not forced into adopting Penner's view of the nihilistic aspect of the bundle of rights model. Native title is designed to meet identified policy aims; it strikes a balance between the rights of the relevant Indigenous Peoples and the interests of wider Australian society. This is achieved by a recognition of native title, subject to it being overridden by interests granted by the Crown which enable more economically productive uses of land, such as commercial mining, agriculture and fishing, to be carried out.[86] Of course, this is not to say that everyone agrees that a proper balance between a respect for Australia's Indigenous People and the security of commercial activity has been struck.[87]

B. Right to Sue in Tort as 'Property'

In *Georgiadis v Australian and Overseas Telecommunications Corporation*,[88] the High Court of Australia had to consider the constitutionality of a Commonwealth statute which extinguished the right of an employee of a Commonwealth instrumentality to sue his employer in negligence for personal injuries. That right to sue for common law damages had been replaced by a right to statutory compensation quantified by a less generous formula. The precise issue in the case was whether the operation of the statute in respect of a common law right that had already accrued effected an acquisition by the Commonwealth of the property of the plaintiff employee. A majority[89] of the High Court held that, for the purposes of section 51(xxxi) of the Australian Constitution, the Commonwealth had acquired property of the employee. Further, because the right to statutory compensation to which the employee was entitled was less generous than the right to common law damages he had lost, the Commonwealth had not provided just terms for the acquisition as

---

[85] Ibid, 59–60.

[86] See the text to nn 24–29.

[87] For a discussion, see S Hepburn, 'Feudal Tenure and Native Title: Revising an Enduring Fiction' (2005) 27 *Sydney Law Review* 49, 81–86.

[88] *Georgiadis v Australian and Overseas Telecommunications Corporation* (1994) 179 CLR 297.

[89] Mason CJ, Deane and Gaudron JJ (in a joint judgment) and Brennan J Dawson, Toohey and McHugh JJ dissented. The view of the majority was applied in a later High Court decision involving a similar law: *Smith v ANL Ltd* (2000) 204 CLR 493.

required by section 51(xxxi). Therefore, the purported extinguishment was invalid insofar as it applied to the common law cause of action that had already accrued.

As part of the majority, Mason CJ, Deane and Gaudron JJ held that in extinguishing its financial liability to pay common law damages to an employee who had been injured through the negligence of its instrumentality, the Commonwealth had acquired a benefit that was 'property' for the purposes of the constitutional provision.[90] In dissenting, Dawson and Toohey JJ decided that the financial benefit acquired by the Commonwealth did not constitute 'property'.[91] Their Honours did not explain why this was the case, but as they believed that some indispensible attribute of property was absent, they were implicitly adopting an essentialist conception of the institution. Brennan J reached the same conclusion as Mason CJ, Deane and Gaudron JJ by a different route. His Honour said that if what the employee had lost through the extinguishment of his common law right to sue could be characterised as 'property', then that which the Commonwealth acquired through the extinguishment should be characterised the same way. Brennan J concluded that because the right to sue was a chose in action, it was proprietary in nature even though for public policy reasons—avoiding the 'evils of champerty'—such a right could not be assigned.[92] His Honour said: 'Assignability is not in all circumstances an essential characteristic of a right of property.'[93]

From an economic perspective, the decision in *Georgiadis* is justified. The Commonwealth had deprived the employee of a valuable right for its own benefit without fully compensating him for his loss. The State, in exercising its power to take property under its prerogative of eminent domain, must be constrained by the requirement of giving full compensation, thereby notionally leaving the deprived citizen indifferent between the compensated taking occurring or not. If such compensation were not provided for the acquisition, there would be no guarantee that the State would only take property when it was efficient to do so (that is, only when the social benefit of the taking would exceed the private cost of the affected citizen). In addition, the threat of the possibility of an uncompensated taking would provide property owners with an incentive to under-invest in their property.[94]

By contrast, Penner would presumably not agree with the right to sue in tort being characterised as property. This is because such a right would be too personal to satisfy his separability thesis: it is too bound up with the person of the purported 'owner'. Further, the right to sue for negligently inflicted harm reflects an interest protected by the law of tort, rather than property, so the holding in *Georgiadis* would infringe the necessity of individuating separate branches of the law.

---

[90] *Georgiadis* (n 88) 305. Such a view would be consistent with the application of either an essentialist or bundle of rights conception of property.

[91] Ibid, 315 (Dawson J), 321 (Toohey J).

[92] Ibid, 311.

[93] Ibid, 311–12, quoting Mason J in *R v Toohey, ex parte Meneling Station Pty Ltd* (1982) 158 CLR 327, 342–43. Dawson J (at 314), Toohey J (at 319–20) and McHugh J (at 325) were prepared to accept that the right to sue in tort was 'property', but stated that this was not relevant as s 51(xxxi) is concerned with whether the Commonwealth had acquired property and not whether the claimant had been deprived of property.

[94] Posner (n 16) 56–59; R Cooter and T Ulen, *Law and Economics*, 6th edn (Boston, MA, Prentice Hall, 2012) 175–76.

The bundle of rights model can accommodate the conception of property that emerges from *Georgiadis*. The right to be compensated for negligently inflicted injury can be seen as a manifestation of one or more of the rights to possess or use (one's bodily integrity) or the right to income (if one's bodily integrity has been exploited by the employer), or the right to security (having immunity from expropriation of one's bodily integrity). The fact that one of the rights usually associated with property—the right to transfer—is missing is certainly not fatal. Further, there is a good reason why the concept of property should in this context be given a more extensive meaning than usual. Section 51(xxxi) is a constitutional guarantee and 'property' is to be 'construed liberally as befits' that purpose.[95] The protection is anti-utilitarian in the sense that it prevents the notion of the public good being used to justify sacrificing the interests of an owner of property for the good of the community at large.[96] If property were given a narrow and very technical meaning in this context, it would be easy for the Commonwealth, by taking a few but important rights, to deprive an owner of significant benefits without providing him or her just compensation. (This is why 'property' in the section 51(xxxi) context has been held to include 'innominate and anomalous' interests.)[97] The meaning given to 'property' in *Georgiadis* is justified, having regard to its objective of constitutional protection.

V. RECENT CASES ON CONTRACTUAL RESTRAINTS

Historically, restraints on alienation were often imposed by transferors as conditions on the grant of property itself. So where the prohibited alienation occurred, the interest granted was purportedly brought to an end by being either revested in the grantor or transferred to another party.[98] In more recent times, however, restraints on alienation have been imposed by contract. One reason for this has been said to be the difficulty in creating exotic interests in registered title land.[99]

In this part we will examine the English and Australian positions regarding contractual restraints on alienation. We will also identify the circumstances in which a contractual provision will be struck down on the basis that it infringes the policy of favouring the free alienability of property.

A. England

The position in England seems to be straightforward. In *Caldy Manor Estate Ltd v Farrell*,[100] the Court of Appeal upheld a contractual provision that prohibited the vendor of a parcel of land from later selling it separately from other land that he

---

[95] *Georgiadis* (n 88) 312.
[96] Ibid, 310–11.
[97] Ibid, 305 (Mason CJ, Deane and Gaudron JJ).
[98] See Sweet (n 2) 240.
[99] See *Bondi Beach Astra Retirement Village Pty Ltd v Gora* [2010] NSWSC 81 [79].
[100] *Caldy Manor Estate Ltd v Farrell* [1974] 1 WLR 1303.

already owned. The Court explained that a threatened breach of the covenant *might* result in the grant of an injunction preventing the sale and that an actual breach would result only in the liability to pay (possibly nominal) damages. In neither case would the breach of covenant result in the termination of the covenantor's estate, which distinguishes this situation from one where the restraint was imposed as a condition of the grant. This was the basis for the Court holding that the restraint was valid and *not* void 'as being an unlawful restraint on alienation'.[101] The decision is regarded as establishing that in English law the doctrine of unlawful restraints does not apply to contractual restraints on the alienability of land.[102]

The position regarding the status of provisions prohibiting the assignment of contractual rights is also clear. In *Linden Gardens Trusts Ltd v Lenestra Sludge Disposal Ltd*,[103] the House of Lords considered a contract for the removal by the contractor of asbestos from the lessee's building. The contract contained a clause which provided that the lessee could not assign the benefit of the contract without the contractor's consent. The House of Lords held that the clause did not offend public policy and that it rendered ineffective a purported assignment by the lessee made without the contractor's consent.[104] In delivering the leading judgment, Lord Browne-Wilkinson stated that a party to a contract might have a genuine commercial interest in ensuring that he or she is bound to render performance only to the party with whom the contract was made.[105] Epstein describes the interest in the following way:

> The reason for the agreement [prohibiting the assignment of contractual rights] is the fear of surcharge—of additional burdens—upon a promisor should the promisee assign the right to a third party. The promisee is a known quantity chosen and selected by the promisor. Even if the legal system gives the promisor the same rights against the promisee's assignee, the value of those rights still might be reduced by the assignment. The promisor may not have the same informal leverage against the assignee ... Preventing the assignment reduces the cost to the promisor by fixing the content of the obligation that would otherwise run to an unidentified party.[106]

The policy concern identified by Lord Browne-Wilkinson was the basis for the contractual prohibition on assignment being given full effect. First, it was held that the prohibition was valid and that it did not offend public policy. Second, the prohibition rendered the purported assignment nugatory; the alternative of giving effect to the attempted transfer of the benefit to the assignee, but holding the assignor lessee liable to the contractor in damages for breach of the prohibition, was rejected.[107]

The decisions in *Caldy* (involving land) and *Linden Gardens* (involving contractual rights) share the position that a contractual restraint on alienation will not be struck down on the basis of public policy. However, they take divergent approaches as to what happens when a purported transfer is made in breach of such a clause.

---

[101] Ibid, 1307.
[102] K Mackie, 'Contractual Restraints on Alienation' (1998) 12 *Journal of Contract Law* 255, 257.
[103] *Linden Gardens* (n 4).
[104] Ibid, 107, 109.
[105] Ibid, 107, 108–09.
[106] Epstein (n 33) 982.
[107] *Linden Gardens* (n 4) 107, 109.

Caldy states that unless restrained by an injunction beforehand (which will not be available as of right), the transfer of land will be effective, but damages will lie against the transferor for breach of contract. By contrast, *Linden Gardens* holds that the attempted transfer of the contractual rights is totally ineffective. Tolhurst explains why a different approach is taken in regard to contractual rights. Because such rights owe their existence entirely to the agreement between the parties, that agreement not only determines the nature and content of the obligations as a matter of contract, but also shapes the attributes of the chose in action constituted by those contractual rights. An agreement prohibiting transfer robs the chose in action of its assignability.[108] This sets contractual rights apart from other forms of property that exist independently of an agreement between certain individuals.

B. Australia

Australia has accepted the English position, as expounded in *Linden Gardens*, that a prohibition on the assignment of *contractual rights* will be respected and will not be regarded as infringing public policy.[109] However, the High Court decision of *Hall v Busst*[110] has periodically generated further judicial consideration of the validity of contractual restrictions on the alienability of land, as well as chattels[111] and shares.[112] In *Hall v Busst*, Dixon CJ stated that a covenant entered into between the vendor and purchaser of land, which prohibited the purchaser from transferring, assigning or leasing the land without the prior written consent of the vendor, was unenforceable on the basis that it contravened the public policy of favouring the free alienability of land.[113]

Chief Justice Dixon's statement has been relied upon in several later cases by parties attempting to escape from a contractual provision they had entered into which prohibited alienation for a particular period,[114] or which granted an option to purchase,[115] or which granted a right of pre-emption.[116] With regard to grants of an option or right of pre-emption, the relevant restraint on alienation was effected by a combination of factors. First, the grantee's right to purchase was activated either by an attempt by the grantor to alienate the property to a third party, or was otherwise

---

[108] G Tolhurst, 'The Efficacy of Contractual Provisions Prohibiting Assignment' (2004) 26 *Sydney Law Review* 161, 179–81.

[109] See, eg, *Owners of Strata Plan 5290 v CGS & Co Pty Ltd* (2011) 281 ALR 575, 588–89, [60]–[61].

[110] *Hall v Busst* (n 4).

[111] *Re MacKay* (1972) 20 FLR 174.

[112] *Reuthlinger v MacDonald* [1976] 1 NSWLR 88.

[113] *Hall v Busst* (n 4) 217–18. Because the restraint was imposed by contract rather than a condition in the grant itself, it was not necessary to consider the argument that restraints on alienation are void because they are repugnant to the grant of a fee simple, a view which would be consistent with an essentialist conception of property.

[114] *Reuthlinger* (n 112); *Elton v Cavill (No 2)* (1994) 34 NSWLR 289; *Southlink Holdings Pty Ltd v Morerand Pty Ltd* [2010] VSC 214.

[115] *Wollondilly Shire Council v Picton Power Lines Pty Ltd* (1994) 33 NSWLR 551 and *Vercorp Pty Ltd v Lin* [2007] 2 Qd R 180; *Noon v Bondi Beach Astra Retirement Village Pty Ltd* (2010) 15 BPR 28,221; *Gora* (n 99).

[116] *John Nitschke Nominees Pty Ltd v Hahndorf Golf Club Inc* (2004) 88 SASR 109; *Moraitis Fresh Packaging (NSW) Pty Ltd v Fresh Express (Australia) Pty Ltd* (2008) 14 BPR 26,339.

protected by an express or implied term that the grantor would not alienate his or her interest in a way that would render the grant ineffective.[117] Second, the price for the exercise of the option or pre-emption was fixed at a level that might be below the market value at the time of exercise.[118]

In the majority of these cases where courts reached a conclusion as to the validity of the restraint, they concluded that the restraint was valid and did not infringe the public policy of favouring the free alienability of property. The courts did so on the basis that the public policy concerns invoked by a restriction on the owner's ability to alienate were overridden by the fact that the restraint served to advance a legitimate collateral interest of the promisee.[119] So, for example, a party who sells land to another on the basis that it will be developed or used in a particular way and, if it is not, the vendor will have the right to repurchase it at the original sale price may have a genuine commercial interest that is served by the restraint. The vendor might be a developer, who retains land that will be benefited if a house of a particular standard is constructed on the relevant land.[120] Or the vendor might be a local council that is trying to promote industrial development in the area.[121] Alternatively, the party benefited and the party burdened might be co-owners of property, and a co-owner has a legitimate interest in controlling the identity of those with whom they are in a relationship of co-ownership.[122] Or the parties may be joint venturers in a project involving the rezoning of land held by one of the parties. As it is central to the workings of the joint venture, for so long as it is on foot, that the land continue in the ownership of that party, the non-owning joint venturer will have a legitimate interest in a restraining the alienation of the land.[123]

The concept of a legitimate collateral purpose has been endorsed, and perhaps even expanded, by the New South Wales Court of Appeal in *Bondi Beach Astra Retirement Village Pty Ltd v Gora*. In this case the Court upheld a restraint which effectively meant that the operator of a retirement village was entitled to repurchase the fee simple in a unit previously sold to an occupant, at the price originally paid by the occupant (which was well below the current market value), whenever the occupant died or attempted to alienate his or her interest. The Court found that a public interest was implicated in such an arrangement:[124] facilitating the provision of housing for the aged.[125] Giles JA said:

> [R]estraints of the present kind in the provision and operation of retirement villages serve sound purposes ... To those who wish it, many or perhaps most of whom will need to take care with their finances, a lesser capital outlay at the cost of restraints of the kind in the

---

[117] *Picton Power Lines* (n 115) 555.

[118] See *Moraitis Fresh Packaging* (n 116) 26, 365, [146] (Hodgson JA). Where the exercise price is equivalent to the current market value, it is unlikely that the restraint will be impeachable: *John Nitschke* (n 116) 371, [124].

[119] The early cases expressly adopting this principle are *Reuthlinger* (n 112) 101 and *Elton* (n 114) 296, 300. The principle itself derives from Sweet (n 2) 246 and was recently endorsed in *Gora* (n 99) [327]–[333].

[120] *Vercorp* (n 115) 192, [57].

[121] *Picton Power Lines* (n 115).

[122] *Elton* (n 114) 296, 300.

[123] *Southlink* (n 114) [43]–[44].

[124] *Gora* (n 99) [4] (Giles JA).

[125] Ibid, [336], [341] (Campbell JA).

present case will be acceptable, if not attractive. As retirement villages are conducted, the result will not be that property is taken out of commerce because it is inalienable. It will be cycled through successive residents of the retirement village. Public policy does not require that the restraints will be struck down.[126]

The existence in Australia of the legitimate collateral interest concept is reminiscent of the policy, articulated by Lord Browne-Wilkinson in *Linden Gardens* and by Richard Epstein, justifying why clauses prohibiting the assignment of contractual rights are upheld. Just as in the context of bare contractual rights, parties who enter into a joint venture or a co-ownership arrangement involving land usually do so on the basis that the identity of the other is important. They are reluctant to be thrust unexpectedly into business with a stranger.[127] More generally, contractual restraints on alienation can make good business sense for the parties involved—as otherwise they would not be voluntarily entered into—and the party agreeing to purchase subject to the restriction will usually benefit from paying a lower purchase price.[128]

From an economic perspective, upholding such restraints on alienation is conducive to efficiency. Of course, when considered at the time of the desired, but prohibited, alienation, the restraint appears to work against the movement of a resource to a higher-valued use. However, it must be remembered that the restraint, where it is of a nature that allows it to be upheld, has served the interest of both the promisor and the promisee.[129] To allow the promisor, who has paid less for the resource because of the restraint, to resile from the bargain is the equivalent of letting him or her have their cake and eat it too.

Penner does briefly consider the effect of restraints on alienation on his understanding of property, but only in the context of governmental restrictions on a class of property rights, such as property in houses generally,[130] and not in the context of restraints imposed by contract on individual objects of property. However, in the context of governmental regulation, Penner thinks that whether the restraint is indictable as an 'attack on property', the subjective purpose behind the regulation is determinative. So, a complete ban on the transfer or sharing of a house would be prima facie colourable as striking at the property-like character of the owner's interest, but not if the purpose were to stop the threat of transmission of an infectious disease.[131] Further, he states that a ban on the selling of houses would be a diminution of an owner's property rights if the intention were to render an owner a mere occupier who needed state approval in order to withdraw from his or her property and take some value from it. But if the intention were to shut down an aspect of the market because it was thought that such dealings produced inequitable results, that would not be a diminution of property rights as the right to sell is not inherent in the right of property.[132] The relevance for Penner of the motivation behind the restraint,

---

[126] Ibid, [5].
[127] Epstein (n 33) 982.
[128] Ibid.
[129] Richard Epstein, 'Past and Future: The Temporal Dimension in the Law of Property' (1986) 64 *Washington University Law Quarterly* 667, 694, 713.
[130] Penner (n 15) 100–03.
[131] Ibid, 102.
[132] Ibid.

and the fact that he sees property and contract as serving different interests, suggests that he would have no difficulty with the Australian position of upholding contractual restraints that meet a legitimate collateral purpose.

VI. CONCLUSION

Most forms of property are, of course, alienable. Our world would be very different if it were otherwise. The economic conception of property does a good job in explaining why: the efficient use of resources requires that it be so. As we have seen, however, the economic perspective also countenances: (1) an obligation to alienate (in the form of a liability rule); and (2) the inability to alienate, based upon the law's imposition of an inalienability rule or because of a private contractual agreement. An economic perspective of law takes a nuanced attitude to alienability because it regards the phenomenon as instrumental in achieving efficiency. However, where a society has made a choice that in a particular context a goal other than efficiency is important, as Australia has done in the area of native title, then the economic model loses some of its explanatory power.

Penner's idea of property takes a rather agnostic view of alienation where it involves sale rather than gift. The right to sell is neither inherent in nor antithetical to the notion that the institution of property serves the distinctive human interest of determining the use of the external things of the world. However, Penner's thesis contains a major weakness. Dividing areas of the law into watertight compartments based upon discrete aspects of human interests splinters both bodies of legal doctrine and human activity in an unrealistic way. It is also reminiscent of the bundle of rights model that he abhors. To break down a legal system into separate rules about using things and selling things, and to say that these are distinct and cannot influence each other, is to see legal rules as existing as separate sticks. Penner's insistence upon the conceptual purity of property denies it being shaped in a way that is socially useful. The innovative way in which property is filled out in the native title and constitutional contexts strikes socially desirable balances: in the former between (i) recognising traditional Indigenous relationships with land and (ii) allowing commercially important exploitation of natural resources, and in the latter between (i) allowing the Commonwealth government to acquire property for the public good and (ii) the protection of individual citizens. What all this means is that the bundle of rights model of property should not be rejected out of hand, as Penner is wont to do. The Australian cases show that if it is employed in a restrained manner, the bundle of rights model is a useful device. In most circumstances the bundle will include the rights identified by the economist as important: use, exclusion and alienability. However, in some contexts, where there is a consensus that the economic paradigm is not completely appropriate, various rights, such as the right of alienation, can be removed from an entitlement in order to allow property to serve a socially constructive purpose.

18

Possession Taken by Theft and the Original Acquisition of Personal Property Rights

ROBIN HICKEY[*]

I. INTRODUCTION

AXIOMATICALLY AT COMMON law, title to goods is relative.[1] Even one who avowedly is not the owner of some thing can bring proceedings in respect of interference with it, provided at least she can prove prior possession.[2] The proceedings available to a prior possessor in these circumstances are the ordinary actions that serve to protect interests in goods, most importantly the tort of conversion. This means that, on the ground of her relatively better title, the possessor can recover the thing possessed or damages representing its full value.[3] While this rule brings fairly uncontroversial procedural advantages to lawful possessors (who by proving possession are spared the potentially onerous burden of proving title),[4] it seems to be a doctrine of general application. Indeed, in *Costello v Chief Constable of Derbyshire*, the Court of Appeal held that even a thief acquires a relative title to sue for conversion of things he has stolen, Lightman J observing that 'as a matter of principle and authority possession means the same thing and is entitled

---

[*] Senior Lecturer in Law, Durham University. I would like to thank Lorna Fox-O'Mahony and the anonymous referee for their very useful comments on the draft.

[1] See generally D Fox, 'Relativity of Title at Law and in Equity' (2006) 65 *CLJ* 330.

[2] *Armory v Delamirie* (1722) 1 Stra 505; *Jeffries v Great Western Railway Company* (1856) E&B 802. See generally ELG Tyler and NE Palmer (eds), *Crossley Vaines' Personal Property*, 5th edn (London, Butterworths, 1973) 46; S Green and J Randall, *The Tort of Conversion* (Oxford, Hart Publishing, 2009) 82, 88, framing title to sue in conversion in terms of the claimant's 'superior possessory right' and observing the ability of actual possession to generate such a right within a system of relative titles. At common law this basic proposition is also true of title to land: see *Asher v Whitlock* (1865–66) LR 1 QB 1. This chapter uses the learning on goods instrumentally to make a general claim about the effects of possession at common law, but so far as it goes, the argument on matters of justification ought to have relevance too in the context of land.

[3] *Armory* (n 2) stands for the proposition that the full value of the goods can be recovered and also for the evidential rule that any doubts about that value will be resolved against the wrongdoer. While damages is the usual remedy for conversion, s 3 of the Torts (Interference with Goods) Act 1977 provides jurisdiction for courts to order delivery up as an alternative. On this, and remedial awards for conversion generally, see Green and Randall (n 2) ch 7.

[4] See *The Winkfield* [1902] P 42, 54–55 (Collins MR).

to the same legal protection, whether or not it has been obtained lawfully or by theft or by other unlawful means'.[5]

In modern texts, this general availability of conversion has been rationalised to a substantive claim about the nature of the relative title acquired by possession. Possession is understood as a causative event, and the right generated in consequence of possession is seen as a general property right with the content of ownership.[6] This right is still understood as a *relative* right, availing against any wrongdoer who comes later in time to the thing, while yielding to the claim of anyone who proves a better right;[7] however, so rendered, the doctrine of relatively of title acquires a very substantive flavour. It is a doctrine about the permissible existence of concurrent but several property rights *of the same kind* in respect of *the same thing*. It is a doctrine about the permissible existence of several and independent *owners* of the same thing,[8] each of whom can point to some basis for their independent claim, and at the very least to some prior possession which has generated their right. These rights will always be judged relatively, but this does not alter the substance of the position. Possession results in the original acquisition of ownership. Or if we prefer the more conventional terminology, possession results in the original acquisition of general property in goods.

Sometimes such original acquisition of property by a possessor seems to be a sensible response. While the first concern of the law must always be to protect the continuing property of those better entitled,[9] matters of policy and justice can nevertheless be served by recognising the creation of relative, independent property. This is especially true in the case of finders, where the acquisition of general property seems to reflect the proper ability of the finder to make interim management decisions about the found thing (eg where it is to be stored, by whom and so on), and also fulfils a secondary redistributive objective, grounding the alternative entitlement of the finder in the event that the loser cannot be traced.[10] More generally, to the extent that possession is the accepted basis of a bailee's interest at common law,[11] it seems fair to regard that possession as generating a property right, since during the currency of even the most basic bailment, the bailee will require ordinary powers of management incidental to a general property right, if for no other reason than to ensure the thing is kept safely and returned intact to the bailor at the end of the bailment. But this kind of acquisition seems much less intuitive in the case

---

[5] *Costello v Chief Constable of Derbyshire* [2001] 1 WLR 1437, 1450.

[6] B McFarlane, *The Structure of Property Law* (Oxford, Hart Publishing, 2008) 144–46; R Hickey, *Property and the Law of Finders* (Oxford, Hart Publishing, 2010) 162–64; S Douglas, *Liability for Wrongful Interferences with Chattels* (Oxford, Hart Publishing, 2011) 24–26, 29–30.

[7] This means that, in modern accounts, 'title' is effectively synonymous with 'property right', or at least might be taken to denote a general property right with certain standard content. As *English Private Law* explains, title is 'derived from "entitlement", that entitlement being a right to exclusive possession of the thing over which it subsists forever': A Burrows (ed), *English Private Law*, 2nd edn (Oxford, Oxford University Press, 2007) [4.131].

[8] McFarlane (n 6) 145–46.

[9] It is clear that an owner's loss of possession, whether casually or by force or theft, effects no change to her property rights. Indeed, it even remains doubtful whether abandonment operates to divest property rights in respect of goods. For interesting recent discussion of the latter issue, see S Thomas, 'Do Freegans Commit Theft?' (2010) 30 *Legal Studies* 98.

[10] Hickey (n 6) 156–57.

[11] *Coggs v Bernard* (1703) 2 Ld Raym 909; *Ashby v Tolhurst* [1937] 2 KB 242; M Bridge, *Personal Property Law*, 3rd edn (Oxford, Clarendon Press, 2002) 33–35.

of a thief.[12] In obvious and important ways, to recognise the acquisitive effect of possession-taken-by-theft is to reward criminal behaviour and to offend commonly accepted juridical principles.[13] Moreover, in this context it makes no difference that the thief's title is merely *relative*, for while it will certainly yield to the prior continuing property right of his victim, its acquisitive significance will be at stake precisely where that person cannot be found. This is very clearly seen on the facts of *Costello* itself, where the police were ordered to redeliver a stolen car to a thief, who thereafter was at liberty to use and enjoy it, subject to the continuing (but unlikely to materialise) claim of the registered keeper.[14] To the extent that we recognise the thief's acquisition of relative title in cases of this kind, we necessarily recognise and invoke the broad potential for redistribution that it entails.

With these general concerns in mind, this chapter queries the soundness of the view that wrongful possession should be protected by the standard actions for interference with goods. It argues that, on closer examination, this is not a proposition that is compelled on the authorities, nor one demanded as a matter of principle. This means of course that there is room for cases like *Costello* to be decided differently, but the real significance of the argument lies at a more general level. For when we examine the authoritative and principled basis of this narrow proposition on possession obtained by theft, we expose great need for development in our basic principles of possessory protection. It is not at all clear that English law is committed to the view that in every case a possessor should acquire a relatively good property right in the possessed thing. Indeed, where the possessor is a wrongdoer, and certainly where he is a thief, the objects of the law might be better served by the creation of a more limited form of possessory protection, achieved through the possessor's acquisition of a personal right. To make this argument, this chapter proceeds in turn to evaluate, and doubt, both the authoritative and the principled bases for Lightman J's observation in *Costello*. It then moves to consider the matter from a general perspective, arguing that the values that underpin and justify our basic rules of possessory protection entail a more nuanced response to matters of acquisition.

II. PROTECTING POSSESSION TAKEN BY THEFT

It is clear that in *Costello*, the Court of Appeal considered that protection of the thief's possession was demanded as a matter of principle and authority. Turning first

[12] See S Barkehall Thomas, 'Thieves, Owners, and the Problem of Title: Part 1.—Chattels' (2011) 5 *Journal of Equity* 228, who doubts that the equation of finders and thieves is possible in Australia.

[13] Specifically the principles that: (a) one ought not to profit from one's own wrongdoing; or (b) found an action on immoral conduct (*ex turpi causa non oritur actio*). For well-known discussion of the former, see the treatment of *Riggs v Palmer*, 115 NY 506 (1889) in R Dworkin, *Law's Empire* (Oxford, Hart Publishing, 1998). For an invocation of the latter in the context of acquisition by theft, see *Solomon v Metropolitan Police Commissioner* [1982] Crim LR 606, discussed further below.

[14] *Costello* (n 5). See also *Gough v Chief Constable of the West Midlands* [2004] EWCA Civ 206. The same problem has arisen where courts have ordered the redelivery of cash seized by the police notwithstanding that, on the balance of probabilities, the cash represented the proceeds of unlawful dealing in drugs: *Webb v Chief Constable of Merseyside Police* [2000] QB 427, 434 (CA); and compare *R (on the application of Morgan) v Dyfed Powys Magistrates' Court* [2003] EWHC 1568 (Admin), where the court found no suspicion of criminal activity on the facts.

to the latter, the leading judgment contains lengthy discussion of applicable cases,[15] stretching back to the well-known decision in *Buckley v Gross*.[16] While the Court was convinced that these authorities were sufficient to resolve the case in favour of the claimant, here we take a more sceptical position, arguing that the cases prior to *Costello* were equivocal at best and reflected a good deal of doubt on the matter.

A. Protecting Possession Taken by Theft as a Matter of Authority

The first point to note is that we will not find any authority before the middle of the nineteenth century which holds conversion available to a wrongful possessor. This is significant because common rules on possession are sometimes supposed to be of great antiquity, but very late in the development of conversion,[17] the position of wrongful possessors remained unresolved. In *Elliott v Kemp*, the Court of Exchequer expressly left open the question of whether possession without more would always make available conversion,[18] and in *Jeffries v Great Western Railway Co*, the same point was the subject of fierce debate between counsel and the bench.[19] While the latter case eventually resolved to allow conversion to a (civil) wrongdoer, the bare existence of the argument reveals doubt about the extent of the basic rules on possession, and these doubts continued to be reflected in later cases. A good example is provided by *Buckley v Gross* itself. There the claimant sought recovery of certain quantities of tallow which he had obtained unlawfully. The police had seized the tallow and sold it to the defendants pursuant to statutory powers of disposal.[20] The claimant was not allowed to maintain conversion against the defendants for the reason that any right which he might have acquired in virtue of his possession had nevertheless been divested by the statutory sale to the defendants.[21] However, the prior question as to the nature of the claimant's title was not settled with certainty. Cockburn CJ expressly left open whether a wrongful possessor might maintain trover,[22] but while Blackburn J doubted that even felonious conduct would make a difference to a possessor's entitlement to proceed,[23]

---

[15] *Costello* (n 5) 1445–50.

[16] *Buckley v Gross* (1863) 3 B&S 566.

[17] Our modern tort of conversion evolved slowly from the old form of trover. Trover was a specialised action on the case, so called because it alleged a 'finding' by the defendant and subsequent conversion to his own use. It supplanted older procedures in trespass and detinue, and in practice was the dominant action for the protection of interests in goods from early in the fifteenth century until its abolition by s 49 of the Common Law Procedure Act 1852. This section provided a new form of declaration by which a claimant alleged conversion, and this gives the form to the modern tort. For a useful historical overview, see JB Ames, 'The History of Trover' (1897–98) 11 *Harvard Law Review* 277 and 374.

[18] *Elliott v Kemp* (1840) 7 M&W 306, 312.

[19] *Jeffries* (n 2).

[20] Specifically s 29 of the Metropolitan Police Act 1839, which provided jurisdiction for a magistrate to make orders disposing of property seized lawfully by the police. The order was for delivery 'to the party who shall appear to be the rightful owner', but in the event that such a person could not be ascertained, there was a supplementary power 'to make such order with respect to such goods or money as to such magistrate shall seem meet'. Today the position is governed, in similar terms, by s 1 of the Police (Property) Act 1897.

[21] *Jeffries* (n 2) 571–72 (Cockburn CJ); 573 (Crompton J); 574 (Blackburn J).

[22] Ibid, 571.

[23] Ibid, 573.

Crompton J insisted that the cases allowing recovery were cases of 'innocent' possession.[24] So we can say with safety that any proposition allowing conversion to a thief or other unlawful possessor is one that arrived rather late in the development of conversion and emerged without any great degree of clarity or conviction. Indeed, as late as 1887, even Sir Frederick Pollock could doubt whether wrongful possession availed in conversion.[25]

Since these tentative beginnings, direct authority on the rights of unlawful possessors has been scarce, and not necessarily supportive of Lightman J's proposition. Indeed, there is one relatively recent decision squarely against the idea that a claimant should be permitted to rely on possession obtained by theft. In *Solomon v Metropolitan Police Commissioner*, conversion was refused where the claimant sought to recover a car that she had purchased with the proceeds of a prior conspiracy to steal.[26] As in *Costello*, the claimant had been arrested and the car lawfully seized by the police, but taking the view that the car was 'stolen property' with the meaning of section 24 of the Theft Act 1968, Milmo J thought that public policy precluded recovery by the claimant.[27] In *Costello*, as we shall see later, for reasons which are not necessarily as persuasive as they first appear, Lightman J ultimately disagreed with this public policy rationale,[28] but he also found equivocation in the supporting authorities post-*Jeffries*,[29] and in this he was entirely right. While there are a few well-known cases which appear to support the decision in *Solomon* (in that possession has not availed the possessor, and judges have taken a dim view of his activities), these are much better explained on grounds other than the existence of special rules about a thief's acquisition of title. For example, in *Buckley v Gross*, as we have seen, the claimant was unable to sustain proceedings for subsequent conversion of the stolen tallow because a statutory order of sale had vested a superior title in the defendant.[30] Any conclusion on the title acquired by a thief, if any, was strictly unnecessary to the resolution of the case.[31] Likewise, in *Hibbert v McKiernan*, while the court was clearly opposed to the idea that it should protect

---

[24] Ibid, 573.

[25] F Pollock, *The Law of Torts* (London, Stevens & Sons, 1887) 300. Pollock was one of the authors of the leading authoritative work on possession at common law, so his doubt on wrongfully acquired possession must be taken very seriously: F Pollock and RS Wright, *An Essay on Possession in the Common Law* (Oxford, Clarendon Press, 1888).

[26] *Solomon* (n 13).

[27] JC Smith expressed agreement in the commentary accompanying the case note: 'This [civil] action is brought exclusively for the benefit of the thief and, if it succeeds, it enables her to enjoy the fruits of her crime. It is not surprising that the judge concluded that it would be contrary to public policy to allow the action to proceed': ibid.

[28] *Costello* (n 5) 1450.

[29] *Jeffries* was not cited to the Court of Appeal in *Costello*, but the earliest case to which Lightman J referred was the closely contemporaneous decision in *Buckley* (n 16), discussed below. This starting reference to *Buckley* impliedly supports the general thesis of this section that there was no authority pre-*Jefrries* squarely allowing a wrongdoer to rely on his possession.

[30] *Buckley* (n 16). See also *Irving v National Provincial Bank Ltd* [1962] 2 QB 73. Susan Barkehall Thomas ((n 12) 242) has suggested that this rehearsal of the ratio depends on a narrow reading of *Buckley*, but from the reports, the operation of the statute seems to have been the major concern of the court. Indeed, the opening lines of Cockburn CJ's judgment declare specifically that 'the case comes within s 29 of the statute': (1863) 3 B&S 566, 571.

[31] *Buckley* (n 16) 571; and to similar effect, *Field v Sullivan* [1923] VLR 70, 83 and *Bird v Fort Frances* [1949] 2 DLR 791, 798–99.

possession that the defendants had acquired by stealthily recovering 'lost' balls from a golf course, their conviction for theft was sustained on the basis of a better title in the members of the club and necessitated no decision about the rights, if any, which the defendants had acquired in respect of the balls.[32] Cases of this kind reflect a very natural antipathy to thieves, but they tell us nothing conclusive about a thief's acquisition of title.

Other cases address the matter more squarely from the other end and appear to hold that a thief does acquire a property right in virtue of his possession. The trouble is that, again, on closer examination, these turn out to be far from unequivocal. In *Parker v British Airways Board*, Donaldson LJ thought that a thief acquired a 'frail title', but did not expound the nature of that title, the determination of which, in any event, would have been well beyond the facts of the case before him.[33] In *Betts v Metropolitan Police District Receiver and Carter Paterson & Co Ltd*,[34] the claimant was allowed to recover 15 bales of cloth. He had been charged with stealing and receiving this cloth, alleged to be the property of the second defendants, and eventually the police receiver had delivered it to the second defendants.[35] The claimant's recovery was premised on his prior possession, with du Parcq J expressly directing the jury that, unless the second defendant could prove its title, the claimant's possession was sufficient 'whatever suspicions might be entertained as to the manner in which the [claimant] had come by the cloth'.[36] The difficulty for our purposes is that there was no clear evidence that the claimant had stolen the cloth.[37] Accordingly, despite the direction that suspicions of wrongdoing ought not to displace the general possession rule, this is not a case where a wrongful possessor successfully sued for recovery, and despite the rehearsal of each of these cases in *Costello*,[38] it is not at all clear that there is express authority to confirm that a thief acquires a property right by possession.

If the authorities are lacking on this point, we might still find that a thief's acquisition coheres with the doctrinal and conceptual structures of our personal property law as more broadly understood. In support of the reasoning in *Costello*, Battersby has argued that the idea that a thief acquires a property right figures implicitly in those provisions of the Limitation Act 1980 which regulate the time limits for conversion claims related to a theft.[39] While section 4(1) of the Act generally suspends

---

[32] See also *R v Rostron* [2003] EWCA Crim 2206; and R Hickey, 'Stealing Abandoned Goods: Possessory Title in Proceedings for Theft' (2006) 26 *Legal Studies* 584, considering a matter conversely related to this chapter, about the extent to which subsisting possessory titles prior to a theft operate to make safe an indictment, notwithstanding the appearance that the goods in question have been abandoned.

[33] *Parker v British Airways Board* [1982] QB 1004, 1010.

[34] *Betts v Metropolitan Police District Receiver and Carter Paterson & Co Ltd* [1932] 2 KB 595.

[35] Du Parcq J allowed the police receiver a complete defence, on the ground that, having reason to believe that the second defendants were the owners of the cloth, by delivering the cloth he could be said to be acting in intended execution of a public duty within the meaning of the Public Authorities Protection Act 1893, and so avail of the advantageous time limits specified in that legislation: ibid, 602–05.

[36] Ibid, 599.

[37] The second defendant failed to identify the cloth as that stolen from its premises, and du Parcq J thought the jury right to find against the second defendant on this point.

[38] *Costello* (n 5) 1448–49.

[39] G Battersby, 'Acquiring Title by Theft' (2002) 65 *MLR* 603, 605–06.

operation of the normal six-year time limit,[40] section 4(2) effectively provides that the limit will begin to run thereafter 'if anyone purchases the stolen chattel in good faith'.[41] Battersby suggests that to contemplate specific rules about purchases following a theft supposes that it is possible for the thief to sell to a buyer, which in turn supposes that the thief has acquired a property right, inasmuch as the legal notion of sale comprises an agreement to transfer the general property in the goods. This is plausible and persuasive, but is not necessarily decisive on the acquisition question. One answer is to observe that the statute does not express the rule in terms of 'sale', framing the provision instead in rather more loose terms of 'purchase'. Saliently, the policy objective (providing a time limit which runs in favour of someone who in good faith gives value for goods which have in fact been stolen) would be sensible and desirable even if the thief had no title to pass, so that technically there could be no sale. So far as protection of the innocent purchaser is concerned, her own possessory title in any event is sufficient to restrain all others except the owner, from whom she is protected (and worth protecting) only once the time limit has expired.

With respect, then, it is far from clear that Lightman J was correct to assert that, as a matter of authority, possession is entitled to the same protection whether acquired lawfully or by theft.[42] So far as they go, the authorities have admitted rather more doubt than certainty on the matter, and at the time *Costello* was decided, the safest view would have described them as equivocal at best.

B. Protecting Possession Taken by Theft as a Matter of Principle

Supposing that prior to *Costello* this matter was open authoritatively, the next question is whether as a matter of principle we should protect possession taken by theft. In *Costello*, notwithstanding the 'natural moral disinclination' to support persons in the position of the claimant, Lightman J thought that the principle did compel protection of the thief's possession.[43] It seems that two arguments were doing the work on this front. The first we might dub the 'no expropriation' argument, since it goes to undesirable political consequences said to follow if we disrupt property acquisition by thieves in the absence of express authorisation under specific legislation; the second follows from the common law's general treatment of illegality as a defence to civil claims in cases such as *Tinsley v Milligan*.[44] These arguments appear to be formidable and need to be addressed, but we will see that they are not in the end sufficient to dispose of the questions of principle at stake. Indeed, in its own

---

[40] That is, the normal time limit of six years from the date of the first conversion: see Limitation Act 1980, s 3(1).

[41] Section 4(2) achieves this effect by providing that good faith purchases and any subsequent conversions shall not be regarded as conversions related to a theft, so as to exclude them from the purview of s 4(1), and thereby render them subject to the normal time limit rules in ss 2 and 3(1).

[42] *Costello* has been followed by the Court of Appeal in the later case of *Gough v Chief Constable of West Midlands Police* (n 14), though with some reluctance on policy grounds, and in dicta which suggest the matter may well be a candidate for review in the future: see [39], [48].

[43] *Costello* (n 5) 1450.

[44] *Tinsley v Milligan* [1994] 1 AC 340.

way, each raises rather than denies the need to evaluate the matter again from first principles.

The 'no expropriation' argument reverses an apparently intuitive public policy objection to the idea that a criminal should acquire title to the proceeds of a crime, emphasising the need to protect and preserve *the criminal's* property rights against the overreaching force of the state. In *Webb*,[45] decided very shortly after the first-instance decision in *Costello*,[46] around £36,000 in cash had lawfully been seized from the claimant on the suspicion that it represented the proceeds of drugs trafficking. The claimant was not prosecuted and subsequently sought recovery of the cash from the police. In the ensuing claim for conversion, he was unsuccessful at first instance, but the Court of Appeal allowed his appeal and ordered redelivery. Giving the leading judgment, May LJ saw good reason to allow recovery, insofar as to hold otherwise would amount to an unjustified expropriation of the claimant's property:

> Although from the Chief Constable's perspective the money is the proceeds of crime, from another perspective the court should not, in my view, countenance expropriation by a public authority of money or property belonging to an individual for which there is no statutory authority. There is statutory machinery for the prosecution of those who deal in drugs and for the confiscation upon conviction of the proceeds of their drug dealing. There is statutory machinery for the confiscation upon conviction of the proceeds of other serious crime ... I recognise that there may be circumstances where for a variety of reasons a prosecution may not take place. But that does not, in my view, justify expropriation by means of a defence to a civil claim for return of money which has been seized from persons who are not convicted.[47]

This extract was reproduced in *Costello*,[48] and later Lightman J intimated that it offered a public policy argument to resist the 'natural moral disinclination' towards recovery by the claimant thief.[49] Superficially this reasoning is persuasive and attractive. It must be right that we should be careful to guard against the expropriation activities of the state and entirely uncontroversial to hold that any such powers should be created specifically with clear parliamentary authorisation.[50] But for present purposes, the argument is flawed insofar it assumes precisely that which is at stake, namely that possession obtained by theft results in the acquisition of a property right by the thief. Unless this premise is correct, it is meaningless to speak of expropriation in this context, for there can be no expropriation without prior subsisting property. Yet, as we have seen, it is far from self-evident that property acquisition is warranted on the authorities, the better view being at least that the common law has declined to commit itself on the matter. Accordingly, a further

---

[45] *Webb* (n 14).
[46] *Costello* (n 5) 1438.
[47] *Webb* (n 14) 446.
[48] *Costello* (n 5) 1443.
[49] Ibid, 1450.
[50] Governments can and do create confiscatory procedures which bite on criminal assets. In the context of theft, courts have powers to compel the restoration of stolen property: Powers of Criminal Courts (Sentencing) Act 2000, s 148; and, as we have seen already, they can also make orders depriving a thief or suspected thief of goods in his possession: Police Property Act 1897, s 1; *Buckley* (n 16). For a recent overview of the operation of confiscation orders generally, see J Ulph, 'Confiscation Orders, Human Rights, and Penal Measures' (2010) 126 *LQR* 251.

analytical step is required before the expropriation argument has any teeth. It will only bite to the extent that we are satisfied that a thief *ought to acquire* a property right in respect of things that he steals. For this reason, the 'no expropriation' argument is not sufficient to settle whether as a matter of principle the possession of a thief should be protected. Conversely, indeed, it invites resolution of that very question, and any attempt to deploy the argument in satisfaction of the principle debate serves only to obscure the need for such resolution.

We will take up this more general argument shortly, but before we do, it is worth noting that a similar result occurs if we approach the question of principle by considering the procedural relevance of the claimant's illegality. In both *Webb* and *Costello*, the Court of Appeal was impressed by the argument that in cases of this kind, the claimant need only allege the facts of his possession to prove an entitlement to protection.[51] He need lay no emphasis on how that possession was acquired, so that in no sense must he rely on his illegal activity to found his action. Presented in such terms, this argument engages the well-known decision in *Tinsley v Milligan*, where an agreement to share the beneficial interest in a home was enforced, notwithstanding the emergence of the fact that the arrangement had been effected in order to perpetrate a benefit fraud.[52] We ought to take care, though, when applying *Tinsley* to cases on acquisition of property by unlawful possession, for at least three reasons.

First, there is still doubt and disagreement about the test to be applied when judging the effect of illegality on civil relationships,[53] and to the extent that the matter remains open, it might yet be premature to allow a 'reliance' incarnation of that test to preclude us from considering the acquisitive effects of illegally obtained possession. Second, even if a reliance test does and should apply to cases involving the acquisition of legal property rights, we might want to press a distinction in its operation in the differing contexts of original and derivative acquisition. It is worth remembering that *Tinsley* itself is an example of the latter, and the decision is explicable on the ground that a property right passes under a contract unenforceable for illegality.[54] It is one thing to hold illegality irrelevant to the transfer of property already subsisting in the claimant, but quite another to hold it irrelevant to original acquisition by the claimant. Third, and for present purposes most significantly, even if both these suppositions are wrong, and *Tinsley* effectively operates to endorse the thief's acquisition of property by excluding any substantive enquiry about how his possession was obtained, there would still be broader value in having discussion about the thief's acquisition. Original acquisition rules are important. In the end, they are the rules that will determine the distribution of resources within a given community.[55] It is plain that if this distribution is generally to be considered just, then rules about how distribution is to be effected must endorse and in the end

---

[51] *Webb* (n 14) 446; *Costello* (n 5) 1443.

[52] *Tinsley* (n 44).

[53] See generally PS Davies, 'The Illegality Defence—Two Steps Forward, One Step Back?' [2009] *Conv* 182; 'The Illegality Defence: Turning Back the Clock' [2010] *Conv* 282.

[54] *Tinsley* (n 44) 370.

[55] This point stands, notwithstanding the obvious everyday importance of rules about derivative acquisitions, since any derivative acquisition of a property right in respect of a particular thing depends ultimately on some historical act by which that thing was first acquired. On the relation of original (or 'independent') and derivative (or 'dependent') acquisition, see McFarlane (n 6) 154 ff.

serve the prevailing principles of justice. A community which takes justice seriously should, at the very least, be able to explain and defend the particular rules it invokes about original acquisition, and this includes (perhaps especially includes) original acquisition which seems to run counter to normally accepted principles of justice, as prima facie appears to be the case where we reward the thief or other wrongdoer.

Accordingly, even if the procedural bar in *Tinsley* precludes us from having to consider in practice the merits of acquisition by a thief, we should still ask the question whether such acquisition is warranted in principle,[56] and so, as with the 'no expropriation' argument, we find ourselves ultimately confronted with the more general matter. In the next section we take up this general discussion and, contrary to the view in *Costello*, we argue that our basic principles of possession and conversion do not entail that a thief acquires a relative title, but point conversely to a lower threshold of personal protection.

III. THE GENERAL RATIONALE FOR PROTECTING POSSESSION AND ITS APPLICATION TO POSSESSION TAKEN BY THEFT

In the context of possession generally, the cases come up short on discussions of principle. While it has long been fashionable in academic circles to offer a priori explanations for why possession should be protected,[57] general questions of justification seem not to have figured prominently in common law adjudication. This is at least in part explained by the common law method, which has allowed the extent of a possessor's protection to be realised slowly, through incremental steps much more readily attributable to the genius of counsel in framing a plea than to any grand, overarching theory of property.[58] This means that if we want to deduce the values and principles which animate our laws of possessory acquisition, we need to pay close attention to the cases, observing the factors that informed the construction of pleas and that influenced the courts in their protection of possession. Here we adopt this method, arguing that the early cases protected the possessor precisely to ensure respect for the continuing property of those better entitled. Inasmuch as this rationale is not necessarily applicable to cases of possession-taken-by-theft, it leads us to doubt that the thief's possession should be protected in the same way as lawful possession.

A. Conversion and 'Special Property'

From its inception, the standard count in conversion alleged that the claimant was 'possessed' of the goods in question 'as his own proper chattels'.[59] It was in substance,

---

[56] See also Barkehall Thomas (n 12) 246.

[57] Generally the scholarship has emerged from the US: for excellent examples, see RA Epstein, 'Possession as the Root of Title' (1978–79) 13 *Georgia Law Review* 1221; C Rose, 'Possession as the Origin of Property' (1985) 52 *University of Chicago Law Review* 73.

[58] See Baker, noting that substantive principles of personal property are 'difficult to perceive' from the medieval cases and comprise a body of learning 'less sophisticated' than the land law: JH Baker, *An Introduction to English Legal History*, 4th edn (London, Butterworths, 2002) 379.

[59] Or in pleaded form: 'ut de bonis propriis'. See generally JW Salmond, 'Observations on Trover and Conversion' (1905) *LQR* 42, 46.

then, a two-part allegation of possession consequent on property. There was required to be some right, some title, which 'coloured' or explained the claimant's possession,[60] and two categories of property were recognised: first, of course, the title or general property of an owner; but, second, special property.[61] Special property was taken to refer broadly to the interest of a bailee.[62] A list of such people could sue for trover (carriers, pledgees, factors, innkeepers),[63] as they might equally have done in detinue or by their appeal in the earlier years. It is well suspected on the structure of the earliest forms that initially this was because the bailee was the only person placed to initiate the action, but later the bailee's recourse to law would be explained on the ground of his responsibility to his bailor.[64] Because the bailee must account to his bailor, and answer her for the value of the goods, the bailee must have his action, and trover was no exception from the earliest days of its availability.

Contemporaneous trover cases fit this pattern and suggest that the concept of special property was doing most of the work in early decisions. In *Wilbraham v Snow*, a sheriff was allowed to recover goods taken out of his possession following their lawful seizure. The court reached its decision by analogy with the legal position of carriers, allowing trover to the sheriff because, by law, he was accountable for the value of the goods seized.[65] Likewise, in *Arnold v Jefferson*, the bailee of a bond recovered it following a subsequent conversion, with the court holding specifically that 'trover and conversion will lie upon a special property, as in case of a carrier'.[66] Less obviously (but more interestingly) to the same effect is the great case of *Armory v Delamirie*.[67] While the report itself is silent on the matter, early accounts of *Armory* treat the claimant boy as a non-trespassory possessor.[68] In the context of the decision, the exclusion of liability for trespass is sensible only on the assumption that the boy had taken the jewel ring for safekeeping, that is, under a voluntarily assumed obligation to its owner.[69] This understanding of *Armory* resonates with the later decision in *Webb v Fox*, where counsel maintained that the availability of trover was

---

[60] *Sutton v Buck* (1810) 2 Taunt 302, 309.

[61] See generally (1845) 2 Wms Saund 47, note 1, being Serjeant Williams' notes on the earlier decision in *Wilbraham v Snow* (1670) 1 Mod 30. These notes provided a summary of the general law on trover, which was accepted and highly influential in the decisions of this period: see especially *Jeffries* (n 2); and also Pollock (n 25) 92. Note that while the following paragraphs consider the old learning on 'special property' insofar as it relates to the availability of actions for trover and conversion, this learning may also have broader implications for the conceptual structures of personal property, including the still-unsettled possibility of a doctrine of estates in chattels. For relatively recent discussion considering the nature of the interest acquired by a pledgee, see N Curwen, 'General and Special Property in Goods' (2000) 20 *Legal Studies* 181.

[62] *Webb v Fox* (1797) 7 TR 391, 396.

[63] See the authorities collected in Williams' notes to *Wilbraham v Snow* (1845) 2 Wms Saund 47; and *Sutton* (n 60) 309.

[64] See OW Holmes, *The Common Law* (Boston, Little Brown, 1881) 166–67.

[65] *Wilbraham* (n 61).

[66] *Arnold v Jefferson* (1697) 1 Ld Raym 275, 276. Green and Randall ((n 2) 20) treat *Wilbraham* and *Arnold* as cases which establish the sufficiency of possession without more to make available conversion. But it is difficult to see how this view can be reconciled with the strict reliance on special property concepts in the reports of these decisions, much less with the view in *Elliott* and *Jeffries* that the point was novel.

[67] *Armory* (n 2).

[68] *Webb v Fox* (n 62) 398 (Lawrence J); *Wilbraham v Snow* (n 63) note 1, text to fn (n).

[69] It was well settled by the time of *Armory* that it was no trespass honestly to take a lost thing in order to redeliver it to its owner: see *Isaack v Clark* (1614) 2 Bulst 306; and generally Hickey (n 6) 16–17.

premised very squarely on the claimant's consensually incurred 'liab[ility] over to the person who has the absolute property for any damage that may be done to it'.[70] The court agreed, Lawrence J explaining more succinctly that special property resulted from 'lawful possession' where the possessor 'holds ... subject to the claims of other persons'.[71] It follows that, for much the greater part of its history, lawful account-ability was an essential element of standing to sue for conversion. Accordingly, there could be no question of a thief bringing trover in respect of subsequent conversions of things he had stolen, because in no way could a thief demonstrate the lawful accountability that was the ordinary premise of the action's availability.

To get to the point where a thief could sue for conversion, the courts would need to allow recovery to be premised on the facts of possession alone, without recourse to the strict understanding of special property. From at least the late eighteenth century, counsel began to plead cases on the footing of the claimant's possession,[72] but the uncertainty of the proposition is shown in that often a special property argument would be laid in the alternative. For example, in *Elliott v Kemp*, counsel argued that the deceased's possession of certain articles of furniture would ground a claim for their recovery by her administratrix outwith the prevailing rules of succession,[73] but alternatively a special property argument was advanced, contend-ing that the deceased's own administration bond served to generate a responsibility to account to her husband's estate, and that such responsibility warranted the avail-ability of trover.[74] Similarly, in *Sutton v Buck*, Lord Mansfield would have allowed the claimant to recover a wrecked ship on proof of possession alone,[75] but on the facts, the claimant was the bailee of the ship's owner, and his Lordship thought it equally clear that the owner's delivery was the source of the claimant's entitlement to recover.[76]

To get unequivocally to the point where a wrongdoer could sue for conversion, the courts would need to go a little further and allow a claimant to recover where no special property could possibly be shown on the facts. This seems to have happened in *Jeffries v Great Western Railway Co*,[77] where the defendants had seized from the claimant certain trucks held by the latter under an assignment from a bankrupt. The Queen's Bench expressly acknowledged the novelty in its decision. Referring to the question left open in *Elliott v Kemp*, Crompton J observed that the court was 'now to decide whether a wrongdoer in actual possession of goods, the property

---

[70] A point which counsel regarded as being 'too clear to be disputed': *Webb v Fox* (n 62) 393.

[71] Ibid, 398.

[72] *Rackham v Jesup* (1772) 3 Wilson KB 332.

[73] Counsel for the claimant relied on *Armory* (n 2) and *Sutton* (n 60) to advance the now-familiar argument that 'as against a wrongdoer, the actual possessor of any chattel may maintain an action for it': (1840) 7 M&W 306, 308.

[74] *Elliott* (n 18) 309–10. Ultimately the case was settled on succession principles.

[75] '[The claimant] was, in every sense of the word, in possession of the ship ... If mere possession will make property, to be sure here is possession, taking it without reference to the register act': (1810) Taunt 302, 308.

[76] '[I]t is clear that [the owner] did deliver her to the [claimant], with intent that the [claimant] should have her and keep her, he was, in every sense of the word, in possession of the ship': ibid.

[77] *Jeffries* (n 2).

of a stranger, can recover their value in trover against a wrongdoer who takes the goods from him'.[78] It speaks to the prevailing momentum of the possession-without-more argument that the court's 'impression ha[d] always been' that a wrongful possessor could avail of trover, but the judgments again acknowledge considerable doubt on the matter,[79] which was far from accepted in argument. Counsel for the claimant moved that 'mere possession is sufficient title against a wrongdoer',[80] but the authorities given were immediately denied by the court;[81] the defendant thought there was no basis at all for such a proposition,[82] and for its own part, the greater goal of the claimant's argument was to deny any fraud and show that he had 'at least a claim of title'.[83] Nonetheless, and on the supposition that the claimant was a wrongdoer, the court thought that the action was available and expressed its decision in language which gives the form to our modern rule. So Lord Campbell CJ confirmed that 'against a wrongdoer possession is title';[84] Wightman J spoke of 'the prima facie right arising from possession';[85] and all denied to the defendants the ability to plead an *ius tertii* defence in denial of the claimant's title.[86]

Jeffries deserves greater recognition as the source of our modern law on possession and in many ways offers a surer foundation than *Armory* for the proposition that a general property right is generated by the facts of possession alone.[87] Nonetheless, *Jeffries* was not a case where there was any suggestion that the claimant's acquisition was tainted by criminal liability, and certainly not theft. So, even if we accept that *Jeffries* allows conversion to a civil wrongdoer, it is not inevitable that we extend this protection to a thief. Indeed, we could only be justified in making this extension if the reasoning in *Jeffries* is equally applicable to cases of theft, and to this issue we now turn.

---

[78] Ibid, 807.

[79] Ibid, 807.

[80] Ibid, 803.

[81] Counsel relied on *Newnham v Stevenson* (1851) 10 CB 713, but as Crompton J observed in *Jeffries* (n 2) 803–04, there the claimant held under a voidable title which had not been avoided at the date of the conversion, and the question on the sufficiency of acquired possession was again left open by the court. Moreover, Jervis CJ specifically noted that trover was premised on the assumption 'that the goods came into the possession of the defendant lawfully': (1851) 10 CB 713, 722.

[82] In reliance on Williams' notes to *Wilbraham v Snow* (n 63), Wightman J put it to the defendants that 'the claimant was in possession; and against a wrongdoer possession is title'. Counsel retorted: 'There is no decision to that effect': (1856) 5 E&B 802, 805.

[83] Ibid, 803. After trial judgment for the claimant, the defendants sought to prove the fraud by certain affidavits and obtained a rule nisi for a new trial on that ground, and also on the ground of a misdirection to the jury in the instruction not to admit an *ius tertii* defence to the claimant's title. The motions on this rule gave rise to the proceedings on the claimant's title considered here, but ultimately the court supported the rule and ordered a new trial on the ground of the affidavits: ibid, 803, 806, 808.

[84] Ibid, 805.

[85] Ibid, 806.

[86] Ibid, 805, 807–08.

[87] Following *Jeffries*, courts and commentators began to reconstruct the earlier cases, treating the decisions on special property as if they had depended on possession all along. So, for example, in the well-known case of *The Winkfield*, Collins MR referred to *Jeffries* and *Armory* in the same paragraph to support the view that 'a long series of authorities' held that in trover 'possession is good against a wrongdoer': [1902] P 42, 54. See also Holmes (n 64) 242–43. Such rendering of *Armory* involves a considerable substantive gloss on the idea of special property and is best viewed as an ex post rationalisation.

B. Possession, Property Rights and Personal Rights

Consistently with the general trend in our law of possession, the judgments in *Jeffries* contain very little express reflection on why wrongful possession should be protected. That said, we do find one evaluative remark, which gives some insight on the judges' view of why they should allow such protection, and the substantive significance of *Jeffries* makes it particularly important that we pay attention to this reasoning. After stating in general terms the proposition that possession gives title to sue for subsequent conversions, Lord Campbell CJ offered this reflection, which seems to capture the mood of the court: 'I think it most reasonable law, and essential for the interests of society, that peaceable possession should not be disturbed by wrongdoers.'[88]

This rationale for the protection of (even wrongfully acquired) possession has been endorsed more recently by the Court of Appeal.[89] It is surely a reasonable proposition, but it is not clear that it is sufficient to support the modern law of possession that has been built upon *Jeffries*. Specifically, the proposition that it is worthwhile to restrain wrongful disturbance of possession does not inevitably entail that such protection should be effected by allowing a possessor to access to the standard procedure for the protection of property rights (in our case, conversion), and thus neither does it entail the correlative substantive proposition that even a wrongful possessor acquires a property right.

To make this clear, we need only show that it is very possible to construct a legal regime that achieves the protection of possession without proprietary consequences. The Roman law of possession provides a ready example. Without more, proof of possession at Roman law had 'only the barest legal consequence—that it was protected'.[90] This protection was achieved through the availability of a set of praetorian procedures, known as the possessory interdicts, the function of which was to correct direct trespassory interferences with the claimant's possession.[91] If C took a horse from B's control, irrespective of any question as to B's property in the horse, B could recover its possession from C; however, beyond correction of the trespass, B's possession gave him no broader claim to the horse. So B could not, for example, recover against D, the subsequent transferee of C, because D had not interfered with B's possession.[92] Summarising this position generally, Savigny would much later explain that the possessory interdicts were premised on the restraint of violence rather than the recognition of property: a Roman citizen in possession of a thing did 'not thereby obtain any right to detention, but ... [had] the right of demanding

---

[88] *Jeffries* (n 2) 805.

[89] *Parker v British Airways Board* [1982] QB 1004, 1010.

[90] B Nicholas, *An Introduction to Roman Law* (Oxford, Clarendon Press, 1962, reprinted 1990) 108.

[91] The interdicts *uti possidetis* (land) and *utrubi* (movables) allowed a possessor to retain and confirm his possession relative to his opponent: D.43.17.2. Where force had been used to take possession from the possessor, he could bring *utrubi* again to recover movables, and the interdicts *unde vi* and *unde armata* for the recovery of land. The last of these only applied where armed force had been used.

[92] Nicholas (n 90) 108–09.

that no-one shall else use force against him'.[93] The chief practical manifestation of this distinction was that, while he had access to the possessory interdicts, a Roman possessor was not entitled to bring a *vindicatio*, the standard Roman remedy for the protection of ownership.[94] Accordingly, we must regard the right which resulted from possession at Roman law as something qualitatively different from ownership.[95] Possession there resulted in obligations, not property.

English law may once have allowed the protection of possession to be structured in similar fashion. In their classical forms, the actions of trespass and trover protected a claimant respectively from direct interferences with physical possession and interferences with a property right.[96] Gradually trover expanded to cover the ground of trespass;[97] indeed, in this respect, the decision in *Jeffries* represented a subsumption of trespass by trover, inasmuch as trover was adjudged to lie on proof of the facts of possession alone. The difficulty is that this procedural move would lead to major substantive elision. The commentators who produced the early treatises on the substance of the common law, following the abolition of the forms of action, relied heavily on those outgoing forms in their exposition of doctrinal propositions.[98] Since trover/conversion was accepted as the principal action for the protection of possession, trover's premise (that the claimant is possessed of some thing as of his own property) became applicable by rationalisation to all cases of possession,[99] and eventually to wrongful possessors just as much as lawful possessors.

Viewed in this light, the common law authorities reflect a rather monistic approach to problems that arise when possession is disturbed, and the system of possessory protection, premised entirely on the availability of the standard action for the protection of property, is fairly easily exposed as a system lacking nuance. We have already seen enough to show that it is not inevitable that all possessors should be treated in the same way. Indeed, even if we agree that all possession should in some way be protected because it is the interests of society to restrain unauthorised disturbance with settled-possession-however-acquired, we might still configure the rights of the possessor differently in order to reflect differing circumstances and priorities. The Roman and English texts point us to two general levels of configuration. Sometimes possession might generate a property right, while sometimes it might generate a personal right. These rights differ markedly in their content. A property right generated by possession must bear the general hallmark of property and comprise a right to exclusive use exigible against anyone who comes later

---

[93] FC von Savigny, *Treatise on Possession; or the Jus Possessionis of the Civil Law* (London, Sweet, trans E Perry, 1848) 6–7.

[94] If in the course of acquisition by *usucapio*, he would be entitled to a modified *vindicatio*, the modifications going to the form of the pleadings rather than the substantive gist of the action. But the availability of such proprietary protection must be attributed to the full range of prerequisites for *usucapio* and must be distinguished sharply from the protection of possession-without-more: see Savingy, ibid, 129.

[95] Hence the well-known observation of Ulpian, 'ownership has nothing in common with possession': D 41.2.12.1.

[96] That the function of trespass was to restrain direct physical interferences is corroborated by its jurisdictional foundations in breaches of the King's peace. As to this, see generally Ames (n 17) 282–83.

[97] Ibid, 383–86; Douglas (n 6) 60–61.

[98] F Pollock and FW Maitland, *History of English Law*, vol 2 (Cambridge, Cambridge University Press, 1898) 31.

[99] Pollock (n 25) 91; and see Holmes (n 64) 211, 241–42, 244.

to the thing, not just against the original interferer.[100] A personal right generated by possession need amount to much less, comprising the right to obtain redress from anyone who wrongfully disturbs the subsisting facts of control of the thing, but no greater entitlement to use or enjoy it.[101]

If, in keeping with *Jeffries* and Savigny, the point of protecting the wrongful possessor is found in society's general interest in preserving the peace, this objective would seem to be met by holding that wrongful possession results in the generation of the personal right just described. This would produce a different outcome on the facts of cases like *Costello*. If Mr Costello had acquired a personal right in respect of the car, he could only have complained about direct, trespassory invasions of his possession. Inasmuch as the initial seizure by the police was lawfully exercised and not trespassory, Mr Costello could not have sued the police successfully in respect of the car. It makes no difference on this front that eventually the police's power to detain the car expired, for the expiration of authorisation does not render the initial seizure trespassory.

One possible difficulty with this approach to possession taken by theft concerns the apparently resultant ability of the police to retain seized assets even after expiration of the statutory power.[102] The Court of Appeal was concerned about this in *Costello* and was evidently uncomfortable with the Chief Constable's argument that the police become 'possessory owners' of assets seized from thieves, subject only to their ability to return such things to their owners who (almost inevitably in cases of this kind) are unlikely to be known.[103] Of course, to the extent that such a person is ascertainable, the police must take reasonable steps to return the goods. However, it does not follow that if such persons are unknown, justice is served by returning the thing to the thief. This option is only sensible and permissible if the thief has acquired property, and since this is in doubt, it seems preferable to seek a third response to redelivery. Susan Barkehall Thomas has made this observation recently, arguing that the rules of *bona vacantia* might offer an interesting solution to cases

---

[100] JE Penner, *The Idea of Property in Law* (Oxford, Clarendon Press 1997); McFarlane (n 6) 22–23.

[101] Fox has argued that where personal property is concerned, the right that results from possession always extends only to this limited form of protection against trespassory interference: Fox (n 1) 344. Previously I have doubted this view in the context of the finding cases by suggesting to the contrary that the right resulting from possession is *always* proprietary: Hickey (n 6) 119–22. The argument here is an intermediate view, allowing for the possibility of different responses to different types of case. This intermediate analysis appears to derive some support from *Field v Sullivan* [1923] VLR 70, where McFarlan J thought that a wrongful possessor should be protected against unlawful interferences with possession, but also recognised that she would not necessarily have a right to seek return of the goods seized lawfully, since an unlawful possessor 'was not entitled to possession': [1923] VLR 70, 86. Note that McFarlan J explained these differing responses to lawful and unlawful possession in terms of a 'presumption' that possession was lawful, which might be rebutted by the defendant: [1923] VLR 70, 84, 86; Barkehall Thomas (n 12) 237–38. This seems fair insofar as it places the burden of establishing the claimant's illegality on the defendant, but as to the substantive question about the acquisitive consequences of possession proven to be unlawfully obtained, it seems preferable to explain the matter squarely in terms of the rights of the parties and to avoid recourse to presumptions when explaining the legal effects of proven facts: see the view of William Swadling in Burrows (n 7) para [4.418].

[102] See D Fox, 'Enforcing a Possessory Title to a Stolen Car' (2002) 61 *CLJ* 27, 29, who observed the fairness of subjecting the police 'to liability in respect of … later dealings with the chattel once [the] statutory authority expires'.

[103] *Costello* (n 5) 1444.

of this kind.[104] This would seem to have the advantage of vindicating the public interest in ensuring that thieves do not profit from their crimes, but if it appears too generous to the state, further intermediate options are also available. In this respect we should recall that, where an owner is unknown, section 1 of the Police (Property) Act 1897 (the successor to the provision at stake in *Buckley v Gross*)[105] allows a magistrate to make such order in respect of the goods 'as may seem meet'. As an alternative to redelivery to a thief, this could plausibly include a charitable donation or public sale. Of course, we may wish such disposals to be governed by updated legislation that depended to a lesser extent on the exercise of judicial discretion, but this gets us exactly to the point. Where an owner is unknown, we need to have a clear debate about the rules that should determine distribution of the goods, and this should result in a fair rule to effect that distribution. It makes little sense to avoid this need by relying in default on the putative proprietary entitlements of thieves, especially when it seems difficult to justify the latter on our general principles on possessory protection.

If we are to go further and ascribe property to the possessor who takes by theft, there must be *reason* to allow the acquisition of a property right as opposed to personal possessory protection. In other words, we must be able to justify a thief's acquisition of property. Now sometimes it does seem to make sense for possession to generate a relatively good property right, and nothing here is meant to deny the possibility of offering a coherent justification for such a step. Indeed, the law as it stands offers plausible cases where property acquisition seems fair, as with our earlier examples of finders and bailees.[106] In evaluating these examples, it is important to recall the special property principle on which the law of trover was premised.[107] This doctrine emphasised the accountability of the possessor (B), and so emphasised the prior and continuing property right of the person to whom he was accountable (A). The recognition of property acquisition by B was premised on and consistent with respect for the continuing property of A, and accordingly A's property must figure in any posited justification for B's acquisition. It can plausibly do so where B is a finder or bailee, but in obvious and important ways, this respect for A's continuing property is missing in the circumstances where B is a thief. By definition, the thief's possession is premised on some high degree of disregard for A's property. It still might not be impossible to construct a justification for property acquisition by B-thief: we might build an explanation around realisation of B's autonomy or around the extent to which the possessed thing contributes to B's personal identify.[108] But any such argument in favour of property acquisition by B risks being inappropriately insensitive to the continuing property rights of A, and the common law would need at least to offer an express account as to why protection is justified, notwithstanding the claimant's obvious disregard for the property of another. As things stand,

---

[104] Barkehall Thomas (n 12) 249.
[105] See n 20 above and accompanying text.
[106] See n 10 above and accompanying text.
[107] See n 61 above and accompanying text.
[108] On the general possibility that property justifications might implicate a plural range of values (such as autonomy, personhood, utility, equality and community), see H Dagan, *Property: Values and Institutions* (Oxford, Oxford University Press, 2010).

this account is supplied only by the general interest in keeping the peace, but this argument is not sufficient to entail the acquisition of property by B-thief. Indeed, the desired protection may just as fully be realised by B's acquisition of a personal right, so that in this context, English law came to resemble the Roman law on possession much more closely than might otherwise be thought the case.

IV. CONCLUSION

The current common law response to possession-taken-by-theft raises acute questions about the values and principles that underlie our basic rules of original acquisition. These questions need to be faced much more squarely in common law adjudication and commentary, which for too long has relied uncritically on substantive rationalisations of the old forms of action as the continuing source of its basic propositions on possession. At the very least, we should acknowledge that the extension of the availability of conversion that occurred in *Jeffries* was not a self-evident one and may not be of universal application. Notwithstanding the very clear judgment in *Costello*, there does seem to be reason to distinguish lawful from wrongful possessors, or perhaps even lawful and some kinds of wrongful possessors from other kinds of wrongful possessors. The point is that each category of claimant should be subject to the general enquiry of whether acquisition of a property right is justified. This enquiry is missing from our law at present, and in accounting for the rights of possessors, we have been much too insensitive to the extent to which they should be protected and to the reasons that underpin the available protection.

19

The Prevalence of Private Takings

EMMA JL WARING[*]

I. INTRODUCTION

THE VICTORIAN RAILWAY boom changed the British landscape forever. Nearly 175 years later, property rights are just as liable to be disrupted and rearranged in the name of progress. Successful infrastructure and regeneration projects frequently rely upon strategically used compulsory purchase powers which allow plots of land to be assembled, whilst avoiding holdout problems. However, the compulsory acquisition or 'taking' of land is rightly viewed as politically and constitutionally sensitive given its draconian effect: homes and businesses may be taken away, neighbourhoods fragmented and personal links with land eroded. In recognition of these potential dangers, many constitutional charters attempt to limit the use of acquisition powers to situations where the taking is deemed to be in the public interest or is for a public use.

Both Article 1 of the First Protocol to the European Convention on Human Rights (hereinafter 'A1-P1') and its long-standing American counterpart in the Fifth Amendment to Constitution of the United States (hereinafter 'the Takings Clause') contain an implicit distinction between constitutionally acceptable public takings and unacceptable private takings.[1] These occur where property rights are transferred compulsorily from one private party to another for that private party's benefit, although some tenuous public benefit may also accrue. Whilst courts have struggled to define the exact boundary of the public/private divide in constitutional property clauses, judges on both sides of the Atlantic have consistently criticised private takings. What is less well appreciated is the historic extent to which private entities have exercised acquisition powers, not only when involved in realising public regeneration schemes, but also for their own benefit.

Despite judicial concerns, the existence and use of privately exercised powers of compulsory acquisition, or 'private takings', in England and the US is nothing new. The noteworthy readjustment of privately held property rights triggered by the canal and railway booms of the eighteenth and nineteenth centuries in England and

[*] Lecturer, York Law School, University of York.
[1] A1-P1 states: 'Every natural or legal person is entitled to the peaceful enjoyment of his possessions. No one shall be deprived of his possessions *except in the public interest* and subject to the conditions provided for by law and by the general principles of international law' (emphasis added). The Takings Clause states: 'nor shall private property be taken *for public use*, without just compensation' (emphasis added).

the US Mill Acts reflect a long-standing governmental reliance on private takings. More recently, however, both the UK and the US Supreme Courts have cautioned against private takings.

The second part of this chapter places current concerns about private takings in their historical urban context by giving an overview of their use in the canal and railway booms in England and the Mill Acts in the US. The historical use of private takings illustrates how frequently these powers were used and the valuable impact that they had on entrepreneurial and industrial growth. Even in their heyday, however, they caused anxiety to courts and legislatures; the third part of the chapter argues that since their earliest days, compulsory acquisition powers have been contentious because their use causes two very different values to collide: (i) the importance of stable and strong property rights; and (ii) a desire to recalibrate property holdings for social, economic or development reasons. Today, equivalent private takings for regeneration purposes are just as common as their historic counterparts. However, as the fourth part demonstrates, by examining two recent Anglo-American private takings cases, the modern usage of these transfers throws up particular challenges. It is concluded that private takings can play an important role in regulating property regimes, but that their earlier acceptability should not lead to an automatic welcome today.

II. HISTORICAL PRIVATE TAKINGS

Compulsory acquisition in England has long been a creature of statute.[2] Even at the time that Blackstone was writing his *Commentaries*, the English had frequent and long experience of compulsory acquisition. This included exposure to private takings under inclosure legislation, whereby individual rights in land were compulsorily extinguished so that the land could be reallocated to other individuals and more efficient farming methods applied. For the present purposes, however, the focus is not on the inclosure movement, but rather on the urban canal and railway booms of the eighteenth and nineteenth centuries.

A. Canal Mania

The use of privately held powers of compulsory acquisition to build toll roads, canals and railways in England began to grow from the 1750s onwards.[3] The availability of new and speedier transport routes played a catalytic role in the Industrial Revolution and the burgeoning canal system opened up previously landlocked isolated areas to the advantages of water transport, thereby shaping the economic geography of the country.[4] In an era of relatively poorly built and maintained roads

---

[2] WD McNulty, 'The Power of "Compulsory Purchase" under the Law of England' (1912) 21 *Yale Law Journal* 639, 643.

[3] W McKay (ed), *Erskine May's Treatise on The Law, Privileges, Proceedings and Usage of Parliament*, 23rd edn (London, LexisNexis, 2004) 965.

[4] MJ Daunton, *Progress and Poverty: An Economic and Social History of Britain 1700–1850* (Oxford, Oxford University Press, 1995) 287.

and animal-driven transport, canals proved to be essential to economic and urban development for almost 100 years.

Whilst the financial gains from canals were high, so were the initial costs, particularly in relation to land. It was understandably rare for an economically useful canal to be built solely across one landowner's property. One notable exception was the pioneering 'canal duke' Francis Egerton, the third Duke of Bridgewater.[5] Whilst on the Grand Tour as a young man, Bridgewater had seen the famous Canal du Midi. He realised that building a similar canal across his estates would enable him to transport coal directly and efficiently from his mines at Worsley to industries in Manchester at a greatly reduced price. Just over 250 years ago, in 1761, the first section of the now famous Bridgewater Canal opened for business. Various additional sections were added at later dates, to the extent that the canal now covers some 39 miles and opened up a route from Worsley to Manchester and on to Liverpool.[6] Despite being initially ridiculed by some, Bridgewater's scheme soon demonstrated the economic gains to be made from building canals. It was, however, exceptional in being built across one landowner's estate. Generally, canals required long strips of land crossing various county boundaries, estates and plots, and thereby affected larger numbers of individuals. Holdout situations were an obvious liability for canal promoters, especially given the engineering difficulties in deviating round intransigent landowners. Fortunately, however, Parliament had an answer.

Most canals were funded by joint-stock companies which, following the Bubble Act of 1720, necessarily required parliamentary approval for their incorporation.[7] Accordingly, it was relatively simple to include an additional request for privately held compulsory purchase powers in the petition for a private bill relating to incorporation as a joint-stock company. Private Acts authorising private takings proved to be particularly useful in preventing holdout problems from landowners affected by proposed canal schemes and required little extra effort on the part of a canal's promoters. Following the economic success of the early 'trunk canals' such as the Trent & Mersey, a deal of financial speculation occurred in a brief period from 1789 to 1796, during which it became increasingly common to reallocate property rights between individuals and privately owned joint-stock companies. However, it was with the growth of the railways that the use of private compulsory purchase powers in England began to explode.

B. The Railway Boom

Although steam-powered railways were first viewed as a novelty, their economic potential was soon appreciated. Following the opening of the Stockton to Darlington railway in 1825, the railways expanded rapidly, to the extent that Kostal describes

---

[5] KR Fairclough, 'Egerton, Francis, Third Duke of Bridgewater (1736–1803)', in *Oxford Dictionary of National Biography* (Oxford, Oxford University Press, 2004); online edn, October 2009, www.oxforddnb.com/view/article/8584.

[6] 33 Geo II, c 2.

[7] The Bubble Act of 1720 (6 Geo I, c 18). R Harris 'The Bubble Act: Its Passage and its Effects on Business Organization' (1994) 54 *Journal of Economic History* 610.

the situation by 1840 as the 'most dramatic infringement of private property rights in England since the Civil War' and a situation where few were 'entirely safe from what contemporary observers justly referred to in the 1840s as the railway "invasion" of the land'.[8] The sheer scale of private takings in England in the mid-nineteenth century can be appreciated best by reference to figures on the private bills presented to Parliament at the time.[9] From 1837 to 1842, around 20 to 25 private railway bills were enacted annually. In 1844 this rose to 66 and in 1845 to 110 such bills, before leaping in 1846 to some 550 railway bills.

Private takings were integral in satisfying the seemingly insatiable 'railway mania' that held sway in the mid-nineteenth century. For many railway investors, the availability of private compulsory acquisition powers was essential to the running and operation of a proposed line. Companies did try to negotiate wayleaves across land rather than acquiring the freehold compulsorily, but the rents charged were often uneconomical. Leases of railway land were also relatively uncommon and difficult to procure unless the railway passed through Crown lands, as in the Forest of Dean. All of these problems could, however, be avoided by the judicious insertion of privately held powers of compulsory acquisition in the Private Act establishing the railway company.[10]

At the height of the railway boom, a new company needed only to place an advertisement of incorporation for it to be flooded with applications for shares. For example, the Great North of Scotland Railway received applications for more than three times the number of its shares in 1845, whilst the Direct Western Railway received 1,400,000 applications for its 120,000 shares.[11] It is against this context of a mass readjustment of private property rights that the contemporary literary preoccupation with references to the railways can be understood.[12] Private takings during the railway boom appear to have generated quite different responses in individuals, depending upon their exact circumstances and personal predilections. For some, particularly rural landowners with mineral deposits, it seems that the railways offered the valuable chance to be both landed gentlemen and also industrial entrepreneurs.[13]

Whatever the political or legal merits of allowing so many private takings to occur during the eighteenth and nineteenth centuries, it seems that this compulsory readjustment of property rights succeeded in encouraging entrepreneurship. Within a relatively short period of time, England achieved a 'dense network of railway lines'

---

[8] RW Kostal, *Law and English Railway Capitalism 1825–1875* (Oxford, Clarendon Press, 1994) 144.

[9] OC Williams, *The Historical Development of Private Bill Procedure—Volume 1* (London, HMSO, 1948) 59.

[10] Geo IV, c 59 (1831), s 4 provided the relevant railway company with a power to take land subject to paying compensation and various limitations relating to specific owners and parcels of land.

[11] H Pollins 'The Marketing of Railway Shares in the First Half of the Nineteenth Century' (1954) 7 *Economic History Review* 230, 233.

[12] I Carter, *Railways and Culture in Britain: The Epitome of Modernity* (Manchester, Manchester University Press, 2001).

[13] D Spring, 'The English Landed Estate in the Age of Coal and Iron: 1830–1880' (1951) 11 *Journal of Economic History* 3, 4.

which facilitated commerce between regions, encouraged social and geographical mobility, and contributed to increased business opportunities.[14]

C. The US Mill Acts

The US has also had long experience of private takings and the need to balance the 'sanctity' of private property against economic development.[15] Its jurisprudence both at a Federal and a State level is instructive about the problems caused by private takings. Since 1791 and the enactment of the Takings Clause, the Federal government has been bound by the prohibition on taking property only where this is for a 'public use'. Even before this, though, six of the first 13 State Constitutions, including those of Delaware, Massachusetts, New Hampshire, Pennsylvania, Vermont and Virginia, contained 'public use' limitations on takings.[16] State constitutions are free to enact more stringent property protection than that found in the Federal law if they wish, and some have done so. Stoebuck notes that 26 out of the 50 US States have provisions in their State constitutions allowing for compensation for 'damaged' property as well as 'takings'.[17]

Some of the earliest examples of statutes promoting private takings are the US Mill Acts. In their original form, these pieces of legislation allowed riparian landowners to construct dams that might potentially flood neighbouring land, or construct structures on their riparian neighbour's banks, in order to create sufficient reserves of water to power mills. The first Mill Act was enacted by Virginia in 1667 and 10 colonies followed suit in adopting such legislation, including Connecticut, Delaware, Maryland, Massachusetts, New Hampshire, North Carolina, Pennsylvania, Rhode Island, South Carolina and Virginia.[18] As might be expected given the different geographical and political contexts, the Mill Acts varied in their terms, with some being more protective than others of existing private property rights.

US courts began to face increased pressure to justify interferences with property rights by private parties, particularly following the dramatic increase in cotton mills after 1815. Mills of this kind required enormous heads and flows of water in order to provide sufficient operational power and led to spirited debates about the nature of property rights. The operation of private mills had to be justified on the grounds that a 'public benefit' was tantamount to 'public use' as required by many State and Federal constitutions protecting property rights. Most frequently, the public benefit referred to was of an explicitly economic nature.[19] For example,

---

[14] JS Foreman-Peck, 'Natural Monopoly and Railway Policy in the Nineteenth Century' (1987) 39 *Oxford Economic Papers* 699.

[15] MJ Horwitz, *The Transformation of American Law, 1780–1860* (Cambridge, MA, Harvard University Press, 1977) 47.

[16] NA Sales, 'Classic Republicanism and the Fifth Amendment's "Public Use" Requirement' (1999) 49 *Duke Law Journal* 339, 367–69 and note 137. Sales also notes at 360–61 that, other than the State Constitutions of Vermont and Massachusetts, no States required compensation to be paid by the State when seizing property.

[17] WB Stoebuck, 'A General Theory of Eminent Domain' (1971) 47 *Washington Law Review* 553, 555.

[18] Sales (n 16) 369, note 149.

[19] *Potlatch Lumber Co v Peterson*, 12 Idaho 769 (1906), 785.

South Carolina's Mill Act refers to the desire that the 'erecting of Mills of all kinds and other Mechanick Engines, will greatly improve the Country itself and its Trade and Navigation'. The obvious difficulty with this type of expansive approach to private takings on the grounds of economic benefit was the impossibility of placing meaningful limits on the exercise of the power. Nearly all entrepreneurial actions may be said to produce some wider public benefit and could thereby justify takings, perhaps with the consequence that the 'property of the citizen would never be safe from invasion'.[20]

In response, some States, such as South Carolina, went so far as to repeal their Mill Acts on the grounds that they represented too great an interference with private interests. The US Supreme Court attempted to avoid the problem of reconciling the Mill Acts with the Takings Clause by unconvincingly treating the Acts as regulations rather than takings, and therefore undeserving of compensation. This argument relied upon interpreting the Acts as controls on the 'manner in which the rights of proprietors of lands ... may be asserted and enjoyed' with due regard to the 'interests of all, and to the public good'.[21]

III. PRIVATE TAKINGS AND PRO-ENTREPRENEURIAL DISCOURSE

The realisation in the US that the equation of private economic gain with a public benefit might have adverse effects on the stability of property rights was bound up with a wider clash between two competing views: on the one hand, the importance of protecting absolute and exclusive dominion over property; and, on the other, the desire to promote industrial development and economic growth. As always with this perennial debate, individuals fall either side of porous boundaries. Those calling for progress and the recognition of novel property rights often find themselves later resisting identical calls from others on the grounds that *their* property rights are now in danger of being adversely affected. Few investors are prepared to commit money to a project without being assured that their property rights will receive legal recognition, and even monopoly protection. Conversely, protecting existing property rights against newcomers can hinder further economic growth and development.

The tension between these approaches in US takings jurisprudence has been noted by Greg Alexander, who contends that whilst there might have been an avowed desire to encourage entrepreneurship, this did not mean that there was agreement about how best to achieve this aim. One of the 'two strands of pro-entrepreneurial discourse'[22] favoured providing legal protection for entrepreneurial activity by granting private investors monopoly privileges in return for constructing infrastructure. Others opposed monopolistic property interests as being anti-developmental and undemocratic.[23] The conflict between these two approaches can be seen in

---

[20] *Chesapeake Stone Co v Moreland*, 104 SW 762 (Ky 1907), 765.
[21] *Head v Amoskeag Manufacturing Co*, 113 US 9 (1885), 20–21.
[22] GS Alexander, *Commodity & Propriety: Competing Visions of Property in American Legal Thought 1776–1970* (Chicago, University of Chicago Press, 1997) 186.
[23] Ibid.

the attempts of the US courts to balance the protection of property rights and the promotion of development. As private takings under the Mill Acts became increasingly common, both the courts and the state legislatures appear to have developed misgivings about the constitutional status of such transfers.[24] These reservations became particularly acute as the public benefit of private takings became more diffuse; it became impossible to know in advance when takings would be classified as for a private use and therefore unconstitutional.[25]

Unlike in the US, where debate raged at the legislative level about the desirability of private powers of compulsory acquisition, Parliament appeared relatively untroubled and focused instead on streamlining the private bills procedure in order to make it more efficient.[26] As a result of this, a series of Consolidation Acts were enacted in the mid-1840s to ensure a greater degree of uniformity between similar bills. The most important statute in relation to property rights was the Lands Clauses Consolidation Act 1845 (hereinafter 'the 1845 Act'), which introduced the first statutory procedure for compulsory acquisition of land in England.[27] Under section 18 of this statute, any promoter or company wishing to purchase land compulsorily had to give notice of the proposals to all interested parties, and the Act also set out detailed compensation procedures.[28] However, it seems that there was some belated discussion about the correct balance to be drawn, partly due to various well-publicised business crashes. By 1844, for example, legislation was introduced which gave the government an option in 1869 to buy out all private railway companies established since 1844.[29]

The legislative delay in acknowledging the potential dangers of excessive disruption to private property rights is likely to have been due to the piecemeal nature of the law in this area. The use of Private Acts, rather than Public Acts of Parliament, may well have allowed the Blackstonian myth of absolute dominion to flourish more strongly than might otherwise have been possible. Those affected by a private statute would be intimately interested in its terms, but wider society would often remain oblivious to the ramifications of the project at stake, unless it was particularly contentious. The Private Bill procedure involves Parliament acting not only in its legislative capacity, but also abiding by a quasi-judicial decision-making process.[30] The constitutional framework surrounding this type of legislation is thus of a fundamentally different character from that existing in the US and has been greatly influenced by historical accident. Most probably, private legislation developed out of a practice, which existed by the reign of Henry IV, of individuals petitioning

---

[24] RA Epstein, *Takings: Private Property and the Power of Eminent Domain* (Cambridge, MA, Harvard University Press, 1985) 172.

[25] P Nichols, 'The Meaning of Public Use in the Law of Eminent Domain' (1940) 20 *Boston University Law Review* 615, 619.

[26] FA Sharman, 'The History of the Lands Clauses Consolidation Act 1845—I' [1986] *Statute Law Review* 13, 17–18. See also [1986] *Statute Law Review* 78, 83.

[27] 8 Vict c 18.

[28] 'On the Rights of Property Connected with Railways' (1848) 9 *Law Review & Quarterly Journal of British & Foreign Jurisprudence* 102, 118 gives an overview of the procedure under the 1845 Act.

[29] Foreman-Peck (n 14) 701.

[30] McKay (n 3) 967.

Parliament for extraordinary and peculiar powers over and above those granted by the common law.[31]

The main legislative focus throughout the canal and railway boom appears to have been shaped by pragmatic concerns relating to streamlined processes rather than broader issues of principle. In the absence of explicit constitutional protection for property rights, it seems probable that the significance of private takings was overlooked until the initial flurry of speculation and activity had ended. If any lesson can be drawn from examining the railway mania of the nineteenth century, it is that modern legislatures would do well to consider the significance of private takings for broader property principles when deciding how best to encourage private development and entrepreneurship.

IV. MODERN PRIVATE TAKINGS

Despite the growth of general or public statutes applicable to the whole community, private legislation continued to play an important role, particularly in relation to property rights. Private Acts continue to be used today in order to execute complex local projects, although far less frequently than was the case in previous centuries. Today, however, private takings occur most frequently as part of urban redevelopment and regeneration schemes rather than transport and infrastructure projects.[32] In addition, they normally occur under the auspices of a general Act of Parliament, particularly the Town and Country Planning Act (TCPA) 1990, rather than under specific private legislation. Two instances of this type of urban-regeneration private taking will be considered in this section: one from the UK and one from the US.

A. Store Wars and Private Takings

In *R (Sainsbury's Supermarkets Ltd) v Wolverhampton City Council*,[33] the UK Supreme Court considered the compulsory acquisition of private property for redevelopment purposes by local authorities under the TCPA 1990. The case is particularly interesting for the present purposes because it involved a private taking. Sainsbury's Supermarkets Ltd and Tesco Stores Ltd are two of the largest UK supermarket chains, with a market share of roughly 16 per cent and 30 per cent respectively. They are both anxious not only to maintain their market share but to increase it, and expansion opportunities are highly sought after. Both companies owned part of a semi-derelict site in Wolverhampton known as the Raglan Street site. Sainsbury's owned 86 per cent of the site and Tesco the remaining 14 per cent. Both companies eventually decided separately that they wanted to develop Raglan Street and build their own large new store on the site. Competing development schemes were submitted and the Council granted planning permission for

---

[31] Williams (n 9) 24.
[32] A Bell, 'Private Takings' (2009) 76 *University of Chicago Law Review* 517, 519–20.
[33] *R (Sainsbury's Supermarkets Ltd) v Wolverhampton City Council* [2010] UKSC 20, [2011] 1 AC 437.

both; neither of the rival schemes could be realised without the use of compulsory purchase powers to take property from the other company.

However, Tesco had one 'decisive advantage' over its competitor, since it also controlled a nearby site called the Royal Hospital Site (RHS) with a large number of listed buildings in poor condition.[34] Wolverhampton City Council had long hoped that the RHS could be regenerated, but had accepted that given the planning constraints, this was unlikely to be financially attractive to potential developers. In a bid to win the Council's support for its Raglan Street site plans, Tesco argued that if it were to be the Council's approved developer for the site, it would also be able to 'cross-subsidise' the redevelopment of the languishing RHS some 850 metres away and balance out the costs involved. The Council was swayed by the attractive proposition of gaining two redeveloped areas and approved in principle the making of a compulsory purchase order (CPO) under section 226(1)(a) of the TCPA 1990 as amended[35] over the land owned by Sainsbury's at the Raglan Street site.[36]

This section gives local authorities[37] the power to acquire compulsorily land in their area for planning purposes. According to a government circular, the powers under section 226 are intended to provide a 'positive tool' and are suitable for use when assembling land 'for regeneration and other schemes' where the 'range of activities or purposes ... mean that no other single specific compulsory purchase power' would be 'appropriate'.[38] Under section 226(1)(a) of the TCPA 1990 (as amended), the authority may compulsorily purchase land where the authority (subjectively) thinks that the acquisition will 'facilitate the carrying out of development, re-development or improvement on or in relation to the land'. Acquisition under this provision is limited by section 226(1A), since the power must not be exercised unless the local authority (again subjectively) thinks that the development, redevelopment or improvement is 'likely to contribute to the achievement' of any one or more of the following objects: the promotion or improvement of the economic well-being of their area; the promotion or improvement of the social well-being of their area; and/or the promotion or improvement of the environmental well-being of their area.

Notably, s 226(4) of the TCPA 1990 expressly authorises the involvement of private entities in achieving the local authority's goals and provides for valid private takings:

> It is immaterial by whom the local authority propose that any activity or purpose mentioned [in s 226(1)] should be undertaken or achieved (and in particular the local authority need not propose to undertake an activity or to achieve that purpose themselves).

The inclusion of this provision demonstrates a positive desire on the part of the legislature to encourage the involvement of private parties where this will encourage

---

[34] Ibid [27].

[35] Amended by s 99 of the Planning and Compulsory Purchase Act 2004.

[36] Once a CPO under s 226 has been made, it must be confirmed by the Secretary of State. An independent inspector will be appointed to conduct a public inquiry if there are objections to the CPO. The inspector's report and recommendation will be considered by the Secretary of State when deciding whether or not to confirm the CPO.

[37] Defined in s 226(8) of the TCPA 1990 as a county, district or London borough council.

[38] ODPM Circular 06/2004, *Compulsory Purchase and the Crichel Down Rules*, Appendix A, c 2.

development and financial investment. Effectively, this authorises private takings, with the local authority providing the power of compulsory acquisition, but using this at the instigation and behest of another private party, here Tesco. It is worth remembering that Sainsbury's actually owned six times as much of the Raglan Street site as Tesco and had its own development plans which had outline planning approval. Thus, it is unsurprising that Sainsbury's challenged the CPO, arguing that the Council had illegitimately had regard to the regeneration of the RHS when considering the merits of the competing Raglan Street proposals. The Council and Tesco argued that developing the other site was a valid consideration when deciding which scheme should be supported. Sainsbury's claim was dismissed both at first instance and before the Court of Appeal. However, the Supreme Court by a majority of four to three found in favour of Sainsbury's.[39]

In the lead judgment for the majority, Lord Collins noted the utility of taking principles applying to planning applications into account when considering compulsory purchase schemes. However, because of the 'serious invasion' of property rights involved in compulsory acquisition, a strict approach to such principles was required.[40] One such was the notion that it would be legitimate for a local authority to take off-site benefits into account when deciding which scheme to favour. However, there needed to be a 'real rather than fanciful or remote connection' between the off-site benefits and the development for which the compulsory acquisition is made.[41] In the present case, there was only a 'connection' between the Raglan Street development and the benefits from developing the RHS. Effectively, Tesco was being tempted to undertake one uncommercial development in order to obtain the development that it did want. Or, to put it another way, the Council was being tempted to facilitate one development to get the other development that it wanted.[42] To those asking why a local authority faced with two almost identical schemes should not look to some 'substantial extraneous benefit' offered by one of the parties, Lord Walker noted with asperity that it was 'simply not the right way' for a local authority to decide how to use its powers of compulsory purchase. To do business this way would be just as wrong as allowing a local authority to 'choose a new chief executive, from a short list of apparently equally well-qualified candidates, by holding a closed auction for the office'.[43]

However, those in the minority took a different view. Lord Phillips argued that the Council should first decide whether compulsory purchase would enable the development to proceed before considering which developer should be preferred. This task was to be undertaken by looking to 'all considerations material to that choice', including: (i) the amount of the site already owned by each developer; and (ii) the benefits offered by them, whether or not connected to the development. The fact that this might have the effect of 'an auction between the two developers for the benefit of the community' did not seem to Lord Phillips to be 'inherently

---

[39] Lord Walker, Lady Hale, Lord Mance and Lord Collins were in the majority, with Lord Phillips, Lord Hope and Lord Brown in the minority.
[40] *Sainsbury's* (n 33) [10].
[41] Ibid [70]–[71].
[42] Ibid [72].
[43] Ibid [87].

objectionable'.[44] Lord Hope concurred with the argument that it was legitimate for the Council when choosing between competing proposals to have 'regard to planning benefits that lie outside the perimeter of the site itself'. The choice as to whose land to acquire was inextricably linked with the choice of the developer to whom the land was later to be disposed of.

Effectively, the whole court agreed that the Council could exercise its powers under section 226 of the TCPA 1990. However, from the minority's point of view, this power could not be exercised unless and until the Council had decided which developer's scheme was to be preferred, and this logically required an appreciation of the off-site benefits offered by Tesco. This approach, whilst initially attractive, fails to take sufficient account of the distinction between compulsory acquisition powers and planning decisions, which are, as Baroness Hale observed, a 'different exercise'.[45] Whilst the factors under consideration in both regimes may be similar, the majority in the *Sainsbury's* case was right to emphasise the long common law tradition of restrictively reading statutes involving deprivations of property. This approach has been further bolstered by the incorporation of A1-P1 into domestic law via the Human Rights Act (HRA) 1998.

Taking someone's property from them, whether an individual or a company, involves a serious readjustment of their rights. These are transmuted from proprietary status, with all of the social recognition and state enforcement that this brings, into rather more quicksilver-like liability rights in the form of monetary compensation. Money may well be sufficient compensation for the taking, but its existence neither justifies it happening in the first place nor justifies the downgrading of property protection to liability protection.[46] This is all the more egregious where the redevelopment use to which the property is to be put is exactly that which the landowner itself wants to carry out. Lord Walker rightly observed that the 'proper consideration of the exercise of powers of compulsory acquisition under section 226' should not 'be telescoped into the exercise of powers of disposal under section 233'.[47] Lord Collins for the majority noted that it was 'wrong for the council to deprive Sainsbury's of its property because the council will derive from disposal of that property benefits wholly unconnected with the acquisition of the property'.[48]

Lord Walker's focus on the parties involved in the *Sainsbury's* case is particularly significant. He noted that this case involved land which was 'to end up, not in public ownership and used for public purposes, but in private ownership and used for a variety of purposes, mainly retail and residential'. This case thus involved a private taking and commented that whilst economic regeneration 'is no doubt a public good ... "private to private" acquisitions by compulsory purchase may also produce large profits for powerful business interests, and courts rightly regard them as particularly sensitive'.[49] Here the exercise of private compulsory acquisition powers in a private takings context 'amounts to a serious invasion of the owner's proprietary

---

[44] Ibid [143].
[45] Ibid [92] and see Lord Mance's comments at [101].
[46] G Calabresi and AD Melamed, 'Property Rules, Liability Rules, and Inalienability: One View of the Cathedral' (1972) 85 *Harvard Law Review* 1089.
[47] *Sainsbury's* (n 33) [88].
[48] Ibid [77].
[49] Ibid [81].

rights ... [and] a stricter approach is therefore called for'.[50] The following section briefly considers the most recent US Supreme Court case on private takings before arguing that Lord Walker was correct in calling for modern private takings to be viewed cautiously.

B. The Little Pink House and Private Takings

The case of *Kelo v City of New London*[51] is now a cause célèbre; the photos of Susette Kelo standing outside her little pink house with the stars and stripes unfurled behind her has entered into the American psyche. In 2000, the economically depressed city of New London (hereinafter 'the City') in Connecticut approved a development plan projected to create more than 1,000 jobs, increase tax and other revenues and revitalize the downtown and waterfront areas of the city.[52] The City had suffered from decades of economic decline and its unemployment rate was nearly double that of the State as a whole. A private non-profit development entity, the New London Development Corporation (NLDC), was reactivated and various bond issues were made to support its activities. At this point, Pfizer Inc., a large pharmaceutical company, announced that it would build a $300 million research facility on a site immediately adjacent to the development area. Understandably, the NLDC intended to capitalise on Pfizer's proposed arrival and the expected business that it would attract. The City authorised NLDC to purchase the properties required for the 90-acre project and to use eminent domain powers in the City's name if required.

Unfortunately for the City, nine home owners challenged the decision to use eminent domain to acquire their properties. None of the properties were blighted or in poor condition, they were just in the wrong place at the wrong time. They argued that the City's plan did not satisfy the 'public use' fetter in the Takings Clause and was therefore unconstitutional.[53] The lead petitioner was Susette Kelo, a registered nurse who had lived in the area since 1997 and loved the water-view from her house. Under the development plans, the petitioners' plots were slated to become office space and 'park support', or parking areas. The petitioners argued that the government could rightly take their homes to build a road or railway or to eliminate some type of harmful property use, but that it could not do so 'simply because the new owners may make more productive use of the property'.

The US Supreme Court struggled with the case, dividing five-four in favour of the City with very strong dissents and highly critical public reactions to the decision. The case was summed up as one of 'conflicting dreams', with the petitioners wanting to keep their homes whilst the City dreamed of a resurgent economy.[54] The majority in the US Supreme Court acknowledged that 'it has long been accepted that

---

[50] Ibid [84].
[51] *Kelo v City of New London* (2005) 545 US 469.
[52] 268 Conn 1 (2004) 5; 843 A2d 500, 507 (2004).
[53] The Takings Clause is made applicable to the States by the Fourteenth Amendment, *Chicago, B & QR Co v Chicago*, 166 US 226 (1897).
[54] Conn Super Ct, 13 March 2002 (not Reported in A2d); (2002 WL 500238).

the sovereign may not take the property of *A* for the sole purpose of transferring it to another private party *B*, even though *A* is paid just compensation'.[55] Following previous expansive readings of the public use test in *Berman v Parker*[56] and *Hawaii Housing Authority v Midkiff*,[57] the majority found that there was sufficient public benefit to be gained from the takings involved in *Kelo* to satisfy the public use requirement. In responding to concerns that cities would be able to transfer property between citizens in order to put land to more productive use, the majority stated that 'such an unusual exercise of government power would certainly raise a suspicion that a private purpose was afoot ... [and could] be confronted if and when they arise'.[58]

In his concurrence, Justice Kennedy observed that courts applying rational-basis review in public use cases 'should strike down a taking that ... is intended to favor a particular private party, with only incidental or pretextual public benefits'.[59] In some circumstances, Justice Kennedy noted that a stricter level of scrutiny might be required due to an acute risk of 'undetected impermissible favoritism of private parties'.[60] However, the situations in which such a presumption might arise were not detailed. Whilst confirming that any 'plausible accusation of impermissible favoritism to private parties' should be treated as a 'serious' objection, Justice Kennedy did not enter into an analysis of why this might matter so much.[61] It seems that his disquiet centred on the possible subversion of the public use clause, but without explaining whether and why there might be any additional reason for concern.

Justice O'Connor dissented from the majority's decision, along with Chief Justice Rehnquist, Justice Scalia and Justice Thomas. She argued that 'under the banner of economic development, all private property is now vulnerable to being taken and transferred to another private owner, so long as it might be upgraded'. In holding that the 'incidental public benefits' resulting from using private property were sufficient to satisfy the public use requirement in the Takings Clause, the distinction between private and public use of property had been unconstitutionally eroded. The dissenters stressed repeatedly the significance of ensuring stable property ownership by 'providing safeguards against excessive, unpredictable, or unfair use of the government's eminent domain power', particularly against owners who might be vulnerable or unable to protect themselves 'in the political process against the majority's will'. As Justice O'Connor warned, the impact of the decision 'will not be random. The beneficiaries are likely to be those citizens with disproportionate influence and power in the political process ... the government now has license to transfer property from those with fewer resources to those with more'. This was a point that Justice Thomas also stressed in his dissent, arguing that interpreting the public use clause broadly so as to allow private takings producing incidental public benefits would guarantee that 'these losses will fall disproportionately on poor

---

[55] *Kelo* (n 51) 477 (Justice Stevens).
[56] *Berman v Parker*, 348 US 26 (1954).
[57] *Hawaii Housing Authority v Midkiff*, 467 US 229 (1984).
[58] *Kelo* (n 51) 486–87.
[59] Ibid, 490.
[60] Ibid, 493.
[61] Ibid, 491.

communities'. The reasons given for this anxiety were that such communities were less likely to put their lands to the 'highest and best social use' and would also be 'the least politically powerful'.[62]

In the dissenters' view, there were three permissible if porous categories of taking: (i) those where private property is transferred to public ownership, such as for a road or hospital; (ii) where private property is transferred to other private parties, such as common carriers who make the property available to the public, for example, a railway or utility; and (iii) exceptional private takings that serve a wider public purpose in removing 'affirmative harm on society', such as blight from extreme poverty or in righting social injustices such as land oligopolies. In these rare instances, a private taking was acceptable because a public purpose was directly realised with the elimination of the harmful use of the property in question. This was not the case with the homes in *Kelo*, where their current use posed no social harm at all. There might be some public benefit in replacing them with a more lucrative property use, but this was not the same as saying that their current use was inherently harmful. Justice O'Connor's views here are surely correct. To say otherwise would make a mockery out the central principle that a property owner has a right to prioritise the resource values in their own property so long as these are not directly harmful to others.[63]

The expansion of public use was significant since it included any situation where the proposed new use of the condemned property would generate some secondary public benefit such as increased tax revenue. As Justice O'Connor noted, all property would be up for grabs since:

> [W]ho among us can say she already makes the most productive or attractive possible use of her property? The specter of condemnation hangs over all property. Nothing is to prevent the State from replacing any Motel 6 with a Ritz–Carlton, any home with a shopping mall, or any farm with a factory.[64]

The majority argued that its decision did not sanction the bare transfer from A to B for B's benefit, but, as the dissenters noted, there were no realistic suggestions about how such transfers would be spotted by the courts. In any event, notions of private benefit and incidental public benefit are merged and mutually reinforced in economic development takings, such that it is difficult to separate these out. As Justice Zarella noted in his partial dissent in the Supreme Court of Connecticut in *Kelo*, economic growth is a 'far more indirect and nebulous benefit than the building of roads and courthouses or the elimination of urban blight'. Plans for hotels and offices that will purportedly add jobs and tax revenue to the economic base of a community are just as likely to be viewed as a bonanza to the developers who build them as they are a benefit to the public.'[65]

---

[62] Ibid, 521 (Justice Thomas).
[63] KJ Gray and SF Gray, *Elements of Land Law*, 5th edn (Oxford, Oxford University Press, 2009) [1.5.39].
[64] *Kelo* (n 51) 503.
[65] *Kelo v City of New London* 268 Conn 1 (2004), 141.

V. PROBLEMATIC MODERN PRIVATE TAKINGS

Bending constitutional principles and conceptions of property may seem like an acceptable trade-off to encourage entrepreneurship and economic development.[66] Governments are often bureaucratic and unable to react speedily and efficiently in designing and managing large-scale infrastructure and regeneration projects. Therefore, it is unsurprising that involving the private sector in projects has long been seen as a potential solution for governmental inefficiency, lack of financial accountability, lack of managerial skills and authority, underperforming assets, unresponsiveness and lack of expertise. Despite the historical use and utility of private takings in encouraging entrepreneurship, there are a number of reasons to be cautious about their modern counterparts if they are not to upset the delicate balance between stability and encouraging development.

First, modern private takings are often justified by indefinable notions such as 'regeneration' or economic progress. Those who are already struggling to make full economic use of their property may question why economic use should be the main, if not the sole, criterion for determining whether or not their property use will be supported. Viewing economic use of property as the main criterion for subjecting it to private taking powers leads to a very narrow, non-holistic view of what it means to be a property owner. There is something 'fundamentally objectionable' about someone's property being expropriated in such a 'predatory' manner where the eviction is 'quite deliberately intended to generate money—very substantial amounts of money—for somebody else'.[67] Gone is the image of property as the fullest bundle of sticks, allowing the owner free rein over the use of their property so long as this does not impinge upon or harm others. In its place is a shadowy image of property as an economic unit, which must be utilised to a particular unknowable capacity, in order to afford any protection for more personal interests. Where property is not being 'used' to this required level, such personal links will not receive sufficient recognition in themselves to protect the status quo of the property allocation.

A second difficulty caused by private takings for economic development or regeneration is that their use and scope are difficult to predict. Individuals may feel especially helpless given that it is often impossible to foresee when or even whether the State may want their property, let alone another wealthier or more determined individual. There is always the possibility that someone else may find a 'better' use for property. Whilst historically private takings promoted geographically discrete and temporally limited projects, such as the building of a railroad or the erection of a specific bridge, this is no longer the case.[68] The need for further economic improvement and development may always, mirage-like, appear to be in the distance. In a situation such as this, property rights may become extremely fragile. Not only are courts likely to focus on the institutional competence of the taking party rather than

---

[66] GS Alexander, 'Property as Propriety' (1998) 77 *Nebraska Law Review* 667.

[67] KJ Gray, 'There's No Place Like Home!' (2007) 11 *Journal of South Pacific Law* 73, 83.

[68] See *Props of the Charles River Bridge v Props of the Warren Bridge*, 36 US 420 (1837). Here, even though private investors were rewarded for building a toll bridge by the granting of a monopoly to collect tolls, the monopoly was limited in time. See Alexander (n 66) 204 ff for further discussion about the case.

the public-private label attached to them, but in addition such takings have no easily discernible and limitable end-point: everything is potentially up for grabs.

Broad interpretations of the public use and public interest fetters on takings can be said to undermine the security of property rights generally. Where property rights are vulnerable to being taken by unknown parties (not only the State but private parties as well) and at unknown times (economic development as a non-bounded concept), it seems as if any feelings of security in property rights are illusory.[69] Not only are monetary losses a potential problem, but security in intangible property 'rights' may be vulnerable too. Where property is taken, individuals are no longer as free as they previously were to satisfy their own preferences. The focus narrows to protecting property and assessing risk rather than enjoying the independent legal and political sphere afforded by property.

Third, whilst historically private takings would have targeted those with the knowledge and influence to alter the terms of the taking involved this is not the case today. Those landowners affected by private takings in the eighteenth and nineteenth centuries were likely to be gentry or to have connections within Parliament, and thus those affected were best able to defend their property rights. Not only did aristocratic landowners stand to gain personally from the growth of the railways, but they could also hold significant political sway over the terms of the Private Act itself. An examination of the terms of railway Acts indicates just how successful some individuals were not only in negotiating compensation but also in avoiding the railway across parts of their estates in the first place. For example, the London & Birmingham Railway bought off opposition from the Earls of Clarendon and Essex by paying nearly £73,000, agreeing to a deviation and building a mile-long tunnel to avoid their parks in an area of land at Watford.[70] This parliamentary influence is no longer available to those generally affected by private takings. Whilst the *Sainsbury's* case is unusual in involving two corporate entities, most private takings affect individuals whose property is in relatively run-down or economically depressed areas. As the dissenters in *Kelo* noted, the impact of the case was not going to be felt equally, but would affect those who were most politically and socially vulnerable first, since their properties would appear most attractive for regeneration schemes.

Fourth, even where the trickle-down public benefits of a taking are sufficient to make it constitutionally acceptable, courts should scrutinise the exercise of the power carefully. Historically, private takings flourished and led to significant readjustments of property rights. However, the use of the private bill procedure in England and the constitutional matrix in the US led to useful scrutiny of the terms of the specific taking. Today's takings are of a different order and magnitude given their prevalence and the breadth of the powers involved.

Both in the *Sainsbury's* case and in *Kelo*, there were calls for a higher level of scrutiny given the serious invasion of property rights involved in compulsory acquisition cases. This is all the more relevant in *Kelo*-type situations where someone's home

---

[69] FI Michelman, 'Property as a Constitutional Right' (1981) 38 *Washington & Lee Law Review* 1097, 1102.

[70] J Simmons and G Biddle (eds), *The Oxford Companion to British Railway History from 1603 to the 1990s* (Oxford, Oxford University Press, 1997) 251.

is threatened. It is axiomatic that English courts may intervene when a decision maker acts ultra vires in exceeding the powers granted to them by Parliament. Whatever the basis for judicial intervention (whether based on legislative intent, judicial creativity, common law principles of good administration or the importance of upholding the rule of law), the courts are well practised at reviewing exercises of jurisdiction. There are, however, at least two significant difficulties faced by the courts when reviewing compulsory purchase decisions: (i) modern general public Acts are cast in subjective and broad terms; and (ii) the increase in privatised and contracted-out services has led to problems with accountability, since private bodies integrally involved with the exercise of compulsory purchase powers may not be amenable to judicial review.

The power under section 226 of the TCPA 1990 at issue in the *Sainsbury's* case is framed in such a subjective manner and requires such a low threshold to be passed by the promoter in demonstrating a need for the scheme that there is little room for the courts to be anything other than deferential in the face of such wide discretion. It is true that the power must be coupled with a more precisely drawn plan and proposals before a CPO will be granted, but this requirement for additional precision can be overstated and in no way acts as a sufficient bulwark against impractical or ill-thought-out exercises of compulsory purchase powers. Decisions may be challenged by way of judicial review proceedings if it is deemed to be *Wednesbury* unreasonable or 'so unreasonable that no reasonable authority could ever have come to it'.[71] However, this is a particularly hard standard of review to satisfy. Private takings may be beneficial to society, but it behoves the courts to be more demanding inquisitors than they have generally proved to be when hearing legal challenges to altered CPOs, or uneconomical schemes.[72] The *Kelo* case itself ended up with Pfizer pulling out of the regeneration scheme and, although the area was razed, none of the planned developments have yet occurred.

In addition, the type of schemes that are likely to be promoted under this section will generally involve areas of policy and economic considerations, in relation to which the courts are likely to be deferential due to concerns about relative institutional competence. Whilst there are encouraging glimmerings in the comments of the majority in the *Sainsbury's* case that private takings are particularly sensitive and may therefore warrant a stricter approach, it is difficult to see how this can be achieved given the express parliamentary approval for private parties in section 226(4) of the TCPA 1990 and the subjective breadth of the statutory powers involved. Similarly, as demonstrated in *Kelo*, the US Supreme Court defers to the legislature's determination of a project as serving a public use 'until it is shown to involve an impossibility'.[73] The Court has refused to depart from this attitude of judicial restraint on the basis that such a move would involve the courts deciding what is, and is not, a governmental function. However, the Court's minimal, rational-based scrutiny is hard to justify given the importance of property rights

---

[71] *Associated Provincial Picture Houses Ltd v Wednesbury Corporation* [1948] 1 KB 223.
[72] See *Chesterfield Properties plc v Secretary of State for the Environment* (1997) 76 P & CR 117.
[73] *Old Dominion Co v United States*, 269 US 55 (1925) 66.

to the exercise of other human rights.[74] State courts have taken a firmer line when scrutinising takings legislation and have even inquired into whether formal mechanisms exist that would ensure that the planned businesses continue to contribute to the local economy, as promised.[75] However, this is not the approach that the US Supreme Court followed in *Kelo* itself, where the majority preferred to avoid 'rigid formulas and intrusive scrutiny' and instead to give legislatures 'broad latitude' in determining what public needs justify the use of the takings power.[76] However, there is a danger that this level of review may involve no real scrutiny at all; at some stage, deference becomes passivity.

As noted above, one of the difficulties of controlling modern private takings is that there is still some uncertainty about the amenability of private parties to both judicial review and claims under the HRA 1998. Whilst it is possible for ostensibly private entities to be subjected to judicial review, this depends on the specific nature of the body and its links with the government.[77] Similarly, under the HRA 1998, not all bodies have a duty to act compatibly with European Convention on Human Rights, just core public authorities or hybrid public authorities carrying out an act of a public nature being so affected.[78] Spotting hybrid public authorities in particular has proved difficult in practice and it is extremely unlikely, given the current restrictive approach taken by the courts, that private developers carrying out regeneration projects could be viewed as any type of public authority under the HRA 1998.[79]

Whilst the courts are under an obligation under section 6 of the HRA 1998 as public authorities to protect European Convention rights and also to apply the law compatibly with the Convention in all cases that come before them,[80] this indirect horizontal effect of the HRA 1998 does not help where the entity in question, eg a private developer, is neither a public authority nor amenable to judicial review.[81] In any event, even if it were possible, it is unrealistic to regard judicial review of privatised bodies as a panacea, since such review is 'subject to all of the usual defects of judicial review generally, together with some peculiar to that area'. Aronson

---

[74] L Mansnerus, 'Public Use, Private Use, and Judicial Review in Eminent Domain' (1983) 58 *New York University Law Review* 409, 428 observes that property rights are just as constitutionally significant as others, given that they may be tied up with concepts of home and community, social and family ties, a way of life and perhaps livelihood.

[75] *Wayne County v Hathcock*, 471 Mich 445 (2004), 477. The Supreme Court of Ohio explicitly refused to follow the *Kelo*-type approach and applied a stricter standard of scrutiny in *Norwood v Horney*, 110 Ohio St 3d 353.

[76] *Kelo* (n 51) 483.

[77] *R v Panel on Takeovers and Mergers, ex p Datafin plc* [1987] QB 815; *R v Disciplinary Committee of the Jockey Club, ex p Aga Khan* [1993] 1 WLR 909; *R v Servite Houses and Wandsworth LBC, ex p Goldsmith* (2000) 3 CCLR 325; *R (on the application of Beer (Trading as Hammer Trout Farm)) v Hampshire Farmers Market Ltd* [2003] EWCA Civ 1056.

[78] HRA 1998, ss 6(1) and 6(3)(b).

[79] *Aston Cantlow and Wilmcote with Billesley PCC v Walbank* [2003] UKHL 37, [2004] 1 AC 546; *YL v Birmingham City Council* [2007] UKHL 27, [2008] 1 AC 95; *Weaver v London and Quadrant Housing Trust* [2009] HRLR 29.

[80] HRA 1998, ss 3 and 6(3)(a).

[81] M Hunt, 'The Horizontal Effect of the Human Rights Act' [1998] *Public Law* 423; W Wade, 'Horizons of Horizontality' [2000] 116 *LQR* 217; D Oliver, 'The Human Rights Act and the Public Law/Private Law Divide' [2000] *European Human Rights Law Review* 343; T Raphael, 'The Problem of Horizontal Effect' [2000] *European Human Rights Law Review* 393; S Palmer, 'Public, Private and the Human Rights Act 1998: An Ideological Divide? [2007] *CLJ* 559.

observes that judicial review can remedy individual grievances but rarely provides systemic relief. In addition, decisions to litigate can be happenstance, and even if review proceedings occur, the respondent is usually free to come to the same result, but in a manner that is impervious to judicial criticism.[82]

VI. CONCLUSION

Carol Rose argues that despite the rhetoric of property security, all regimes 'routinely "build in" a variety of rights disruptions that amount to expropriations' so as to ensure that a system will not 'collapse of its own brittleness'.[83] These 'rights disruptions' are based primarily on the need to: (i) remove obsolete or uncertain claims in a 'housekeeping' role; and (ii) control congestion and common pool losses through 'regulatory' disruptions.[84] Pragmatism and familiarity with property reallocations made on these grounds mean that these disruptions often go unnoticed. It is therefore often only when Rose's third category of 'extraordinary' disruption occurs, namely those motivated by revolutions, warfare and other upheavals, that cognisance is taken of the deeper property issues revealed by takings. The third category of takings can play an extremely valuable role in rebalancing societal needs and prioritising particular property uses. Both England and the US have shown themselves historically to be willing to allow compulsory private takings transfers of property rights where this has served an entrepreneurial aim. Such an approach is not in itself injurious to property rights, in that it can stimulate development and remove holdouts or monopolies, thereby encouraging competition to develop. It is argued that historically this approach has been kept within manageable bounds due to the temporal and geographical limitations of the schemes and projects involved in such forced transfers.

Today, however, such limits appear to be disappearing without sufficient attention being paid to the potential consequences of the prevalence and extent of private takings. The involvement of the private sector in these circumstances may be seen as an important means of reducing the cost of government, generating revenue, supplying infrastructure or other facilities that government cannot provide and doing so quickly, introducing competition and reducing the role of central government in society. However, this is not an unalloyed good. There are also opportunities for potential abuse, decreasing service quality, a loss of social equity and a lack of incentives for private firms to take on unprofitable governmental functions. Historical examples of private takings demonstrate the collision between two very different aims: securing the stability of property rights and encouraging development. In order to maintain this difficult and contentious balance, it is argued that modern private takings should be scrutinised carefully and used sparingly so that their benefits are not outweighed by their potential deleterious effect on the stability of property.

---

[82] M Aronson, 'A Public Lawyer's Response to Privatisation and Outsourcing' in M Taggart (ed), *The Province of Administrative Law* (Oxford, Hart Publishing, 1997).

[83] CM Rose 'Property and Expropriation: Themes and Variations in American Law' (2000) *Utah Law Review* 1, 5.

[84] Ibid, 8–14.

Index